The Norton Book of American Short Stories
edited by Peter Prescott

The Norton Book of Light Verse
edited by Russell Baker

The Norton Book of Nature Writing
edited by Robert Finch and John Elder

The Norton Book of the Sea
edited by John O. Coote

The Norton Book of Travel
edited by Paul Fussell

The Norton Book of Modern War

THE NORTON BOOK OF
MODERN WAR

Edited by PAUL FUSSELL

W·W·NORTON & COMPANY·NEW YORK·LONDON

Printed in the United States of America.

The text of this book is composed in Avanta (Electra),
with the display set in Bernhard Modern.
Composition and Manufacturing by
The Haddon Craftsmen, Inc.
Book design by Antonina Krass.

First Edition

Library of Congress Cataloging-in-Publication Data
The Norton book of modern war / edited by Paul Fussell.
          p.   cm.
1. War—Literary collections.   2. Liberature, Modern—20th
century.   3. Literature, Modern—Translations into English.
4. English literature—Translations from foreign languages.
          I. Fussell, Paul, 1924–
              PN6071.W35N67   1991
          808.8'0358–dc20   90-36495

ISBN 0-393-02909-3

W.W. Norton & Company, Inc., 500 Fifth Avenue, New York, N.Y. 10110
W.W. Norton & Company, Ltd., 10 Coptic Street, London WC1A 1PU
          1 2 3 4 5 6 7 8 9 0

CONTENTS

II THE SPANISH CIVIL WAR · 207

Authors Take Sides

III THE SECOND WORLD WAR · 305

Almost Beyond Human Conception

IV THE WARS IN ASIA · 647

V AFTERWORDS · 811

Acknowledgments

I am indebted to Ted Dow, Linda Healey, John Keegan, Donald S. Lamm, John Scanlan, Eugene B. Sledge, Roger J. Spiller, and Russell F. Weigley for information and suggestions; to Judith Pascoe and Kay Whittle for research and technical help; and to Harriette Behringer for her company.

I have been unable to locate the dates for some of the authors in this book. I would be grateful for such informaton sent to me in care of the publishers for use in subsequent printings.

PAUL FUSSELL

INTRODUCTION

On Modern War

The propensity of the twentieth century to generate wars more extensive, destructive, and cruel than any in history must shake the confidence of those like economists and other social scientists, city planners, public health authorities, jurists, legislators, and actuaries, whose work obliges them to assume that people are rational, by their nature free of the urge to self-destruction, and that the general tendency of society is progressive—toward ever greater enlightenment and decency. One need not be a cynic to understand that modern history delivers very different news, and that the modern union of neurotic nationalism and complex technology has defined *war* in a way unknown before.

It could be said that the American Civil War was the first modern one, for it was the first mass war fought in the industrial age, the first to rely on railroads and the telegraph, armored battleships, fast-firing ordnance, and mass-produced, machine-made weapons, uniforms, and shoes—for both men and horses. In the defeat of the South you could read a future in which courage, skill, agility, and persistence would matter much less than access to raw materials and manufacturing capacity. This is what William Tecumseh Sherman warned a friend in the South in 1860. Defeat of the South was inevitable, he told him, because "the North can make a steam engine, locomotive or railway car; hardly a yard of cloth or pair of shoes can you make. You are rushing into war with one of the most powerful, ingeniously mechanical and determined people on earth—right at your doors. You are bound to fail." That is a virtual prophecy of the industrial superiority which assisted the Allied victory in the Second World War. As Louis Simpson has said of one battle near Düsseldorf,

> For every shell Krupp fired,
> General Motors sent back four.

Implicit also in the Civil War was a future in which wars would largely cease to be wars of movement, like Napoleon's, and would become wars of attrition, like the Great War in Flanders and Picardy. Some of the trenches dug for the Civil War are virtually indistinguishable from those bespeaking the stalemate of 1914–1918.

But the Civil War was not really a "modern" war because the later twentieth-century technology of terror and destruction had not yet been devised. Crude forms of the machine gun did appear in the 1860s, and as the nineteenth century went on the products of Gatling, Maxim, and Browning became increasingly sophisticated and available, but the armies, conservative as always, at first seemed little interested in such novelties, preferring to remain with well-tried instruments like man and horse, rifle and bayonet and saber. There was even a sense that the use of the machine gun was rather unsporting. It was all right to try it out on rebellious natives in colonial Africa, but to aim it at gentlemen was not quite appropriate. Cavalry was real soldiering, and General Sir Douglas Haig, in the First World War, thought two machine guns per battalion more than sufficient. The machine gun expended ammunition so incontinently that ammunition supply became critical, and the supply forces in the rear had to grow larger than the fighting forces in the front. And because the machine gun tended to prevent troops, and horses, from crossing open ground safely, it made digging in, cowering in holes below the surface of the ground, inevitable. Once the machine gun achieved its vogue, the soldiers' entrenching shovel became a standard item of issue, and defenders paradoxically became more powerful than attackers. Defenders were strengthened in addition by another product of modern industry, barbed wire. An attacking force now had to expend almost as much artillery fire trying to destroy barbed wire as it had previously spent against human beings.

Because the machine gun counted for more than such former military virtues as "pluck" and "will," it operated as one of the mechanisms of the depersonalization which is the stigma of modern war. Now, you seldom even see the enemy, and it is that which makes the bombing of Dresden and Hiroshima psychologically easy. Diehard officers in early twentieth-century warfare felt suspicious of many more technological developments than the machine gun. Some disliked even the telephone, preferring to use runners bearing written orders and reports. Military technology was at first associated with plebeian vulgarity: it constituted a threat to chivalric and aristocratic usages, and it is this that kept the horse cavalry alive until the first years of the Second World War.

Just as deep entrenchment was one defense against the machine gun, another was the tank, a device developed by the British to protect men crossing ground under fire. At first the tank carried only its own machine guns, but soon, following the inexorable military axiom that with time and experience everything intensifies, it carried cannon as well. After thirty years of technological development, the tank, which once carried a

37 mm gun, hypertrophied to the 45-ton German Tiger of the Second World War, which mounted an 88 mm gun. And the gun of a recent Soviet model fires a shell of 125 mm (almost 5 inches). In the First World War several thousand tanks were produced. The Second World War brought forth around 250,000. In the year 1943 alone American assembly lines produced 21,000 Sherman heavy tanks. Technology constantly improved the tanks' power and effectiveness as radios were added for control and gyroscopes for steadying the gun despite movement over rough ground.

Modern technology would seem to have greatly increased the cruelty and viciousness of war, although actually it may be just as shocking to have your foot shot off by a solid cannonball as to have it blown off by a German *Schü* mine. Great things were hoped for from the development of poison gas, used first by the Germans in the Great War and soon aped by the British. But neither had expected winds to shift, and gas was finally abandoned as a major weapon because it tended to drift back on the side that deployed it, and not at all because it was considered an atrocity. The gas expedient devised by clever chemists in the First World War reappeared in the Zyklon-B the Germans used to kill Jews in the Second, and anyone recalling Du Pont's self-congratulatory slogan, "Better Things for Better Living Through Chemistry," can hardly resist a sardonic view of modern technology and its once attractive promises. Certainly such technological triumphs as anti-personnel mines and booby traps have added significantly to the miseries of modern war, not to mention flamethrowers which spew out napalm and incendiary aerial bombs and rockets which spread it over large areas. Anti-tank and anti-vehicle mines used to require pressure to set them off: now they can be detonated by radio, and from a distance.

The list of bellicose devices spawned by modern technology is virtually endless. It would include such naval accessories as magnetic mines and torpedoes and the degaussing apparatus to frustrate them, submarines and snorkels, radar and sonar and automatic fire controls, and such items as Hitler's V-1s and V-2s, hand-held recoilless artillery, infrared gun sights, defoliants, electronic devices for sensing an enemy's presence, proximity fuses, extensive "air mobility" (use of helicopters), and the ultimate contribution (so far) of technology, the hydrogen bomb. The relative inefficacy of many of these in the most recent of modern wars, the one against the restive peasants of Vietnam, suggests that modern technology has its distinct limits, as well as providing an occasion for ironic backfires—for example, the incident in the Persian Gulf where the United States Navy depended too naively on its advanced missile technology and too little on its courage and capacity for skepticism and good sense and shot down a civilian airliner.

But if technology has augmented the horror, at the same time it has

greatly improved the daily life of soldiers. Modern techniques of refriger-
ation and food preservation have largely eliminated the former military
staple of rotten meat. And technology has also mitigated some of the
agony. Modern anesthetics—first ether and chloroform, then sodium
pentathol—are an improvement on whiskey during amputations. Peni-
cillin and sulfanilimide and streptomycin have all but conquered that
time-honored military scourge, gas gangrene, and the use of aircraft for
removing wounded rapidly from the battlefield is an improvement on
litter-bearers and carts. Not to mention X-ray for locating metal fragments in human tissue: better than probing or guessing.

The air is of course an additional theater of belligerence opened up by
modern war, the clumsy Zeppelins and fragile fighters of 1914–1918
evolving into the supersonic nuclear bombers and radar-evading fighters
of the 1990s. Aerial bombing of civilians is now such a natural part of
modern war that no one any longer would think of wasting time debating its morality, as some people did even so recently as the Second
World War. Clearly "modern" also is aerial envelopment of an enemy
by means of paratroops or by infantry delivered by gliders, which can be
opposed by stout poles dug into the ground at close intervals. That
illustrates the point that every new weapon and device inspires a defense
against it. The machine gun created the tank, the tank the anti-tank
mine and the bazooka and the *Panzerfaust.* So the use of radar created
"Window," strips of metal foil thrown out of planes to confuse radar
sets. Aerial bombing created flak. And the aerial battlefield has brought
with it modern phenomena that would have been unthinkable earlier,
like the Japanese kamikaze suicide planes. Indeed, the totalitarian tradition of suicide following upon military defeat or disgrace or attending
fears of destruction must be designated "modern" as well. Contemporary history swarms with horrifying examples of a practice one had
thought defunct since the days of the ancient Romans and Hebrews: the
civilians on Okinawa who killed themselves to avoid capture by the
Americans; the self-destruction of German General von Kluge and Field
Marshal Rommel; even Leonard and Virginia Woolf, who provided
themselves with poison against an anticipated German invasion of Britain and a subsequent roundup and massacre of Jews. Not to mention the
suicidal, sacrificial Japanese defense of the Pacific islands, rendering obsolete such traditional military concepts as "tactics" and "maneuver." In
a truly modern war, suicide has become almost a weapon, and the cya-
nide capsule has become nearly as familiar as the hand grenade.

Modern also is the practice of "combined operations"—most notably,
amphibious landings on enemy beaches. The technique has been improved by repeated experience of disasters like Gallipoli and Dieppe, and
it is now clear that landings must be assisted by massive offshore bombardment, as in the landings at Salerno, Anzio, and Normandy in the

Second World War and at Inchon in the Korean War, and by virtually complete air superiority. But against defenders determined on suicide, even these don't guarantee easy victories, as such appalling battles as Tarawa, Peleliu, and Iwo Jima indicate. When Rommel used the word *modern* to modify *war,* he meant *armored,* but when his Allied enemies used the term they tended to imply *possessing air superiority,* which they had abundantly during the battle of Normandy and its sequels. Their modern element overcame Rommel's, forcing his tanks to move only at night and thus too slowly to mount a satisfactory armored defense. For another German general of the Second World War the concept *modern* implies an intelligent soldiery capable of independent thought and action. The Russian, says Major General F. W. von Mellenthin, makes an excellent soldier never to be underestimated, "even though," what with his habit of acting merely en masse, "somehow he does not quite fit into the picture of a modern war fought by modern soldiers."

"Force and fraud," said Thomas Hobbes, "are in war the two cardinal virtues." From the days of the Trojan horse, war has necessitated ruses, espionage, deceptions, misrepresentations, and other elements of fiction, and a modern war can be distinguished from others by the extent, depth, sophistication, and technological expertise of these operations. Since the First World War, propaganda has developed into an industry (a figure like Joseph Goebbels would hardly be thinkable before the days of radio), and a whole military and naval specialty, that of the public relations officer, has arisen to provide the "credit" required to motivate soldiers lacking any powerful ideological impulse, as well as to contrive the euphemisms demanded by the distant, respectable, and credulous civilian audience. Technology, especially the development of the computer, has been indispensable in cryptology, and in the Second World War, just as General Motors overcame Krupp, the Americans used their superior technology to read the coded messages conveyed by German military radio and to interpret the Japanese naval code. This last achievement made possible the murder of Admiral Yamamoto, the flight plan of whose plane in the South Pacific became available to American cryptanalysts. For all its brutality, modern war seems more "intellectual" than ever before, dependent on mathematics and the computer, and relying on language with all its well-known resources for projecting the nonliteral and the flagrantly untrue. "Modern" too is the convention of complex duplicity involved in "turning around" enemy spies by inviting them to trade their lives for misleading reports radioed back to their unsuspecting superiors. In addition, it's doubtful that in any period earlier than the Second World War technological capacities were such as to manufacture explosive animal droppings to be placed on remote roads used by enemy traffic.

The use of radio to convey military orders has had profound and eminently "modern" consequences on the self-respect and dignity of the high-ranking officer. Rapidity of communication tends to transform him from a self-reliant individual commander into a mere obeyer of orders received by radio. As Second World War German General Frido von Senger has written, "In modern war, a commander in the field, with his complete system of communications, is so much the executive agent for directives already received that he cannot claim the mantle of fame." Thus the outrage of German commanders at having to obey orders from the Führer that not an inch of ground was to be yielded—making maneuver and any display of real military talent impossible. Indeed, if radio had not been invented, the Germans might have done better in the Second World War. That sort of "totalitarian" obedience suggests the way modern wars, at least before the nuclear bomb gave new weight to the word *total,* tended to become totalitarian exercises that augmented the misery and multiplied the sacrifices. The Allies' insistence on "unconditional surrender," in its way surely a totalitarian demand, guaranteed that the war became total, with, on all sides, total conscription, total industrialization for war, and total propaganda, as well as total resistance by guerrillas in the Soviet Union, Yugoslavia—and Vietnam. Total war requires that such former subtleties as diplomacy and politics and even bribery yield to uncompromising, insensate, merely brutal power, making modern war an institution as damaging to thought and discrimination and judgment and criticism as it is to bodies and buildings, aircraft, ships, and landscapes.

The contributions of both cunning technology and the hysterias of runaway nationalism have added considerable irony to the formerly simple notions of "winning" and "losing" wars. As military historian Peter Young has observed, in twentieth-century wars "modern technology [has] combined with national ambitions to broaden the scope—and the expense—of conflict to a point where it could be almost as costly to win a war as it was to lose it, as the course of history in France after the First World War and in Britain after 1945 both demonstrate."

An ironic understanding like that is now inevitably an element and a consequence of modern wars, which seem to end without at all achieving their announced purpose or worse, achieve a purpose quite opposite to the one proposed. The First World War was said (by Woodrow Wilson) to be undertaken to make the world safe for democracy, but what it made the world safe for was Hitler. The Second World War, ostensibly begun to safeguard the independence of Poland, ended, after six years of brutality and destruction, in the delivery of Poland to the control of the Soviet Union.

This is to observe that in modern war as in few other contemporary phenomena there is a wide gap between actuality and the language invoked to describe it. One repeated motif in modern war writing, indeed, is the disclosure of the unpleasant actuality lurking beneath such popular euphemisms as *casualty, traumatic amputation, pacification, combat fatigue* (madness), and *collective indiscipline* (mutiny). In days when one's fighting was done by other people or entrusted to a special military caste, there was less occasion for the brutal truth-telling to which modern war writing aspires. For example, William Howard Russell of the London *Times* could describe with no one much the wiser the disastrous Charge of the Light Brigade this way: "They swept proudly past, glittering in the morning sun in all the pride and splendor of war." That whole heroic idiom must be accounted one of the main "casualties" of modern war. Too many people now have had personal experience of its falsity, although outright lies about armies and what they are for are still being told which the slightest acquaintance with human actuality will expose. A recent Soviet history of the Red Army, designed for schools, notes that when in 1918 the government decided that it would have to impose a military draft, "The working people, and especially the youth, enthusiastically welcomed the introduction of obligatory military service."

Modern war takes place within a context of cultural "modernism" and indeed is one of its causes. To the degree that conscripts become alienated from official culture, with its rationalizations and heroic fictions, they enact one of cultural modernism's main gestures, visible in such figures as Joyce, D. H. Lawrence, the early T. S. Eliot, Robert Graves, Pound, and W. C. Williams. A disillusion resembling that of soldiers who have fought is one of the most noticeable motifs in modernist culture, and so is the war between the generations—the older clinging to myths of idealism, the younger practiced in skepticism and proficient in rude plain-speaking. Another contribution of modern war to cultural modernism is its projection of the essential modernist anti-hero, the man things are done to or the person whose power of action is severely restricted. The victim of mass conscription and military discipline is a version of Kafka's Gregor Samsa, Hemingway's Jake Barnes, Eliot's Prufrock, or Beckett's Krapp. Although not all of these fought in modern war, heaven and similar comforts and certainties have been withdrawn from them, and they resemble the beat-up, "existential" troops Frederic Manning recalls in his novel about the First World War, *Her Privates We:*

> They turned from the wreckage and misery of life to an empty heaven, and from an empty heaven to the silence of their own hearts. They had been brought to the last extremity of hope, and yet they put their hands on each

other's shoulders and said . . . that it would be all right, though they had
faith in nothing, but in themselves and in each other.

Cultural modernism and its corollary, anti-military skepticism, have so
transformed former concepts of "the hero" that now it's hard not to
agree with Lionel Trilling's "test" for an attractive degree of "modernism" in a contemporary novel or play: "Do you want to be the hero? If
you do, the work is bad." Modern war also proposes the menacing environment from which modernist sensibilities are in flight: on the one
hand the battlefield, during and after the conflict, on the other Eliot's
Waste Land, Joyce's culturally ruined Dublin, Mauberley's cynically
philistine London, and the battered, useless Auden country:

> . . . damaged bridges, rotting wharves and choked canals,
> Tramlines buckled, smashed trucks lying on their side across the rails;
> . . . Pylons fallen or subsiding, trailing dead high-tension wires,

and the vacant scene of Beckett's *Waiting for Godot*. But the most
pervasive contribution of modern war to modernist culture is irony,
widely perceived to be, as Monroe Engel has pointed out, the "norma-
tive mentality" of modern art, just as it is the expected tone in modern
war writing.

One element of modernist culture that makes modern war so much
harder to bear than earlier wars is the attenuation of religious belief since
the nineteenth century. The warrior could once solace himself with the
conviction that his death, painful as it might be, was merely a passage
into a glorious afterlife or Valhalla, where he would be reunited with his
forebears and recently deceased loved ones. No such comfort for most
modern troops, destined to struggle until relieved by wounds or a death
which promises only a black oblivion. Thus modern attitudes have con-
spired with modern technology to make modern war more ghastly than
the wars of the past.

In addition, to fight a war conscious of all the modern arguments for
pacifism, international control of violence, and decent social behavior is
to fight with a painful ironic consciousness little known to soldiers a
couple of centuries ago. If soldiers have not always been literate, in the
modern period they certainly have been, and one notable characteristic
of modern war is that the troops have had access to the appropriate
anti-war books—films too, of course. Thus the psychological conflicts
unique to modern soldiering. For the intelligent, sensitive, and highly
literate especially, each modern war becomes harder to fight than the
one before because of the constant augmentation of anti-war writing.
The soldiers of the First World War had at the outset very little writing
to inform them how vile war is, although gradually Siegfried Sassoon and

Wilfred Owen revealed some of the actuality. Such writings, together with later prose exposés of the war like Graves's *Good-bye to All That,* Hemingway's *A Farewell to Arms,* and Remarque's *All Quiet on the Western Front,* were available in 1939 to disenchant the troops just entering on the Second World War. And those sent to Vietnam could discover before arrival what war was like by consulting Second World War classics like Kurt Vonnegut's *Slaughterhouse-Five* and Joseph Heller's *Catch-22.* In the same way, the innocents waiting offstage for service in some future Vietnam can now instruct themselves and make their task harder by adding to all those monitory texts' accounts of criminality and madness by Seymour Hersh, John Ketwig, and Michael Herr.

No government is happy to have the actualities of modern war disclosed, aware that recruiting and conscription are the more threatened the more modern war writing focuses on blown-off legs and arms and stupid orders and belly wounds and mistaken "political" purposes. All governments impose, or try to impose, some form of censorship in wartime, but censorship cannot be imposed forever, and finally the truth will leak out. Thus, if modern war is a catastrophe for humanity in general, because of writers who will not be silenced it represents a triumph, ironic to be sure, for the civilized principles of impassioned free expression, as the selections in this book suggest.

The drift of modern history seems to imply that the power of the human mind to learn principles of humane restraint and reform from modern wars is extremely limited. What people learn from wars seems to be this: the techniques for making each increasingly efficient—that is, destructive and vicious. Or one learns merely what the cartoonist Bill Mauldin has learned, who says: "One of the startling things you learn in wars is how much blood can come from a human body." But those are adept students of war who learn what Ernest Hemingway learned from his lifetime of observing men at war: "Never think that war, no matter how necessary, nor how justified, is not a crime."

Part I

The First World War

"Never Such Innocence Again"

Although many of its usages now seem archaic to the point of quaintness, the First World War (called the Great War or simply The War until the outbreak of the Second necessitated a name-change) remains the prototype of modern wars. For one thing, it killed and wounded a great many people, over 37 million of them, in fact, more than three times the population of the state of Pennsylvania. It was also the first to make significant use of machine guns, and by the tens of thousands, as well as to feature barbed wire, steel helmets, tanks and flamethrowers, poison gas and gas masks, and fighter planes and aerial bombardment (1,413 people were killed in Zeppelin raids over England), and it was the first war to use the telephone to convey reports from the front lines to the rear and orders from the rear to the front, making possible the very "modern" assumption—i.e., skeptical and adversarial—that the staff doesn't know what's going on. This war also established unevadable conscription as the national means for waging war with mass armies, thus providing civilians with a novel insight, formerly limited to the military, into the experience of socially sanctioned murder. The result was a literature of shock and outrage, a product of horror impinging on optimism and innocence.

"Never such innocence again," writes Philip Larkin. He is thinking of the rush to the British recruiting stations in August 1914. England had not been in a major war for a century, and people were unaware of the potential effects of industrialism on an activity conceived largely in terms of cavalry, chivalry, and "honor." Most British and French expected the war to be over by Christmas 1914, and the men in the training camps were anxious to do their bit with enthusiasm and "pep." The novelty of escaping offices and classrooms for tents in the field and a boyish life of athleticism and good fellowship was a heady experience, and as Rupert Brooke stressed in his famous sonnet "Peace," at the outset the war seemed to offer an invigorating flight from a tired, cynical society. "I adore war," wrote the young poet Julian Grenfell. "It's like a big picnic. . . . I've never been so well or happy." He went on to write about "joy of battle," but in 1915 he was killed at Ypres. In her poem

"Flower of Youth" Katharine Tynan sought optimistic solace in the idea
that the war was making heaven a more wholesome and cheerful place,
populating it now with clean and laughing lads.

At the beginning there was a great flux of social idealism. The Hun
was to be severely punished for overrunning poor little Belgium, and
Europe was to be redeemed from selfishness, cunning, and arbitrary
force. As C. E. Montague remembered, "All the air was ringing with
rousing assurances. France to be saved, Belgium righted, freedom and
civilization rewon, a sour, soiled, crooked old world to be rid of bullies
and crooks and reclaimed for straightness, decency, good-nature. . . .
What a chance!" At the training camps

> real, constitutional lazy fellows would buy little cram-books of drill out of
> their pay and sweat them up at night so as to get on the faster. Men warned
> for a guard next day would agree among themselves to get up an hour
> before the pre-dawn winter Réveillé to practice among themselves the
> beautiful symbolic ritual of mounting guard in the hope of approaching the
> far-off, longed-for ideal of smartness, the passport to France.

Montague's words appear in his book significantly titled *Disenchantment*—published four years after the war. Those who had once been
enchanted were now either dead, maimed, insane, or cynical. "The generous youth of the war . . . was pretty well gone. . . .The authentic flame
. . . was as dead as the half-million of good fellows whom it had fired four
years ago, whose credulous hearts the maggots were now eating under so
many shining and streaming square miles of wet Flanders and Picardy."

It had all begun in June 1914, when Archduke Francis Ferdinand,
heir to the throne of Austria-Hungary, was assassinated in Sarajevo,
Bosnia-Herzogovina, by a Serbian patriot fed up with Austrian domi-
nation of his country. Austria-Hungary used the occasion to pick a long-
desired quarrel with Serbia and to issue an ultimatum that could only
produce war. At this point the system of European alliances, negotiated
over many decades, had to be honored: Russia came to the aid of Serbia,
whereupon Germany jumped in on the side of Austria-Hungary. France
then honored her treaty with Russia, Britain hers with France. By October 1914, Turkey had joined the side of Germany and Austria-Hungary
(the "Central Powers"). By the end of the year the notorious trench
system was emplaced in Belgium and France, running 400 miles from its
northern anchor at the North Sea to its southern end at the Swiss border,
while in the east, another front developed along the Russian border with
Austria-Hungary. Italy came in on the side of the Allies in 1915, opening
a front against Austria. And in April 1917, the United States, exasperated by German sinking of its ships, joined the Allies, although it
took many months for an American army to be assembled, supplied,

trained, shipped to Europe, and installed in the line. The Americans arrived so late in the war that although they fought impressively and were generally credited with supplying the needed weight to win the war, they suffered only about one-tenth the casualties of the British, and more American soldiers died from influenza than from gas and bullets and shells.

Stalemate and *attrition* are terms inseparable from the memory of the First World War. Because massed, quick-firing artillery and machine guns employed by the thousands gave the defense an unprecedented advantage, both the Allies and the Central Powers found themselves virtual prisoners of their trenches for months on end. Indeed, from the winter of 1914 until the spring of 1918, the trench system seemed fixed, moving now and then a few hundred yards forward or back, on great occasions moving as much as a few miles. Theoretically it would have been possible to walk from the North Sea beaches all the way to the Alps entirely below ground, but actually the trench system was not absolutely continuous. It was broken here and there, with mere shell holes or fortified strong points serving as connecting links. A little more than half the Allied line was occupied by the French. The rest was British, consisting of about 800 battalions of some 1,000 men each. The two main concentrations of Allied strength were the Ypres Salient in Flanders and the Somme area in Picardy. These are the places most often recalled in these selections.

Ideally, there were three parallel lines of trenches facing the enemy, with the front-line trench fifty yards to a mile or so from its hostile counterpart across the way. Several yards behind the front-line trench was the support trench, and several yards behind that the reserve. These were "firing" trenches, connected by communication trenches running perpendicular. "Saps," shallower trenches, ran out into No Man's Land, giving access to forward observation and listening posts, as well as grenade ("bomb") throwing positions and machine gun nests. Coming up to the trenches from the rear, you might walk in a communication trench a mile or more long. It often began in a town and gradually deepened, and by the time it reached the reserve trench it would be eight feet deep. Into the sides of the trenches were dug "funk holes," where one or two men would crouch when shelling became particularly heavy. There were also deep dugouts, reached by crude stairways, used as officers' quarters and command posts. The floor of a well-constructed trench was covered with wooden duckboards because the bottom of a trench was usually wet and the walls, always crumbling, had to be reinforced by sandbags, corrugated iron, or bundles of reeds. A trench was protected on the enemy side by copious entanglements of barbed wire, placed far enough out to prevent the enemy's crawling up to grenade-throwing range. The normal way of using the trenches was for a unit to occupy the front trench for a week or so, then, replaced by fresh men from the rear, to move back to the support trench, and so, after another week, to the reserve. Then perhaps a few days in a battered town way back, and then the sequence all over again.

British optimism and complacency guaranteed that their trenches were especially miserable. As one soldier explained,

> The whole conduct of our trench warfare seemed to be based on the concept that we, the British, were not stopping in the trenches for long, but were tarrying a while on the way to Berlin and that very soon we would be chasing Jerry across country. The result, in the long term, meant that we lived a mean and impoverished sort of existence in lousy scratch holes.

And *lousy* there is literal. The men's hair and clothing bred colonies of lice, which the delousing stations and baths behind the line, used when the troops were at rest, repressed only temporarily. The trenches also harbored millions of rats, which fed largely on the flesh of corpses. The stench of rotting meat was everywhere, and you could smell the front lines miles before you reached them. Remedies for this unpleasantness were offered by the British instructions for military hygiene, issued after the war had been in progress a while:

> *Treatment of Bodies Exposed in the Open which cannot be Buried or Cremated.* —Bodies in a state of putrefaction lying out in advance of the trenches which cannot be buried or cremated owing to hostile fire, or bodies uncovered in parapets of trenches where they have been hastily buried, often give rise to considerable nuisance. They should be dealt with in the following manner:—(i) *Bodies in the Open.* —Deodorants will be found useful. The bodies may be sprayed with solution C, and if sufficient time is available the clothes should be ripped up so that the solution may be applied to the whole body, particularly in the region of the abdomen, or the bodies can be covered with quick-lime. . . .
> (ii) *Bodies in Walls of Trenches, &c.* —Dead bodies and remains of animals in the sides and walls of trenches, mine craters, &c., . . . should be treated with chloride of lime, quick-lime, or sprayed with oresol or solution C and then isolated either by means of boarding filled in with earth and chloride of lime or by sand bags soaked in heavy petroleum oil.

A day in a front-line trench, amid such phenomena as bodies sprayed with solution C, began about an hour before first light—say, 4:30. This was the moment for the invariable ritual of morning stand-to, when everyone stared across No Man's Land, weapon ready, and prepared to repel attack. After the dawn danger had passed, the men stood down and prepared breakfast in small groups, frying bacon and heating tea over small, preferably smokeless fires. In British trenches the daily rum ration of about two tablespoonful was then doled out to each man. Before attacking, when the troops would have to climb out of the trench on ladders and cross No Man's Land, larger doses would be vouchsafed. One medical officer deposed after the war was over, "Had it not been for the rum ration I do not think we should have won the war."

During the day everyone stayed below the top of the trench and cleaned weapons or repaired those parts of the trench damaged by the night's artillery fire. But when nighttime came the real work began. Wiring parties went out in front to repair the wire and to install new entanglements. Digging parties went forward in saps to extend them. Carrying parties negotiated the communication trenches, bringing up rations and ammunition and mail. All this night work was likely to be illuminated suddenly by enemy flares, and it was often interrupted by machine-gun and artillery fire. The British trenches, where this murderous parody of the normal world of "work" was going on, were just seventy miles from London, and the absurd proximity of the wartime existence to real life was ironic and poignant, for one could breakfast in the trenches and be back in London for dinner in the evening, and not just dinner but dinner at a classy setting like one's club or the Café Royal. One officer, returned to the trenches after an evening spent at a London musical show with his wife, commented: "Christ! . . . I was at *Chu Chin Chow* last night with my wife. Hard to believe, isn't it? Hard to believe. Impossible to believe. That other life, so near in time and distance, was something led by different men. Two lives that bore no relation to each other."

But now and then trench routine would be dramatically violated by an attempt at a large-scale advance. Most of these proved futile and disastrous, none more so than the battle of the Somme, which the British fought from July to November 1916. Planned meticulously for over six months—new railway lines were laid, masses of ammunition and supplies were laid in, a seven-to-one superiority in troops was assured, the German lines were deluged with a full week's artillery fire from over 1,500 guns—the Somme attack had every reason to succeed. At 7:30 on the morning of July 1, 1916, the attacking waves of eleven British divisions left their trenches and, filled with hope, began walking, their rifles at port arms, toward the German trenches. A minute later the machine-gun units of the six German divisions facing them carried their weapons upstairs from their deep dugouts and simply hosed down the attackers. One astonished German machine-gunner recalled, "We were very surprised to see them walking. We had never seen that before. . . . When we started firing we just had to load and reload. They went down in their hundreds. You didn't have to aim, we just fired into them." Of the 110,000 who attacked, 60,000 were killed or wounded before the day was over. More than 20,000 lay dead between the lines, and it was days before the wounded in No Man's Land stopped crying out. The failure of the attack seemed to encapsulate all the bizarre anomalies and frustrations of the First World War. Trying to make sense of the events of July 1, 1916, Edmund Blunden concluded that the stalemate was hopeless, the war ridiculously static, triumphal breakthrough impossible. "By the end of the day," he wrote, "both sides had seen, in a sad scrawl of broken earth and murdered men, the answer to the question. No road. No thoroughfare. Neither race had won, nor could win, the War. The War had won, and would go on winning."

This sense of despair verging on the absurd became the dominant tone of the writing that emerged from the First World War. Among the troops, hatred for the kept and censored press was widespread, fueling anger that their friends and families at home had little idea of the horrors being enacted in their name. In public rhetoric like sermons and editorials, terms like *gallant, steed,* and *warrior* were still to be heard. The war was being mediated through the language of a dead chivalry rather than that of the new industrialized murder. "Pluck" was now irrelevant: the artillery shell found you whether you were brave or cowardly, and no amount of courage or swank kept the machine-gun bullet from going through you.

Of all writers, it can be assumed that poets are especially sensitive to the adequacy of language to register honest experience, and it was the poets of the Great War who protested most effectively against human debasement and verbal fraud. Perceiving that the protest on behalf of sense and humanity was largely the work of poets, Hemingway has reasoned that "poets are not arrested as quickly as prose writers would be if they wrote critically." Indeed, among the untutored, who may have dimly remembered the reputations of such as Oscar Wilde, Ernest Dowson, and Algernon Charles Swinburne, poets were regarded as dreamy, if not hopelessly effeminate or half-mad. When the young infantry officers Robert Graves and Siegfried Sassoon wanted to meet and talk about the poems they were writing, they did so secretly, since discussing such stuff was considered "a disgrace to the battalion." One reason Sassoon performed so bravely at the front, according to Arnold Bennett, was that he was "jealous for the military reputation of poets."

But to be effective as protest, poetry must be read, and by large numbers of people. The soldier poets of the First World War happened to write at a moment remarkably favorable to both the writing and reading of poetry. Both they and readers who were sophisticated assumed that major public awareness could find a lodging in lyric poetry. There was deep respect for literature in those days, and it was this respect that invited these young trench-horrified privates and junior officers like Isaac Rosenberg, Ivor Gurney, and Sassoon to couch their views of the war not in journalism, polemic pamphlets, or works of exposition and argument, but in poems.

And it's notable that while others, like Eliot and Pound and Joyce, were writing "experimentally," the poets of the First World War tended to write in a traditional style. An example is the way Wilfred Owen proceeds in his famous *"Dulce et Decorum Est."* What one encounters in the poem—the soldier choking to death in a gas attack, exhibited by Owen to shock some sentimental and ignorant stay-at-home "friend"— is so compelling and "modern" (in the nasty way) that it's easy to overlook the poem's nonmodern form. Owen writes it not in any novel style as a correlative of the novel message but in quite standard iambic-pentameter lines arranged in formal quatrains. Owen seems to eschew bolder modernisms because he wants desperately to communicate—not his technical cleverness but his point, and he knew he had to reach that well-bred literary audience he wanted to shock into a new understanding. These readers respected the appearance of order in poetry, and to convey news of disorder and scandal, he had to remain within a formal technique bespeaking traditional ideas of order. Indeed, a large part of the ironic effect of First World War poems, those dwelling on meaningless slaughters, fatuous errors, and appalling mess and hopelessness, results from their being conducted with so high a regard for order. Collapsing so seldom into the hysteria one might think appropriate, they remain conventional in means, and their conventionality doubly emphasizes the awfulness of what they convey. The British social habit of understatement was luckily available to suggest the method. It's curious that the anxieties of the trenches impelled the poets toward an apparently retrograde formalism, while safely at home, far from the carnage, Edgar Lee Masters, Hilda Doolittle, and Carl Sandburg were practicing writing poems without rhyme or meter, William Carlos Williams was freeing himself from inherited poetic forms, and Ezra Pound was finding rhyme largely irrelevant to the task of the *Cantos.* Front-line mess and trauma seem to invite a compensatory reliance on form as a buttress.

Familiar by now, so familiar as to have attained the status of an instructive insight applicable to all modern wars, is the ironic "plot" described by events and emotions from 1914 to 1918. If the war began in jubilation and innocence, an ironic reversal to horror and disillusion was triggered first by the misadventure of Gallipoli, then by the battle of the Somme, and then by the battle of Passchendaele. As Joseph Cohen has noted in his biography of Isaac Rosenberg, Rupert Brooke's death in 1915 could serve as an emblem of "the brave sacrifices of the young," but three years later, Rosenberg's death—on April Fool's Day 1918— became the symbol of the futility of such sacrifices. As late as 1917, Edmund Blunden recalled,

> there were still . . . poets who kept something of the idealism of 1914 in their outlook and their poems. But [1917] was the Passchendaele year, and to me it seems that the Passchendaele drive was murder—not only to the

troops but to their singing faiths and hopes. From then on the voice of those who found strength and interval enough merely for penning their visions was generally a cry.

In July 1917, Siegfried Sassoon issued his famous public statement in which he declared his refusal to serve any longer in the brutal, purposeless shambles the war had become. A month earlier, T. S. Eliot had sent the *Nation* "a letter lately received from a young officer . . . [who] entered the army directly from a Public School and began his service in the trenches before he was nineteen." The young officer, angry because no one at home seems sufficiently aware of the realities of the front, offers civilians

> a picture of a leprous earth, scattered with the swollen and blackened corpses of hundreds of young men. The appalling stench of rotting carrion. . . . Mud like porridge, trenches like shallow and sloping cracks in the porridge—porridge that stinks in the sun. Swarms of flies and bluebottles clustering on pits of offal. Wounded men lying in the shell holes among the decaying corpses: helpless under the scorching sun and bitter nights, under repeated shelling. Men with bowels dropping out, lungs shot away, with blinded, smashed faces, or limbs blown into space. Men screaming and gibbering. Wounded men hanging in agony on the barbed wire, until a friendly spout of liquid fire shrivels them up like a fly in a candle.

"But these are only words," says the young officer, "and probably convey only a fraction of their meaning to the hearers. They shudder, and it is forgotten."

When the war finally ended, Sassoon, watching the hysterical flag-waving crowds celebrating in London, said: "It is a loathsome ending to the loathsome tragedy of the last four years." Sensitive observers knew now that winning is losing, and that "victory" is now as archaic a myth as "valor," and both as hollow as "glory." When four years after the Armistice the Treaty of Versailles was signed, Vera Brittain, whose brother and fiancé were both destroyed in France, couldn't even bring herself to read the text. As she says, "I was beginning already to suspect that my generation had been deceived, its young courage cynically exploited, its idealism betrayed, and I did not want to know the details of that betrayal." Sensing that the treaty simply invited a renewed war ("It is not peace," said Ferdinand Foch, "it is an armistice for twenty years"), Vera Brittain threw herself into pacifist agitation and saw her prophecies of nonsensical disaster fulfilled when the Second World War broke out in 1939.

RUPERT BROOKE
1887 – 1915

Educated at Rugby and Cambridge, Brooke traveled in the United States and the South Seas and became the darling of stylish British literary society. When the war broke out he enlisted in the Royal Naval Division and was about to go ashore at Gallipoli when he died of blood poisoning. His group of five sonnets titled 1914 (of which this is the first) were wildly popular at the beginning of the war.

PEACE
(1914)

Now, God be thanked Who has matched us with His hour,
    And caught our youth, and wakened us from sleeping,
With hand made sure, clear eye, and sharpened power,
    To turn, as swimmers into cleanness leaping,

Glad from a world grown old and cold and weary,
    Leave the sick hearts that honour could not move,
And half-men, and their dirty songs and dreary,
    And all the little emptiness of love!

Oh! we, who have known shame, we have found release there,
    Where there's no ill, no grief, but sleep has mending,
      Naught broken save this body, lost but breath;
Nothing to shake the laughing heart's long peace there
    But only agony, and that has ending;
      And the worst friend and enemy is but Death.

PHILIP LARKIN
1922–1985

Larkin was born in Coventry, went to Oxford, and became the librarian of the University of Hull. He published this poem in 1964.

MCMXIV

Those long uneven lines
Standing as patiently
As if they were stretched outside
The Oval or Villa Park,
The crowns of hats, the sun
On moustached archaic faces
Grinning as if it were all
An August Bank Holiday lark;

And the shut shops, the bleached
Established names on the sunblinds,
The farthings and sovereigns,
And dark-clothed children at play
Called after kings and queens,
The tin advertisements
For cocoa and twist, and the pubs
Wide open all day;

And the countryside not caring:
The place-names all hazed over
With flowering grasses, and fields
Shadowing Domesday lines
Under wheat's restless silence;
The differently-dressed servants

With tiny rooms in huge houses,
The dust behind limousines;

Never such innocence,
Never before or since,
As changed itself to past
Without a word—the men
Leaving the gardens tidy,
The thousands of marriages
Lasting a little while longer:
Never such innocence again.

A. E. HOUSMAN
1859–1936

Housman celebrated the professional British soldiers killed in the first months of the war, before conscription.

Epitaph on an Army of Mercenaries

These, in the day when heaven was falling,
   The hour when earth's foundations fled,
Followed their mercenary calling
   And took their wages and are dead.

Their shoulders held the sky suspended;
   They stood, and earth's foundations stay;
What God abandoned, these defended,
   And saved the sum of things for pay.

HUGH MACDIARMID
1892-1978

MacDiarmid, pen-name of the Scottish nationalist, Marxist, and Anglo-phobe Christopher M. Grieve, took up Housman's challenge.

ANOTHER EPITAPH ON AN ARMY OF MERCENARIES

It is a God-damned lie to say that these
Saved, or knew, anything worth any man's pride.
They were professional murderers and they took
Their blood money and impious risks and died.
In spite of all their kind some elements of worth
With difficulty persist here and there on earth.

R. A. SCOTT MACFIE
1868-?

Macfie was in his mid-forties when he served in France with the Liverpool Scottish Regiment, winning the Military Medal and rising to the rank of Regimental Quartermaster Sergeant.

To His Father

Wed. 23 Dec. 1914

My dear Father,

Before I forget I had better mention that some of my recent letters have not been posted on the day when they were written. Generally I have no time for writing until we are on the point of marching off, & then it is too late to hand letters to the censor.

We have had a very unfortunate day and I can only congratulate myself that I have got through with nothing worse than very wet and dirty clothes and curiously swelled but painless hands. We left our muddy farm at one o'clock on Monday to march to the trenches, about six or seven miles away, it being E & F Co.'s turn to go in the front firing line. We are none of us particularly well, and the whole battalion is weakened by an epidemic of diarrhoea which has been going on for several weeks. The roads were pretty bad, and as we went a pitiable number of men dropped out, unable to keep up. Among them were both my clerk and my batman, & I am now without assistance. I don't even know what has become of them.

To reach the trenches we had to end our march by a long walk across incredibly muddy fields, worked into a deep viscous sea of slime by the constant passing of troops. I was wearing new boots without nails, and my first misfortune was to fall into a deep ditch full of water, right up to the waist. A little later I tumbled on my face in the deep slime, and with a heavy pack on my back, containing two days' rations in addition to my ordinary property, had some difficulty in extricating myself and regaining my balance.

The trenches turned out to be very difficult to approach even in the dark, and unfortunately there was a small but brilliantly bright moon. To reach them we had to cross a very muddy field, studded with the pits shells make on explosion, pass through a gate into another field and cross it under still closer and heavier fire. At the gate the mud was 18 ins. to 2 ft. deep and so sticky that it was difficult to get one's feet out, and men who fell (as many, including myself, did) had a hard struggle to regain an upright position even with assistance.

It was pretty obvious that the way to get into the trenches was to creep in as silently as possible and hope to escape the notice of the Germans, who were only 50 to 100 yards away. We were relieving a regular battalion, and their officers spoiled everything by making the first arrivals from among our men fire as fast as they could. This of course gave the game away, magnesium rockets galore went up, & a fusilade of bullets raked the area we had to cross.

My place is in the rear of the company—the last man of all. There was, of course a check at the gate and a number of men in front of me foolishly bunched themselves together in a group. Suddenly a man rolled over on the ground moaning: "My back, my back!" All the men threw themselves flat on the muddy ground, huddled in a disorderly heap. There were shell-pits full of water on each side and I could not get the men to make room for me to walk through, so I walked over the top of them. An F Co. man, member of the maxim gun team had been badly wounded in the back, apparently by an explosive bullet. While reporting the casualty at a "dug out" close by, where our officers were waiting, one of my own men was brought in similarly wounded. It was impossible to carry him, the stretchers were not with us, so they simply had to drag the poor fellow sliding over the mud. You can imagine the condition in which he arrived. It was no joke being wounded there.

One of my serjeants passed, with a bandage round his head, slightly wounded and seeking the way to the dressing station a couple of miles away.

When all the men had passed the gate the last officer and I crossed the field together. Of course I fell into a small ditch and increased again the thickness of the layer of clay that covered me, and then tripped over some loose barbed wire and made matters still worse.

There was a communicating trench from the gate to the firing trenches through which we should have been able to walk under cover. But, for want of a small pump or a simple drain, it was quite full of water. So was the first section of the firing trench, but the second bit was separated from it by a clay dam and contained only a few inches of water and mud which we baled out the next day.

They were trenches which had been made by, and taken from, the Germans. My end the left was not bad, though the parapet, made of wet clay, allowed bullets to pass pretty freely. However, we were able to make it comparatively dry and habitable when dawn came, and if we had had materials for a fire it might have become almost comfortable though it was too small to stretch oneself in at full length. Further up the trenches were dreadfully bad—uncomfortable and insecure. Some were far too shallow, so that the men had to lie down to obtain cover; others had a foot or 18 ins. of water in them; in others dead and decaying bodies had been used in building the walls. We had plenty of rum and jars of cold tea, as well as the provisions we carried in our valises, but it was impossible to send them to some of the men after daybreak—difficult even at night.

Soon messages came in that other casualties had resulted while entering the trenches. Vance, a recently promoted lance corporal, killed; an F Co. piper badly wounded; Beach, one of my men shot through the knee; etc. The stretcher-bearers arrived and I challenged them: "Halt, who goes there?"—"Liverpool Scottish stretcher-bearers"—"Is Faulkner there?"—"No"—"Citrine?"—"Yes"—"How are you doing Citrine?" "Fine, Colours!" Citrine was the sole euphonium player in the band, a good man. He wanted to go out as an ordinary private but, being intelligent, the doctor had persuaded him to be a stretcher bearer. Fifteen minutes later, they returned past me. "Well, who have you got?"— "Citrine, shot dead." It gave me a great shock.

I wanted to go up the lines to see if anything could be done for the other wounded, but the officers near me refused permission because there had been already casualties enough. I asked leave to go to headquarters or to a telephone station to try to get a stretcher to take away the wounded piper. They allowed me to go back to the gate of the field, near which were "dug outs" in which our maxim gun was kept in reserve. I reached it after falling, as usual, three times and wallowing in the mud. Luckily there was a telephone. The stretcher bearers were sent for and arrived some time before dawn. The officer refused to allow them to proceed because it was too late. The poor piper died of bleeding & exposure during the forenoon, in a trench full of water, and without anything to eat or drink, and another wounded man had to lie on his corpse. It was all rather ghastly.

We were supposed to stay in at least 2, and possibly 3 days, and at my end where we were fairly comfortable and not in serious danger, we felt fit for it. But at the other end the conditions were worse, and the officer in charge sent down messages that his men could not possibly stand another night. Arrangements were therefore made to relieve us at 1 to 2 A.M. (we were in for about 30 hours).

The Germans were waiting their opportunity, and from dusk onwards sent up periodical magnesium rockets to catch us during the change. By great care and good luck it was effected almost without their knowledge. We got out, and the others got in, with only a small addition to our casualty list. One of my serjeants was wounded in the foot, several men were scratched, etc. The total cost of this unfortunate day to us is not yet known: 4 men are certainly killed, and 8 or 9 seriously wounded. In addition we shall have a lot of rheumatism and illness. That all our clothes are soaked, that we shall not have an opportunity of drying them for weeks, that half our equipment is lost, our rifles clogged with mud, etc., is not counted seriously. Deficiencies can be indented for and replaced, and if we get rheumatism from wet boots and kilts there is a doctor to send us to hospital.

There will not be much left of the Liverpool Scottish soon. About 120–130 left the farm, belonging to the double company E & F and representing 240 who came to France. A dozen dropped out on the road, another dozen were killed and wounded and the billet in which we slept last night is now full of sick men. I do not think there are 50 men left in

E Co., and it is amazing to me that I am among the survivors considering my age, infirmities, and general want of muscular power.

Your affectionate Son
R. A. Scott Macfie

KATHARINE TYNAN
1861–1931

Active with William Butler Yeats in the Irish literary revival, Tynan published this poem in the Spectator *on December 26, 1914. The Bishop of London quoted it often in his wartime sermons.*

FLOWER OF YOUTH

Lest Heaven be thronged with grey-beards hoary,
    God, who made boys for His delight,
Stoops in a day of grief and glory
    And calls them in, in from the night.

Heaven's thronged with gay and careless faces,
    New-waked from dreams of dreadful things,
They walk in green and pleasant places
    And by the crystal water-springs.

Dear boys! They shall be young forever:
God who made boys so clean and good
Smiles with the eyes of fatherhood.

Now Heaven is by the young invaded;
    Their laughter's in the House of God.
Stainless and simple as He made it,
    God keeps the heart o' the boy unflawed.

W. N. HODGSON
1893–1916

*Hodgson was moved to enlist because he'd read one of Rupert Brooke's
1914 sonnets. He won a commission and ultimately the Military Cross.
He wrote this poem two days before he was killed at the jump-off on the
Somme, July 1, 1916.*

BEFORE ACTION

By all the glories of the day
   And the cool evening's benison,
By that last sunset touch that lay
   Upon the hills when day was done,
By beauty lavishly outpoured
   And blessings carelessly received,
By all the days that I have lived
   Make me a soldier, Lord.

By all of man's hopes and fears,
   And all the wonders poets sing,
The laughter of unclouded years,
   And every sad and lovely thing;
By the romantic ages stored
   With high endeavour that was his,
By all his mad catastrophes
   Make me a man, O Lord.

I, that on my familiar hill
   Saw with uncomprehending eyes
A hundred of Thy sunsets spill
   Their fresh and sanguine sacrifice,

Ere the sun swings his noonday sword
Must say goodbye to all of this; —
By all delights that I shall miss,
Help me to die, O Lord.

DANIEL J. SWEENEY

Private Daniel J. Sweeney took part in the battle of the Somme, which he described for his fiancée, Ivy Williams.

To Ivy Williams

Pte D. J. Sweeney
8081 D Coy
1st Lincoln Regt
B.E.F.

My Dearest Ivy

I am still alive and kicking also I am as happy as anybody out here, but so hungry but that cannot be helped. Well darling I expect by now you know all about the great battle. I told you when I was at home it would only be a few weeks but I am glad to say that the date of the attack was kept a secret until the very last minute also there were very few men out here who knew at what time we were to charge the Germans, that being kept a secret has meant this success. I am sure. Well dearest I know that you would like to know all about this Great Battle and I will tell you what I know and saw of this murder. I think I am allowed to tell you but it will be a truer storey than what you have read in the papers at least I think so. (I have not seen any papers for two weeks now)

Well dear on the 20 of June my Regt. were ordered to proceed into the trenches for how long we did not know. Well everything went fairly well until midnight of the 24. I was one of a party of men who were to go out with an officer (who is dead now I believe) to go over to the German lines and try and find out how strong they were and if possible try and spring a surprise bomb attack on them, but just as we were going to start we received orders that the Great Bombardment was going to start that night so that was cancelled. Well our artillery and trench mortars started and so did Fritz's artillery he did get the wind up he sent all his shells into our trenches and at last he stopped but we still carried on up to 4 o ck. of the morning of the 25th June then our trench mortars stopped and the artillery fired a few shells every now and again. Well Fritz began to puzzle us as he only fired a very few rounds that day. Well I have nothing of interest to say of rest of the day but just as it was getting dark the R. Engineers came into our trenches and uncovered the gass cilinders which we had brought into the trench a few days before and they began to fix the pipes into them. At 11 ock that night our artillery started and so did our gas (we had our gas helmets on) then when the gas started and had gone as far as it is to go before we attack then our artillery stopped but as soon as we stopped old Fritz's artillery opened out THINKING that we were attacking but we were not, we were all under what cover we could get, of course we had a few wounded and killed but that could not be helped as he was sending some very big shells over. Well everything quietened down about 3.30 A.M. On the 26th the remainder of the day was not so noisy, that night we kept him awake but his artillery did not retalliate much. Well the morning of the 27th came and the boys of my regiment also myself were beginning to feel the strain as this was our 7th day in the trenches well there were no signs of us getting relieved so we had to stick it. That night 27th Lieut. Kirk, the best officer we had in this coy called for volunteers to go with him over to see Fritz and to see what damage our artillery had done. Well every man in the coy would follow this officer anywhere but he only took ten of us, they always expect us Regulars to go on these "trips" as we are experts or supposed to be experts at the game. Well we took 8 bombs each and got on top of our trenches in line and a pice of string running from the left hand man up to the right so as we would not get in front of each other, well we crawled up to what was once barbed wire but now it was only little bits (and well we knew it as our hands were torn to pices with it, but that was nothing. Well the officer pulled the string that was the order for us to lie still while he went forward, he came back and we crawled on a little further and at last got very near looking into his trenches we could not see much but I received an awful shock which nearly made me give the show away—I heard someone in the trench and I saw him put his hand on the top of the trench and then bang and a flash that nearly blinded me—this is what happened—the man was a German Officer and at night each side fire a sort of rocket up into the air out of a pistol and it bursts into flame and shows all the "no man's land" up. I did get a shock and I was shaking like a jelly but our officer then pulled the string 3 times and we stood up and threw 2 bombs each into the trench and ran back to our own trenches as quickly as we could. We all got back before the Germans recovered from the surprise except 5, I was one of them I tripped over something and fell into a big shell hole and stayed there until Fritz had finished his rapid fire. We had 2 wounded but not bad I crawled in an hour afterwards a bit shook up but quite happy. Well dear the morning of the 28th came and our artillery and trench mortars gave them shocks all day but Old Fritz did not retalliate much at all we were greatly surprised. Well that night we gassed him again and he never fired hardly any shells back, and we never attacked but I bet poor Old Fritz was hanging in for us to do so. Well dear we were about done up as it was a terrible strain on anyones nerves, no sleep, and nothing else but shells day and night, but at last the order came that we were getting relieved. We were relieved at 3.30 A.M. on the morning of the 29th, and we were not sorry. The C.O.Y.L.I. that is the regiment that relieved us told us that they were making the charge but did not know when. Well we left the trench and went into some big dugouts about 2 miles behind the firing line and slept nearly all day on the 30th we cleaned up and had a wash and shave, the first wash for ten days, my word it was a treat "Sunlight" was "Bon" soap, some of the boys had scented soap but any old soap does out here we don't have time to study our complexion. Well dearest the 30th June was a very busy day for us we received orders that greatly surprised all of my Regt, and this is what it was, the attack was going to be made on the 1st July and we were in supports. On our way to the firing line every man had to carry something, some would get tools and water cans. I was rather unlucky I had to carry a box of 4 Stokes Shells which were no light weight. Well the morning of the 1st July came and I was very tired as we had not had much rest but it had to be done and no one knew even on the morning of the 1st what time the attack was being made but the artillery started at 6.30 and at 7.30 we heard the C.O. shout "The boys are going over" and where we was by getting on the hill near us we could see the boys going like mad across "no mans land" but we could not look for long as Fritz's artillery observers might have spotted us. At 8 o'c we began to move up and we had to go very slowly up the communication trenches as Fritz was shelling all of them, well we got our loads and after a very hot time we came into our own fire trench, now was the worst part of the job as we had to get up the ladders and get across to the German trench with our loads as quick as we could, how I managed it I shall never be able to say, but as soon as we were all on top the Germans started sending shrapnell shells—terrible things—well I heard when we got into the German 1st line of trenches that 15 of our boys were killed and wounded coming across, well we got into his first line and there we lost 24 men killed by 1 shell, buried them all I was blown against the back of the trench and just managed to get into a German dugout before 3 more big ones came. Well that night we had to go into the firing line and relieve the boys who had made the charge. We captured 4 lines of trenches that day not so bad. Well we got into them safe and we were there a few hours when he started his counter attack. We mowed them down in hundreds and never got within 20 yards of our trench he soon got fed up and did not try again that night. Well Dear we were in the fire line all night of the 1st also 2nd and we were relieved on the night of the 3rd by the 10th Division. Well we all came out by way of a road and we were lucky in not getting one man wounded. Well my Darling we are now out of hearing of the guns as we have had a 26 mile train ride, but when I dont think it will be long before we are into them again but at present we are not strong enough. I told you Dear that I was happy well so I am but I think of my poor dear old chums who have fallen I could cry. I have had to cry in the trench with one of my chums poor old Jack Nokes he has been out here since the very beginning of the war and has not received a scratch, he has never been home on leave because of a small crime, his home is at Wimbledon. Poor lad he died game with his mother's name his last word. I cryed like a child, not only him but a lot more of my poor comrades have gone. Ivy My Darling I am sure it is you and my poor sister praying for me that God has spared me. I said my prayers at least a 1,000 times a day (please God spare me to get out of this war safely for my dear Ivy's and my sister's sake). Ivy I cannot tell you the horrors of this war. You cannot realise what it is like to see poor lads lying about with such terrible wounds and we cannot help them. Well My Darling do not think that I am downhearted but it makes me sad when I think of these poor lads. Well My Dear I must finish this letter tomorrow as it is getting too dark now I know you will excuse the writing but I have only my knee and a little bit of wood to write on. We have come out of action with 4 officers out of 26 and 435 men out of 1150. I am glad to say that most of them are wounded, and I can say that for every 1 of our dead there are 10 German soldiers dead. I have accounted for 14 I am certain of but I believe I killed 12 in one dugout. I gave them 8 bombs one for Kitchner and the others for my chums. One German very nearly proved himself a better man than myself and he might have had me only for 2 of our men coming on the scene, we took him prisoner so he could not grumble, ("Mercy Cammerand") is all we could get out of him and "English very good". Well we took hundreds of prisoners that day and they were glad to be prisoners. but we made them work like slaves, we made them carry water and ammunition up to the firing line and some of them could not stand when we had finished with them. I have forgotten to tell you about the charge my regt made on the morning of the 3 July. There was only one piece of his last line of trenches which we wanted taken and the 1st Lincolns were picked to do it and we did it to we had to charge into a big wood and a wood is a terrible place to take. Well after ten minutes bombardment we went off towards their trench and we were met by a terrible machine gun fire which knocked a lot of our boys over as soon as they saw us coming they left their trench and ran into the wood then we had some terrible fighting with bombs and bayonets the Germans had a machine gun in this wood and we could see it and only 1 man with it but he was a brave man we could not get near him. As soon as some of the boys got to close he started throwing bombs but at last he was shot in the head but he must have killed a lot of our boys before he went under. Well when we got into their trenches and looked around we were surprised there was a big dugout with an electric dinamo in it just like an electric station all the dugouts had electric lights in them this turned out to be a general headquarters. We captured 2 Generals and 1100 men in this charge not so bad for the old Lincs was it. Our General did not know how to thank us he was pleased. Well dear we left the trenches that night and next day we were in the train all our divisions and now we are getting fitted out again but I dont think we will be in action again for a few weeks. This division is the same one that was anialated at Loos and now it has got its name back again 21 Division 62nd Brigade. Well Dearest that is all I can tell you this time. I am afraid that you will not be able to understand half of it as the writing is very bad but I know that My Dear little Ivy will excuse me. Well Dear Ivy I received your letter of the 26 June also your card of the 20, and they made me so happy. I am glad to hear that Frank is in a better place tell him I wish that I was with him. Well darling I think your photo is splendid and I shall value it more than any other photo I have got in my book. I do not know when I shall be able to have mine done but I will at the first opportunity. Yes dear tell Flo I should very much like to have one of her photos. I think her a very nice girl and I am sure it must be nice for you to have a friend like her to work with I wish Flo would change places with me but I believe she would if she could. Give her my very best wishes and I wish her the very best of health.

Well My Dearest I think I must close now as I shall be in parade very soon. I have not the time to answer all your letter so please excuse. Give my fondest love to mother and dad and my very best wishes to Olive and Charles and Frank also your next door neighbors. So sorry I have not time to write more but I know Dear that you will excuse this SHORT letter this time. I have heard from my French lady and she is very pleased to hear that I am (engaged). I have also received a letter from Elsie and her mother, they are old friends of mine. Well Dearest I will now close hoping to be able to write again soon. Cheerio My Dearest. I close with fondest love and thousand of kisses I remain.

xxxxxxxx	Your Loving
xxx	Boy
xxx	Jack

SIEGFRIED SASSOON
1886–1967

After his experience in the war, this fox hunter, poet, and aesthete wrote a distinguished fictionalized autobiography, The Memoirs of George Sherston, *based largely on his diaries. These record his front-line moments as a junior officer in the Royal Welch Fusiliers. He was a brave and able soldier, but gradually perceived that the war had become a meaningless waste. This view he registered in many satiric poems, and he finally issued a public statement condemning the war and refusing further duty. Expecting to be court-martialled, he was instead sent to a mental hospital. Guilt at so easily escaping the trenches sent him back to the front, where in July 1918, he was wounded badly and sent home for good.*

From DIARIES

January 25 [1916]

Riding out this morning in sunshine and stillness—the landscape like a bowl of wine, golden; light spreading across the earth, and earth drinking its fill of light; down by Warlus the village shepherd stamps up and down the fallows on his numb feet, with his hood over his head; alone with his flock and his dogs and his two goats, and a hundred busy black rooks, and a few hares popping up and scuttling across the wheat, stopping to listen, and then away again—big sandy ones.

Since January 18, when R. Ormrod went on leave, I am Transport Officer; why does this safe job come my way when I wanted danger and hardship? But there is no way out of it, without looking a fool, so I must take it. And it is better fun than with the company. The old nags want a bit of looking after—and the whole show wants tidying up.

Last Sunday (January 23) I left here to go to Amiens on a sunny morning, which had turned dull and cheerless by 1 o'clock. The train rambles in to Amiens in one and a half hours, about eighteen miles.

The Cathedral, as one stands in the nave, gives an impression of clear whiteness; the massive columns seem slender, so vast is the place; and the windows beyond the altar are high and delicate, with a little central colour, blue, violet and amber, and the rest white, with a touch of grass-green in the sombre-glowing glass lower down.

The architecture of the place, leading the eye upward, soars above the gaudy insignia of the service—shrines and candles and pictures (like the great idea of religion—outshining all formulae of office and celebration). The rose-windows are full of dusky flames; with touches of scarlet, apple-green, sapphire, violet, and orange.

The noble arches and pillars are lifted up toward heaven to break into flowers, lilies of clear light, and the gorgeous hues of richer petals and clusters. And the voices of the great organ shout and mingle their raptures high overhead, shaking the roofs with glory.

Beyond the great wrought-iron gate, where the marvellously carven stalls are, the choir are a black bevy against the stars of the altar-lights. They fill the cathedral with their antiphons, while the French are at their meek orisons, old women and tired soldiers in blue-grey, children and white-haired men.

But the invader is here; a Japanese officer flits in with curious eyes; the Army Service Corps and Red Cross men are everywhere, walking up and down with the foolish looks of sightseers, who come neither to watch nor to pray. And the Jocks, the kilted ones, their arrogance is overweening, they move with an air of conquest; have we conquered France? For the old English knights and squires and varlets must have moved up and down just as these do, elbowing the fantastic Frenchmen against the wall; their eyes had the same veiled insolence five hundred years ago, I am certain. These wear long capes or cloaks which give them a mediaeval look.

*   *   *

March 30

7 o'clock on a frosty white morning with a lark shaking his little wings above the trenches, and an airplane droning high up in the soft early sunlight. At 5 it was quite light, with a sickle-moon low in the west and the dawn a delicate flush of faint pink and submerged radiance above a mist-swathed country, peeping out from tree or roof, all white, misty-white and frosty-white, men stamp their feet and rats are about on the crannied rime-frosted parapets. Folds of mist, drifting in a dense blur; above them the white shoals and chasms of the sky.

Here life is audacious and invincible—until it is whirled away in enigmatic helplessness and ruin; and then it is only the bodies that are smashed and riddled; for the profound and purposeful spirit of renascence moves in and rests on all things—imperceptible between the scarred and swarming earth and noble solitudes of sky—the spirit that triumphs over visible destruction, as leaping water laughs at winds and rocks and shipwrecked hulks.

Their temper is proven, the fibre of their worth is tested and revealed; these men from Welsh farms and Midland cities, from factory and shop and mine, who can ever give them their meed of praise for the patience and tender jollity which seldom forsake them?

The cheerless monotony of their hourly insecurity, a monotony broken only by the ever-present imminence of death and wounds—the cruelty and malice of these things that fall from the skies searching for men, that they may batter and pierce the bodies and blot the slender human existence.

As I sit in the sun in a nook among the sandbags and chalky debris, with shells flying overhead in the blue air, a lark sings high up, and a little weasel comes and runs past me within a foot of my outstretched feet, looking at me with tiny bright eyes. Bullets sing and whistle and hum; so do bits of shell; rifles crack; some small guns and trench-mortars pop and thud; big shells burst with a massive explosion, and the voluminous echoes roll along the valleys, to fade nobly and without haste or consternation.

Bullets are deft and flick your life out with a quick smack. Shells rend and bury, and vibrate and scatter, hurling fragments and lumps and jagged splinters at you; they lift you off your legs and leave you huddled and bleeding and torn and scorched with a blast straight from the pit. Heaven is furious with the smoke and flare and portent of shells, but bullets are a swarm of whizzing hornets, mad, winged and relentless, undeviating in their malicious onset.

The big guns roar their challenge and defiance; but the machine-guns rattle with intermittent bursts of mirthless laughter.

There are still pools in the craters; they reflect the stars like any lovely water, but nothing grows near them; snags of iron jut from their banks, tin cans and coils of wire, and other trench-refuse. If you search carefully, you may find a skull, eyeless, grotesquely matted with what was once hair; eyes once looked from those detestable holes, they made the fabric of a passionate life, they appealed for justice, they were lit with triumph, and beautiful with pity.

How good it is to get the savour of time past; what living skies, what crowds of faces, what unending murmur of voices, mingle with the sounds of visions of to-day; for to-day is always the event; and all the yesterdays are windows looking out on unbounded serenity, and dreams written on the darkness; and suspended actions re-fashion themselves in silence, playing the parts they learned, at a single stroke of thought.

* * *

April 13

We came away and reached Morlancourt about 1.30. Heavy firing on our right between 2 and 3 A.M. Then the dawn broke quiet and chilly, the cloudy sky whitening, and the country below appearing sad and stricken; I could see the ruined villages of Fricourt and Mametz down below on our left, and the long seams of trenches on the other side of the valley, and the still-leafless trees, shivering sentries of the unhappy countryside.

And the larks were singing high up before the light began. And later on the voice of a thrush came to me from a long way off, muffled by the gusts of wind, a thrush singing behind the German lines.

Looking across the parapet at the tangle of wire and the confusion of mine-craters and old fortifications, the prospect is not cheerful. Nothing grows; everything is there for destruction. What eyes have stared across there while their brains and bodies were longing for sleep and home and desirable things! Eyes that see nothing now. But this moralising is in very bad taste indeed. We came back in a half-gale of wind from the northwest. Dandelions are flowering along the edges of the communication-trenches. And then I slept and slept, and woke dreaming of English landscapes.

* * *

April 25

There was a great brawny Highland Major here to-day, talking of the Bayonet. For close on an hour he talked, and all who listened caught fire from his enthusiasm: for he was prophesying; he had his message to deliver.

When he had finished, I went up the hill to my green wood where the half-built mansion stands. And there it was quite still except for a few birds; robins, and thrushes, and lesser notes. The church-bells were ringing in the town, deep and mellow. A pigeon cooed. Phrases from the bayonet lecture came back to me. Some midges hummed around my head. The air was still warm with the sun that had quite disappeared behind the hills. A rook cawed in the trees. A woodpecker laughed, harsh and derisive. "The bullet and the bayonet are brother and sister." "If you don't kill him, he'll kill you!" "Stick him between the eyes, in the throat, in the chest, or round the thighs." "If he's on the run, there's only one place; get your bayonet into his kidneys; it'll go in as easy as butter." "Kill them, kill them: there's only one good Bosche and that's a dead 'un!" "Quickness, anger, strength, good fury, accuracy of aim. Don't waste good steel. Six inches are enough—what's the use of a foot of steel sticking out at the back of a man's neck? Three inches will do him, and when he coughs, go and find another." And so on.

I told the trees what I had been hearing; but they hate steel, because axes and bayonets are the same to them. They are dressed in their fresh green, every branch showing through the mist of leaves, and the straight stems most lovely against the white and orange sky beyond. And a blackbird's song cries aloud that April cannot understand what war means.

THE KISS

To these I turn, in these I trust—
Brother Lead and Sister Steel.
To this blind power I make appeal,
I guard her beauty clean from rust.

He spins and burns and loves the air,
And splits a skull to win my praise;
But up the nobly marching days
She glitters naked, cold and fair.

Sweet Sister, grant your soldier this:
That in good fury he may feel
The body where he sets his heel
Quail from your downward darting kiss.

* * *

May 23   6.15 P.M.

On Crawley Ridge. A very still evening. Sun rather hazy but sky mostly clear. Looking across to Fricourt: trench-mortars bursting in the cemetery: clouds of dull white vapour slowly float away over grey-green grass with yellow buttercup-smears, and saffron of weeds. Fricourt, a huddle of reddish roofs, skeleton village—church-tower white—almost demolished, a patch of white against the sombre green of the Fricourt wood (full of German batteries). Away up the hill the white seams and heapings of trenches dug in the chalk. The sky full of lark-songs. Sometimes you can count thirty slowly and hear no sound of a shot: then the muffled pop of a rifle-shot a long way off, or a banging 5.9, or our eighteen-pounder—then a burst of machine-gun westward, the yellow sky with a web of whitish filmy cloud half across the sun; and the ridges rather blurred with outlines of trees; an airplane droning overhead. A thistle sprouting through the chalk on the parapet; a cockchafer sailing through the air a little way in front.

Down the hill, and on to the old Bray-Fricourt road, along by the railway; the road white and hard; a partridge flies away calling; lush grass everywhere, and crops of nettles; a large black slug out for his evening walk (doing nearly a mile a month, I should think).

Stansfield talking about Canada and times when he was hard up—this afternoon (twelve and a half cents a meal). Two Manchester officers this morning.

May 25

Twenty-seven men with faces blackened and shiny—Christy-minstrels—with hatchets in their belts, bombs in pockets, knobkerries— waiting in a dug-out in the reserve line. At 10.30 they trudge up to Battalion H.Q. splashing through mire and water in the chalk trench, while the rain comes steadily down. The party is twenty-two men, five N.C.O.s and one officer (Stansfield). From H.Q. we start off again, led by Compton-Smith: across the open to the end of 77 Street. A red flashlight winks a few times to guide us thither. Then up to the front line—the men's feet making a most unholy tramp and din; squeeze along to the starting-point, where Stansfield and his two confederates (Sergeant Lyle and Corporal O'Brien) loom over the parapet from above, having successfully laid the line of lime across the craters to the Bosche wire. In a few minutes the five parties have gone over—and disappear into the rain and darkness—the last four men carry ten-foot light ladders. It is 12 midnight. I am sitting on the parapet listening for something to happen—five, ten, nearly fifteen minutes—not a sound— nor a shot fired—and only the usual flare-lights, none very near our party. Then through the hazy dripping skies the 5.9 shells begin to drone across in their leisurely way, a few at first, and then quite a flock of them. I am out with the rear party by now—about twenty yards in front of our trench (the wire has been cut of course), the men (evacuating party) are lying half-down a crater on the left, quite cheery. In the white glare of a flare-light I can see the rest of the column lying straight down across the ridge between the craters. Then a few whizz-bangs fizz over to our front trench and just behind the raiders. After twenty minutes there is still absolute silence in the Bosche trench; the raid is obviously held up by their wire, which we thought was so easy to get through. One of the bayonet-men comes crawling back; I follow him to our trench and he tells me that they can't get through: O'Brien says it's a failure; they're all going to throw a bomb and retire.

A minute or two later a rifle-shot rings out and almost simultaneously several bombs are thrown by both sides: a bomb explodes right in the water at the bottom of left crater close to our men, and showers a pale spume of water; there are blinding flashes and explosions, rifle-shots, the scurry of feet, curses and groans, and stumbling figures loom up from below and scramble awkwardly over the parapet—some wounded— black faces and whites of eyes and lips show in the dusk; when I've counted sixteen in, I go forward to see how things are going, and find Stansfield wounded, and leave him there with two men who soon get

him in: other wounded men crawl in; I find one hit in the leg; he says
"O'Brien is somewhere down the crater badly wounded." They are still
throwing bombs and firing at us: the sinister sound of clicking bolts
seems to be very near; perhaps they have crawled out of their trench and
are firing from behind their advanced wire. Bullets hit the water in the
craters, and little showers of earth patter down on the crater. Five or six
of them are firing into the crater at a few yards' range. The bloody sods
are firing down at me at point-blank range. (I really wondered whether
my number was up.) From our trenches and in front of them I can hear
the mumble of voices—most of them must be in by now. After minutes
like hours, with great difficulty I get round the bottom of the crater and
back toward our trench; at last I find O'Brien down a very deep (about
twenty-five feet) and precipitous crater on my left (our right as they went
out). He is moaning and his right arm is either broken or almost shot off:
he's also hit in the right leg (body and head also, but I couldn't see that
then). Another man (72 Thomas) is with him; he is hit in the right arm.
I leave them there and get back to our trench for help, shortly afterwards
Lance-Corporal Stubbs is brought in (he has had his foot blown off).
Two or three other wounded men are being helped down the trench; no
one seems to know what to do; those that are there are very excited and
uncertain: no sign of any officers—then Compton-Smith comes along (a
mine went up on the left as we were coming up at about 11.30 and thirty
(R.E.s) men were gassed or buried). I get a rope and two more men and
we go back to O'Brien, who is unconscious now. With great difficulty we
get him half-way up the face of the crater; it is now after one o'clock and
the sky beginning to get lighter. I make one more journey to our trench
for another strong man and to see to a stretcher being ready. We get him
in, and it is found that he has died, as I had feared. Corporal Mick
O'Brien (who often went patrolling with me) was a very fine man and
had been with the Battalion since November 1914. He was at Neuve
Chapelle, Festubert and Loos.

I go back to a support-line dug-out and find the unwounded men of
the raiding-party refreshing themselves: everyone is accounted for now;
eleven wounded (one died of wounds) and one killed, out of twenty-
eight. I see Stansfield, who is going on all right, but has several bomb-
wounds. On the way down I see the Colonel, sitting on his bed in a
woollen cap with a tuft on top, and very much upset at the non-success
of the show, and the mine disaster; but very pleased with the way our
men tried to get through the wire. I get down to 71 North about 2.15,
with larks beginning to sing in the drizzling pallor of the sky. (Covered
with mud and blood, and no tunic on!) I think it was lucky the Colonel
refused to allow me to go out with the raiding party, as I meant to get
through that wire somehow, and it seems to have been almost impossible
(we had bad wire-cutters) and the Bosches were undoubtedly ready for

us, and no one could have got into their trench and got out alive, as there were several of them. They certainly showed great ability and cunning, but I suppose they generally do. This morning I woke up *feeling as if I'd been to a dance*—awful mouth and head.

There was no terror there—only men with nerves taut and courage braced—then confusion and anger and—failure. I think there was more delight than dread in the prospect of the dangers; certainly I saw no sign of either. But on the left where the mine-explosion took place at 11.30 there were gassed men lying about in the trench in dark rain and all sorts of horrors being gallantly overcome.

From G.H.Q. communiqué—Friday May 26: "At Mametz we raided hostile trenches. Our party *entered without difficulty* [!!!] and maintained a spirited bombing fight, and finally withdrew at the end of twenty-five minutes." The truth which is (less than) half a truth!!!

May 26   8.15 P.M.

Looking west from the support line; the brown, shell-pitted ground gloomy in the twilight—beyond, the receding country, dim-blue and solemn, a distant group of thick-topped trees on a ridge dark against the low colour of fading sunset, deep-glowing-ruddy-amber, fading higher to pale orange and yellow; above that a long dove-coloured bar of cloud faintly fringed with crimson. And over all the proper star of dusk.

The guns rumble miles and miles away, carts can be heard on the roads behind Fricourt. Everything is very still, until a canister comes over and bursts, throwing up a cloud of purple-black smoke that drifts across the half-lit sky, and "the blue vaporous end of day." A rat comes out and nips across among the tin cans and burst sandbags and rubbish. And I turn away and go down the fifteen steps to a dark candle-yellow dug-out to fetch my bally revolver.

May 27

Sitting on the firestep in warm weather and sunshine about 10 A.M. with the lark above and the usual airmen. Can't remember Thursday night's show very clearly: it seems mostly rain and feeling chilled, and the flash of rifles in the gloom; and O'Brien's shattered limp body propped up down that infernal bank—face ghastly in the light of a flare, clothes torn, hair matted over the forehead—nothing left of the old cheeriness and courage and delight in any excitement of Hun-chasing. Trying to lift him up the side of the crater, the soft earth kept giving way under one's feet: he was a heavy man too, fully six feet high. But he was a dead man when at last we lowered him over the parapet on to a stretcher: and one of the stretcher-bearers examined his wounds and felt for the life that wasn't there, and then took off his round helmet with a sort of reverence—or it may have been only a chance gesture. I would have given a lot if he could have been alive, but it was a hopeless case—a bomb had given him its full explosion. But when I go out on patrols his ghost will surely be with me; he'll catch his breath and grip his bomb just as he used to do.

*　*　*

July 1   7.30 A.M.
   [Opening of the battle of the Somme]
   Last night was cloudless and starry and still. The bombardment went on steadily. We had breakfast at 6. The morning is brilliantly fine, after a mist early. Since 6.30 there has been hell let loose. The air vibrates with the incessant din—the whole earth shakes and rocks and *throbs*—it is one continuous roar. Machine-guns tap and rattle, bullets whistling overhead—small fry quite outdone by the gangs of hooligan-shells that dash over to rend the German lines with their demolition-parties. The smoke-cloud is cancelled as the wind is wrong since yesterday. Attack should be starting now, but one can't look out, as the machine-gun bullets are skimming.
   Inferno—inferno—bang—smash!
   7.45 A.M. The artillery barrage is now working to the right of Fricourt and beyond. I have seen the 21st Division advancing on the left of Fricourt; and some Huns apparently surrendering—about three-quarters of a mile away. Our men advancing steadily to the first line. A haze of smoke drifting across the landscape—brilliant sunshine. Some York-shires on our left (50th Brigade) watching the show and cheering as if at a football match. The noise as bad as ever.
   9.30 A.M. Came back to dug-out and had a shave. Just been out to have another look. The 21st Division are still going across the open on the left, apparently with no casualties. The sun flashes on bayonets, and the tiny figures advance steadily and disappear behind the mounds of trench-debris. A few runners come back, and the ammunition-parties are going across. Trench-mortars etc are knocking hell out of Sunken Road Trench and the ground where 22nd Brigade will go across soon. The noise is not as bad, and the Huns aren't firing much now.
   9.50 A.M. Fricourt is half-hidden by clouds of drifting smoke—brown, blue, pinkish, and grey; shrapnel bursting in small blue-white puffs, with tiny flashes. The smoke drifts across our front on a south-east wind, just a breeze.
   The birds seem bewildered; I saw a lark start to go up, and then flutter along as if he thought better of it. Others were fluttering above the trench with querulous cries, weak on the wing.
   The uproar isn't as bad as it was an hour ago. I can see seven of our balloons, half-right, and close together. Seven or eight aeroplanes are

above our lines and the German front-trenches, also half-right. Our men still advancing in twenties and thirties in file, about a mile to the left. Another huge explosion in Fricourt, and cloud of brown-pink smoke. Some bursts are yellowish.

10.5 A.M. I can see the Manchesters in our front trench getting ready to go over. Figures filing down the trench. Two Hun shells just burst close to our trench-mortar positions at 84 Street. Two of the Manchesters gone out to look at our wire-gaps (which I made night before last).

Just eaten my last orange. I am looking at a sunlit picture of Hell. And still the breeze shakes the yellow charlock, and the poppies glow below Crawley ridge where a few Hun shells have fallen lately. Manchesters are sending forward a few scouts. A bayonet glitters. A runner comes back across the open to their Battalion H.Q. in 84 Street. (I am about five hundred yards behind the front trenches, where Sandown Avenue joins Kingston Road.) The Huns aren't shelling or firing machine-guns. 21st still trotting along the skyline toward La Boiselle. Barrage going strong to right of Contalmaison ridge. Heavy shelling by us of Hun trenches toward Mametz.

12.15 P.M. Things have been quieter the last hour: 20th Manchesters not gone across yet. Germans putting over a few shrapnel-shells. Weather hot and cloudless. A lark singing overhead.

1.30 P.M. 20th Manchester attack at 2.30. Mametz and Montauban reported taken; Mametz consolidated.

2.30 P.M. 20th Manchester left New Trench and took Sunken Road Trench. We could see about four hundred. Many walked across with sloped arms. About twenty-five casualties on the left (from a machine-gun in Fricourt). I could see one man moving his left arm up and down as he lay on his side: his head was a crimson patch. The others lay still. Then the swarm of ants disappeared over the hill. Fricourt was a cloud of pinkish smoke. Hun machine-guns were firing on the other side of the hill. At 2.50 no one to be seen in no-man's-land except the casualties (about half-way across).

5.30 P.M. I saw about twenty or thirty men of A. Company, Second R.W.F., crawling across to Sunken Road, from same place as the 20th Manchesters, and lit a red signal. Huns put a few big shells on to the cemetery—and traversed Kingston Road with machine-gun bursts. Manchesters' wounded still out there. Remainder of A. went over after, about a hundred in all. I was in dug-out till 6, nothing to be seen meanwhile. At 7.15 P.M. people could be seen moving about the Hun lines beyond Sunken Road, and crossing the craters by 82 Street. Very little firing was going on. Yorkshires (50th Brigade) reported to have made a mess of clearing Fricourt: the Sixth Dorsets (two companies; C.O., Adjutant, and Major) came along Kingston Road, evidently got to finish the

job. Weather clear and warm and still. Our dug-out heavily shelled with
five-nines between 1.30 and 2.30.

8 P.M. Situation as reported by Staff Captain of 22nd Brigade to
Greaves. Montauban and Mametz taken and consolidated. 20th Brigade
(on our right) got their objective with some difficulty.

20th Manchesters are held up behind Sunken Road Trench. 50th
Brigade have done badly in clearing Fricourt. 21st Division have done
very well, and reached north-east corner of Fricourt Wood. A good
number of prisoners have been brought in on our sector (reported several
hundred).

9.30 P.M. Our A. Company holds Rectangle and Sunken Road: Manchesters Bois Français Support. C.O. 20th Manchesters killed. Greaves
and I stay in Kingston Road: Garnons-Williams gone with carrying-
party, so C. Company is reduced to six runners, two stretcher-bearers,
Company Sergeant Major, Signallers, and Ryder! Things are quiet at
present. Sky cloudy westward; five grey wisps: red sunset.

10.45 P.M. Heavy gunfire on the left round La Boiselle. Fairly quiet
opposite us. Some of the Sixth Dorsets are in Kingston Road. That
battalion attacks Fricourt in the morning.

July 2   11.15 A.M.

A quiet night. Fine sunny morning. Nothing happening at present.
Fricourt and Rose Trench to be attacked again to-day. Everything all
right on rest of XV Corps front. Greaves and I are to remain in Kingston
Road.

2.30 P.M. Adjutant just been up here, excited, optimistic and unshaven. Fricourt and Rose Trench have been occupied without resistance (there was no bombardment). Over two thousand prisoners taken
by Seventh Division alone. First R.W.F. took over two hundred. Germans have gone back to their second line.

I am lying out in front of our trench in the long grass, basking in
sunshine where yesterday morning one couldn't show a finger. The Germans are shelling our new front line. Fricourt is full of British soldiers
seeking souvenirs. The place was a ruin before; now it is a dust-heap.
Everywhere the news seems good: I only hope it will last.

A gunner Forward Observation Officer just been along with a Hun
helmet; says the Huns in Fricourt were cut off and their trenches demolished. Many dead lying about—he saw one dead officer lying across a
smashed machine-gun with his head smashed in—"a fine-looking chap"
he said (with some emotion).

Next thing is to hang on to the country we've taken. We move up
to-night. Seventh Division has at any rate done all that was asked of it
and reached the ground just short of Mametz Wood; the Second

Queens are said to have legged it as usual when the Bosch made a poorish counter-attack.

July 3   11.15 A.M.

Greaves, self and party left Kingston Road at 6.45 A.M. The battalion assembled at 71 North and we marched across to a point north-west of Carnoy where the 22nd Brigade concentrated. The four battalions piled arms and lay down in an open grassy hollow south of the Carnoy-Mametz road, with a fine view of the British and (late) Bosche lines where the 91st Brigade attacked on Saturday, about six hundred yards away. Everyone very cheery—no officer-casualties yet. C. D. Morgan, Dobell and Peter with A.: H. B. Williams, Alexander, Smith B.: C. self and Greaves and Lomax. Hanmer-Jones and Baynes with D.: Stevens and Newton with Bombers. Anscombe (Lewis guns), C.O., Medical Officer and Reeves—Brunicardi (observing for Brigade) and E. Dadd. Weather still, warm, sky rather cloudy. Sorry to say most of C. Company are on special parties—carrying etc; poor old Molyneux will be in an awful state at not being near his master. I think we move up this evening and probably attack Mametz Wood to-morrow. (This is only a guess.) If so, we'll probably get cut up. Greaves and I are lucky to have had such an easy time lately. A. and B. Companies have had no sleep for two nights.

5.45 P.M. Everyone has been dozing in the sun all day. Minshull Ford rode round after lunch, and bucked from his horse about what his Brigade had been doing. K. Fry took his M.C. ribbon off and sewed it on me. R. W. F. about four hundred and twenty strong.

20th Manchesters reduced to about two hundred and fifty. Second Warwicks and Royal Irish haven't been in action yet. As I dozed I could hear the men all round talking about the things they'd looted from the Bosche trenches.

Evening falls calm and hazy; an orange sunset, blurred at the last. At 8.45 I'm looking down from the hill, a tangle of long grass and thistles and some small white weed like tiny cow-parsley. The four battalions are in four groups. A murmur of voices comes up—one or two mouth-organs playing—a salvo of our field-guns on the right—and a few droning airplanes overhead. A little smoke drifting from tiny bivouac-fires. At the end of the hollow the road to Mametz (where some captured German guns came along two hours since). Beyond that the bare ground rising to the Bazentin ridge, with seams of our trench-lines and those taken from the enemy—grey-green and chalk-white stripes.

AT CARNOY
JULY 3

Down in the hollow there's the whole Brigade
Camped in four groups: through twilight falling slow
I hear a sound of mouth-organs, ill-played,
And murmur of voices, gruff, confused, and low.
Crouched among thistle-tufts I've watched the glow
Of a blurred orange sunset flare and fade;
And I'm content. To-morrow we must go
To take some cursèd Wood . . . O world God made!

July 4   4.30 A.M.
   The Battalion started at 9.15 P.M. yesterday and, after messing about
for over four hours, got going with tools, wire, etc. and went through
Mametz, up a long communication-trench with three very badly mangled corpses lying in it: a man, short, plump, with turned-up moustaches,
lying face downward and half sideways with one arm flung up as if
defending his head, and a bullet through his forehead. A doll-like figure.
Another hunched and mangled, twisted and scorched with many days'
dark growth on his face, teeth clenched and grinning lips. Came down
across the open hillside looking across to Mametz Wood, and out at the
end of Bright Alley. Found that the Royal Irish were being bombed and
machine-gunned by Bosches in the wood, and had fifteen wounded. A
still grey morning; red east; everyone very tired.
   12.30 P.M. These dead are terrible and undignified carcases, stiff and
contorted. There were thirty of our own laid in two ranks by the Ma-
metz-Carnoy road, some side by side on their backs with bloody clotted
fingers mingled as if they were handshaking in the companionship of
death. And the stench undefinable. And rags and shreds of blood-stained
cloth, bloody boots riddled and torn.

                              *   *   *
July 13
   Still we remain in this curious camp, which leaves a jumbled impression of horse-lines and waggons and men carrying empty deal shell-
boxes, and tents, and bivouacs, and red poppies and blue cornflowers,
and straggling Méaulte village a little way off among the dark-green July
trees, with pointed spire in the middle, and a general atmosphere of
bustle while we remain idle at this caravanserai for supplies and men and
munitions. There is a breeze blowing and grey weather.
   Sitting at the tent-door last night about 9.30 I was watching a group of
our officers and three from the Second R.W.F. who have arrived from
Béthune. All were voluble—their faces indistinct but their heads loom-

ing against the last grey luminous gleam of evening.

I keep reading *Tess* and *The Return of the Native*—they fit in admirably with my thoughts.

Here with me are Dobell and Newton, fresh from Sandhurst, cheery and attractive, and old Julian Dadd—the good soul, and Hawes, full of jokes, and Hanmer-Jones, blundering old thing, as stupid as an owl, but kind, and two others.

The Battalion are still waiting at the Citadel, three-quarters of a mile away, over the thistled slopes. Haven't seen Robert Graves yet: he is near, with the Second Battalion—unpopular, of course, poor dear.

Indian cavalry ride past along the Méaulte–Bray road. The landscape looks grey and withered to-day, and the poppies leap at one in harsh spots of flame, hectic and cruel.

This life begets a condition of mental stagnation unless one keeps trying to get outside it all. I try to see everything with different eyes to my companions, but their unreasoning mechanical outlook is difficult to avoid. Often their words go past me like dead leaves on the wind; one gets used to them, like banging guns that scourge the landscape and raise huge din; and then, after being merely irritated by them, they are suddenly dear and friendly, not to be lost.

> The quicksilvery glaze on the rivers and pools vanished; from broad mirrors of light they changed to lustreless sheets of lead. *(Return of the Native)*

Sometimes when I see my companions lying asleep or resting, rolled in their blankets, their faces turned to earth or hidden by the folds, for a moment I wonder whether they are alive or dead. For at any hour I may come upon them, and find that long silence descended over them, their faces grey and disfigured, dark stains of blood soaking through their torn garments, all their hope and merriment snuffed out for ever, and their voices fading on the winds of thought, from memory to memory, from hour to hour, until they are no more to be recalled. So does the landscape grow dark at evening, embowered with dusk, and backed with a sky full of gun-flashes. And then the night falls and the darkness of death and sleep.

* * *

January 17 [1917]

A draft of a hundred and fifty "proceeded" to France to-night. Most of them half-tight, except those who had been in the guard-room to stop them bolting (again), and the Parson's speech went off, to the usual asides and witticisms. He ended: "And God go with you. I shall go as far as the station with you." Then the C.O. stuttered a few inept and ungracious remarks. "You are going out to the Big Push which will end the war" etc (groans). And away they marched to beat of drums—a pathetic scene of humbug and cant. How much more impressive if they went in silence, with no foolishness of "God Speed"—like Hardy's "men who march away . . . To hazards whence no tears can win us."

*   *   *

15 February

Left Waterloo 12 noon. Irish Hussar in carriage. Sunshine at Southampton. Skite by Haig in daily papers: "we shall demolish the enemy" etc.

Left London feeling nervous and rattled; but the worried feeling wears off once aboard the *Archangel*. People seem to become happy in a bovine way as soon as they are relieved of all responsibility for the future. Soldiers going to the war are beasts of burden, probably condemned to death. They are not their own masters in any way except in their unconquerable souls.

Yet, when they have left their relatives and friends blinking and swallowing sobs on Waterloo platform, after a brief period of malaise (while watching the Blighty landscape flitting past) they recover. When the train has left Woking and the Necropolis in the rear they begin to "buck themselves up." After all, becoming a military serf or trench galley-slave is a very easy way out of the difficulties of life. No more perplexities there. A grateful Patria transports them inexpensively away from their troubles—nay, rewards them for their acquiescence with actual money and medals. But nevertheless they are like cabbages going to Covent Garden, or beasts driven to market. Hence their happiness. They have no worries, because they have no future; they are only alive through an oversight—of the enemy. They are not "going out" to *do* things, but to have things *done* to them.

*   *   *

April 14

At 9 P.M. we started off to relieve the 13th Northumberland Fusiliers in Hindenburg support (Second R.W.F. being in support to the First Cameronians). It was only an hour's walk, but our Northumberland Fusilier guides lost themselves and we didn't arrive and complete the relief until 4 A.M. Luckily it was fine. I went to bed at 5 A.M., after patrolling our 900-yard front *alone!*—in a corridor of the underground communication-trench of the Hindenburg Line—a wonderful place. Got up at 9.30 after a miserable hour's sleep—cold as hell—and started off at 10.45 with a fatigue-party to carry up trench-mortar bombs from dump between St Martin-Cojeul and Croisilles. Got back very wet and tired about 4.30. Rained all day—trenches like glue.

Was immediately told I'd got to take command of a hundred bombers (the Battalion is only 270 strong!) to act as reserve for the First Cameronians in to-morrow's attack. The Cameronians are to bomb down the two Hindenburg Lines, which they tried to do on Saturday and had rather a bad time. We may not be wanted. If we are it will be bloody work I know. I haven't slept for more than an hour at a time since

Tuesday night, but I am feeling pretty fit and cheery. I have seen the
most ghastly sights since we came up here. The dead bodies lying about
the trenches and in the open are beyond description—especially after
the rain. (A lot of the Germans killed by our bombardment last week are
awful.) Our shelling of the line—and subsequent bombing etc—has left
a number of mangled Germans—they will haunt me till I die. And
everywhere one sees the British Tommy in various states of dismember-
ment—most of them are shot through the head—so not so fearful as the
shell-twisted Germans. Written at 9.30 sitting in the Hindenburg underground tunnel on Sunday night, fully expecting to get killed on Monday morning.

April 16
   At 3 A.M. the attack began on Fontaine-les-Croisilles. I sat in the First
Cameronians H.Q. down in the tunnel until nearly 6, when I was told to
despatch twenty-five bombers to help their B. Company in the Hindenburg front line. I took them up myself and got there just as they had been
badly driven back after taking several hundred yards of the trench. They
seemed to have run out of bombs, failing to block the trench etc, and
were in a state of wind-up. However the sun was shining, and the trench
was not so difficult to deal with as I had expected.
   My party (from A. Company) were in a very jaded condition owing to
the perfectly bloody time they've been having lately, but they pulled
themselves together fine and we soon had the Bosches checked and
pushed them back nearly four hundred yards. When we'd been there
about twenty-five minutes I got a sniper's bullet through the shoulder
and was no good for about a quarter of an hour. Luckily it didn't bleed
much. Afterwards the rest of our men came up and the Cameronians
were recalled, leaving me to deal with the show with about seventy men
and a fair amount of bombs, but no Lewis-guns.
   I was just preparing to start bombing up the trench again when a
message came from Colonel Chaplin saying we must not advance any
more owing to the people on each side having failed to advance, and
ordering me to come away, as he was sending someone up to take over. I
left the trench about 9.45. Got wound seen to at our Aid Post in the
tunnel, walked to Hénin—and was told to walk on to Boyelles. Got there
very beat, having foot-slogged about four kilometres through mud. Was
put on a motor-bus and jolted for an hour and a half to Warlencourt
(20th Casualty Clearing Station) and told to expect to go to England.
Written about 7.30 P.M., with rain pelting on the roof and wind very
cold. I hate to think of the poor old Battalion being relieved on such a
night after the ghastly discomforts of the last six days. The only blessing
is that our losses have been very slight. Only about a dozen of my party
to-day—most of them slight. No one killed. My wound is hurting like
hell, the tetanus injection has made me very chilly and queer, and I am

half-dead for lack of sleep, sitting in a chair in my same old clothes—
puttees and all—and not having been offered even a wash. Never
mind—"For I've sped through. O Life! O Sun!"

April 17

After a blessed eight hours' sleep (more than I'd had since last
Wednesday) I waited till 3 o'clock reading *Far from the Madding
Crowd*, when we got on board a Red Cross train of serpentine length.
Five hundred men and thirty-two officers on board. Warlencourt is eighteen kilometres from Arras—quite near Saulty, where we stayed on April
7. We passed through Doullens about 6 P.M. and Abbeville at 8.30 and
reached Camières at midnight.

An officer called Kerr is with me—one of the First Cameronians. He
was hit in the bombing show about an hour before I got up there on
Monday morning, so I've got some sidelights on what really happened.

At present I am still feeling warlike, and quite prepared to go back to
the line in a few weeks. My wound is fairly comfortable, and will be
healed in a fortnight, they say. I know it would be best for me *not* to go
back to England, where I should probably be landed for at least three
months, and return to the line in July or August, with all the hell and
wrench of coming back and settling down to be gone through again. I
think I've established a very strong position in the Second Battalion in
the five weeks I was with them. My luck never deserts me; it seems
inevitable for me to be cast for the part of "leading hero"!

THINGS TO REMEMBER

The dull red rainy dawn on Sunday April 15, when we had relieved the
13th Northumberland Fusiliers—our Company of eighty men taking
over a frontage of nine hundred yards.

During the relief—stumbling along the trench in the dusk, dead men
and living lying against the sides of the trench—one never knew which
were dead and which living. Dead and living were very nearly one, for
death was in all our hearts. Kirby shaking dead German by the shoulder
to ask him the way.

On April 14 the 19th Brigade attacked at 5.30 A.M. I looked across at
the hill where a round red sun was coming up. The hill was deeply
shadowed and grey-blue, and all the country was full of shell-flashes and
drifting smoke. A battle picture.

Scene in the Hénin Dressing Station. The two bad cases—abdomen
(hopeless) and ankle. The pitiful parson. My walk with Mansfield.

Sergeant Baldwin (A. Company) his impassive demeanour—like a
well-trained footman. "My officer's been hit." He bound up my wound.

* * *

"Blighters"

The House is crammed: tier beyond tier they grin
And cackle at the Show, while prancing ranks
Of harlots shrill the chorus, drunk with din;
"We're sure the Kaiser loves our dear old Tanks!"

I'd like to see a Tank come down the stalls,
Lurching to rag-time tunes, or "Home, sweet Home,"
And there'd be no more jokes in Music-halls
To mock the riddled corpses round Bapaume.

How To Die

Dark clouds are smouldering into red
    While down the craters morning burns.
The dying soldier shifts his head
    To watch the glory that returns;
He lifts his fingers toward the skies
    Where holy brightness breaks in flame;
Radiance reflected in his eyes,
    And on his lips a whispered name.

You'd think, to hear some people talk,
    That lads go West with sobs and curses,
And sullen faces white as chalk,
    Hankering for wreaths and tombs and hearses.
But they've been taught the way to do it
    Like Christian soldiers; not with haste
And shuddering groans; but passing through it
    With due regard for decent taste.

The General

"Good-morning; good-morning!" the General said
When we met him last week on our way to the line.
Now the soldiers he smiled at are most of 'em dead,
And we're cursing his staff for incompetent swine.
"He's a cheery old card," grunted Harry to Jack

As they slogged up to Arras with rifle and pack.

    .   .   .   .

But he did for them both by his plan of attack.

LAMENTATIONS

I found him in the guard-room at the Base.
From the blind darkness I had heard his crying
And blundered in. With puzzled, patient face
A sergeant watched him; it was no good trying
To stop it; for he howled and beat his chest.
And, all because his brother had gone west,
Raved at the bleeding war; his rampant grief
Moaned, shouted, sobbed, and choked, while he was kneeling
Half-naked on the floor. In my belief
Such men have lost all patriotic feeling.

GLORY OF WOMEN

You love us when we're heroes, home on leave,
Or wounded in a mentionable place.
You worship decorations; you believe
That chivalry redeems the war's disgrace.
You make us shells. You listen with delight,
By tales of dirt and danger fondly thrilled.
You crown our distant ardours while we fight,
And mourn our laurelled memories when we're killed.
You can't believe that British troops "retire"
When hell's last horror breaks them, and they run,
Trampling the terrible corpses—blind with blood.
    O German mother dreaming by the fire,
    While you are knitting socks to send your son
    His face is trodden deeper in the mud.

DAVID JONES
1895-1974

Painter and poet, Jones enlisted in the Royal Welch Fusiliers and put in twenty-eight months as a private on the Western Front. In 1937, after meditating on the meaning of the war for almost twenty years, he published his long poem In Parenthesis. *Here he depicted a typical British soldier, Private John Ball, experiencing the events at the Somme on July 1, 1916, against an elaborate background of ancient and medieval religious and military motifs.*

From IN PARENTHESIS

    . . . Mr. Jenkins takes them over
and don't bunch on the left
for Christ's sake.

        Riders on pale horses loosed
and vials irreparably broken
an' Wat price bleedin' Glory
Glory
Glory Hallelujah
and the Royal Welsh sing:
Jesu
        lover of me soul . . . to *Aberystwyth.*
But that was on the right with
the genuine Taffies
        but we are rash levied
from Islington and Hackney
and the purlieus of Walworth
flashers from Surbiton
men of the stock of Abraham

from Bromley-by-Bow
Anglo-Welsh from Queens Ferry
rosary-wallahs from Pembrey Dock
lighterman with a Norway darling
from Greenland Stairs
and two lovers from Ebury Bridge,
Bates and Coldpepper
that men called the Lily-white boys.
Fowler from Harrow and the House who'd lost his way into
this crush who was gotten in a parsonage on a maye.
Dynamite Dawes the old 'un
and Diamond Phelps his batty
from Santiago del Estero
and Bulawayo respectively,
both learned in ballistics
            and wasted on a line-mob.

Of young gentlemen wearing the Flash,
from reputable marcher houses
with mountain-squireen first-borns
prince-pedigreed
from Meirionedd and Cyfeiliog.
C. of E. on enlistment eyes grey with mark above left nipple
probably Goidelic from length of femur.
Heirs also of tin-plate lords
from the Gower peninsula,
detailed from the womb
            to captain Industry
if they dont cop a packet this day
nor grow more wise.
Whereas C.S.M. Tyler was transferred from the West Kents
whose mother sang for him
at Mary-Cray
if he would fret she sang for lullaby:
            We'll go to the Baltic with Charlie Napier
she had that of great uncle Tyler
Eb Tyler, who'd got away with the Inkerman bonus.
Every one of these, stood, separate, upright, above ground,
blinkt to the broad light
risen dry mouthed from the chalk
vivified from the Nullah without commotion
and to distinctly said words,
moved in open order and keeping admirable formation

and at the high-port position
walking in the morning on the flat roof of the world
and some walked delicately
sensible of their particular judgment.

Each one bearing in his body the whole apprehension of that
innocent, on the day he saw his brother's votive smoke diffuse
and hang to soot the fields of holocaust; neither approved nor
ratified nor made acceptable but lighted to everlasting parti-
tion.
Who under the green tree
had awareness of his dismembering, and deep-bowelled damage; for whom the green tree bore scarlet memorial, and herb
and arborage waste.

Skin gone astrictive
              for fear gone out to meet half-way—
bare breast for—
to welcome—who gives a bugger for
the Dolorous Stroke.

But sweet sister death has gone debauched today and stalks
on this high ground with strumpet confidence, makes no coy
veiling of her appetite but leers from you to me with all her
parts discovered.
    By one and one the line gaps, where her fancy will—how-
soever they may howl for their virginity
she holds them—who impinge less on space
sink limply to a heap
nourish a lesser category of being
like those other who fructify the land
like Tristram
Lamorak de Galis
Alisand le Orphelin
Beaumains who was youngest
or all of them in shaft-shade
at strait Thermopylae
or the sweet brothers Balin and Balan
embraced beneath their single monument.
    Jonathan my lovely one
on Gelboe mountain
and the young man Absalom.
White Hart transfixed in his dark lodge.
Peredur of steel arms

and he who with intention took grass of that field to be for
him the Species of Bread.
    Taillefer the maker,
and on the same day,
thirty thousand other ranks.
And in the country of Béarn—Oliver
and all the rest—so many without memento
beneath the tumuli on the high hills
and under the harvest places.

But how intolerably bright the morning is where we who are
alive and remain, walk lifted up, carried forward by an effective word.

But red horses now—blare every trump without economy,
burn boat and sever every tie every held thing goes west and
tethering snapt, bolts unshot and brass doors flung wide and
you go forward, foot goes another step further.
The immediate foreground sheers up, tilts toward,
like an high wall falling.
There she breaches black perpendiculars
where the counter-barrage warms to the seventh power where
the Three Children walk under the fair morning
and the Twin Brother
and the high grass soddens through your puttees
and dew asperges the freshly dead.

There doesn't seem a soul about yet surely we walk already
near his preserves; there goes old Dawes as large as life and
there is Lazarus Cohen like on field-days, he always would
have his entrenching-tool-blade-carrier hung low, jogging on
his fat arse.
    They pass a quite ordinary message about keeping aligned
with No. 8.

You drop apprehensively—the sun gone out,
strange airs smite your body
and muck rains straight from heaven
and everlasting doors lift up for '02 Weavel.
    You cant see anything but sheen on drifting particles and
you move forward in your private bright cloud like
one assumed
who is borne up by an exterior volition.

You stumble on a bunch of six with Sergeant Quilter getting
them out again to the proper interval, and when the chemical
thick air dispels you see briefly and with great clearness what
kind of a show this is.

The gentle slopes are green to remind you
of South English places, only far wider and flatter spread and
grooved and harrowed criss-cross whitely and the disturbed
subsoil heaped up albescent.

Across upon this undulated board of verdure chequered
bright
when you look to left and right
small, drab, bundled pawns severally make effort
moved in tenuous line
and if you looked behind—the next wave came slowly, as successive surfs creep in to dissipate on flat shore;
and to your front, stretched long laterally,
and receded deeply,
the dark wood.

And now the gradient runs more flatly toward the separate
scarred saplings, where they make fringe for the interior thicket
and you take notice.
    There between the thinning uprights
at the margin
straggle tangled oak and flayed sheeny beech-bole, and fragile
birch whose silver queenery is draggled and ungraced
and June shoots lopt
and fresh stalks bled
            runs the Jerry trench.
And cork-screw stapled trip-wire
to snare among the briars
and iron warp with bramble weft
with meadow-sweet and lady-smock
for a fair camouflage.

Mr. Jenkins half inclined his head to them—he walked just
barely in advance of his platoon and immediately to the left of
Private Ball.
    He makes the conventional sign
and there is the deeply inward effort of spent men who would
make response for him,
and take it at the double.

He sinks on one knee
and now on the other,
his upper body tilts in rigid inclination
this way and back;
weighted lanyard runs out to full tether,
         swings like a pendulum
         and the clock run down.
Lurched over, jerked iron saucer over tilted brow,
clampt unkindly over lip and chin
nor no ventaille to this darkening
         and masked face lifts to grope the air
and so disconsolate;
enfeebled fingering at a paltry strap—
buckle holds,
holds him blind against the morning.
    Then stretch still where weeds pattern the chalk predella
—where it rises to his wire—and Sergeant T. Quilter takes
over.

Sergeant Quilter is shouting his encouragements, you can almost
hear him, he opens his mouth so wide.
    Sergeant Quilter breaks into double-time
and so do the remainder.
    You stumble in a place of tentacle
you seek a place made straight
you unreasonably blame the artillery
you stand waist-deep
you stand upright
you stretch out hands to pluck at Jerry wire as if it were bramble mesh.
    No. 3 section inclined a little right where a sequence of 9.2's
have done well their work of preparation and cratered a plain
passage. They bunch, a bewildered half dozen, like sheep where
the wall is tumbled—but high-perched Brandenburgers
from their leafy vantage-tops observe
that kind of folly:
nevertheless, you and one other walk alive before his para
pets.
    Yet a taut prehensile strand gets you at the instep, even so,
and sprawls you useless to the First Objective. But Private Watcyn takes it with blameless technique, and even remembers to
halloo the official blasphemies.
    The inorganic earth where your body presses seems it self to
pulse deep down with your heart's acceleration . . . but you go on

living, lying with your face bedded in neatly folded, red-piped, greatcoat and yet no cold cleaving thing drives in between ex-pectant shoulder-blades, so you get to your feet, and the sun-lit chalk is everywhere absorbing fresh stains.

Dark gobbets stiffen skewered to revetment-hurdles and dyed garments strung-up for a sign;
       but the sun shines also
on the living
and on Private Watcyn, who wears a strange look under his iron brim, like a small child caught at some bravado in a garden, and old Dawes comes so queerly from the thing he saw in the next bay but one.

But for all that it is relatively pleasant here under the first trees and lying in good cover.

But Sergeant Quilter is already on the parados. He sorts them out a bit
they are five of No. 1
six of No. 2
two of No. 3
four of No. 4
a lance-jack, and a corporal.

So these nineteen deploy
between the rowan and the hazel,
go forward to the deeper shades.

And now all the wood-ways live with familiar faces and your mate moves like Jack o' the Green: for this season's fertility gone unpruned, & this year's renewing sap shot up fresh tendrils to cumber greenly the heaped decay of last fall, and no forester to tend the paths, nor strike with axes to the root of selected boles, nor had come Jacqueline to fill a pinafore withmay-thorn.

But keepers who engineer new and powerful devices,
forewarned against this morning
prepared with booby-trap beneath
and platforms in the stronger branches
like main-top for an arbalestier,
precisely and competently advised and all in the know,
as to this hour
      when unicorns break cover
and come down
and foxes flee, whose warrens know the shock,
and birds complain in flight—for their nests fall like stars
      and all their airy world gone crazed
and the whole woodland rocks where these break their horns.

It was largely his machine guns in Acid Copse that did it, and our own heavies firing by map reference, with all lines phut and no reliable liaison.

So you just lay where you were and shielded what you could of your body.

It slackened a little and they try short rushes and you find yourself alone in a denseness of hazel-brush and body high bramble and between the bright interstices and multifarious green-stuff, grey textile, scarlet-edged goes and comes—and there is another withdrawing-heel from the thicket.

His light stick-bomb winged above your thorn-bush, and aged oak-timbers shiver and leaves shower like thrown blossom for a conqueror. You tug at rusted pin—
it gives unexpectedly and your fingers pressed to released flange.
You loose the thing into the underbrush.

Dark-faced iron oval lobs heavily to fungus-cushioned dank, wobbles under low leaf to lie, near where the heel drew out just now; and tough root-fibres boomerang to top-most
green filigree and earth clods flung disturb fresh fragile shoots
that brush the sky.

You huddle closer to your mossy bed
you make yourself scarce
you scramble forward and pretend not to see,
but ruby drops from young beech-sprigs—
are bright your hands and face.

And the other one cries from the breaking-buckthorn.

He calls for Elsa, for Manuela
for the parish priest of Burkersdorf in Saxe Altenburg.

You grab his dropt stick-bomb as you go, but somehow you don't fancy it and anyway you forget how it works. You definitely like the coloured label on the handle, you throw it to the tall wood-weeds.

So double detonations, back and fro like well-played-up-to service at a net, mark left and right the forcing of the groves.

But there where a small pathway winds and sun shafts play, a dozen of them walk toward, they come in file, their lifted armslike Jansenist Redeemers, who would save, at least, themselves. Some come furtively who peer sideways, inquisitive of their captors, and one hides a face twisted for intolerable pain and one other casts about him, acutely, as who would take his opportunity, but for the most part they come as sleepwalkers whose bodies go unbidden of the mind, without malevolence, seeking only rest.

But the very young one

who walks apart
whose wide-lidded eyes monstrate immeasurable fatigue—his
greatcoat fits superbly at the waist and its tailored skirts have
distinction; he comes to the salute for Mr. Trevor with more
smartness than anything Mr. Trevor had imagined possible.
    (and conscript-rookies in '17
got so bored with this tale.)
'89 Jones
'99 Thomas
    are detailed for escort.
They spring to it, very well pleased.

    Perhaps they had forgotten his barrage down on the ap-
proaches, storming in the valley, reducing the reserves by one in
three. Impaling this park on all sides but one, at which north
gate his covering parties tactically disposed themselves:
        from digged-pits and chosen embushments
they could quite easily train dark muzzles
to fiery circuit
and run with flame stabs to and fro among
stammer a level traversing
and get a woeful cross-section on
stamen-twined and bruised pistilline
steel-shorn of style and ovary
leaf and blossoming
with flora-spangled khaki pelvises
and where rustling, where limbs thrust—
        from nurturing sun hidden,
late-flowering dog-rose spray let fly like bowyer's ash,
disturbed for the movement
for the pressing forward, bodies in the bower
where adolescence walks the shrieking wood.

He watches where you lift a knee joint gingerly, to avoid low
obstacles,
with flexed articulation poked
from young leaves parted
      —and plug and splinter
shin and fibula
and twice-dye with crimson moistening
for draggled bloodwort and the madder sorrel.
    And covering every small outlet and possible sally-way and
playing old harry with any individual or concerted effort of these
to debouch or even get a dekko of his dispositions.

Now you looked about you for what next to do, or you fired
blindly among the trees and ventured a little further inward; but
already, diagonally to your front, they were coming back in ones
and twos.

You wished you could see people you knew better than the
"C" Company man on your right or the bloke from "A" on your
left, there were certainly a few of No. 8, but not a soul of your
own—which ever way.

No mess-mates at call in cool interior aisles, where the light
came muted, filtered from high up traceries, varied a refracted
lozenge-play on pale cheeks turned; on the bowels of Sergeant
Quilter,
and across feet that hasted
and awkward for anxiety,
        and behind your hurrying
you could hear his tripod's clank nearer than just now.
But where four spreading beeches stood in line and the ground
shelved away about splayed-out roots to afford them cover
Dawes and Diamond Phelps
and the man from Rotherhithe
with five more from "D," and two H.Q. details, and two from
some other unit altogether.

And next to Diamond, and newly dead the lance-jack from
No. 5, and three besides, distinguished only in their variant mutilation.

But for the better discipline of the living,
a green-gilled corporal,
returned to company last Wednesday
from some Corps sinecure,
who'd lost his new tin-hat, his mousey hair and pendulous red
ears like the grocery bloke at the Dry
said his sentences.
His words cut away smartly, with attention to the prescribed
form, so that when he said do this they bloody did it, for all his
back-area breeze-up high.

For Christ knows he must persuade old sweats with more than
sewn-on chevrons or pocket his legatine prestige and lie doggo.

But he'd got them into line at the prone, and loosing off with
economy; and he himself knelt at the further beech bole
to control their fire.

He gathered stragglers as they fell back and John Ball took his
position next to Private Hopkins and they filled the green wood
about them with their covering musketry; till Captain Marlowe
came all put out and withdrew them another forty yards—then

you had to assemble your entrenching-tool parts and dig-in
where you stood, for: Brigade will consolidate positions on
line:—V, Y, O & K.

And who's all this medley and where's Joe Pollock and he saw
Bobby Saunders get it early on and the Brigadier's up with
Aunty Bembridge and all with their Conduit Street bandboxed
shirtings, to flash beige and vermilion at the lapels' turn and neat
sartorial niceties down among the dead men and: It's only right
he should be with the boys the fire-eating old bastard.

Bring meats proper to great lords in harness and: I say Calthrop,
have a bite of this perfectly good chocolate you can eat the stuff
with your beaver up, this Jackerie knows quite well that organis-
ing brains must be adequately nourished
    But O Dear God and suffering Jesus
why dont they bring water from a well
rooty and bully for a man on live
and mollifying oil poured in
and hands to bind with gentleness.
    Fetch those quickly
whose linened bodies leaning over
with anti-toxic airs
would change your pillow-slip—
for the best part of them.
And potent words muttered, and
an anaesthetist's over-dose for gaped viscera.

But why is Father Larkin talking to the dead?

But where's Fatty and Smiler—and this Watcyn boasts he'd
seen the open land beyond the trees, with Jerry coming on in
mass—
and they've left Diamond between the beech boles
and old Dawes blaspheming quietly;
and there's John Hales with Wop Castello cross legged under
the sallies, preoccupied with dead lines—gibbering the formulae of their profession—
Wop defends the D III converted;
and Bates without Coldpepper
digs like a Bunyan muck-raker for his weight of woe.

But it's no good you cant do it with these toy spades, you want
axes, heavy iron for tough anchoring roots, tendoned deep down.

When someone brought up the Jerry picks it was better, and you did manage to make some impression. And the next one to you, where he bends to delve gets it in the middle body. Private Ball is not instructed, and how could you stay so fast a tide, it would be difficult with him screaming whenever you move him ever so little, let alone try with jack-knife to cut clear the hampering cloth.

The First Field Dressing is futile as frantic seaman's shift bunged to stoved bulwark, so soon the darking flood percolates and he dies in your arms.
    And get back to that digging can't yer—
this aint a bloody Wake
        for these dead, who soon will have their dead
for burial clods heaped over.
Nor time for halsing
nor to clip green wounds
nor weeping Maries bringing anointments
neither any word spoken
nor no decent nor appropriate sowing of this seed
nor remembrance of the harvesting
of the renascent cycle
and return
nor shaving of the head nor ritual incising for these *viriles* under each tree.
    No one sings: Lully lully
for the mate whose blood runs down.

IVOR GURNEY
1890–1937

A composer and poet whose early eccentricity ended in insanity, Gurney was confined to an asylum for his last fifteen years. During the war he was a private in the Gloucester Regiment and was gassed and "shell-shocked" at Passchendaele.

THE SILENT ONE

Who died on the wires, and hung there, one of two—
Who for his hours of life had chattered through
Infinite lovely chatter of Bucks accent:
Yet faced unbroken wires; stepped over, and went
A noble fool, faithful to his stripes—and ended.
But I weak, hungry, and willing only for the chance
Of line—to fight in the line, lay down under unbroken
Wires, and saw the flashes and kept unshaken,
Till the politest voice—a finicking accent, said:
"Do you think you might crawl through there: there's a hole."
Darkness, shot at: I smiled, as politely replied—
"I'm afraid not, Sir." There was no hole no way to be seen
Nothing but chance of death, after tearing of clothes.
Kept flat, and watched the darkness, hearing bullets whizzing—
And thought of music—and swore deep heart's deep oaths
(Polite to God) and retreated and came on again,
Again retreated—and a second time faced the screen.

THE BOHEMIANS

Certain people would not clean their buttons,
Nor polish buckles after latest fashions,
Preferred their hair long, putties comfortable,
Barely escaping hanging, indeed hardly able;
In Bridge and smoking without army cautions
Spending hours that sped like evil for quickness,
(While others burnished brasses, earned promotions).
These were those ones who jested in the trench,
While others argued of army ways, and wrenched
What little soul they had still further from shape,
And died off one by one, or became officers.
Without the first of dream, the ghost of notions
Of ever becoming soldiers, or smart and neat,
Surprised as ever to find the army capable
Of sounding "Lights out" to break a game of Bridge,
As to fear candles would set a barn alight:
In Artois or Picardy they lie—free of useless fashions.

BRITISH SOLDIERS' SONGS

The Reason Why

TUNE: *"AULD LANG SYNE"*

We're here because we're here,
Because we're here Because we're here.
We're here because we're here,
Because we're here, Because we're here.
Oh, here we are, oh, here we are,
Oh, here we are again.
Oh, here we are, oh, here we are,
Oh, here we are again.

For You But Not For Me
(The Bells of Hell)

The Bells of Hell go ting-a-ling-a-ling
For you but not for me;
And the little devils how they sing-a-ling-a-ling
For you but not for me.
O Death, where is thy sting-a-ling-a-ling,
O Grave, thy victory?
The Bells of Hell go ting-a-ling-a-ling
For you but not for me.

THE OLD BATTALION

If you want to find the sergeant,
I know where he is, I know where he is;
If you want to find the sergeant,
I know where he is:
He's lying on the canteen floor.
I've seen him, I've seen him,
Lying on the canteen floor.
I've seen him,
Lying on the canteen floor.

If you want to find the quarter-bloke,
I know where he is, I know where he is;
If you want to find the quarter-bloke,
I know where he is:
He's miles and miles behind the line.
I've seen him, I've seen him,
Miles and miles behind the line.
I've seen him,
Miles and miles behind the line.

If you want to find the sergeant-major,
I know where he is, I know where he is;
If you want to find the sergeant-major,
I know where he is:
He's boozing up the privates' rum.
I've seen him, I've seen him,
Boozing up the privates' rum.
I've seen him,
Boozing up the privates' rum.

If you want to find the CO,
I know where he is, I know where he is;
If you want to find the CO,
I know where he is:
He's down in the deep dugouts.
I've seen him, I've seen him,
Down in the deep dugouts.
I've seen him,
Down in the deep dugouts.

If you want to find the old battalion,
I know where they are, I know where they are;
If you want to find the old battalion,
I know where they are:
They're hanging on the old barbed wire.
I've seen them, I've seen them,
Hanging on the old barbed wire.
I've seen them,
Hanging on the old barbed wire.

WILFRID GIBSON
1878–1962

A minor poet and friend of Rupert Brooke, Gibson served as a private on the Western Front and after the war as a social worker in London.

IN THE AMBULANCE

Two rows of cabbages,
Two of curly-greens,
Two rows of early peas,
Two of kidney-beans.

That's what he keeps muttering,
Making such a song,
Keeping other chaps awake
The whole night long.

Both his legs are shot away,
And his head is light,
So he keeps on muttering
All the blessed night:

> *Two rows of cabbages,*
> *Two of curly-greens,*
> *Two rows of early peas,*
> *Two of kidney-beans.*

BACK

> They ask me where I've been,
> And what I've done and seen.
> But what can I reply
> Who know it wasn't I,
> But someone just like me,
> Who went across the sea
> And with my head and hands
> Killed men in foreign lands . . .
> Though I must bear the blame,
> Because he bore my name.

ISAAC ROSENBERG
1890–1918

A talented young painter studying at the Slade School, Rosenberg en-
listed in the King's Own Royal Lancaster Regiment and was killed on a
night patrol on the Western Front seven months before the Armistice.

BREAK OF DAY IN THE TRENCHES

> The darkness crumbles away.
> It is the same old druid Time as ever,
> Only a live thing leaps my hand,
> A queer sardonic rat,

As I pull the parapet's poppy
To stick behind my ear.
Droll rat, they would shoot you if they knew
Your cosmopolitan sympathies.
Now you have touched this English hand
You will do the same to a German
Soon, no doubt, if it be your pleasure
To cross the sleeping green between.
It seems you inwardly grin as you pass
Strong eyes, fine limbs, haughty athletes,
Less chanced than you for life,
Bonds to the whims of murder,
Sprawled in the bowels of the earth,
The torn fields of France.
What do you see in our eyes
At the shrieking iron and flame
Hurled through still heavens?
What quaver—what heart aghast?
Poppies whose roots are in man's veins
Drop, and are ever dropping;
But mine in my ear is safe—
Just a little white with the dust.

HERBERT READ
1893-1968

*Best known as an art critic, Read was an infantry company commander
at Ypres and elsewhere. Recalling Wordsworth's poem of the same title
celebrating the noble character of the "man in arms," Read, who found
nothing at the front but "primitive filth, lice, boredom, and death,"
produced this modern version.*

The Happy Warrior

His wild heart beats with painful sobs,
His strain'd hands clench an ice-cold rifle,
His aching jaws grip a hot parch'd tongue,
His wide eyes search unconsciously.

He cannot shriek.

Bloody saliva
Dribbles down his shapeless jacket.

I saw him stab
And stab again
A well-killed Boche.

This is the happy warrior,
This is he . . .

ROBERT GRAVES
1895–1986

During the war Graves, later the copious novelist, poet, critic, translator, and essayist, was a brave, if satiric and difficult, young officer with the Royal Welch Fusiliers. Recalling wartime events a decade later, he tended to see them—even such serious disasters as the battle of Loos— as versions of stage farce. As soon as he finished writing his memoir Good-bye to All That *(1929), he departed for the island of Majorca, "resolved never to make England my home again."*

From Good-bye to All That

On September 19th we relieved the Middlesex Regiment at Cambrin, and were told that these would be the trenches from which we attacked. The preliminary bombardment had already started, a week in advance. As I led my platoon into the line, I recognized with some disgust the same machine-gun shelter where I had seen the suicide on my first night in trenches. It seemed ominous. This was by far the heaviest bombardment from our own guns we had yet seen. The trenches shook properly, and a great cloud of drifting shell-smoke obscured the German line. Shells went over our heads in a steady stream; we had to shout to make our neighbours hear. Dying down a little at night, the racket began again every morning at dawn, a little louder each time. "Damn it," we said, "there can't be a living soul left in those trenches." But still it went on. The Germans retaliated, though not very vigorously. Most of their heavy artillery had been withdrawn from this sector, we were told, and sent across to the Russian front. More casualties came from our own shorts and blow-backs than from German shells. Much of the ammunition that our batteries were using was made in the United States and contained a high percentage of duds; the driving bands were always coming off. We had fifty casualties in the ranks and three officer casualties, including Buzz Off—badly wounded in the head. This happened before steel helmets were issued; we would not have lost nearly so many with those. I got two insignificant wounds on the hand, which I took as an omen of the right sort.

On the morning of the 23rd, Thomas came back from Battalion Headquarters carrying a note-book and six maps, one for each of us company officers. "Listen," he said, "and copy out all this skite on the back of your maps. You'll have to explain it to your platoons this afternoon. Tomorrow morning we go back to dump our blankets, packs and greatcoats in Béthune. The next day, that's Saturday the 25th, we attack." This being the first definitive news we had been given, we looked up half startled, half relieved. I still have the map, and these are the orders as I copied them down:—

First Objective—*Les Briques Farm*—The big house plainly visible to our front, surrounded by trees. To reach this it is necessary to cross three lines of enemy trenches. The first is three hundred yards distant, the second four hundred, and the third about six hundred. We then cross two railways. Behind the second railway line is a German trench called the Brick Trench. Then comes the Farm, a strong place with moat and cellars and a kitchen garden strongly staked and wired.

Second Objective—*The Town of Auchy*—This is also plainly visible from our trenches. It is four hundred yards beyond the Farm and defended by a first line of trench half-way across, and a second line immediately in front of the town. When we have occupied the first line our direction is half-right, with the left of the Battalion directed on Tall Chimney.

Third Objective—*Village of Haisnes*—Conspicuous by high-spired church. Our eventual line will be taken up on the railway behind this village, where we will dig in and await reinforcements.

When Thomas had reached this point, The Actor's shoulders were shaking with laughter.

"What's up?" asked Thomas irritably.

The Actor giggled: "Who in God's name is responsible for this little effort?"

"Don't know," Thomas said. "Probably Paul the Pimp, or someone like that." (Paul the Pimp was a captain on the Divisional Staff, young, inexperienced and much disliked. He "wore red tabs upon his chest. And even on his undervest.") "Between the six of us, but you youngsters must be careful not to let the men know, this is what they call a 'subsidiary attack.' There will be no troops in support. We've just got to go over and keep the enemy busy while the folk on our right do the real work. You notice that the bombardment is much heavier over there. They've knocked the Hohenzollern Redoubt to bits. Personally, I don't give a damn either way. We'll get killed whatever happens."

We all laughed.

"All right, laugh now, but by God, on Saturday we've got to carry out this funny scheme." I had never heard Thomas so talkative before.

"Sorry," The Actor apologized, "carry on with the dictation."

Thomas went on:

The attack will be preceded by forty minutes' discharge of the accessory, which will clear the path for a thousand yards, so that the two railway lines will be occupied without difficulty. Our advance will follow closely behind the accessory. Behind us are three fresh divisions and the Cavalry Corps. It is expected we shall have no difficulty in breaking through. All men will parade with their platoons; pioneers, servants, etc., to be warned. All platoons to be properly told off under N.C.O's. Every N.C.O. is to know exactly what is expected of him, and when to take over command in case of casualties. Men who lose touch must join up with the nearest company or regiment and push on. Owing to the strength of the accessory, men should be warned against remaining too long in captured trenches where the accessory is likely to collect, but to keep to the open and above all to push on. It is important that if smoke-helmets have to be pulled down they must be tucked in under the shirt.

The Actor interrupted again. "Tell me, Thomas, do you believe in this funny accessory?"

Thomas said: "It's damnable. It's not soldiering to use stuff like that, even though the Germans did start it. It's dirty, and it'll bring us bad luck. We're sure to bungle it. Look at those new gas-companies—sorry, excuse me this once, I mean accessory-companies—their very look makes me tremble. Chemistry-dons from London University, a few lads straight from school, one or two N.C.O's of the old-soldier type, trained together for three weeks, then given a job as responsible as this. Of course they'll bungle it. How could they do anything else? But let's be merry. I'm going on again:

> Men of company: what they are to carry:
>> Two hundred rounds of ammunition (bomb-throwers fifty, and signallers one hundred and fifty rounds).
>> Heavy tools carried in sling by the strongest men.
>> Waterproof sheet in belt.
>> Sandbag in right tunic-pocket.
>> Field-dressing and iodine.
>> Emergency ration, including biscuit.
>> One tube-helmet, to be worn when we advance, rolled up on the head. It must be quite secure and the top part turned down. If possible each man will be provided with an elastic band.
>> One smoke-helmet, old pattern, to be carried for preference behind the back, where it is least likely to be damaged by stray bullets, etc.
>> Wire-cutters, as many as possible, by wiring party and others; hedging gloves by wire party.
>> Platoon screens, for artillery observation, to be carried by a man in each platoon who is not carrying a tool.
>> Packs, capes, greatcoats, blankets will be dumped, not carried.
>> No one is to carry sketches of our position or anything to be likely of service to the enemy.

"That's all. I believe we're going over first with the Middlesex in support. If we get through the German wire I'll be satisfied. Our guns don't seem to be cutting it. Perhaps they're putting that off until the intense bombardment. Any questions?"

That afternoon I repeated the whole rigmarole to the platoon, and told them of the inevitable success attending our assault. They seemed to believe it. All except Sergeant Townsend. "Do you say, Sir, that we have three divisions and the Cavalry Corps behind us?" he asked.

"Yes," I answered.

"Well, excuse me, Sir, I'm thinking it's only those chaps on the right that'll get reinforcements. If we get half a platoon of Mons Angels, that's about all we will get."

"Sergeant Townsend," I said, "you're a well-known pessimist. This is going to be a really good show."

We spent the night repairing damaged trenches.

When morning came we were relieved by the Middlesex, and marched back to Béthune, where we dumped our spare kit at the Montmorency barracks. The Battalion officers messed together in the château near by. This billet was claimed at the same time by the staff of a New Army division, due to take part in the fighting next day. The argument ended amicably with the Division and Battalion messing together. It was, someone pointed out, like a brutal caricature of The Last Supper in duplicate. In the middle of the long table sat the two pseudo-Christs, our Colonel and the Divisional General. Everybody was drinking a lot; the subalterns, allowed whiskey for a treat, grew rowdy. They raised their glasses with: "Cheerio, we will be messing together tomorrow night in La Bassée!" Only the company commanders were looking worried. I remember "C" Company Commander especially, Captain A. L. Samson, biting his thumb and refusing to join in the excitement. I think it was Childe-Freeman of "B" Company who said that night: "The last time the Regiment visited these parts we were under decent leadership. Old Marlborough had more sense than to attack the La Bassée lines; he masked them and went around."

The G.S.O. 1 of the New Army division, a staff-colonel, knew the Adjutant well. They had played polo together in India. I happened to be sitting opposite them. The G.S.O. 1 said, rather drunkenly: "Charley, see that silly old woman over there? Calls himself General Commanding! Doesn't know where he is; doesn't know where his division is; can't even read a map properly. He's marched the poor sods off their feet and left his supplies behind, God knows how far back. They've had to use their iron rations and what they could pick up in the villages. And tomorrow he's going to fight a battle. Doesn't know anything about battles; the men have never been in trenches before, and tomorrow's going to be a glorious balls-up, and the day after tomorrow he'll be sent home." Then he ended, quite seriously: "Really, Charley, it's just as I say, no exaggeration. You mark my words!"

That night we marched back again to Cambrin. The men were singing. Being mostly from the Midlands, they sang comic songs rather than Welsh hymns: "Slippery Sam," "When We've Wound up the Watch on the Rhine," and "I Do Like a S'nice S'mince Pie," to concertina accompaniment. The tune of the "S'nice S'mince Pie" ran in my head all next day, and for the week following I could not get rid of it. The Second Welsh would never have sung a song like "When We've Wound up the Watch on the Rhine." Their only songs about the War were defeatist:

> I want to go home,
> I want to go home.
> The coal-box and shrapnel they whistle and roar,
> I don't want to go to the trenches no more,
> I want to go over the sea
> Where the Kayser can't shoot bombs at me.
> Oh, I
> Don't want to die,
> I want to go home.

There were several more verses in the same strain. Hewitt, the Welsh machine-gun officer, had written one in a more offensive spirit:

> I want to go home,
> I want to go home.
> One day at Givenchy the week before last
> The Allmands attacked and they nearly got past.
> They pushed their way up to the Keep,
> Through our maxim-gun sights we did peep,
> Oh, my!
> They let out a cry,
> They never got home.

But the men would not sing it, though they all admired Hewitt.

The Béthune-La Bassée road was choked with troops, guns and transport, and we had to march miles north out of our way to circle round to Cambrin. Even so, we were held up two or three times by massed cavalry. Everything radiated confusion. A casualty clearing-station had been planted astride one of the principal cross-roads, and was already being shelled. By the time we reached Cambrin, the Battalion had marched about twenty miles that day. Then we heard that the Middlesex would go over first, with us in support; and to their left the Second Argyll and Sutherland Highlanders, with the Cameronians in support. The junior Royal Welch officers complained loudly at our not being given the honour of leading the attack. As the senior regiment, they protested, we were entitled to the "Right of the Line." An hour or so past midnight we moved into trench sidings just in front of the village. Half a mile of communication trench, known as "Maison Rouge Alley," separated us from the firing line. At half-past five the gas would be discharged. We were cold, tired, sick, and not at all in the mood for a battle, but tried to snatch an hour or two of sleep squatting in the trench. It had been raining for some time.

A grey, watery dawn broke at last behind the German lines; the bombardment, surprisingly slack all night, brisked up a little. "Why the devil don't they send them over quicker?" The Actor complained. "This isn't my idea of a bombardment. We're getting nothing opposite us. What little there seems to be is going into the Hohenzollern."

"Shell shortage. Expected it," was Thomas's laconic reply.

We were told afterwards that on the 23rd a German aeroplane had bombed the Army Reserve shell-dump and sent it up. The bombardment on the 24th, and on the day of the battle itself, compared very poorly with that of the previous days. Thomas looked strained and ill. "It's time they were sending that damned accessory off. I wonder what's doing."

The events of the next few minutes are difficult for me now to sort out. I found it more difficult still at the time. All we heard back there in the sidings was a distant cheer, confused crackle of rifle-fire, yells, heavy shelling on our front line, more shouts and yells, and a continuous rattle of machine-guns. After a few minutes, lightly wounded men of the Middlesex came stumbling down Maison Rouge Alley to the dressing-station. I stood at the junction of the siding and the Alley.

"What's happened? What's happened?" I asked.

"Bloody balls-up," was the most detailed answer I could get.

Among the wounded were a number of men yellow-faced and choking, their buttons tarnished green—gas cases. Then came the badly wounded. Maison Rouge Alley being narrow, the stretchers had difficulty in getting down. The Germans started shelling it with five-point-nines.

Thomas went back to Battalion Headquarters through the shelling to ask for orders. It was the same place that I had visited on my first night in the trenches. This cluster of dug-outs in the reserve line showed very plainly from the air as Battalion Headquarters, and should never have been occupied during a battle. Just before Thomas arrived, the Germans put five shells into it. The Adjutant jumped one way, the Colonel another, the R.S.M. a third. One shell went into the signals dug-out, killed some signallers and destroyed the telephone. The Colonel, slightly cut on the hand, joined the stream of wounded and was carried back as far as the base with it. The Adjutant took command.

Meanwhile "A" Company had been waiting in the siding for the rum to arrive; the tradition of every attack being a double tot of rum beforehand. All the other companies got theirs. The Actor began cursing: "Where the bloody hell's that storeman gone?" We fixed bayonets in readiness to go up and attack as soon as Captain Thomas returned with orders. Hundreds of wounded streamed by. At last Thomas's orderly appeared. "Captain's orders, Sir: 'A' Company to move up to the front line." At that moment the storeman arrived, without rifle or equipment, hugging the rum-bottle, red-faced and retching. He staggered up to The Actor and said: "There you are, Sir!," then fell on his face in the thick mud of a sump-pit at the junction of the trench and the siding. The stopper of the bottle flew out and what remained of the three gallons bubbled on the ground. The Actor made no reply. This was a crime that deserved the death penalty. He put one foot on the storeman's neck, the other in the small of his back, and trod him into the mud. Then he gave the order "Company forward!" The Company advanced with a clatter of steel, and this was the last I ever heard of the storeman.

It seems that at half-past four an R.E. captain commanding the gas-company in the front line phoned through to Divisional Headquarters: "Dead calm. Impossible discharge accessory." The answer he got was: "Accessory to be discharged at all costs." Thomas had not over-es-timated the gas-company's efficiency. The spanners for unscrewing the cocks of the cylinders proved, with two or three exceptions, to be misfits. The gas-men rushed about shouting for the loan of an adjustable span-ner. They managed to discharge one or two cylinders; the gas went whistling out, formed a thick cloud a few yards off in No Man's Land, and then gradually spread back into our trenches. The Germans, who had been expecting gas, immediately put on their gas-helmets: semi-rigid ones, better than ours. Bundles of oily cotton-waste were strewn along the German parapet and set alight as a barrier to the gas. Then their batteries opened on our lines. The confusion in the front trench must have been horrible; direct hits broke several of the gas-cylinders, the trench filled with gas, the gas-company stampeded.

No orders could come through because the shell in the signals dug-out at Battalion Headquarters had cut communication not only between companies and Battalion, but between Battalion and Division. The of-ficers in the front trench had to decide on immediate action; so two companies of the Middlesex, instead of waiting for the intense bombard-ment which would follow the advertised forty minutes of gas, charged at once and got held up by the German wire—which our artillery had not yet cut. So far it had only been treated with shrapnel, which made no effect on it; barbed wire needed high-explosive, and plenty of it. The Germans shot the Middlesex men down. One platoon is said to have found a gap and got into the German trench. But there were no survivors of the platoon to confirm this. The Argyll and Sutherland Highlanders went over, too, on the Middlesex left; but two companies, instead of charging at once, rushed back out of the gas-filled assault trench to the support line, and attacked from there. It will be recalled that the trench system had been pushed forward nearer the enemy in preparation for the battle. These companies were therefore attacking from the old front line, but the barbed-wire entanglements protecting it had not been removed, so that the Highlanders got caught and machine-gunned between their own assault and support lines. The other two companies were equally unsuccessful. When the attack started, the German N.C.O's had jumped up on the parapet to encourage their men. These were Jägers, famous for their musketry.

The survivors of the two leading Middlesex companies now lay in shell-craters close to the German wire, sniping and making the Germans keep their heads down. They had bombs to throw, but these were nearly all of a new type issued for the battle. The fuses were lighted on the match-box principle, and the rain had made them useless. The other two companies of the Middlesex soon followed in support. Machine-gun fire stopped them half-way. Only one German machine-gun remained in action, the others having been knocked out by rifle- or trench-mortar fire. Why the single gun survived is a story in itself.

It starts with the privilege granted British colonial governors and high-commissioners of nominating one or two officers from their countries for attachment in wartime to the Regular Army. Under this scheme, the officers began as full lieutenants. The Captain-General of Jamaica (if that is his correct style) nominated the eighteen-year-old son of a rich planter, who went straight from Kingston to the First Middlesex. He was good-hearted enough, but of little use in the trenches, having never been out of the island in his life or, except for a short service with the West India militia, seen any soldiering. His company commander took a fatherly interest in "Young Jamaica," and tried to teach him his duties. This Company Commander was known as "The Boy." He had twenty years' service with the Middlesex, and the unusual boast of having held every rank from "boy" to captain in the same company. His father, I believe, had been the regimental sergeant-major. But "Jamaica," as a full lieutenant, ranked senior to the other experienced subalterns in the company, who were only second-lieutenants.

The Middlesex Colonel decided to shift Jamaica off on some course of extra-regimental appointment at the earliest opportunity. Somewhere about May or June, when instructed to supply an officer for the brigade trench-mortar company, he had sent Jamaica. Trench-mortars, being then both dangerous and ineffective, the appointment seemed suitable. At the same time, the Royal Welch had also been asked to detail an officer, and the Colonel had sent Tiley, an ex-planter from Malaya, and what is called a "fine natural soldier." Tiley was chosen because, when attached to us from a Lancashire regiment, he had showed his resentment at the manner of his welcome somewhat too plainly. But, by September, mortars had improved in design and become an important infantry arm; so Jamaica, being senior to Tiley, held the responsible position of Brigade Mortar Officer.

When the Middlesex charged, The Boy fell mortally wounded as he climbed over the parapet. He tumbled back and began crawling down the trench to the stretcher-bearers' dug-out, past Jamaica's trench-mortar emplacement. Jamaica had lost his gun-team, and was boldly serving the trench-mortars himself. On seeing The Boy, however, he deserted his post and ran off to fetch a stretcher-party. Tiley, meanwhile, on the other flank opposite Mine Point, had knocked out all the machine-guns within range. He went on until his mortar burst. Only one machine-gun in the Pope's Nose, a small salient facing Jamaica, remained active.

At this point the Royal Welch Fusiliers came up Maison Rouge Alley. The Germans were shelling it with five-nines (called "Jack Johnsons" because of their black smoke) and lachrymatory shells. This caused a continual scramble backwards and forwards, to cries of: "Come on!" "Get back, you bastards!" "Gas turning on us!" "Keep your heads, you men!" "Back like hell, boys!" "Whose orders?" "What's happening?" "Gas!" "Back!" "Come on!" "Gas!" "Back!" Wounded men and stretcher-bearers kept trying to squeeze past. We were alternately putting on and taking off our gas-helmets, which made things worse. In many places the trench had caved in, obliging us to scramble over the top. Childe-Freeman reached the front line with only fifty men of "B" Company; the rest had lost their way in some abandoned trenches halfway up.

The Adjutant met him in the support line. "Ready to go over, Freeman?" he asked.

Freeman had to admit that most of his company were missing. He felt this disgrace keenly; it was the first time that he had commanded a company in battle. Deciding to go over with his fifty men in support of the Middlesex, he blew his whistle and the company charged. They were stopped by machine-gun fire before they had got through our own entanglements. Freeman himself died—oddly enough, of heart-failure—as he stood on the parapet.

A few minutes later, Captain Samson, with "C" Company and the remainder of "B," reached our front line. Finding the gas-cylinders still whistling and the trench full of dying men, he decided to go over too— he could not have it said that the Royal Welch had let down the Middlesex. A strong, comradely feeling bound the Middlesex and the Royal Welch, intensified by the accident that the other three battalions in the Brigade were Scottish, and that our Scottish Brigadier was, unjustly no doubt, accused of favouring them. Our Adjutant voiced the extreme non-Scottish view: "The Jocks are all the same; both the trousered kind and the bare-arsed kind: they're dirty in trenches, they skite too much, and they charge like hell—both ways." The First Middlesex, who were the original "Diehards," had more than once, with the Royal Welch, considered themselves let down by the Jocks. So Samson charged with "C" and the remainder of "B" Company.

One of "C" officers told me later what happened. It had been agreed to advance by platoon rushes with supporting fire. When his platoon had gone about twenty yards, he signalled them to lie down and open covering fire. The din was tremendous. He saw the platoon on his left flopping down too, so he whistled the advance again. Nobody seemed to hear. He jumped up from his shell-hole, waved and signalled "Forward!"

Nobody stirred.

He shouted: "You bloody cowards, are you leaving me to go on alone?"

His platoon-sergeant, groaning with a broken shoulder, gasped: "Not cowards, Sir. Willing enough. But they're all f—ing dead." The Pope's Nose machine-gun, traversing, had caught them as they rose to the whistle.

"A" Company, too, had become separated by the shelling. I was with the leading platoon. The Surrey-man got a touch of gas and went coughing back. The Actor accused him of skrimshanking. This I thought unfair; the Surreyman looked properly sick. I don't know what happened to him, but I heard that the gas-poisoning was not serious and that he managed, a few months later, to get back to his own regiment in France. I found myself with The Actor in a narrow communication trench between the front and support lines. This trench had not been built wide enough for a stretcher to pass the bends. We came on The Boy lying on his stretcher, wounded in the lungs and stomach. Jamaica was standing over him in tears, blubbering: "Poor old Boy, poor old Boy, he's going to die; I'm sure he is. He's the only one who treated me decently."

The Actor, finding that we could not get by, said to Jamaica: "Take that poor sod out of the way, will you? I've got to get my company up. Put him into a dug-out, or somewhere."

Jamaica made no answer; he seemed paralyzed by the horror of the occasion and could only repeat: "Poor old Boy, poor old Boy!"

"Look here," said The Actor, "if you can't shift him into a dug-out we'll have to lift him on top of the trench. He can't live now, and we're late getting up."

"No, no," Jamaica shouted wildly.

The Actor lost his temper and shook Jamaica roughly by the shoulders. "You're the bloody trench-mortar wallah, aren't you?" he shouted.

Jamaica nodded miserably.

"Well, your battery is a hundred yards from here. Why the hell aren't you using your gas-pipes to some purpose? Buzz off back to them!" And he kicked him down the trench. Then he called over his shoulder: "Sergeant Rose and Corporal Jennings! Lift this stretcher up across the top of the trench. We've got to pass."

Jamaica leaned against a traverse. "I do think you're the most heartless beast I've ever met," he said weakly.

We went up to the corpse-strewn front line. The captain of the gas-company, who was keeping his head, and wore a special oxygen respirator, had by now turned off the gas-cocks. Vermorel-sprayers had cleared out most of the gas, but we were still warned to wear our masks. We climbed up and crouched on the fire-step, where the gas was not so thick—gas, being heavy stuff, kept low. Then Thomas arrived with the remainder of "A" Company and with "D," we waited for the whistle to follow the other two companies over. Fortunately at this moment the Adjutant appeared. He was now left in command of the Battalion, and told Thomas that he didn't care a damn about orders; he was going to cut his losses and not send "A" and "D" over to their deaths until he got definite orders from Brigade. He had sent a runner back, and we must wait.

Meanwhile, the intense bombardment that was to follow the forty minutes' discharge of gas began. It concentrated on the German front trench and wire. A good many shells fell short, and we had further casualties from them. In No Man's Land, the survivors of the Middlesex and of our "B" and "C" Companies suffered heavily.

My mouth was dry, my eyes out of focus, and my legs quaking under me. I found a water-bottle full of rum and drank about half a pint; it quieted me, and my head remained clear. Samson lay groaning about twenty yards beyond the front trench. Several attempts were made to rescue him. He had been very badly hit. Three men got killed in these attempts; two officers and two men, wounded. In the end his own orderly managed to crawl out to him. Samson sent him back, saying that he was riddled through and not worth rescuing; he sent his apologies to the Company for making such a noise.

We waited a couple of hours for the order to charge. The men were silent and depressed; only Sergeant Townsend was making feeble, bitter jokes about the good old British Army muddling through, and how he thanked God we still had a Navy. I shared the rest of my rum with him, and he cheered up a little. Finally a runner arrived with a message that the attack had been postponed. . . .

My memory of that day is hazy. We spent it getting the wounded down to the dressing-station, spraying the trenches and dug-outs to get rid of the gas, and clearing away the earth where trenches were blocked. The trenches stank with a gas-blood-lyddite-latrine smell. Late in the afternoon we watched through our field-glasses the advance of reserves under heavy shell-fire towards Loos and Hill 70; it looked like a real break-through. They were troops of the New Army division whose staff we had messed with the night before. Immediately to the right of us we had the Highland Division. Ian Hay has celebrated their exploits on that day in *The First Hundred Thousand;* I suppose that we were "the flat caps on the left" who "let down" his comrades-in-arms.

FRANK RICHARDS
1884–1961

For fifteen years before the war, Private Frank Richards was a professional soldier with the British army in India. During the war he served with the Second Battalion of the Royal Welch Fusiliers, whose junior officers included both Siegfried Sassoon and Robert Graves. Years afterward, wondering whether an account of his experience he'd written was worth reading, he sent it to Graves, who assured him it was and helped him publish it. Richards' book, Old Soldiers Never Die, *published in 1933, Graves called "without exception the most valuable account of World War One written from the ranks." Among its merits, he found, is "its humorous restraint in describing unparalleled horrors."*

From OLD SOLDIERS NEVER DIE

We moved to a little village not far from Soissons where my company was billeted in a linseed-cake factory. Whilst there a General Army Order from the Commander-in-Chief, General Sir John French, was read out, in which he thanked the officers and men for the magnificent spirit they had shown since the twenty-third of August and also said that it was only a question of hours or days before they would be in pursuit of a beaten enemy. Twenty-four hours later another General Army Order from Sir John French was read out, in which he stated that it had been brought to his notice that men did not salute their superior officers, and that the men were probably of the opinion that they did not have to salute their superior officers whilst on active service. But officers must be saluted on active service the same as in peace time, and officers commanding units must see that this is carried out. Ever since we had landed in France we had been under the impression that we did not have to salute officers now; our officers were under the same impression and never pulled us up for not saluting them: we simply stood to attention and answered "Sir" when they were speaking to us. The following day we were on saluting drill, and each one of us tried to outdo the other in our flow of language. There were two parades. The old pre-War soldier heartily disliked saluting parade and church parade. Duffy said we didn't have a ghost of a chance under this sort of conditions and that we were bound to lose the War. I have often thought since then that our time would have far better been employed if we had been learned something about a machine-gun.

During the time we were on the Aisne our brigade were in reserve and during our leisure hours we played Kitty Nap, Pontoon, Brag, and Crown and Anchor. A pukka old soldier's Bible was his pack of cards. Corporal Pardoe of my section and I won quite a lot of money. Mine came in handy afterwards for having a good time, but Corporal Pardoe was thrifty with his winnings, and didn't spend hardly a penny. Duffy told me I was in God's pocket but that he had no doubt in his own mind that I would get killed during the next action I was in, and that all men who were lucky at gambling very soon had their lights put out. Duffy was a pessimist in his way but a first-class soldier and good all-round chap.

CHRISTMAS, 1914

On Christmas morning we stuck up a board with "A Merry Christmas" on it. The enemy had stuck up a similar one. Platoons would sometimes go out for twenty-four hours rest—it was a day at least out of the trench and relieved the monotony a bit—and my platoon had gone out in this way the night before, but a few of us stayed behind to see what would happen. Two of our men then threw their equipment off and jumped on the parapet with their hands above their heads. Two of the Germans done the same and commenced to walk up the river bank, our two men going to meet them. They met and shook hands and then we all got out of the trench. Buffalo Bill rushed into the trench and endeavoured to prevent it, but he was too late: the whole of the Company were now out, and so were the Germans. He had to accept the situation, so soon he and the other company officers climbed out too. We and the Germans met in the middle of no-man's-land. Their officers was also now out. Our officers exchanged greetings with them. One of the German officers said that he wished he had a camera to take a snapshot, but they were not allowed to carry cameras. Neither were our officers.

We mucked in all day with one another. They were Saxons and some of them could speak English. By the look of them their trenches were in as bad a state as our own. One of their men, speaking in English, mentioned that he had worked in Brighton for some years and that he was fed up to the neck with this damned war and would be glad when it was all over. We told him that he wasn't the only one that was fed up with it. We did not allow them in our trench and they did not allow us in theirs. The German Company-Commander asked Buffalo Bill if he would accept a couple of barrels of beer and assured him that they would not make his men drunk. They had plenty of it in the brewery. He accepted the offer with thanks and a couple of their men rolled the barrels over and we took them into our trench. The German officer sent one of his men back to the trench, who appeared shortly after carrying a tray with bottles and glasses on it. Officers of both sides clinked glasses and drunk one another's health. Buffalo Bill had presented them with a plum pudding just before. The officers came to an understanding that the unofficial truce would end at midnight. At dusk we went back to our respective trenches.

We had a decent Christmas dinner. Each man had a tin of Maconochie's and a decent portion of plum pudding. (A tin of Maconochie's consisted of meat, potatoes, beans and other vegetables and could be eaten cold, but we generally used to fry them up in the tin on a fire. I don't remember any man ever suffering from tin or lead poisoning through doing them in this way. The best firms that supplied them were Maconochie's and Moir Wilson's, and we could always depend on having a tasty dinner when we opened one of their tins. But another firm that supplied them at this time must have made enormous profits out of the British Government. Before ever we opened the first tins that were supplied by them we smelt a rat. The name of the firm made us suspicious. When we opened them our suspicions were well founded. There was nothing inside but a rotten piece of meat and some boiled rice. The head of that firm should have been put against the wall and shot for the way they sharked us troops.) The two barrels of beer were drunk, and the German officer was right: if it was possible for a man to have drunk the two barrels himself he would have bursted before he had got drunk. French beer was rotten stuff.

Just before midnight we all made it up not to commence firing before they did. At night there was always plenty of firing by both sides if there were no working parties or patrols out. Mr. Richardson, a young officer who had just joined the Battalion and was now a platoon officer in my company, wrote a poem during the night about the Briton and the Bosche meeting in no-man's-land on Christmas day, which he read out to us. A few days later it was published in *The Times* or *Morning Post*, I believe. During the whole of Boxing Day we never fired a shot, and they the same, each side seemed to be waiting for the other to set the ball a-rolling. One of their men shouted across in English and inquired how we had enjoyed the beer. We shouted back and told him it was very weak but that we were very grateful for it. We were conversing off and on during the whole of the day. We were relieved that evening at dusk by a battalion of another brigade. We were mighty surprised as we had heard no whisper of any relief during the day. We told the men who relieved us how we had spent the last couple of days with the enemy, and they told us that by what they had been told the whole of the British troops in the line, with one or two exceptions, had mucked in with the enemy. They had only been out of action themselves forty-eight hours after being twenty-eight days in the front-line trenches. They also told us that the French people had heard how we had spent Christmas day and were saying all manner of nasty things about the British Army.

Going through Armentières that night some of the French women were standing in the doors spitting and shouting at us: "You no bon, you English soldiers, you boko kamerade Allemenge." We cursed them back until we were blue in the nose, and the Old Soldier, who had a wonderful command of bad language in many tongues, excelled himself. We went back to Erquinghem on the outskirts of Armentières and billeted in some sheds. Not far from the sheds was a large building which had been converted into a bath-house for the troops. We had our first bath one day in the latter end of November, and on the twenty-seventh of December we had our second. Women were employed in the bathhouse to iron the seams of our trousers, and each man handed in his shirt, underpants and socks and received what were supposed to be clean ones in exchange; but in the seams of the shirts were the eggs, and after a man had his clean shirt on for a few hours the heat of his body would hatch them and he would be just as lousy as ever he had been. I was very glad when I had that second bath, because I needed a pair of pants. A week before whilst out in the village one night I had had a scrounge through a house and found a magnificent pair of ladies' bloomers. I thought it would be a good idea to discard my pants, which were skin-tight, and wear these instead, but I soon discovered that I had made a grave mistake. The crawlers, having more room to manœuvre in, swarmed into those bloomers by platoons, and in a few days time I expect I was the lousiest man in the company. When I was stripping for the bath Duffy and the Old Soldier noticed the bloomers, and they both said that I looked sweet enough to be kissed.

* * *

At Bray Dunes I got in conversation with a Canadian officer who was in charge of some men building a light railway. He said it was a good job that the States came in the War as the French were ready to throw the sponge up. A few days later two of our signallers overheard a full colonel of the Staff telling our Colonel that he did not know what would have happened if the United States had not come in when they did. It was common knowledge among the Staff that the whole of the French Army were more or less demoralized, and the States coming in had to a great extent been the means of restoring their morale. We got wind that our Division and another had been sent up the coast to try and break through the German Front and capture Ostend. This was freely discussed by the officers, but no break through was attempted owing to so little progress being made on the Ypres front.

One of the largest concentration prison camps I ever saw was erected in this area. It was estimated to hold between ten and fifteen thousand prisoners, but all I saw in it were two solitary prisoners who must have been very lonely in so large a place.

On the night the Battalion went in the line I went on leave. It was eighteen months since I had the last one and as usual I made the most of it. I didn't spend the whole of it in pubs: I spent two days going for long tramps in the mountains, which I thoroughly enjoyed after being so long in a flat country. I was presented with a gold watch, in recognition of winning the D.C.M., which I still have, but it has been touch-and-go with it several times since the War. Probably if there hadn't been an inscription on it I should have parted with it. This time every man of military age that I met wanted to shake hands with me and also ask my advice on how to evade military service, or, if they were forced to go, which would be the best corps to join that would keep them away from the firing line. They were wonderfully patriotic at smoking concerts given in honour of soldiers returning from the Front, but their patriotism never extended beyond that.

When I landed back at Boulogne I came across the man who had been shot through his cheeks at Bois Grenier in April 1915. If anything, that bullet had improved his appearance. He now had a nice little dimple on each side of his face. We had a chat. I asked what he was doing now and he said that he had a Staff job, as a military policeman around the Docks. He told me very seriously that if it was possible, and he had the name and address of the German that shot him, he would send him the largest parcel he could pack and a hundred-franc note as well. He was having the time of his life on his present job and had one of the smartest fillies in Boulogne, who was the goods in every way. As I left him I could not help thinking how lucky some men were and how unlucky were others.

When I arrived back I found that the Division had left the coastal area on short notice. All returning leave men of the Division were in a little camp outside Dunkirk. One night some German planes came over bombing and one of our searchlights kept a plane in its rays for some time. Anti-aircraft guns, machine-guns and Lewis guns, and we with our rifles were all banging at him, but he got away with it. Whilst everyone was busy firing at that one, his friends were busy dropping their bombs on Dunkirk. It was very rare that a plane flying at any height was brought down by anti-aircraft guns or rifle-fire but we lost a lot of planes on the Somme by rifle-fire when they came down very low, machine-gunning the enemy before our troops attacked. German planes used to do the same thing and seldom got away with it either.

I rejoined the Battalion in a village near Ypres and guessed that we would soon be in the blood tub. Ricco and Paddy had been made full corporals but Paddy had taken a lot of persuading before he consented to be made an N.C.O. He was sent back to Division Headquarters for a special course of signalling and was lucky enough to miss the next show we were in. Our Colonel went on leave and missed the show too. The name of our Acting-Colonel was Major Poore. He was not an old regimental officer but had been posted to us some six months before from the Yeomanry, I believe. He was a very big man, about fifty years of age, slightly deaf, and his favourite expression was "What, what!" He was a very decent officer. A tall, slender young lieutenant who had just returned from leave was made Assistant-Adjutant for the show. I believe he was given that job because he was an excellent map-reader. As we were marching along the road, Sealyham asked him if he had come across Mr. Sassoon during his leave. He replied that he hadn't and that he had spent a good part of his leave trying to find out where he was but had failed to get any news at all. This young officer had joined the Battalion about the same time as Mr. Sassoon and we old hands thought he was a man and a half to spend his leave looking for a pal. His name was Casson. I wrote it down first here as Carson, but an old soldiering pal tells me that I had it wrong. Mr. Casson was said to be a first-class pianist, but trench warfare did not give him much opportunity to show his skill at that. If he was as good a pianist as he was a cool soldier he must have been a treat to hear.

During the night we passed through a wood where a Very-light dump had been exploded by a German shell. It was like witnessing a fireworks display at home. We stayed in the wood for the night. Our Brigade were in reserve and ready to be called upon at any moment. Orders were given that no fires were to be lit. September 26th, 1917, was a glorious day from the weather point of view and when dawn was breaking Ricco and I who were crack hands at making smokeless fires had found a dump of pick-handles which when cut up in thin strips answered very well. We soon cooked our bacon and made tea for ourselves and the bank clerk and architect, and made no more smoke than a man would have done smoking a cigarette. We had at least made sure of our breakfast which might be the last we would ever have.

At 8 A.M. orders arrived that the Battalion would move off to the assistance of the Australians who had made an attack early in the morning on Polygon Wood. Although the attack was successful they had received heavy casualties and were now hard pressed themselves. Young Mr. Casson led the way, as cool as a cucumber. One part of the ground we travelled over was nothing but lakes and boggy ground and the whole of the Battalion were strung out in Indian file walking along a track about eighteen inches wide. We had just got out of this bad ground but were still travelling in file when the enemy opened out with a fierce bombardment. Just in front of me half a dozen men fell on the side of the track: it was like as if a Giant Hand had suddenly swept them one side. The Battalion had close on a hundred casualties before they were out of that valley. If a man's best pal was wounded he could not stop to dress his wounds for him.

We arrived on some rising ground and joined forces with the Australians. I expected to find a wood but it was undulating land with a tree dotted here and there and little banks running in different directions. About half a mile in front of us was a ridge of trees, and a few concrete pillboxes of different sizes. The ground that we were now on and some of the pillboxes had only been taken some hours previously. I entered one pillbox during the day and found eighteen dead Germans inside. There was not a mark on one of them; one of our heavy shells had made a direct hit on the top of it and they were killed by concussion, but very little damage had been done to the pillbox. They were all constructed with reinforced concrete and shells could explode all round them but the flying pieces would never penetrate the concrete. There were small windows in the sides and by jumping in and out of shell holes attacking troops could get in bombing range: if a bomb was thrown through one of the windows the pillbox was as good as captured.

There was a strong point called Black Watch Corner which was a trench facing north, south, east and west. A few yards outside the trench was a pillbox which was Battalion Headquarters. The bank clerk, architect and I got in the trench facing our front, and I was soon on friendly terms with an Australian officer, whom his men called Mr. Diamond. He was wearing the ribbon of the D.C.M., which he told me he had won in Gallipoli while serving in the ranks and had been granted a commission some time later. About a hundred yards in front of us was a bank which extended for hundreds of yards across the ground behind which the Australians were. Our chaps charged through them to take a position in front and Captain Mann, our Adjutant, who was following close behind, fell with a bullet through his head. The enemy now began to heavily bombard our position and Major Poore and Mr. Casson left the pillbox and got in a large shell hole which had a deep narrow trench dug in the bottom of it. They were safer there than in the pillbox, yet in less than fifteen minutes an howitzer shell had pitched clean in it, killing the both of them.

During the day shells fell all around the pillbox but not one made a direct hit on it. The ground rocked and heaved with the bursting shells. The enemy were doing their best to obliterate the strong point that they had lost. Mr. Diamond and I were mucking-in with a tin of Maconochies when a dud shell landed clean in the trench, killing the man behind me, and burying itself in the side of the trench by me. Our Maconochie was spoilt but I opened another one and we had the luck to eat that one without a clod of earth being thrown over it. If that shell had not been a dud we should have needed no more Maconochies in this world. I had found eight of them in a sandbag before I left the wood and brought them along with me. I passed the other six along our trench, but no one seemed to want them with the exception of the bank clerk and architect who had got into my way of thinking that it was better to enter the next world with a full belly than an empty one.

The bombardment lasted until the afternoon and then ceased. Not one of us had hardly moved a yard for some hours but we had been lucky in our part of the trench, having only two casualties. In two other parts of the strong point every man had been killed or wounded. The shells had been bursting right on the parapets and in the trenches, blowing them to pieces. One part of the trench was completely obliterated. The fourth part of the strong point had also been lucky, having only three casualties. Mr. Diamond said that we could expect a counter attack at any minute. He lined us up on the parapet in extended order outside the trench and told us to lie down. Suddenly a German plane swooped very low, machine-gunning us. We brought him down but not before he had done some damage, several being killed including our Aid Post Sergeant.

A few minutes later Dr. Dunn temporarily resigned from the Royal Army Medical Corps. He told me to get him a rifle and bayonet and a bandolier of ammunition. I told him that he had better have a revolver but he insisted on having what he had asked me to get. I found them for him and slinging the rifle over his shoulder he commenced to make his way over to the troops behind the bank. I accompanied him. Just before we reached there our chaps who were hanging on to a position in front of it started to retire back. The doctor barked at them to line up with the others. Only Captain Radford and four platoon officers were left in the Battalion and the Doctor unofficially took command.

We and the Australians were all mixed up in extended order. Everyone had now left the strong point and were lined up behind the bank, which was about three feet high. We had lent a Lewis-gun team to the 5th Scottish Rifles on our right, and when it began to get dark the Doctor sent me with a verbal message to bring them back with me, if they were still in the land of the living. When I arrived at the extreme right of our line I asked the right-hand man if he was in touch with the

5th Scottish. He replied that he had no more idea than a crow where they were, but guessed that they were somewhere in front and to the right of him. I now made my way very carefully over the ground. After I had walked some way I began to crawl. I was liable any moment to come in contact with a German post or trench. I thought I saw someone moving in front of me, so I slid into a shell hole and landed on a dead German. I waited in that shell hole for a while trying to pierce the darkness in front. I resumed my journey and, skirting one shell hole, a wounded German was shrieking aloud in agony: he must have been hit low down but I could not stop for no wounded man. I saw the forms of two men in a shallow trench and did not know whether they were the 5th Scottish or the Germans until I was sharply challenged in good Glasgow English. When I got in their trench they told me that they had only just spotted me when they challenged. The Lewis-gun team were still kicking and my journey back with them was a lot easier than the outgoing one.

I reported to the Doctor that there was a gap of about one hundred yards between the 5th Scottish Rifles and we; and he went himself to remedy it. The whole of the British Front that night seemed to be in a semi-circle. We had sent up some S O S rockets and no matter where we looked we could see our S O S rockets going up in the air: they were only used when the situation was deemed critical and everybody seemed to be in the same plight as ourselves. The bank clerk and I got into a shell hole to snatch a couple of hours rest, and although there were two dead Germans in it we were soon fast asleep. I was woke up to guide a ration party to us who were on their way. Dawn was now breaking and I made my way back about six hundred yards, where I met them. We landed safely with the rations.

Major Kearsley had just arrived from B Echelon to take command of the Battalion. The Brigadier-General of the Australians had also arrived and was sorting his men out. It was the only time during the whole of the War that I saw a brigadier with the first line of attacking troops. Some brigadiers that I knew never moved from Brigade Headquarters. It was also the first time I had been in action with the Australians and I found them very brave men. There was also an excellent spirit of comradeship between officers and men.

We were moving about quite freely in the open but we did not know that a large pillbox a little over an hundred yards in front of us was still held by the enemy. They must have all been having a snooze, otherwise some of us would have been riddled. Major Kearsley, the Doctor and I went out reconnoitring. We were jumping in and out of shell holes when a machine-gun opened out from somewhere in front, the bullets knocking up the dust around the shell holes we had just jumped into. They both agreed that the machine-gun had been fired from the pillbox about a hundred yards in front of us. We did some wonderful jumping and hopping, making our way back to the bank. The enemy's artillery had also opened out and an hour later shells were bursting all over our front and in the rear of us.

A sapping platoon of one sergeant and twenty men under the command of The Athlete were on the extreme left of the bank, and the Major and I made our way towards them. We found the men but not the officer and sergeant, and when the Major inquired where they were they replied that they were both down the dug-out. There was a concrete dug-out at this spot which had been taken the day before. I shouted down for them to come up, and the Major gave the young officer a severe reprimand for being in the dug-out, especially as he knew our men had just started another attack. Our chaps and the 5th Scottish Rifles had attacked on our right about fifteen minutes previously. The Major gave The Athlete orders that if the pillbox in front was not taken in fifteen minutes he was to take his platoon and capture it and then dig a trench around it. If the pillbox was captured during that time he was still to take his platoon and sap around it. I felt very sorry for The Athlete. This was the first real action he had been in and he had the most windy sergeant in the Battalion with him. Although The Athlete did not know it, this sergeant had been extremely lucky after one of the Arras stunts that he had not been court-martialled and tried on the charge of cowardice in face of the enemy.

We arrived back at our position behind the bank. We and the Australians were in telephone communication with no one; all messages went by runners. Ricco, the bank clerk and the architect were running messages, the majority of our Battalion runners being casualties. Sealyham was still kicking and Lane was back in B Echelon; it was the first time for over two years he had been left out of the line. The Sapping-Sergeant came running along the track by the bank and informed the Major that The Athlete had sent him for further instructions as he was not quite certain what he had to do. The Major very nearly lost his temper and told me to go back with the Sergeant and tell him what he had to do. Just as we arrived at the sapping-platoon we saw some of our chaps rushing towards the pillbox, which surrendered, one officer and twenty men being inside it.

C and D Companies were now merged into one company. They advanced and took up a position behind a little bank about a hundred yards in front of the pillbox. I informed The Athlete that he had to take his platoon and sap around the pillbox, and that this was a verbal message which Major Kearsley had given me for him. I left him and the Sergeant conferring together and made my way back by a different route.

The enemy were now shelling very heavily and occasionally the track was being sprayed by machine-gun bullets. I met a man of one of our companies with six German prisoners whom he told me he had to take back to a place called Clapham Junction, where he would hand them over. He then had to return and rejoin his company. The shelling was worse behind us than where we were and it happened more than once that escort and prisoners had been killed making their way back. I had known this man about eighteen months and he said, "Look here, Dick. About an hour ago I lost the best pal I ever had, and he was worth all these six Jerries put together. I'm not going to take them far before I put them out of mess." Just after they passed me I saw the six dive in one large shell hole and he had a job to drive them out. I expect being under their own shelling would make them more nervous than under ours. Some little time later I saw him coming back and I knew it was impossible for him to have reached Clapham Junction and returned in the time, especially by the way his prisoners had been ducking and jumping into shell holes. As he passed me again he said: "I done them in as I said, about two hundred yards back. Two bombs did the trick." He had not walked twenty yards beyond me when he fell himself: a shell-splinter had gone clean through him. I had often heard some of our chaps say that they had done their prisoners in whilst taking them back but this was the only case I could vouch for, and no doubt the loss of his pal had upset him very much.

During the afternoon the Major handed me a message to take to A Company, which consisted of the survivors of two companies now merged into one under the command of a young platoon officer. They had to advance and take up a position about two hundred yards in front of them. The ground over which I had to travel had been occupied by the enemy a little while before and the Company were behind a little bank which was being heavily shelled. I slung my rifle, and after I had proceeded some way I pulled my revolver out for safety. Shells were falling here and there and I was jumping in and out of shell holes. When I was about fifty yards from the Company, in getting out of a large shell hole I saw a German pop up from another shell hole in front of me and rest his rifle on the lip of the shell hole. He was about to fire at our chaps in front who had passed him by without noticing him. He could never have heard me amidst all the din around: I expect it was some instinct made him turn around with the rifle at his shoulder. I fired first and as the rifle fell out of his hands I fired again. I made sure he was dead before I left him. If he hadn't popped his head up when he did no doubt I would have passed the shell hole he was in. I expect he had been shamming death and every now and then popping up and sniping at our chaps in front. If I hadn't spotted him he would have soon put my lights out after I had passed him and if any of his bullets had found their mark it would not have been noticed among the Company, who were getting men knocked out now and then by the shells that were bursting around them. This little affair was nothing out of the ordinary in a runner's work when in attacks.

The shelling was very severe around here and when I arrived I shouted for the officer. A man pointed along the bank. When I found him and delivered the message he shouted above the noise that he had not been given much time; I had delivered the message only three minutes before they were timed to advance. During the short time they had been behind the bank one-third of the Company had become casualties. When I arrived back I could only see the Major. All the signallers had gone somewhere on messages and the Doctor was some distance away attending wounded men whom he came across. He seemed to be temporarily back in the R.A.M.C.

The Major asked me how my leg was. I replied that it was all right when I was moving about, but it became very stiff after I had been resting. During the two days many pieces and flying splinters of shells and bullets must have missed me by inches. But when a small piece of spent shrapnel had hit me on the calf of the leg I knew all about it. I thought at the time that someone had hit me with a coal hammer. I had the bottom of my trousers doubled inside the sock on the calf and also my puttee doubled in the same place which, no doubt, had helped to minimize the blow. If it had not been a spent piece it would have gone clean through the calf and given me a beautiful blighty wound, which I don't mind admitting I was still hoping for.

Ricco in returning from running a message to Brigade had come across the ration party of another battalion who had all been killed, and he had brought back with him a lovely sandbag full of officers' rations. There were several kinds of tinned stuffs and three loaves of bread. The bank clerk, architect and Sealyham had also arrived back and we all had a muck in. The way the bank clerk and architect got a tin of cooked sausages across their chests made me wonder whether their forefathers had not been pure-bred Germans. The officers who the bag of rations were intended for could never have enjoyed them better than we did.

Just as we finished our feed Major Kearsley called me and told me to follow him. I could see we were making our way towards where we had visited the sapping-platoon, but I could not see any men sapping around the pillbox and was wondering if they had been knocked out. When we arrived at the concrete dug-out some of the sapping-platoon were still outside it and some had become casualties, but The Athlete and the Sergeant were still down in the dug-out. I shouted down and told them to come up and the Major asked The Athlete the reason why he had not carried out his orders. He replied that the shelling had been so intense around the pillbox after it was taken that he decided to stop where he was until it slackened. Then he had seen our troops advance again and he was under the impression that the trench would not be needed. The Major again gave him a severe reprimand and told him to take what men he had left and sap around the pillbox as he had been ordered at first.

Shortly after, the major said he was going to visit the positions our companies had lately taken. We set off on our journey and when we passed through the Australians they started shouting, "Come back, you bloody fools! They've got everything in line with machine-gun fire." We took no notice and by jumping in shell holes now and again we reached halfway there. We had only advanced a few yards further when in jumping into a large shell hole an enemy machine-gun opened out and the ground around us was sprayed with bullets. The Major was shot clean through the leg just above the ankle. As I dressed his wound we discussed the possibility of returning to the bank. I said that it would be dusk in two hours' time and that we had better wait until then. He replied that he could not do that as he would have to hand over the command of the Battalion, and also wanted to discuss matters with the Commanding Officer of the 5th Scottish Rifles, and that we would make our way back at once. He clambered out of the shell hole and I followed. He hopped back to the bank, taking a zig-zag course and I the same. How we were not riddled was a mystery: the machine-gun had been playing a pretty tune behind us.

We met the Doctor and Captain Radford, who had been sent for some time before, advancing along the bank. They had decided to shift Battalion Headquarters more on the left of the bank and they had just shifted in time. The spot where Battalion Headquarters had been was now being blown to pieces. Shells were bursting right along the bank and for a considerable way back and men were being blowed yards in the air. The Major said that the Battalion would be relieved at dusk and he would try to stick it until then; but the Doctor warned him, if he did, that it might be the cause of him losing his leg.

He then handed over the command to Captain Radford, who said that he would much prefer the Doctor taking command, as he seemed to have a better grip of the situation than what he had. But the Major said he could not do that as the Doctor was a non-combatant, but that they could make any arrangements they liked when he had left. We made our way to the 5th Scottish Rifles and met their colonel outside a little dug-out. He mentioned that only three young platoon-officers were left in his battalion. They went in the dug-out to discuss matters and when we left the Major had a difficult job to walk. The Casualty Clearing Station was at Clapham Junction and all along the track leading down to it lay stretcher-bearers and bandaged men who had been killed making their way back. Many men who had received what they thought were nice blighty wounds had been killed along this track. The previous day the track, in addition to being heavily shelled had also been under machine-gun fire. As we were moving along I counted over twenty of our tanks which had been put out of action. Mr. Diamond, whom I had not seen since the previous day, passed us with his arm in a sling and said, "Hello. I'm glad to see you alive." He had been hit through the muscle of his arm. Shells were bursting here and there and we could sniff gas. We put our gas helmets on for a little while and it was twilight when we reached Clapham Junction.

The Major told me that the Battalion was going back to Dickiebusch after it was relieved and that I had no need to return. He wrote me out a note to take back to the transport. He then said that he would have liked to have remained with the Battalion until they were relieved but he thought it best to follow the Doctor's advice, especially when he said that he might lose his leg. I told him not to take too much notice of the Doctor, who would have made a better general than a doctor, and that I had seen worse bullet-wounds than what he had which had healed up in a fortnight's time. I hoped he would be back with the Battalion inside a couple of months. We shook hands and wished one another the best of luck and I made my way back to the transport.

The enemy bombed Dickiebusch that night but it was such a common occurrence around this area and I was so dead-beat that I took no notice of it. The following morning I rejoined the remnants of the Battalion and found that Ricco, the bank clerk, the architect and Sealyham were still kicking. They thought I had gone West and were as delighted to see me as I was them. We had lost heavily in signallers, but Tich was still hale and hearty.

ERICH MARIA REMARQUE
1898–1970

Few pre-war assumptions about the dignity and glory of battle survived the fictional exposé All Quiet on the Western Front, *by the German ex-soldier Erich Maria Remarque. Appearing in 1929, the same year as Hemingway's* A Farewell to Arms *and Graves's* Good-bye to All That, *it helped disillusion a whole between-the-wars generation, persuading*

them that the Great War, viewed from whichever side, was as stupid, cruel, and meaningless as the most experienced of its combatants said. Remarque went on to write many more novels, but none was as success-ful. He came to the United States in 1939 and became a naturalized citizen in 1947.
The speaker here is a young German infantryman, Paul Bäumer.

From ALL QUIET ON THE WESTERN FRONT

We are at rest five miles behind the front. Yesterday we were relieved, and now our bellies are full of beef and haricot beans. We are satisfied and at peace. Each man has another mess-tin full for the evening; and, what is more, there is a double ration of sausage and bread. That puts a man in fine trim. We have not had such luck as this for a long time. The cook with his carroty head is begging us to eat; he beckons with his ladle to everyone that passes, and spoons him out a great dollop. He does not see how he can empty his stew-pot in time for coffee. Tjaden and Müller have produced two wash-basins and had them filled up to the brim as a reserve. In Tjaden this is voracity, in Müller it is foresight. Where Tjaden puts it all is a mystery, for he is and always will be as thin as a rake.

What's more important still is the issue of a double ration of smokes. Ten cigars, twenty cigarettes, and two quids of chew per man; now that is decent. I have exchanged my chewing tobacco with Katczinsky for his cigarettes, which means I have forty altogether. That's enough for a day.

It is true we have no right to this windfall. The Prussian is not so generous. We have only a miscalculation to thank for it.

Fourteen days ago we had to go up and relieve the front line. It was fairly quiet on our sector, so the quartermaster who remained in the rear had requisitioned the usual quantity of rations and provided for the full company of one hundred and fifty men. But on the last day an astonish-ing number of English field-guns opened up on us with high-explosive, drumming ceaselessly on our position, so that we suffered heavily and came back only eighty strong.

Last night we moved back and settled down to get a good sleep for once: Katczinsky is right when he says it would not be such a bad war if only one could get a little more sleep. In the line we have had next to none, and fourteen days is a long time at one stretch.

It was noon before the first of us crawled out of our quarters. Half an hour later every man had his mess-tin and we gathered at the cook-house, which smelt greasy and nourishing. At the head of the queue of course were the hungriest—little Albert Kropp, the clearest thinker among us and therefore the first to be lance-corporal; Müller, who still carries his school textbooks with him, dreams of examinations, and during a bombardment mutters propositions in physics; Leer, who wears a full beard and has a preference for the girls from officers' brothels. And as the fourth, myself, Paul Bäumer. All four are nineteen years of age, and all four joined up from the same class as volunteers for the war.

Close behind us were our friends: Tjaden, a skinny lock-smith of our own age, the biggest eater of the company. He sits down to eat as thin as a grasshopper and gets up as big as a bug in the family way; Haie Westhus, of the same age, a peat-digger, who can easily hold a ration-loaf in his hand and say: Guess what I've got in my fist; then Detering, a peasant, who thinks of nothing but his farmyard and his wife; and finally Stanislaus Katczinsky, the leader of our group, shrewd, cunning, and hard-bitten, forty years of age, with a face of the soil, blue eyes, bent shoulders, and a remarkable nose for dirty weather, good food, and soft jobs.

Our gang formed the head of the queue before the cook-house. We were growing impatient, for the cook paid no attention to us.

Finally Katczinsky called out to him: "Say, Heinrich, open up the soup-kitchen. Anyone can see the beans are done."

He shook his head sleepily: "You must all be there first." Tjaden grinned: "We are all here."

The sergeant-cook still took no notice. "That may do for you," he said. "But where are the others?"

"They won't be fed by you to-day. They're either in the dressing-station or pushing up daisies."

The cook was quite disconcerted as the facts dawned on him. He was staggered. "And I have cooked for one hundred and fifty men—"

Kropp poked him in the ribs. "Then for once we'll have enough. Come on, begin!"

Suddenly a vision came over Tjaden. His sharp, mousey features began to shine, his eyes grew small with cunning, his jaws twitched, and he whispered hoarsely: "Man! then you've got bread for one hundred and fifty men too, eh?"

The sergeant-cook nodded, absent-minded and bewildered.

Tjaden seized him by the tunic. "And sausage?"

Ginger nodded again.

Tjaden's chaps quivered. "Tobacco too?"

"Yes, everything."

Tjaden beamed: "What a bean-feast! That's all for us! Each man gets—wait a bit—yes, practically two issues."

Then Ginger stirred himself and said: "That won't do."

Then we got excited and began to crowd around.

"Why won't that do, you old carrot?" demanded Katczinsky.

"Eighty men can't have what is meant for a hundred and fifty."

"We'll soon show you," growled Müller.

"I don't care about the stew, but I can only issue rations for eighty men," persisted Ginger.

Katczinsky got angry. "You might be generous for once. You haven't drawn food for eighty men. You've drawn it for the Second Company. Good. Let's have it then. We are the Second Company."

We began to jostle the fellow. No one felt kindly toward him, for it was his fault that the food twice came up to us in the line too late and cold. Under shell-fire he wouldn't bring his kitchen up near enough, so that our soup-carriers had to go much farther than those of the other companies. Now Bulcke of the First Company is a much better fellow. He is as fat as a hamster in winter, but he trundles his pots when it comes to that right up to the very front line.

We were in just the right mood, and there would certainly have been a dust-up if our company commander had not appeared. He informed himself of the dispute, and only remarked: "Yes, we did have heavy losses yesterday."

He looked in the dixie. "The beans look good."

Ginger nodded. "Cooked with meat and fat."

The lieutenant looked at us. He knew what we were thinking. And he knew many other things too, because he came to the company as a non-com. and was promoted from the ranks. He lifted the lid from the dixie again and sniffed. Then passing on he said: "Serve out the whole issue. We can do with it. And bring me a plate full too."

Ginger looked sheepish as Tjaden danced round him.

"It doesn't cost you anything! One would think the quartermaster's store belonged to him! And now get on with it, you old blubber-sticker, and don't you miscount either."

"You be hanged!" spat out Ginger. When things get beyond him he throws up the sponge altogether; he just goes to pieces. And as if to show that all things were now the same to him, of his own free will he shared out half a pound of synthetic honey equally among us.

To-day is wonderfully good. The mail has come, and almost every man has a couple of letters.

Kropp pulls out one. "Kantorek sends you all his best wishes."

We laugh. Müller throws his cigarette away and says: "I wish he was here."

Kantorek had been our schoolmaster, an active little man in a grey tail-coat, with a face like a shrew-mouse. He was about the same size as

Corporal Himmelstoss, the "Terror of Klosterberg." It is very queer that the unhappiness of the world is so often brought on by small men. They are so much more energetic and uncompromising than the big fellows. I have always taken good care to keep out of sections with small company commanders. They are mostly confounded little martinets.

During drill-time Kantorek gave us long lectures until the whole of our class went under his shepherding to the District Commandant and volunteered. I can see him now, as he used to glare at us through his spectacles and say in a moving voice: "Won't you join up, Comrades?"

These teachers always carry their feelings ready in their waistcoat pockets, and fetch them out at any hour of the day. But we didn't think of that then.

There was, indeed, one of us who hesitated and did not want to fall into line. That was Josef Behm, a plump, homely fellow. But he did allow himself to be persuaded, otherwise he would have been ostracized. And perhaps more of us thought as he did, but no one could very well stand out, because at that time even one's parents were ready with the word "coward;" no one had the vaguest idea what we were in for. The wisest were just the poor and simple people. They knew the war to be a misfortune, whereas people who were better off were beside themselves with joy, though they should have been much better able to judge what the consequences would be.

Katczinsky said that was a result of their upbringing. It made them stupid. And what Kat said, he had thought about.

Strange to say, Behm was one of the first to fall. He got hit in the eye during an attack, and we left him lying for dead. We couldn't bring him with us, because we had to come back helter-skelter. In the afternoon suddenly we heard him call, and saw him outside creeping towards us. He had only been knocked unconscious. Because he could not see, and was mad with pain, he failed to keep under cover, and so was shot down before anyone could go and fetch him in.

Naturally we couldn't blame Kantorek for this. Where would the world be if one brought every man to book? There were thousands of Kantoreks, all of whom were convinced that there was only one way of doing well, and that way theirs.

And that is just why they let us down so badly.

For us lads of eighteen they ought to have been mediators and guides to the world of maturity, the world of work, of duty, of culture, of progress—to the future. We often made fun of them and played jokes on them, but in our hearts we trusted them. The idea of authority, which they represented, was associated in our minds with a greater insight and a manlier wisdom. But the first death we saw shattered this belief. We had to recognize that our generation was more to be trusted than theirs.

They surpassed us only in phrases and in cleverness. The first bombardment showed us our mistake, and under it the world as they had taught it to us broke in pieces.

While they continued to write and talk, we saw the wounded and dying. While they taught that duty to one's country is the greatest thing, we already knew that death-throes are stronger. But for all that we were no mutineers, no deserters, no cowards—they were very free with all these expressions. We loved our country as much as they; we went courageously into every action; but also we distinguished the false from the true, we had suddenly learned to see. And we saw that there was nothing of their world left. We were all at once terribly alone; and alone we must see it through.

Before going over to see Kemmerich we pack up his things: he will need them on the way back.

In the dressing-station there is great activity; it reeks as ever of carbolic, ether, and sweat. Most of us are accustomed to this in the billets, but here it makes one feel faint. We ask for Kemmerich. He lies in a large room and receives us with feeble expressions of joy and helpless agitation. While he was unconscious someone had stolen his watch.

Müller shakes his head: "I always told you that nobody should carry as good a watch as that."

Müller is rather crude and tactless, otherwise he would hold his tongue, for anybody can see that Kemmerich will never come out of this place again. Whether he finds his watch or not will make no difference. At the most one will only be able to send it to his people.

"How goes it, Franz?" asks Kropp.

Kemmerich's head sinks.

"Not so bad . . . but I have such a damned pain in my foot."

We look at his bed covering. His leg lies under a wire basket. The bed covering arches over it. I kick Müller on the shin, for he is just about to tell Kemmerich what the orderlies told us outside: that Kemmerich has lost his foot. The leg is amputated. He looks ghastly, yellow, and wan. In his face there are already the strained lines that we know so well, we have seen them now hundreds of times. They are not so much lines as marks. Under the skin the life no longer pulses, it has already pressed out to the boundaries of the body. Death is working through from within. It already has command in the eyes. Here lies our comrade, Kemmerich, who a little while ago was roasting horse-flesh with us and squatting in the shell-holes. He it is still and yet it is not he any longer. His features have become uncertain and faint, like a photographic plate on which two pictures have been taken. Even his voice sounds like ashes.

I think of the time when we went away. His mother, a good plump matron, brought him to the station. She wept continually, her face was bloated and swollen. Kemmerich felt embarrassed, for she was the least composed of all; she simply dissolved into fat and water. Then she caught sight of me and took hold of my arm again and again, and implored me to look after Franz out there. Indeed he did have a face like a child, and such frail bones that after four weeks pack-carrying he already had flat feet. But how can a man look after anyone in the field!

"Now you will soon be going home," says Kropp. "You would have had to wait at least three or four months for your leave."

Kemmerich nods. I cannot bear to look at his hands, they are like wax. Under the nails is the dirt of the trenches, it shows through blue-black like poison. It strikes me that these nails will continue to grow like long fantastic cellar-plants long after Kemmerich breathes no more. I see the picture before me. They twist themselves into corkscrews and grow and grow, and with them the hair on the decayed skull, just like grass in a good soil, just like grass, how can it be possible—

Müller leans over. "We have brought your things, Franz."

Kemmerich signs with his hand. "Put them under the bed."

Müller does so. Kemmerich starts on again about the watch. How can one calm him without making him suspicious?

Müller reappears with a pair of airman's boots. They are fine English boots of soft, yellow leather which reach to the knee and lace all the way—they are things to be coveted.

Müller is delighted at the sight of them. He matches their soles against his own clumsy boots and says: "Will you be taking them with you, Franz?"

We all three have the same thought; even if he should get better, he would be able to use only one—they are no use to him. But as things are now it is a pity that they should stay here; the orderlies will of course grab them as soon as he is dead.

"Won't you leave them with us?" Müller repeats.

Kemmerich doesn't want to. They are his most prized possessions.

"Well, we could exchange," suggests Müller again. "Out here one can make some use of them." Still Kemmerich is not to be moved.

I tread on Müller's foot; reluctantly he puts the fine boots back again under the bed.

We talk a little more and then take our leave.

"Cheerio, Franz."

I promise him to come back in the morning. Müller talks of doing so too. He is thinking of the lace-up boots and means to be on the spot.

Kemmerich groans. He is feverish. We get hold of an orderly outside and ask him to give Kemmerich a dose of morphia.

He refuses. "If we were to give morphia to everyone we would have to have tubs full—"

"You only attend to officers properly," says Kropp viciously.

I hastily intervene and give him a cigarette. He takes it.
"Are you usually allowed to give it, then?" I ask him.
He is annoyed. "If you don't think so, then why do you ask?"
I press a couple more cigarettes into his hand. "Do us the favour—"
"Well, all right," he says.
Kropp goes in with him. He doesn't trust him and wants to see. We wait outside.
Müller returns to the subject of the boots. "They would fit me perfectly. In these boots I get blister after blister. Do you think he will last till to-morrow after drill? If he passes out in the night, we know where the boots—"
Kropp returns. "Do you think—?" he asks.
"Done for," says Müller emphatically.
We go back to the huts. I think of the letter that I must write to-morrow to Kemmerich's mother. I am freezing. I could do with a tot of rum. Müller pulls up some grass and chews it. Suddenly little Kropp throws his cigarette away, stamps on it savagely, and looking round him with a broken and distracted face, stammers: "Damned swine, the damned swine!"
We walk on for a long time. Kropp has calmed himself; we understand: he sees red, out here every man gets like that sometime.
"What has Kantorek written to you?" Müller asks him.
He laughs. "We are the Iron Youth."
We all three smile bitterly. Kropp rails: he is glad that he can speak.
Yes, that's the way they think, these hundred thousand Kantoreks! Iron Youth. Youth! We are none of us more than twenty years old. But young? Youth? That is long ago. We are old folk.

It is strange to think that at home in the drawer of my writing table there lies the beginning of a play called "Saul" and a bundle of poems. Many an evening I have worked over them—we all did something of the kind—but that has become so unreal to me that I cannot comprehend it any more. Our early life is cut off from the moment we came here, and that without our lifting a hand. We often try to look back on it and to find an explanation, but never quite succeed. For us young men of twenty everything is extraordinarily vague, for Kropp, Müller, Leer, and me, for all of us whom Kantorek calls the "Iron Youth." All the older men are linked up with their previous life. They have wives, children, occupations, and interests, they have a background which is so strong that the war cannot obliterate it. We young men of twenty, however, have only our parents, and some, perhaps, a girl—that is not much, for at our age the influence of parents is at its weakest and girls have not yet got a hold over us. Besides this there was little else—some enthusiasm, a few hobbies, and our school. Beyond this our life did not extend. And of this nothing remains.

Kantorek would say that we stood on the threshold of life. And so it would seem. We had as yet taken no root. The war swept us away. For the others, the older men, it is but an interruption. They are able to think beyond it. We, however, have been gripped by it and do not know what the end may be. We know only that in some strange and melancholy way we have become a waste land. All the same, we are not often sad.

Though Müller would be delighted to have Kemmerich's boots, he is really quite as sympathetic as another who could not bear to think of such a thing for grief. He merely sees things clearly. Were Kemmerich able to make any use of the boots, then Müller would rather go barefoot over barbed wire than scheme how to get hold of them. But as it is the boots are quite inappropriate to Kemmerich's circumstances, whereas Müller can make good use of them. Kemmerich will die; it is immaterial who gets them. Why, then, should Müller not succeed to them? he has more right than a hospital-orderly. When Kemmerich is dead it will be too late. Therefore Müller is already on the watch.

We have lost all sense of other considerations, because they are artificial. Only the facts are real and important for us. And good boots are scarce.

Once it was different. When we went to the District Commandant to enlist, we were a class of twenty young men, many of whom proudly shaved for the first time before going to the barracks. We had no definite plans for our future. Our thoughts of a career and occupation were as yet of too unpractical a character to furnish any scheme of life. We were still crammed full of vague ideas which gave to life, and to the war also, an ideal and almost romantic character. We were trained in the army for ten weeks and in this time more profoundly influenced than by ten years at school. We learned that a bright button is weightier than four volumes of Schopenhauer. At first astonished, then embittered, and finally indifferent, we recognized that what matters is not the mind but the boot brush, not intelligence but the system, not freedom but drill. We became soldiers with eagerness and enthusiasm, but they have done everything to knock that out of us. After three weeks it was no longer incomprehensible to us that a braided postman should have more authority over us than had formerly our parents, our teachers, and the whole gamut of culture from Plato to Goethe. With our young, awakened eyes we saw that the classical conception of the Fatherland held by our teachers resolved itself here into a renunciation of personality such as one would not ask of the meanest servant—salutes, springing to attention, parade-marches, presenting arms, right wheel, left wheel, clicking the heels, insults, and a thousand pettifogging details. We had fancied our task would be different, only to find we were to be trained for heroism as though we were circus-ponies. But we soon accustomed ourselves to it. We learned in fact that some part of these things was necessary, but the rest merely show. Soldiers have a fine nose for such distinctions.

By threes and fours our class was scattered over the platoons amongst Frisian fishermen, peasants, and labourers with whom we soon made friends. Kropp, Müller, Kemmerich, and I went to No. 9 platoon under Corporal Himmelstoss.

He had the reputation of being the strictest disciplinarian in the camp, and was proud of it. He was a small undersized fellow with a foxy, waxed moustache, who had seen twelve years' service and was in civil life a postman. He had a special dislike for Kropp, Tjaden, Westhus, and me, because he sensed a quiet defiance.

I have remade his bed fourteen times in one morning. Each time he had some fault to find and pulled it to pieces. I have kneaded a pair of prehistoric boots that were as hard as iron for twenty hours—with intervals of course—until they became as soft as butter and not even Himmelstoss could find anything more to do to them; under his orders I have scrubbed out the Corporals' Mess with a tooth-brush. Kropp and I were given the job of clearing the barrack-square of snow with a handbroom and a dust-pan, and we would have gone on till we were frozen had not a lieutenant accidentally appeared who sent us off, and hauled Himmelstoss over the coals. But the only result of this was to make Himmelstoss hate us more. For six weeks consecutively I did guard every Sunday and was hut-orderly for the same length of time. With full pack and rifle I have had to practise on a soft, wet, newly ploughed field the "Prepare to advance, advance!" and the "Lie down!" until I was one lump of mud and finally collapsed. Four hours later I had to report to Himmelstoss with my clothes scrubbed clean, my hands chafed and bleeding. Together with Kropp, Westhus, and Tjaden I have stood at attention in a hard frost without gloves for a quarter of an hour at a stretch, while Himmelstoss watched for the slightest movement of our bare fingers on the steel barrel of the rifle. I have run eight times from the top floor of the barracks down to the courtyard in my shirt at two o'clock in the morning because my drawers projected three inches beyond the edge of the stool on which one had to stack all one's things. Alongside me ran the corporal, Himmelstoss, and trod on my bare toes. At bayonet-practice I had constantly to fight with Himmelstoss, I with a heavy iron weapon whilst he had a handy wooden one with which he easily struck my arms till they were black and blue. Once, indeed, I became so infuriated that I ran at him blindly and gave him a mighty jab in the stomach and knocked him down. When he reported me the company commander laughed at him and told him he ought to keep his eyes open; he understood Himmelstoss, and apparently was not displeased at his discomfiture. I became a past master on the horizontal bars and strove to surpass my instructor at physical jerks;—we have trembled at the mere sound of his voice, but this runaway post-horse never got the better of us.

One Sunday as Kropp and I were lugging a latrine-bucket on a pole across the barrack-yard, Himmelstoss came by, all polished up and spry for going out. He planted himself in front of us and asked how we liked the job. In spite of ourselves we tripped and emptied the bucket over his legs. He raved, but the limit had been reached.

"That means clink," he yelled.

But Kropp had had enough. "There'll be an inquiry first," he said, "and then we'll unload."

"Mind how you speak to a non-commissioned officer!" bawled Himmelstoss. "Have you lost your senses? You wait till you're spoken to. What will you do, anyway?"

"Show you up, Corporal," said Kropp, his thumbs in line with the seams of his trousers.

Himmelstoss saw what we meant and went off without saying a word. But before he disappeared he growled: "You'll drink this!"—but it was the end of his authority. He tried it on once more in the ploughed field with his "Prepare to advance, advance" and "Lie down." We obeyed each order, since an order's an order and has to be obeyed. But we did it so slowly that Himmelstoss became desperate. Carefully we went down on our knees, then on our hands, and so on; in the meantime, quite infuriated, he had given another command. But before we had even begun to sweat he was hoarse. After that he left us in peace. He did indeed always refer to us as swine, but there was, nevertheless, a certain respect in his tone.

There were many other staff corporals, the majority of whom were more decent. But above all each of them wanted to keep his good job there at home as long as possible, and that he could do only by being strict with the recruits.

Practically every conceivable polishing job in the entire camp fell to us and we often howled with rage. Many of us became ill through it; Wolf actually died of inflammation of the lung. But we would have felt ridiculous had we hauled down our colours. We became hard, suspicious, pitiless, vicious, tough—and that was good; for these attributes had been entirely lacking in us. Had we gone into the trenches without this period of training most of us would certainly have gone mad. Only thus were we prepared for what awaited us. We did not break down, but endured; our twenty years, which made many another thing so grievous, helped us in this. But by far the most important was that it awakened in us a strong, practical sense of *esprit de corps*, which in the field developed into the finest thing that arose out of the war—comradeship.

I sit by Kemmerich's bed. He is sinking steadily. Around us is a great commotion. A hospital train has arrived and the wounded fit to be moved are being selected. The doctor passes by Kemmerich's bed without once looking at him.

"Next time, Franz," I say.

He raises himself on the pillow with his elbows. "They have amputated my leg."

He knows it too then. I nod and answer: "You must be thankful you've come off with that."

He is silent.

I resume: "It might have been both legs, Franz. Wegeler has lost his right arm. That's much worse. Besides, you will be going home." He looks at me. "Do you think so?"

"Of course."

"Do you think so?" he repeats.

"Sure. Once you've got over the operation."

He beckons me to bend down. I stoop over him and he whispers: "I don't think so."

"Don't talk rubbish, Franz, in a couple of days you'll see for yourself. What is it anyway—an amputated leg? Here they patch up far worse things than that."

He lifts one hand. "Look here though, these fingers."

"That's the result of the operation. Just eat decently and you'll soon be well again. Do they look after you properly?"

He points to a dish that is still half full. I get excited. "Franz, you must eat. Eating is the main thing. That looks good too."

He turns away. After a pause he says slowly: "I wanted to become a head-forester once."

"So you may still," I assure him. "There are splendid artificial limbs now, you'd hardly know there was anything missing. They are fixed on to the muscles. You can move the fingers and work and even write with an artificial hand. And besides, they will always be making new improvements."

For a while he lies still. Then he says: "You can take my lace-up boots with you for Müller."

I nod and wonder what to say to encourage him. His lips have fallen away, his mouth has become larger, his teeth stick out and look as though they were made of chalk. The flesh melts, the forehead bulges more prominently, the cheek-bones protrude. The skeleton is working itself through. The eyes are already sunken in. In a couple of hours it will be over.

He is not the first I have seen thus; but we grew up together and that always makes it a bit different. I have copied his essays. At school he used to wear a brown coat with a belt and shiny sleeves. He was the only one of us, too, who could do the giant's turn on the parallel bars. His hair flew in his face like silk when he did it. Kantorek was proud of him for it. But he couldn't endure cigarettes. His skin was very white; he had something of the girl about him.

I glance at my boots. They are big and clumsy, the breeches are tucked into them, and standing up one looks well-built and powerful in these great drain-pipes. But when we go bathing and strip, suddenly we have slender legs again and slight shoulders. We are no longer soldiers but little more than boys; no one would believe that we could carry packs. It is a strange moment when we stand naked; then we become civilians, and almost feel ourselves to be so. When bathing Franz Kemmerich looked as slight and frail as a child. There he lies now—but why? The whole world ought to pass by this bed and say: "That is Franz Kemmerich, nineteen and a half years old, he doesn't want to die. Let him not die!"

My thoughts become confused. This atmosphere of carbolic and gangrene clogs the lungs, it is a thick gruel, it suffocates.

It grows dark. Kemmerich's face changes colour, it lifts from the pillow and is so pale that it gleams. The mouth moves slightly. I draw near to him. He whispers: "If you find my watch, send it home—"

I do not reply. It is no use any more. No one can console him. I am wretched with helplessness. This forehead with its hollow temples, this mouth that is now merely a slit, this sharp nose! And the fat, weeping woman at home to whom I must write. If only the letter were sent off already!

Hospital-orderlies go to and fro with bottles and pails. One of them comes up, casts a glance at Kemmerich and goes away again. You can see he is waiting, apparently he wants the bed.

I bend over Franz and talk to him as though that could save him: "Perhaps you will go to the convalescent home at Klosterberg, among the villas, Franz. Then you can look out from the window across the fields to the two trees on the horizon. It is the loveliest time of the year now, when the corn ripens; at evening the fields in the sunlight look like mother-of-pearl. And the lane of poplars by the Klosterbach, where we used to catch sticklebacks! You can build an aquarium again and keep fish in it, and you can go out without asking anyone, you can even play the piano if you want to."

I lean down over his face which lies in the shadow. He still breathes, lightly. His face is wet, he is crying. What a fine mess I have made of it with my foolish talk!

"But Franz"—I put my arm round his shoulders and put my face against his. "Will you sleep now?"

He does not answer. The tears run down his cheeks. I would like to wipe them away but my handkerchief is too dirty.

An hour passes. I sit tensely and watch his every movement in case he may perhaps say something. What if he were to open his mouth and cry out! But he only weeps, his head turned aside. He does not speak of his mother or his brothers and sisters. He says nothing; all that lies behind him; he is entirely alone now with his little life of nineteen years, and cries because it leaves him. This is the most disturbing and hardest parting that ever I have seen, although it was pretty bad too with Tiedjen, who called for his mother—a big bear of a fellow who, with wild eyes full of terror, held off the doctor from his bed with a dagger until he collapsed.

Suddenly Kemmerich groans and begins to gurgle.

I jump up, stumble outside and demand: "Where is the doctor? Where is the doctor?"

As I catch sight of the white apron I seize hold of it: "Come quick, Franz Kemmerich is dying."

He frees himself and asks an orderly standing by: "Which will that be?"

He says: "Bed 26, amputated thigh."

He sniffs: "How should I know anything about it, I've amputated five legs to-day;" he shoves me away, says to the hospital-orderly "You see to it," and runs off to the operating room.

I tremble with rage as I go along with the orderly. The man looks at me and says: "One operation after another since five o'clock this morning. You know to-day alone there have been sixteen deaths—yours is the seventeenth. There will probably be twenty altogether—"

I become faint, all at once I cannot do any more. I won't revile any more, it is senseless, I could drop down and never rise up again.

We are by Kemmerich's bed. He is dead. The face is still wet from the tears. The eyes are half open and yellow like old horn buttons.

The orderly pokes me in the ribs. "Are you taking his things with you?" I nod.

He goes on: "We must take him away at once, we want the bed. Outside they are lying on the floor."

I collect the things, untie Kemmerich's identification disc and take it away. The orderly asks about the pay-book. I say that it is probably in the

Orderly Room, and go. Behind me they are already hauling Franz on to a waterproof sheet.

Outside the door I am aware of the darkness and the wind as a deliverance. I breathe as deep as I can, and feel the breeze in my face, warm and soft as never before. Thoughts of girls, of flowery meadows, of white clouds suddenly come into my head. My feet begin to move forward in my boots, I go quicker, I run. Soldiers pass by me, I hear their voices without understanding. The earth is streaming with forces which pour into me through the soles of my feet. The night crackles electrically, the front thunders like a concert of drums. My limbs move supplely, I feel my joints strong, I breathe the air deeply. The night lives, I live. I feel a hunger, greater than comes from the belly alone.

Müller stands in front of the hut and waits for me. I give him the boots. We go in and he tries them on. They fit well.

He roots among his supplies and offers me a fine piece of saveloy. With it goes hot tea and rum.

* * *

We have to go up on wiring fatigue. The motor lorries roll up after dark. We climb in. It is a warm evening and the twilight seems like a canopy under whose shelter we feel drawn together. Even the stingy Tjaden gives me a cigarette and then a light.

We stand jammed in together, shoulder to shoulder, there is no room to sit. But we do not expect that. Müller is in a good mood for once; he is wearing his new boots.

The engines drone, the lorries bump and rattle. The roads are worn and full of holes. We dare not show a light so we lurch along and are often almost pitched out. That does not worry us, however. It can happen if it likes; a broken arm is better than a hole in the guts, and many a man would be thankful enough for such a chance of finding his way home again.

Beside us stream the munition-columns in long files. They are making the pace, they overtake us going forward. We joke with them and they answer back.

A wall becomes visible, it belongs to a house which lies on the side of the road. I suddenly prick up my ears. Am I deceived? Again I hear distinctly the cackle of geese. A glance at Katczinsky—a glance from him to me; we understand one another.

"Kat, I hear some aspirants for the frying-pan over there."

He nods. "It will be attended to when we come back. I have their number."

Of course Kat has their number. He knows all about every leg of goose within a radius of fifteen miles.

The lorries arrive at the artillery lines. The gun-emplacements are camouflaged with bushes against aerial observation, and look like a kind of military Feast of the Tabernacles. These branches might seem gay and cheerful were not cannon embowered there.

The air becomes acrid with the smoke of the guns and the fog. The fumes of powder taste bitter on the tongue. The roar of the guns makes our lorry stagger, the reverberation rolls raging away to the rear, everything quakes. Our faces change imperceptibly. We are not, indeed, in the front-line, but only in the reserves, yet in every face can be read: This is the Front, now we are within its embrace.

It is not fear. Men who have been up as often as we have become thick skinned. Only the young recruits are agitated. Kat explains to them: "That was a twelve-inch. You hear the explosion first and afterwards comes the sound of the gun."

But the hollow sound of the firing does not reach us. It is swallowed up in the general murmur of the front. Kat listens: "There'll be a bombardment to-night."

We all listen. The front is restless. "The Tommies are firing already," says Kropp.

The shelling can be heard distinctly. It is the English batteries to the right of our section. They are beginning an hour too soon. According to us they start punctually at ten o'clock.

"What's got them?" says Müller, "their clocks must be fast."

"There'll be a bombardment, I tell you, I can feel it in my bones." Kat shrugs his shoulders.

Three shells land beside us. The burst of flame shoots across the fog, the fragments howl and drone. We shiver and are glad to think that we shall be back in the huts early in the morning.

Our faces are neither paler nor more flushed than usual; they are not more tense nor more flabby—and yet they are changed. We feel that in our blood a contact has shot home. That is no figure of speech; it is fact. It is the front, the consciousness of the front, that makes this contact. The moment that the first shells whistle over and the air is rent with the explosions, there is suddenly in our veins, in our hands, in our eyes, a tense waiting, a watching, a profound growth, a strange sharpening of the senses. The body with one bound is in full readiness.

It often seems to me as though it were the vibrating, shuddering air that with a noiseless leap springs upon us; or as though the front itself emitted an electric current which awakened unknown nerve-centres.

Every time it is the same. We start out for the front plain soldiers, either cheerful or gloomy; then come the first gun-emplacements and every word of our speech has a new ring.

When Kat stands in front of the hut and says: "There'll be a bombardment," that is merely his own opinion; but if he says it here, then the sentence has the sharpness of a bayonet in the moonlight, it cuts clean through the thought, it thrusts nearer and speaks to this unknown thing that is awakened in us, a dark meaning—"There'll be a bombardment." Perhaps it is our inner and most secret life that shivers and falls on guard.

To me the front is a mysterious whirlpool. Though I am in still water far away from its centre, I feel the whirl of the vortex sucking me slowly, irresistibly, inescapably into itself.

From the earth, from the air, sustaining forces pour into us—mostly from the earth. To no man does the earth mean so much as to the soldier. When he presses himself down upon her long and powerfully, when he buries his face and his limbs deep in her from the fear of death by shell-fire, then she is his only friend, his brother, his mother; he stifles his terror and his cries in her silence and her security; she shelters him and gives him a new lease of ten seconds of life, receives him again and often for ever.

Earth!—Earth!—Earth!

Earth with thy folds, and hollows and holes, into which a man may fling himself and crouch down! In the spasm of terror, under the hailing of annihilation, in the bellowing death of the explosions, O Earth, thou grantest us the great resisting surge of new-won life. Our being, almost utterly carried away by the fury of the storm, streams back through our hands from thee, and we, thy redeemed ones, bury ourselves in thee, and through the long minutes in a mute agony of hope bite into thee with our lips!

At the sound of the first droning of the shells we rush back, in one part of our being, a thousand years. By the animal instinct that is awakened in us we are led and protected. It is not conscious; it is far quicker, much more sure, less fallible, than consciousness. One cannot explain it. A man is walking along without thought or heed;—suddenly he throws himself down on the ground and a storm of fragments flies harmlessly over him;—yet he cannot remember either to have heard the shell coming or to have thought of flinging himself down. But had he not abandoned himself to the impulse he would now be a heap of mangled flesh. It is this other, this second sight in us, that has thrown us to the ground and saved us, without our knowing how. If it were not so, there would not be one man alive from Flanders to the Vosges.

We march up, moody or good-tempered soldiers—we reach the zone where the front begins and become on the instant human animals.

An indigent looking wood receives us. We pass by the soup-kitchens. Under cover of the wood we climb out. The lorries turn back. They are to collect us again in the morning, before dawn.

Mist and the smoke of guns lie breast-high over the fields. The moon is shining. Along the road troops file. Their helmets gleam softly in the moonlight. The heads and the rifles stand out above the white mist, nodding heads, rocking carriers of guns.

Farther on the mist ends. Here the heads become figures; coats, trousers, and boots appear out of the mist as from a milky pool. They become a column. The column marches on, straight ahead, the figures resolve themselves into a block, individuals are no longer recognizable, the dark wedge presses onward, fantastically topped by the heads and weapons floating off on the milky pool. A column—not men at all.

Guns and munition wagons are moving along a cross-road. The backs of the horses shine in the moonlight, their movements are beautiful, they toss their heads, and their eyes gleam. The guns and the wagons float before the dim background of the moonlit landscape, the riders in their steel helmets resemble knights of a forgotten time; it is strangely beautiful and arresting.

We push on to the pioneer dump. Some of us load our shoulders with pointed and twisted iron stakes; others thrust smooth iron rods through rolls of wire and go off with them. The burdens are awkward and heavy.

The ground becomes more broken. From ahead come warnings: "Look out, deep shell-holes on the left"—"Mind, trenches"—

Our eyes peer out, our feet and our sticks feel in front of us before they take the weight of the body. Suddenly the line halts; I bump my face against the roll of wire carried by the man in front and curse.

There are some shell-smashed lorries in the road. Another order: "Cigarettes and pipes out." We are getting near the line.

In the meantime it has become pitch dark. We skirt a small wood and then have the front line immediately before us.

An uncertain, red glow spreads along the sky line from one end to the other. It is in perpetual movement, punctuated with the bursts of flame from the muzzles of the batteries. Balls of light rise up high above it, silver and red spheres which explode and rain down in showers of red, white, and green stars. French rockets go up, which unfold a silk parachute to the air and drift slowly down. They light up everything as bright as day, their light shines on us and we see our shadows sharply outlined on the ground. They hover for the space of a minute before they burn out. Immediately fresh ones shoot up to the sky, and again green, red, and blue stars.

"Bombardment," says Kat.

The thunder of the guns swells to a single heavy roar and then breaks up again into separate explosions. The dry bursts of the machine-guns rattle. Above us the air teems with invisible swift movement, with howls, piping, and hisses. They are the smaller shells;—and amongst them, booming through the night like an organ, go the great coal-boxes and the heavies. They have a hoarse, distant bellow like a rutting stag and make their way high above the howl and whistle of the smaller shells. It reminds me of flocks of wild geese when I hear them. Last autumn the wild geese flew day after day across the path of the shells.

The searchlights begin to sweep the dark sky. They slide along it like gigantic tapering rulers. One of them pauses, and quivers a little. Immediately a second is beside him, a black insect is caught between them and tries to escape—the airman. He hesitates, is blinded and falls.

At regular intervals we ram in the iron stakes. Two men hold a roll and the others spool off the barbed wire. It is that awful stuff with close-set, long spikes. I am not used to unrolling it and tear my hand.

After a few hours it is done. But there is still some time before the lorries come. Most of us lie down and sleep. I try also, but it has turned too chilly. Near to the sea one is constantly waked by the cold.

Once I fall fast asleep. Then waking suddenly with a start I do not know where I am. I see the stars, I see the rockets, and for a moment have the impression that I have fallen asleep at a garden fête. I don't know whether it is morning or evening, I lie in the pale cradle of the twilight, and listen for soft words which will come, soft and near—am I crying? I put my hand to my eyes, it is so fantastic; am I a child? Smooth skin;—it lasts only a second, then I recognize the silhouette of Katczinsky. The old veteran, he sits quietly and smokes his pipe—a covered pipe of course. When he sees I am awake, he says: "That gave you a fright. It was only a nose-cap, it landed in the bushes over there."

I sit up, I feel myself strangely alone. It's good Kat is there. He gazes thoughtfully at the front and says:

"Mighty fine fire-works if they weren't so dangerous."

One lands behind us. Two recruits jump up terrified. A couple of minutes later another comes over, nearer this time. Kat knocks out his pipe. "It makes a glow."

Then it begins in earnest. We crawl away as well as we can in our haste. The next lands fair among us. Two fellows cry out. Green rockets shoot up on the sky-line. Barrage. The mud flies high, fragments whizz past. The crack of the guns is heard long after the roar of the explosions.

Beside us lies a fair-headed recruit in utter terror. He has buried his face in his hands, his helmet has fallen off. I fish hold of it and try to put it back on his head. He looks up, pushes the helmet off and like a child creeps under my arm, his head close to my breast. The little shoulders heave. Shoulders just like Kemmerich's. I let him be. So that the helmet should be of some use I stick it on his behind;—not for a jest, but out of consideration, since that is his highest part. And though there is plenty of meat there, a shot in it can be damned painful. Besides, a man has to lie a whole month on his belly in the hospital, and afterwards he would be almost sure to have a limp.

It's got someone pretty badly. Cries are heard between the explosions. At last it grows quiet. The fire has lifted over us and is now dropping on the reserves. We risk a look. Red rockets shoot up to the sky. Apparently there's an attack coming.

Where we are it is still quiet. I sit up and shake the recruit by the shoulder. "All over, kid! It's all right this time."

He looks round him dazedly. "You'll get used to it soon," I tell him.

He sees his helmet and puts it on. Gradually he comes to. Then suddenly he turns fiery red and looks confused. Cautiously he reaches his hand to his behind and looks at me dismally.

I understand at once: Gun-shy. That wasn't the reason I had stuck his helmet over it. "That's no disgrace," I reassure him: "Many's the man before you has had his pants full after the first bombardment. Go behind that bush there and throw your underpants away. Get along—"

He goes off. Things become quieter, but the cries do not cease. "What's up, Albert?" I ask.

"A couple of columns over there have got it in the neck."

The cries continue. It is not men, they could not cry so terribly.

"Wounded horses," says Kat.

It's unendurable. It is the moaning of the world, it is the martyred creation, wild with anguish, filled with terror, and groaning.

We are pale. Detering stands up. "God! For God's sake! Shoot them!"

He is a farmer and very fond of horses. It gets under his skin. Then as if deliberately the fire dies down again. The screaming of the beasts becomes louder. One can no longer distinguish whence in this now quiet, silvery landscape it comes; ghostly, invisible, it is everywhere, between heaven and earth it rolls on immeasurably. Detering raves and yells out: "Shoot them! Shoot them, can't you? damn you again!"

"They must look after the men first," says Kat quietly.

We stand up and try to see where it is. If we could only see the animals we should be able to endure it better. Müller has a pair of glasses. We see a dark group, bearers with stretchers, and larger black clumps moving about. Those are the wounded horses. But not all of them. Some gallop away in the distance, fall down, and then run on farther. The belly of one is ripped open, the guts trail out. He becomes tangled in them and falls, then he stands up again.

Detering raises his gun and aims. Kat hits it up in the air. "Are you mad—?"

Detering trembles and throws his rifle on the ground.

We sit down and hold our ears. But this appalling noise, these groans and screams penetrate, they penetrate everywhere.

We can bear almost anything. But now the sweat breaks out on us.

We must get up and run, no matter where, but where these cries can no longer be heard. And it is not men, only horses.

From the dark group stretchers move off again. Then single shots crack out. The black heap is convulsed and becomes thinner. At last! But still it is not the end. The men cannot overtake the wounded beasts which fly in their pain, their wide open mouths full of anguish. One of the men goes down on his knee, a shot—one horse drops—another. The last one props himself on his forelegs and drags himself round in a circle like a merry-go-round; squatting, it drags round in circles on its stiffened forelegs, apparently its back is broken. The soldier runs up and shoots it. Slowly, humbly it sinks to the ground.

We take our hands from our ears. The cries are silenced. Only a long-drawn, dying sigh still hangs on the air.

Then again only the rockets, the singing of the shells, and the stars—and they shine out wonderfully.

Detering walks up and down cursing: "Like to know what harm they've done." He returns to it once again. His voice is agitated, it sounds almost dignified as he says: "I tell you it is the vilest baseness to use horses in the war."

We go back. It is time we returned to the lorries. The sky is become a bit brighter. Three o'clock in the morning. The breeze is fresh and cool, the pale hour makes our faces look grey.

We trudge onward in single file through the trenches and shell-holes and come again to the zone of mist. Katczinsky is restive, that's a bad sign.

"What's up, Kat?" says Kropp.

"I wish I were back home." Home—he means the huts.

"It won't last much longer, Kat."

He is nervous. "I don't know, I don't know—"

We come to the communication-trench and then to the open fields. The little wood reappears; we know every foot of ground here. There's the cemetery with the mounds and the black crosses.

That moment it breaks out behind us, swells, roars, and thunders. We duck down—a cloud of flame shoots up a hundred yards ahead of us.

The next minute under a second explosion part of the wood rises slowly in the air, three or four trees sail up and then crash to pieces. The shells begin to hiss like safety-valves—heavy fire—

"Take cover!" yells somebody—"Cover!"

The fields are flat, the wood is too distant and dangerous—the only cover is the graveyard and the mounds. We stumble across in the dark and as though spirited away every man lies glued behind a mound.

Not a moment too soon. The dark goes mad. It heaves and raves. Darknesses blacker than the night rush on us with giant strides, over us

and away. The flames of the explosions light up the graveyard.
There is no escape anywhere. By the light of the shells I try to get a
view of the fields. They are a surging sea, daggers of flame from the
explosions leap up like fountains. It is impossible for anyone to break
through it.

The wood vanishes, it is pounded, crushed, torn to pieces. We must
stay here in the graveyard.

The earth bursts before us. It rains clods. I feel a smack. My sleeve is
torn away by a splinter. I shut my fist. No pain. Still that does not
reassure me: wounds don't hurt till afterwards. I feel the arm all over. It
is grazed but sound. Now a crack on the skull, I begin to lose consciousness. Like lightning the thought comes to me: Don't faint, sink down in
the black broth and immediately come up to the top again. A splinter
slashes into my helmet, but has travelled so far that it does not go
through. I wipe the mud out of my eyes. A hole is torn up in front of me.
Shells hardly ever land in the same hole twice, I'll get into it. With one
bound I fling myself down and lie on the earth as flat as a fish; there it
whistles again, quickly I crouch together, claw for cover, feel something
on the left, shove in beside it, it gives way, I groan, the earth leaps, the
blast thunders in my ears, I creep under the yielding thing, cover myself
with it, draw it over me, it is wood, cloth, cover, cover, miserable cover
against the whizzing splinters.

I open my eyes—my fingers grasp a sleeve, an arm. A wounded man? I
yell to him—no answer—a dead man. My hand gropes farther, splinters
of wood—now I remember again that we are lying in the graveyard.

But the shelling is stronger than everything. It wipes out the sensibilities, I merely crawl still deeper into the coffin, it should protect me, and
especially as Death himself lies in it too.

Before me gapes the shell-hole. I grasp it with my eyes as with fists.
With one leap I must be in it. There, I get a smack in the face, a hand
clamps on to my shoulder—has the dead man waked up?—The hand
shakes me, I turn my head, in the second of light I stare into the face of
Katczinsky, he has his mouth wide open and is yelling. I hear nothing, he
rattles me, comes nearer, in a momentary lull his voice reaches me:
"Gas—Gaas—Gaaas—Pass it on."

I grab for my gas-mask. Some distance from me there lies someone. I
think of nothing but this: That fellow there must know: Gaaas—
Gaaas—

I call, I lean toward him, I swipe at him with the satchel, he doesn't
see—once again, again—he merely ducks—it's a recruit—I look at Kat
desperately, he has his mask ready—I pull out mine too, my helmet falls
to one side, it slips over my face, I reach the man, his satchel is on the
side nearest me, I seize the mask, pull it over his head, he understands, I
let go and with a jump drop back into the shell-hole.

The dull thud of the gas-shells mingles with the crashes of the high explosives. A bell sounds between the explosions, gongs, and metal clappers warning everyone—Gas—Gas—Gaas.

Someone plumps down behind me, another. I wipe the goggles of my mask clear of the moist breath. It is Kat, Kropp, and someone else. All four of us lie there in heavy, watchful suspense and breathe as lightly as possible.

These first minutes with the mask decide between life and death: is it tightly woven? I remember the awful sights in the hospital: the gas patients who in day-long suffocation cough their burnt lungs up in clots.

Cautiously, the mouth applied to the valve, I breathe. The gas still creeps over the ground and sinks into all hollows. Like a big, soft jelly-fish it floats into our shell-hole and lolls there obscenely. I nudge Kat, it is better to crawl out and lie on top than to stay here where the gas collects most. But we don't get as far as that; a second bombardment begins. It is no longer as though the shells roared; it is the earth itself raging.

With a crash something black bears down on us. It lands close beside us; a coffin thrown up.

I see Kat move and I crawl across. The coffin has hit the fourth man in our hole on his out-stretched arm. He tries to tear off his gas-mask with the other hand. Kropp seizes him just in time, twists the hand sharply behind his back and holds it fast.

Kat and I proceed to free the wounded arm. The coffin lid is loose and bursts open, we are easily able to pull it off, we toss the corpse out, it slides down to the bottom of the shell-hole, then we try to loosen the under-part.

Fortunately the man swoons and Kropp is able to help us. We no longer have to be careful, but work away till the coffin gives with a sigh before the spade that we have dug in under it.

It has grown lighter. Kat takes a piece of the lid, places it under the shattered arm, and we wrap all our bandages round it. For the moment we can do no more.

Inside the gas-mask my head booms and roars—it is nigh bursting. My lungs are tight, they breathe always the same hot, used-up air, the veins on my temples are swollen, I feel I am suffocating.

A grey light filters through to us. I climb out over the edge of the shell-hole. In the dirty twilight lies a leg torn clean off; the boot is quite whole, I take that all in at a glance. Now someone stands up a few yards distant. I polish the windows, in my excitement they are immediately dimmed again, I peer through them, the man there no longer wears his mask.

I wait some seconds—he has not collapsed—he looks around and makes a few paces—rattling in my throat I tear my mask off too and fall

down, the air streams into me like cold water, my eyes are bursting, the
wave sweeps over me and extinguishes me.

The shelling has ceased. I drag myself to the crater and tell the others.
They take off their masks. We lift up the wounded man, one taking his
splintered arm. And so we stumble off hastily.

The graveyard is a mass of wreckage. Coffins and corpses lie strewn
about. They have been killed once again; but each of them that was flung
up saved one of us.

The hedge is destroyed, the rails of the light railway are torn up and
rise stiffly in the air in great arches. Someone lies in front of us. We stop;
Kropp goes on alone with the wounded man.

The man on the ground is a recruit. His hip is covered with blood; he
is so exhausted that I feel for my water-bottle where I have rum and tea.
Kat restrains my hand and stoops over him.

"Where's it got you, comrade?"

His eyes move. He is too weak to answer.

We cut off his trousers carefully. He groans. "Gently, gently, it is
much better—"

If he has been hit in the stomach he oughtn't to drink anything.
There's no vomiting, that's a good sign. We lay the hip bare. It is one
mass of mincemeat and bone splinters. The joint has been hit. This lad
won't walk any more.

I wet his temples with a moistened finger and give him a swig. His
eyes move again. We see now that the right arm is bleeding as well.

Kat spreads out two wads of dressing as wide as possible so that they
will cover the wound. I look for something to bind loosely round it. We
have nothing more, so I slit up the wounded man's trouser leg still
farther in order to use a piece of his underpants as a bandage. But he is
wearing none. I now look at him closely. He is the fair-headed boy of a
little while ago.

In the meantime Kat has taken a bandage from a dead man's pocket
and we carefully bind the wound. I say to the youngster who looks at us
fixedly: "We're going for a stretcher now—"

Then he opens his mouth and whispers: "Stay here—"

"We'll be back again soon," says Kat. "We are only going to get a
stretcher for you."

We don't know if he understands. He whimpers like a child and
plucks at us: "Don't go away—"

Kat looks around and whispers: "Shouldn't we just take a revolver and
put an end to it?"

The youngster will hardly survive the carrying, and at the most he will
only last a few days. What he has gone through so far is nothing to what

he's in for till he dies. Now he is numb and feels nothing. In an hour he will become one screaming bundle of intolerable pain. Every day that he can live will be a howling torture. And to whom does it matter whether he has them or not—

I nod. "Yes, Kat, we ought to put him out of his misery."

He stands still a moment. He has made up his mind. We look round—but we are no longer alone. A little group is gathering, from the shell-holes and trenches appear heads.

We get a stretcher.

Kat shakes his head. "Such a kid—" He repeats it: "Young innocents—"

Our losses are less than was to be expected—five killed and eight wounded. It was in fact quite a short bombardment. Two of our dead lie in the upturned graves. We had merely to throw the earth in on them.

We go back. We trot off silently in single file one behind the other. The wounded are taken to the dressing-station. The morning is cloudy. The bearers make a fuss about numbers and tickets, the wounded whimper. It begins to rain.

An hour later we reach our lorries and climb in. There is more room now than there was.

The rain becomes heavier. We take out waterproof sheets and spread them over our heads. The rain rattles down, and flows off at the sides in streams. The lorries bump through the holes, and we rock to and fro in a half-sleep.

Two men in the front of the lorry have long forked poles. They watch for telephone wires which hang crosswise over the road so densely that they might easily pull our heads off. The two fellows take them at the right moment on their poles and lift them over behind us. We hear their call "Mind—wire—," dip the knee in a half-sleep and straighten up again.

Monotonously the lorries sway, monotonously come the calls, monotonously falls the rain. It falls on our heads and on the heads of the dead up in the line, on the body of the little recruit with the wound that is so much too big for his hip; it falls on Kemmerich's grave; it falls in our hearts.

An explosion sounds somewhere. We wince, our eyes become tense, our hands are ready to vault over the side of the lorry into the ditch by the road.

It goes no farther—only the monotonous cry: "Mind—wire,"—our knees bend—we are again half asleep.

EDMUND BLUNDEN
1896-1974

Poet, teacher, scholar, editor, and man of letters, Blunden was one whose whole life was powerfully dominated by his wartime experience as a shy company officer in some of the worst of the fighting, including the battle of Passchendaele, also known as Third Ypres. His quietly ironic memoir Undertones of War *(1928) is one of the classics.*

CONCERT PARTY: BUSSEBOOM

The stage was set, the house was packed,
    The famous troop began;
Our laughter thundered, act by act;
    Time light as sunbeams ran.

Dance sprang and spun and neared and fled,
    Jest chirped at gayest pitch,
Rhythm dazzled, action sped
    Most comically rich.

With generals and lame privates both
    Such charms worked wonders, till
The show was over—lagging loth
    We faced the sunset chill;

And standing on the sandy way,
    With the cracked church peering past,
We heard another matinée,
    We heard the maniac blast

Of barrage south by Saint Eloi,
    And the red lights flaming there

Called madness: Come, my bonny boy,
  And dance to the latest air.

To this new concert, white we stood;
  Cold certainty held our breath;
While men in the tunnels below Larch Wood
  Were kicking men to death.

PILLBOX

Just see what's happening, Worley!—Worley rose
And round the angled doorway thrust his nose
And Serjeant Hoad went too to snuff the air.
Then war brought down his fist, and missed the pair!
Yet Hoad was scratched by a splinter, the blood came,
And out burst terrors that he'd striven to tame,
A good man, Hoad, for weeks. *I'm blown to bits,*
He groans, he screams. *Come, Bluffer, where's your wits?*
Says Worley, *Bluffer, you've a blighty, man!*
And in the pillbox urged him, here began
His freedom: *Think of Eastbourne and your dad.*
The poor man lay at length and brief and mad
Flung out his cry of doom; soon ebbed and dumb
He yielded. Worley with a tot of rum
And shouting in his face could not restore him.
The ship of Charon over channel bore him.
All marvelled even on that most deathly day
To see this life so spirited away.

THIRD YPRES

Triumph! How strange, how strong had triumph come
On weary hate of foul and endless war
When from its grey gravecloths awoke anew
The summer day. Among the tumbled wreck

Of fascined lines and mounds the light was peering,
Half-smiling upon us, and our newfound pride;
The terror of the waiting night outlived,
The time too crowded for the heart to count

All the sharp cost in friends killed on the assault.
No hook of all the octopus had held us,
Here stood we trampling down the ancient tyrant.
So shouting dug we among the monstrous pits.

Amazing quiet fell upon the waste,
Quiet intolerable to those who felt
The hurrying batteries beyond the masking hills
For their new parley setting themselves in array
In crafty forms unmapped.
                     No, these, smiled faith,
Are dumb for the reason of their overthrow.
They move not back, they lie among the crews
Twisted and choked, they'll never speak again.
Only the copse where once might stand a shrine
Still clacked and suddenly hissed its bullets by.
The War would end, the Line was on the move,
And at a bound the impassable was passed.
We lay and waited with extravagant joy.

Now dulls the day and chills; comes there no word
From those who swept through our new lines to flood
The lines beyond? but little comes, and so
Sure as a runner time himself's accosted.
And the slow moments shake their heavy heads,
And croak, "They're done, they'll none of them get through,
They're done, they've all died on the entanglements,
The wire stood up like an unplashed hedge and thorned
With giant spikes—and there they've paid the bill."

Then comes the black assurance, then the sky's
Mute misery lapses into trickling rain,
That wreathes and swims and soon shuts in our world.
And those distorted guns, that lay past use,
Why—miracles not over!—all a-firing!
The rain's no cloak from their sharp eyes. And you,
Poor signaller, you I passed by this emplacement,
You whom I warned, poor daredevil, waving your flags,
Amid this screeching I pass you again and shudder
At the lean green flies upon the red flesh madding.
Runner, stand by a second. Your message.—He's gone,
Falls on a knee, and his right hand uplifted
Claws his last message from his ghostly enemy,
Turns stone-like. Well I liked him, that young runner,

But there's no time for that. O now for the word
To order us flash from these drowning roaring traps
And even hurl upon that snarling wire?
Why are our guns so impotent?
                                    The grey rain,
Steady as the sand in an hourglass on this day,
Where through the window the red lilac looks,
And all's so still, the chair's odd click is noise—
The rain is all heaven's answer, and with hearts
Past reckoning we are carried into night
And even sleep is nodding here and there.

The second night steals through the shrouding rain.
We in our numb thought crouching long have lost
The mockery triumph, and in every runner
Have urged the mind's eye see the triumph to come,
The sweet relief, the straggling out of hell
Into whatever burrows may be given
For life's recall. Then the fierce destiny speaks.
This was the calm, we shall look back for this.
The hour is come; come, move to the relief!
Dizzy we pass the mule-strewn track where once
The ploughman whistled as he loosed his team;
And where he turned home-hungry on the road,
The leaning pollard marks us hungrier turning,
We crawl to save the remnant who have torn
Back from the tentacled wire, those whom no shell
Has charred into black carcasses—Relief!
They grate their teeth until we take their room,
And through the churn of moonless night and mud
And flaming burst and sour gas we are huddled
Into the ditches where they bawl sense awake
And in a frenzy that none could reason calm,
(Whimpering some, and calling on the dead)
They turn away: as in a dream they find
Strength in their feet to bear back that strange whim,
Their body.
                    At the noon of the dreadful day
Our trench and death's is on a sudden stormed
With huge and shattering salvoes, the clay dances
In founts of clods around the concrete sties,
Where still the brain devises some last armour
To live out the poor limbs.
                              This wrath's oncoming

Found four of us together in a pillbox,
Skirting the abyss of madness with light phrases,
White and blinking, in false smiles grimacing.
The demon grins to see the game, a moment
Passes, and—still the drum-tap dongs my brain
To a whirring void—through the great breach above me
The light comes in with icy shock and the rain
Horridly drops. Doctor, talk, talk! if dead
Or stunned I know not; the stinking powdered concrete,
The lyddite turns me sick—my hair's all full
Of this smashed concrete. O I'll drag you, friends,
Out of the sepulchre into the light of day,
For this is day, the pure and sacred day.
And while I squeak and gibber over you,
Look, from the wreck a score of field-mice nimble,
And tame and curious look about them; (these
Calmed me, on these depended my salvation).

There comes my sergeant, and by all the powers
The wire is holding to the right battalion,
And I can speak—but I myself first spoken
Hear a known voice now measured even to madness
Call me by name.
                    "For God's sake send and help us,
Here in a gunpit, all headquarters done for,
Forty or more, the nine-inch came right through,
All splashed with arms and legs, and I myself
The only one not killed, not even wounded.
You'll send—God bless you!" The more monstrous fate
Shadows our own, the mind swoons doubly burdened,
Taught how for miles our anguish groans and bleeds,
A whole sweet countryside amuck with murder;
Each moment puffed into a year with death.
Still swept the rain, roared guns,
Still swooped into the swamps of flesh and blood,
All to the drabness of uncreation sunk,
And all thought dwindled to a moan, Relieve!
But who with what command can now relieve
The dead men from that chaos, or my soul?

EDWARD THOMAS
1878-1917

Born in London and educated at Oxford, Thomas was an unhappy reviewer and miscellaneous writer until galvanized by a reading of the early poems of Robert Frost, whose lack of pretentious "poetic" rhetoric he found "revolutionary," and in his own poems he tried to equal their calm surfaces. Only six of his poems were published before he was killed on the Western Front.

IN MEMORIAM (EASTER, 1915)

The flowers left thick at nightfall in the wood
This Eastertide call into mind the men,
Now far from home, who, with their sweethearts, should
Have gathered them and will do never again.

THIS IS NO CASE OF PETTY RIGHT OR WRONG

This is no case of petty right or wrong
That politicians or philosophers
Can judge. I hate not Germans, nor grow hot
With love of Englishmen, to please newspapers.
Beside my hate for one fat patriot
My hatred of the Kaiser is love true:—
A kind of god he is, banging a gong.
But I have not to choose between the two,
Or between justice and injustice. Dinned
With war and argument I read no more
Than in the storm smoking along the wind
Athwart the wood. Two witches' cauldrons roar.

From one the weather shall rise clear and gay;
Out of the other an England beautiful
And like her mother that died yesterday.
Little I know or care if, being dull,
I shall miss something that historians
Can rake out of the ashes when perchance
The phoenix broods serene above their ken.
But with the best and meanest Englishmen
I am one in crying, God save England, lest
We lose what never slaves and cattle blessed.
The ages made her that made us from dust:
She is all we know and live by, and we trust
She is good and must endure, loving her so:
And as we love ourselves we hate her foe.

A PRIVATE

This ploughman dead in battle slept out of doors
Many a frozen night, and merrily
Answered staid drinkers, good bedmen, and all bores:
"At Mrs. Greenland's Hawthorn Bush," said he,
"I slept." None knew which bush. Above the town,
Beyond "The Drover," a hundred spot the down
In Wiltshire. And where now at last he sleeps
More sound in France—that, too, he secret keeps.

ERIC HISCOCK
1900–1986

Hiscock was a schoolboy in Oxford and an assistant in the Bodleian Library there when, underage, he managed to join the Royal Fusiliers, and by the spring of 1918 he was fighting near Ypres. After the war he became a journalist on the Evening Standard, *where he specialized in book news. More than a half-century after the war, in 1976, he published*

The Bells of Hell Go Ting-a-ling-a-ling, *a vivid memoir of the war which some have thought not as factually accurate as it pretends to be.*

From THE BELLS OF HELL GO TING-A-LING-A-LING

At dusk we stood-to on the trench firesteps as we had done for so many nights in "Bellevue." I must have slept standing up with my rifle in my right hand, because I was suddenly hearing a hoarse voice, choked with emotion, saying to me: "Asleep on duty in the front line, Hiscock. I could shoot you for this," and I could feel the barrel of a revolver pressing into my stomach. The voice belonged to Sergeant Hall, and he went on: "And if you hadn't been on that raid I bloody well would have done." Sergeant Hall was absolutely within his rights, especially so with the enemy fully expected to send over a raiding party as a reprisal for the morning's pillbox adventure. I noticed, even in my rather drunken, tired state, that he kept his voice low. This was because Lieutenant Clarke was not many yards away and Hall was fully aware that between the Lieutenant and me there was little love lost. . . . Clarke was a thwarted homosexual who viewed my friendship with Brook and Jackson with envy and suspicion. His envy of such a close-knit triumvirate was not difficult to understand. We *were* close-knit, but as heterosexual as it was possible to be in such a man-made man-populated community as the 26th Battalion, Royal Fusiliers, in Flanders. Obviously, we masturbated (but not each other), and the affection that existed between us was confined to the sharing of duties, the opening of parcels from home, and appreciation of what Rupert Brooke once referred to as the "rough male kiss of blankets." But Lieutenant Clarke thought otherwise and he was especially drawn towards Brook whose golden hair, laughing face, and tall slim body might have stirred any trench-bound male even more disciplined, sexually, than Clarke. Sergeant Hall was fully conscious of Clarke's dislike of me and knew well enough that had he found me asleep on duty instead of himself he would have had little compunction in shooting me.

Sergeant Hall put his revolver away in its holster and, patting me lightly on the shoulder, he said: "Don't be a cunt," and passed on down the trench.

*   *   *

We moved into the line again, dangerously enough, under the notorious Kemmel Hill. Outgoing were the French and long before we took over from them we knew we would inherit dirty, ill-protected dug-outs from men who strenuously believed in doing nothing to draw the enemy's fire. The journey to the line was long and arduous and it was no consolation to find, at journey's end, that the French troops had been satisfied with so-called dug-outs consisting of a hole in the ground protected from shell-fire by no more than a sheet of rusty corrugated iron resting on two obsolete rifles. Not only were they unsafe but they were lice-ridden and a damned disgrace. The line was fully observed by the Germans from somewhere on the Hill, and the slightest movement by day brought on machine-gun fire and the irritatingly dangerous "Whizz-bangs" so beloved by the enemy. It was impossible to hear them coming: all one knew was the short, sharp "whizz" of arrival followed by the immediate "bang" of the explosion, and in the French-vacated holes in the ground that we were being forced to occupy there was little or no shelter from them. No movement by day meant that everything, including the apportioning of rations, had to be done at night.

My section, as cabin'd and confin'd as any other, took care not to excite attention from the Hill, but we knew well enough that the time would come when bloody-mindedness would settle in up the Hill and our numbers might very well be up. The daytime watchfulness and the night's activity robbed us of sleep and everybody, from Lieutenant Clarke (in charge of "C" Company while Captain Mason stayed behind the line at Battalion H.Q.) down to Acting L/C Hiscock, became moody, ill-tempered and jumpy. Towards dawn of our tenth day's residence in front of Kemmel a pair of nervous Lewis gunners, spurred on by the sounds of what might have been an enemy raiding party, let loose with a couple of drums each and brought a reply in the shape of a hail of trench mortars. Our own mortar men, slightly behind us, sent *their* reply over and by dawn's light, when all should have been quiet (would have been quiet had the French been in occupation) the heavy stuff started to come over. The lice-ridden, corrugated iron shelters were no places to stay in during such bombardment and during a brief lull I gathered my section together, picked up the day's rations in a sandbag and ordered them to make for some deep shell holes about fifty yards away. With Garstone I flung myself down in the one furthest away from the shallow trenches which were now becoming real danger spots and we both lay at the bottom of it, covered with mud but with the day's rations intact and a feeling of hopefulness that we might survive.

As the morning became lighter and a pale watery sun worked hard at penetrating the rain-clouds over the Hill I noticed that in the exodus from the slip trenches with their useless dug-outs I had covered a fair part of my Lee-Enfield rifle with mud. I had started to pick off as much as possible when *bang* the damned thing went off. I had touched the trigger, hidden by Kemmel Hill mud, and a bullet had missed my stupid head but gone through the Lance-Corporal stripe on my greatcoat and done exactly the same thing on the tunic sleeve beneath. It had also penetrated my arm near some old vaccination marks between the shoulder and elbow, narrowly missing the bone. Stunned by the suddenness of it all, I hardly heard Garstone say: "What the hell have you done? You've shot yourself," and he crawled nearer to me to see for himself just how much damage had been done. He cut out the sleeves of my greatcoat and tunic, extracted the emergency field dressing pack sewn inside the bottom left-hand corner of my tunic, broke open the iodine phial, poured it over the two bullet holes (one each side of the arm) and then bound up the wound, using the gauze and bandage supplied with the pack. All day we stayed where we were and at nightfall prepared to make our way back to the shallow trenches which still appeared to be intact. We had hardly slipped down into them when an irate, blustering Lieutenant Clarke, his eyes blazing, his pale, spotty face twitching with rage, appeared in front of us, brandishing his service revolver.

"Consider yourself under arrest, Lance-Corporal Hiscock. Self-inflicted wound. They'll court martial you for this. And you'll be lucky if they don't shoot you."

Lieutenant Clarke was, of course, nearly right. I had inflicted a wound on myself, but *I* knew—and fortunately for me, Garstone knew—that it had been done accidentally. The charge-sheet description of my "crime," *Self-inflicted Wound,* was one of the most heinous in the calendar (*Buggery* was pretty bad, too, as Lieutenant Clarke knew well enough) and if such wounded lived, a Field General Court Martial followed their hospitalisation. I had no illusions that I was not in dire trouble and found it hard to appreciate Private Percival's wry comment after he had been ordered, along with Garstone, to fall in and escort me from the trench to a Casualty Clearing Station: "Tha'd best write 'ome and tell them tha's got a permanent job at Base, lad!" Uselessly I insisted to Lieutenant Clarke that my muddied rifle had gone off accidentally for he brushed such a plea roughly aside with: "You ran away from the shelling. You couldn't take it, could you? Then in what you thought was a nice quiet shell hole you gave yourself a Blighty. There'll be no Blighty for you, my boy. Self-inflicted wounds never get sent home. You'll stay at the Base and then you'll be court martialled, and serve you bloody-well right." For Lieutenant Clarke the future looked rosy. With me out of the way, there would only be Jackson to prevent him making play for Brook's favours (as some wise-cracking comic was to say half a century later in some uninhibited movie: "A really dirty old man never gives up") and if I got prison at Etaples he would have unlimited time to pursue his prey. It was a strange, unrewarding obsession on Lieutenant Clarke's part and as Garstone and Percival fell in as my escort I failed to see why he bothered. Brook, despite his glamour, his fair hair, and his rather feminine traits, was wholly heterosexual. The fact that he had not left a girl behind him (a fact carefully noted by Lieutenant Clarke as he censored letters home) meant nothing and helped Clarke's cause not one iota. He had left his Public School to enlist in the Royal Fusiliers and his monasticism had only changed backgrounds and locale. It was all as simple as that. My trip down the line towards an ultimate Etaples was going to be very uncomfortable for me but unrewarding to my persecutor.

With Garstone and Percival I waited for the Company's stretcher-bearers and after they arrived we all made our way through a maze of shallow trenches to an ambulance that stood at a corner of very dangerous-looking crossroads. Shells were dropping in a desultory, fairly futile fashion and it wasn't long before we moved off and it was impossible not to wonder whether a direct hit might save me, Lieutenant Clarke, the Canadian Clearing Station we were heading for, a quorum of officers at some future Field General Court Martial, and my poor parents back in Oxford, a hell of a lot of heartache, fuss and bother. About twenty miles behind the line the ambulance men, and Garstone and Percival, delivered me to an orderly who inspected my wounds, signed some papers that went with my body, tied a green docket on me with my particulars under an ominous looking D.I. in large black capital letters, and told me I would be going down to a Base Hospital the following evening. A nursing Sister came and inspected my arm, told a nurse what to do with it, then I heard her say: "Poor boy. I don't wonder he's a D.I. He ought still to be at school." They left me alone with my thoughts until an orderly brought me a cup of heavily sugared tea, free of the hated chlorinated-water flavour, and I asked him: "What does D.I. mean?" He gave me a queer look, an amalgam in expression of pity and incredulity. "Self-inflicted wound. That's what you've done, isn't it? Up at Kemmel Hill?" I told him of my stupid accident, but nothing about Lieutenant Clarke, and he said: "Too bad, son. You're down on the books as a D.I., and that's how you'll stay. You'll be all right at Wimereux. At least you're not going to the D.I. hospital at Havre." He added, ominously enough: "You're bound to get a Field General. You can tell 'em what happened then."

The train at the railhead seemed fairly full of stretcher-cases and after my night at the Clearing Station I became a more comfortable walking case. But from my good shoulder hung that incriminating green label and the derisive looks I got from orderlies and other walking cases made me nervous, inhibited, and I hung my stupid head in shame. Was this what I had joined the University & Public Schools Battalion of the Royal Fusiliers in Oxford for? Was this to be my war? And my still lively imagination saw again that accusing recruiting-poster of the children asking their father (was it perpetrated by John Hassall, R.I.? I think so):

"What did you do in the Great War, daddy?" And my answer, would it have to be: "I shot myself and got sentenced to death!" It all seemed downbeat to me and I remained in my lonely shell until, two nights later, I was delivered to the 53rd General Hospital at Wimereux. There I was again interrogated but a bed with incredible white linen sheets followed and a nurse with red hair and a Birmingham accent gave me a blanket bath, dressed my wounds, and told me that the M.O. would see me in the morning. That night, despite a certain throbbing in my arm (had it turned gangrenous?—remembering poor old Ramsden's bullet-holed hand) I slept well, waking only when, with a scuffle and the setting-up of screens round the bed of the man next to me in the ward, nurses decided that he had died of wounds. He had, I learned later, put a Mills bomb under his right leg after a bombardment at Ypres that had lasted for most of a day, and if that wasn't a theme for Siegfried Sassoon, I don't know what was.

After early tea, early bed-making followed by breakfast, the ward was walked by the M.O. who had my bandages removed for inspection. He was gruff, but not a bad chap, and whatever he thought about my green card hanging with my temperature and defecation record-card, he never commented on it to me. I heard him murmur to the Sister accompanying him that the wound looked dirty and that she'd better watch it. Or did he say wash it? Either way, my nervous self at once jumped to the conclusion that gangrene was setting in and, like the murderer whose heart stopped in the condemned cell, I feared I might cheat Lieutenant Clarke and his Field General Court Martial yet. A nurse, the one from Birmingham with the red hair and freckled face, followed fussily in the M.O. and Sister's wake and did what a good soldier in the line should do to his rifle's barrel every day: she pulled it through. She used some heavily impregnated gauze threaded through what looked like a bodkin, and when I flinched she cried: "It's no use running away, I shall only come after you." She pursued this cleansing course morning and evening for about a week, at the end of which I was allowed up and out, with my arm in an impressive-looking sling.

"Up" meant perambulation in the ward, helping in a mild way with the orderlies' and nurses' fetch-and-carry chores and "Out" meant a stroll along the sand-dunes which encompassed the hospital. Frustration is liable to set in wherever you are and although I had experienced no sexual urges since I had shot myself at Kemmel my presence in Ward D at the 53rd General Hospital stirred something more than a mothering instinct in the breast of my red-haired nurse from Birmingham. On one of my wanderings along the sand-dunes I came across Maud sitting on an Army blanket between two dunes and to my surprise she asked me to stop and sit down beside her. It was her half-day (unless there was a new troop train with wounded arriving) and she had put on a civilian dress which reminded me of earlier days with Doris at Oxford. It was short and full and the neckline plunged deeply. With the early summer sun lighting up her freckled face and burnishing her crown of red hair, and with a faint hint of flesh above her black lisle stockings, she stirred something in me that hadn't been stirred for a long time. As I accepted her invitation and flopped down on the blanket beside her my left arm in its sling caught her a slight blow on the shoulder and she fell back, at the same time clutching at me with her right hand. We found ourselves facing each other, lying full length on the blanket overlooking the sea, and together we laughed and the next thing I knew was that her lips were on mine and she was crying: "You're a quiet one, but I like you. Have you ever done this before?" And she put my good hand down her dress on to one of her breasts. It was firm yet soft, and very warm, and the impertinent nipple nudged itself into the centre of my palm. Before I could answer her question, her tongue was exploring deep into my mouth and I was trembling with what an older man would have recognized as desire. But Maud was wanting only cosy, friendly fun with sex overtones, and I was, that afternoon, to be her source of supply. She was as lonely as I was, the Birmingham blood coursed warmly through her veins and it wasn't every day that a safe young soldier with little or no experience of sex, and no licentious longings, dropped into her hard-working life. As the sun moved slowly and down across the sky Maud and I, with Maud in command, forgot war and troop trains full of wounded men, forgot green identification labels with D.I. markings on them, forgot imminent Field General Courts Martial, and enjoyed each other. Collegiates on American campuses, some years later, were to call what we did at Wimereux "deep petting." It was nothing new. What we did that afternoon in wartime was discover that Adam and Eve's disease— loneliness—could be assuaged simply enough by the touching of hands, the feel of mouth on mouth and the exploration of hitherto hidden delights. That such delights were found beneath a shabby suit of hospital blue and a surprisingly gay dress with a plunging neckline, and that even as flesh touched flesh two enemy aeroplanes suddenly dived out of the sky to drop their light bombs in the vicinity of the hospital, only added to the hedonism of the two people so haphazardly thrown together.

My wound healed and, completely ambulant, I was transferred to the hospital kitchen. Coping with such daily chores as washing plates, peeling potatoes, making interminable cups of tea was obviously to be my lot instead of any period of convalescence. "Self-inflicted wounds" rarely reached Con Camps and I stayed at Wimereux until I was directed to Etaples for my Field General Court Martial.

* * *

On arrival at Etaples I was sent to a hutment containing about thirty other ranks all of whom had been in hospitals or Casualty Clearing

Stations with self-inflicted wounds, had recovered and were either waiting for a Field General Court Martial or the result of one. On the whole,
despite many disabilities (some were minus an arm or a leg, one had an
ugly-looking scar reaching from his right eye to his mouth caused by a
razor-slash, another was learning to write letters home with his left
hand—three fingers and a thumb were missing from his right, due to a
deliberately too long association with a Mills bomb after the pin had
been withdrawn) there was an infectious friendliness in the hut. Something to do, no doubt, with the theory that comrades in distress can't do
better than stick together. Beds were trestles on which three boards and
palliasses rested and although sheets were not supplied we were allowed
plenty of clean, lice-free Army blankets. Lights Out came at nine o'clock
but discipline from outside was fairly lax, and most nights a macabre
entertainment took place. We had no access to musical accompaniment,
so the performers (and, surprisingly enough, there were plenty) hammed
their way through their material unaided. One inmate who was awaiting
the verdict on his self-destruction of the big toe on his left foot (he had
deliberately slashed it with an Army razor and cynics in the hut opined
that the Army razor capable of such destruction hadn't been issued yet)
had recovered enough to limp up and down the ward strumming a small
banjo (was it called a banjolele—a hybrid of a banjo and a ukelele?) and
singing an old music-hall ballad which had been made famous by G. H.
Chirgwin—*The White-Eye Kaffir*. Chirgwin, a Cockney-born serio-
comic, like most Victorian-Edwardian popular performers, had made his
reputation out of one or two songs, and the one that the razor-slashing
inmate of the hospital at Etaples entertained us with was Chirgwin's
most famous. It went something like this:

> My fiddle is my Sweetheart, *yes!*
> And I'm her faithful beau.
> I take her to my bosom, *yes!*
> Because I love her so.

At the end of each verse and chorus the performer, following Chirgwin's
example, went into a yodelling act, and the hut's inmates followed him,
vociferously enough. Other amateur acts followed (one, very persistent
performer who had held up his arm above the trench he was supposed
to be guarding somewhere on the Somme and had been observed by
his Commanding Officer just when a sniper's bullet had penetrated
his right wrist) persisted in reciting, with actions, the whole of that
maudlin musical monologue, *The Green Eye of The Little Yellow God*,
and I, a captive audience if ever there was one, learnt it by heart. I can
still recite it faultlessly, verse by verse, line by line, from the dramatic
opening:

> There's a one-eyed yellow idol to the north of Katmandu,
> There's a little marble cross below the town,
> There's a broken-hearted woman tends the grave of Mad Karoo,
> And the little god forever gazes down,

to the penultimate verse, after Karoo has stolen the idol's green eye for the Colonel's daughter and suffered the consequences of his rash act, the author, Milton Hayes, tells how he died and how his girl-friend found his body.

> As she crossed the barrack-square
> She could hear the dreamy air
> Of a waltz tune, stealing softly through the gloom.
> His door was open wide,
> Silver moonlight shining through,
> The place was wet and slippy where she trod,
> An ugly knife lay buried in the heart of Mad Karoo...
> 'Twas the vengeance of the little Yellow God. .

Such bathos cuts little emotional ice with me today but in the hospital ward at Etaples, as the story was unfolded by the man who had suffered a German bullet through his wrist, it all seemed wonderful and we cheered him to the echo.

But the White-Eyed Kaffir and Mad Karoo were only delaying tactic-characters. Soon, my fate would be decided along with the other, more maimed inmates of the hut. There were daily parades on the Etaples square and there it was that some men were warned of their imminent Field General Courts Martial while others, sadly enough, listened to the sentences that had been decided at their trials some days before.

The morning came when I was detailed to appear in front of a quorum of officers consisting of a Major from the Royal Army Service Corps, a Captain of the Oxfordshire and Buckinghamshire Light Infantry, a Captain of the Royal Artillery, and a Lieutenant of the Royal Warwickshire Regiment.

The comic artist *manqué* in me warmed towards the Lieutenant, for was his not the same regiment that had Captain Bruce Bairnsfather fighting for it? And, happily enough, drawing those imperishable pictures, for the *Bystander*, of walrus-moustached Old ("If you knows of a better 'ole, go to it") Bill? A Lieutenant in Bairnsfather's regiment would in no way help me but I immediately liked having him there.

The R.A.S.C. Major, officer-in-charge of the trial, was rotund, well-fed (as might be expected of a Major in the R.A.S.C.) and pink of face. He looked as though he had never missed an early morning shave since landing in France (had certainly never tried to shave in cold tea, in the front line at dawn, instead of drinking it for breakfast) and was certainly

ignorant of what it was like to try and cut a small loaf of bread into eight
identically-sized pieces. I hated him on sight.

The O.B.L.I. Captain I might have known from earlier, happier days
in the city that helped title his regiment but the thin-lipped, stern-eyed
man with a limp (he sported three blue war-service chevrons, one red
one signifying he was almost certainly a regular officer risen from the
ranks who had fought at Mons in 1914, and three gold wound-bars) was
a complete stranger and, obviously, was going to be no help at all.

The R.A. Captain was youngish, handsome in a florid way, and his
Sam Browne belt and leggings signified only too plainly to me that he
was a tyrant to his batman. A stickler for discipline if ever there was one
and hardly likely to take pity on a stupid acting Lance-Corporal (unpaid)
who had shot himself in the arm, in the front line.

I felt utterly lost and despondent and bitterly regretted I had ever
succumbed to the spurious glamour of wearing khaki back in those far-
off days in Oxford's St. Giles.

Like Jesus, I could have wept.

With the well-fed R.A.S.C. Major in charge of my trial there was a
slow start to the proceedings and I had time to analyse my feelings.
Oddly enough, my mind went back to a morning at St. Frideswide's
Infant School, when I was a timid tot of five. The paper bag my mother
had wrapped some bread and butter in for my mid-morning break was
empty and I blew it up and burst it with a bang.

"Stand up the boy or girl who did that!" shouted a furious Miss
Hardcastle, and as no one obeyed I pointed an accusing finger at some
quite innocent child who promptly denied that she was the culprit. Then
retribution for my misdeed set in: at least half the class stood up and told
Miss Hardcastle that I was the miscreant. She pulled me out of my seat
and stood me in the corner for the rest of the morning and threatened
me that she would tell my sister (in an upper classroom) what I had done
and that my father would whip some sense into me. The bottom of my
stomach felt like falling out, and I wet my trousers.

There was no trouser wetting as the R.A.S.C. Major slowly and ominously read out the charge from the sheet he held in his pudgy hand, but
my stomach felt extremely loose as though I had taken a dose of salts.

"That Acting Lance-Corporal Hiscock, 59333, of the 26th Battalion
of the Royal Fusiliers did, while on duty in the front line at Kemmel Hill,
inflict upon himself a gunshot wound in the left arm," and as he threw
the charge-sheet down on the desk he glared at his po-faced mates who
were such a terrifying part of my inquisition.

"Do you have anything to say, Lance-Corporal Hiscock?" he snarled.
Then, dropping his voice a little, he asked: "Are you represented or do
you wish to conduct your own defence?"

Such sentences, such questions . . . Christ! was I, the boy from St. Giles, Oxford, a bloody criminal?

I looked round at the rest of the quorum before answering. The R.A. Captain was glaring straight ahead of him, fingering his khaki tie that had been knotted so carefully. I could detect no pity there. The O.B.L.I. Captain was just as unforthcoming as I might have expected from the wearer of a uniform that boasted one red and three blue service chevrons. He had probably sat in on many a poor sod's fate. The Lieutenant belonging to the Warwickshires caught my eye as I was about to speak. Was there just a glimmer of sympathy there? Perhaps, and a faint, hopeful feeling spread through me, that was to last no more than a second as I told them all that I had no one to defend me (I nearly added: "Not even God") and that I was prepared to talk about the affair in my own way.

"We don't want speeches, Lance-Corporal Hiscock," said the R.A.S.C. Major, "just the facts."

"Yes sir," I said meekly, then launched into a fairly halting description of what had happened that sad morning in the grim shadow of Kemmel Hill. I told how the shelling had been too hot for those of us crouching in such badly constructed trenches and how I had taken shelter, with Private Garstone and the day's rations, in a deep shell-hole some yards away.

Then I added, looking the well-fed R.A.S.C. Major straight in the eyes: "I fail to see what Lieutenant Clarke has to complain about."

I could feel the shock-waves that rose from the quorum as they fiddled with pieces of paper before them where they sat in judgement on me.

"Why in heaven's name do you stress the name of Lieutenant Clarke? Don't you know that he is only doing his duty by reporting your alleged behaviour in the face of the enemy?" The speaker's face, always flushed, now looked positively choleric.

I wanted to say: "Shit, the man's a bugger, and all he wanted was to get rid of me so that he could fuck my friend Brook." Instead, I said meekly: "He misunderstood the whole situation, sir. He accused me of a self-inflicted wound whereas what actually happened was that I brushed some caked mud off my rifle, and my finger, in taking off the mud, pulled the hidden trigger and the gun went off. I was lucky not to kill myself." I wondered how many more times I would have to repeat the story: I was getting word-perfect.

I then added: "I wouldn't have killed myself intentionally, would I?" adding "Sir," just before I went on with: "If you agree about that then I am not the willing victim of a self-inflicted wound."

It wasn't going well. I felt a cold sweat starting to run down my spine, and a fear gripped me. I looked at the inquisitors again. The Lieutenant from the Warwickshires was leaning across the Oxford & Bucks Captain and speaking quietly but urgently to the R.A.S.C. Major. The Captain in the Royal Artillery stopped doodling on a pad of Army-issue paper and scribbled a hasty note which he handed to the Major.

It was the Major's turn to speak, and his mouth turned down sourly at its corners.

"There was present in the shell-hole you mention in your evidence a member of your own section, wasn't there? He was Private Garstone." He turned to an orderly: "Bring in Private Garstone."

Garstone, looking thin and frightened but able to retain a certain composure, was marched in between two men and came to a halt in front of the quorum.

The Major: "You are Private Garstone?"

Garstone: "Yes, sir."

The Major: "And you were present when Lance-Corporal Hiscock shot himself?"

I couldn't keep silent over such a blatant piece of misdirection and I shouted:

"Sir, I object to that question," and the O.B.L.I. Captain shouted back: "We don't want any bloody barrack-room lawyers here." The heat was on, and it was, I felt forlornly, up to Garstone now.

The Major shouted that the objection was over-ruled, and told Garstone to answer the question.

Garstone, quietly but in a convincing manner that I considered was likely to help me rather than hinder, did as he was directed.

"We occupied a shell-hole after leaving the trench due to heavy shelling. We stayed there all night. In the morning I noticed that Lance-Corporal Hiscock's Lee-Enfield was covered with mud. I saw him endeavour to rub some of the mud off and then I heard an explosion. I saw that Lance-Corporal Hiscock was holding his left arm, high up. He had a very surprised expression on his face."

I liked those last words, "a very surprised expression on his face." For heaven's sake, I was shocked beyond reason, and could hardly realise what had happened.

The Major: "And what happened then, Private Garstone?"

"I managed to tend his wound, sir. I got his field-dressing out of his tunic, put iodine on both the bullet-holes" ("quite right," interpolated the O.B.L.I. Lieutenant) "then wrapped the arm up with the small bandage supplied."

The quorum seemed satisfied with Garstone's quiet and efficiently told tale, and the Major asked him if he had said anything to me.

"Yes, sir," replied Garstone, "I said: 'You bloody fool, you've shot yourself!' "

I thought that was rather an ambiguous statement on Garstone's part but was powerless to say anything before the Major came out with a sharply delivered question:

"And, of course, you thought he had done it deliberately?"

Full marks then went from me to Garstone who replied, standing stiff as a ramrod to attention: "No, sir, of course not. I saw it happen. It was an accident, no matter what Lieutenant Clarke says," and the Major shot back with: "Why do you say, 'no matter what Lieutenant Clarke says.' Have you any reason to believe he would tell a lie?"

Then it all came out, with Garstone winning medals from me, and some astonished looks from the quorum.

"He's a bugger, sir. He's been after one or two of us and he's very fond of Lance-Corporal Hiscock's friend, Lance-Corporal Brook."

A Sunday paper reporter, following a public trial, would have noted down at this point the words "Sensation in Court."

The O.B.L.I. Captain, the Warwickshire Lieutenant, and the Captain from the Royal Artillery started scribbling like mad. They handed the result to the Major who solemnly studied what had been written.

Then he ordered: "Call Lieutenant Clarke."

He was known in the Company as "Pox-Doctor's Clarke," and when he arrived in front of the quorum he looked like one. His pale, spotted-with-acne face, with its red-rimmed eyes under a head of mouse-colored hair, was certainly no hero's visage and as he stood, shamblingly, at attention in front of the Bench even I, who hated his guts, felt sorry for him. And then I discovered within myself something strange. I didn't hate him because he was homosexual, I hated him because he was a cad, and the most uncomfortable man ever to appear in my young life so far. I had known many homosexuals during my choirboy days in Oxford (and although I didn't know it as I stood in front of the quorum at Etaples I was to meet and get to like many in Fleet Street and publishing later on) and had rarely hated them. Lieutenant Clarke I loathed for what he was as a *man in uniform*, and I knew he was now to get his come-uppance, and almost felt sorry for him.

The Major asked him: "Lieutenant Clarke, would you say that the charge of self-inflicted wound which you have brought against Lance-Corporal Hiscock, was completely disinterested?"

"I'm sorry, sir, but I'm afraid I don't know what you mean."

"Don't be a bloody fool, Clarke. You know what I mean. I am asking you, in effect, would it be to your advantage if Lance-Corporal Hiscock was removed from the immediate proximity of Lance-Corporals Brook and Jackson?"

Clarke remained impassively stupid. But surely he knew where these questions of the Major's were leading.

"I'm sorry, sir, but I don't know what you mean."

Then all hell broke loose. The Major stood up and fixed Lieutenant Clarke with unblinking eyes, and his lip curled. His right hand pointed accusingly at the wretched man in front of him. "Then I'll tell you, Lieutenant Clarke. It has become known to us, in evidence, that Lance-Corporal Hiscock was a close friend of one Lance-Corporal Brook. And of one Lance-Corporal Jackson. We believe that these three were a well-knit trio in and out of the line, in and out of France, and we also believe that you would have preferred such a relationship not to be. In that way you would have had easier access to Lance-Corporal Brook's body. When you charged Lance-Corporal Hiscock with deliberately shooting himself you believed—hoped, perhaps, might be a better word—that he would be sent out of the line, and out of Lance-Corporal Brook's daily existence, and that you would then be better able to make perverted advances to Lance-Corporal Brook."

Clarke seemed to shrink within his officer's uniform as he struggled to say: "But this is preposterous. I have never made perverted advances to Lance-Corporal Brook."

The Major, now quite choleric in appearance, and with his eyes bulging from their sockets, said: "You are not accused of doing so. I only *suggested* you have been *scheming* to do so, and that you accuse Lance-Corporal Hiscock of shooting himself in order to remove him from Lance-Corporal Brook's side. I put it to you, Lieutenant Clarke, that you did not in any way observe Lance-Corporal Hiscock shooting himself, that you did not truly believe he *had* shot himself, and that this case is a complete tissue of lies originated by yourself."

Lieutenant Clarke seemed to shrink even further into his uniform, and he stuttered: "I—I—must have been mistaken, sir. I—I—withdraw any charge on the sheet attributed to me. Completely, sir."

My heart gave a joyous leap. Garstone's evidence, which had confirmed all that I had said, had won the day. Lieutenant Clarke had lost, and would be lucky not to be cashiered.

The R.A.S.C. Major half-smiled at me as he gave orders for me to be returned to my Battalion without further ado, and so it was I went back to the Etaples hutment until, after a few mess-and-cookhouse parades, I was paraded one chilly morning with about half a dozen others to hear the result of my trial.

Eventually my turn came, after I had stood there at attention and heard one poor sod sentenced to five years imprisonment for shooting three fingers off his right hand, and another awarded Field Punishment No. I for desertion from the front line during a particularly nasty bombardment by Jerry.

Field Punishment No. I, the barrack-room gossips insisted, meant being strung up on a gun-carriage wheel for hours on end and beaten at regular intervals (like gongs, Noël Coward would have said) with a cat-o'-

nine tails, but I doubt if that really happened. It smacked too much of the Boer War to be true. But it was certainly no light and pleasant fatigue-duty, such as cleaning out latrines.

The officer-in-charge who was resolutely reading out the results of Field General Courts Martial came to my name.

"Lance-Corporal Hiscock," he announced, "ten days' pay stopped," and I found myself crossing my heart and thanking Michael and all his angels. Visions (nay, nightmares) of eternal jankers at Etaples—with an incarcerated son writing home to fond parents to say that, for the next two or three years, he had a safe job at the Base, disappeared as if by magic and I stepped back gratefully and smartly (I hope) into the ranks of delinquent soldiers I had left a few apprehensive moments before.

To all intents and purposes I was a free man again.

* * *

The first few days following my repatriation passed smoothly enough. The Company was housed in Nissen huts, leisure was fairly plentiful when the dress rehearsals of the mass-attack hand grenade bombing were over, and my stupid adventure in front of Kemmel Hill seemed to be forgotten.

Brook and Jackson were to be made full-Corporals but if I had any hopes of joining them I was soon to be disillusioned.

Lieutenant Clarke, grinning maliciously, came up to me one afternoon as I sat reading a letter from home, and informed me with ill-concealed pleasure that Captain Mason wanted to see me, privately.

I found him in the Company H.Q. hut, drinking whisky.

"All right, Hiscock, stand at ease, I want to talk to you. Your F.G.C.M. didn't do you any harm, did it, and I can't say I'm not glad. I think you had a bad time. But there's something I've got to tell you. Lieutenant Clarke tells me that men in the Company are complaining about your Lance-Corporal's stripe."

"But, sir," I said, "I wasn't broke. I was docked ten days' pay."

"Exactly, and that's what Lieutenant Clarke says the men are complaining about. They feel you are no longer fit to look after a section."

"You mean, sir, that Lieutenant Clarke says so?"

"Look, Hiscock, don't bloody well argue. You talk too much. You were bloody lucky to get off with ten days' pay stopped, and personally I'm all for the quiet life. I suggest you go away quietly and take your stripe down yourself. Nothing will appear in Company Orders. You are acting unpaid, anyway, and if you break yourself nobody will worry. And Lieutenant Clarke will be happy."

Captain Mason was dead right. What, for God's sake, had I to lose but an unpaid lancejack's stripe which had a bullet through it anyway? I had no ambitions for advancement and looking back down the more adult years I doubt very much whether I would have made an adequate Sergeant.

Brook and Jackson were of different material, and were made for promotion. Brook's Public School education had fitted him for command. His sunny disposition kept him from glooming over the often dire circumstances he found himself in, and although some of the men ribbed him by imitating his "posh" accent ("crepe-soled," they called it) they worked willingly enough for him and often followed him into danger with the brave-looking carelessness that was his khaki-clad characteristic.

Jackson's brash Cockney approach to trench life had something of the Old Contemptibles' quality. Quite fearless, he strutted into war on his slightly bandy legs with a total disregard for his own comfort.

While he deprecated discipline on the one hand he demanded it implacably when it was necessary and it never surprised me, when, later on, he took command of an entire officerless Company under fire and was awarded the Military Medal. Those oft-repeated cries of his: "Roll on my ticket," "Blimey, why did I ever leave civvy street?", "Gawd stone the bleeding crows, I must have been fucking daft the day I joined up," may have hidden his solid worth from those who knew him only vaguely.

Since his semi-permanent mess-orderly days at Dover he had covered himself with glory, had become a remarkably fine soldier with the ability and built-in desire to set an example to all who served with him.

The only comment he made on my return to the Battalion was: "Blimey, chum, we'll get that bastard Clarke yet, you see," words that were prophetic, when the time came.

Brook ran true to friendly form.

"My dear old boy," he said as he put an arm round my narrow shoulders, "who would have thought Lance-Corporal Hiscock, acting unpaid, would have managed to cheat the hangman's rope with such efficiency? Let no one say you won't yet make an efficient soldier," and he produced a fifty-franc note, the result of parental patronage from Ross-on-Wye. We walked half-a-dozen kilometers to an *estaminet* and there we splurged most of it on some very drunk-making champagne.

"Pity Lieutenant Clarke wasn't here to share it," he said with his high-pitched giggle, as we staggered back to our billets.

"Never mind," he added, "perhaps he will get his later on."

But it wasn't all champagne and preparation for mass bomb-throwing. From where we were we soon moved up the line again, journeying by night, loaded with wire, rations and ammunition (along with Lewis guns and the more deadly, and heavier, Vickers guns).

It is difficult, at this distance from the dread reality of those front-line nights, to communicate what it was like for a youngster still well under the age of enlistment to be included in such hazardous fatigues. Most journeys were made in single file, on treacherous duckboard tracks perched precariously across the sinister, stinking, death-filled mud flats. Darkness was our only protection as, weighed down with full marching order and the cumbersome impedimenta of trench warfare, we struggled on towards the front line, losing a man every few yards.

As we picked our fear-filled way along the duckboards the desolate scene would be lit eerily and repeatedly by the enemy's Verey lights. As they rose and hovered in the midnight air every man below froze into uneasy immobility. It wasn't difficult to simulate a blasted, much-shelled tree trunk in this shell-blasted hell, but I have often wondered since how many boys who have fetched me tea in Fleet Street offices could have done what I did (however unwillingly) without breaking out into a mad sweat and a heartfelt cry for mother.

I don't know what happened mentally, but physically I occasionally broke down under the sheer weight of equipment that had to be carried, lack of sleep, and the intolerable discipline that was necessary in 1918 to keep tired and bored soldiers up to something like scratch, and away from mutiny.

The ever-present dreamlike quality of the days and nights (nights when I heard men gasping for breath as death enveloped them in evil-smelling mud-filled shell-holes as they slipped from the duckboard tracks as they struggled towards the front line) filled me with an intense loathing of man-made war. I wanted home with all my being.

It was scarifying to journey, night after night, across that mud-filled ocean of death. The slow, halting progress as messages were passed down from man to man ("broken duckboard here, pass it on," or "Minnie coming over, pass it on") were often punctuated with desperate cries of drowning men as, with their loads, they slipped from the treacherous track and floundered to finality in seemingly bottomless shell-holes filled with black slime already serving as graveyards for earlier unfortunates. Nothing could be done for such desperate men and the procession passed them by regardless of their pitiful cries before, choking to death, they drowned in Flanders' erstwhile peaceful plains.

Two nights of such awesome fatigues remain in my memory, resolutely refusing to be eradicated. One is linked in my mind with somewhere called Starcross Corner but today no map shows where such a place was positioned. On this particular night it was next door to Hell.

The journey with the night's load had been particularly hazardous and everybody's nerves were frayed when, suddenly, the enemy's bloody-mindedness showed up in an intense machine-gun barrage. Experts in such uncomfortable things estimated later that a concentration of at least fifty guns were directing their death-dealing lead at one and the same time on Starcross Corner. The object, obviously, was complete decimation of the whole outfit. The trajectory was at all levels so that men standing upright on the duckboards covering the mud would almost certainly be hit in the head or the chest. There was no dividend to be gained through the time-honoured act of throwing oneself flat on the ground on account of the inescapable fact that the ground in this instance was a narrow duckboard track perched precariously on mud. Horrifyingly enough, streams of bullets were sweeping the duckboards at the level of a man's head had he risked sliding off the wretched things into a nearby shell-hole. There was little or no escape.

I decided to throw myself to the boarded ground and at once realised I wasn't low enough. I have often joked in later, more peaceful days, when walking in St. James's Park, about the evening swallows "parting my hair," as they swooped across the water towards Pall Mall and the Ritz Hotel.

The difference between London swallows diving towards their dinner *via* pedestrians' heads, and German bullets sweeping Starcross Corner was well-directed death, and I fully expected to die.

Uppermost in my mind was the thought that I might be permanently disfigured. I had seen enough scarred warriors minus a leg or an arm, or men with their jaws shot off, or blinded, or once virile citizens now paralysed from the waist down, not to hope that when a bullet or exploding shell had my name and number on it I would either be killed outright or wounded in such a way that when recovery came there would be no ugly remembrancing mark.

Terrified, I clawed the stinking mud as the bullets whistled round my head and shoulders and I waited for death.

Two bullets whipped into the duckboards within an inch of my face, splashing sodden splinters on to my steel helmet, and mud into my eyes. I was caught with near-panic when more bullets thudded into the place where my head had been only a few moments before and I knew damned well there was nowhere to go, no retreat.

Suddenly I felt a boot up my arse.

Looking round I could just recognise in the dark the pallid features of Lieutenant Clarke. He was standing fairly erect, and carrying a revolver at the end of a lanyard attached to his scrawny neck.

"Private Hiscock, you'll never get to base like that," and as he said it a Verey light showed, terrifyingly awful, a *minenwerfer* trundling towards where he was standing and I was lying.

"No, sir," I managed to say, "but at this moment we both stand an excellent chance of getting blown to hell or heaven."

Horrified, Lieutenant Clarke dropped on the duckboard behind me, and from the loose mouth set in his now ashen face he groaned:

"For Christ's sake let it go over. Let it go over."

As my mother used to say when she found that I, at the tender age of twelve, had been betting on a horse that had won: "The devil, surely enough, looks after his own."

The air filled with the ever-increasing train-like rumble of the *minenwerfer* tumbling over and as it progressed towards its haphazard target, Lieutenant Clarke and I clawed our way even closer to the sodden earth that might soon cover us for ever.

Nearer the damnable thing came and no Earthman will ever tremble before some flying saucer from Outer Space the way Lieutenant Clarke and I trembled before that monstrous example of German frightfulness.

From Lieutenant Clarke there came another, louder groan, then a sound as of cloth being rent asunder and a smell that permeated the air even more than the stinking earth we were seeking as a refuge.

Lieutenant Clarke had shit himself.

Out of a corner of my eye I saw enough to cause my frightened heart to miss a beat with joy. Minnie seemed to be retaining enough power to miss our particular corner of Belgium and was heading for the wasteland that lay beyond.

"She's going over, sir," I shouted to Lieutenant Clarke who was moving about on the duckboard in an uncomfortable way and even as I spoke, Monstrous Minnie gave a sudden lurch and dived to ground level. Well, what would once have been ground level before two armies over the years had destroyed it forever, ploughing up what had been peacefully ploughed up previously. Into the mud and slime of four years' man-made hell Minnie fell and exploded, and if a London bus today could be transported in time and space to where she fell it would fit the hole she made exactly. Then gradually sink below until, like thousands of once-living English and German fighting men, it would be lost to sight forever.

* * *

Brook died with a machine-gun bullet through his lovely head, a few dreadful days before it all ended on November 11th. Never was there such a waste of a young life. He had intelligence, charm, a body the Greek gods might have envied, and he exuded friendship wherever he went. I never met any man from Dover to Brook's death who hadn't a kind word for him, despite the occasional ribbing he brought down on his blond head on account of what Noël Coward would have called his "la-de-bloody-da" manner. No wonder Lieutenant Clarke coveted him. There is a strain of homosexuality in most men. Some want to keep it under control, others let it rip and behave like Oscar Wilde looking on slim golden youths with lips that entice the love that knew no name until it was dragged through the courts, and into Reading Gaol. Brook had a feminine streak in him, but not enough to allow him to yield to such pursuers as Lieutenant Clarke, which made Lieutenant Clarke more avid for conquest than ever. Brook, Jackson and myself all had some homosexual tendencies (despite Jacko's infatuation with his Croydon belle) and in the days and nights of stress we masturbated, but kisses on unshaved faces were rare, and then only in moments of acute danger. When we were sent off on the prisoner-getting raid from the "Bellevue" trench in the Ypres Salient Brook kissed me a fond farewell and hoped we'd get back safely. Jackson, seeing such endearments taking place on the duckboards covering the ghastly evil-smelling mud that was our temporary High Street, would grimace and say: "Blimey, you blokes. I can't think why you don't get married," but his arms would encircle both of us with all the energy of an Arsenal half-back who had watched his friend on the outside-left score a goal that might take the team to Wembley.

Trench warfare bred a monasticism not unlike which was lived at Eton (or any other Public School) and in Oxford and Cambridge where susceptible undergraduates yearned for favours from choirboys singing *Hear My Prayer* with all the passion of a Spring morning thrush greeting an early worm. Many a soldier died and was mourned by his fellow men with even more intensity than by some bereft wife at home in England. But the Lieutenant Clarkes were a wholly different cup of tea. They were destroyers, devoid of the feelings that, probably, kept the brave boys of Arthur's Round Table together. No wonder such people often come to a dramatic end. Not unlike the parson I knew who, forever pursuing the sordid impossible, ended up with his penis cut off and stuck on his nose in some dank alley within the environs of his own parish.

WILFRED OWEN
1893–1918

Owen was a lieutenant in the Manchester Regiment whose literary career was encouraged by Siegfried Sassoon. A week before the Armistice, this sensitive, shy, affectionate creature, already the winner of the Military Cross, was leading his men in an attack on the Western Front when he was machine-gunned to death.

INSENSIBILITY

1

Happy are men who yet before they are killed
Can let their veins run cold.
Whom no compassion fleers
Or makes their feet
Sore on the alleys cobbled with their brothers.
The front line withers.
But they are troops who fade, not flowers,
For poets' tearful fooling:
Men, gaps for filling:
Losses, who might have fought
Longer; but no one bothers.

2

And some cease feeling
Even themselves or for themselves.
Dullness best solves
The tease and doubt of shelling,
And Chance's strange arithmetic
Comes simpler than the reckoning of their shilling.
They keep no check on armies' decimation.

3

Happy are these who lose imagination:
They have enough to carry with ammunition.
Their spirit drags no pack.
Their old wounds, save with cold, can not more ache.
Having seen all things red,
Their eyes are rid
Of the hurt of the colour of blood for ever.
And terror's first constriction over,
Their hearts remain small-drawn.
Their senses in some scorching cautery of battle
Now long since ironed,
Can laugh among the dying, unconcerned.

4

Happy the soldier home, with not a notion
How somewhere, every dawn, some men attack,
And many sighs are drained.

Happy the lad whose mind was never trained:
His days are worth forgetting more than not.
He sings along the march
Which we march taciturn, because of dusk,
The long, forlorn, relentless trend
From larger day to huger night.

5

We wise, who with a thought besmirch
Blood over all our soul,
How should we see our task
But through his blunt and lashless eyes?
Alive, he is not vital overmuch;
Dying, not mortal overmuch;
Nor sad, nor proud,
Nor curious at all.
He cannot tell
Old men's placidity from his.

6

But cursed are dullards whom no cannon stuns,
That they should be as stones.
Wretched are they, and mean
With paucity that never was simplicity.
By choice they made themselves immune
To pity and whatever moans in man
Before the last sea and the hapless stars;
Whatever mourns when many leave these shores;
Whatever shares
The eternal reciprocity of tears.

ANTHEM FOR DOOMED YOUTH

What passing-bells for these who die as cattle?
    —Only the monstrous anger of the guns.
    Only the stuttering rifles' rapid rattle
Can patter out their hasty orisons.
No mockeries now for them; no prayers nor bells;
    Nor any voice of mourning save the choirs,—
The shrill, demented choirs of wailing shells;
    And bugles calling for them from sad shires.

What candles may be held to speed them all?
Not in the hands of boys but in their eyes
Shall shine the holy glimmers of goodbyes.
The pallor of girls' brows shall be their pall;
Their flowers the tenderness of patient minds,
And each slow dusk a drawing-down of blinds.

DULCE ET DECORUM EST

Bent double, like old beggars under sacks,
Knock-kneed, coughing like hags, we cursed through sludge,
Till on the haunting flares we turned our backs
And towards our distant rest began to trudge.
Men marched asleep. Many had lost their boots
But limped on, blood-shod. All went lame; all blind;
Drunk with fatigue; deaf even to the hoots
Of tired, outstripped Five-Nines that dropped behind.

Gas! GAS! Quick, boys!—An ecstasy of fumbling,
Fitting the clumsy helmets just in time;
But someone still was yelling out and stumbling,
And flound'ring like a man in fire or lime . . .
Dim, through the misty panes and thick green light,
As under a green sea, I saw him drowning.

In all my dreams, before my helpless sight,
He plunges at me, guttering, choking, drowning.

If in some smothering dreams you too could pace
Behind the wagon that we flung him in,
And watch the white eyes writhing in his face,
His hanging face, like a devil's sick of sin;
If you could hear, at every jolt, the blood
Come gargling from the froth-corrupted lungs,
Obscene as cancer, bitter as the cud
Of vile, incurable sores on innocent tongues,—
My friend, you would not tell with such high zest
To children ardent for some desperate glory,
The old Lie: Dulce et decorum est
Pro patria mori.

FUTILITY

Move him into the sun—
Gently its touch awoke him once,
At home, whispering of fields half-sown.
Always it woke him, even in France,
Until this morning and this snow.
If anything might rouse him now
The kind old sun will know.

Think how it wakes the seeds—
Woke once the clays of a cold star.
Are limbs, so dear achieved, are sides
Full-nerved, still warm, too hard to stir?
Was it for this the clay grew tall?
—O what made fatuous sunbeams toil
To break earth's sleep at all?

THE SEND-OFF

Down the close darkening lanes they sang their way
To the siding-shed,
And lined the train with faces grimly gay.

Their breasts were stuck all white with wreath and spray
As men's are, dead.

Dull porters watched them, and a casual tramp
Stood staring hard,
Sorry to miss them from the upland camp.

Then, unmoved, signals nodded, and a lamp
Winked to the guard.

So secretly, like wrongs hushed-up, they went.
They were not ours:
We never heard to which front these were sent,

Nor there if they yet mock what women meant
Who gave them flowers.

Shall they return to beating of great bells
In wild train-loads?
A few, a few, too few for drums and yells,

May creep back, silent, to village wells,
Up half-known roads.

ROBERT C. HOFFMAN
1897–1985

Hoffman fought in France as a nineteen-year-old infantry sergeant in the U.S. 28th Division. Wounded several times, he survived to become a champion weightlifter and physical-culture entrepreneur, an executive of the York (Pennsylvania) Bar Bell Co., and the publisher of the magazine Strength and Health, *as well as the author of books like* Big Arms: How To Develop Them *and* How To Be Strong, Healthy, and Happy. *In 1940 he wrote* I Remember the Last War *to caution against American involvement in another one.*

From I REMEMBER THE LAST WAR

The ward of the hospital I was in was a huge affair with row after row of iron beds filled with wounded. I believe there must have been five hundred wounded in the huge room in which I was placed. It is doubtful if this building was originally a hospital; it had been pressed into service for that purpose. The song "Madelon" was popular at this time and a boy about fourteen came daily to sing for us. He thought that he was doing his bit to cheer us up. At the age of puberty which he was passing through, any boy will have far from an attractive voice—an occasional near bass, alternating with a high falsetto, and all degrees of tones in between. But this young fellow had a particularly terrible voice aside from going through the period of changing voices—a piercing, penetrating, rasping voice which would have done credit to an east side fishmonger.

It was very trying and the fellows who were less badly wounded would chase him out every day by throwing everything they could find at him. Singing was one thing; his type of shouting was another.

In my first few days in the hospital I walked around quite a bit to see what I could see and to get acquainted. Later I was confined to my bed, when I had the fever, by the simple process of taking the lower part of my pajamas. Even a young man who had passed through what I had already encountered could not walk around with only a pajama coat. But the first few days things were quite interesting.

I walked down into the inner court or garden where soldiers of several nationalities who had been severely wounded, and had been at this hospital for many months, were convalescing. They told me many tales of the fighting of former years. It was truly a league of nations there. No wonder it was called the Mixed Hospital. At least a dozen different races were represented. French, German, American, Turkish, Russian, Belgian, Roumanian, Montenegrin, Austrian, and a French Senegalese warrior or two were there.

There were men badly enough wounded in my ward. Most of them were wounded only in the arm or the leg. I knew there were more seriously wounded men somewhere. I wandered one day into another ward similar to the one we occupied, but with much more seriously wounded men occupying its beds. There were men who had their faces marred almost past recognition as anything human. Some had lost noses, jaws or ears. The records prove that men who lived had been shot through every single part of the body, every organ, even all parts of the brain. Men normally die who are shot through an important internal organ—heart, intestines, or liver. Usually a head shot kills the man instantly; but many have lived when shot through the head.

Few have any idea of the horrible cripples left by the last war. Even in the years which have intervened since the ending of that war, hundreds of thousands of men have been kept in hospitals—some of these men so severely wounded that they are never permitted to be seen by others. While it is no harder to lose a nose than a finger, what a horrible thing it does to a man's face. I could not help but think how I would have looked from the bullet which left its mark on my cheek if I had not turned my head just at the right instant. I might have been here with these men, having only half a face of my own.

There were many good surgeons in the war, but there were others who found in it an opportunity to try experiments, theories of their own, on sorely wounded men—men who did not have strength enough to argue back. Some worthy work of plastic surgery was done, but most of them, when the operation was ended, were no better looking than Frankenstein. There were doctors there who thought they could cure flat feet. They tried their experiments on any men who would submit, and certainly they didn't do them any good, but did harm to many. There was considerable faulty setting of bones and rebreaking of these bones, in an endeavor to do a better job of setting them the next time.

Surgical skill improves. In the time of the Civil War amputation was the chief method of treating the wounded. I often pass a point on the Lincoln Highway two miles this side of Gettysburg. That is one of the first stone monuments the interested person sees when passing the battlefield. This stone monument marks the site of a field hospital which was located there during and immediately after the great battle. Years ago an old man who was in that battle, and at that time lived in Gettysburg, serving as a battlefield guide, told me that there was a pile of arms and legs outside of that hospital six feet high and ten feet across the base. I can believe it too, for sanitation and medical skill had not advanced so far at that time (nearly eighty years ago). Amputate the limb first, think about it afterwards seemed to be the plan.

There were constant operations in this part of the hospital. But most sinister of all, and perhaps most important of all, was a small room, which contained a few beds, in which the very worst patients were placed. Many called this the morgue, the "dead room," or the "dying room." Men were dying every day in spite of the fact that the more seriously wounded usually died before they reached a base hospital. In spite of all medical skill, tetanus—lockjaw—would set in; gangrene could not always be prevented. Some of these men had lost a great amount of blood, and many of them, even during the summer season, already had contracted Flu, which in their weakened state was fatal.

When a man was dying they would move him out. It was bad enough for him to die without his comrades, who did not know when their own turn might come, having to watch him die. Some of the men went out screaming when they were moved. The nurses would try to ease their going by telling them that they were only going to the operating room for minor treatment or to the dressing room, to have their bandages changed. The fellows soon learned to observe whether the little bag which held their personal belongings—sometimes a helmet or a coat— came with them. If it remained behind they could expect to come back; but if it too was moved, then they were sure that worse was in store for them. Some begged to be left there to die with their friends around them, not to be placed with a lot of near corpses who were complete strangers.

The more pitifully wounded did not wish to live. They constantly begged doctors and nurses, sometimes at the top of their voices, to put an end to them. Some made attempts to end their lives with a knife or fork. It became necessary to feed these wounded and never leave a knife or fork with them. One of the orderlies told me that a blinded man who was suffering greatly and did not wish to live had killed himself at one time with a fork. It was hard to drive it deep enough through his chest to end his life, and he kept hitting it with his clenched fist to drive it deeper.

There was a limit to how many pain tablets could be given to any man—how many his heart would stand. But most of them begged for another tablet the minute they recovered sufficiently from the former tablets and once again felt severe pain.

Most of the nurses back at the base were older women. I am sure the long hours they had to work and the demands of their patients shortened their lives considerably. The younger and stronger girls were up nearer the front, where even more labor and more difficult duties were encountered. It was interesting, although somewhat gruesome, to stand in the lobbies and watch the traffic going by: wheeled carts containing men who were going up into wards such as mine; men who were hurt worse than they had expected and were going downstairs in the ward with the worst cases; many men expecting to die being moved to the living morgue and men who had died being taken out for burial. Some of them were better off; at least I would rather be dead than as horribly crippled as many—a lifelong dependent upon others—living dead. I have always felt that life would not be worth living if constant pain and suffering, being confined to pain-ridden beds and wheel chairs, was to be one's lot until death. But humans cling to life. They want to see loved ones, their home, the sun rise the next day, see the spring again. They seem willing to live in spite of all suffering. It is a good old world, after all. So we may change our minds if we must face the stern realization that death is finally at hand.

Five or six men a day were dying. They were taken right out in the fields back of the hospital and buried. Bugles sounding taps, and the firing of guns, as each man was buried with military honors, became familiar sounds. Normal death is not so bad. I've seen a lot of death of one sort and another. I've really died several times myself—by drowning, unconscious four days after an automobile accident, knocked to unconsciousness in the Argonne; not a bit different than actual death as far as one's feelings are concerned. The difference is the fact that in real death one never wakes up, never opens his eyes to the light of the world again. But I was brought back each time to life. I am sure that I experienced real death at one time; although in my prime, my life before me, everything to live for, I had absolutely no desire to live. I felt this way when I first became conscious four days after an auto accident in which I was involved. Dying under those circumstances could not be so bad. And dying of old age must not be so bad either. Under those circumstances one has lived his or her life. There is a slow losing of the faculties, a dulling of the mind; finally one has no realization of whether he is alive or not. That would be a nice way to die. Some of my relatives died that way, really of old age. But others died horrible deaths from cancer, Bright's disease, dropsy, or diabetes. Sudden death from heart trouble would be quick—like a bullet that ends things.

But many of these men were doomed to a life of slow and painful death. The doctors and nurses, of course, told them that they would become completely cured in time, but the fellows talked among themselves and didn't quite believe it. I admired their courage, for many of them were smiling and calm under the circumstances. I wondered if they were not more deserving of medals for bravery than was I. It is one thing to be brave when one's body is whole, one's comrades around, and a stirring fight is in progress; but still another thing to be torn to pieces, in pain, little more than half a man lying in a hard bed, in dark and miserable surroundings, without one's friends and loved ones nearby. But I suppose it is worse to die, as so many died, in the mud, in front of our lines, unable to get medical attention as so many were to die a bit later in our part of the war.

These brave young fellows, like the young German I had seen in the field hospital, knew that they must die, were soon to leave this world, friends, hopes, prospects, many of them never having had the opportunity to live. They had been studying, working, training, striving for better things to come. But there were to be no better things for some. Their lives were all but ended, their candle of life had all but burned away.

Far from pleasant moments I spent in this ward below ours. It was bad enough in our section, and I could tell even the most sorely wounded of the men whose beds were around mine how lucky they were. It is hard to feel lucky when a rifle or machine gun bullet has gone through the bones of the shin; when it has gone entirely through the huge muscles of the thigh (for there it is difficult to heal. It must be kept open, forced to heal from the center first. Drainage tubes must be constantly kept in it, so that it will remain clean within and not become infected in any manner. It was necessary to reopen so many of these hastily cared for wounds that had grown shut while not quite clean inside); a shot through the elbow or the knee, a wound that would usually leave the bone stiff for the remainder of life; or through the hand or the foot. Such wounds might take years to heal. The men who merely had a hole in an arm or a shoulder were lucky enough.

And I was so lucky that I was ashamed to be in the hospital with men who were really hurt. But the doctors had insisted that I go there. They must have known whether it was necessary or not. I believe that they thought some of the bits of iron, sand, and gravel, which had made my face so terrible to look at, might have penetrated the flesh or even the skull to a point where they would be removed some time later. But it turned out that my wounds were only superficial. You can be sure I was pleased when I saw what the doctor was doing to other men around me. I was lucky.

It is not pleasant to lie on one's back with a leg suspended in the air high above one's head—perhaps to have it enclosed in splints for long weeks and months; or to have closed eyes, as so many hundreds in that hospital had, from gas; to lie there in absolute darkness, having no idea whether they would be able to see again or not. There were no radios in those days—nothing to do but lie there in darkness until the doctor and the nurse made one of their two trips a day; until the orderly brought a bed pan or one of the meals.

And speaking about meals—they were mighty poor in this hospital. They may have sufficed for a small man who was sorely wounded; but I was perpetually hungry. I became a pest in the kitchen—until my pajamas were commandeered. Then my only redress was to complain orally. During the entire war I wondered what became of the food that was sent to France. The people at home were doing without it so that the men who were doing the fighting would have it. The men in the rear didn't have it; they said it was at the front. It wasn't at the front; we had just enough to exist on; it wasn't at the big camps. Where could it be? I often wondered. Later I was to learn that much of it was at the base ports. The marine guards at those ports, even the colored stevedores, lived royally— it not being unusual to have roast beef and chicken, five or six kinds of vegetables, one or two desserts besides ice cream—and not on Christmas either. That's where the food was—in the hands of the men who took it off the ship. The more desirable portions stayed there; we at the front got only what was left.

The days dragged along. I helped where I could—talking to the more seriously wounded, helping the orderlies feed a badly-wounded man, even aiding the nurses in making beds. I wasn't a pretty sight as I went around in my pajamas and with slippers of the Oriental type. With my head shaved in front, with my face still swollen and bloated, I looked like an accident that had happened or at least a cross between a Chinaman and a misspent life.

I had been getting out of bed too much, and it did seem about this time that comrades, doctors and nurses who had warned me to go to bed and take things easy had been right. I broke out with a fever and a rash, and then I was kept in bed. I could look out the window and see the French people fishing for a tiny flat, sardine-like fish. They frequently popped these fish into their mouths and ate them raw. There was a rowing club near, and soldiers who had been invalided home due to wounds would row along the river in a four-oared shell. I had been an oarsman at home and longed to be out there with them.

We heard stories of what was going on at the front. Our own Fourth of July had passed while we were at the evacuation hospital at Collumieres. And now came the equivalent in France of our Fourth of July—Bastille Day. The Germans had selected that day as the beginning of their big drive to Paris. Things looked gloomy at first. There was talk of the possible necessity of moving the wounded in this hospital still farther south if the German drive continued. Then came the Americans' counter attack on July 18th. We soon learned that they had driven in on the flanks of both sides of the large pocket which extended to Chateau Thierry and in a surprisingly short time had caused a great German retreat which was to continue until the cessation of hostilities. It was the turning point. Nurses, doctors, patients and visitors were elated.

The hospital was already filled. Great numbers of men were dying and being wounded in the terrific battles at the front. A place had to be found for them. Doctors came through examining each bed case carefully to see which of them could be moved or were able to get out of bed and perhaps be conveyed to some other location—other public buildings, or the homes of French people. I told the doctor when my turn came that I was anxious to leave and get back to my comrades at the front. He refused to even let me out of bed. I was particularly chagrined, for I yearned to go out in the yard and walk along the river. He told me that I would be required to remain in bed for at least a week. Then he would see.

Many men were evacuated. Comrades I had come to know were gone. That's one thing about the war—you meet people one day, come to know them well, and to like them, and in another day they are gone, never to appear in your life again. I am carrying some scores of fellows around in my memory that I came to like and have never seen since. While our original company was made up entirely of men who lived in Pennsylvania, notably Pittsburgh and Pottstown, many of our men were from the smaller cities around Pittsburgh—men who had enlisted while we were guarding bridges, factories and tunnels—Beaver, Beaver Falls, New Brighton, Elwood City, Wampum and other places. We had men from Texas, from Montana and from other parts of the West and South, men who, if they survived the war, lived so far away that I could never see them again.

The fresh wounded started to come in about this time, and by some coincidence in came a man from my very own company who was placed in the next bed to mine. He had been shot through the leg and was to spend many long weary weeks lying upon his back, with his leg in splints, suspended in the air, with a pulley-like arrangement to raise and lower it, with a drainage tube to keep the wound open. He was able to tell me what had happened to our organization in the days of my absence, and as he was unable to sleep much, we talked about the war.

The wounded that came in now were particularly serious cases—men who had been wounded by tremendous shells. There was much screaming and anguish displayed by these sorely-wounded men. Seldom was it quiet at night. Men whose nerves broke would be screaming all night. There were many cases of shell shock—men who had their maniacal moments when they felt that they were still at the front, being subjected to shell fire. They were out of their minds and there was nothing that could be done about it; but it made it most unpleasant for the other wounded. Horrible cases of mustard gas were everywhere. Some of these men were blinded and had to lie for endless days with their heads covered with bandages. Some of the men later were able to walk spraddle-legged down the aisles. I was told that their testicles had in some cases shrivelled up like dry peas in a pod. Certainly they were in a bad way.

About the 21st of July the doctors at the base hospital decided that I was fit to go back to the front. It was nice to have my uniform again after several weeks in pajamas. I bade all the nurses, doctors and patients good-bye and was off to St. Agnain for equipment and shipment to my organization. A single day's trip, two days at the camp, new uniform, rifle and complete equipment and I was off again. But this time I went through Paris. I spent two days in the great city and saw the sights.

And the next day I was to have one of the busiest days of my life. Early in the morning I entrained for Chateau Thierry. It wasn't a long trip—perhaps three hours with the slow French trains. Long before I reached Chateau Thierry I saw signs of the war—chiefly shattered trains, which had been used to haul troops to the front. The windows were smashed; there were holes in the roofs—principally from shrapnel; but there had been considerable machine gunning of these trains by the German aviation. As usual the Germans had control of the air and could do as they willed. I could see the blood on the cushions of the cars as we passed, and knew that the men who had occupied those coaches had had a bad time.

About eleven o'clock I arrived at the station in Chateau Thierry. I disembarked and was met by a transportation officer who examined my pass, looked in his book to see where our organization was, and made arrangements for me to ride toward the front in a French truck. There were hundreds of cots lined up on the station platform, chiefly gas patients, waiting their turn to be sent to the base hospitals. They lay there as if dead, with bandages covering their eyes. There were a host of gas casualties on this front.

This was my first time in Chateau Thierry. I had seen it at a distance from the heights of Hill 204, when it was occupied by the Germans. Now the Germans were many miles away. The people were already coming back to the city. There were a few women and children, a few elderly men, and soldiers in abundance—both from the American and French armies.

After a reasonable wait the truck on which I was to ride drew up to the station and I was off. Apparently I was the only one going back to the front at this time. I saw something of Chateau Thierry as we drove through it. It must have been a beautiful town before it had been shelled and occupied by the Germans, for even in its partly-shattered state it still showed signs of beauty. In a short time we were out on the country road, going north. Before long I could hear the muttering of the guns. There were plenty of signs of the war that had passed. In the first stages of the journey, the dead had been buried. Crosses lined the roads and the edges of the fields. A great many of our engineers were working on the road, trying to make it passable for large bodies of troops as soon as possible. There were many places where we had to detour through the fields as a shell hole had made the road impassable. The bridges along the creeks had been destroyed, and temporary bridges had been set up so that we could cross.

In a surprisingly short time, at about two o'clock, we were close enough to the front that we started to see the dead soldiers of both armies along the way. The American soldiers had been buried hastily in the holes they had dug along the road as they were advancing. But there were still many of them lying in the fields. I could see their khaki uniforms and their white faces as we passed.

As we went along we came to many dead Germans. Some had been pulled off the road. At one place we saw many of them lined up for burial. They smelled quite dead, but the driver of the truck insisted upon stopping to look them over. "Boche, mort, bon," he said over and over. I would translate this as "dead Boche, or German, is a good German." French soldiers standing alongside the road held their noses and laughed and said, "Tomorrow." They weren't in a hurry to put their enemies under the ground.

Sanitary crews and engineers were cleaning up as fast as they could, but a bit farther on we started to pass dead soldiers—Germans—still lying upon the road. They had remained too long in their endeavor to stop the forward progress of our troops, and they had paid with their lives. I saw German soldiers sitting beside the road quite dead. Their arms and heads were bandaged. They had had a bit of attention but had died anyway.

My driver had a hatred for the Germans and a strong stomach too, for he ran over every dead German he could reach with his truck. He zigzagged along from dead German to dead German, driving his huge truck over them and smashing them as completely as the rabbits and skunks we see killed along our own roads so often. Then he would stop and look at them and laugh. It was a rather trying ordeal for me. For days I had been back with human beings, in reasonable comfort and safety. Only that morning I had left one of the world's gayest cities (although Paris in war time was a great deal quieter than usual, it was still a gay city); the night before I had visited the Folies Bergere, had strolled down the Boulevard Italians, and out of the thousands of—how shall I say it— femmes de nuit (I hope that no masters of French read this book, for my American army French is twenty years behind me. But I am trying to say, "ladies of the evening," as they were called in Paris) I had found a very nice little girl and had enjoyed being with her.

And here I was back at the front with a vengeance. The truck drove perilously near the front, finally stopped and let me off. I asked a military policeman on guard at a crossroads where the 111th was stationed. He told me that they were up at the front and directed me. I asked everyone I saw along the way for directions and about four o'clock I was so close to the front that I could see the action up ahead. Machine gun and rifle bullets were whizzing overhead. Seventy-sevens were falling all around, and the stretcher bearers were coming back in bunches. I walked, and then I crawled, to get back with my outfit. And when I got there I found it was not the 111th, but the 112th regiment of our division. I admit frankly I was relieved and pleased to learn that our regiment was not at this time in the lines. I went back, glad enough to get away from the raging inferno I had found at the front. Three or four kilometers away I found our regiment, and our company camped in a wood. Everyone was glad to see me and I was glad to see them. They had not expected me back—had heard that I was much more seriously wounded than I actually was. The captain told me that he had heard great things about me, and was glad to have me back as casualties had been so heavy that few capable men were left. It seemed to me that I hardly knew the men in the company. Most of the original members were gone. New men had joined the company and I had to get acquainted all over again. It is difficult to understand why men who have been at the front—who had been, perhaps, badly wounded—are so anxious to come up again. People may wonder if it is an irresistible impulse like that which draws the moth again and again to the flame when it has already been burnt, or is it the same feeling some people get to jump from a high place? Scores have jumped over the brink at Niagara Falls. The magnet that drew me back to the front was the desire to see my friends again—to see what they were doing, to learn what they had done, to find what had happened to so and so, to be glad that another friend was still alive and well. All the men had had narrow escapes and were glad to be alive.

I learned here what had occurred in my absence. After the two platoons had marched away, the regiment had continued to a small town named Le Petit Villiers. This little village was well behind the front but there was considerable air activity nearby. Bombing squadrons constantly passed as well as observation planes. It was believed that the Germans were preparing for a big drive. What was left of the two platoons came back to their companies at this little town. Prior to their return there had been many rumors about them, but now for the first time there was first-hand information. While most of the wounded had passed through the French first-aid station, some had gone through our own regimental hospital as they were sent to the rear. Only a few men from A Company had returned, and they received a tremendous ovation as they arrived.

The entire company stayed up that night until very late listening to the wonderful stories of the "veterans." Excitement and enthusiasm remained at fever heat all during that evening. And from hearing of the exploits of these men—the first to engage in battle—a new spirit was born which was to carry our troops to heroic exploits in the weeks and months to come.

The story those who returned told was a wonderful story, a story of mad adventure, of wounds, pain, death by bombs, bayonets, snipers and machine guns. Any man who returned was alive only through a series of miracles. The survivors' faces were still flushed, their eyes wide and starry from the excitement which they still felt. They were enthusiastic concerning the behavior of our troops in action, of the long-remembered meal the French general had given them after the battle, of his praise for their fine work, of the decorations which had been promised to them. They told particularly of how certain men had died, and of Jim Early, Bill Felix, and Bob Hoffman who had reached the farthermost point; of the prisoners who had been captured. And they showed a great number of souvenirs to commemorate the first experience in battle. The men were proud of their organization.

There was drilling for the next day or two at this place until one day a group of officers from the regiment climbed into a light truck and journeyed forward several miles to look over a new position to which our regiment was to move. A hike of five kilos nearer the front was made at this time. It had started to rain and the next day there was a march of more miles. At that point the colonel called the officers of the regiment together and read the message of congratulation the French general had sent concerning the action of the two platoons, and a citation from divisional headquarters concerning their fine work. Our regiment remained a full week at this point and then moved up to positions at the front. There was a great deal of gas at this point, constant gas alarms, many of which heralded genuine gas attacks. Our organization lost men heavily from gas near here for they had two rather unpleasant assignments to perform. One was the burying of the dead soldiers who had lain for two or three weeks under the July sun, and the other was the digging up of dead Germans to remove their identification tags.

In a woods nearby the soldiers were still lying who had helped stop the German advance toward Paris. They had sold their lives dearly in many cases, for a great many Germans had died too. Three weeks these men had lain in the sun and our troops set out to bury them. Americans and Germans alike were put under the sod. There were horses too and they were a problem. Horses are huge when they become bloated, swell to twice their normal size. Their legs are thrust out like steel posts and it requires a hole about ten feet square and six feet deep to put a horse under. If the legs were off, a hole hardly more than half that size is required. At times we succeeded in using an axe and saw to cut off the horses' legs. It was a hard task and an unpleasant one, but it had to be done.

Finally the fields were cleared but there was still another gruesome task to perform. It is a law of war that the names of enemy dead be sent back through a neutral country to their homeland. The identification tags had been taken from the dead Americans but the Germans had been buried just as they were. There was the task to dig them up again—enough to remove half of their oval-shaped identification tags. That was a much more disagreeable job than the first. Gas came over and owing to the terrific odor even the powerful-smelling mustard gas could not be detected. Our men were working hard in the mid-July heat, perspiring, just in the right condition for mustard gas. Nearly half the remainder of our company, sixty-seven in all, were gassed badly enough to be sent to the hospital. Many of them died; most of them were out for the duration of the war—all reasons why I never saw any of the men who made the attack on Hill 204 at the front again.

Did you ever smell a dead mouse? This will give you about as much idea of what a group of long dead soldiers smell like as will one grain of sand give you an idea of Atlantic City's beaches. A group of men were sent to Hill 204 to make a reconnaissance, to report on conditions there as well as to bury the dead. The story was a very pathetic one. The men were still lying there nearly two weeks later just as they had fallen. I knew all of these men intimately and it was indeed painful to learn of their condition. Some had apparently lived for some time; had tried to dress their own wounds, or their comrades had dressed them; but later they had died there. I was especially pleased that the capture of the German soldiers had made it possible to bring back all the wounded in our sector. Many of the men had been pumped full of machine gun bullets—shot almost beyond recognition. A hundred or so bullets, even in a dead man's body, is not a pretty sight. One of our men was lying with a German bayonet through him—not unlike a pin through a large beetle.

Bayonets are hard to remove when once they have been caught between the ribs, especially the saw-tooth bayonets many of the Germans carried. To dislodge them it is usually necessary to shoot once or more to loosen the bayonet. This German had not waited, but had left his gun and passed on. The little Italian boy was still lying on the barbed wire, his eyes open and his helmet hanging back on his head. There had been much shrapnel and some of the bodies were torn almost beyond recognition. This was the first experience at handling and burying the dead for many of our men. It was a trying experience as I was to personally find somewhat later. The identification tags removed from the dead were corroded white, and had become imbedded in the putrid flesh. Even after the burial, when these tags were brought back to the company, they smelled so horribly that some of the officers became extremely sick. One huge man—a giant of a man—who was shot cleanly between the eyes was lying among a group of dead Americans and Germans (that must have been Corporal Graves); and a middle-aged sergeant, who must have been Sergeant George Amole. There is nothing much more pitiful than a battlefield after a battle.

There are two chief reasons why a soldier feels fear: First, that he will not get home to see his loved ones again; but, most of all, picturing himself in the same position as some of the dead men we saw. They lay there face up, usually in the rain, their eyes open, their faces pale and chalk-like, their gold teeth showing. That is in the beginning. After that they are usually too horrible to think about. We buried them as fast as we could—Germans, French and Americans alike. Get them out of sight, but not out of memory. I can remember hundreds and hundreds of dead men. I would know them now if I were to meet them in a hereafter. I could tell them where they were lying and how they were killed— whether with shell fire, gas, machine gun or bayonet. In the town of Varennes there were scores of dead Germans lying around. They had held their positions until the last moment. Many of them had been killed by the tremendous bombardment as they tried to leave. Others had been killed by our advance troops. I spent three days in this town as our battalion was in reserve and I came to know all the dead Germans as I walked around. Later perhaps a hundred of them were laid out for burial. I saw them lying there and I am sure that I could have taken every one of them back to the point where he had died and put him in the exact position in which he had lain.

In the beginning we had a fear of the dead. We hated to touch them. Some of the hardest experiences of my life were taking the identification tags from my dead friends. The first dead man I touched was Philip Beketich, an Austrian baker who was with our company. He was wounded in the battle of Fismes. I had tried to save his life by carrying him through the heavy enemy fire and putting him in one of the cellars of the French houses. He was shot in my arms as I carried him. A few hours later I found time to go round and find how he was. He was dead—stiff and cold. He had quite a splendid development of the pectoral muscles—the big muscles of the chest. Working as a baker had apparently been responsible for that. I had to remove his identification tags, and they had slipped down between his collar bones and the flesh of his chest. They were held there, and it took an effort to get them out. I thrilled and chilled with horror as I touched him. Just a bit later I had to touch my very good friend Lester Michaels, a fine young fellow who had been a star football player on our company team, and a good piano player who entertained us when such an instrument was available. He had been walking past me in Fismes, bent well over. "Keep down, Mike," I said. "There's a sniper shooting through here." Just then Mike fell, with a look of astonishment on his face. "What's the matter, Mike?" I asked. He replied, "They've got me," shook a few times and lay dead upon his face with his legs spread apart—shot through the heart. He lay there for more than a day. There was a terrific battle on and we had no chance to help the wounded—certainly not the dead. I was running short of ammunition and I needed the cartridges in Mike's belt. I tried to unfasten his belt, but I could not reach it. Finally I had to turn him completely over. It was quite an effort owing to the spread-eagle manner in which he lay. His body was hard and cold, and I saw his dead face—difficult to describe the feeling I had. But necessity demanded that I unloosen his belt and take his ammunition and still later his identification tag. After the war I heard from his relatives who wanted to know exactly how he had died.

There are many people who sought this information. They liked to know whether the soldier was killed by shell fire, whether while fighting hand to hand, while running to the attack, or in some phase of defensive work. It was hard to touch these dead men at first. My people at home, hearing of what I was passing through, expected me to come back hard, brutal, callous, careless. But I didn't even want to take a dead mouse out of a trap when I was home. Yet over there I buried seventy-eight men one morning. I didn't dig the holes for them, of course, but I did take their personal belongings from them to return to their people—their rings, trinkets, letters and identification tags. They were shot up in a great variety of ways, and it was not pleasant, but I managed to eat my quota of bread and meat when it came up with no opportunity to wash my hands.

One night I was hiking along through the darkness going into the Argonne battle. We fell out for a moment at the side of the road, and I sat on what I thought was a partially buried sand bag. After resting there for a time a comrade told me that I was sitting on a dead man. I didn't even move. I didn't think he would mind. At times men died in such a position that they were hard to bury. The ground was hard; there was danger of shell fire as long as we were on a burial detail. We'd try hard to make the graves as shallow as possible. So often men were buried in the holes other men had dug along the side of the road as they advanced. A rifle or bayonet would be thrust in the ground at the head of the grave, and a man's identification tag placed upon it. Soon the remainder of the army would be moving up—the machine gunners, the artillery, the supply trucks. They would have to pass on a narrow road. The truck would run over the grave and knock down the improvised cross; there was no further way to identify the dead man. For this and a score of other reasons it was folly to bring back the men who had died in France. I am sure that few of them had been properly identified and were actually the men they were supposed to be. Later in the war we always left one tag upon the dead man and turned the other in to headquarters after making a report of the death. A cross would be erected and marked. These men could be identified. We had a coordinated position on the map so that the body could be found. But earlier in the war when both tags were placed outside the grave, and later lost, the body could not be identified.

When a man died in a sitting or kneeling position it was impossible to straighten him out—difficult to dig a deep enough hole to cover him. More than once I would try to straighten out the body—stand on the legs and the head would come up; stand on the head and the legs would come up; finally compromise by burying the upper body, letting the legs stick up for a cross, and hanging the helmet and gas mask to the human cross. Other times it was necessary to put a big man in a comparatively small hole. We would step on his middle to bend it sufficiently to make him fit the hole.

One of my most poignant memories of the war took place in the battle of Fismes. . . . For several days we had been crawling around the town, firing from windows, cellars, attics and from behind the stone wall in the back of the house yards. This got tiresome, and finally the fellow next to me—a candidate by the name of Vaugn (a man who had qualified for a commission through a special course of schooling, and was waiting only a vacancy to receive it)—raised up, laid his gun upon the top of the wall and started to shoot over the wall. That was more comfortable and it was much easier to see what was being shot at. It was the method used by the old Indian fighters as they fired over the stockades of their forts. I should have known better with my previous battle experience, but I thought, "If Vaugn can shoot over the wall, I can too." Soon we were banging away merrily. But after several shots each I suddenly saw Vaugn's helmet go sailing down over the slight hill. I looked at him and the entire top of his head was off—apparently a dum dum type of bullet (one in which the lead had been cut so that it would spread the instant it struck, tearing a terrific hole in the object it hit) had flattened against his helmet or tin hat, and had taken off his head to a level with his eyes and ears. He had been kneeling; his buttocks went back a bit, his head forward and his brains ran out there in front of me like soup from a pot. I did not fire over another wall. The sniper had his choice to pick one or the other of us. For some unknown reason he chose Vaugn. I'm here and he's gone. Vaugn lay there for a couple of days; finally he was carried down and stored in the room where we had the other dead piled up like logs of wood; but he had to have his own place in the corner. It was gruesome enough.

JAMES MILNE

Company Sergeant-Major James Milne of the Gordon Highlanders wrote this letter expecting to be killed within a few hours. He survived not just the forthcoming battle but the whole war.

To His Wife

B.E.F.
Sat 20th July 1917

My own Beloved Wife,
    I do not know how to start this letter or not. The circumstances are different from any under which I ever wrote before. I am not to post it but will leave it in my pocket and if anything happens to me someone will perhaps post it. We are going over the top this forenoon and only God in Heaven knows who will come out of it alive. I am going into it now Dearest sure that I am in His hands and that whatever happens I look to Him, in this world and the world to come. If I am called my regret is that I leave you and my Bairns but I leave you all to His great mercy and goodness, knowing that he will look over you all and watch you. I trust in Him to bring me through but should He decree otherwise then though we do not know His reasons we know it must be best. I go to

Him with your dear face the last vision on earth I shall see and your name upon my lips. You, the best of Women. You will look after my Darling Bairns for me and tell them how their Daddy died. Oh! how I love you all and as I sit here waiting I wonder what you are doing at home. I must not do that. It is hard enough sitting waiting. We may move at any minute. When this reaches you for me there will be no more war, only eternal peace and waiting for you. You must be brave my Darling for my sake for I leave you the bairns. It is a legacy of struggle for you but God will look after you and we shall meet again when there will be no more parting. I am to write no more Sweetheart. I know you will read my old letters and keep them for my sake and that you will love me or my memory till we meet again.

Kiss the Bairns for me once more. I dare not think of them, My Darlings.

Good Bye, you best of Women and best of Wives my beloved sweetheart.

May God in His Mercy look over you and bless you all till that day we shall meet again in His own Good time.

May He in that same Mercy preserve me today. Goodbye Meg

xxxx   Eternal love from
xxxx   Yours for Ever and Ever
                                                                    Jim

VERA BRITTAIN
1893–1970

Brittain was an ambitious, intensely feminist student at Somerville College, Oxford. During the war, she served as a nurse in the Volunteer Aid Detachment. The deaths on the Western Front of her fiancé Roland Leighton, her brother Edward, and her friends Geoffrey Thurlow and Victor Richardson (he was cruelly blinded first) left her devastated, and she devoted the rest of her life to outrage, elegy, and pacifism. She told her story in her memoir Testament of Youth *(1933), which she understood as "the indictment of a civilization."*

From TESTAMENT OF YOUTH

Roland and his mother and I went up together to London, where he had arranged to spend the rest of his leave. At Heather Cliff he said good-bye to Clare and his brother, and at the station to his father; in spite of these farewells he seemed preoccupied, as though living in an inner world from which experience excluded even those whom he dearly loved.

All day I felt inordinately tired, and so, I think, did Roland. His mother and I had sat up till 3 A.M. the previous night talking about him and our possible future; we had been obliged to get up early to catch the London train, so that none of us had spent more than three hours in bed. Roland and I, weary and depressed, passed most of the day in shops, renewing his equipment for the winter. To the disappointment of his mother, who thought a ring the only true symbol of union between a man and a woman, and to the subsequent surprised incredulity of other engaged Buxton girls—who used to remove their gloves in church in order to display a diamond half-hoop on the conspicuous third finger of their left hands—we both reacted violently against the idea of an engagement ring, Roland saying that he "detested the obvious," and I fiercely determined to exhibit no "token of possession." I could not endure the thought of displaying a conventional jewel in order to indicate to other men that I was "appropriated" and to suggest to other women that I had won a long-sought prize after a successful hunt; it seemed too typical of the old inequality.

Throughout the remaining hours the shadow of the approaching end of day—and perhaps of so much more—lay heavily upon us. I made Roland go to Dunlop's and choose himself a pipe, and he bought me an extravagant bouquet of deep red roses, but despite these lover-like transactions we felt jarred and irritated by the knowledge that the little time left to us had to be spent in the noise and tantalising publicity of shops and streets. At Savory & Moore's he restocked his medical case with morphia; I was glad, later, to remember that he had bought a good supply.

After tea—for both of us a sullen, subdued meal, at which we had joined his mother and an old novelist friend—I had to go to St. Pancras to catch my train back to Buxton. I felt sadder and more listless than ever; so much that I had meant to say to him was still unsaid, and yet it seemed of no use to say anything more. He told me at last, very bitterly, that he didn't want to go back to the front; he had come to loathe its uncongenial monotony, and this glimpse of England and "real life" had made him hate it more than before.

At St. Pancras there was no empty carriage in which we could talk for the few moments left to us, so we had perforce to walk up and down the noisy platform, saying nothing of importance, and ferociously detesting the cheerful, chattering group round my carriage door.

"I wish to God there weren't other people in the world!" he exclaimed irritably.

"I agree," I said, and remarked wearily that I should have to put up with their pleasant company in a lighted dining-car all the way to Buxton.

"Oh, *damn!*" he responded.

But when, suddenly, the shriek of the whistle cut sharply through the tumult of sound, our resolution not to kiss on a crowded platform vanished with our consciousness of the crowd's exasperating presence. Too angry and miserable to be shy any more, we clung together and kissed in forlorn desperation.

"I shan't look out of the window and wave to you," I told him, and he replied incoherently: "No—don't; I can't!"

To my amazement, taut and tearless as I was, I saw him hastily mop his eyes with his handkerchief, and in that moment, when it was too late to respond or to show that I understood, I realised how much more he cared for me than I had supposed or he had ever shown. I felt, too, so bitterly sorry for him because he had to fight against his tears while I had no wish to cry at all, and the intolerable longing to comfort him when there was no more time in which to do it made me furious with the frantic pain of impotent desire.

And then, all at once, the whistle sounded again and the train started. As the noisy group moved away from the door he sprang on to the footboard, clung to my hand and, drawing my face down to his, kissed my lips in a sudden vehemence of despair. And I kissed his, and just managed to whisper "Good-bye!" The next moment he was walking rapidly down the platform, with his head bent and his face very pale. Although I had said that I would not, I stood by the door as the train left the station and watched him moving through the crowd. But he never turned again.

* * *

Certainly the stage seemed perfectly set for his leave. Now that my parents had at last migrated temporarily to the Grand Hotel at Brighton, our two families were so near; the Matron had promised yet again that my own week's holiday should coincide with his, and even Edward wrote cheerfully for once to say that as soon as the actual date was known, he and Victor would both be able to get leave at the same time.

"Very wet and muddy and many of the communication trenches are quite impassable," ran a letter from Roland written on December 9th. "Three men were killed the other day by a dug-out falling in on top of them and one man was drowned in a sump hole. The whole of one's world, at least of one's visible and palpable world, is mud in various

stages of solidity or stickiness. . . . I can be perfectly certain about the
date of my leave by to-morrow morning and will let you know."

And, when the final information did come, hurriedly written in pencil
on a thin slip of paper torn from his Field Service note-book, it brought
the enchanted day still nearer than I had dared to hope.

"Shall be home on leave from 24th Dec.—31st. Land Christmas Day.
R."

Even to the unusual concession of a leave which began on Christmas
morning after night-duty the Matron proved amenable, and in the encouraging quietness of the winter's war, with no Loos in prospect, no
great push in the west even possible, I dared to glorify my days—or
rather my nights—by looking forward. In the pleasant peace of Ward
25, where all the patients, now well on the road to health, slept soundly,
the sympathetic Scottish Sister teased me a little for my irrepressible
excitement.

"I suppose you won't be thinking of going off and getting married? A
couple of babies like you!"

It was a new and breath-taking thought, a flame to which Roland's
mother—who approved of early marriages and believed that ways and
means could be left to look after themselves far better than the average
materialistic parent supposed—added fuel when she hinted mysteri-
ously, on a day off which I spent in Brighton, that *this* time Roland
might not be content to leave things as they were. . . . Suppose, I
meditated, kneeling in the darkness beside the comforting glow of the
stove in the silent ward, that during this leave we *did* marry as suddenly,
as, in the last one, we became "officially" engaged? Of course it would be
what the world would call—or did call before the War—a "foolish"
marriage. But now that the War seemed likely to be endless, and the
chance of making a "wise" marriage had become, for most people, so
very remote, the world was growing more tolerant. No one—not even
my family now, I thought—would hold out against us, even though we
hadn't a penny beyond our pay. What if, after all, we did marry thus
foolishly? When the War was over we could still go back to Oxford, and
learn to be writers—or even lecturers; if we were determined enough
about it we could return there, even though—oh, devastating, sweet
speculation!—I might have had a baby.

I had never much cared for babies or had anything to do with them;
before that time I had always been too ambitious, too much interested in
too many projects, to become acutely conscious of a maternal instinct.
But on those quiet evenings of night-duty as Christmas approached, I
would come, half asleep, as near to praying as I had been at any time,
even when Roland first went to France or in the days following Loos.

"Oh, God!" my half-articulate thoughts would run, "do let us get
married and let me have a baby—something that is Roland's very own,

something of himself to remember him by if he goes. . . . It shan't be a burden to his people or mine for a moment longer than I can help, I promise. I'll go on doing war-work and give it all my pay during the War—and as soon as ever the War's over I'll go back to Oxford and take my Finals so that I can get a job and support it. So *do* let me have a baby, dear God!"

The night before Christmas Eve, I found my ward transformed into the gay semblance of a sixpenny bazaar with Union Jacks, paper streamers, crinkled tissue lampshades and Christmas texts and greetings, all carried out in staggering shades of orange and vivid scarlet and brilliant green. In the cheerful construction of red paper bags, which I filled with crackers and sweets for the men's Christmas stockings, I found that the hours passed quickly enough. Clipping, and sewing, and opening packets, I imagined him reading the letter that I had written him a few days earlier, making various suggestions for meeting him, if he could only write or wire me beforehand, when the Folkestone train arrived at Victoria, and travelling down with him to Sussex.

"And shall I really see you again, and so soon?" it had concluded. "And it will be the anniversary of the week which contained another New Year's Eve—and *David Copperfield,* and two unreal and wonderful days, and you standing alone in Trafalgar Square, and thinking of—well, what *were* you thinking of? When we were really both children still, and my connection with any hospital on earth was unthought-of, and your departure for the front merely the adventurous dream of some vaguely distant future date. And life was lived, at any rate for two days, in the Omar Khayyámesque spirit of

> Unborn to-morrow and dead yesterday—
> Why fret about them if To-day be sweet?

But we are going to better that—even that—*this* time. Au revoir."

When I went to her office for my railway-warrant in the morning, the Matron smiled kindly at my bubbling impatience, and reminded me how lucky I was to get leave for Christmas. At Victoria I inquired what boat trains arrived on Christmas Day, and learnt that there was only one, at 7.30 in the evening. The risk, I decided, of missing him in the winter blackness of a wartime terminus was too great to be worth taking: instead, I would go straight to Brighton next morning and wait for him there.

As Christmas Eve slipped into Christmas Day, I finished tying up the paper bags, and with the Sister filled the men's stockings by the exiguous light of an electric torch. Already I could count, perhaps even on my fingers, the hours that must pass before I should see him. In spite of its tremulous eagerness of anticipation, the night again seemed short; some of the convalescent men wanted to go to early services, and that meant beginning temperatures and pulses at 3 A.M. As I took them I listened to the rain pounding on the tin roof, and wondered whether, since his leave ran from Christmas Eve, he was already on the sea in that wild, stormy darkness. When the men awoke and reached for their stockings, my whole being glowed with exultant benevolence; I delighted in their pleasure over their childish home-made presents because my own mounting joy made me feel in harmony with all creation.

At eight o'clock, as the passages were lengthy and many of the men were lame, I went along to help them to the communion service in the chapel of the college. It was two or three years since I had been to such a service, but it seemed appropriate that I should be there, for I felt, wrought up as I was to a high pitch of nervous emotion, that I ought to thank whatever God might exist for the supreme gift of Roland and the love that had arisen so swiftly between us. The music of the organ was so sweet, the sight of the wounded men who knelt and stood with such difficulty so moving, the conflict of joy and gratitude, pity and sorrow in my mind so poignant, that tears sprang to my eyes, dimming the chapel walls and the words that encircled them: "I am the Resurrection and the Life: he that believeth in Me, though he were dead, yet shall he live: and whosoever liveth and believeth in Me shall never die."

Directly after breakfast, sent on my way by exuberant good wishes from Betty and Marjorie and many of the others, I went down to Brighton. All day I waited there for a telephone message or a telegram, sitting drowsily in the lounge of the Grand Hotel, or walking up and down the promenade, watching the grey sea tossing rough with white surf-crested waves, and wondering still what kind of crossing he had had or was having.

When, by ten o'clock at night, no news had come, I concluded that the complications of telegraph and telephone on a combined Sunday and Christmas Day had made communication impossible. So, unable to fight sleep any longer after a night and a day of wakefulness, I went to bed a little disappointed, but still unperturbed. Roland's family, at their Keymer cottage, kept an even longer vigil; they sat up till nearly midnight over their Christmas dinner in the hope that he would join them, and, in their dramatic, impulsive fashion, they drank a toast to the Dead.

The next morning I had just finished dressing, and was putting the final touches to the pastel-blue crêpe-de-Chine blouse, when the expected message came to say that I was wanted on the telephone. Believing that I was at last to hear the voice for which I had waited for twenty-four hours, I dashed joyously into the corridor. But the message was not from Roland but from Clare; it was not to say that he had arrived home that morning, but to tell me that he had died of wounds at a Casualty Clearing Station on December 23rd.

                                    *   *   *

And now there were no more disasters to dread and no friends left to
wait for; with the ending of apprehension had come a deep, nullifying
blankness, a sense of walking in a thick mist which hid all sights and
muffled all sounds. I had no further experience to gain from the War;
nothing remained except to endure it.

It had not, however, to be endured much longer. I had only been at
Millbank for a few days when it became obvious even to me that something unusual and important was happening all over Europe. For a long
time, although I read spasmodically about the German retreat, my mind
refused to take in its significance; I had ceased to think of the War as
ever ending, and much less as ending in victory. But now the growing
crescendo of triumphant battle, the rapid withdrawal of the Germans on
the Western Front to the Hindenburg line and beyond while Turkey
and Austria were collapsing in the East, penetrated even my torpid
consciousness, and I awoke with a fearful start to the astonishing fact
that, up at Ypres, the Allies had required only one day to gain as much
territory as had been taken in three months during the costly and all too
bitterly memorable offensive round Passchendaele in 1917.

After November 3rd, when the Germans were left alone to face the
united strength of their old enemies reinforced by the exultant, inexhaustible Americans, when Valenciennes fell and the British Army
struck its ultimate blow on the Sambre, I realised that the end had
become a matter of days. But I could still call up only a languid interest
when I read that the Canadians, by capturing Mons, had picturesquely
finished the War where it began, and I neither knew nor cared that a day
or two afterwards a section of the recovered territory was occupied by a
new battalion of the London Rifle Brigade, which had crossed the Channel just in time to see the fighting reach its incredible conclusion.

                                    *   *   *

When the sound of victorious guns burst over London at 11 A.M. on
November 11th, 1918, the men and women who looked incredulously
into each other's faces did not cry jubilantly: "We've won the War!"
They only said: "The War is over."

From Millbank I heard the maroons crash with terrifying clearness,
and, like a sleeper who is determined to go on dreaming after being told
to wake up, I went on automatically washing the dressing bowls in the
annex outside my hut. Deeply buried beneath my consciousness there
stirred the vague memory of a letter that I had written to Roland in
those legendary days when I was still at Oxford, and could spend my
Sundays in thinking of him while the organ echoed grandly through
New College Chapel. It had been a warm May evening, when all the city
was sweet with the scent of wallflowers and lilac, and I had walked back

to Micklem Hall after hearing an Occasional Oratorio by Handel, which described the mustering of troops for battle, the lament for the fallen and the triumphant return of the victors.

"As I listened," I told him, "to the organ swelling forth into a final triumphant burst in the song of victory, after the solemn and mournful dirge over the dead, I thought with what mockery and irony the jubilant celebrations which will hail the coming of peace will fall upon the ears of those to whom their best will never return, upon whose sorrow victory is built, who have paid with their mourning for the others' joy. I wonder if I shall be one of those who take a happy part in the triumph—or if I shall listen to the merriment with a heart that breaks and ears that try to keep out the mirthful sounds."

And as I dried the bowls I thought: "It's come too late for me. Somehow I knew, even at Oxford, that it would. Why couldn't it have ended rationally, as it might have ended, in 1916, instead of all that trumpet-blowing against a negotiated peace, and the ferocious talk of secure civilians about marching to Berlin? It's come five months too late—or is it three years? It might have ended last June, and let Edward, at least, be saved! Only five months—it's such a little time, when Roland died nearly three years ago."

But on Armistice Day not even a lonely survivor drowning in black waves of memory could be left alone with her thoughts. A moment after the guns had subsided into sudden, palpitating silence, the other V.A.D. from my ward dashed excitedly into the annex.

"Brittain! Brittain! Did you hear the maroons? It's over—it's all over! Do let's come out and see what's happening!"

Mechanically I followed her into the road. As I stood there, stupidly rigid, long after the triumphant explosions from Westminster had turned into a distant crescendo of shouting, I saw a taxicab turn swiftly in from the Embankment towards the hospital. The next moment there was a cry for doctors and nurses from passers-by, for in rounding the corner the taxi had knocked down a small elderly woman who in listening, like myself, to the wild noise of a world released from nightmare, had failed to observe its approach.

As I hurried to her side I realized that she was all but dead and already past speech. Like Victor in the mortuary chapel, she seemed to have shrunk to the dimensions of a child with the sharp features of age, but on the tiny chalk-white face an expression of shocked surprise still lingered, and she stared hard at me as Geoffrey had stared at his orderly in those last moments of conscious silence beside the Scarpe. Had she been thinking, I wondered, when the taxi struck her, of her sons at the front, now safe? The next moment a medical officer and some orderlies came up, and I went back to my ward.

But I remembered her at intervals throughout that afternoon, during which, with a half-masochistic notion of "seeing the sights," I made a circular tour to Kensington by way of the intoxicated West End. With aching persistence my thoughts went back to the dead and the strange irony of their fates—to Roland, gifted, ardent, ambitious, who had died without glory in the conscientious performance of a routine job; to Victor and Geoffrey, gentle and diffident, who, conquering nature by resolution, had each gone down bravely in a big "show"; and finally to Edward, musical, serene, a lover of peace, who had fought courageously through so many battles and at last had been killed while leading a vital counter-attack in one of the few decisive actions of the War. As I struggled through the waving, shrieking crowds in Piccadilly and Regent Street on the overloaded top of a 'bus, some witty enthusiast for contemporary history symbolically turned upside down the signboard "Seven Kings."

Late that evening, when supper was over, a group of elated V.A.D.s who were anxious to walk through Westminster and Whitehall to Buckingham Palace prevailed upon me to join them. Outside the Admiralty a crazy group of convalescent Tommies were collecting specimens of different uniforms and bundling their wearers into flag-strewn taxis; with a shout they seized two of my companions and disappeared into the clamorous crowd, waving flags and shaking rattles. Wherever we went a burst of enthusiastic cheering greeted our Red Cross uniform, and complete strangers adorned with wound stripes rushed up and shook me warmly by the hand. After the long, long blackness, it seemed like a fairy-tale to see the street lamps shining through the chill November gloom.

I detached myself from the others and walked slowly up Whitehall, with my heart sinking in a sudden cold dismay. Already this was a different world from the one that I had known during four life-long years, a world in which people would be light-hearted and forgetful, in which themselves and their careers and their amusements would blot out political ideals and great national issues. And in that brightly lit, alien world I should have no part. All those with whom I had really been intimate were gone; not one remained to share with me the heights and the depths of my memories. As the years went by and youth departed and remembrance grew dim, a deeper and ever deeper darkness would cover the young men who were once my contemporaries.

For the first time I realised, with all that full realisation meant, how completely everything that had hitherto made up my life had vanished with Edward and Roland, with Victor and Geoffrey. The War was over; a new age was beginning; but the dead were dead and would never return.

RUDYARD KIPLING
1865-1936

Kipling wrote, among many other works, The Irish Guards in the Great War *(1923), a two-volume history of that unit, in which his son was killed. These Epitaphs, which he published in 1919, he once designated "naked cribs of the Greek Anthology."*

From EPITAPHS OF THE WAR

A SON

My son was killed while laughing at some jest. I would I knew
What it was, and it might serve me in a time when jests are few.

AN ONLY SON

I have slain none except my Mother. She
(Blessing her slayer) died of grief for me.

THE COWARD

I could not look on Death, which being known,
Men led me to him, blindfold and alone.

THE BEGINNER

On the first hour of my first day
In the front trench I fell.
(Children in boxes at a play
Stand up to watch it well.)

R.A.F. (AGED EIGHTEEN)

Laughing through clouds, his milk-teeth still unshed,
Cities and men he smote from overhead.
His deaths delivered, he returned to play
Childlike, with childish things not put away.

THE REFINED MAN

I was of delicate mind. I stepped aside for my needs,
　Disdaining the common office. I was seen from afar and killed. . . .
How is this matter for mirth? Let each man be judged by his deeds.
　I have paid my price to live with myself on the terms that I willed.

BOMBED IN LONDON

On land and sea I strove with anxious care
To escape conscription. It was in the air!

THE SLEEPY SENTINEL

Faithless the watch that I kept: now I have none to keep.
I was slain because I slept: now I am slain I sleep.
Let no man reproach me again, whatever watch is unkept—
I sleep because I am slain. They slew me because I slept.

BATTERIES OUT OF AMMUNITION

If any mourn us in the workshop, say
We died because the shift kept holiday.

COMMON FORM

If any question why we died,
Tell them, because our fathers lied.

A DEAD STATESMAN

I could not dig: I dared not rob:
Therefore I lied to please the mob.
Now all my lies are proved untrue
And I must face the men I slew.
What tale shall serve me here among
Mine angry and defrauded young?

A DRIFTER OFF TARENTUM

He from the wind-bitten North with ship and companions descended,
Searching for eggs of death spawned by invisible hulls.
Many he found and drew forth. Of a sudden the fishery ended
In flame and a clamorous breath known to the eye-pecking gulls.

DESTROYERS IN COLLISION

For Fog and Fate no charm is found
    To lighten or amend.
I, hurrying to my bride, was drowned—
    Cut down by my best friend.

UNKNOWN FEMALE CORPSE

Headless, lacking foot and hand,
Horrible I come to land.
I beseech all women's sons
Know I was a mother once.

THE BRIDEGROOM

Call me not false, beloved,
    If, from thy scarce-known breast
So little time removed,
    In other arms I rest.

For this more ancient bride,
    Whom coldly I embrace,
Was constant at my side
    Before I saw thy face.

Our marriage, often set—
By miracle delayed—
At last is consummate,
And cannot be unmade.

Live, then, whom Life shall cure,
Almost, of Memory,
And leave us to endure
Its immortality.

IVOR GURNEY
1890–1937

Locked in his mental asylum, Gurney continued writing poetry about the war until his death.

STRANGE HELLS

There are strange hells within the minds war made
Not so often, not so humiliatingly afraid
As one would have expected—the racket and fear guns made.
One hell the Gloucester soldiers they quite put out:
Their first bombardment, when in combined black shout

Of fury, guns aligned, they ducked lower their heads
And sang with diaphragms fixed beyond all dreads,
That tin and stretched-wire tinkle, that blither of tune:
"Après la guerre fini," till hell all had come down,
Twelve-inch, six-inch, and eighteen pounders hammering hell's
      thunders.

Where are they now, on state-doles, or showing shop-patterns
Or walking town to town sore in borrowed tatterns
Or begged. Some civic routine one never learns.
The heart burns—but has to keep out of face how heart burns.

WAR BOOKS

What did they expect of our toil and extreme
Hunger—the perfect drawing of a heart's dream?
Did they look for a book of wrought art's perfection,
Who promised no reading, nor praise, nor publication?
Out of the heart's sickness the spirit wrote
For delight, or to escape hunger, or of war's worst anger,
When the guns died to silence and men would gather sense
Somehow together, and find this was life indeed,
And praise another's nobleness, or to Cotswold get hence.
There we wrote—Corbie Ridge—or in Gonnehem at rest—
Or Fauquissart—our world's death songs, ever the best.
One made sorrows' praise passing the church where silence
Opened for the long quivering strokes of the bell—
Another wrote all soldiers' praise, and of France and night's stars,
Served his guns, got immortality, and died well.
But Ypres played another trick with its danger on me,
Kept still the needing and loving-of-action body,
Gave no candles, and nearly killed me twice as well,
And no souvenirs, though I risked my life in the stuck tanks.
Yet there was praise of Ypres, love came sweet in hospital,
And old Flanders went under to long ages of plays' thought in my
    pages.

PHILIP JOHNSTONE

*Even before the war was over, Johnstone imagined the way it would soon
be turned into a harmless "subject" and published this poem in the*
Nation *on February 16, 1918.*

High Wood

Ladies and gentlemen, this is High Wood,
Called by the French, Bois des Fourneaux,
The famous spot which in Nineteen-Sixteen,
July, August and September was the scene
Of long and bitterly contested strife,
By reason of its High commanding site.
Observe the effect of shell-fire in the trees
Standing and fallen; here is wire; this trench
For months inhabited, twelve times changed hands;
(They soon fall in), used later as a grave.
It has been said on good authority
That in the fighting for this patch of wood
Were killed somewhere above eight thousand men,
Of whom the greater part were buried here,
This mound on which you stand being . . .
                        Madame, please,

You are requested kindly not to touch
Or take away the Company's property
As souvenirs; you'll find we have on sale
A large variety, all guaranteed.
As I was saying, all is as it was,
This is an unknown British officer,
The tunic having lately rotted off.
Please follow me—this way . . .
                       the *path,* sir, *please,*

The ground which was secured at great expense
The Company keeps absolutely untouched,
And in that dug-out (genuine) we provide
Refreshments at a reasonable rate.
You are requested not to leave about
Paper, or ginger-beer bottles, or orange-peel,
There are waste-paper baskets at the gate.

SIEGFRIED SASSOON
1886–1967

Like Edmund Blunden, Sassoon found it impossible to forget the war and devoted the rest of his life to remembering it and reminding others of its terrors and its costs.

Aftermath
March 1919

Have you forgotten yet? . . .
For the world's events have rumbled on since those gagged days,
Like traffic checked while at the crossing of city-ways:
And the haunted gap in your mind has filled with thoughts that flow

Like clouds in the lit heaven of life; and you're a man reprieved to go,
Taking your peaceful share of Time, with joy to spare.
But the past is just the same—and War's a bloody game . . .
Have you forgotten yet? . . .
Look down, and swear by the slain of the War that you'll never forget.

Do you remember the dark months you held the sector at Mametz—
The nights you watched and wired and dug and piled sandbags on
    parapets?
Do you remember the rats; and the stench
Of corpses rotting in front of the front-line trench—
And dawn coming, dirty-white, and chill with a hopeless rain?
Do you ever stop and ask, "Is it all going to happen again?"

Do you remember that hour of din before the attack—
And the anger, the blind compassion that seized and shook you then
As you peered at the doomed and haggard faces of your men?
Do you remember the stretcher-cases lurching back

With dying eyes and lolling heads—those ashen-grey
Masks of the lads who once were keen and kind and gay?

Have you forgotten yet? . .
Look up, and swear by the green of the spring that you'll never forget.

EZRA POUND
1885–1972

The poem sequence Hugh Selwyn Mauberley (Life and Contacts), *published by Pound in 1920, is a complex, often wryly comic, refraction of the fine sensibility of a fictional minor man of letters, but at one point, Pound darkens the poem as he contemplates the Great War and its meaning for his generation.*

From HUGH SELWYN MAUBERLEY (LIFE AND CONTACTS)

IV

These fought in any case,
and some believing,
    pro domo, in any case . . .

Some quick to arm,
some for adventure,
some from fear of weakness,
some from fear of censure,
some for love of slaughter, in imagination,
learning later . . .
some in fear, learning love of slaughter;
Died some, pro patria,
   non "dulce" non "et decor" . . .
walked eye-deep in hell
believing in old men's lies, then unbelieving
came home, home to a lie,
home to many deceits,

home to old lies and new infamy;
usury age-old and age-thick
and liars in public places.

Daring as never before, wastage as never before.
Young blood and high blood,
fair cheeks, and fine bodies;

fortitude as never before

frankness as never before,
disillusions as never told in the old days,
hysterias, trench confessions,
laughter out of dead bellies.

V

There died a myriad,
And of the best, among them.
For an old bitch gone in the teeth,
For a botched civilization.

Charm, smiling at the good mouth,
Quick eyes gone under earth's lid,

For two gross of broken statues
For a few thousand battered books.

E. E. CUMMINGS
1894–1963

*Like many college-age Americans, Cummings served in France in the
Norton-Harjes Ambulance Corps.*

i sing of Olaf glad and big
whose warmest heart recoiled at war:
a conscientious object-or

his wellbelovéd colonel (trig
westpointer most succinctly bred)
took erring Olaf soon in hand;
but—though an host of overjoyed
noncoms (first knocking on the head
him) do through icy waters roll
that helplessness which others stroke
with brushes recently employed
anent this muddy toiletbowl,
while kindred intellects evoke
allegiance per blunt instruments—
Olaf (being to all intents
a corpse and wanting any rag
upon what God unto him gave)
responds, without getting annoyed
"I will not kiss your fucking flag"

straightway the silver bird looked grave
(departing hurriedly to shave)

but—though all kinds of officers
(a yearning nation's blueeyed pride)
their passive prey did kick and curse
until for wear their clarion
voices and boots were much the worse,
and egged the firstclassprivates on
his rectum wickedly to tease
by means of skilfully applied
bayonets roasted hot with heat—
Olaf (upon what were once knees)
does almost ceaselessly repeat
"there is some shit I will not eat"

our president,being of which
assertions duly notified
threw the yellowsonofabitch
into a dungeon, where he died

Christ(of His mercy infinite)
i pray to see; and Olaf, too

preponderatingly because
unless statistics lie he was
more brave than me: more blond than you.

         *   *   *

my sweet old etcetera
aunt lucy during the recent

war could and what
is more did tell you just
what everybody was fighting

for,
my sister

isabel created hundreds
(and
hundreds)of socks not to
mention shirts fleaproof earwarmers

etcetera wristers etcetera, my
mother hoped that

i would die etcetera
bravely of course my father used
to become hoarse talking about how it was
a privilege and if only he
could meanwhile my

self etcetera lay quietly
in the deep mud et

cetera
(dreaming,
et
     cetera, of
Your smile
eyes knees and of your Etcetera)

                    *   *   *

"next to of course god america i
love you land of the pilgrims' and so forth oh
say can you see by the dawn's early my
country 'tis of centuries come and go
and are no more what of it we should worry
in every language even deafanddumb
thy sons acclaim your glorious name by gorry
by jingo by gee by gosh by gum
why talk of beauty what could be more beautiful than these heroic happy dead

who rushed like lions to the roaring slaughter
they did not stop to think they died instead
then shall the voice of liberty be mute?"

He spoke. And drank rapidly a glass of water

VERNON SCANNELL
1922-

Scannell fought with the Gordon Highlanders in the Second World War.

THE GREAT WAR

Whenever war is spoken of
I find
The war that was called Great invades the mind:
The grey militia marches over land
A darker mood of grey
Where fractured tree-trunks stand
And shells, exploding, open sudden fans
Of smoke and earth.
Blind murders scythe
The deathscape where the iron brambles writhe;
The sky at night
Is honoured with rosettes of fire,
Flares that define the corpses on the wire
As terror ticks on wrists at zero hour.
These things I see,
But they are only part
Of what it is that slyly probes the heart:
Less vivid images and words excite
The sensuous memory
And, even as I write,

Fear and a kind of love collaborate
To call each simple conscript up
For quick inspection:
Trenches' parapets
Paunchy with sandbags; bandoliers, tin-hats,
Candles in dug-outs,
Duckboards, mud and rats.
Then, like patrols, tunes creep into the mind:
*A Long Long Trail, The Rose of No-Man's Land,
Home Fires* and *Tipperary;*
And through the misty keening of a band
Of Scottish pipes the proper names are heard
Like fateful commentary of distant guns:
Passchendaele, Bapaume, and Loos, and Mons.
And now,
Whenever the November sky
Quivers with a bugle's hoarse, sweet cry,
The reason darkens; in its evening gleam
Crosses and flares, tormented wire, grey earth
Splattered with crimson flowers,
And I remember,
Not the war I fought in
But the one called Great
Which ended in a sepia November
Four years before my birth.

PART II
THE SPANISH CIVIL WAR

Authors Take Sides

Like the young enthusiasts who rushed to the colors in the First World War, the Americans and Europeans who joined the anti-Fascist side in the Spanish Civil War from 1936 to 1939 were motivated by idealism and a sense of justice. And like their predecessors, most ended in severe disillusion and despair, this time caused not so much by the intensification of horror occasioned by industrialism and by stupid generalship as by the surprising political perception that communism, of the sort administered by the ideological commissars from the Soviet Union, could as easily end in unfairness, brutality, and inhumanity as capitalism, or for that matter, monarchy. It was as if the volunteers had to relearn the disillusioning lessons of 1914–1918, notably the point that modern war very seldom attains its announced purposes. The purpose of fighting the Fascists in Spain was to restore liberal, democratic government, and it was just this that the brighter American and European volunteers perceived the Communists would not permit. The British Communist Christopher Caudwell wrote a friend in 1936, "You know how I feel about the whole mad business of war," but added, "you know also how I feel about the importance of democratic freedom." It was precisely democratic freedom that was efficiently subverted by the ideologues who came to dominate the "liberal" side, using all the old familiar devices of the absolute repression of dissent, political murder, and flagrant lies. Although the Spanish Civil War hardly advanced the technique of warfare, it qualifies as thoroughly "modern" because of the rigidity and intensity of the dogmas professed on each side. The war established the principle that troops require political advisers to maintain their ideological purity, thus foreshadowing the presence of commissars (costumed as military officers) overseeing the thinking of Soviet soldiers in the Second World War while National Socialist political officers did a similar office for German troops.

For many years before 1936 Spain had experienced strong divisions between conservative and radical opinion. In elections in the early 1930s monarchist candidates were soundly defeated. King Alfonso fled the country, and a republic was proclaimed. It set to work changing conditions which for centuries had identified Spain as a backward country: it embarked on bold land reform; it sought to improve conditions for industrial workers; and boldest of all, it severely limited the role of the Catholic church in education and diminished the size and influence of the army's officer corps. The rightists, sensing the new threat from both anti-clericalism and socialism, were not slow to react. Landowners, the clergy, industrialists, and the upper-middle class resisted these reforms, and when in 1934 there were uprisings among miners and ill-paid workers, the army, directed by General Francisco Franco, killed over a thousand demonstrators. The intellectual left still had enough votes to win the election of 1936, whereupon the government of the Republic, increasingly radicalized, began to entertain notions of soviets and workers' governments.

The tradition in Hispanic countries (like those in Central and South America) is that when democratic governments go too far with reforms, the army must step in to preserve Christianity, private property, and order. Thus, the army in Spanish Morocco began rebelling against the elected socialist government in Madrid, and the army in Spain soon took the cue, emerging from its barracks to shoot disobedient workers and peasants. Soon it was reinforced by the rebellious troops in Morocco, who were air-lifted (another "modernism") to Spain in transport planes provided by Germany and Italy. The situation was now a full-fledged civil war, fought between the "Loyalists," adherents of the democratically elected government, and the "Nationalists," who conceived they were defending "the real Spain." The names each side called each other were, respectively, Communists (or Reds) and Fascists: less inflammatory terms were Republicans and Insurgents. If the Loyalists included large numbers of atheists and anti-clericals, the Nationalists assumed that they were defending the Church. If the Loyalists could seem "internationalist" and therefore rather intellectual, the Nationalists could seem what the term implied—provincial, narrow, superstitious. Until almost the end of the war the Loyalists held onto Barcelona, the Manhattan of Spain, as distinguished from Madrid, the Washington. The Loyalists were assumed to represent the poor and agricultural south of the country, the Nationalists the richer, more highly industrialized north. When the Nationalists captured Loyalist territory they prohibited labor unions and political parties, and when the Loyalists (less often) captured Nationalist territory they seized the land of the rich and gave it to the peasants.

Since Germany and Italy had assisted the Nationalist army, it was reasonable for the Soviet Union to assist the Loyalists. America and Britain declared their neutrality, although the British Labor party sided enthusiastically with the anti-Franco forces. A vigorous European war was now conducted in Spain between men and women representing the ideologies that would find themselves in conflict on the Eastern Front in a later war, from June 1941, to May 1945, and in this preliminary struggle about one million people were killed. "This terrible round figure," says Hugh Thomas, the distinguished historian of the war, "suits both [Nationalist] victors and [Loyalist] vanquished. The former can argue that they saved Spain from atheism and communism at the cost of a million dead. The latter can allege that General Franco climbed to power over a million corpses."

The two sides were by no means evenly matched. The Nationalists had a trained army equipped with modern weapons and assisted by German and Italian troops, tanks, and aircraft. The Loyalists were not merely untrained: they were badly disunified, divided into uncoordinated local militias (some armed with hunting shotguns) as well as competing ideological factions—communists, anarchists, socialists, what-have-you—which did not scruple to kill each other in the quest for power. Some Republican soldiers had uniforms. More had armbands, or nothing. Common was an outfit of corduroy breeches and tall hunting boots or leather puttees, with any sort of warm jacket on top and here and there a steel helmet. Weapons were equally scarce and ad hoc, and ammunition was often severely rationed. The Loyalists did have the help of some Soviet tanks and guns and of some 40,000 foreigners who came to Spain to fight "against fascism." These volunteers came from France, Germany, and Austria, Yugoslavia, Hungary, Italy, and the Scandinavian countries—and, despite official prohibitions on their presence, Britain and the United States. Most were organized (if that's the word) in the International Brigades, which included the Abraham Lincoln Battalion, consisting largely of American blacks, student members of the Young Communist League, merchant seamen, and shipyard and steel workers and other union members. There were political commissars also to keep everyone up to ideological snuff.

"Which side are you on?" (that is, management or labor) was the refrain of a popular union song of the period, and it was a time when Americans and Britons, even those not accustomed to the adversarial assumptions of union politics, felt a need to declare loyalty—almost always to the Loyalists. In 1937 a number of writers and cultural figures, including W. H. Auden, Pablo Neruda, and Stephen Spender, circulated a questionnaire among their peers asking, "Are you for, or against, the legal government and the People of Republican Spain?" The results were published as the book *Authors Take Sides on the Spanish Civil War*, edited by Louis Aragon. Of the 145 respondents, only 5 supported the Franco side. One was Evelyn Waugh, who had been received into the Catholic church seven years earlier. Another champion of the Nationalist cause was the poet Roy Campbell, who declared of Britons favoring the Loyalists,

> The Sodomites are on your side,
> The cowards and the cranks.

Regardless, the roster of those opposing Franco included British Communists like Anthony Blunt, Hugh MacDiarmid, C. Day Lewis, and Kim Philby, who shrewdly disguised his sympathies and his secret services to Soviet intelligence by operating as a news correspondent on the Nationalist side, as well as such distinguished Continental thinkers as André Malraux and Arthur Koestler. Among British enthusiasts were Rosamund Lehmann, Rex Warner, Rose Macaulay, David Gascoyne, Helen Waddell, Cyril Connolly, Rebecca West, George Orwell, and Auden ("Famous Poet to Drive Ambulance in Spain."—*Daily Worker.*) The murder of Spanish poet Federico Garcia Lorca by the political right did not help the Nationalist cause abroad, and many literary and intellectual young people flocked to Spain, some to be destroyed, like Christopher Caudwell, John Cornford, and Julian Bell, the nephew of Virginia Woolf, killed after one month in Spain. As one who had observed the disaster of the First World War, Woolf could not understand why a new generation of young men chose to go off to be killed. "I suppose it's a fever in the blood of the younger generation," she wrote, "which we can't possibly understand. . . . We were all CO's in the Great War. . . . The moment force is used it becomes meaningless and unreal to me." The Americans who fought for the Loyalists included few authors, but those who agitated at home or went to Spain to report on the war included Hemingway and Dos Passos, Lillian Hellman, Martha Gellhorn, Archibald MacLeish, Sherwood Anderson, William Faulkner, John Steinbeck, Theodore Dreiser, and John Dewey. Ring Lardner's son Jim was killed fighting on the Loyalist side.

When Franco arrived in Spain with his Moroccan forces, he aimed for Madrid. Although his forces controlled half the country, the Loyalists in Madrid held out for forty-three months while they were bombed from the air and bombarded from the nearby hills. It was a siege foreshadowing events in the Second World War—the siege of Leningrad, for example—and was attended with similar hunger and agony. Meanwhile the Nationalists chewed away at Loyalist strength elsewhere, and the destruction was appalling. At the battle of Jarama in February 1937, the Abraham Lincoln Battalion was introduced to combat. Led by an incompetent Russian officer, over half the men were killed the first day. Slaughtered likewise was the battalion of British volunteers, 225 men remaining out of 600.

The usual atrocities were committed by both sides. Hemingway, during the war fervent in his support of the Republic and silent about its crimes, admitted afterward that the war could be regarded as a "carnival of treachery and rottenness on both sides." At the outset especially, the various factions comprising the Republican side were hard on religion, torturing and killing bishops and priests, monks and nuns, and burning churches. (It was Auden's shock at seeing churches destroyed that began to sour him on the leftist cause.) For their part, the Nationalists murdered unruly civilians, usually laborers and farmers, when they felt like it. One time they herded 1,800 suspected revolutionaries into the bullring at Badajoz and machine-gunned them all. The best-known Nationalist atrocity was the bombing of the town of Guernica, near Bilbao, on April 26, 1937. It was market day, and the town's population of 7,000 was swollen by people coming in from the countryside. Planes flown by German crews suddenly appeared and bombed the town for over three hours, machine-gunning people who tried to run away. The center of the town was destroyed and 1,654 civilians killed. The horror of Guernica produced not just Picasso's famous protest painting. It increased international sympathy with the Loyalists, persuading, for example, *Time, Life,* and *Newsweek* to side with the Republic. With the saturation bombing of Guernica, says Philip Knightley, modern "total war" may be said to begin, characterized by "the indiscriminate bombing of a civilian target as a deliberate experiment in terror." True enough, although the German Zeppelin raids on England in the First World War should not be overlooked.

"The Spanish bourgeoisie saw their chance of crushing the labor movement," says George Orwell, "and took it." It was in essence, he says, a class war. A cause conceived in those terms is hard to articulate in any but language inseparable from that Marxist concept, and although the Spanish War produced memorable journalism from foreign observers, rigid Loyalist ideology lay heavily on the poetry. What Cyril Connolly said about authors' answers to the question, Which side were they on?, suggests why so few poems from this war have persisted as rereadable works of art. As a subtle literary intelligence, Connolly was depressed by the dull uniformity of the leftist authors' responses, and even more, as he wrote, "by the poverty of diction, the clichés, the absence of distinction," and the readiness of the writers to speak in language indistinguishable from that of slogans. If the best poetry from 1914–1918 was anti–war, and with a vengeance, most of the poems from 1936–1939 were, at least implicitly, pro-war, and so busy being politically and emotionally correct that they forgot to be memorable. Sentimental terms like *valor, pride, the vanguard,* and *our glorious dead,* which one might have expected the First World War to have quashed forever, came swarming back into the poetry, and rarely attended by the irony so essential a part of the adult modern consciousness. The literary problem was one common in revolutions, as Stephen Spender saw. It was "an identity of the ideas of public policy and poetry," a situation experience has shown is fatal to specifically modern poetry, with its quasi-subversive habits. But people who found nothing comic or inappropriate in addressing perfect strangers as *comrade* and who invoked *ad nauseam* the buzz-word *solidarity* could not be expected to be very exquisite managers of diction in their writing. Even poets normally as able as C. Day Lewis could produce with apparent insensitivity poems constructed almost entirely of clichés, like *base coinage, hiding behind the skirts of,* and *indelibly stamped with.* There were a great many English-speaking poets of the Spanish War: Edgell Rickword, John Lepper, T.A.R. Hyndman, Alan McDade, Tom Wintringham, Charles Donnelly, Margot Heinemann, H. B. Mallalieu, and Charlotte Haldane, among others. But the poems they wrote, inspired by contemporary orthodoxy, are now as unknown as most of their authors: they were too uncomplex, too inert.

The dehumanization a pro-war poetry will invite is well illustrated by Auden's poem "Spain," which he wrote in 1937. Originally this poem was published as a pamphlet sold to aid Spanish Republican relief. While admitting that "Spain" was "one of the few decent things that have been written about the Spanish war," George Orwell pointed to the problem for the sensitive reader of accepting the revolutionary premise, or cliché, that you can't make an omelet without breaking eggs. Orwell was particularly struck by one stanza in Auden's poem devoted to the sacrifices necessary to bring on the new world of socialist rectitude:

> Today the deliberate increase in the chances of death,
> The conscious acceptance of guilt in the necessary murder;
> Today the expending of powers
> On the flat ephemeral pamphlet and the boring meeting.

Orwell comments that those words suggest

> a sort of thumb-nail sketch of a day in the life of a "good party-man." In the morning a couple of political murders, a ten-minutes' interlude to stifle "bourgeois" remorse, and then a hurried luncheon and a busy afternoon and evening chalking walls and distributing leaflets. All very edifying. But notice the phrase "necessary murder." It could only be written by a person to whom murder is at most a *word. . . .* The Hitlers and Stalins find murder necessary, but they don't advertise their callousness. . . . Mr. Auden's brand of amoralism is only possible if you are the kind of person who is always somewhere else when the trigger is pulled.

(In 1940 Auden revised his text, changing "the necessary murder" to "the fact of murder.")

Stephen Spender is one of the few poets who viewed the war with his compassion uncorrupted by politics. He was extremely sensitive to human suffering, regardless of causes, slogans, positions, manifestos, and all the journalistic justifications of modern war. He wrote a friend from Spain, "The war is often terrible." Indeed, he reported, "A man who had been all through the Great War said he had seen nothing more awful than the first four days of fighting at Morata [near Jarama], without trenches or any defense except olive trees." In his poem "Two Armies" especially, Spender does justice to "the common suffering" and perceives the war as a disaster registering a universal human meaning. In the Spanish War, as in all wars, there were two armies, and it is not clear why one should be thought of as suffering more than the other.

LUIS BUÑUEL
1900–1983

Born in Calanda, Spain, and educated at Jesuit schools, Buñuel became a well-known avant-garde filmmaker who fled Spain after the defeat of the Loyalist forces. In his memoir My Last Sigh *(1983) he recalled his experience of the war.*

From My Last Sigh

In July 1936, Franco arrived in Spain with his Moroccan troops and the firm intention of demolishing the Republic and re-establishing "order." My wife and son had gone back to Paris the month before, and I was alone in Madrid. Early one morning, I was jolted awake by a series of explosions and cannon fire; a Republican plane was bombing the Montaña army barracks.

At this time, all the barracks in Spain were filled with soldiers. A group of Falangists had ensconced themselves in the Montaña and had been firing from its windows for several days, wounding many civilians. On the morning of July 18, groups of workers, armed and supported by Azaña's Republican assault troops, attacked the barracks. It was all over by ten o'clock, the rebel officers and Falangists executed. The war had begun.

It was hard to believe. Listening to the distant machine-gun fire from my balcony, I watched a Schneider cannon roll by in the street below, pulled by a couple of workers and some gypsies. The revolution we'd felt gathering force for so many years, and which I personally had so ardently desired, was now going on before my eyes. All I felt was shock.

Two weeks later, Elie Faure, the famous art historian and an ardent supporter of the Republican cause, came to Madrid for a few days. I went to visit him one morning at his hotel and can still see him standing at his window in his long underwear, watching the demonstrations in the street below and weeping at the sight of the people in arms. One day, we watched a hundred peasants marching by, four abreast, some armed with hunting rifles and revolvers, some with sickles and pitchforks. In an obvious effort at discipline, they were trying very hard to march in step. Faure and I both wept.

It seemed as if nothing could defeat such a deep-seated popular force, but the joy and enthusiasm that colored those early days soon gave way to arguments, disorganization, and uncertainty—all of which lasted until November 1936, when an efficient and disciplined Republican organization began to emerge. I make no claims to writing a serious account of the deep gash that ripped through my country in 1936. I'm not a historian, and I'm certainly not impartial. I can only try to describe what I saw and what I remember. At the same time, I do see those first months in Madrid very clearly. Theoretically, the city was still in the hands of the Republicans, but Franco had already reached Toledo, after occupying other cities like Salamanca and Burgos. Inside Madrid, there was constant sniping by Fascist sympathizers. The priests and the rich landowners—in other words, those with conservative leanings, whom we assumed would support the Falange—were in constant danger of being executed by the Republicans. The moment the fighting began, the anarchists liberated all political prisoners and immediately incorporated them into the ranks of the Confederación Nacional de Trabajo, which was under the direct control of the anarchist federation. Certain members of this federation were such extremists that the mere presence of a religious icon in someone's room led automatically to Casa Campo, the public park on the outskirts of the city where the executions took place. People arrested at night were always told that they were going to "take a little walk."

It was advisable to use the intimate *"tu"* form of address for everyone, and to add an energetic *compañero* whenever you spoke to an anarchist, or a *camarada* to a Communist. Most cars carried a couple of mattresses tied to the roof as protection against snipers. It was dangerous even to hold out your hand to signal a turn, as the gesture might be interpreted as a Fascist salute and get you a fast round of gunfire. The *señoritos,* the sons of "good" families, wore old caps and dirty clothes in order to look as much like workers as they could, while on the other side the Communist party recommended that the workers wear white shirts and ties.

Ontañon, who was a friend of mine and a well-known illustrator, told me about the arrest of Sáenz de Heredia, a director who'd worked for me on *La hija de Juan Simón* and *Quién me quiere a mí?* Sáenz, Primo de Rivera's first cousin, had been sleeping on a park bench because he was afraid to go home, but despite his precautions he had been picked up by a group of Socialists and was now awaiting execution because of his fatal family connections. When I heard about this, I immediately went to the

Rotpence Studios, where I found that the employees, as in many other enterprises, had formed a council and were holding a meeting. When I asked how Sáenz was, they all replied that he was "just fine," that they had "nothing against him." I begged them to appoint a delegation to go with me to the Calle de Marqués de Riscál, where he was being held, and to tell the Socialists what they'd just told me. A few men with rifles agreed, but when we arrived, all we found was one guard sitting at the gate with his rifle lying casually in his lap. In as threatening a voice as I could muster, I demanded to see his superior, who turned out to be a lieutenant I'd had dinner with the evening before.

"Well, Buñuel," he said calmly, "what're you doing here?"

I explained that we really couldn't execute *everyone,* that of course we were all very aware of Sáenz's relationship to Primo de Rivera, but that the director had always acted perfectly correctly. The delegates from the studio also spoke in his favor, and eventually he was released, only to slip away to France and later join the Falange. After the war, he went back to directing movies, and even made a film glorifying Franco! The last I saw of him was at a long, nostalgic lunch we had together in the 1950s at the Cannes Festival.

During this time, I was very friendly with Santiago Carrillo, the secretary of the United Socialist Youth. Finding myself unarmed in a city where people were firing on each other from all sides, I went to see Carrillo and asked for a gun.

"There are no more," he replied, opening his empty drawer.

After a prodigious search, I finally got someone to give me a rifle. I remember one day when I was with some friends on the Plaza de la Independencia and the shooting began. People were firing from rooftops, from windows, from behind parked cars. It was bedlam, and there I was, behind a tree with my rifle, not knowing where to fire. Why bother having a gun, I wondered, and rushed off to give it back.

The first three months were the worst, mostly because of the total absence of control. I, who had been such an ardent subversive, who had so desired the overthrow of the established order, now found myself in the middle of a volcano, and I was afraid. If certain exploits seemed to me both absurd and glorious—like the workers who climbed into a truck one day and drove out to the monument to the Sacred Heart of Jesus about twenty kilometers south of the city, formed a firing squad, and executed the statue of Christ—I nonetheless couldn't stomach the summary executions, the looting, the criminal acts. No sooner had the people risen and seized power than they split into factions and began tearing one another to pieces. This insane and indiscriminate settling of accounts made everyone forget the essential reasons for the war.

I went to nightly meetings of the Association of Writers and Artists for the Revolution, where I saw most of my friends—Alberti, Bergamín, the journalist Corpus Varga, and the poet Altolaguirre, who believed in God and who later produced my *Mexican Bus Ride*. The group was constantly erupting in passionate and interminable arguments, many of which concerned whether we should just act spontaneously or try to organize ourselves. As usual, I was torn between my intellectual (and emotional) attraction to anarchy and my fundamental need for order and peace. And there we sat, in a life-and-death situation, but spending all our time constructing theories.

Franco continued to advance. Certain towns and cities remained loyal to the Republic, but others surrendered to him without a struggle. Fascist repression was pitiless; anyone suspected of liberal tendencies was summarily executed. But instead of trying to form an organization, we debated—while the anarchists persecuted priests. I can still hear the old cry: "Come down and see. There's a dead priest in the street." As anticlerical as I was, I couldn't condone this kind of massacre, even though the priests were not exactly innocent bystanders. They took up arms like everybody else, and did a fair bit of sniping from their bell towers. We even saw Dominicans with machine guns. A few of the clergy joined the Republican side, but most went over to the Fascists. The war spared no one, and it was impossible to remain neutral, to declare allegiance to the utopian illusion of a *tercera España*.

Some days, I was very frightened. I lived in an extremely bourgeois apartment house and often wondered what would happen if a wild bunch of anarchists suddenly broke into my place in the middle of the night to "take me for a walk." Would I resist? How could I? What could I say to them?

The city was rife with stories; everyone had one. I remember hearing about some nuns in a convent in Madrid who were on their way to chapel and stopped in front of the statue of the Virgin holding the baby Jesus in her arms. With a hammer and chisel, the mother superior removed the child and carried it away.

"We'll bring him back," she told the Virgin, "when we've won the war."

The Republican camp was riddled with dissension. The main goal of both Communists and Socialists was to win the war, while the anarchists, on the other hand, considered the war already won and had begun to organize their ideal society.

"We've started a commune at Torrelodones," Gil Bel, the editor of the labor journal *El Sindicalista*, told me one day at the Café Castilla. "We already have twenty houses, all occupied. You ought to take one."

I was beside myself with rage and surprise. Those houses belonged to people who'd fled or been executed. And as if that weren't enough, Torrelodones stood at the foot of the Sierra de Guadarrama, only a few kilometers from the Fascist front lines. Within shooting distance of Franco's army, the anarchists were calmly laying out their utopia.

On another occasion, I was having lunch in a restaurant with the musician Remacha, one of the directors of the Filmófono Studios where I'd once worked. The son of the restaurant owner had been seriously wounded fighting the Falangists in the Sierra de Guadarrama. Suddenly, several armed anarchists burst into the restaurant yelling, *"Salud compañeros!"* and shouting for wine. Furious, I told them they should be in the mountains fighting instead of emptying the wine cellar of a good man whose son was fighting for his life in a hospital. They sobered up quickly and left, taking the bottles with them, of course.

Every evening, whole brigades of anarchists came down out of the hills to loot the hotel wine cellars. Their behavior pushed many of us into the arms of the Communists. Few in number at the beginning of the war, they were nonetheless growing stronger with each passing day. Organized and disciplined, focused on the war itself, they seemed to me then, as they do now, irreproachable. It was sad but true that the anarchists hated them more than they hated the Fascists. This animosity had begun several years before the war when, in 1935, the Federación Anarquista Ibérica (FAI) announced a general strike among construction workers. The anarchist Ramón Acín, who financed *Las Hurdes,* told me about the time a Communist delegation went to see the head of the strike committee.

"There are three police stoolies in your ranks," they told him, naming names.

"So what?" the anarchist retorted. "We know all about it, but we like stoolies better than Communists."

Despite my ideological sympathies with the anarchists, I couldn't stand their unpredictable and fanatical behavior. Sometimes, it was sufficient merely to be an engineer or to have a university degree to be taken away to Casa Campo. When the Republican government moved its headquarters from Madrid to Barcelona because of the Fascist advance, the anarchists threw up a barricade near Cuenca on the only road that hadn't been cut. In Barcelona itself, they liquidated the director and the engineers in a metallurgy factory in order to prove that the factory could function perfectly well when run by the workers. Then they built a tank and proudly showed it to a Soviet delegate. (When he asked for a parabellum and fired at it, it fell apart.)

Despite all the other theories, a great many people thought that the anarchists were responsible for the death of Durutti, who was shot while getting out of his car on the Calle de la Princesa, on his way to try to ease the situation at the university, which was under siege. They were the kind of fanatics who named their daughters Acracia (Absence of Power) or Fourteenth September, and couldn't forgive Durutti the discipline he'd imposed on his troops.

We also feared the arbitrary actions of the POUM (Partido Obrero de Unificación Marxista), which was theoretically a Trotskyite group. Members of this movement, along with anarchists from the FAI, built barricades in May 1937 in the streets of Barcelona against the Republican army, which then had to fight its own allies in order to get through. My friend Claudio de la Torre lived in an isolated house outside of Madrid. His grandfather had been a freemason, the quintessential abomination in the eyes of the Fascists. In fact, they despised freemasons as heartily as they did the Communists. Claudio had an excellent cook whose fiancé was fighting with the anarchists. One day I went to his house for lunch, and suddenly, out there in the open country, a POUM car drove up. I was very nervous, because the only papers I had on me were Socialist and Communist, which meant less than nothing to the POUM. When the car pulled up to the door, the driver leaned out and . . . asked for directions. Claudio gave them readily enough, and we both heaved a great sigh of relief as he drove away.

All in all, the dominant feeling was one of insecurity and confusion, aggravated, despite the threat of fascism on our very doorstep, by endless internal conflicts and diverging tendencies. As I watched the realization of an old dream, all I felt was sadness.

And then one day I learned of Lorca's death, from a Republican who'd somehow managed to slip through the lines. Shortly before *Un Chien andalou*, Lorca and I had had a falling-out; later, thin-skinned Andalusian that he was, he thought (or pretended to think) that the film was actually a personal attack on him.

"Buñuel's made a little film, just like that!" he used to say, snapping his fingers. "It's called *An Andalusian Dog*, and I'm the dog!"

By 1934, however, we were the best of friends once again; and despite the fact that I sometimes thought he was a bit too fond of public adulation, we spent a great deal of time together. With Ugarte, we often drove out into the mountains to relax for a few hours in the Gothic solitude of El Paular. The monastery itself was in ruins, but there were a few spartan rooms reserved for people from the Fine Arts Institute. If you brought your own sleeping bag, you could even spend the night.

It was difficult, of course, to have serious discussions about painting and poetry while the war raged around us. Four days before Franco's arrival, Lorca, who never got excited about politics, suddenly decided to leave for Granada, his native city.

"Federico," I pleaded, trying to talk him out of it. "Horrendous things are happening. You can't go down there now; it's safer to stay right here."

He paid no attention to any of us, and left, tense and frightened, the following day. The news of his death was a terrific shock. Of all the human beings I've ever known, Federico was the finest. I don't mean his plays or his poetry; I mean him personally. He was his own masterpiece. Whether sitting at the piano imitating Chopin, improvising a pantomime, or acting out a scene from a play, he was irresistible. He read beautifully, and he had passion, youth, and joy. When I first met him, at the Residencia, I was an unpolished rustic, interested primarily in sports. He transformed me, introduced me to a wholly different world. He was like a flame.

His body was never found. Rumors about his death circulated freely, and Dali even made the ignoble suggestion that there'd been some homosexual foul play involved. The truth is that Lorca died because he was a poet. "Death to the intelligentsia" was a favorite wartime slogan. When he got to Granada, he apparently stayed with the poet Rosales, a Falangist whose family was friendly with Lorca's. I guess he thought he was safe with Rosales, but a group of men (no one knows who they were, and it doesn't really matter, anyway) led by someone called Alonso appeared one night, arrested him, and drove him away in a truck with some workers. Federico was terrified of suffering and death. I can imagine what he must have felt, in the middle of the night in a truck that was taking him to an olive grove to be shot. I think about it often.

At the end of September, the Republican minister of foreign affairs, Alvarez del Vayo, asked to see me. Curious, I went to his office and was told only that I'd find out everything I wanted to know when I got to Geneva. I left Madrid in an overcrowded train and found myself sitting next to a POUM commander, who kept shouting that the Republican government was garbage and had to be wiped out at any cost. (Ironically, I was to use this commander later, as a spy, when I worked in Paris.) When I changed trains in Barcelona, I ran into José Bergamín and Muñoz Suaï, who were going to Geneva with several students to attend a political convention. They asked me what kind of papers I was carrying.

"But you'll never get across the border," Suaï cried, when I told him. "You need a visa from the anarchists to do that!"

The first thing I saw when we arrived at Port Bou was a group of soldiers ringing the station, and a table where three somber-faced anarchists, led by a bearded Italian, were holding court like a panel of judges.

"You can't cross here," they told me when I showed them my papers.

Now the Spanish language is capable of more scathing blasphemies than any other language I know. Curses elsewhere are typically brief and punctuated by other comments, but the Spanish curse tends to take the form of a long speech in which extraordinary vulgarities—referring chiefly to the Virgin Mary, the Apostles, God, Christ, and the Holy Spirit, not to mention the Pope—are strung end to end in a series of impressive scatological exclamations. In fact, blasphemy in Spain is truly an art; in Mexico, for instance, I never heard a proper curse, whereas in my native land, a good one lasts for at least three good-sized sentences. (When circumstances require, it can become a veritable hymn.)

It was with a curse of this kind, uttered in all its seemly intensity, that I regaled the three anarchists from Port Bou. When I'd finished, they stamped my papers and I crossed the border. (What I've said about the importance of the Spanish curse is no exaggeration; in certain old Spanish cities, you can still see signs like "No Begging or Blaspheming— Subject to Fine or Imprisonment" on the main gates. Sadly, when I returned to Spain in 1960, the curse seemed much rarer; or perhaps it was only my hearing.)

In Geneva, I had a fast twenty-minute meeting with the minister, who asked me to go to Paris and start work for the new ambassador, who turned out to be my friend Araquistán, a former journalist, writer, and left-wing Socialist. Apparently, he needed men he could trust. I stayed in Paris until the end of the war; I had an office on the rue de la Pépinière and was officially responsible for cataloguing the Republican propaganda films made in Spain. In fact, however, my job was somewhat more complicated. On the one hand, I was a kind of protocol officer, responsible for organizing dinners at the embassy, which meant making sure that André Gide was not seated next to Louis Aragon. On the other hand, I was supposed to oversee "news and propaganda." This job required that I travel—to Switzerland, Antwerp (where the Belgian Communists gave us their total support), Stockholm, London—drumming up support for various Republican causes. I also went to Spain from time to time, carrying suitcases stuffed with tracts that had been printed in Paris. Thanks to the complicity of certain sailors, our tracts once traveled to Spain on a German ship.

While the French government steadfastly refused to compromise or to intervene on behalf of the Republic, a move that would certainly have changed the direction of things, the French people, particularly the workers who belonged to the Confédération Générale de Travail, helped us enormously. It wasn't unusual, for instance, for a railroad employee or a taxi driver to come see me and tell me that two Fascists had arrived the previous night on the eight-fifteen train and had gone to such-and-such a hotel. I passed all information of this kind directly to Araquistán, who was proving to be by far our most efficient ambassador.

The nonintervention of France and the other democratic powers was fatal to the Republican cause. Although Roosevelt did declare his support, he ceded to the pressure from his Catholic constituency and did not intervene. Neither did Léon Blum in France. We'd never hoped for direct participation, but we had thought that France, like Germany and Italy, would at least authorize the transport of arms and "volunteers." In fact, the fate of Spanish refugees in France was nothing short of disastrous. Usually, they were simply picked up at the border and thrown directly into camps. Later, many of them fell into the hands of the Nazis and perished in Germany, mainly in Mauthausen.

The International Brigades, organized and trained by the Communists, were the only ones who gave us real aid, but there were others who simply appeared on their own, ready to fight. Homage should also be paid to Malraux, albeit some of the pilots he sent were little more than mercenaries. In my Paris office, I issued safe-conduct passes to Hemingway, Dos Passos, and Joris Ivens, so they could make a documentary on the Republican army.

There was a good deal of frustrating intrigue going on while we were making a propaganda film in Spain with the help of two Russian cameramen. This particular film was to have worldwide distribution, but after I returned to Paris, I heard nothing for several months on the progress of the shoot. Finally, I made an appointment with the head of the Soviet trade delegation, who kept me waiting for an hour until I began shouting at his secretary. The man finally received me icily.

"And what are *you* doing in Paris?" he asked testily.

I retorted that he had absolutely no right to evaluate my activities, that I only followed orders, and that I only wanted to know what had happened to the film. He refused to answer my question and showed me rather unceremoniously to the door. As soon as I got back to my office, I wrote four letters—one to *L'Humanité,* one to *Pravda,* one to the Russian ambassador, and the last to the Spanish minister—denouncing what seemed to be sabotage inside the Soviet trade delegation itself (a charge that was eventually confirmed by friends in the French Communist party, who told me that it was "the same all over"). It seemed that the Soviet Union had enemies, even within its own official circles, and indeed, some time later, the head of the delegation became one of the victims of the Stalinist purges.

Another strange story, which sheds a curious light on the French police (not to mention police all over the world), concerns three mysterious bombs. One day, a young and very elegant Colombian walked into my office. He'd asked to see the military attaché, but since we no longer had one, I suppose someone thought I was the next best thing. He put a small suitcase on my desk, and when he opened it, there lay three little bombs.

"They may be small," he said to me, "but they're powerful. They're the ones we used in the attacks on the Spanish consulate in Perpignan and on the Bordeaux-Marseille train."

Dumbfounded, I asked him what he wanted and why he'd come to me. He replied that he had no intention of hiding his Fascist sympathies (he was a member of the Condor Legion) but that he was doing this because he despised his superior!

"I want him arrested," he said simply. "Why is none of your business. But if you want to meet him, come to La Coupole tomorrow at five o'clock. He'll be the man on my right. I'll just leave these with you, then."

As soon as he'd gone, I told Araquistán, who phoned the prefect of police. When their bomb experts got through with their analysis, it turned out that our terrorist had been right; they were more potent than any others of that size.

The next day, I invited the ambassador's son and an actress friend of mine to have a drink with me at La Coupole. The Colombian was exactly where he said he'd be, sitting on the terrace with a group of people. And as incredible as it may sound, I knew the man on his right, and so did my friend. He was a Latin American actor, and we all shook hands quite amicably as we walked by. (His treacherous colleague never moved a muscle.)

Since I now knew the name of the leader of this terrorist group, as well as the hotel in Paris where he lived, I contacted the prefect, who was a Socialist, as soon as I got back to the embassy. He assured me that they'd pick him right up; but time went by, and nothing happened. Later, when I ran into the boss sitting happily with his friends at the Select on the Champs-Elysées, I wept with rage. What kind of world is this? I asked myself. Here's a known criminal, and the police don't want any part of him!

Shortly afterward, I heard from my Colombian informant again, who told me that his leader would be at our embassy the next day applying for a visa to Spain. Once again, he was correct. The actor had a diplomatic passport and got his visa with no trouble whatsoever. On his way to Madrid, however, he was arrested at the border by the Republican police, who'd been warned ahead of time; but he was released almost immediately on the protest of his government. He went on to Madrid, carried out his mission, and then calmly returned to Paris. Was he invulnerable? What kind of protection did he have? I was desperate to know.

Around that time, I left on a mission to Stockholm, where I read in a newspaper that a bomb had leveled a small apartment building near the Etoile that had been the headquarters of a labor union. I remember the article saying quite precisely that the bomb was so powerful the building had simply crumbled to dust, and that two agents had died in the blast. It was obvious which terrorist had done the job.

Again, nothing happened. The man continued to pursue his activities, protected by the careful indifference of the French police, who seemed to support whomever had the upper hand. At the end of the war, the actor, a member of the Fifth Column, was decorated for his services by Franco.

While my terrorist was cheerfully going about his dirty work in Paris, I

was being violently attacked by the French right wing, who—believe it
or not—had not forgotten *L'Age d'or.* They wrote about my taste for
profanity and my "anal complex," and the newspaper *Gringoire* (or was
it *Candide?*) reminded its readers that I'd come to Paris several years
before in an effort to "corrupt French youth."

One day, Breton came to see me at the embassy.

"Mon cher ami," he began, "there seem to be some disagreeable
rumors about the Republicans' executing Péret because he belonged to
POUM."

POUM had inspired some adherence among the surrealists. In fact,
Benjamin Péret had left for Barcelona, where he could be seen every day
on the Plaza Cataluña surrounded by people from POUM. On Breton's
request, I asked some questions and learned that Péret had gone to the
Aragón front in Huesca; apparently, he'd also criticized the behavior of
certain POUM members so openly and vociferously that many had announced their firm intention of shooting him. I guaranteed Breton that
Péret hadn't been executed by the Republicans, however, and he returned to France soon afterward, safe and sound.

From time to time, I met Dali for lunch at the Rôtisserie Périgourdine
on the place St.-Michel. One day, he made me a bizarre offer.

"I can introduce you to an enormously rich Englishman," he said.
"He's on your side, and he wants to give you a bomber!"

The Englishman, Edward James, had just bought all of Dali's 1938
output, and did indeed want to give the Republicans an ultramodern
bomber which was then hidden in a Czechoslovakian airport. Knowing
that the Republic was dramatically short of air strength, he was making
us this handsome present—in exchange for a few masterpieces from the
Prado. He wanted to set up an exhibition in Paris, as well as in other
cities in France; the paintings would be placed under the warranty of the
International Tribunal at The Hague, and after the war there would be
two options: If the Republicans won, the paintings would be returned to
the Prado, but if Franco was victorious, they'd remain the property of
the Republican government in exile.

I conveyed this unusual proposition to Alvarez del Vayo, who admitted that a bomber would be very welcome, but that wild horses couldn't
make him take paintings out of the Prado. "What would they say about
us?" he demanded. "What would the press make of this? That we traded
our patrimony for arms? No, no, it's impossible. Let's have no further
talk about it."

(Edward James is still alive and is the owner of several châteaus, not to
mention a large ranch in Mexico.)

My secretary was the daughter of the treasurer of the French Communist party. He'd belonged to the infamous Bande à Bonnot, and his
daughter remembers taking walks as a child on the arm of the notorious

Raymond-la-Science. I myself knew two old-timers from the band—Rirette Maîtrejean and the gentleman who did cabaret numbers and called himself the "innocent convict." One day, a communiqué arrived asking for information about a shipment of potassium from Italy to a Spanish port then in the hands of the Fascists. My secretary called her father.

"Let's go for a little drive," he said to me two days later, when he arrived in my office. "I want you to meet someone."

We stopped in a café outside of Paris, and there he introduced me to a somber but elegantly dressed American, who seemed to be in his late thirties and who spoke French with a strong accent.

"I hear you want to know about some potassium," he inquired mildly.

"Yes," I replied.

"Well, I think I just might have some information for you about the boat."

He did indeed give me very precise information about both cargo and itinerary, which I immediately telephoned to Negrín. Several years later, I met the man again at a cocktail party at the Museum of Modern Art in New York. We looked at each other across the room, but never exchanged a word. Later still, after the Second World War, I saw him at La Coupole with his wife. This time, we had a chat, during which he told me that he used to run a factory in the outskirts of Paris and had supported the Republican cause in various ways, which is how my secretary's father knew him.

During this time I was living in the suburb of Meudon. When I got home at night, I'd always stop, one hand on my gun, and check to make sure I hadn't been followed. We lived in a climate of fear and secrets and unknown forces, and as we continued to receive hourly bulletins on the progress of the war, we watched our hopes slowly dwindle and die.

It's not surprising that Republicans like myself didn't oppose the Nazi-Soviet pact. We'd been so disappointed by the Western democracies, who still treated the Soviet Union with contempt and refused all meaningful contact with its leaders, that we saw Stalin's gesture as a way of gaining time, of strengthening our forces, which, no matter what happened in Spain, were sure to be thrown into World War II. Most of the French Communist party also approved of the pact; Aragon made that clear more than once. One of the rare voices raised in protest within the party was that of the brilliant Marxist intellectual Paul Nizan. Yet we all knew that the pact wouldn't last, that, like everything else, it too would fall apart.

I remained sympathetic to the Communist party until the end of the 1950s, when I finally had to confront my revulsion. Fanaticism of any kind has always repelled me, and Marxism was no exception; it was like any other religion that claims to have found *the* truth. In the 1930s, for instance, Marxist doctrine permitted no mention of the unconscious mind or of the numerous and profound psychological forces in the individual. Everything could be explained, they said, by socioeconomic mechanisms, a notion that seemed perfectly derisory to me. A doctrine like that leaves out at least half of the human being.

I know I'm digressing; but, as with all Spanish picaresques, digression seems to be my natural way of telling a story. Now that I'm old and my memory is weaker, I have to be very careful, but I can't seem to resist beginning a story, then abandoning it suddenly for a seductive parenthesis, and by the time I finish, I've forgotten where I began. I'm always asking my friends: "Why am I telling you this?" And now I'm afraid I'll have to give in to one last digression.

There were all kinds of missions I had to carry out, one being that of Negrín's bodyguard from time to time. Armed to the teeth and backed up by the Socialist painter Quintanilla, I used to watch over Negrín at the Gare d'Orsay without his being aware of it. I also often slipped across the border into Spain, carrying "special" documents. It was on one of those occasions that I took a plane for the first time in my life, along with Juanito Negrín, the prime minister's son. We'd just flown over the Pyrenees when we saw a Fascist fighter plane heading toward us from the direction of Majorca. We were terrified, until it veered off suddenly and turned around, dissuaded perhaps by the DC-8 from Barcelona.

During a trip to Valencia, I went to see the head of agitprop to show him some papers that had come to us in Paris and which we thought might be useful to him. The following morning, he picked me up and drove me to a villa a few kilometers outside the city, where he introduced me to a Russian, who examined my documents and claimed to recognize them. Like the Falangists and the Germans, the Republicans and the Russians had dozens of contacts like this—the secret services were doing their apprenticeships everywhere. When a Republican brigade found itself besieged from the other side of the Gavarnie, French sympathizers smuggled arms to them across the mountains. In fact, throughout the war, smugglers in the Pyrenees transported both men and propaganda. In the area of St.-Jean-de-Luz, a brigadier in the French gendarmerie gave the smugglers no trouble if they were crossing the border with Republican tracts. I wish there'd been a more official way to show my gratitude, but I did give him a superb sword I'd bought near the place de la République, on which I'd had engraved: "For Services Rendered to the Spanish Republic."

Our relationship with the Fascists was exceedingly complex, as the García incident illustrates so well. García was an out-and-out crook who claimed to be a Socialist. During the early months of the war, he set up his racket in Madrid under the sinister name of the Brigada del Amanecer—the Sunrise Brigade. Early in the morning, he'd break into the houses of the well-to-do, "take the men for a walk," rape the women, and steal whatever he and his band could get their hands on. I was in Paris when a French union man who was working in a hotel came to tell me that a Spaniard was getting ready to take a ship for South America and that he was carrying a suitcase full of stolen jewels. It seemed that García had made his fortune, left Spain, and was skipping the continent altogether under an assumed name.

García was a terrible embarrassment to the Republic, but the Fascists were also desperate to catch him. The boat was scheduled for a stopover at Santa Cruz de Tenerife, which at that time was occupied by Franco. I passed my information along to the ambassador, and without a moment's hesitation he relayed it to the Fascists via a neutral embassy. When García arrived in Santa Cruz, he was picked up and hanged.

One of the strangest stories to emerge from the war was the Calanda pact. When the agitation began, the civil guard was ordered to leave Calanda and concentrate at Saragossa. Before leaving, however, the officers gave the job of maintaining order in the town to a sort of council made up of leading citizens, whose first venture was to arrest several notorious activists, including a well-known anarchist, a few Socialist peasants, and the only Communist. When the anarchist forces from Barcelona reached the outskirts of town at the beginning of the war, these notable citizens decided to pay a visit to the prison.

"We've got a proposition for you," they told the prisoners. "We're at war, and heaven only knows who's going to win. We're all Calandians, so we'll let you out on the condition that, whatever happens, all of us promise not to engage in any acts of violence whatsoever."

The prisoners agreed, of course, and were immediately released; a few days later, when the anarchists entered Calanda, their first act was to execute eighty-two people. Among the victims were nine Dominicans, most of the leading citizens on the council, some doctors and landowners, and even a few poor people whose only crime was a reputation for piety.

The deal had been made in the hope of keeping Calanda free from the violence that was tearing the rest of the country apart, to make the town a kind of no man's land; but neutrality was a mirage. It was fatal to believe that anyone could escape time or history.

Another extraordinary event that occurred in Calanda, and probably in many other villages as well, began with the anarchist order to go to the main square, where the town crier blew his trumpet and announced: "From today on, it is decreed that there will be free love in Calanda." As you can imagine, the declaration was received with utter stupefaction, and the only consequence was that a few women were harassed in the streets. No one seemed to know what free love meant, and when the women refused to comply with the decree, the hecklers let them go on their way with no complaints. To jump from the perfect rigidity of Catholicism to something called free love was no easy feat; the entire town was in a state of total confusion. In order to restore order, in people's minds more than anywhere else, Mantecon, the governor of Aragón, made an extemporaneous speech one day from the balcony of our house in which he declared that free love was an absurdity and that we had other, more serious things to think about, like a civil war.

By the time Franco's troops neared Calanda, the Republican sympathizers in the town had long since fled. Those who stayed to greet the Falangists had nothing to worry about. Yet if I can believe a Lazarist father who came to see me in New York, about a hundred people in Calanda were executed, so fierce was the Fascists' desire to remove any possible Republican contamination.

My sister Conchita was arrested in Saragossa after Republican planes had bombed the city (in fact, a bomb fell on the roof of the basilica without exploding, which gave the church an unparalleled opportunity to talk about miracles), and my brother-in-law, an army officer, was accused of having been involved in the incident. Ironically, he was in a Republican jail at that very moment. Conchita was finally released, but not before a very close brush with execution.

(The Lazarist father who came to New York brought me the portrait Dali had painted of me during our years at the Residencia. After he told me what had happened in Calanda, he said to me earnestly, "Whatever you do, don't go back there!" I had no desire whatsoever to go back, and many years were to pass before I did in fact return.)

In 1936, the voices of the Spanish people were heard for the first time in their history; and, instinctively, the first thing they attacked was the Church, followed by the great landowners—their two ancient enemies. As they burned churches and convents and massacred priests, any doubts anyone may have had about hereditary enemies vanished completely.

I've always been impressed by the famous photograph of those ecclesiastical dignitaries standing in front of the Cathedral of Santiago de Compostela in full sacerdotal garb, their arms raised in the Fascist salute toward some officers standing nearby. God and Country are an unbeatable team; they break all records for oppression and bloodshed.

I've never been one of Franco's fanatical adversaries. As far as I'm concerned, he wasn't the Devil personified. I'm even ready to believe that he kept our exhausted country from being invaded by the Nazis. Yes, even in Franco's case there's room for some ambiguity. And in the cocoon of my timid nihilism, I tell myself that all the wealth and culture on the Falangist side ought to have limited the horror. Yet the worst excesses came from them; which is why, alone with my dry martini, I have my doubts about the benefits of money and culture.

F. G. TINKER
1910–1939

Frank Glasgow Tinker was born in Arkansas and after attending Annapolis became a naval aviator. He resigned his commission in 1935 to become second mate on a Gulf Oil tanker, and in 1936, under the name Francisco Gomez Trejo, he flew for the Spanish Loyalists, an experience he recalled in his book Some Still Live *(1938). He died not in combat but by suicide, shooting himself in a hotel room in Little Rock, surrounded by relics of the Spanish Civil War.*

From SOME STILL LIVE

THE ITALIAN DEBACLE

On March eighth we received two more replacement pilots—Lecha and Blanche. They were each given about an hour in which to practise take-offs and landings so that they could get used to the rather rough landing field. Also to give LaCalle a chance to see what kind of pilots they were. Blanche turned out to be an exceptionally good pilot. Lecha was only fair, having had very little previous flying time.

That night Chang told us a very interesting story about Blanche. He had been over in Spanish Morocco when the rebellion broke out, had pretended to be a Fascist sympathizer, and was assigned to the job of copiloting a large seaplane bomber, the chief pilot being a Spanish Rebel captain. One of the plane's two mechanics was also a Loyalist sympathizer, so the two of them got together and did a little secret plotting. At the first favorable opportunity, Blanche gave the signal by shooting the chief pilot dead and taking over the controls himself. While he was doing this, his consort was busy shooting up the other mechanic and the rear machine gunner. Whereupon Blanche set a course for Loyalist territory and landed the plane in the harbor at Valencia, where he was received with wild acclaim. The grateful Government immediately made him a first lieutenant in the Loyalist Air Force, and he flew seaplanes for a while until he decided to try his hand in fighting planes. The Government immediately granted his request and sent him to Los Alcázares for training. When he completed the course there he was sent to the Escuadrilla de LaCalle, and we were certainly glad to have him.

At that particular time LaCalle was having a bit of trouble finding someone to lead the third patrol, which Berthial had been leading. He wanted to give me the job, but I fell back on my ignorance of the Spanish language as an excuse for staying with Whitey and Chang. When he saw the way in which Blanche handled his plane, he immediately made him the third patrol leader. All hands concurred in the opinion that he had made a very wise choice.

On this day we received word that the enemy had started a drive on the front to the north of us—the Guadalajara front. The attack was started from the Fascist-held town of Sigüenza, which is forty-odd miles northeast of Guadalajara. It consisted of three columns, highly mechanized, advancing down the main highway connecting Madrid and Zaragoza. It was, as we found out later, the beginning of the famous Italian offensive on the Guadalajara front. At any rate, they managed to advance several miles before nightfall that day. The Government troops put up a strong resistance with machine guns and light field pieces, but they were gradually forced back by Mussolini's tanks.

March ninth was a rather eventful day. Early in the morning our alarm flares started us off, and hardly had the last plane cleared the ground when we saw three bimotored Junkers coming out of a low-lying layer of clouds which began just north of the field and extended northward as far as the eye could see. They also saw us climbing up, and the sight so rattled them that they dropped their bombs in the river and fled. We managed to get in a few long-distance shots at them, but they were too fast for us to overtake.

The Italian troops made considerable headway that day. Early in the morning they captured three small towns near the main highway—Almadrones, Argecilla, and Ledanca—and continued their advance. All this time it was raining heavily, which was to our advantage. Their central column was pushing down the main highway sweeping all opposition before it. Our soldiers lacked the equipment for combatting tanks and armored cars; but after about a third of this column had crossed a bridge near an important crossroad, the bridge was washed out by the flood due to the unusually heavy rains. This kept the majority of this most important column out of action for several hours during the most critical part of the advance while the bridge was being repaired. The vanguard of the central column continued its advance for three or four miles, but it was not strong enough to consolidate its newly-captured positions and was forced to retreat. The washing-out of this bridge was a great blow to the Italians, since it frustrated the entire advantage of their mechanized army—speed and surprise.

In the meantime the Italians to the east of the main highway had also been making considerable progress. They surrounded the town of Brihuega and captured it shortly after nightfall. They had advanced so rapidly that they were within the city limits before the Government commander was even aware that they were in the vicinity. As Brihuega is only about fifteen miles from Guadalajara, there were some awfully long faces around our dining table that night. And our spirits weren't at all uplifted by the two- or three-hour bombardment we were treated to that night. That was the only occasion I can remember when there was no singing or laughing in a bomb shelter during a bombardment. Even the usually cheerful Cristina and Maria were looking a little sad and thoughtful that night.

The following morning was dismal and rainy, with clouds almost down on the valley floor. However, the ceiling lifted for a while, so LaCalle sent Whitey out on a reconnaissance flight over the Italian territory. When he returned he reported that many troops were moving on enemy roads back of the lines. We immediately loaded up with bombs and got all set to take off. Just about that time, though, the ceiling dropped back to zero again and stayed there the rest of the day. All we could do was sit there grinding our teeth and listening to the heavy artillery booming away in the distance. LaCalle would come around every now and then and give us the latest news from the front.

The news on this day wasn't as disheartening as that of the day before. Our high command had taken advantage of the enemy's delay, caused by the bridge washout, to send up reinforcements as fast as they could get them there. Among these reinforcements were the eleventh and twelfth brigades of the international column, which were sent up during the night. They immediately entrenched themselves in the valleys and arroyos which extended westward from Brihuega. Our espionage system also discovered that Italian headquarters had been moved up to the little town of Trijueque, located on the main highway due west of Brihuega. It rained so heavily and continuously on this day that neither side was able to do very much fighting.

Whitey, Chang, and I went into Madrid that night and almost got bombed on our way back at the little town of Torrejón de Ardoz. The Junkers were trying to bomb the railroad station there, but instead they hit the area about halfway between the station and the highway, which were about two hundred yards apart. We just barely had time to jump into the ditch before the bombs started falling. We stayed there for about half an hour before continuing on our way to Azuqueca, where we were bawled out by LaCalle for being twenty minutes late; but we had the shrapnel-slashed top of our car to back up our story, so we were exonerated.

The eleventh of March was another wet day, with occasional heavy clouds coming along scraping the ground. About the middle of the morning we loaded up with bombs, nevertheless, and took off between rain squalls for our first look at the Guadalajara front. We cruised along over the very low clouds, with only an occasional glimpse of the ground below, and fortunately found an opening just over the place we were supposed to bomb, so down we went. We dropped our bombs at an altitude of about 600 feet and then went the rest of the way down with all four machine guns hammering away. The Italian troops were certainly in a bad way down there. The continual rains had made a regular quagmire out of that entire section of the country, and they were practically without protection from our aerial attack. What trenches they had been able to dig filled up with water almost as soon as they were dug. They didn't seem to have any anti-aircraft guns at all at that time, although a few of their field guns opened up an ineffective fire on us. We could see the poor devils scurrying through the mud in all directions as we came down spraying them with bullets. We made only one pass at them, as we had instructions to hurry back to the field before the ceiling fell to zero again.

That afternoon we learned that there was very little fighting going on at the front. The adverse weather conditions kept the Italians from using their machinery, so they were practically stalled. Their trucks, armored cars, and even their tanks were forced to stay on the main highways. Our side was taking advantage of the situation to rush in reinforcements and armament. The Government had managed to get in some modern, rapid-fire, large-caliber guns, enabling our men to play havoc with the enemy's stalled motor units. These guns would have done much more damage but for the fact that the men were unaccustomed to their operation.

About two hours before sundown we loaded up with bombs and took off again. This proved to be a tactical error; hardly had we left the ground when the clouds converged and we found ourselves right in the middle of a terrific thunder, lightning, and hail storm. LaCalle gave the landing signal and went over to the river and dropped his bombs—we had orders never to land with bombs, as several pilots had been killed that way—the rest of us doing likewise. By that time there were planes all over the sky—flying through the rain, hail, and lightning flashes. Our patrol stayed in formation until Chang pulled his head down in his cockpit so that he could reach his bomb release. He then slid over and

almost rammed my plane, missing it by about six feet. This rattled him
so much that he sheered off into the rain and never did find Whitey and
me again.

LaCalle landed safely, but the rest of them were having difficulties;
two or three were trying to land at the same time and nearly had colli-
sions. Whitey and I watched this performance for a while, the storm
getting worse all the time, and then decided to head for Albacete while
we still had a chance. Neither one of us had a map, but somehow or
other we managed to get there. We landed about an hour later, wondering how many of our squadron mates had got down safely.

As soon as we identified ourselves we were taken to the pilots' house,
which was about two miles from the field. There we met the Russian
Commander-in-chief, General Douglas, and several of our Russian
friends whom we had met at Alcalá. They located a Russo-English interpreter, and when they heard our story called up Alcalá immediately to
tell them that the two Americans were safe. They also told them to pass
the word along to LaCalle at Azuqueca. After that we were led down to
the very sumptuous dining room. The place had formerly been a duke's
hunting lodge and was furnished and decorated like a palace. After an
excellent meal we sat around talking to the American wife—Mrs. Rose-
Marie—of an American pilot who was flying transport planes for the
Government. She could also speak Russian, so our Russian friends were
able to join in the conversation. After a couple of hours of this we were
shown to our quarters and turned in for the night.

Early the next morning we went out to the field and discovered that
we were to fly back to Alcalá with no less a personage than General
Douglas himself. We naturally assumed that we would be assigned to the
job of flying protection over some slow-moving transport plane. Our eyes
almost popped out of our heads when we saw the general come out and
climb into a fighting plane just like the ones we were flying ourselves.
We had heard of generals in the United States flying—but they merely
flew long enough to qualify for the 50 per cent extra pay to be derived
thereby. But here was a general actually flying himself up to the front in
a single-seater fighting plane!

Anyway, we took off with the general, in V formation, and were over
Alcalá about an hour later. When he gave the break-up signal we sheered
off, as previously instructed, and headed for Guadalajara. When we
landed there, it was just as though two prodigal sons had returned. Our
two mechanics, Chamorro and Juanas, were overjoyed to see us. They
had given us up for lost when we failed to return the day before, and had
only halfway believed LaCalle when he told them that we were safe in
Albacete. They even had brand-new packages of American cigarettes
ready for us; and American cigarettes were rather scarce at that time.

When we went in to make our report to LaCalle we received a half-hearted calling-down for leaving the vicinity of the field so soon. However, we could see that he was pleased to see us back safely. In fact, Chang later informed us that he had heard LaCalle bragging to the Russians about how two of his pilots had been able to find the field at Albacete in such adverse weather conditions without a map. We also found out that the rest of the boys had climbed up above the clouds and flown around until the squall passed. Then they had all come down and landed safely, with the exception of Chang, who had got himself lost and finally tried to land in some farmer's newly-plowed field. Naturally, his plane had nosed over. He was not hurt in the crash, however, and had been retrieved shortly before midnight.

The squadron had already made one flight across the lines that morning, and we had arrived just in time for the second one. On this flight we had a double mission to fulfil. We were to protect a squadron of our heavy bombers while they bombed, and then, when they finished, go down and do our dive-bombing and machine-gunning; or, in other words, mop up after them. We climbed to 8,000 feet directly over our field and waited until the heavy bombers came along. They were flying at about 3,200 feet, so we came down to 6,500 feet and accompanied them across the lines. Even from that height we could see that a great battle was in progress down below. The flashes of field artillery from both sides were almost continuous. The appearance of our aerial fleet turned out to be the beginning of the end as far as the already-retreating Italians were concerned.

Three of our heavy bombers made a direct hit on and around the crossroad northwest of Brihuega and completely ruined it. They also wrecked fifteen or twenty trucks and cars which were trying to retreat and had become involved in a traffic jam there. A huge truck, whirling end over end through the air, made a most impressive sight. As soon as our bombers were safely back in our territory we dove down on the poor devils ourselves and cut loose with both bombs and machine guns. After that we went up to about 1,000 feet and started cruising around.

This crossroad was the only avenue of retreat for the motorized units of the central and part of the eastern Italian columns. The fields were so muddy that they were forced to stay on the two roads leading from this crossroad to Brihuega and Trijueque. Even the foot soldiers had trouble retreating through the mud, which, being very sticky, accumulated in large lumps on their feet.

As no enemy planes appeared, we had nothing at all to do except watch the progress of the battle below and help to demoralize the Italians. Immediately after the aerial bombardment, our tanks (Russian) started to advance slowly through the mire, followed by cavalry, which proved to be worth its weight in gold in this engagement. By that time the Italians were so demoralized that it was almost terrible to behold. Rifles and ammunition belts were abandoned to facilitate running and away they went. That misery loves company was illustrated by the way the fleeing wretches tended to group together as they ran. That was very bad judgment indeed, because at the first sign of a group of men, down would come one of our fighting planes with all four guns chattering away. That was part of the instructions we had received before leaving the field. A description of one of these murderous dives will give you an idea of what the foot soldiers may expect in the war to come.

I spotted one especially large group of Italians in wild retreat before a couple of tanks. My first move was to maneuver my plane to a down-wind position from them—the wind was blowing in the same direction they were running—and then push its nose over into about a sixty-degree dive. At that altitude—1,000 feet—the men looked like a mass of ants on the ground, even through my telescopic sight. At about 700 feet I opened fire with one upper and one lower machine gun. This was so that I could see, by the tracer bullets, whether or not I was on the target. The stream of bullets was just ahead of the fleeing group, so I opened up with the other two guns and pulled the plane's nose up a little.

By this time I could see the individuals plainly; they had also become aware of my presence. Then they did the worst thing they could have done—started running in the opposite direction. I could see dead-white faces swivel around and, at sight of the plane, comprehension would turn them even whiter. I could see their lips drawing back from their teeth in stark terror. Some of them tried to run at right angles, but it was too late; already they were falling like grain before a reaper. I pushed the rudder back and forth gently, so that the bullets would cover a wider area, then pulled back on the stick—just as gently—thus lengthening the swath. I pulled out of the dive about twenty feet off the ground, zoomed up to rejoin the squadron, and started looking for more victims. We kept this up until our gasoline and bullets were so low that we were forced to return to the field.

Late in the afternoon the weather cleared up enough for us to make another trip across the lines. Once more we loaded up with bombs and climbed above the lower layer of clouds. Just as we got into position for bombing, we spotted a squadron of Italian fighting planes—Fiats—headed in our direction. LaCalle failed to see them and went right on about his bombing. We thought he was merely ignoring them, so we followed him down and did our bombing and machine-gunning. When we got back to the field we found that both our patrol and the third patrol had been fired on—one plane in each patrol coming back full of holes.

Chang's plane was the one shot up in our patrol—it had thirty-five or forty bullet holes in it. He had been, as usual, lagging back out of position in the formation. The funny thing about it was that he thought someone in the third patrol had been shooting at him; he had not seen the Fiats at all. In fact, he didn't even know that he had been under fire until he landed and his mechanic pointed out that his plane was full of holes. Then he immediately wanted to go over and fight everyone in the third patrol. It took all of Whitey's eloquence and mine to convince him that he had actually been under fire from enemy planes.

That night we received very good news from the front lines. Our troops had advanced as far as the crossroad and were busy consolidating their positions. They had captured a large number of enemy cars and trucks which had been unable to get past the bombed crossroad. The territory the Italians still held on the west of the main highway was so mountainous that the use of anything on wheels was out of the question. We had inflicted an enormous amount of damage on the enemy that morning. Our heavy bombers had destroyed several columns of trucks on the highways and our own bombardment and machine gunnery had entirely broken the morale of the Italian first-line troops.

The same bad weather was in evidence the next day. In the morning LaCalle sent Whitey and me across the lines on a reconnaissance flight to check up on the movements of the enemy. We spotted several convoys of trucks and two or three long freight trains between Jadraque and Sigüenza. We also discovered that they now had anti-aircraft guns, as we were fired at several times. All of this we marked down on our maps so there would be no chance of forgetting anything. On our way back to the field we saw three bombers off in the distance headed toward enemy territory. Whether they were ours or theirs we never did find out. We had had strict instructions from LaCalle to do nothing except reconnoiter and protect ourselves.

That afternoon we loaded up with bombs, and just as we were getting ready to take off, our two red flares went floating up. Fortunately, we were all sitting in our planes with our motors idling, so we all went off at once—except two or three who habitually lagged behind. Just as Whitey and I came around in our first turn we saw three bimotored Junkers come out from behind the clouds overhead. They saw us at once, and their gunners immediately opened fire, although they were a good 4,800 feet above us. The pilot of the Junkers on the right was evidently a bit nervous, because he deserted the formation and started for his own territory full blast. (I have often wondered what happened to him when he reached his camp.) The other two held course and speed, and tried to carry out their mission. They were trying to hit the railroad station, but they overshot, and their bombs landed right in the middle of the old Hispano-Suiza buildings at the end of the field—just as the above-mentioned laggards were taking off over that area.

Although we were weighed down with bombs, Whitey and I started
climbing at once, and were soon up to the level of the two remaining
planes; but as soon as we got up to their level they dived into the thick
clouds and started for home. We finally saw one of them streaking
through the clouds below and went after it—opening fire as soon as we
lined up our sights on it. Its rear machine gunner also opened fire on us:
we could see his tracer bullets coming our way. However, we hit either
him or his gun, because after about ten seconds of firing his stream of
tracer bullets ended abruptly. We fired at that plane until it scrambled
to safety in the next cloud. Then we went back to rejoin the formation.

The rest of the squadron had all tried to close in with the single plane
which had left the formation, but it had too great a start. Blanche, the
new leader of the third patrol, managed to fire at it a few seconds before
one of its gunners shot the tail off his plane. He immediately bailed out
and pulled his parachute rip cord. Then we were horrified to see the
parachute string out above him and fail to open. The entire squadron
saw him strike the ground, about 6,500 feet below, with terrific force.
LaCalle re-formed the squadron and we went on across the lines and
carried out our bombing mission—using up the rest of our bullets on the
enemy troops as we were returning.

Chang had gone down to the spot where Blanche struck and had
memorized the location thoroughly before returning to the field. By the
time we returned he had already started out after the body in our patrol
car. They returned about half an hour later. For the rest of the time
during which we used that particular car we had a rather grim reminder
of our ex-squadron mate in the form of a large bloodstain on the rear
cushion. His parachute had failed to open because it had been wet, so
they immediately started checking up on all our parachutes.

The front-line reports we received that night were more cheering than
ever. It seemed that our infantry had made two very effective counterat-
tacks. The first had been made against the town of Trijueque and had
been supported by tanks and planes. The support from the air had consisted of two squadrons of bombers protected by a squadron of mono-
planes. They had made five trips across the lines that day and had done
outstanding work. The tanks, as usual, had advanced after each bombardment. The second attack, above Brihuega, had cut the enemy lines
between Brihuega and Torija. This placed the Italians occupying
Brihuega in the most dangerous position.

That night Whitey, Chang, and I took a run in to Madrid after the
evening meal. We met all our American newspaper friends and indulged
in another hot bath. When we got back home we discovered that we had
missed an unusually good bombardment. Three houses on the edge of
the little town had been destroyed. In fact, the more timid of the town's
citizens were still in bed when we got there an hour after it happened.

Before we turned in, LaCalle came around and told me that I was going to lead the third patrol whether I wanted to or not. Blanche's death that day had again left it without a leader.

JOHN DOS PASSOS
1896-1970

During the First World War, Dos Passos served in the French Ambulance Service and the U.S. Army Medical Corps. His novel Three Soldiers *(1921) was one of the first to deglorify the American army, and in his trilogy* U.S.A. *(1938) he continued his procedure of looking beneath the surface, exposing this time American commercial and political corruption. His interest in socialism as an antidote brought him to Spain to observe various left factions, but their brutality and power hunger finally disillusioned him. This article he sent back to* Esquire *in January 1938.*

Room and Bath at the Hotel Florida

I wake up suddenly with my throat stiff. It's not quite day. I am lying in a comfortable bed, in a clean well-arranged hotel room staring at the light indigo oblong of the window opposite. I sit up in bed. Again there's the hasty loudening shriek, the cracking roar, the rattle of tiles and a tinkling shatter of glass and granite fragments. Must have been near because the hotel shook. My room is seven or eight stories up. The hotel is on a hill. From the window I can look out at all the old part of Madrid over the crowded tiled roofs, soot-color flecked with pale yellow and red under the metal blue before dawn gloaming. The packed city stretches out sharp and still as far as I can see, narrow roofs, smokeless chimney-pots, buffcolored towers with cupolas and the pointed slate spires of seventeenthcentury Castile. Everything is cut out of metal in the steely brightening light. Again the shriek, the roar, rattle, tinkle of a shell bursting somewhere. Then silence again, cut only by the thin yelps of a hurt dog, and very slowly from one of the roofs below a smudge of dirty yellow smoke forms, rises, thickens and spreads out in the still air under the low indigo sky. The yelping goes weakly on and on.

It's too early to get up. I try going to bed again, fall asleep to wake almost immediately with the same tight throat, the same heavy feeling in my chest. The shells keep coming in. They are small but they are damn close. Better get dressed. The water's running in the bathroom, though the hot's not on yet. A man feels safe shaving, sniffing the little customary odor of the usual shaving soap in the clean bathroom. After a bath and a shave I put on my bathrobe, thinking after all this is what the Madrileños have been having instead of an alarmclock for five months now, and walk downstairs to see what the boys are up to. The shells keep coming in. The hotel, usually so quiet at this time, is full of scamper and confusion.

Everywhere doors fly open onto the balconies round the central glassed-over well. Men and women in various stages of undress are scuttling out of front rooms, dragging suitcases and mattresses into back rooms. There's a curlyhaired waiter from the restaurant who comes out of several different doors in succession each time with his arm round a different giggling or sniveling young woman. Great exhibitions of dishevelment and lingerie.

Downstairs the correspondents are stirring about sleepily. An Englishman is making coffee on an electric coffeepot that speedily blows out the fuse at the same time melting the plug. A Frenchman in pajamas is distributing grapefruit to all and sundry from the door of his room. The shells keep coming in. Nobody seems to know how to get at the coffee until a completely dressed woman novelist from Iowa takes charge of it and distributes it around in glasses with some scorched toast and halves of the Frenchman's grapefruit. Everybody gets lively and talkative until there's no more coffee left. By that time the shelling has died down a little and I go back to bed to sleep for an hour.

When I woke up again everything was quiet. There was hot water in the bathroom. From somewhere among the closepacked roofs under the window there drifted up a faint taste of sizzling olive oil. Round the balconies in the hotel everything was quiet and normal. The pleasant-faced middleaged chambermaids were there in their neat aprons, quietly cleaning. On the lower floor the waiters were serving the morning coffee. Outside on the Plaza de Callao there were some new dents in the pavement that hadn't been there the night before. Somebody said an old newsvendor at the corner had been killed. Yesterday the doorman at the hotel got a spent machinegun bullet in the thigh.

The midmorning sunlight was hot on the Gran Via in spite of the frigid dry wind of Castilian springtime. Stepping out of doors into the bustling jangle of the city I couldn't help thinking of other Madrids I'd known, twenty years ago, eighteen years ago, four years ago. The streetcars are the same, the longnose sallow Madrileño faces are the same, with the same mixture of brown bulletheaded countrymen, the women in the dark-colored shawls don't look very different. Of course you don't see the Best People any more. They are in Portugal and Seville or in their graves. Never did see many this early anyway. The shellholes and the scars made by flying fragments and shrapnel have not changed the general look of the street, nor have the political posters pasted up on every bare piece of wall, or the fact that people are so scrappily dressed and that there's a predominance of uniforms in khaki and blue denim. It's the usualness of it that gives it this feeling of nightmare. I happen to look up at the hotel my wife and I stayed in the last time we were here. The entrance on the street looks normal and so does the departmentstore next door, but the upper stories of the building, and the story where our room was, are shot as full of holes as a Swiss cheese.

Nobody hurries so fast along the street, and hardly anybody passes along the Gran Via these days without speeding his pace a little because it's the street where most shells fall, without pausing to glance up at the tall NewYorkish telephone building to look for new shellholes. It's funny how the least Spanish building in Madrid, the baroque tower of Wall Street's International Tel and Tel, the symbol of the colonizing power of the dollar, has become in the minds of the Madrileños the symbol of the defense of the city. Five months of intermittent shellfire have done remarkably little damage. There are a few holes and dents but nothing that couldn't be repaired in two weeks. On the side the shelling comes from, the windows of several stories have been bricked up. The pompous period ornamentation has hardly been chipped.

Inside you feel remarkably safe. The whole apparatus of the telephone service still goes on in the darkened offices. The elevators run. There's a feeling like Sunday in a New York downtown building. In their big quiet office you find the press censors, a cadaverous Spaniard and a plump little pleasant voiced Austrian woman. They say they are going to move their office to another building. It's too much to ask the newspapermen on the regular services to duck through a barrage every time they have to file a story, and the censors are beginning to feel that Franco's gunners are out after them personally. Only yesterday the Austrian woman came back to find that a shellfragment had set her room on fire and burned up all her shoes, and the censor had seen a woman made mincemeat of beside him when he stepped out to get a bite of lunch. It's not surprising that the censor is a nervous man; he looks underslept and underfed. He talks as if he understood, without taking too much personal pleasure in it, the importance of his position of guardian of those telephones that are the link with happier countries where the civil war is still being carried on by means of gold credits on bankledgers and munitions contracts and conversations on red plush sofas in diplomatic anterooms instead of with six-inch shells and firing squads. He doesn't give the impression of being complacent about his job. But it's hard for one who is more or less of a free agent from a country at peace to talk about many things with men who are chained to the galley benches of a war.

It's a relief to get away from the switchboards of power and walk out in the sunny streets again. If you follow the Gran Via beyond the Plaza de Callao down the hill towards the North station, stopping for a second in an excellent bookshop that's still open for business, you run into your first defense barricade. It is solidly built of cemented pavingstones laid in regular courses high as your head. That's where men will make a last stand and die if the fascists break through.

I walk on down the street. This used to be the pleasantest and quickest way to walk out into the country, down into the shady avenue along the Manzanares where the little fat church stands that has Goya's frescoes in it, and out through the iron gate into the old royal domain of El Pardo. Now it's the quickest way to the front.

At the next barricade there's a small beadyeyed sentry who smilingly asks to see my pass. He's a Cuban. As Americans we talk. Somehow there's a bond between us as coming from the western world.

There are trenches made with sandbags in the big recently finished Plaza de España. The huge straggling bronze statues of Don Quixote and Sancho Panza look out oddly towards the enemy position in Carabanchel. At a barracks building on the corner a bunch from the International Brigade is waiting for chow. French faces, Belgian faces, North of Italy faces; German exiles, bearded men blackened with the sun, young boys; a feeling of energy and desperation comes from them. The dictators have stolen their world from them; they have lost their homes, their families, their hopes of a living or a career; they are fighting back.

Up another little hill is the burned shell of the Montaña Barracks where the people of Madrid crushed the military revolt last July. Then we're looking down the broad rimedge street of the Paseo de Rosales. It used to be one of the pleasantest places in Madrid to live because the four and fivestory apartmenthouses overlooked the valley of the Manzanares and the green trees of the old royal parks and domains. Now it's no man's land. The lines cross the valley below, but if you step out on the Paseo you're in the full view of the enemy on the hills opposite, and the Moors are uncommonly good riflemen.

With considerable speed the sightseers scuttled into a house on the corner. There's the narrow hall and the row of bells and the rather grimy dark stairs of the regular Madrid apartmenthouse, but instead of the apartment of Señor Fulano de Tal on the third floor you open a ground glass door and find . . . the front. The rest of the house has been blown away. The ground glass door opens on air, at your feet a well opens full of broken masonry and smashed furniture, then the empty avenue and beyond across the Manzanares, a magnificent view of the enemy. On the top floor there's a room on that side still intact; looking carefully through the half-shattered shutters we can make out trenches and outposts at the top of the hill, a new government trench halfway up the hill and closing the picture, as always, the great snowy cloudtopped barrier of the Guadarrama. The lines are quiet; not a sound. Through the glasses we can see some militiamen strolling around behind a clump of trees. After all it's lunchtime. They can't be expected to start a battle for the benefit of a couple of sightseers.

Walking back to the hotel through the empty streets of the wrecked quarter back of the Paseo we get a chance to see all the quaint possibilities of shellfire and airbombing among dwelling houses. The dollhouse effect is the commonest, the front or a side of a house sliced off and touchingly revealing parlors, bedrooms, kitchens, dining rooms, twisted iron beds dangling, elaborate chandeliers hanging over void, a piano suspended in the air, a sideboard with dishes still on it, a mirror with a gilt stucco frame glittering high up in a mass of wreckage where everything else has been obliterated.

After lunch I walk out into the northern part of the city to see the mother of an old friend of mine. It's the same apartment where I have been to visit them in various past trips. The same old maid in black with a starched apron opens the door into the dim white rooms with the old oak and walnut furniture that remind me a little of Philip II's rooms in the Escorial. My friend's mother is much older than when I saw her last, but her eyes under the handsomely arched still dark eyebrows are as fine as ever, they have the same black flash when she talks. With her is an older sister from Andalusia, a very old whitehaired woman, old beyond conversation. They have been in Madrid ever since the movement, as they call it, started. Her son has tried to get her to go to Valencia where he has duties but she doesn't like to leave her apartment and she wouldn't like the fascists to think they'd scared her into running away. Of course getting food is a nuisance but they are old now and don't need much, she says. She could even invite me to lunch if I'd come someday and wouldn't expect to get too much to eat. She tells me which of the newspapers she likes; then we fall to talking about the old days when they lived at El Pardo and her husband the doctor was alive and I used to walk out to see them through the beautiful park of liveoaks that always made me feel as if I were walking through the backgrounds of Velasquez's paintings. The park was a royal hunting preserve and was protected, in those days of the Bourbons, by mantraps and royal game keepers in Goya costumes. The deer were tame. Over the tea and the almond paste cakes we talked of walks in the sierra and skiing and visits to forgotten dried-up Castilian villages and the pleasure of looking at the construction of old buildings and pictures and the poems of Antonio Machado.

As I stepped out into the empty street I heard shelling in the distance again. As a precaution I walked over to the metrostation and took the crowded train down to the Gran Via. When I got out of the elevator at the station I found that there weren't so many people as usual walking down towards the Calle de Alcalá. There was a tendency to stand in doorways.

I was thinking how intact this part of the town was when, opposite Molinero's, the pastry shop where we used to go in the intermissions of the symphony concerts at the Price Circus and stuff with almond paste and eggyolk and whipped cream pastry in the old days, I found myself stepping off the curb into a pool of blood. Water had been sloshed over it but it remained in red puddles among the cobbles. So much blood must have come from a mule, or several people hit at one time. I walked round it. But what everybody was looking at was the division El Campesino in new khaki uniforms parading up the Calle de Alcalá with flags and Italian guns and trucks captured at Brihuega. The bugles blew and the drums rattled and the flags rippled in the afternoon sunlight and the young men and boys in khaki looked healthy and confident walking by tanned from life at the front and with color stung into their faces by the lashing wind off the sierras. I followed them into the Puerta del Sol that, in spite of the two blocks gutted by incendiary bombs, looked remarkably normal in the late afternoon bustle, full of shoeshine boys and newsvendors and people selling shoelaces and briquets and paper covered books.

On the island in the middle where the metrostation is, an elderly man shined my shoes.

A couple of shells came in behind me far up a street. The dry whacking shocks were followed by yellow smoke and the smell of granite dust that drifted slowly past in the wind. There were no more. Groups of men chatting on the corners went on chatting. Perhaps a few more people decided to take the metro instead of the streetcar. An ambulance passed. The old man went on meticulously shining my shoes.

I began to feel that General Franco's gunner, smoking a cigarette as he looked at the silhouette of the city from the hill at Carabanchel, was taking aim at me personally. At last the old man was satisfied with his work, and sat down on his box again to wait for another customer while I walked across the halfmoonshaped square through the thinning crowd, to the old Café de Lisboa. Going in through the engraved glass swinging doors and sitting down on the faded chartreusecolored plush and settling down to read the papers over a glass of vermouth was stepping back twenty-one years to the winter when I used to come out from my cold room at the top of a house on the other corner of the Puerta del Sol and warm up with coffee there during the morning. The papers, naturally, were full of victories; this is wartime. When I come out of the café at seven o'clock closing, and head for the Hotel Florida it's already almost dark. For some reason the city seems safer at night.

The correspondents take their meals in the basement of the Hotel Gran Via almost opposite the Telephone Building. You go in through the unlit lobby and through a sort of pantry and down some back stairs past the kitchen into a cavelike place that still has pink lights and an air of night club jippery about it. There at a long table sit the professional foreign correspondents and the young worldsaviours and the members of foreign radical delegations. At the small tables in the alcoves there tend to be militiamen and internationals on sprees and a sprinkling of young ladies of the between the sheets brigade.

This particular night there's a group of British parliamentary bigwigs, including a duchess at a special table. It's been a big day for them, because General Franco's gunners have bagged more civilians than usual. Right outside of the hotel, in fact under the eyes of the duchess, two peaceful Madrileños were reduced to a sudden bloody mess. A splatter of brains had to be wiped off the glassless revolving doors of the hotel. But stuffed with horrors as they were, the British bigwigs had eaten supper.

In fact they'd eaten up everything there was, so that when the American correspondents began to trickle in with nothing in their stomachs but whiskey and were fed each a sliver of rancid ham, there was a sudden explosion of the spirit of Seventy-six. Why should a goddamn lousy etcetera duchess eat three courses when a hardworking American newspaperman has to go hungry.

A slightly punchdrunk little ex-bantamweight prizefighter who was often in the joint wearing a snappy militiaman's uniform, and who had tended in the past to be chummy with the members of the gringo contingent who were generous with their liquor, became our champion and muttered dark threats about closing the place up and having the cooks and waiters sent to the front, lousy profiteers hiding under the skirts of the C.N.T. who were all sons of loose women and saboteurs of the war and worse than fascists, mierda. In the end the management produced a couple of longdead whitings and a plate of spinach which they'd probably been planning to eat themselves, and the fires of revolt died down.

Still in Madrid the easiest thing to get, though it's high in price, is whiskey; so it's on that great national fooddrink that the boys at the other end of the wires tend to subsist. One of the boys who'd been there longest leaned across the table and said plaintively, "Now you won't go home and write about the drunken correspondents, will you?"

Outside the black stone city was grimly flooded with moonlight that cut each street into two oblique sections. Down the Gran Via I could see the flashlight of a patrol and hear them demanding in low voices the password for the night of whoever they met on the sidewalk.

From the west came a scattered hollow popping, soft perforations of the distant horizon. Somewhere not very far away men with every nerve tense were crawling along the dark sides of walls, keeping their heads down in trenches, yanking their right arms back to sling a hand grenade at some creeping shadow opposite. And in all the black houses the children we'd seen playing in the streets were asleep, and the grownups were lying there thinking of lost friends and family and ruins and people they'd loved and of hating the enemy and of hunger and how to get a little more food tomorrow, feeling in the numbness of their blood, in spite of whatever scorn in the face of death, the low unending smoulder of apprehension of a city under siege. And I couldn't help feeling a certain awe, as I took off my clothes in my quiet clean room with electric light and running water and a bathtub, in the face of all these people in this city. I lay down on the bed to read a book but instead stared at the ceiling and thought of the pleasantfaced middleaged chambermaid who'd cleaned my room that morning and made the bed and put everything in order and who'd been coming regularly every day, doing the job ever since the siege began just as she'd done it in the days of Don Alfonso, and wondered where she slept and what about her family and her kids and her man, and how perhaps tomorrow coming to work there'd be that hasty loudening shriek and the street full of dust and splintered stone and instead of coming to work the woman would be just a mashed-out mess of blood and guts to be scooped into a new pine coffin and hurried away. And they'd slosh some water over the cobbles and the death of Madrid would go on. A city under siege is not a very good place for a sightseer. It's a city without sleep.

ANTOINE DE SAINT-EXUPÉRY
1900–1944

French aviator, novelist, and lyricist of the air, Saint-Exupéry was born in Lyons and served with the French air force between the wars, flying also as an air mail pilot in Africa and South America. During the Spanish Civil War he was in Barcelona with the anarchists, sending back despa-

tches to L'Intransegeant, *and he recaptured his days in Spain in his popular autobiography* Wind, Sand, and Stars *(1939). Although aging in the Second World War, he was allowed to fly still, for the Free French Air Force. In July 1944, he was shot down and killed over southern France.*

From WIND, SAND, AND STARS

I was sitting on the pavement of a café, sipping my drink surrounded by light-hearted men and women, when suddenly four armed men stopped where I sat, stared at a man at the next table, and without a word pointed their guns at his stomach. Streaming with sweat the man stood up and raised leaden arms above his head. One of the militiamen ran his hands over his clothes and his eyes over some papers he found in the man's pockets, and ordered him to come along.

The man left his half-emptied glass, the last glass of his life, and started down the road. Surrounded by the squad, his hands stuck up like the hands of a man going down for the last time.

"Fascist!" A woman behind me said it with contempt. She was the only witness who dared betray that anything out of the ordinary had taken place. Untouched, the man's glass stood on the table, a mute witness to a mad confidence in chance, in forgiveness, in life. I sat watching the disappearance in a ring of rifles of a man who five minutes before, within two feet of me, had crossed the invisible firing line.

My guides were anarchists. They led me to the railway station where troops were being entrained. Far from the platforms built for tender farewells, we were walking in a desert of signal towers and switching points, stumbling in the rain through a labyrinthine yard filled with blackened goods wagons where tarpaulins the color of lard were spread over carloads of stiffened forms. This world had lost its human quality, had become a world of iron, and therefore uninhabitable. A ship remains a living thing only so long as man with his brushes and oils swabs an artificial layer of light over it. Leave them to themselves a couple of weeks and the life dies out of your ship, your factory, your railway; death covers their faces. After six thousand years the stones of a temple still vibrate with the passage of man; but a little rust, a night of rain, and this railway yard is eaten away to its very skeleton.

Here are our men. Cannon and machine-guns are being loaded on board with the straining muscles and the hoarse gaspings that are always drawn from men by these monstrous insects, these fleshless insects, these lumps of carapace and vertebra. What is startling here is the silence. Not a note of song, not a single shout. Only, now and then, when a gun-carriage lands, the hollow thump of a steel plate. Of human voices no sound.

No uniforms, either. These men are going off to be killed in their working garb. Wearing their dark clothes stiff with mud, the column heaving and sweating at their work look like the denizens of a night shelter. They fill me with the same uneasiness I felt when the yellow fever broke out among us at Dakar, ten years ago.

The chief of the detachment had been speaking to me in a whisper. I caught the end of his speech:

". . . and we move up to Saragossa."

Why the devil did he have to whisper! The atmosphere of this yard made me think of a hospital. But of course! That was it. A civil war is not a war, it is a disease. These men were not going up to the front in the exultation of certain victory; they were struggling blindly against infection.

And the same thing was going on in the enemy camp. The purpose of this struggle was not to rid the country of an invading foreigner but to eradicate a plague. A new faith is like a plague. It attacks from within. It propagates in the invisible. Walking in the streets, whoever belongs to a Party feels himself surrounded by secretly infected men.

This must have been why these troops were going off in silence with their instruments of asphyxiation. There was not the slightest resemblance between them and regiments that go into battle against foreign armies and are set out on the chessboard of the fields and moved about by strategists. These men had gathered together haphazardly in a city filled with chaos.

There was not much to choose between Barcelona and its enemy, Saragossa: both were composed of the same swarm of communists, anarchists, and fascists. The very men who collected on the same side were perhaps more different from one another than from their enemies. In civil war the enemy is inward; one as good as fights against oneself.

What else can explain the particular horror of this war in which firing squads count for more than soldiers of the line? Death in this war is a sort of quarantine. Purges take place of germ-carriers. The anarchists go from house to house and load the plague-stricken into their tumbrils, while on the other side of the barricade Franco is able to utter that horrible boast: "There are no more communists among us."

The conscripts are weeded out by a kind of medical board; the officer in charge is a sort of army doctor. Men present themselves for service with pride shining in their eyes and the belief in their hearts that they have a part to play in society.

"Exempt from service for life!" is the decision.

Fields have been turned into charnel-houses and the dead are burned in lime or petroleum. Respect for the dignity of man has been trampled under foot. Since on both sides the political parties spy upon the stirrings of man's conscience as upon the workings of a disease, why should the urn of his flesh be respected? This body that clothes the spirit, that moves with grace and boldness, that knows love, that is apt for self-sacrifice—no one now so much as thinks of giving it decent burial.

I thought of our respect for the dead. I thought of the white sanatorium where the light of a man's life goes quietly out in the presence of those who love him and who garner as if it were an inestimable treasure his last words, his ultimate smile. How right they are! Seeing that this same whole is never again to take shape in the world. Never again will be heard exactly that note of laughter, that intonation of voice, that quality of repartee. Each individual is a miracle. No wonder we go on speaking of the dead for twenty years.

Here, in Spain, a man is simply stood up against a wall and he gives up his entrails to the stones of the courtyard. You have been captured. You are shot. Reason: your ideas were not our ideas.

This entrainment in the rain is the only thing that rings true about their war. These men stand round and stare at me, and I read in their eyes a mournful sobriety. They know the fate that awaits them if they are captured. I begin to shiver with the cold and observe of a sudden that no woman has been allowed to see them off.

The absence of women seems to me right. There is no place here for mothers who bring children into the world in ignorance of the faith that will some day flare up in their sons, in ignorance of the ideologist who, according to his lights, will prop up their sons against a wall when they have come to their twenty years of life.

We went up by motor into the war zone. Barricades became more frequent, and from place to place we had to negotiate with revolutionary committees. Passes were valid only from one village to the next.

"Are you trying to get closer to the front?"

"Exactly."

The chairman of the local committee consulted a large-scale map.

"You won't be able to get through. The rebels have occupied the road four miles ahead. But you might try swinging left here. This road ought to be free. Though there was talk of rebel cavalry cutting it this morning."

It was very difficult in those early days of the revolution to know one's way about in the vicinity of the front. There were loyal villages, rebel villages, neutral villages, and they shifted their allegiance between dawn and dark. This tangle of loyal and rebel zones made me think the push must be pretty weak. It certainly bore no resemblance to a line of trenches cutting off friend from enemy as cleanly as a knife. I felt as if I

were walking in a bog. Here the earth was solid beneath our feet: there
we sank into it. We moved in a maze of uncertainty. Yet what space,
what air between movements! These military operations are curiously
lacking in density.

Once again we reached a point beyond which we were told we could
not advance. Six rifles and a low wall of paving stones blocked the road.
Four men and two women lay stretched on the ground behind the wall. I
made a mental note that the women did not know how to hold a rifle.
  "This is as far as you can go."
  "Why?"
  "Rebels."
  We got out of the car and sat down with the militiamen upon the
grass. They put down their rifles and cut a few slices of fresh bread.
  "Is this your village?" we asked.
  "No, we are Catalans, from Barcelona. Communist Party."
  One of the girls stretched herself and sat up on the barricade, her hair
blowing in the wind. She was rather thick-set, but young and healthy.
Smiling happily she said:
  "I am going to stay in this village when the war is over. I didn't know
it, but the country beats the city all hollow."
  She cast a loving glance round at the countryside, as if stirred by a
revelation. Her life had been the gray slums, days spent in a factory, and
the sordid compensation afforded by the cafés. Everything that went on
here seemed to her as jolly as a picnic. She jumped down and ran to the
village well. Probably she believed she was drinking at the very breast of
mother earth.
  "Have you done any fighting here?"
  "No. The rebels kick up a little dust now and then, but . . . We see a
lorryload of men from time to time and hope that they will come along
this road. But nothing has come by in two weeks."
  They were awaiting their first enemy. In the rebel village opposite sat
another half-dozen militiamen awaiting a first enemy. Twelve warriors
alone in the world.
  Each side was waiting for something to be born in the invisible. The
rebels were waiting for the host of hesitant people in Madrid to declare
themselves for Franco. Barcelona was waiting for Saragossa to waken out
of an inspired dream, declare itself Socialist, and fall. It was the thought
more than the soldier that was besieging the town. The thought was the
great hope and the great enemy.
  It seemed to me that the bombers, the shells, the militiamen under
arms, by themselves had no power to conquer. On each side a single man
entrenched behind his line of defense was better than a hundred besieg-
ers. But thought might worm its way in.

From time to time there is an attack. From time to time the tree is shaken. Not to uproot it, but merely to see if the fruit is yet ripe. And if it is, a town falls.

II

Back from the front, I found friends in Barcelona who allowed me to join in their mysterious expeditions. We went deep into the mountains and were now in one of those villages which are possessed by a mixture of peace and terror.

"Oh, yes, we shot seventeen of them."

They had shot seventeen "fascists." The parish priest, the priest's housekeeper, the sexton, and fourteen village notables. Everything is relative, you see. When they read in their provincial newspaper the story of the life of Basil Zaharoff, master of the world, they transpose it into their own language. They recognize in him the nurseryman, or the pharmacist. And when they shoot the pharmacist, in a way they are shooting Basil Zaharoff. The only one who does not understand is the pharmacist.

"Now we are all Loyalists together. Everything has calmed down."

Almost everything. The conscience of the village is tormented by one man whom I have seen at the tavern, smiling, helpful, so anxious to go on living! He comes to the pub in order to show us that, despite his few acres of vineyard, he too is part of the human race, suffers with rheumatism like it, mops his face like it with a blue handkerchief. He comes, and he plays billiards. Can one shoot a man who plays billiards? Besides, he plays badly with his great trembling hands. He is upset; he still does not know whether he is a fascist or not. He puts me in mind of those poor monkeys who dance before the boa-constrictor in the hope of softening it.

There was nothing we could do for the man. For the time being we had another job in hand. Sitting on a table and swinging my legs at committee headquarters, while my companion, Pépin, pulled a bundle of soiled papers out of his pocket, I had a good look at these terrorists. Their looks belied their name: honorable peasants with frank eyes and sober attentive faces, they were the same everywhere we went; and though we were foreigners possessing no authority, we were everywhere received with the same grave courtesy.

"Yes, here it is," said Pépin, a document in his hand. "His name is Laporte. Any of you know him?"

The paper went from hand to hand and the members of the committee shook their heads.

"No. Laporte? Never heard of him."

I started to explain something to them, but Pépin motioned me to be silent. "They won't talk," he said, "but they know him well enough."

Pépin spread his references before the chairman, saying casually: "I am a French socialist. Here is my party card."

The card was passed round and the chairman raised his eyes to us: "Laporte. I don't believe. . . ."

"Of course you know him. A French monk. Probably in disguise. You captured him yesterday in the woods. Laporte, his name is. The French consulate wants him."

I sat swinging my legs. What a strange session! Here we were in a mountain village sixty miles from the French frontier, asking a revolutionary committee that shot even parish priests' housekeepers to surrender to us in good shape a French monk. Whatever happened to us, we would certainly have asked for it. Nevertheless, I felt safe. There was no treachery in these people. And why, as a matter of fact, should they bother to play tricks? We had absolutely no protection; we meant no more to them than Laporte; they could do anything they pleased.

Pépin nudged me. "I've an idea we have come too late," he said.

The chairman cleared his throat and made up his mind.

"This morning," he said, "we found a dead man on the road just outside the village. He must be there still."

And he pretended to send off for the dead man's papers.

"They've already shot him," Pépin said to me. "Too bad! They would certainly have turned him over to us. They are good kind people."

I looked straight into the eyes of these curious "good kind people." Strange: there was nothing in their eyes to upset me. There seemed nothing to fear in their set jaws and the blank smoothness of their faces. Blank, as if vaguely bored. A rather terrible blankness. I wondered why, despite our unusual mission, we were not suspect to them. What difference had they established in their minds between us and the "fascist" in the neighboring tavern who was dancing his dance of death before the unavailing indifference of these judges? A crazy notion came into my head, forced upon my attention by all the power of my instinct: If one of those men yawned I should be afraid. I should feel that all human communication had snapped between us.

After we left, I said to Pépin:

"That is the third village in which we have done this job and I still cannot make up my mind whether the job is dangerous or not."

Pépin laughed and admitted that although he had saved dozens of men on these missions, he himself did not know the answer.

"Yesterday," he confessed, "I had a narrow squeak. I snaffled a Carthusian monk away from them just as they were about to shoot the fellow. The smell of blood was in the air, and . . . Well, they growled a bit, you know."

I know the end of that story. Pépin, the socialist and notorious anti-church political worker, having staked his life to get that Carthusian, had hustled him into a motor-car and there, by way of compensation, he sought to insult the priest by the finest bit of blasphemy he could summon:

"You . . . you . . . you triple damned monk!" he had finally spluttered. This was Pépin's triumph. But the monk, who had not been listening, flung his arms round Pépin's neck and wept with happiness.

In another village they gave up a man to us. With a great air of mystery, four militiamen dug him up out of a cellar. He was a lively bright-eyed monk whose name I have already forgotten, disguised as a peasant and carrying a long gnarled stick scarred with notches.

"I kept track of the days," he explained. "Three weeks in the woods is a long time. Mushrooms are not specially nourishing, and they grabbed me when I came near a village."

The mayor of the village, to whom we owed this gift, was very proud of him.

"We shot at him a lot and thought we had killed him," he said. And then, by way of excuse for the bad marksmanship, he added: "I must say it was at night."

The monk laughed.

"I wasn't afraid."

We put him into the car, and before we threw in the clutch everybody had to shake hands all round with these terrible terrorists. The monk's hand was shaken hardest of all and he was repeatedly congratulated on being alive. To all these friendly sentiments he responded with a warmth of unquestionably sincere appreciation.

As for me, I wish I understood mankind.

We went over our lists. At Sitges lived a man who, we had been told, was in danger of being shot. We drove round and found his door wide open. Up a flight of stairs we ran into our skinny young man.

"It seems that these people are likely to shoot you," we told him. "Come back to Barcelona with us and you will be shipped home to France in the *Duquesne.*"

The young man took a long time to think this over and then said: "This is some trick of my sister's."

"What?"

"She lives in Barcelona. She would never pay for the child's keep and I always had to. . . ."

"Your family troubles are none of our affair. Are you in danger here, yes or no?"

"I don't know. I tell you, my sister . . ."

"Do you want to get away, yes or no?"

"I really don't know. What do you think? In Barcelona, my sister . . ."
The man was carrying on his family quarrel through the revolution.
He was going to stay here in order to do his sister in the eye.
"Do as you please," we said, finally, and we left him where he was.

We stopped the car and got out. A volley of rifle-shot had crackled in
the still country air. From the top of the road we looked down upon a
clump of trees out of which, a quarter of a mile away, stuck two tall
chimneys. A squad of militiamen came up and loaded their guns. We
asked what was going on. They looked round, pointed to the chimneys,
and decided that the firing must have come from the factory.

The shooting died down almost immediately, and silence fell again.
The chimneys went on smoking peacefully. A ripple of wind ran over the
grass. Nothing had changed visibly, and we ourselves were unchanged.
Nevertheless, in that clump of trees someone had just died.

One of the militiamen said that a girl had been killed at the factory,
together with her brothers, but there was still some uncertainty about
this. What excruciating simplicity! Our own peace of mind had not been
invaded by those muffled sounds in the clump of greenery, by that brief
partridge drive. The angelus, as it were, that had rung out in that foliage
had left us calm and unrepentant.

Human events display two faces, one of drama and the other of indifference. Everything changes according as the event concerns the individual or the species. In its migrations, in its imperious impulses, the
species forgets its dead. This, perhaps, explains the unperturbed faces of
these peasants. One feels that they have no special taste for horror; yet
they will come back from that clump of trees on the one hand content to
have administered their kind of justice, and on the other hand quite
indifferent to the fate of the girl who stumbled against the root of the
tree of death, who was caught by death's harpoon as she fled, and who
now lies in the wood, her mouth filled with blood.

Here I touch the inescapable contradiction I shall never be able to
resolve. For man's greatness does not reside merely in the destiny of the
species: each individual is an empire. When a mine caves in and closes
over the head of a single miner, the life of the community is suspended.

His comrades, their women, their children, gather in anguish at the
entrance to the mine, while below them the rescue party scratch with
their picks at the bowels of the earth. What are they after? Are they
consciously saving one unit of society? Are they freeing a human being as
one might free a horse, after computing the work he is still capable of
doing? Ten other miners may be killed in the attempted rescue: what
inept cost accounting! Of course it is not a matter of saving one ant out
of the colony of ants! They are rescuing a consciousness, an empire
whose significance is incommensurable with anything else.

Inside the narrow skull of the miner pinned beneath the fallen timber, there lives a world. Parents, friends, a home, the hot soup of evening, songs sung on feast days, loving kindness and anger, perhaps even a social consciousness and a great universal love, inhabit that skull. By what are we to measure the value of a man? His ancestor once drew a reindeer on the wall of a cave; and two hundred thousand years later that gesture still radiates. It stirs us, prolongs itself in us. Man's gestures are an eternal spring. Though we die for it, we shall bring up that miner from his shaft. Solitary he may be; universal he surely is.

In Spain there are crowds in movement, but the individual, that universe, calls in vain for help from the bottom of the mine.

III

Machine-gun bullets cracked against the stone above our heads as we skirted the moonlit wall. Low-flying lead thudded into the rubble of an embankment that rose on the other side of the road. Half a mile away a battle was in progress, the line of fire drawn in the shape of a horse-shoe ahead of us and on our flanks.

Walking between wall and parapet on the white highway, my guide and I were able to disregard the spatter of missiles in a feeling of perfect security. We could sing, we could laugh, we could strike matches, without drawing upon ourselves the direct fire of the enemy. We went forward like peasants on their way to market. Half a mile away the iron hand of war would have set us inescapably upon the black chessboard of battle; but here, out of the game, ignored, the Republican lieutenant and I were as free as air.

Shells filled the night with absurd parabolas during their three seconds of freedom between release and exhaustion. There were the duds that dove without bursting into the ground; there were the travelers in space that whipped straight overhead, elongated in their race to the stars. And the leaden bullets that ricocheted in our faces and tinkled curiously in our ears were like bees, dangerous for the twinkling of an eye, poisonous but ephemeral.

Walking on, we reached a point where the embankment had collapsed.

"We might follow the cross-trench from here," my guide suggested.

Things had suddenly turned serious. Not that we were in the line of machine-gun fire, or that a roving searchlight was about to spot us. It was not as bad as that. There had simply been a rustling overhead; a sort of celestial gurgle had sounded. It meant no harm to us, but the lieutenant remarked suddenly, "That is meant for Madrid," and we went down into the trench.

The trench ran along the crest of a hill a little before reaching the suburb of Carabanchel. In the direction of Madrid a part of the parapet had crumbled and we could see the city in the gap, white, strangely white, under the full moon. Hardly a mile separated us from those tall structures dominated by the tower of the Telephone Building.

Madrid was asleep—or rather Madrid was feigning sleep. Not a light; not a sound. Like clockwork, every two minutes the funereal fracas that we were henceforth to hear roared forth and was dissolved in a dead silence. It seemed to waken no sound and no stirring in the city, but was swallowed up each time like a stone in water.

Suddenly in the place of Madrid I felt that I was staring at a face with closed eyes. The hard face of an obstinate virgin taking blow after blow without a moan. Once again there sounded overhead that gurgling in the stars of a newly uncorked bottle. One second, two seconds, five seconds went by. There was an explosion and I ducked involuntarily. There goes the whole town, I thought.

But Madrid was still there. Nothing had collapsed. Not an eye had blinked. Nothing was changed. The stone face was as pure as ever.

"Meant for Madrid," the lieutenant repeated mechanically. He taught me to tell these celestial shudders apart, to follow the course of these sharks rushing upon their prey:

"No, that is one of our batteries replying. . . . That's theirs, but firing somewhere else. . . . There's one meant for Madrid."

Waiting for an explosion is the longest passage of time I know. What things go on in that interminable moment! An enormous pressure rises, rises. Will that boiler ever make up its mind to burst? At last! For some that meant death, but there are others for whom it meant escape from death. Eight hundred thousand souls, less half a score of dead, have won a last-minute reprieve. Between the gurgling and the explosion eight hundred thousand lives were in danger of death.

Each shell in the air threatened them all. I could feel the city out there, tense, compact, a solid. I saw them all in the mind's eye—men, women, children, all that humble population crouching in the sheltering cloak of stone of a motionless virgin. Again I heard the ignoble crash and was gripped and sickened by the downward course of the torpedo. . . . Torpedo? I scarcely knew what I was saying. "They . . . they are torpedoing Madrid." And the lieutenant, standing there counting the shells, said:

"Meant for Madrid. Sixteen."

I crept out of the trench, lay flat on my stomach on the parapet, and stared. A new image has wiped out the old. Madrid with its chimney-pots, its towers, its portholes, now looks like a ship on the high seas. Madrid all white on the black waters of the night. A city outlives its inhabitants. Madrid, loaded with emigrants, is ferrying them from one shore to the other of life. It has a generation on board. Slowly it navigates through the centuries. Men, women, children fill it from garret to hold. Resigned or quaking with fear, they live only for the moment to come. A vessel loaded with humanity is being torpedoed. The purpose of the enemy is to sink Madrid as if she were a ship.

Stretched out on the parapet I do not care a curse for the rules of war. For justifications or for motives. I listen. I have learned to read the course of these gurglings among the stars. They pass quite close to Sagittarius. I have learned to count slowly up to five. And I listen. But what tree has been sundered by this lightning, what cathedral has been gutted, what poor child has just been stricken, I have no means of knowing.

That same afternoon I had witnessed a bombardment in the town itself. All the force of this thunder-clap had to burst on the Gran Via in order to uproot a human life. One single life. Passers-by had brushed rubbish off their clothes; others had scattered on the run; and when the light smoke had risen and cleared away, the betrothed, escaped by miracle without a scratch, found at his feet his *novia*, whose golden arm a moment before had been in his, changed into a blood-filled sponge, changed into a limp packet of flesh and rags.

He had knelt down, still uncomprehending, had nodded his head slowly, as if saying to himself, "Something very strange has happened."

This marvel spattered on the pavement bore no resemblance to what had been his beloved. Misery was excruciatingly slow to engulf him in its tidal wave. For still another second, stunned by the feat of the invisible prestidigitator, he cast a bewildered glance round him in search of the slender form, as if it at least should have survived. Nothing was there but a packet of muck.

Gone was the feeble spark of humanity. And while in the man's throat there was brewing that shriek which I know not what deferred, he had the leisure to reflect that it was not those lips he had loved but their pout, not them but their smile. Not those eyes, but their glance. Not that breast, but its gentle swell. He was free to discover at last the source of the anguish love had been storing up for him, to learn that it was the unattainable he had been pursuing. What he had yearned to embrace was not the flesh but a downy spirit, a spark, the impalpable angel that inhabits the flesh.

I do not care a curse for the rules of war and the law of reprisal. As for the military advantage of such a bombardment, I simply cannot grasp it. I have seen housewives disemboweled, children mutilated; I have seen the old itinerant market crone sponge from her treasures the brains with which they were spattered. I have seen a janitor's wife come out of her cellar and douse the sullied pavement with a bucket of water, and I am still unable to understand what part these humble slaughterhouse accidents play in warfare.

A moral rôle? But a bombardment turns against the bombarder! Each shell that fell upon Madrid fortified something in the town. It persuaded the hesitant neutral to plump for the defenders. A dead child weighs heavily in the balance when it is one's own. It was clear to me that a bombardment did not disperse—it unified. Horror causes men to clench their fists, and in horror men join together.

The lieutenant and I crawled along the parapet. Face or ship, Madrid stood erect, receiving blows without a moan. But men are like this: slowly but surely, ordeal fortifies their virtues.

Because of the ordeal my companion's heart was high. He was thinking of the hardening of Madrid's will. He stood up with his fists on his hips, breathing heavily. Pity for the women and the children had gone out of him.

"That makes sixty," he counted grimly.

The blow resounded on the anvil. A giant smith was forging Madrid.

One side or the other would win. Madrid would resist or it would fall. A thousand forces were engaged in this mortal confusion of tongues from which anything might come forth. But one did not need to be a Martian, did not need to see these men dispassionately in a long perspective, in order to perceive that they were struggling against themselves, were their own enemy. Mankind perhaps was being brought to bed of something here in Spain; something perhaps was to be born of this chaos, this disruption. For indeed not all that I saw in Spain was horror, not all of it filled my mouth with a taste of ashes.

GEORGE ORWELL
1903–1950

Born Eric Blair, Orwell went to Spain in 1936 and joined the militia of the POUM (United Marxist Workers party). A brave if eccentric soldier, in 1937 he was shot through the neck and returned to England disillusioned with the behavior of the international Communists who had captured the Spanish workers' movement and forced it into their mold. He registered his experiences in Homage to Catalonia *(1938).*

From HOMAGE TO CATALONIA

In the Lenin Barracks in Barcelona, the day before I joined the militia, I saw an Italian militiaman standing in front of the officers' table. He was a tough-looking youth of twenty-five or six, with reddish-yellow hair and powerful shoulders. His peaked leather cap was pulled fiercely over one eye. He was standing in profile to me, his chin on his breast, gazing with a puzzled frown at a map which one of the officers had open on the table. Something in his face deeply moved me. It was the face of a man who would commit murder and throw away his life for a friend—the kind of face you would expect in an Anarchist, though as likely as not he was a Communist. There were both candour and ferocity in it; also the pathetic reverence that illiterate people have for their supposed superiors. Obviously he could not make head or tail of the map; obviously he regarded map-reading as a stupendous intellectual feat. I hardly know why, but I have seldom seen anyone—any man, I mean—to whom I have taken such an immediate liking. While they were talking round the table some remark brought it out that I was a foreigner. The Italian raised his head and said quickly:

"Italiano?"

I answered in my bad Spanish: "No, Inglés. Y tú?"

"Italiano."

As we went out he stepped across the room and gripped my hand very hard. Queer, the affection you can feel for a stranger! It was as though his spirit and mine had momentarily succeeded in bridging the gulf of language and tradition and meeting in utter intimacy. I hoped he liked me as well as I liked him. But I also knew that to retain my first impression of him I must not see him again; and needless to say I never did see him again. One was always making contacts of that kind in Spain.

I mention this Italian militiaman because he has stuck vividly in my memory. With his shabby uniform and fierce pathetic face he typifies for me the special atmosphere of that time. He is bound up with all my memories of that period of the war—the red flags in Barcelona, the gaunt trains full of shabby soldiers creeping to the front, the grey war-stricken towns farther up the line, the muddy, ice-cold trenches in the mountains.

This was in late December, 1936, less than seven months ago as I write, and yet it is a period that has already receded into enormous distance. Later events have obliterated it much more completely than they have obliterated 1935, or 1905, for that matter. I had come to Spain with some notion of writing newspaper articles, but I had joined the militia almost immediately, because at that time and in that atmosphere it seemed the only conceivable thing to do. The Anarchists were still in virtual control of Catalonia and the revolution was still in full swing. To anyone who had been there since the beginning it probably seemed even in December or January that the revolutionary period was ending; but when one came straight from England the aspect of Barcelona was something startling and overwhelming. It was the first time that I had ever been in a town where the working class was in the saddle. Practically every building of any size had been seized by the workers and was draped with red flags or with the red and black flag of the Anarchists; every wall was scrawled with the hammer and sickle and with the initials of the revolutionary parties; almost every church had been gutted and its images burnt. Churches here and there were being systematically demolished by gangs of workmen. Every shop and café had an inscription saying that it had been collectivized; even the bootblacks had been collectivized and their boxes painted red and black. Waiters and shopwalkers looked you in the face and treated you as an equal. Servile and even ceremonial forms of speech had temporarily disappeared. Nobody said "Señor" or "Don" or even "Usted"; everyone called everyone else "Comrade" and "Thou," and said "Salud!" instead of "Buenos días." Tipping had been forbidden by law since the time of Primo de Rivera; almost my first experience was receiving a lecture from an hotel manager for trying to tip a lift-boy. There were no private motor cars, they had all been commandeered, and all the trams and taxis and much of the other transport were painted red and black. The revolutionary posters were everywhere, flaming from the walls in clean reds and blues that made the few remaining advertisements look like daubs of mud. Down the Ramblas, the wide central artery of the town where crowds of people streamed constantly to and fro, the loud-speakers were bellowing revolutionary songs all day and far into the night. And it was the aspect of the crowds that was the queerest thing of all. In outward appearance it was a town in which the wealthy classes had practically ceased to exist. Except for a small number of women and foreigners there were no "well-dressed" people at all. Practically everyone wore rough working-class clothes, or blue overalls or some variant of the militia uniform. All this was queer and moving. There was much in it that I did not understand, in some ways I did not even like it, but I recognized it immediately as a state of affairs worth fighting for. Also I believed that things were as they appeared, that this was really a workers' State and that the entire bourgeoisie had either fled, been killed, or voluntarily come over to the workers' side; I did not realize that great numbers of well-to-do bourgeois were simply lying low and disguising themselves as proletarians for the time being.

Together with all this there was something of the evil atmosphere of war. The town had a gaunt untidy look, roads and buildings were in poor repair, the streets at night were dimly lit for fear of air-raids, the shops

were mostly shabby and half-empty. Meat was scarce and milk practically unobtainable, there was a shortage of coal, sugar, and petrol, and a
really serious shortage of bread. Even at this period the bread-queues
were often hundreds of yards long. Yet so far as one could judge the
people were contented and hopeful. There was no unemployment, and
the price of living was still extremely low; you saw very few conspicuously
destitute people, and no beggars except the gipsies. Above all, there was
a belief in the revolution and the future, a feeling of having suddenly
emerged into an era of equality and freedom. Human beings were trying
to behave as human beings and not as cogs in the capitalist machine. In
the barbers' shops were Anarchist notices (the barbers were mostly Anarchists) solemnly explaining that barbers were no longer slaves. In the
streets were coloured posters appealing to prostitutes to stop being prostitutes. To anyone from the hard-boiled, sneering civilization of the
English-speaking races there was something rather pathetic in the literal-
ness with which these idealistic Spaniards took the hackneyed phrases of
revolution. At that time revolutionary ballads of the naïvest kind, all
about proletarian brotherhood and the wickedness of Mussolini, were
being sold on the streets for a few centimes each. I have often seen an
illiterate militiaman buy one of these ballads, laboriously spell out the
words, and then, when he had got the hang of it, begin singing it to an
appropriate tune.

All this time I was at the Lenin Barracks, ostensibly in training for the
front. When I joined the militia I had been told that I should be sent to
the front the next day, but in fact I had to wait while a fresh *centuria* was
got ready. The workers' militias, hurriedly raised by the trade unions at
the beginning of the war, had not yet been organized on an ordinary
army basis. The units of command were the "section," of about thirty
men, the *centuria,* of about a hundred men, and the "column," which in
practice meant any large number of men. The Lenin Barracks was a
block of splendid stone buildings with a riding-school and enormous
cobbled courtyards; it had been a cavalry barracks and had been captured during the July fighting. My *centuria* slept in one of the stables,
under the stone mangers where the names of the cavalry chargers were
still inscribed. All the horses had been seized and sent to the front, but
the whole place still smelt of horse-piss and rotten oats. I was at the
barracks about a week. Chiefly I remember the horsy smells, the quaver-
ing bugle-calls (all our buglers were amateurs—I first learned the Spanish
bugle-calls by listening to them outside the Fascist lines), the tramp-
tramp of hobnailed boots in the barrack yard, the long morning parades
in the wintry sunshine, the wild games of football, fifty a side, in the
gravelled riding-school. There were perhaps a thousand men at the barracks, and a score or so of women, apart from the militiamen's wives who
did the cooking. There were still women serving in the militias, though

not very many. In the early battles they had fought side by side with the men as a matter of course. It is a thing that seems natural in time of revolution. Ideas were changing already, however. The militiamen had to be kept out of the riding-school while the women were drilling there, because they laughed at the women and put them off. A few months earlier no one would have seen anything comic in a woman handling a gun.

The whole barracks was in the state of filth and chaos to which the militia reduced every building they occupied and which seems to be one of the by-products of revolution. In every corner you came upon piles of smashed furniture, broken saddles, brass cavalry-helmets, empty sabre-scabbards, and decaying food. There was frightful wastage of food, especially bread. From my barrack-room alone a basketful of bread was thrown away at every meal—a disgraceful thing when the civilian population was short of it. We ate at long trestle-tables out of permanently greasy tin pannikins, and drank out of a dreadful thing called a *porrón*. A *porrón* is a sort of glass bottle with a pointed spout from which a thin jet of wine spurts out whenever you tip it up; you can thus drink from a distance, without touching it with your lips, and it can be passed from hand to hand. I went on strike and demanded a drinking-cup as soon as I saw a *porrón* in use. To my eyes the things were altogether too like bed-bottles, especially when they were filled with white wine.

By degrees they were issuing the recruits with uniforms, and because this was Spain everything was issued piecemeal, so that it was never quite certain who had received what, and various of the things we most needed, such as belts and cartridge-boxes, were not issued till the last moment, when the train was actually waiting to take us to the front. I have spoken of the militia "uniform," which probably gives a wrong impression. It was not exactly a uniform. Perhaps a "multiform" would be the proper name for it. Everyone's clothes followed the same general plan, but they were never quite the same in any two cases. Practically everyone in the army wore corduroy knee-breeches, but there the uniformity ended. Some wore puttees, others corduroy gaiters, others leather leggings or high boots. Everyone wore a zipper jacket, but some of the jackets were of leather, others of wool and of every conceivable colour. The kinds of cap were about as numerous as their wearers. It was usual to adorn the front of your cap with a party badge, and in addition nearly every man wore a red or red and black handkerchief round his throat. A militia column at that time was an extraordinary-looking rabble. But the clothes had to be issued as this or that factory rushed them out, and they were not bad clothes considering the circumstances. The shirts and socks were wretched cotton things, however, quite useless against cold. I hate to think of what the militiamen must have gone through in the earlier months before anything was organized. I remember coming upon a newspaper of only about two months earlier in which one of the P.O.U.M. leaders, after a visit to the front, said that he would try to see to it that "every militiaman had a blanket." A phrase to make you shudder if you have ever slept in a trench.

On my second day at the barracks there began what was comically called "instruction." At the beginning there were frightful scenes of chaos. The recruits were mostly boys of sixteen or seventeen from the back streets of Barcelona, full of revolutionary ardour but completely ignorant of the meaning of war. It was impossible even to get them to stand in line. Discipline did not exist; if a man disliked an order he would step out of the ranks and argue fiercely with the officer. The lieutenant who instructed us was a stout, fresh-faced, pleasant young man who had previously been a Regular Army officer, and still looked like one, with his smart carriage and spick-and-span uniform. Curiously enough he was a sincere and ardent Socialist. Even more than the men themselves he insisted upon complete social equality between all ranks. I remember his pained surprise when an ignorant recruit addressed him as "Señor." "What! Señor! Who is that calling me Señor? Are we not all comrades?" I doubt whether it made his job any easier. Meanwhile the raw recruits were getting no military training that could be of the slightest use to them. I had been told that foreigners were not obliged to attend "instruction" (the Spaniards, I noticed, had a pathetic belief that all foreigners knew more of military matters than themselves), but naturally I turned out with the others. I was very anxious to learn how to use a machine-gun; it was a weapon I had never had a chance to handle. To my dismay I found that we were taught nothing about the use of weapons. The so-called instruction was simply parade-ground drill of the most antiquated, stupid kind; right turn, left turn, about turn, marching at attention in column of threes and all the rest of that useless nonsense which I had learned when I was fifteen years old. It was an extraordinary form for the training of a guerrilla army to take. Obviously if you have only a few days in which to train a soldier, you must teach him the things he will most need; how to take cover, how to advance across open ground, how to mount guards and build a parapet—above all, how to use his weapons. Yet this mob of eager children, who were going to be thrown into the front line in a few days' time, were not even taught how to fire a rifle or pull the pin out of a bomb. At the time I did not grasp that this was because there were no weapons to be had. In the P.O.U.M. militia the shortage of rifles was so desperate that fresh troops reaching the front always had to take their rifles from the troops they relieved in the line. In the whole of the Lenin Barracks there were, I believe, no rifles except those used by the sentries.

After a few days, though still a complete rabble by any ordinary standard, we were considered fit to be seen in public, and in the mornings we were marched out to the public gardens on the hill beyond the Plaza de España. This was the common drill-ground of all the party militias, besides the Carabineros and the first contingents of the newly formed Popular Army. Up in the public gardens it was a strange and heartening sight. Down every path and alley-way, amid the formal flower-beds, squads and companies of men marched stiffly to and fro, throwing out their chests and trying desperately to look like soldiers. All of them were unarmed and none completely in uniform, though on most of them the militia uniform was breaking out in patches here and there. The procedure was always very much the same. For three hours we strutted to and fro (the Spanish marching step is very short and rapid), then we halted, broke the ranks and flocked thirstily to a little grocer's shop which was halfway down the hill and was doing a roaring trade in cheap wine. Everyone was very friendly to me. As an Englishman I was something of a curiosity, and the Carabinero officers made much of me and stood me drinks. Meanwhile, whenever I could get our lieutenant into a corner, I was clamouring to be instructed in the use of a machine-gun. I used to drag my Hugo's dictionary out of my pocket and start on him in my villainous Spanish:

"Yo sé manejar fusil. No sé manejar ametralladora. Quiero aprender ametralladora. Cuándo vamos aprender ametralladora?"

The answer was always a harassed smile and a promise that there should be machine-gun instruction *mañana*. Needless to say *mañana* never came. Several days passed and the recruits learned to march in step and spring to attention almost smartly, but if they knew which end of a rifle the bullet came out of, that was all they knew. One day an armed Carabinero strolled up to us when we were halting and allowed us to examine his rifle. It turned out that in the whole of my section no one except myself even knew how to load the rifle, much less how to take aim.

All this time I was having the usual struggles with the Spanish language. Apart from myself there was only one Englishman at the barracks, and nobody even among the officers spoke a word of French. Things were not made easier for me by the fact that when my companions spoke to one another they generally spoke in Catalan. The only way I could get along was to carry everywhere a small dictionary which I whipped out of my pocket in moments of crisis. But I would sooner be a foreigner in Spain than in most countries. How easy it is to make friends in Spain! Within a day or two there was a score of militiamen who called me by my Christian name, showed me the ropes and overwhelmed me with hospitality. I am not writing a book of propaganda and I do not want to idealize the P.O.U.M. militia. The whole militia-system had serious faults, and the men themselves were a mixed lot, for by this time voluntary recruitment was falling off and many of the best men were already at the front or dead. There was always among us a certain percentage who were completely useless. Boys of fifteen were being brought up for enlistment by their parents, quite openly for the sake of the ten pesetas a day which was the militiaman's wage; also for the sake of the bread which the militia received in plenty and could smuggle home to their parents. But I defy anyone to be thrown as I was among the Spanish working class—I ought perhaps to say the Catalan working class, for apart from a few Aragonese and Andalusians I mixed only with Catalans—and not be struck by their essential decency; above all, their straightforwardness and generosity. A Spaniard's generosity, in the ordinary sense of the word, is at times almost embarrassing. If you ask him for a cigarette he will force the whole packet upon you. And beyond this there is generosity in a deeper sense, a real largeness of spirit, which I have met with again and again in the most unpromising circumstances. Some of the journalists and other foreigners who travelled in Spain during the war have declared that in secret the Spaniards were bitterly jealous of foreign aid. All I can say is that I never observed anything of the kind. I remember that a few days before I left the barracks a group of men returned on leave from the front. They were talking excitedly about their experiences and were full of enthusiasm for some French troops who had been next to them at Huesca. The French were very brave, they said; adding enthusiastically: "Más valientes que nosotros"—"Braver than we are!" Of course I demurred, whereupon they explained that the French knew more of the art of war—were more expert with bombs, machine-guns, and so forth. Yet the remark was significant. An Englishman would cut his hand off sooner than say a thing like that.

Every foreigner who served in the militia spent his first few weeks in learning to love the Spaniards and in being exasperated by certain of their characteristics. In the front line my own exasperation sometimes reached the pitch of fury. The Spaniards are good at many things, but not at making war. All foreigners alike are appalled by their inefficiency, above all their maddening unpunctuality. The one Spanish word that no foreigner can avoid learning is *mañana*—"tomorrow" (literally, "the morning"). Whenever it is conceivably possible, the business of today is put off until *mañana*. This is so notorious that even the Spaniards themselves make jokes about it. In Spain nothing, from a meal to a battle, ever happens at the appointed time. As a general rule things happen too late, but just occasionally—just so that you shan't even be able to depend on their happening late—they happen too early. A train which is due to leave at eight will normally leave at any time between nine and ten, but perhaps once a week, thanks to some private whim of the engine-driver, it leaves at half-past seven. Such things can be a little trying. In theory I rather admire the Spaniards for not sharing our Northern time-neurosis; but unfortunately I share it myself.

After endless rumours, *mañanas*, and delays we were suddenly ordered to the front at two hours' notice, when much of our equipment was still unissued. There were terrible tumults in the quartermaster's store; in the end numbers of men had to leave without their full equipment. The barracks had promptly filled with women who seemed to have sprung up from the ground and were helping their men-folk to roll their blankets and pack their kit-bags. It was rather humiliating that I had to be shown how to put on my new leather cartridge-boxes by a Spanish girl, the wife of Williams, the other English militiaman. She was a gentle, dark-eyed, intensely feminine creature who looked as though her life-work was to rock a cradle, but who as a matter of fact had fought bravely in the street-battles of July. At this time she was carrying a baby which was born just ten months after the outbreak of war and had perhaps been begotten behind a barricade.

The train was due to leave at eight, and it was about ten past eight when the harassed, sweating officers managed to marshal us in the barrack square. I remember very vividly the torchlit scene—the uproar and excitement, the red flags flapping in the torchlight, the massed ranks of militiamen with their knapsacks on their backs and their rolled blankets worn bandolier-wise across the shoulder; and the shouting and the clatter of boots and tin pannikins, and then a tremendous and finally successful hissing for silence; and then some political commissar standing beneath a huge rolling red banner and making us a speech in Catalan. Finally they marched us to the station, taking the longest route, three or four miles, so as to show us to the whole town. In the Ramblas they halted us while a borrowed band played some revolutionary tune or other. Once again the conquering-hero stuff—shouting and enthusiasm, red flags and red and black flags everywhere, friendly crowds thronging the pavement to have a look at us, women waving from the windows. How natural it all seemed then; how remote and improbable now! The train was packed so tight with men that there was barely room even on the floor, let alone on the seats. At the last moment Williams's wife came rushing down the platform and gave us a bottle of wine and a foot of that bright red sausage which tastes of soap and gives you diarrhoea. The train crawled out of Catalonia and on to the plateau of Aragon at the normal war-time speed of something under twenty kilometres an hour.

*   *   *

In trench warfare five things are important: firewood, food, tobacco, candles and the enemy. In winter on the Zaragoza front they were important in that order, with the enemy a bad last. Except at night, when a surprise-attack was always conceivable, nobody bothered about the enemy. They were simply remote black insects whom one occasionally saw hopping to and fro. The real preoccupation of both armies was trying to keep warm.

I ought to say in passing that all the time I was in Spain I saw very little fighting. I was on the Aragon front from January to May, and between January and late March little or nothing happened on that front, except at Teruel. In March there was heavy fighting round Huesca, but I personally played only a minor part in it. Later, in June, there was the disastrous attack on Huesca in which several thousand men were killed in a single day, but I had been wounded and disabled before that happened. The things that one normally thinks of as the horrors of war seldom happened to me. No aeroplane ever dropped a bomb anywhere near me, I do not think a shell ever exploded within fifty yards of me, and I was only in hand-to-hand fighting once (once is once too often, I may say). Of course I was often under heavy machine-gun fire, but usually at longish ranges. Even at Huesca you were generally safe enough if you took reasonable precautions.

Up here, in the hills round Zaragoza, it was simply the mingled boredom and discomfort of stationary warfare. A life as uneventful as a city clerk's, and almost as regular. Sentry-go, patrols, digging; digging, patrols, sentry-go. On every hill-top, Fascist or Loyalist, a knot of ragged, dirty men shivering round their flag and trying to keep warm. And all day and night the meaningless bullets wandering across the empty valleys and only by some rare improbable chance getting home on a human body.

Often I used to gaze round the wintry landscape and marvel at the futility of it all. The inconclusiveness of such a kind of war! Earlier, about October, there had been savage fighting for all these hills; then, because the lack of men and arms, especially artillery, made any large-scale operation impossible, each army had dug itself in and settled down on the hill-tops it had won. Over to our right there was a small outpost, also P.O.U.M., and on the spur to our left, at seven o'clock of us, a P.S.U.C. position faced a taller spur with several small Fascist posts dotted on its peaks. The so-called line zigzagged to and fro in a pattern that would have been quite unintelligible if every position had not flown a flag. The P.O.U.M. and P.S.U.C. flags were red, those of the Anarchists red and black; the Facists generally flew the monarchist flag (red-yellow-red), but occasionally they flew the flag of the Republic (red-yellow-purple). The scenery was stupendous, if you could forget that every mountain-top was occupied by troops and was therefore littered with tin cans and crusted with dung. To the right of us the sierra bent south-eastwards and made way for the wide, veined valley that stretched across to Huesca. In the middle of the plain a few tiny cubes sprawled like a throw of dice; this was the town of Robres, which was in

Loyalist possession. Often in the mornings the valley was hidden under seas of cloud, out of which the hills rose flat and blue, giving the landscape a strange resemblance to a photographic negative. Beyond Huesca there were more hills of the same formation as our own, streaked with a pattern of snow which altered day by day. In the far distance the monstrous peaks of the Pyrenees, where the snow never melts, seemed to float upon nothing. Even down in the plain everything looked dead and bare. The hills opposite us were grey and wrinkled like the skins of elephants. Almost always the sky was empty of birds. I do not think I have ever seen a country where there were so few birds. The only birds one saw at any time were a kind of magpie, and the coveys of partridges that startled one at night with their sudden whirring, and, very rarely, the flights of eagles that drifted slowly over, generally followed by rifleshots which they did not deign to notice.

At night and in misty weather patrols were sent out in the valley between ourselves and the Fascists. The job was not popular, it was too cold and too easy to get lost, and I soon found that I could get leave to go out on patrol as often as I wished. In the huge jagged ravines there were no paths or tracks of any kind; you could only find your way about by making successive journeys and noting fresh landmarks each time. As the bullet flies the nearest Fascist post was seven hundred metres from our own, but it was a mile and a half by the only practicable route. It was rather fun wandering about the dark valleys with the stray bullets flying high overhead like redshanks whistling. Better than nighttime were the heavy mists, which often lasted all day and which had a habit of clinging round the hill-tops and leaving the valleys clear. When you were anywhere near the Fascist lines you had to creep at a snail's pace; it was very difficult to move quietly on those hill-sides, among the crackling shrubs and tinkling limestones. It was only at the third or fourth attempt that I managed to find my way to the Fascist lines. The mist was very thick, and I crept up to the barbed wire to listen. I could hear the Fascists talking and singing inside. Then to my alarm I heard several of them coming down the hill towards me. I cowered behind a bush that suddenly seemed very small, and tried to cock my rifle without noise. However, they branched off and did not come within sight of me. Behind the bush where I was hiding I came upon various relics of the earlier fighting—a pile of empty cartridge-cases, a leather cap with a bullet-hole in it, and a red flag, obviously one of our own. I took it back to the position, where it was unsentimentally torn up for cleaning-rags.

I had been made a corporal, or *cabo*, as it was called, as soon as we reached the front, and was in command of a guard of twelve men. It was no sinecure, especially at first. The *centuria* was an untrained mob composed mostly of boys in their teens. Here and there in the militia you came across children as young as eleven or twelve, usually refugees from

Fascist territory who had been enlisted as militiamen as the easiest way of providing for them. As a rule they were employed on light work in the rear, but sometimes they managed to worm their way to the front line, where they were a public menace. I remember one little brute throwing a hand-grenade into the dug-out fire "for a joke." At Monte Pocero I do not think there was anyone younger than fifteen, but the average age must have been well under twenty. Boys of this age ought never to be used in the front line, because they cannot stand the lack of sleep which is inseparable from trench warfare. At the beginning it was almost impossible to keep our position properly guarded at night. The wretched children of my section could only be roused by dragging them out of their dug-outs feet foremost, and as soon as your back was turned they left their posts and slipped into shelter; or they would even, in spite of the frightful cold, lean up against the wall of the trench and fall fast asleep. Luckily the enemy were very unenterprising. There were nights when it seemed to me that our position could be stormed by twenty Boy Scouts armed with air-guns, or twenty Girl Guides armed with battledores, for that matter.

At this time and until much later the Catalan militias were still on the same basis as they had been at the beginning of the war. In the early days of Franco's revolt the militias had been hurriedly raised by the various trade unions and political parties; each was essentially a political organization, owing allegiance to its party as much as to the central Government. When the Popular Army, which was a "non-political" army organized on more or less ordinary lines, was raised at the beginning of 1937, the party militias were theoretically incorporated in it. But for a long time the only changes that occurred were on paper; the new Popular Army troops did not reach the Aragon front in any numbers till June, and until that time the militia-system remained unchanged. The essential point of the system was social equality between officers and men. Everyone from general to private drew the same pay, ate the same food, wore the same clothes, and mingled on terms of complete equality. If you wanted to slap the general commanding the division on the back and ask him for a cigarette, you could do so, and no one thought it curious. In theory at any rate each militia was a democracy and not a hierarchy. It was understood that orders had to be obeyed, but it was also understood that when you gave an order you gave it as comrade to comrade and not as superior to inferior. There were officers and N.C.O.s, but there was no military rank in the ordinary sense; no titles, no badges, no heel-clicking and saluting. They had attempted to produce within the militias a sort of temporary working model of the classless society. Of course there was not perfect equality, but there was a nearer approach to it than I had ever seen or than I would have thought conceivable in time of war.

But I admit that at first sight the state of affairs at the front horrified

me. How on earth could the war be won by an army of this type? It was
what everyone was saying at the time, and though it was true it was also
unreasonable. For in the circumstances the militias could not have been
much better than they were. A modern mechanized army does not
spring up out of the ground, and if the Government had waited until it
had trained troops at its disposal, Franco would never have been resisted.
Later it became the fashion to decry the militias, and therefore to pretend that the faults which were due to lack of training and weapons were
the result of the equalitarian system. Actually, a newly raised draft of
militia was an undisciplined mob not because the officers called the
privates "Comrade" but because raw troops are *always* an undisciplined
mob. In practice the democratic "revolutionary" type of discipline is
more reliable than might be expected. In a workers' army discipline is
theoretically voluntary. It is based on class-loyalty, whereas the discipline
of a bourgeois conscript army is based ultimately on fear. (The Popular
Army that replaced the militia was midway between the two types.) In
the militias the bullying and abuse that go on in an ordinary army would
never have been tolerated for a moment. The normal military punish-
ments existed, but they were only invoked for very serious offences.
When a man refused to obey an order you did not immediately get him
punished; you first appealed to him in the name of comradeship. Cynical
people with no experience of handling men will say instantly that this
would never "work," but as a matter of fact it does "work" in the long
run. The discipline of even the worst drafts of militia visibly improved as
time went on. In January the job of keeping a dozen raw recruits up to
the mark almost turned my hair grey. In May for a short while I was
acting-lieutenant in command of about thirty men, English and Spanish. We had all been under fire for months, and I never had the slightest
difficulty in getting an order obeyed or in getting men to volunteer for a
dangerous job. "Revolutionary" discipline depends on political consciousness—on an understanding of *why* orders must be obeyed; it takes
time to diffuse this, but it also takes time to drill a man into an automaton on the barrack-square. The journalists who sneered at the militia-
system seldom remembered that the militias had to hold the line while
the Popular Army was training in the rear. And it is a tribute to the
strength of "revolutionary" discipline that the militias stayed in the field
at all. For until about June 1937 there was nothing to keep them there,
except class loyalty. Individual deserters could be shot—were shot, occasionally—but if a thousand men had decided to walk out of the line
together there was no force to stop them. A conscript army in the same
circumstances—with its battle-police removed—would have melted
away. Yet the militias held the line, though God knows they won very
few victories, and even individual desertions were not common. In four

or five months in the P.O.U.M. militia I only heard of four men deserting, and two of those were fairly certainly spies who had enlisted to obtain information. At the beginning the apparent chaos, the general lack of training, the fact that you often had to argue for five minutes before you could get an order obeyed, appalled and infuriated me. I had British Army ideas, and certainly the Spanish militias were very unlike the British Army. But considering the circumstances they were better troops than one had any right to expect.

Meanwhile, firewood—always firewood. Throughout that period there is probably no entry in my diary that does not mention firewood, or rather the lack of it. We were between two and three thousand feet above sea-level, it was mid-winter and the cold was unspeakable. The temperature was not exceptionally low, on many nights it did not even freeze, and the wintry sun often shone for an hour in the middle of the day; but even if it was not really cold, I assure you that it seemed so. Sometimes there were shrieking winds that tore your cap off and twisted your hair in all directions, sometimes there were mists that poured into the trench like a liquid and seemed to penetrate your bones; frequently it rained, and even a quarter of an hour's rain was enough to make conditions intolerable. The thin skin of earth over the limestone turned promptly into a slippery grease, and as you were always walking on a slope it was impossible to keep your footing. On dark nights I have often fallen half a dozen times in twenty yards; and this was dangerous, because it meant that the lock of one's rifle became jammed with mud. For days together clothes, boots, blankets, and rifles were more or less coated with mud. I had brought as many thick clothes as I could carry, but many of the men were terribly underclad. For the whole garrison, about a hundred men, there were only twelve great-coats, which had to be handed from sentry to sentry, and most of the men had only one blanket. One icy night I made a list in my diary of the clothes I was wearing. It is of some interest as showing the amount of clothes the human body can carry. I was wearing a thick vest and pants, a flannel shirt, two pull-overs, a woollen jacket, a pigskin jacket, corduroy breeches, puttees, thick socks, boots, a stout trench-coat, a muffler, lined leather gloves, and a woollen cap. Nevertheless I was shivering like a jelly. But I admit I am unusually sensitive to cold.

Firewood was the one thing that really mattered. The point about the firewood was that there was practically no firewood to be had. Our miserable mountain had not even at its best much vegetation, and for months it had been ranged over by freezing militiamen, with the result that everything thicker than one's finger had long since been burnt. When we were not eating, sleeping, on guard or on fatigue-duty we were in the valley behind the position, scrounging for fuel. All my memories of that time are memories of scrambling up and down the almost perpendicular slopes, over the jagged limestone that knocked one's boots to pieces, pouncing eagerly on tiny twigs of wood. Three people searching for a couple of hours could collect enough fuel to keep the dug-out fire alight for about an hour. The eagerness of our search for firewood turned us all into botanists. We classified according to their burning qualities every plant that grew on the mountain-side; the various heaths and grasses that were good to start a fire with but burnt out in a few minutes, the wild rosemary and the tiny whin bushes that would burn when the fire was well alight, the stunted oak tree, smaller than a gooseberry bush, that was practically unburnable. There was a kind of dried-up reed that was very good for starting fires with, but these grew only on the hill-top to the left of the position, and you had to go under fire to get them. If the Fascist machine-gunners saw you they gave you a drum of ammunition all to yourself. Generally their aim was high and the bullets sang overhead like birds, but sometimes they crackled and chipped the limestone uncomfortably close, whereupon you flung yourself on your face. You went on gathering reeds, however; nothing mattered in comparison with firewood.

Beside the cold the other discomforts seemed petty. Of course all of us were permanently dirty. Our water, like our food, came on mule-back from Alcubierre, and each man's share worked out at about a quart a day. It was beastly water, hardly more transparent than milk. Theoretically it was for drinking only, but I always stole a pannikinful for washing in the mornings. I used to wash one day and shave the next; there was never enough water for both. The position stank abominably, and outside the little enclosure of the barricade there was excrement everywhere. Some of the militiamen habitually defecated in the trench, a disgusting thing when one had to walk round it in the darkness. But the dirt never worried me. Dirt is a thing people make too much fuss about. It is astonishing how quickly you get used to doing without a handkerchief and to eating out of the tin pannikin in which you also wash. Nor was sleeping in one's clothes any hardship after a day or two. It was of course impossible to take one's clothes and especially one's boots off at night; one had to be ready to turn out instantly in case of an attack. In eighty nights I only took my clothes off three times, though I did occasionally manage to get them off in the daytime. It was too cold for lice as yet, but rats and mice abounded. It is often said that you don't find rats and mice in the same place, but you do when there is enough food for them.

In other ways we were not badly off. The food was good enough and there was plenty of wine. Cigarettes were still being issued at the rate of a packet a day, matches were issued every other day, and there was even an issue of candles. They were very thin candles, like those on a Christmas cake, and were popularly supposed to have been looted from churches. Every dug-out was issued daily with three inches of candle, which would burn for about twenty minutes. At that time it was still possible to buy candles, and I had brought several pounds of them with me. Later on the famine of matches and candles made life a misery. You do not realize the importance of these things until you lack them. In a night-alarm, for instance, when everyone in the dug-out is scrambling for his rifle and treading on everybody else's face, being able to strike a light may make the difference between life and death. Every militiaman possessed a tinder-lighter and several yards of yellow wick. Next to his rifle it was his most important possession. The tinder-lighters had the great advantage that they could be struck in a wind, but they would only smoulder, so that they were no use for lighting a fire. When the match famine was at its worst our only way of producing a flame was to pull the bullet out of a cartridge and touch the cordite off with a tinder-lighter.

It was an extraordinary life that we were living—an extraordinary way to be at war, if you could call it war. The whole militia chafed against the inaction and clamoured constantly to know why we were not allowed to attack. But it was perfectly obvious that there would be no battle for a long while yet, unless the enemy started it. Georges Kopp, on his periodical tours of inspection, was quite frank with us. "This is not a war," he used to say, "it is a comic opera with an occasional death." As a matter of fact the stagnation on the Aragon front had political causes of which I knew nothing at that time; but the purely military difficulties—quite apart from the lack of reserves of men—were obvious to anybody.

To begin with, there was the nature of the country. The front line, ours and the Fascists', lay in positions of immense natural strength, which as a rule could only be approached from one side. Provided a few trenches have been dug, such places cannot be taken by infantry, except in overwhelming numbers. In our own position or most of those round us a dozen men with two machine-guns could have held off a battalion. Perched on the hill-tops as we were, we should have made lovely marks for artillery; but there was no artillery. Sometimes I used to gaze round the landscape and long—oh, how passionately!—for a couple of batteries of guns. One could have destroyed the enemy positions one after another as easily as smashing nuts with a hammer. But on our side the guns simply did not exist. The Fascists did occasionally manage to bring a gun or two from Zaragoza and fire a very few shells, so few that they never even found the range and the shells plunged harmlessly into the empty ravines. Against machine-guns and without artillery there are only three things you can do: dig yourself in at a safe distance—four hundred yards, say—advance across the open and be massacred, or make small-scale night-attacks that will not alter the general situation. Practically the alternatives are stagnation or suicide.

And beyond this there was the complete lack of war materials of every description. It needs an effort to realize how badly the militias were armed at this time. Any public school O.T.C. in England is far more like a modern army than we were. The badness of our weapons was so astonishing that it is worth recording in detail.

For this sector of the front the entire artillery consisted of four trench-mortars with *fifteen rounds* for each gun. Of course they were far too precious to be fired and the mortars were kept in Alcubierre. There were machine-guns at the rate of approximately one to fifty men; they were oldish guns, but fairly accurate up to three or four hundred yards. Beyond this we had only rifles, and the majority of the rifles were scrap-iron. There were three types of rifle in use. The first was the long Mauser. These were seldom less than twenty years old, their sights were about as much use as a broken speedometer, and in most of them the rifling was hopelessly corroded; about one rifle in ten was not bad, however. Then there was the short Mauser, or *mousqueton*, really a cavalry weapon. These were more popular than the others because they were lighter to carry and less nuisance in a trench, also because they were comparatively new and looked efficient. Actually they were almost useless. They were made out of reassembled parts, no bolt belonged to its rifle, and three-quarters of them could be counted on to jam after five shots. There were also a few Winchester rifles. These were nice to shoot with, but they were wildly inaccurate, and as their cartridges had no clips they could only be fired one shot at a time. Ammunition was so scarce that each man entering the line was only issued with fifty rounds, and most of it was exceedingly bad. The Spanish-made cartridges were all refills and would jam even the best rifles. The Mexican cartridges were better and were therefore reserved for the machine-guns. Best of all was the German-made ammunition, but as this came only from prisoners and deserters there was not much of it. I always kept a clip of German or Mexican ammunition in my pocket for use in an emergency. But in practice when the emergency came I seldom fired my rifle; I was too frightened of the beastly thing jamming and too anxious to reserve at any rate one round that would go off.

We had no tin hats, no bayonets, hardly any revolvers or pistols, and not more than one bomb between five or ten men. The bomb in use at this time was a frightful object known as the "F.A.I. bomb," it having been produced by the Anarchists in the early days of the war. It was on the principle of a Mills bomb, but the lever was held down not by a pin but a piece of tape. You broke the tape and then got rid of the bomb with the utmost possible speed. It was said of these bombs that they were "impartial"; they killed the man they were thrown at and the man who threw them. There were several other types, even more primitive but probably a little less dangerous—to the thrower, I mean. It was not till late March that I saw a bomb worth throwing.

And apart from weapons there was a shortage of all the minor necessities of war. We had no maps or charts, for instance. Spain has never been fully surveyed, and the only detailed maps of this area were the old military ones, which were almost all in the possession of the Fascists. We had no range-finders, no telescopes, no periscopes, no field-glasses except a few privately-owned pairs, no flares or Very lights, no wire-cutters, no armourers' tools, hardly even any cleaning materials. The Spaniards seemed never to have heard of a pull-through and looked on in surprise when I constructed one. When you wanted your rifle cleaned you took it to the sergeant, who possessed a long brass ramrod which was invariably bent and therefore scratched the rifling. There was not even any gun oil. You greased your rifle with olive oil, when you could get hold of it; at different times I have greased mine with vaseline, with cold cream, and even with bacon-fat. Moreover, there were no lanterns or electric torches—at this time there was not, I believe, such a thing as an electric torch throughout the whole of our sector of the front, and you could not buy one nearer than Barcelona, and only with difficulty even there.

As time went on, and the desultory rifle-fire rattled among the hills, I began to wonder with increasing scepticism whether anything would ever happen to bring a bit of life, or rather a bit of death, into this cock-eyed war. It was pneumonia that we were fighting against, not against men. When the trenches are more than five hundred yards apart no one gets hit except by accident. Of course there were casualties, but the majority of them were self-inflicted. If I remember rightly, the first five men I saw wounded in Spain were all wounded by our own weapons—I don't mean intentionally, but owing to accident or carelessness. Our worn-out rifles were a danger in themselves. Some of them had a nasty trick of going off if the butt was tapped on the ground; I saw a man shoot himself through the hand owing to this. And in the darkness the raw recruits were always firing at one another. One evening when it was barely even dusk a sentry let fly at me from a distance of twenty yards; but he missed me by a yard—goodness knows how many times the Spanish standard of marksmanship has saved my life. Another time I had gone out on patrol in the mist and had carefully warned the guard commander beforehand. But in coming back I stumbled against a bush, the startled sentry called out that the Fascists were coming, and I had the pleasure of hearing the guard commander order everyone to open rapid fire in my direction. Of course I lay down and the bullets went harmlessly over me. Nothing will convince a Spaniard, at least a young Spaniard, that fire-arms are dangerous. Once, rather later than this, I was photographing some machine-gunners with their gun, which was pointed directly towards me.

"Don't fire," I said half-jokingly as I focused the camera.

"Oh, no, we won't fire."

The next moment there was a frightful roar and a stream of bullets tore past my face so close that my cheek was stung by grains of cordite. It was unintentional, but the machine-gunners considered it a great joke. Yet only a few days earlier they had seen a mule-driver accidentally shot by a political delegate who was playing the fool with an automatic pistol and had put five bullets in the mule-driver's lungs.

The difficult passwords which the army was using at this time were a minor source of danger. They were those tiresome double passwords in which one word has to be answered by another. Usually they were of an elevating and revolutionary nature, such as *Cultura—progreso,* or *Seremos—invencibles,* and it was often impossible to get illiterate sentries to remember these highfalutin words. One night, I remember, the password was *Cataluña—heroica,* and a moon-faced peasant lad named Jaime Domenech approached me, greatly puzzled, and asked me to explain.

"Heroica—what does heroica mean?"

I told him that it meant the same as valiente. A little while later he was stumbling up the trench in the darkness, and the sentry challenged him:

"Alto! Cataluña!"

"Valiente!" yelled Jamie, certain that he was saying the right thing. Bang!

However, the sentry missed him. In this war everyone always did miss everyone else, when it was humanly possible.

* * *

One afternoon Benjamin told us that he wanted fifteen volunteers. The attack on the Fascist redoubt which had been called off on the previous occasion was to be carried out tonight. I oiled my ten Mexican cartridges, dirtied my bayonet (the things give your position away if they flash too much), and packed up a hunk of bread, three inches of red sausage, and a cigar which my wife had sent from Barcelona and which I had been hoarding for a long time. Bombs were served out, three to a man. The Spanish Government had at last succeeded in producing a decent bomb. It was on the principle of a Mills bomb, but with two pins instead of one. After you had pulled the pins out there was an interval of seven seconds before the bomb exploded. Its chief disadvantage was that one pin was very stiff and the other very loose, so that you had the choice of leaving both pins in place and being unable to pull the stiff one out in a moment of emergency, or pulling out the stiff one beforehand and being in a constant stew lest the thing should explode in your pocket. But it was a handy little bomb to throw.

A little before midnight Benjamin led the fifteen of us down to Torre Fabian. Ever since evening the rain had been pelting down. The irrigation ditches were brimming over, and every time you stumbled into one you were in water up to your waist. In the pitch darkness and sheeting rain in the farm-yard a dim mass of men was waiting. Kopp addressed us, first in Spanish, then in English, and explained the plan of attack. The Fascist line here made an L-bend and the parapet we were to attack lay on rising ground at the corner of the L. About thirty of us, half English and half Spanish, under the command of Jorge Roca, our battalion commander (a battalion in the militia was about four hundred men), and Benjamin, were to creep up and cut the Fascist wire. Jorge would fling the first bomb as a signal, then the rest of us were to send in a rain of bombs, drive the Fascists out of the parapet and seize it before they could rally. Simultaneously seventy Shock Troopers were to assault the next Fascist "position," which lay two hundred yards to the right of the other, joined to it by a communication-trench. To prevent us from shooting each other in the darkness white armlets would be worn. At this moment a messenger arrived to say that there were no white armlets. Out of the darkness a plaintive voice suggested: "Couldn't we arrange for the Fascists to wear white armlets instead?"

There was an hour or two to put in. The barn over the mule stable was so wrecked by shell-fire that you could not move about in it without a light. Half the floor had been torn away by a plunging shell and there was a twenty-foot drop on to the stones beneath. Someone found a pick and levered a burst plank out of the floor, and in a few minutes we had got a fire alight and our drenched clothes were steaming. Someone else produced a pack of cards. A rumour—one of those mysterious rumours that are endemic in war—flew round that hot coffee with brandy in it was about to be served out. We filed eagerly down the almost-collapsing staircase and wandered round the dark yard, enquiring where the coffee was to be found. Alas! there was no coffee. Instead, they called us together, ranged us into single file, and then Jorge and Benjamin set off rapidly into the darkness, the rest of us following.

It was still raining and intensely dark, but the wind had dropped. The mud was unspeakable. The paths through the beet-fields were simply a succession of lumps, as slippery as a greasy pole, with huge pools everywhere. Long before we got to the place where we were to leave our own parapet everyone had fallen several times and our rifles were coated with mud. At the parapet a small knot of men, our reserves, were waiting, and the doctor and a row of stretchers. We filed through the gap in the parapet and waded through another irrigation ditch. Splash-gurgle! Once again in water up to your waist, with the filthy, slimy mud oozing over your boot-tops. On the grass outside Jorge waited till we were all through. Then, bent almost double, he began creeping slowly forward. The Fascist parapet was about a hundred and fifty yards away. Our one chance of getting there was to move without noise.

I was in front with Jorge and Benjamin. Bent double, but with faces raised, we crept into the almost utter darkness at a pace that grew slower at every step. The rain beat lightly in our faces. When I glanced back I could see the men who were nearest to me, a bunch of humped shapes like huge black mushrooms gliding slowly forward. But every time I raised my head Benjamin, close beside me, whispered fiercely in my ear: "To keep ze head down! To keep ze head down!" I could have told him that he needn't worry. I knew by experiment that on a dark night you can never see a man at twenty paces. It was far more important to go quietly. If they once heard us we were done for. They had only to spray the darkness with their machine-gun and there was nothing for it but to run or be massacred.

But on the sodden ground it was almost impossible to move quietly. Do what you would your feet stuck to the mud, and every step you took was slop-slop, slop-slop. And the devil of it was that the wind had dropped, and in spite of the rain it was a very quiet night. Sounds would carry a long way. There was a dreadful moment when I kicked against a tin and thought every Fascist within miles must have heard it. But no, not a sound, no answering shot, no movement in the Fascist lines. We crept onwards, always more slowly. I cannot convey to you the depth of my desire to get there. Just to get within bombing distance before they heard us! At such a time you have not even any fear, only a tremendous hopeless longing to get over the intervening ground. I have felt exactly the same thing when stalking a wild animal; the same agonized desire to get within range, the same dreamlike certainty that it is impossible. And how the distance stretched out! I knew the ground well, it was barely a hundred and fifty yards, and yet it seemed more like a mile. When you are creeping at that pace you are aware as an ant might be of the enormous variations in the ground; the splendid patch of smooth grass here, the evil patch of sticky mud there, the tall rustling reeds that have got to be avoided, the heap of stones that almost makes you give up hope because it seems impossible to get over it without noise.

We had been creeping forward for such an age that I began to think we had gone the wrong way. Then in the darkness thin parallel lines of something blacker were faintly visible. It was the outer wire (the Fascists had two lines of wire). Jorge knelt down, fumbled in his pocket. He had our only pair of wire-cutters. Snip, snip. The trailing stuff was lifted delicately aside. We waited for the men at the back to close up. They seemed to be making a frightful noise. It might be fifty yards to the Fascist parapet now. Still onwards, bent double. A stealthy step, lowering your foot as gently as a cat approaching a mousehole; then a pause to listen; then another step. Once I raised my head; in silence Benjamin put his hand behind my neck and pulled it violently down. I knew that the inner wire was barely twenty yards from the parapet. It seemed to me inconceivable that thirty men could get there unheard. Our breathing was enough to give us away. Yet somehow we did get there. The Fascist parapet was visible now, a dim black mound, looming high above us. Once again Jorge knelt and fumbled. Snip, snip. There was no way of cutting the stuff silently.

So that was the inner wire. We crawled through it on all fours and rather more rapidly. If we had time to deploy now all was well. Jorge and Benjamin crawled across to the right. But the men behind, who were spread out, had to form into single file to get through the narrow gap in the wire, and just at this moment there was a flash and a bang from the Fascist parapet. The sentry had heard us at last. Jorge poised himself on one knee and swung his arm like a bowler. Crash! His bomb burst somewhere over the parapet. At once, far more promptly than one would have thought possible, a roar of fire, ten or twenty rifles, burst out from the Fascist parapet. They had been waiting for us after all. Momentarily you could see every sandbag in the lurid light. Men too far back were flinging their bombs and some of them were falling short of the parapet. Every loophole seemed to be spouting jets of flame. It is always hateful to be shot at in the dark—every rifle-flash seems to be pointed straight at yourself—but it was the bombs that were the worst. You cannot conceive the horror of these things till you have seen one burst close to you and in darkness; in the daytime there is only the crash of explosion, in the darkness there is the blinding red glare as well. I had flung myself down at the first volley. All this while I was lying on my side in the greasy mud, wrestling savagely with the pin of a bomb. The damned thing *would* not come out. Finally I realized that I was twisting it in the wrong direction. I got the pin out, rose to my knees, hurled the bomb, and threw myself down again. The bomb burst over to the right, outside the parapet; fright had spoiled my aim. Just at this moment another bomb burst right in front of me, so close that I could feel the heat of the explosion. I flattened myself out and dug my face into the mud so hard that I hurt my neck and thought that I was wounded. Through the din I heard an English voice behind me say quietly: "I'm hit." The bomb had, in fact, wounded several people round about me without touching myself. I rose to my knees and flung my second bomb. I forget where that one went.

The Fascists were firing, our people behind were firing, and I was very conscious of being in the middle. I felt the blast of a shot and realized that a man was firing from immediately behind me. I stood up and shouted at him: "Don't shoot at me, you bloody fool!" At this moment I saw that Benjamin, ten or fifteen yards to my right, was motioning to me with his arm. I ran across to him. It meant crossing the line of spouting loopholes, and as I went I clapped my left hand over my cheek; an idiotic gesture—as though one's hand could stop a bullet!—but I had a horror of being hit in the face. Benjamin was kneeling on one knee with a pleased, devilish sort of expression on his face and firing carefully at the rifle-flashes with his automatic pistol. Jorge had dropped wounded at the first volley and was somewhere out of sight. I knelt beside Benjamin, pulled the pin out of my third bomb and flung it. Ah! No doubt about it that time. The bomb crashed inside the parapet, at the corner, just by the machine-gun nest.

The Fascist fire seemed to have slackened very suddenly. Benjamin leapt to his feet and shouted: "Forward! Charge!" We dashed up the short steep slope on which the parapet stood. I say "dashed"; "lumbered" would be a better word; the fact is that you can't move fast when you are sodden and mudded from head to foot and weighted down with a heavy rifle and bayonet and a hundred and fifty cartridges. I took it for granted that there would be a Fascist waiting for me at the top. If he fired at that range he could not miss me, and yet somehow I never expected him to fire, only to try for me with his bayonet. I seemed to feel in advance the sensation of our bayonets crossing, and I wondered whether his arm would be stronger than mine. However, there was no Fascist waiting. With a vague feeling of relief I found that it was a low parapet and the sandbags gave a good foothold. As a rule they are difficult to get over. Everything inside was smashed to pieces, beams flung all over the place, and great shards of uralite littered everywhere. Our bombs had wrecked all the huts and dug-outs. And still there was not a soul visible. I thought they would be lurking somewhere underground, and shouted in English (I could not think of any Spanish at the moment): "Come on out of it! Surrender!" No answer. Then a man, a shadowy figure in the half-light, skipped over the roof of one of the ruined huts and dashed away to the left. I started after him, prodding my bayonet ineffectually into the darkness. As I rounded the corner of the hut I saw a man—I don't know whether or not it was the same man as I had seen before—fleeing up the communication-trench that led to the other Fascist position. I must have been very close to him, for I could see him clearly. He was bareheaded and seemed to have nothing on except a blanket which he was clutching round his shoulders. If I had fired I could have blown him to pieces. But for fear of shooting one another we had been ordered to use only bayonets once we were inside the parapet, and in any case I never even thought of firing. Instead, my mind leapt backwards twenty years, to our boxing instructor at school, showing me in vivid pantomime how he had bayoneted a Turk at the Dardanelles. I gripped my rifle by the small of the butt and lunged at the man's back. He was just out of my reach. Another lunge: still out of reach. And for a little distance we proceeded like this, he rushing up the trench and I after him on the ground above, prodding at his shoulder-blades and never quite getting there—a comic memory for me to look back upon, though I suppose it seemed less comic to him.

Of course, he knew the ground better than I and had soon slipped away from me. When I came back the position was full of shouting men. The noise of firing had lessened somewhat. The Fascists were still pouring a heavy fire at us from three sides, but it was coming from a greater distance. We had driven them back for the time being. I remember saying in an oracular manner: "We can hold this place for half an hour, not more." I don't know why I picked on half an hour. Looking over the right-hand parapet you could see innumerable greenish rifle-flashes stabbing the darkness; but they were a long way back, a hundred or two hundred yards. Our job now was to search the position and loot anything that was worth looting. Benjamin and some others were already scrabbling among the ruins of a big hut or dug-out in the middle of the position. Benjamin staggered excitedly through the ruined roof, tugging at the rope handle of an ammunition box.

"Comrades! Ammunition! Plenty ammunition here!"

"We don't want ammunition," said a voice, "we want rifles."

This was true. Half our rifles were jammed with mud and unusable. They could be cleaned, but it is dangerous to take the bolt out of a rifle in the darkness; you put it down somewhere and then you lose it. I had a tiny electric torch which my wife had managed to buy in Barcelona, otherwise we had no light of any description among us. A few men with good rifles began a desultory fire at the flashes in the distance. No one dared fire too rapidly; even the best of the rifles were liable to jam if they got too hot. There were about sixteen of us inside the parapet, including one or two who were wounded. A number of wounded, English and Spanish, were lying outside. Patrick O'Hara, a Belfast Irishman who had had some training in first-aid, went to and fro with packets of bandages, binding up the wounded men and, of course, being shot at every time he returned to the parapet, in spite of his indignant shouts of "Poum!"

We began searching the position. There were several dead men lying about, but I did not stop to examine them. The thing I was after was the machine-gun. All the while when we were lying outside I had been wondering vaguely why the gun did not fire. I flashed my torch inside the machine-gun nest. A bitter disappointment! The gun was not there. Its tripod was there, and various boxes of ammunition and spare parts, but the gun was gone. They must have unscrewed it and carried it off at the first alarm. No doubt they were acting under orders, but it was a stupid and cowardly thing to do, for if they had kept the gun in place they could have slaughtered the whole lot of us. We were furious. We had set our hearts on capturing a machine-gun.

We poked here and there but did not find anything of much value. There were quantities of Fascist bombs lying about—a rather inferior type of bomb, which you touched off by pulling a string—and I put a couple of them in my pocket as souvenirs. It was impossible not to be struck by the bare misery of the Fascist dug-outs. The litter of spare clothes, books, food, petty personal belongings that you saw in our own dug-outs was completely absent; these poor unpaid conscripts seemed to own nothing except blankets and a few soggy hunks of bread. Up at the far end there was a small dug-out which was partly above ground and had a tiny window. We flashed the torch through the window and instantly raised a cheer. A cylindrical object in a leather case, four feet high and six inches in diameter, was leaning against the wall. Obviously the machine-gun barrel. We dashed round and got in at the doorway, to find that the thing in the leather case was not a machine-gun but something which, in our weapon-starved army, was even more precious. It was an enormous telescope, probably of at least sixty or seventy magnifications, with a folding tripod. Such telescopes simply did not exist on our side of the line and they were desperately needed. We brought it out in triumph and leaned it against the parapet, to be carried off later.

At this moment someone shouted that the Fascists were closing in. Certainly the din of firing had grown very much louder. But it was obvious that the Fascists would not counter-attack from the right, which meant crossing no man's land and assaulting their own parapet. If they had any sense at all they would come at us from inside the line. I went round to the other side of the dug-outs. The position was roughly horseshoe-shaped, with the dug-outs in the middle, so that we had another parapet covering us on the left. A heavy fire was coming from that direction, but it did not matter greatly. The danger-spot was straight in front, where there was no protection at all. A stream of bullets was passing just overhead. They must be coming from the other Fascist position farther up the line; evidently the Shock Troopers had not captured it after all. But this time the noise was deafening. It was the unbroken, drum-like roar of massed rifles which I was used to hearing from a little distance; this was the first time I had been in the middle of it. And by now, of course, the firing had spread along the line for miles around. Douglas Thompson, with a wounded arm dangling useless at his side, was leaning against the parapet and firing one-handed at the flashes. Someone whose rifle had jammed was loading for him.

There were four or five of us round this side. It was obvious what we must do. We must drag the sand-bags from the front parapet and make a barricade across the unprotected side. And we had got to be quick. The fire was high at present, but they might lower it at any moment; by the flashes all round I could see that we had a hundred or two hundred men against us. We began wrenching the sand-bags loose, carrying them twenty yards forward and dumping them into a rough heap. It was a vile job. They were big sand-bags, weighing a hundredweight each and it took every ounce of your strength to prise them loose; and then the rotten sacking split and the damp earth cascaded all over you, down your neck and up your sleeves. I remember feeling a deep horror at everything: the chaos, the darkness, the frightful din, the slithering to and fro in the mud, the struggles with the bursting sand-bags—all the time encumbered with my rifle, which I dared not put down for fear of losing it. I even shouted to someone as we staggered along with a bag between us: "This is war! Isn't it bloody?" Suddenly a succession of tall figures came leaping over the front parapet. As they came nearer we saw that they wore the uniform of the Shock Troopers, and we cheered, thinking they were reinforcements. However, there were only four of them, three Germans and a Spaniard. We heard afterwards what had happened to the Shock Troopers. They did not know the ground and in the darkness had been led to the wrong place, where they were caught on the Fascist wire and numbers of them were shot down. These were four who had got lost, luckily for themselves. The Germans did not speak a word of English, French, or Spanish. With difficulty and much gesticulation we explained what we were doing and got them to help us in building the barricade.

The Fascists had brought up a machine-gun now. You could see it spitting like a squib a hundred or two hundred yards away; the bullets came over us with a steady, frosty crackle. Before long we had flung enough sand-bags into place to make a low breastwork behind which the few men who were on this side of the position could lie down and fire. I was kneeling behind them. A mortar-shell whizzed over and crashed somewhere in no man's land. That was another danger, but it would take them some minutes to find our range. Now that we had finished wrestling with those beastly sand-bags it was not bad fun in a way; the noise, the darkness, the flashes approaching, our own men blazing back at the flashes. One even had time to think a little. I remember wondering whether I was frightened, and deciding that I was not. Outside, where I was probably in less danger, I had been half sick with fright. Suddenly there was another shout that the Fascists were closing in. There was no doubt about it this time, the rifle-flashes were much nearer. I saw a flash hardly twenty yards away. Obviously they were working their way up the communication-trench. At twenty yards they were within easy bombing range; there were eight or nine of us bunched together and a single well-placed bomb would blow us all to fragments. Bob Smillie, the blood running down his face from a small wound, sprang to his knee and flung a bomb. We cowered, waiting for the crash. The fuse fizzled red as it sailed through the air, but the bomb failed to explode. (At least a quarter of these bombs were duds.) I had no bombs left except the Fascist ones and I was not certain how these worked. I shouted to the others to know if anyone had a bomb to spare. Douglas Moyle felt in his pocket and passed one across. I flung it and threw myself on my face. By one of those strokes of luck that happen about once in a year I had managed to drop the bomb almost exactly where the rifle had flashed. There was the roar of the explosion and then, instantly, a diabolical outcry of screams and groans. We had got one of them, anyway; I don't know whether he was killed, but certainly he was badly hurt. Poor wretch, poor wretch! I felt a vague sorrow as I heard him screaming. But at the same instant, in the dim light of the rifle-flashes, I saw or thought I saw a figure standing near the place where the rifle had flashed. I threw up my rifle and let fly. Another scream, but I think it was still the effect of the bomb. Several more bombs were thrown. The next rifle-flashes we saw were a long way off, a hundred yards or more. So we had driven them back, temporarily at least.

Everyone began cursing and saying why the hell didn't they send us some supports. With a sub-machine-gun or twenty men with clean rifles we could hold this place against a battalion. At this moment Paddy Donovan, who was second-in-command to Benjamin and had been sent back for orders, climbed over the front parapet.

"Hi! Come on out of it! All men to retire at once!"

"What?"

"Retire! Get out of it!"

"Why?"

"Orders. Back to our own lines double-quick."

People were already climbing over the front parapet. Several of them were struggling with a heavy ammunition box. My mind flew to the telescope which I had left leaning against the parapet on the other side of the position. But at this moment I saw that the four Shock Troopers, acting I suppose on some mysterious orders they had received beforehand, had begun running up the communication-trench. It led to the other Fascist position and—if they got there—to certain death. They were disappearing into the darkness. I ran after them, trying to think of the Spanish for "retire"; finally I shouted, "Atrás! Atrás!", which perhaps conveyed the right meaning. The Spaniard understood it and brought the others back. Paddy was waiting at the parapet.

"Come on, hurry up."

"But the telescope!"

"B—— the telescope! Benjamin's waiting outside."

We climbed out. Paddy held the wire aside for me. As soon as we got away from the shelter of the Fascist parapet we were under a devilish fire that seemed to be coming at us from every direction. Part of it, I do not doubt, came from our own side, for everyone was firing all along the line. Whichever way we turned a fresh stream of bullets swept past; we were driven this way and that in the darkness like a flock of sheep. It did not make it any easier that we were dragging a captured box of ammunition—one of those boxes that hold 1,750 rounds and weigh about a hundredweight—besides a box of bombs and several Fascist rifles. In a few minutes, although the distance from parapet to parapet was not two hundred yards and most of us knew the ground, we were completely lost. We found ourselves slithering about in a muddy field, knowing nothing except that bullets were coming from both sides. There was no moon to go by, but the sky was growing a little lighter. Our lines lay east of Huesca; I wanted to stay where we were till the first crack of dawn showed us which was east and which was west; but the others were against it. We slithered onwards, changing our direction several times and taking it in turns to haul at the ammunition-box. At last we saw the low flat line of a parapet looming in front of us. It might be ours or it might be the Fascists'; nobody had the dimmest idea which way we were going. Benjamin crawled on his belly through some tall whitish weed till he was about twenty yards from the parapet and tried a challenge. A shout of "Poum!" answered him. We jumped to our feet, found our way along the parapet, slopped once more through the irrigation ditch—splash-gurgle!—and were in safety.

Kopp was waiting inside the parapet with a few Spaniards. The doctor and the stretchers were gone. It appeared that all the wounded had been got in except Jorge and one of our own men, Hiddlestone by name, who were missing. Kopp was pacing up and down, very pale. Even the fat folds at the back of his neck were pale; he was paying no attention to the bullets that streamed over the low parapet and cracked close to his head. Most of us were squatting behind the parapet for cover. Kopp was muttering. "Jorge! Congo! Jorge!" And then in English. "If Jorge is gone it is terreeble, terreeble!" Jorge was his personal friend and one of his best officers. Suddenly he turned to us and asked for five volunteers, two English and three Spanish, to go and look for the missing men. Moyle and I volunteered with three Spaniards.

As we got outside the Spaniards murmured that it was getting dangerously light. This was true enough; the sky was dimly blue. There was a tremendous noise of excited voices coming from the Fascist redoubt. Evidently they had reoccupied the place in much greater force than before. We were sixty or seventy yards from the parapet when they must have seen or heard us, for they sent over a heavy burst of fire which made us drop on our faces. One of them flung a bomb over the parapet—a sure sign of panic. We were lying in the grass, waiting for an opportunity to move on, when we either heard or thought we heard—I have no doubt it was pure imagination, but it seemed real enough at the time—that the Fascist voices were much closer. They had left the parapet and were coming after us. "Run!" I yelled to Moyle, and jumped to my feet. And heavens, how I ran! I had thought earlier in the night that you can't run when you are sodden from head to foot and weighted down with a rifle and cartridges; I learned now you can *always* run when you think you have fifty or a hundred armed men after you. But if I could run fast, others could run faster. In my flight something that might have been a shower of meteors sped past me. It was the three Spaniards, who had been in front. They were back to our own parapet before they stopped and I could catch up with them. The truth was that our nerves were all to pieces. I knew, however, that in a half light one man is invisible where five are clearly visible, so I went back alone. I managed to get to the outer wire and searched the ground as well as I could, which was not very well, for I had to lie on my belly. There was no sign of Jorge or Hiddlestone, so I crept back. We learned afterwards that both Jorge and Hiddlestone had been taken to the dressing-station earlier. Jorge was lightly wounded through the shoulder. Hiddlestone had received a dreadful wound—a bullet which travelled right up his left arm, breaking the bone in several places; as he lay helpless on the ground a bomb had burst near him and torn various other parts of his body. He recovered, I am glad to say. Later he told me that he had worked his way some distance lying on his back, then had clutched hold of a wounded Spaniard and they had helped one another in.

It was getting light now. Along the line for miles around a ragged meaningless fire was thundering, like the rain that goes on raining after a storm. I remember the desolate look of everything, the morasses of mud, the weeping poplar trees, the yellow water in the trench-bottoms; and men's exhausted faces, unshaven, streaked with mud and blackened to the eyes with smoke. When I got back to my dug-out the three men I shared it with were already fast asleep. They had flung themselves down with all their equipment on and their muddy rifles clutched against them. Everything was sodden, inside the dug-out as well as outside. By long searching I managed to collect enough chips of dry wood to make a tiny fire. Then I smoked the cigar which I had been hoarding and which, surprisingly enough, had not got broken during the night.

Afterwards we learned that the action had been a success, as such things go. It was merely a raid to make the Fascists divert troops from the other side of Huesca, where the Anarchists were attacking again. I had judged that the Fascists had thrown a hundred or two hundred men into the counter-attack, but a deserter told us later on that it was six hundred. I dare say he was lying—deserters, for obvious reasons, often try to curry favour. It was a great pity about the telescope. The thought of losing that beautiful bit of loot worries me even now.

ERNEST HEMINGWAY
1899–1961

Among the crowd of writers involving themselves with the cause of the Spanish Republic was Ernest Hemingway, who covered the war in 1937 and 1938 for the North American Newspaper Alliance. Back home in Cuba in 1939, while a new war was breaking out in Europe, he used his "absolutely invaluable" impressions of the Spanish war in his novel For Whom the Bell Tolls *(1940).*

From FOR WHOM THE BELL TOLLS

El Sordo was making his fight on a hilltop. He did not like this hill and when he saw it he thought it had the shape of a chancre. But he had had no choice except this hill and he had picked it as far away as he could see it and galloped for it, the automatic rifle heavy on his back, the horse laboring, barrel heaving between his thighs, the sack of grenades swinging against one side, the sack of automatic rifle pans banging against the other, and Joaquín and Ignacio halting and firing, halting and firing to give him time to get the gun in place.

There had still been snow then, the snow that had ruined them, and when his horse was hit so that he wheezed in a slow, jerking, climbing stagger up the last part of the crest, splattering the snow with a bright, pulsing jet, Sordo had hauled him along by the bridle, the reins over his shoulder as he climbed. He climbed as hard as he could with the bullets spatting on the rocks, with the two sacks heavy on his shoulders, and then, holding the horse by the mane, had shot him quickly, expertly, and tenderly just where he had needed him, so that the horse pitched, head forward down to plug a gap between two rocks. He had gotten the gun to firing over the horse's back and he fired two pans, the gun clattering, the empty shells pitching into the snow, the smell of burnt hair from the burnt hide where the hot muzzle rested, him firing at what came up to the hill, forcing them to scatter for cover, while all the time there was a chill in his back from not knowing what was behind him. Once the last of the five men had reached the hilltop the chill went out of his back and he had saved the pans he had left until he would need them.

There were two more horses dead along the slope and three more were dead here on the hilltop. He had only succeeded in stealing three horses last night and one had bolted when they tried to mount him bareback in the corral at the camp when the first shooting had started.

Of the five men who had reached the hilltop three were wounded. Sordo was wounded in the calf of his leg and in two places in his left arm. He was very thirsty, his wounds had stiffened, and one of the wounds in his left arm was very painful. He also had a bad headache and as he lay waiting for the planes to come he thought of a joke in Spanish. It was, *"Hay que tomar la muerte como si fuera aspirina,"* which means, "You will have to take death as an aspirin." But he did not make the joke aloud. He grinned somewhere inside the pain in his head and inside the nausea that came whenever he moved his arm and looked around at what there was left of his band.

The five men were spread out like the points of a five-pointed star. They had dug with their knees and hands and made mounds in front of their heads and shoulders with the dirt and piles of stones. Using this cover, they were linking the individual mounds up with stones and dirt. Joaquín, who was eighteen years old, had a steel helmet that he dug with and he passed dirt in it.

He had gotten this helmet at the blowing up of the train. It had a bullet hole through it and every one had always joked at him for keeping it. But he had hammered the jagged edges of the bullet hole smooth and driven a wooden plug into it and then cut the plug off and smoothed it even with the metal inside the helmet.

When the shooting started he had clapped this helmet on his head so hard it banged his head as though he had been hit with a casserole and, in the last lung-aching, leg-dead, mouth-dry, bullet-spatting, bullet-cracking, bullet-singing run up the final slope of the hill after his horse was killed, the helmet had seemed to weigh a great amount and to ring his bursting forehead with an iron band. But he had kept it. Now he dug with it in a steady, almost machinelike desperation. He had not yet been hit.

"It serves for something finally," Sordo said to him in his deep, throaty voice.

"Resistir y fortificar es vencer," Joaquín said, his mouth stiff with the dryness of fear which surpassed the normal thirst of battle. It was one of the slogans of the Communist party and it meant, "Hold out and fortify, and you will win."

Sordo looked away and down the slope at where a cavalryman was sniping from behind a boulder. He was very fond of this boy and he was in no mood for slogans.

"What did you say?"

One of the men turned from the building that he was doing. This man was lying flat on his face, reaching carefully up with his hands to put a rock in place while keeping his chin flat against the ground.

Joaquín repeated the slogan in his dried-up boy's voice without checking his digging for a moment.

"What was the last word?" the man with his chin on the ground asked.

"*Vencer,*" the boy said. "Win."

"*Mierda,*" the man with his chin on the ground said.

"There is another that applies to here," Joaquín said, bringing them out as though they were talismans, "Pasionaria says it is better to die on your feet than to live on your knees."

"*Mierda* again," the man said and another man said, over his shoulder, "We're on our bellies, not our knees."

"Thou. Communist. Do you know your Pasionaria has a son thy age in Russia since the start of the movement?"

"It's a lie," Joaquín said.

"*Qué va,* it's a lie," the other said. "The dynamiter with the rare name told me. He was of thy party, too. Why should he lie?"

"It's a lie," Joaquín said. "She would not do such a thing as keep a son hidden in Russia out of the war."

"I wish I were in Russia," another of Sordo's men said. "Will not thy Pasionaria send me now from here to Russia, Communist?"

"If thou believest so much in thy Pasionaria, get her to get us off this hill," one of the men who had a bandaged thigh said.

"The fascists will do that," the man with his chin in the dirt said.

"Do not speak thus," Joaquín said to him.

"Wipe the pap of your mother's breasts off thy lips and give me a hatful of that dirt," the man with his chin on the ground said. "No one of us will see the sun go down this night."

El Sordo was thinking: It is shaped like a chancre. Or the breast of a young girl with no nipple. Or the top cone of a volcano. You have never seen a volcano, he thought. Nor will you ever see one. And this hill is like a chancre. Let the volcanos alone. It's late now for the volcanos.

He looked very carefully around the withers of the dead horse and there was a quick hammering of firing from behind a boulder well down the slope and he heard the bullets from the submachine gun thud into the horse. He crawled along behind the horse and looked out of the angle between the horse's hindquarters and the rock. There were three bodies on the slope just below him where they had fallen when the fascists had rushed the crest under cover of the automatic rifle and submachine gunfire and he and the others had broken down the attack by throwing and rolling down hand grenades. There were other bodies that he could not see on the other sides of the hill crest. There was no dead ground by which attackers could approach the summit and Sordo knew that as long as his ammunition and grenades held out and he had as many as four men they could not get him out of there unless they brought up a trench mortar. He did not know whether they had sent to La Granja for a trench mortar. Perhaps they had not, because surely, soon, the planes would come. It had been four hours since the observation plane had flown over them.

This hill is truly like a chancre, Sordo thought, and we are the very pus of it. But we killed many when they made that stupidness. How could they think that they would take us thus? They have such modern armament that they lose all their sense with overconfidence. He had killed the young officer who had led the assault with a grenade that had gone bouncing and rolling down the slope as they came up it, running, bent half over. In the yellow flash and gray roar of smoke he had seen the officer dive forward to where he lay now like a heavy, broken bundle of old clothing marking the farthest point that the assault had reached. Sordo looked at this body and then, down the hill, at the others.

They are brave but stupid people, he thought. But they have sense enough now not to attack us again until the planes come. Unless, of course, they have a mortar coming. It would be easy with a mortar. The mortar was the normal thing and he knew that they would die as soon as a mortar came up, but when he thought of the planes coming up he felt as naked on that hilltop as though all of his clothing and even his skin had been removed. There is no nakeder thing than I feel, he thought. A flayed rabbit is as well covered as a bear in comparison. But why should they bring planes? They could get us out of here with a trench mortar easily. They are proud of their planes, though, and they will probably bring them. Just as they were so proud of their automatic weapons that they made that stupidness. But undoubtedly they must have sent for a mortar, too.

One of the men fired. Then jerked the bolt and fired again, quickly.

"Save thy cartridges," Sordo said.

"One of the sons of the great whore tried to reach that boulder," the man pointed.

"Did you hit him?" Sordo asked, turning his head with difficulty.

"Nay," the man said. "The fornicator ducked back."

"Who is a whore of whores is Pilar," the man with his chin in the dirt said. "That whore knows we are dying here."

"She could do no good," Sordo said. The man had spoken on the side of his good ear and he had heard him without turning his head. "What could she do?"

"Take these sluts from the rear."

"Qué va," Sordo said. "They are spread around a hillside. How would she come on them? There are a hundred and fifty of them. Maybe more now."

"But if we hold out until dark," Joaquín said.

"And if Christmas comes on Easter," the man with his chin on the ground said.

"And if thy aunt had *cojones* she would be thy uncle," another said to him. "Send for thy Pasionaria. She alone can help us."

"I do not believe that about the son," Joaquín said. "Or if he is there he is training to be an aviator or something of that sort."

"He is hidden there for safety," the man told him.

"He is studying dialectics. Thy Pasionaria has been there. So have Lister and Modesto and others. The one with the rare name told me."

"That they should go to study and return to aid us," Joaquín said.

"That they should aid us now," another man said. "That all the cruts of Russian sucking swindlers should aid us now." He fired and said, *"Me cago en tal;* I missed him again."

"Save thy cartridges and do not talk so much or thou wilt be very thirsty," Sordo said. "There is no water on this hill."

"Take this," the man said and rolling on his side he pulled a wineskin that he wore slung from his shoulder over his head and handed it to Sordo. "Wash thy mouth out, old one. Thou must have much thirst with thy wounds."

"Let all take it," Sordo said.

"Then I will have some first," the owner said and squirted a long stream into his mouth before he handed the leather bottle around.

"Sordo, when thinkest thou the planes will come?" the man with his chin in the dirt asked.

"Any time," said Sordo. "They should have come before."

"Do you think these sons of the great whore will attack again?"

"Only if the planes do not come."

He did not think there was any need to speak about the mortar. They would know it soon enough when the mortar came.

"God knows they've enough planes with what we saw yesterday."

"Too many," Sordo said.

His head hurt very much and his arm was stiffening so that the pain of moving it was almost unbearable. He looked up at the bright, high, blue early summer sky as he raised the leather wine bottle with his good arm. He was fifty-two years old and he was sure this was the last time he would see that sky.

He was not at all afraid of dying but he was angry at being trapped on this hill which was only utilizable as a place to die. If we could have gotten clear, he thought. If we could have made them come up the long valley or if we could have broken loose across the road it would have been all right. But this chancre of a hill. We must use it as well as we can and we have used it very well so far.

If he had known how many men in history have had to use a hill to die on it would not have cheered him any for, in the moment he was passing through, men are not impressed by what has happened to other men in similar circumstances any more than a widow of one day is helped by the knowledge that other loved husbands have died. Whether one has fear of it or not, one's death is difficult to accept. Sordo had accepted it but there was no sweetness in its acceptance even at fifty-two, with three wounds and him surrounded on a hill.

He joked about it to himself but he looked at the sky and at the far mountains and he swallowed the wine and he did not want it. If one must die, he thought, and clearly one must, I can die. But I hate it.

Dying was nothing and he had no picture of it nor fear of it in his mind. But living was a field of grain blowing in the wind on the side of a hill. Living was a hawk in the sky. Living was an earthen jar of water in the dust of the threshing with the grain flailed out and the chaff blowing. Living was a horse between your legs and a carbine under one leg and a hill and a valley and a stream with trees along it and the far side of the valley and the hills beyond.

Sordo passed the wine bottle back and nodded his head in thanks. He leaned forward and patted the dead horse on the shoulder where the muzzle of the automatic rifle had burned the hide. He could still smell the burnt hair. He thought how he had held the horse there, trembling, with the fire around them, whispering and cracking, over and around them like a curtain, and had carefully shot him just at the intersection of the cross-lines between the two eyes and the ears. Then as the horse pitched down he had dropped down behind his warm, wet back to get the gun to going as they came up the hill.

"*Eras mucho caballo,*" he said, meaning, "Thou wert plenty of horse."

El Sordo lay now on his good side and looked up at the sky. He was lying on a heap of empty cartridge hulls but his head was protected by the rock and his body lay in the lee of the horse. His wounds had stiffened badly and he had much pain and he felt too tired to move.

"What passes with thee, old one?" the man next to him asked.

"Nothing. I am taking a little rest."

"Sleep," the other said. "*They* will wake us when they come."

Just then some one shouted from down the slope.

"Listen, bandits!" the voice came from behind the rocks where the closest automatic rifle was placed. "Surrender now before the planes blow you to pieces."

"What is it he says?" Sordo asked.

Joaquín told him. Sordo rolled to one side and pulled himself up so that he was crouched behind the gun again.

"Maybe the planes aren't coming," he said. "Don't answer them and do not fire. Maybe we can get them to attack again."

"If we should insult them a little?" the man who had spoken to Joaquín about La Pasionaria's son in Russia asked.

"No," Sordo said. "Give me thy big pistol. Who has a big pistol?"

"Here."

"Give it to me." Crouched on his knees he took the big 9 mm. Star and fired one shot into the ground beside the dead horse, waited, then fired again four times at irregular intervals. Then he waited while he counted sixty and then fired a final shot directly into the body of the dead horse. He grinned and handed back the pistol.

"Reload it," he whispered, "and that every one should keep his mouth shut and no one shoot."

"*Bandidos!*" the voice shouted from behind the rocks.

No one spoke on the hill.

"*Bandidos!* Surrender now before we blow thee to little pieces."

"They're biting," Sordo whispered happily.

As he watched, a man showed his head over the top of the rocks. There was no shot from the hilltop and the head went down again. El Sordo waited, watching, but nothing more happened. He turned his head and looked at the others who were all watching down their sectors of the slope. As he looked at them the others shook their heads.

"Let no one move," he whispered.

"Sons of the great whore," the voice came now from behind the rocks again.

"Red swine. Mother rapers. Eaters of the milk of thy fathers."

Sordo grinned. He could just hear the bellowed insults by turning his good ear. This is better than the aspirin, he thought. How many will we get? Can they be that foolish?

The voice had stopped again and for three minutes they heard nothing and saw no movement. Then the sniper behind the boulder a hundred yards down the slope exposed himself and fired. The bullet hit a rock and ricocheted with a sharp whine. Then Sordo saw a man, bent double, run from the shelter of the rocks where the automatic rifle was across the open ground to the big boulder behind which the sniper was hidden. He almost dove behind the boulder.

Sordo looked around. They signalled to him that there was no movement on the other slopes. El Sordo grinned happily and shook his head. This is ten times better than the aspirin, he thought, and he waited, as happy as only a hunter can be happy.

Below on the slope the man who had run from the pile of stones to the shelter of the boulder was speaking to the sniper.

"Do you believe it?"

"I don't know," the sniper said.

"It would be logical," the man, who was the officer in command, said. "They are surrounded. They have nothing to expect but to die."

The sniper said nothing.

"What do you think?" the officer asked.

"Nothing," the sniper said.

"Have you seen any movement since the shots?"

"None at all."

The officer looked at his wrist watch. It was ten minutes to three o'clock.

"The planes should have come an hour ago," he said. Just then another officer flopped in behind the boulder. The sniper moved over to make room for him.

"Thou, Paco," the first officer said. "How does it seem to thee?"

The second officer was breathing heavily from his sprint up and across the hillside from the automatic rifle position.

"For me it is a trick," he said.

"But if it is not? What a ridicule we make waiting here and laying siege to dead men."

"We have done something worse than ridiculous already," the second officer said. "Look at that slope."

He looked up the slope to where the dead were scattered close to the top. From where he looked the line of the hilltop showed the scattered rocks, the belly, projecting legs, shod hooves jutting out, of Sordo's horse, and the fresh dirt thrown up by the digging.

"What about the mortars?" asked the second officer.

"They should be here in an hour. If not before."

"Then wait for them. There has been enough stupidity already."

"*Bandidos!*" the first officer shouted suddenly, getting to his feet and putting his head well up above the boulder so that the crest of the hill looked much closer as he stood upright. "Red swine! Cowards!"

The second officer looked at the sniper and shook his head. The sniper looked away but his lips tightened.

The first officer stood there, his head all clear of the rock and with his hand on his pistol butt. He cursed and vilified the hilltop. Nothing happened. Then he stepped clear of the boulder and stood there looking up the hill.

"Fire, cowards, if you are alive," he shouted. "Fire on one who has no fear of any Red that ever came out of the belly of the great whore."

This last was quite a long sentence to shout and the officer's face was red and congested as he finished.

The second officer, who was a thin sunburned man with quiet eyes, a thin, long-lipped mouth and a stubble of beard over his hollow cheeks, shook his head again. It was this officer who was shouting who had ordered the first assault. The young lieutenant who was dead up the slope had been the best friend of this other lieutenant who was named Paco Berrendo and who was listening to the shouting of the captain, who was obviously in a state of exaltation.

"Those are the swine who shot my sister and my mother," the captain said. He had a red face and a blond, British-looking moustache and there was something wrong about his eyes. They were a light blue and the lashes were light, too. As you looked at them they seemed to focus slowly. Then "Reds," he shouted. "Cowards!" and commenced cursing again.

He stood absolutely clear now and, sighting carefully, fired his pistol at the only target that the hilltop presented: the dead horse that had belonged to Sordo. The bullet threw up a puff of dirt fifteen yards below the horse. The captain fired again. The bullet hit a rock and sung off.

The captain stood there looking at the hilltop. The Lieutenant Berrendo was looking at the body of the other lieutenant just below the summit. The sniper was looking at the ground under his eyes. Then he looked up at the captain.

"There is no one alive up there," the captain said. "Thou," he said to the sniper, "go up there and see."

The sniper looked down. He said nothing.

"Don't you hear me?" the captain shouted at him.

"Yes, my captain," the sniper said, not looking at him.

"Then get up and go." The captain still had his pistol out. "Do you hear me?"

"Yes, my captain."

"Why don't you go, then?"

"I don't want to, my captain."

"You don't want to?" The captain pushed the pistol against the small of the man's back. "You don't want to?"

"I am afraid, my captain," the soldier said with dignity.

Lieutenant Berrendo, watching the captain's face and his odd eyes, thought he was going to shoot the man then.

"Captain Mora," he said.

"Lieutenant Berrendo?"

"It is possible the soldier is right."

"That he is right to say he is afraid? That he is right to say he does not want to obey an order?"

"No. That he is right that it is a trick."

"They are all dead," the captain said. "Don't you hear me say they are all dead?"

"You mean our comrades on the slope?" Berrendo asked him. "I agree with you."

"Paco," the captain said, "don't be a fool. Do you think you are the only one who cared for Julián? I tell you the Reds are dead. Look!"

He stood up, then put both hands on top of the boulder and pulled himself up, kneeing-up awkwardly, then getting on his feet.

"Shoot," he shouted, standing on the gray granite boulder and waved both his arms. "Shoot me! Kill me!"

On the hilltop El Sordo lay behind the dead horse and grinned. What a people, he thought. He laughed, trying to hold it in because the shaking hurt his arm.

"Reds," came the shout from below. "Red canaille. Shoot me! Kill me!"

Sordo, his chest shaking, barely peeped past the horse's crupper and saw the captain on top of the boulder waving his arms. Another officer stood by the boulder. The sniper was standing at the other side. Sordo kept his eye where it was and shook his head happily.

"Shoot me," he said softly to himself. "Kill me!" Then his shoulders shook again. The laughing hurt his arm and each time he laughed his head felt as though it would burst. But the laughter shook him again like a spasm.

Captain Mora got down from the boulder.

"Now do you believe me, Paco?" he questioned Lieutenant Berrendo.

"No," said Lieutenant Berrendo.

"*Cojones!*" the captain said. "Here there is nothing but idiots and cowards."

The sniper had gotten carefully behind the boulder again and Lieutenant Berrendo was squatting beside him.

The captain, standing in the open beside the boulder, commenced to shout filth at the hilltop. There is no language so filthy as Spanish. There are words for all the vile words in English and there are other words and expressions that are used only in countries where blasphemy keeps pace with the austerity of religion. Lieutenant Berrendo was a very devout Catholic. So was the sniper. They were Carlists from Navarra and while both of them cursed and blasphemed when they were angry they regarded it as a sin which they regularly confessed.

As they crouched now behind the boulder watching the captain and listening to what he was shouting, they both disassociated themselves from him and what he was saying. They did not want to have that sort of talk on their consciences on a day in which they might die. Talking thus will not bring luck, the sniper thought. Speaking thus of the *Virgen* is bad luck. This one speaks worse than the Reds.

Julián is dead, Lieutenant Berrendo was thinking. Dead there on the slope on such a day as this is. And this foul mouth stands there bringing more ill fortune with his blasphemies.

Now the captain stopped shouting and turned to Lieutenant Berrendo. His eyes looked stranger than ever.

"Paco," he said, happily, "you and I will go up there."

"Not me."

"What?" The captain had his pistol out again.

I hate these pistol brandishers, Berrendo was thinking. They cannot give an order without jerking a gun out. They probably pull out their pistols when they go to the toilet and order the move they will make.

"I will go if you order me to. But under protest," Lieutenant Berrendo told the captain.

"Then I will go alone," the captain said. "The smell of cowardice is too strong here."

Holding his pistol in his right hand, he strode steadily up the slope. Berrendo and the sniper watched him. He was making no attempt to take any cover and he was looking straight ahead of him at the rocks, the dead horse, and the fresh-dug dirt of the hilltop.

El Sordo lay behind the horse at the corner of the rock, watching the captain come striding up the hill.

Only one, he thought. We get only one. But from his manner of speaking he is *caza mayor*. Look at him walking. Look what an animal. Look at him stride forward. This one is for me. This one I take with me on the trip. This one coming now makes the same voyage I do. Come on, Comrade Voyager. Come striding. Come right along. Come along to meet it. Come on. Keep on walking. Don't slow up. Come right along. Come as thou art coming. Don't stop and look at those. That's right. Don't even look down. Keep on coming with your eyes forward. Look, he has a moustache. What do you think of that? He runs to a moustache, the Comrade Voyager. He is a captain. Look at his sleeves. I said he was *caza mayor*. He has the face of an *Inglés*. Look. With a red face and blond hair and blue eyes. With no cap on and his moustache is yellow. With blue eyes. With pale blue eyes. With pale blue eyes with something wrong with them. With pale blue eyes that don't focus. Close enough. Too close. Yes, Comrade Voyager. Take it, Comrade Voyager.

He squeezed the trigger of the automatic rifle gently and it pounded back three times against his shoulder with the slippery jolt the recoil of a tripoded automatic weapon gives.

The captain lay on his face on the hillside. His left arm was under him. His right arm that had held the pistol was stretched forward of his head. From all down the slope they were firing on the hill crest again.

Crouched behind the boulder, thinking that now he would have to sprint across that open space under fire, Lieutenant Berrendo heard the deep hoarse voice of Sordo from the hilltop.

"Bandidos!" the voice came. *"Bandidos!* Shoot me! Kill me!"

On the top of the hill El Sordo lay behind the automatic rifle laughing so that his chest ached, so that he thought the top of his head would burst.

"Bandidos," he shouted again happily. "Kill me, *bandidos!"* Then he shook his head happily. We have lots of company for the Voyage, he thought.

He was going to try for the other officer with the automatic rifle when he would leave the shelter of the boulder. Sooner or later he would have to leave it. Sordo knew that he could never command from there and he thought he had a very good chance to get him.

Just then the others on the hill heard the first sound of the coming of the planes.

El Sordo did not hear them. He was covering the down-slope edge of the boulder with his automatic rifle and he was thinking: when I see him he will be running already and I will miss him if I am not careful. I could shoot behind him all across that stretch. I should swing the gun with him and ahead of him. Or let him start and then get on him and ahead of him. I will try to pick him up there at the edge of the rock and swing just ahead of him. Then he felt a touch on his shoulder and he turned and saw the gray, fear-drained face of Joaquín and he looked where the boy was pointing and saw the three planes coming.

At this moment Lieutenant Berrendo broke from behind the boulder and, with his head bent and his legs plunging, ran down and across the slope to the shelter of the rocks where the automatic rifle was placed.

Watching the planes, Sordo never saw him go.

"Help me to pull this out," he said to Joaquín and the boy dragged the automatic rifle clear from between the horse and the rock.

The planes were coming on steadily. They were in echelon and each second they grew larger and their noise was greater.

"Lie on your backs to fire at them," Sordo said. "Fire ahead of them as they come."

He was watching them all the time. *"Cabrones! Hijos de puta!"* he said rapidly.

"Ignacio!" he said. "Put the gun on the shoulder of the boy. Thou!" to Joaquín, "Sit there and do not move. Crouch over. More. No. More."

He lay back and sighted with the automatic rifle as the planes came on steadily.

"Thou, Ignacio, hold me the three legs of that tripod," They were dangling down the boy's back and the muzzle of the gun was shaking from the jerking of his body that Joaquín could not control as he crouched with bent head hearing the droning roar of their coming.

Lying flat on his belly and looking up into the sky watching them come, Ignacio gathered the legs of the tripod into his two hands and steadied the gun.

"Keep thy head down," he said to Joaquín. "Keep thy head forward."

"Pasionaria says 'Better to die on thy——' " Joaquín was saying to himself as the drone came nearer them. Then he shifted suddenly into "Hail Mary, full of grace, the Lord is with thee; Blessed art thou among women and Blessed is the fruit of thy womb, Jesus. Holy Mary, Mother of God, pray for us sinners now and at the hour of our death. Amen. Holy Mary, Mother of God," he started, then he remembered quickly as the roar came now unbearably and started an act of contrition racing in it, "Oh my God, I am heartily sorry for having offended thee who art worthy of all my love——"

Then there were the hammering explosions past his ears and the gun barrel hot against his shoulder. It was hammering now again and his ears were deafened by the muzzle blast. Ignacio was pulling down hard on the tripod and the barrel was burning his back. It was hammering now in the roar and he could not remember the act of contrition.

All he could remember was at the hour of our death. Amen. At the hour of our death. Amen. At the hour. At the hour. Amen. The others all were firing. Now and at the hour of our death. Amen.

Then, through the hammering of the gun, there was the whistle of the air splitting apart and then in the red black roar the earth rolled under his knees and then waved up to hit him in the face and then dirt and bits of rock were falling all over and Ignacio was lying on him and the gun was lying on him. But he was not dead because the whistle came again and the earth rolled under him with the roar. Then it came again and the earth lurched under his belly and one side of the hilltop rose into the air and then fell slowly over them where they lay.

The planes came back three times and bombed the hilltop but no one on the hilltop knew it. Then the planes machine-gunned the hilltop and went away. As they dove on the hill for the last time with their machine guns hammering, the first plane pulled up and winged over and then each plane did the same and they moved from echelon to V-formation and went away into the sky in the direction of Segovia.

Keeping a heavy fire on the hilltop, Lieutenant Berrendo pushed a patrol up to one of the bomb craters from where they could throw grenades onto the crest. He was taking no chances of any one being alive and waiting for them in the mess that was up there and he threw four grenades into the confusion of dead horses, broken and split rocks, and torn yellow-stained explosive-stinking earth before he climbed out of the bomb crater and walked over to have a look.

No one was alive on the hilltop except the boy Joaquín, who was unconscious under the dead body of Ignacio. Joaquín was bleeding from the nose and from the ears. He had known nothing and had no feeling since he had suddenly been in the very heart of the thunder and the breath had been wrenched from his body when the one bomb struck so close and Lieutenant Berrendo made the sign of the cross and then shot him in the back of the head, as quickly and as gently, if such an abrupt movement can be gentle, as Sordo had shot the wounded horse.

Lieutenant Berrendo stood on the hilltop and looked down the slope at his own dead and then across the country seeing where they had galloped before Sordo had turned at bay here. He noticed all the dispositions that had been made of the troops and then he ordered the dead men's horses to be brought up and the bodies tied across the saddles so that they might be packed in to La Granja.

"Take that one, too," he said. "The one with his hands on the automatic rifle. That should be Sordo. He is the oldest and it was he with the gun. No. Cut the head off and wrap it in a poncho." He considered a minute. "You might as well take all the heads. And of the others below on the slope and where we first found them. Collect the rifles and pistols and pack that gun on a horse."

Then he walked down to where the lieutenant lay who had been killed in the first assault. He looked down at him but did not touch him.

"Qué cosa más mala es la guerra," he said to himself, which meant, "What a bad thing war is."

Then he made the sign of the cross again and as he walked down the hill he said five Our Fathers and five Hail Marys for the repose of the soul of his dead comrade. He did not wish to stay to see his orders being carried out.

STEPHEN SPENDER
1909–

The British poet Stephen Spender went to Spain during the war and wrote propaganda for the Republican side. He is the author of many volumes of poetry, criticism, literary history, and memoirs and is well known as a lecturer in England and the United States.

Two Armies

Deep in the winter plain, two armies
Dig their machinery, to destroy each other.
Men freeze and hunger. No one is given leave
On either side, except the dead, and wounded.
These have their leave; while new battalions wait
On time at last to bring them violent peace.

All have become so nervous and so cold
That each man hates the cause and distant words
That brought him here, more terribly than bullets.
Once a boy hummed a popular marching song,
Once a novice hand flapped their salute;
The voice was choked, the lifted hand fell,
Shot through the wrist by those of his own side.

From their numb harvest, all would flee, except
For discipline drilled once in an iron school
Which holds them at the point of the revolver.
Yet when they sleep, the images of home
Ride wishing horses of escape
Which herd the plain in a mass unspoken poem.

Finally, they cease to hate: for although hate
Bursts from the air and whips the earth with hail
Or shoots it up in fountains to marvel at,
And although hundreds fall, who can connect
The inexhaustible anger of the guns
With the dumb patience of those tormented animals?

Clean silence drops at night, when a little walk
Divides the sleeping armies, each
Huddled in linen woven by remote hands.
When the machines are stilled, a common suffering
Whitens the air with breath and makes both one
As though these enemies slept in each other's arms.

Only the lucid friend to aerial raiders
The brilliant pilot moon, stares down
Upon this plain she makes a shining bone
Cut by the shadows of many thousand bones.
Where amber clouds scatter on No-Man's-Land

She regards death and time throw up
The furious words and minerals which destroy.

ULTIMA RATIO REGUM

The guns spell money's ultimate reason
In letters of lead on the Spring hillside.
But the boy lying dead under the olive trees
Was too young and too silly
To have been notable to their important eye.
He was a better target for a kiss.

When he lived, tall factory hooters never summoned him
Nor did restaurant plate-glass doors revolve to wave him in.
His name never appeared in the papers.
The world maintained its traditional wall
Round the dead with their gold sunk deep as a well,
Whilst his life, intangible as a Stock Exchange rumour, drifted outside.

O too lightly he threw down his cap
One day when the breeze threw petals from the trees.
The unflowering wall sprouted with guns,
Machine-gun anger quickly scythed the grasses;
Flags and leaves fell from hands and branches;
The tweed cap rotted in the nettles.

Consider his life which was valueless
In terms of employment, hotel ledgers, news files.
Consider. One bullet in ten thousand kills a man.
Ask. Was so much expenditure justified
On the death of one so young, and so silly
Lying under the olive trees, O world, O death?

Part III
The Second World War

Almost Beyond
Human Conception

Conveying an adequate idea of the Second World War is close to impossible because, as war correspondent Robert Goralski has said, "What we did to each other is almost beyond human conception." For one thing, the sheer numbers defeat attempts to flesh them out with actual, unique human beings. Killed and wounded were over 78 million people, more of them civilians than soldiers. Close to 6 million Jews were beaten, shot, or gassed to death by the Germans. One million people died of starvation and despair in the siege of Leningrad. Over 50 million young men and women worldwide were mustered into armies, navies, and air forces, 12 million in both the Soviet Union and the United States, 10 million in Germany, 6 million in Japan, 4.5 million in both Italy and Britain. If the battle of the Somme constitutes a scandal because 20,000 British soldiers were killed in one day, twice that number of civilians were asphyxiated and burned to death in the bombing of Hamburg. Seventy thousand died at Hiroshima, 35,000 at Nagasaki, and the same at Dresden. Among British bomber crews, over 55,000 were killed, more than all the British officers killed and wounded in the First World War. When the Germans invaded the Soviet Union, they did so with 165 divisions, and the Soviets finally threw them back with 800. The number of Germans who surrendered at Stalingrad was 91,000. (The number surviving years of captivity to return home was 6,000.) Two million men were engaged in the battle of Kursk, in the Soviet Union. Fought in 1943, it remains the greatest land battle in history. Six thousand tanks fought each other, and four thousand planes. "At times," says Robert Leckie, "the smoke from burning tanks blotted out the sun," and "out of the blackened sky fell shrieking, burning airplanes." It was like something supernatural: "Frightened peasants screaming in terror ran for the forests with their hands over their ears." In such circumstances, only small numbers and a few actual names can resume human significance, like the number three—three men came out alive when, on May 24, 1941, the British battle cruiser *Hood* blew up. The rest of the crew,

1,418 men, disappeared. Only Signalman Briggs, Midshipman Dundas, and Seaman Tilburn survived.

No easier than imagining its magnitude is specifying the starting point of the Second World War. Some would say it began back in 1919 with the Treaty of Versailles, when Germany was branded as the instigator of the First World War and was shortly to be charged with "reparations," humiliating and unpayable. German re-armament and aggressive national self-justification seem an inevitable reaction. Others might point to Japanese aggression in China beginning in 1931. The worldwide economic depression of the 1930s assisted the rise to power of Hitler's National Socialists, who contrived the re-militarization of the Rhineland in 1936 and the annexation of Austria and parts of Czechoslovakia in 1938. Meanwhile, Japan was flexing nationalist muscles and preparing to lead an anti-colonialist effort expelling Britain, the Netherlands, and the United States from their traditional possessions in the Far East. Up to this time, Britain, still horrified by her massive losses in the First World War, tried by numerous expedients of compromise and persuasion to satisfy Hitler's territorial hunger, but when the Germans demanded Poland too and invaded it on September 1, 1939, Britain and France finally drew the line, declaring war on Germany three days later. For several months little happened, French and German troops regarding each other from behind their border fortifications of the Maginot and Siegfried lines. But in May 1940, the Germans simply flanked the Maginot Line to the north and swept through Holland, Belgium, Luxembourg, and finally France. A British Expeditionary Force sent to assist the French army was forced back and fled across the Channel from Dunkirk, leaving all its heavy equipment behind. British propaganda tried to salvage what hope it could from this debacle, but it was now apparent that Germany could do what it wanted on the Continent until there was a change in international dynamics. Although clearly distressed by these European events, the United States had so far displayed no great willingness to come to Britain's defense. Its neutrality puzzled and angered many Britons. As Philip Warner has said, at this time

> the British opinion of the United States was that at heart it was really still a part of the British Empire. The fact that it had been an independent country for over 150 years and that Americans included millions of people whose ancestors had migrated from European countries such as Italy, Germany, Yugoslavia, and even Russia, and thus had no feelings of affinity towards Britain, did not break into the consciousness of the average Briton. . . . In fact most Americans hardly gave a thought to Britain.

Not to mention the outright hostility to Britain among many Irish Americans, as well as the opposition to British colonialism habitual among American liberals. Britain's problems were now multiplied by

Italy's declaring war on her and invading Egypt. Soon General Rommel's Afrika Corps was pressing against the British in North Africa. On June 22, 1941, Germany surprisingly turned eastward and invaded its erstwhile ally, the Soviet Union, at first with dramatic success, plunging hundreds of miles into unsuspecting and unready Russian defenses. And if the war spread in that direction in 1941, in early 1942 it became genuinely a world war when Japan seized the Philippines and Malaya and Burma and advanced in the Pacific right up to Australia. Germany had an understanding with Japan, and when, reacting to the attack on Pearl Harbor, the United States declared war on Japan, Germany responded by declaring war on the United States. This, together with its invasion of the Soviet Union, proved a terrible mistake, but it required years for the obviously superior industrial capacity of the United States to get into gear and for America to muster and train an army capable of joining the British in recapturing the Continent and entering Germany. Ultimately American forces outnumbered British, the reason Eisenhower was designated Supreme Allied Commander. Getting American tanks and planes to Europe was not easy, for U-boats sank trans-Atlantic vessels virtually at will until radar, the convoy system, and extended air protection shifted the advantage to the Allies. For Germany the turning point of the war was probably the battle of Stalingrad, in February 1943. After that, German forces were engaged in practically full-time retreat. To add to Germany's troubles, the Allies invaded Italy and began a slow, painful advance north.

It was clear to the Allies that getting back onto the Continent would be costly. When they had raided the French coastal town of Dieppe in August 1942, they suffered 50 percent casualties and achieved nothing. Although the Soviets insisted that the Allies invade the Continent in 1943, the United States and Britain required a year more to build the landing craft and to achieve the absolute air superiority required for invasion. Despite the relative success of the landings in Normandy, conquering the still powerful and energetically officered German army took almost another year, during which Hitler's "secret weapons," the V-1 and V-2 self-propelled bombs and rockets, killed many civilians in England and Belgium. In the final year of the European war the Allies overran what earlier had been only the substance of terrible rumors, the extermination camps in which the Germans killed millions of "subhumans"—Jews, Poles, Slavs, gypsies, and homosexuals.

In the Far East Japanese power had been eroding ever since the naval battle of Midway, in 1942, but it was clear that given the suicidal Japanese resistance as island after island was seized by the Americans, the home islands would have to be invaded. To provide bases for the ultimate infantry and marine battle on the Japanese homeland, the Philippines were recaptured and Okinawa occupied. Incendiary bombings of civilians prepared the way for invasion: more people (180,000) were killed in "conventional" attacks on Tokyo in April 1945, than in both the atomic bombings. After the German surrender in May 1945, the Americans began shifting troops and supplies to the Pacific, but the atom bombs made invasion unnecessary. When the Japanese surrendered in August 1945, General MacArthur expressed the understanding of billions when he designated the war "a great tragedy." A tragedy generates fear and pity, and there had been plenty of fear and pity for the past six years. The main cities of Japan were ashes, and if years of bombing had ironically stiffened rather than softened the German will to resist, there was scarcely a German city of any size that was not in ruins, with people starving in holes. (Although in the Third Reich irony, the normal attendant of modern war, was rare, there were occasional outcrops. After the bombing of Dresden, someone painted on the sidewalk, "Thank you, dear Führer.") Millions of suddenly freed foreign workers, enslaved for years by the Germans, wandered across Europe, many of them looting and raping in revenge. It would be decades before civilized conditions would be half-restored, and to this day, if you look past the façades of new buildings in Warsaw to the areas behind, you will see war ruins standing there just as in 1945.

It was not until the Second World War that the relative civility of the First was apparent. Most of the atrocity stories imputing extraordinary cruelty to the Germans then were revealed to have been concocted by Allied propagandists. Not so the appalling narratives emanating from this war, telling of Japanese bayoneting of nurses and hospital patients in Hong Kong and of their inexplicably cruel treatment of helpless prisoners of war. In Britain today, there are still thousands of former prisoners of the Japanese who will refuse forever to buy anything bearing the name Sony or Toyota. Unthinkable in the First World War would have been the German *Einsatzgruppen,* special SS units accompanying the army as it conquered Eastern Europe, whose duty it was to murder commissars, Jews, intellectuals, and peasants slack in obedience. Unknown in the First World War was an institution like the Gestapo, which tortured and killed freely while trying to repress civilian resistance in German-occupied countries. And although the Spanish Civil War had made familiar the idea of "partisans" and guerrillas, the hatred of the Germans among ordinary people, as well as among confirmed communists, occasioned large risings of irregular forces all over Europe, but especially in France, Russia, Yugoslavia, and Greece. These were kept supplied by air-drops from Allied planes and were sometimes led and abetted by Allied officers parachuted at the same time. Partisan units, which ambushed the Germans, blew up railway tracks, roads, bridges, and vehicles, paid heavily for their patriotism and daring: in Yugoslavia alone over 300,000 were killed and over 400,000 wounded. Those the Germans captured—"bandits," they called them—were unceremoniously shot or hanged, their bodies left dangling to discourage others. Widespread was the German practice of rounding up admittedly innocent people chosen at random—the local schoolteacher, the pharmacist, an adopted child, the town drunk—as hostages against partisan attack in the district, ten hostages to be shot for each German soldier killed. It was hard to decide whether the world in general, increasingly uninhibited by former scruples deriving from religion, had grown more cruel since the First World War or whether the Germans, nourished on the adolescent and pathological imperatives of National Socialism, had accomplished a unique breakthrough into a new anti-ethics of pedantic viciousness. When the German surrender was finally consummated at Rheims, General Eisenhower felt so revolted by the recently disclosed death camps that he refused even to be present when the surrender was signed by General Jodl, later hanged at Nuremburg.

Faced with events so unprecedented and so inaccessible to normal models of humane understanding, literature spent a lot of time standing silent and aghast. Journalism was different. Even though it was either officially censored or self-censored (usually both), it performed its normal task of registering the facts, and practiced by a correspondent like Martha Gellhorn it delivered a credible, useful version of events. But a version not only credible but morally and artistically significant sometimes seemed beyond the power of literature to deliver. One impediment was suggested by the poets. It is demoralizing to be called on to fight the same enemy twice in the space of twenty-one years, and what is there to say except what has been said the first time? Canadian poet Milton Acorn put it this way:

> This is where we came in; this has happened before
> Only the last time there was cheering.

British poet Keith Douglas, in his poem "Desert Flowers," refers to Isaac Rosenberg's "Break of Day in the Trenches" from the First World War and admits, "Rosenberg I only repeat what you were saying." Herbert Read's poem "To a Conscript of 1940" exhibits a similar weariness at this replay of a former disaster. The time for idealism, Read notes, is long past. The soldiers of the Second World War can perform satisfactorily, he observes, only if they know in advance that no social good will come from the war.

Another problem for literature was the difficulty of making moral sense out of circumstances and behavior so destructive of normal moral assumptions. Barbara Foley has defined the problem while commenting on the Holocaust. It's not, she says, that its data are "unknowable." The impediment to understanding the Holocaust is that "its full dimensions are inaccessible to the ideological frameworks that we have inherited from the liberal era."

   Almost entirely absent from the Second World War were those gung-ho celebrations uttered at the beginning of the First War by Rupert Brooke and W. N. Hodgson. By the time Hitler had invaded Poland and the Allies knew they would have to fight, the old illusion that war was anything but criminal and messy was largely in tatters. As Robert E. Sherwood said, the Second World War was "the first in American history [and of course even more so in British history] in which the general disillusionment preceded the firing of the first shot." Or as one Briton remembered the national state of mind at the outbreak of the war, "We were all conscientious objectors, and all in [the war]." When E. M. Forster was asked in 1940 what he felt about the war, he replied, "I don't want to lose it. I don't expect Victory (with a big V!), and I can't join in any build-a-new-world stuff. Once in a lifetime one can swallow that, but not twice." As a motive for self-immolation among the Allies, patriotism seemed close to obsolete. "Who the hell dies for King and Country anymore?" asked a Canadian soldier. "That crap went out in the First World War."

   Consequently, regardless of its danger, for those implicated in it the Second War could seem almost boring. One of the best and most representative poems from the Second War is Alun Lewis's "All Day It Has Rained," which catches the sense that while ultimate significance may be possible, at the moment the war is a great emptiness. A sigh, not a scream of pain or a shout of outrage, seems a typical sound of this war. Unlike the loquacity which is one of the cultural attendants of the First War, silence is the stigma of experience in the Second. Writers as articulate as Wallace Stevens, T. S. Eliot, Robert Frost, and Samuel Beckett had little to say about the war, and Edmund Wilson, John Berryman, and Delmore Schwartz sometimes acted as if it were not taking place. The Allied troops likewise tended to silence, or at least to a brevity suggesting severe disenchantment. Once the war was over, for most of the participants there was little to be said either. "When I came back," one soldier said, "I didn't realize how silent I had been through those four years, and I . . . continued silent. It was funny." Soldiers who were writers became silent too. As Karl Shapiro says, speaking of John Ciardi and other young writers who'd been in combat and had plenty to testify about, "We all came out of the same army and joined the same generation of silence."

   This time, less said the better, as John Pudney writes in his poem "Missing," deploring the death of his friend "Smith":

No roses at the end
Of Smith, my friend.

Words will not fill the post
Of Smith, the ghost.

That suggests the exhaustion by modern war of elegiac language and imagery. Gavin Ewart implies as much by avoiding traditional elegiac procedures in his poem "When a Beau Goes In." The destruction of a pilot in his airplane has become so routine and meaningless that "Nobody says, 'Poor lad.' " The irony of Second World War poetry seems effortless, inevitable, natural, as in Randall Jarrell's "The Death of the Ball Turret Gunner"—representative also in its brevity. This unwillingness to embroider suggests a world where sensitive users of language have been virtually forced into the laconic mode by the excesses of propaganda, advertising, publicity, and nationalistic lying.

Because of both censorship and the desire to win the war on its own contemporary terms, it's not easy to find people writing interestingly of the war while it's going on. Given the sentimentality of much patriotic wartime journalism and the deceptiveness of official emissions, and given the false conceptions of character and motivation nourished by Hollywood and by writing aimed at Hollywood, one turns with relief to the letters and diaries of soldiers. These admit a reader to something like actuality, that is, the soldier's war. As the historian Roger J. Spiller has said,

> Because the soldier's history of war does not readily submit to the orderly requirements of history, and because, when uncovered, it often challenges the orderly traditions by which military history has shaped our understanding of warfare, the soldier's war has been the great secret of military history. And within this special, secret history of war, the darkest corner of all has had to do with war's essential, defining feature—combat, what it is like to have lived through it, and to have lived with one's own combat history for the rest of one's life.

There is no more illuminating testimony about the soldier's war in the selections that follow than that of United States Marine Eugene B. Sledge, whose memoir, *With the Old Breed at Peleliu and Okinawa,* has become a classic of modesty, honesty, and simplicity, more telling than any amount of literary sophistication. And from the Axis side there is Guy Sajer's memorable account of his soldier's war in *The Forgotten Soldier.* American Private First Class Mitchell Sharpe, who fought the Germans with the infantry in France and Germany, gets the soldier's war right when he tells his mother,

If you could only see us kids killed at eighteen, nineteen and twenty fighting in a country that means nothing to us, fighting because it means either kill or be killed, not because you're making the world safe for democracy or destroying Nazism.

The death of his friend Neal, killed near him and left by the side of the path "with eyes and mouth open," has shown him "what a hopeless and senseless mockery this war is." That perception seems to arise only from experience, and experience in the library, film theater, debating society, or classroom will not seem to suffice.

HERBERT READ
1893–1968

Read learned in 1914–1918 (see his poem "The Happy Warrior," page 881) that modern war is very likely to subvert its proclaimed purposes, reducing its actors to fighting without any aim nobler than survival. In 1940 he was shocked to see the operation beginning all over again.

To a Conscript of 1940

Qui n'a pas une fois désespéré de l'honneur, ne sera
jamais un héros.
                                    Georges Bernanos

A soldier passed me in the freshly fallen snow,
His footsteps muffled, his face unearthly grey;
And my heart gave a sudden leap
As I gazed on a ghost of five-and-twenty years ago.

I shouted Halt! and my voice had the old accustomed ring
And he obeyed it as it was obeyed
In the shrouded days when I too was one
Of an army of young men marching

Into the unknown. He turned towards me and I said:
"I am one of those who went before you
Five-and-twenty years ago: one of the many who never
    returned,
Of the many who returned and yet were dead.

"We went where you are going, into the rain and the mud;
We fought as you will fight

With death and darkness and despair;
We gave what you will give—our brains and our blood.

"We think we gave in vain. The world was not renewed.
There was hope in the homestead and anger in the streets
But the old world was restored and we returned
To the dreary field and workshop, and the immemorial feud

"Of rich and poor. Our victory was our defeat.
Power was retained where power had been misused
And youth was left to sweep away
The ashes that the fires had strewn beneath our feet.

"But one thing we learned: there is no glory in the deed
Until the soldier wears a badge of tarnished braid;
There are heroes who have heard the rally and have seen
The glitter of a garland round their head.

"Theirs is the hollow victory. They are deceived.
But you, my brother and my ghost, if you can go
Knowing that there is no reward, no certain use
In all your sacrifice, then honour is reprieved.

"To fight without hope is to fight with grace,
The self reconstructed, the false heart repaired."
Then I turned with a smile, and he answered my salute
As he stood against the fretted hedge, which was like white
    lace.

ALUN LEWIS
1915–1944

*Born in Wales and educated there and in Manchester as a teacher of
history, Lewis joined the army in 1940. His vision and writings reflect
the influence of Edward Thomas (1878–1917), the quiet poet who
brought understatement and obliqueness to bear on the realities of the*

Great War. Lewis died of a gunshot wound in Burma in circumstances
which have never been publicly clarified.

ALL DAY IT HAS RAINED

All day it has rained, and we on the edge of the moors
Have sprawled in our bell-tents, moody and dull as boors,
Groundsheets and blankets spread on the muddy ground
And from the first grey wakening we have found
No refuge from the skirmishing fine rain
And the wind that made the canvas heave and flap
And the taut wet guy-ropes ravel out and snap.
All day the rain has glided, wave and mist and dream,
Drenching the gorse and heather, a gossamer stream
Too light to stir the acorns that suddenly
Snatched from their cups by the wild south-westerly
Pattered against the tent and our upturned dreaming faces.
And we stretched out, unbuttoning our braces,
Smoking a Woodbine, darning dirty socks,
Reading the Sunday papers—I saw a fox
And mentioned it in the note I scribbled home;—
And we talked of girls, and dropping bombs on Rome,
And thought of the quiet dead and the loud celebrities
Exhorting us to slaughter, and the herded refugees;
—Yet thought softly, morosely of them, and as indifferently
As of ourselves or those whom we
For years have loved, and will again
Tomorrow maybe love; but now it is the rain
Possesses us entirely, the twilight and the rain.
And I can remember nothing dearer or more to my heart
Than the children I watched in the woods on Saturday
Shaking down burning chestnuts for the schoolyard's merry play,
Or the shaggy patient dog who followed me
By Sheet and Steep and up the wooded scree
To the Shoulder O' Mutton where Edward Thomas brooded long
On death and beauty—till a bullet stopped his song.

HENRY REED
1914–1986

Reed graduated from the University of Birmingham and became a teacher, journalist, and author of popular radio plays. His experience of being lectured at by non-commissioned officers while an army cadet he recalled sardonically when the war was over, a reminder of the amount of wartime spent listening to (useless) instruction.

LESSONS OF THE WAR
To Alan Michell

Vixi duellis nuper idoneus
Et militavi non sine gloria

I. NAMING OF PARTS

To-day we have naming of parts. Yesterday,
We had daily cleaning. And to-morrow morning,
We shall have what to do after firing. But to-day,
To-day we have naming of parts. Japonica
Glistens like coral in all of the neighbouring gardens,
       And to-day we have naming of parts.

This is the lower sling swivel. And this
Is the upper sling swivel, whose use you will see,
       When you are given your slings. And this is the piling
                                                    swivel,
Which in your case you have not got. The branches
Hold in the gardens their silent, eloquent gestures,
       Which in our case we have not got.

This is the safety-catch, which is always released
With an easy flick of the thumb. And please do not let me

See anyone using his finger. You can do it quite easy
If you have any strength in your thumb. The blossoms
Are fragile and motionless, never letting anyone see
    Any of them using their finger.

And this you can see is the bolt. The purpose of this
Is to open the breech, as you see. We can slide it
Rapidly backwards and forwards: we call this
Easing the spring. And rapidly backwards and forwards
The early bees are assaulting and fumbling the flowers:
    They call it easing the Spring.
They call it easing the Spring: it is perfectly easy
If you have any strength in your thumb: like the bolt,
And the breech, and the cocking-piece, and the point of
                                                balance,
Which in our case we have not got; and the almond-blossom
Silent in all of the gardens and the bees going backwards
                                        and forwards,
    For to-day we have naming of parts.

II. JUDGING DISTANCES

Not only how far away, but the way that you say it
Is very important. Perhaps you may never get
The knack of judging a distance, but at least you know
How to report on a landscape: the central sector,
The right of arc and that, which we had last Tuesday,
    And at least you know

That maps are of time, not place, so far as the army
Happens to be concerned—the reason being,
Is one which need not delay us. Again, you know
There are three kinds of tree, three only, the fir and the
                                                poplar,
And those which have bushy tops to; and lastly
    That things only seem to be things.

A barn is not called a barn, to put it more plainly,
Or a field in the distance, where sheep may be safely
                                                grazing.
You must never be over-sure. You must say, when
                                            reporting:
At five o'clock in the central sector is a dozen

Of what appear to be animals; whatever you do,
Don't call the bleeders *sheep*.

I am sure that's quite clear; and suppose, for the sake of
                                                    example,
The one at the end, asleep, endeavours to tell us
What he sees over there to the west, and how far away,
After first having come to attention. There to the west,
On the fields of summer the sun and the shadows bestow
    Vestments of purple and gold.
The still white dwellings are like a mirage in the heat,
And under the swaying elms a man and a woman
Lie gently together. Which is, perhaps, only to say
That there is a row of houses to the left of arc,
And that under some poplars a pair of what appear to be
                                                    humans
    Appear to be loving.

Well that, for an answer, is what we might rightly call
Moderately satisfactory only, the reason being,
Is that two things have been omitted, and those are
                                                    important.
The human beings, now: in what direction are they,
And how far away, would you say? And do not forget
    There may be dead ground in between.

There may be dead ground in between; and I may not have
                                                    got
The knack of judging a distance; I will only venture
A guess that perhaps between me and the apparent lovers,
(Who, incidentally, appear by now to have finished,)
At seven o'clock from the houses, is roughly a distance
    Of about one year and a half.

III. UNARMED COMBAT

In due course of course you will all be issued with
Your proper issue; but until to-morrow,
You can hardly be said to need it; and until that time,
We shall have unarmed combat. I shall teach you.
The various holds and rolls and throws and breakfalls
    Which you may sometimes meet.

And the various holds and rolls and throws and breakfalls
Do not depend on any sort of weapon,
But only on what I might coin a phrase and call
The ever-important question of human balance,
And the ever-important need to be in a strong
    Position at the start.

There are many kinds of weakness about the body,
Where you would least expect, like the ball of the foot.
But the various holds and rolls and throws and breakfalls
Will always come in useful. And never be frightened
To tackle from behind: it may not be clean to do so,
    But this is global war.

So give them all you have, and always give them
As good as you get; it will always get you somewhere.
(You may not know it, but you can tie a Jerry
Up without rope; it is one of the things I shall teach you.)
Nothing will matter if only you are ready for him.
    The readiness is all.

The readiness is all. How can I help but feel
I have been here before? But somehow then,
I was the tied-up one. How to get out
Was always then my problem. And even if I had
A piece of rope I was always the sort of person
    Who threw the rope aside.

And in my time I have given them all I had,
Which was never as good as I got, and it got me nowhere.
And the various holds and rolls and throws and breakfalls
Somehow or other I always seemed to put
In the wrong place. And as for war, my wars
    Were global from the start.

Perhaps I was never in a strong position,
Or the ball of my foot got hurt, or I had some weakness
Where I had least expected. But I think I see your point.
While awaiting a proper issue, we must learn the lesson
Of the ever-important question of human balance.
    It is courage that counts.

Things may be the same again; and we must fight
Not in the hope of winning but rather of keeping

Something alive: so that when we meet our end,
It may be said that we tackled wherever we could,
That battle-fit we lived, and though defeated,
Not without glory fought.

JOHN PUDNEY
1909-1977

Pudney, a journalist, was an intelligence officer with the RAF. "The twelve lines of 'For Johnny,' " he said, "were first written on the back of an envelope in London during an air raid alert in 1941." He added: "There never was a particular Johnny. The twelve lines, which forced themselves on me virtually intact at one go, were meant for them all."

FOR JOHNNY

Do not despair
For Johnny-head-in-air;
He sleeps as sound
As Johnny under ground.

Fetch out no shroud
For Johnny-in-the-cloud;
And keep your tears
For him in after years.

Better by far
For Johnny-the-bright-star,
To keep your head,
And see his children fed.

MISSING

Less said the better.
The bill unpaid, the dead letter,
No roses at the end
Of Smith, my friend.

Last words don't matter,
And there are none to flatter.
Words will not fill the post
Of Smith, the ghost.

For Smith, our brother,
Only son of loving mother,
The ocean lifted, stirred,
Leaving no word.

GAVIN EWART
1916–

Ewart is best known as a poet of rowdy comic verse, but during the war, serving in the British army in North Africa and Italy, he witnessed events grim enough to supply a dark, ironic shading to even his funniest capers. A Beau is a Beaufighter, a heavy two-man British observation plane and fighter. The event in "Incident, Second World War" actually occurred. A cousin of Ewart's, to whom the poem is dedicated, was present and was killed.

WHEN A BEAU GOES IN

When a Beau goes in,
Into the drink,
It makes you think,

Because, you see, they always sink
But nobody says "Poor lad"
Or goes about looking sad
Because, you see, it's war,
It's the unalterable law.

Although it's perfectly certain
The pilot's gone for a Burton
And the observer too
It's nothing to do with you
And if they both should go
To a land where falls no rain nor hail nor driven snow—
Here, there or anywhere,
Do you suppose *they* care?

You shouldn't cry
Or say a prayer or sigh.
In the cold sea, in the dark,
It isn't a lark
But it isn't Original Sin—
It's just a Beau going in.

INCIDENT, SECOND WORLD WAR
(In Memoriam P.M.B. Matson)

It was near the beginning of that war. 1940 or '41,
when everything was fairly new to almost everyone.
The bombing of cities we understood, and blackouts; and certainly,
    thanks
to the German Army and Air Force, we'd seen dive-bombers and tanks.
But when the fighters came in to strafe with hedge-hopping low attacks
how many bits and pieces would be picked up to fill the sacks?
Aircraft cannon were not much fun for the weary grounded troops
and there wasn't much entertainment when the Stukas were looping
    loops
but nobody knew for certain the percentage who wouldn't get up,
how many would be donating their arms or their legs to Krupp.
So somebody in an office had the very bright idea,
why not set up an Exercise: machine-gunning from the air?
The War Office would know exactly the kind of figures involved,
an exciting statistical problem could be regarded as solved.

In a field, they put khaki dummies, on the reverse side of a hill.
And afterwards, they reckoned, they could estimate the kill.
Opposite these was the audience, to watch the total effect,
a sort of firework display—but free—the RAF being the architect.
All arms were represented? I think so. A grandstand seat
was reserved for top brass and others, a healthy open-air treat;
enclosed, beyond the dummies, they stood (or sat?) and smoked
or otherwise passed the time of day, relaxed as they talked and joked.

An experienced Spitfire pilot was briefed to fly over low
and give those dummies all he'd got—the star turn of the show,
with all the verisimilitude of a surprise attack.
Then to his fighter station he would whizz round and back.
They waited. And suddenly, waiting, they saw that angel of death
come at them over the hillside. Before they could draw breath
he passed with all guns firing; some fell on their faces, flat,
but the benefit was minimal that anyone had from that.
He reckoned that *they* were the dummies, in his slap-happy lone-wolf
　　way,
that trigger-crazy pilot. He might have been right, some say.
But bitterness and flippancy don't compensate for men's lives
and official notifications posted to mothers and wives.

Nevertheless, there *were* results; percentages were worked out,
how 10 per cent could be written off, the wounded would be about
50 per cent or so. Oh yes, they got their figures all right.
Circulated to units. So at least that ill-omened flight
was a part of the Allied war effort, and on the credit side—
except for those poor buggers who just stood there and died.

JAMES JONES
1921–1977

Jones was an enlisted man in the United States Army before the war. His outfit landed on Guadalcanal in January 1943, but after two days on the line Jones was wounded, and the rest of the war he spent in hospitals or absent without leave, disturbed and alcoholic. The Guadalcanal campaign is the context of his novel The Thin Red Line, *published in 1962. In 1975 a publisher persuaded Jones to supply a text for a book exhibiting the art—paintings, drawings, and cartoons—of the war. Jones made of the job an occasion to deliver not just a brief history of the war but a memorable personal deposition about the psychology, the hopes and fears and neuroses and complaints, of the Second World War infantry soldier. The book is laconically titled* WWII.

From THE THIN RED LINE

"Grab holt and prepare to land!" the barge pilot shouted at them. Doll did. In a couple of moments the barge grated, cleared and rushed on, grated again, lurched, ground on noisily a few more feet and stopped, and Doll was on Guadalcanal. So were the rest of the men in the same barge, but Doll did not consider that. The front ramp, handled by the talkative assistant pilot, had already begun to fall almost before the barge was stopped.

"Everybody out!" the barge pilot shouted. "No transfer slips!"

There still remained two feet of water beyond the end of the ramp, but it was easy enough to jump; and only one man, who slipped on the metal of the ramp, landed in the water and got one foot wet. It wasn't Doll. The ramp was already rising, as the barge went into reverse and pulled back out to go for another load. Then they were trudging through the sand up the long beach, trying to pick their way across it through the streams of men, to where Bugger Stein and Lieutenant Band were assembling the company.

Corporal Fife had, of course, been in the barge which brought off the company headquarters. Their barge pilot had told them substantially the same thing Doll's had: "Your outfit's lucky. The Jap's on his way." The transports must have been spotted, he said. But they were getting off just ahead of time, he said, so they'd be safe. The main thought uppermost in Fife's mind was that everything was so organized, and handled with such matter-of-fact dispatch. Like a business. Like a regular business. And yet at the bottom of it was blood: blood, mutilation, death. It seemed weird, wacky, to Fife. The air strip had got the news, by radio from a plane apparently, and had transmitted it to the beach, where the barge pilots were all informed—or else informed themselves and each other—and presumably the crews as well as the army commanders, if not the troops themselves, on board the ships were told, too. And yet there was nothing anybody could do about it, apparently. Except wait. Wait and see what happened. Fife had looked around at the faces in the barge covertly.

Bugger Stein betrayed his nervousness by continually adjusting his glasses, over and over, with the thumb and fingers of his right hand on the frame. Lieutenant Band betrayed his by repeatedly licking his lips. Storm's face was too impassively set. The second cook Dale's eyes were snapping bright, and he blinked them over and over. Welsh's eyes, through the narrow slits to which they were closed in the bright sun, betrayed nothing of anything. Neither amusement nor anything else, this time; not even cynicism. Fife hoped his own face looked all right, but he felt as though his eyebrows might be too high up on his forehead. Once they got ashore, and the guide had led them to their assigned spot in the edge of the coconut trees which came right down to the beach itself, Fife kept saying over and over to himself what the barge pilot had told them on the way in: "Your outfit's lucky. You're getting off ahead of time."

And in a way, it was quite right too. When the planes came, they were after the ships, not the shore. As a result, Fife, and all the rest of C-for-Charlie had a perfectly safe grandstand, ringside seat for the whole show. Actually Fife at least, who loved humanity, was going to find that he wished he hadn't had a seat at all, after it was over. But he had to admit it fascinated him, with a morbid fascination.

Apparently the news had not affected the beach very much at all. The LCIs and a welter of other types of barges still came roaring, jamming in to unload their cargoes of men or supplies, while others were in process of pulling back out to rejoin the shuttle. The beach was literally alive with men, all moving somewhere, and seemed to undulate with a life of its own under their mass as beaches sometimes appear to do when invaded by armies of fiddler crabs. Lines, strings and streams of men crossed and recrossed it with hot-footed and apparently unregulated alacrity. They were in all stages of dress and undress, sleeveless shirts, legless pants, no shirts at all, and in some few cases, particularly those working in or near the water, they worked totally stark naked or in their white government issue underpants through which the dark hairiness of their genitals showed plainly. There were no women anywhere around here at all anyway, and there were not likely to be any either for quite some little time. They wore all sorts of fantastic headgear, issue, civilian, and homemade, so that one might see a man working in the water totally naked with nothing adorning his person except his identity tags around his neck and a little red beany, turned-up fatigue hat, or a hat of banana leaves on his head. The supply barges were unloaded by gangs of men immediately, right at the water's edge, so that the barge could go back for more. Then lines of other men carried these boxes, cases, cans back up the beach into the trees, or formed chains and passed them from hand to hand, trying to clear the space at the water's edge. Further away down the beach the heavier matériel, trucks, anti-tank guns, artillery, were being unloaded, driven by their own drivers, or hauled up by Marine tractors. And still further away, this whole operation was being conducted a second time for the second transport, anchored quite a few hundred yards behind the first.

All of this activity had been going on at this same pace since very early morning apparently, and the news of the impending air raid did not appear to affect it one way or the other. But as the minutes crept by one after the other, there was a noticeable change in the emotional quality and excitement of the beach. C-for-Charlie, from its vantage point at the edge of the trees, could sense the tautening of the emotional tenor. They watched a number of men who had been calmly bathing waistdeep in the sea in the midst of all this hectic activity, look at their watches and then get out and walk naked up to their clothes in the edge of the trees. Then, just a few moments after this, someone at the water's edge flung up an arm and cried out, "There they are!" and the cry was taken up all up and down the beach.

High up in the sunbright sky a number of little specks sailed serenely along toward the channel where the two ships lay. After a couple of minutes when they were closer, a number of other specks, fighter planes, could be seen above them engaging each other. Below on the beach the men with jobs and the working parties had already gone back to their work; but as the others, including C-for-Charlie company, watched, about half the engaged fighter planes broke off and turned back to the north, apparently having reached the limit of their fuel range. Only a couple of the remaining fighters started out to chase them, and they almost at once gave it up and turned back, and with the others began to attack the bombers. On they all came, slowly getting larger. The tiny mosquitoes dipped and swirled and dived in a mad, whirling dance around the heavier, stolid horseflies, who nevertheless kept serenely and sedately on. Now the bombers began to fall, first one here, trailing a great plume of smoke soon dissipated by the winds of the upper air, then another one there, trailing no smoke at all and fluttering down. No parachutes issued from them. Still the bombers kept on. Then one of the little mosquitoes fell, and a moment later, in another place, another. Parachutes appeared from both, floating in the sunbright air. Still the mosquitoes darted and swirled. Another injured horsefly fell. But it was surprising, at least to C-for-Charlie and the other newcomers, how many did not fall. Considering the vehemence and numbers of the attack, it appeared that they must all go down. But they didn't, and the whole concerted mass moved slowly on toward the ships in the channel, the changing tones of the motors as the fighters dived or climbed clearly discernible now.

Below on the beach the minutes, and then the seconds, continued to tick by. There were no cheers when a bomber fell. When the first one had fallen, another new company nearby to C-for-Charlie had made an attempt at a feeble cheer, in which a few men from C-for-Charlie had joined. But it soon died from lack of nourishment, and after that it was not again attempted. Everybody watched in silence, rapt, fascinated. And the men down on the beach continued to work, though more excitedly now.

To Corporal Fife, standing tensely in the midst of the silent company headquarters, the lack of cheering only heightened his previous impression of its all being like a business. A regular business venture, not war at all. The idea was horrifying to Fife. It was weird and wacky and somehow insane. It was even immoral. It was as though a clerical, mathematical equation had been worked out, as a calculated risk: Here were two large, expensive ships and, say, twenty-five large aircraft had been sent out after them. These had been given protection as long as possible by smaller aircraft, which were less expensive than they, and then sent on alone on the theory that all or part of twenty-five large aircraft was worth all or part of two large ships. The defending fighters, working on the same principle, strove to keep the price as high as possible, their ultimate hope being to get all twenty-five large aircraft without paying all or any of either ship. And that there were men in these expensive machines which were contending with each other, was unimportant—except for the fact that they were needed to manipulate the machines. The very idea itself, and what it implied, struck a cold blade of terror into Fife's essentially defenseless vitals, a terror both of unimportance, his unimportance, and of powerlessness: his powerlessness. He had no control or sayso in any of it. Not even where it concerned himself, who was also a part of it. It was terrifying. He did not mind dying in a war, a real war—at least, he didn't think he did—but he did not want to die in a regulated business venture.

Slowly and inexorably the contending mass high up in the air came on. On the beach the work did not stop. Neither did the LCIs and other barges. When the planes had almost reached the ships, one more bomber fell, crashing and exploding in smoke and flames in the channel in full view of everybody. Then they began to pass over the ships. A gentle sighing became audible through the air. Then a geyser of water, followed by another, then another, popped high up out of the sea. Seconds later the sounds of the explosions which had caused them swept across the beach and on past them into the coconut trees, rustling them. The gentle sighing noise grew louder, carrying a fluttery overtone, and other geysers began to pop up all over the sea around the first ship, and then a few seconds later, around the second. It was no longer possible to distinguish the individual sticks of bombs, but they all saw the individual stick of three bombs which made the hit. Like probing fingers, the first lit some distance in front of the first ship, the second coming closer. The third fell almost directly alongside. An LCI was just putting off from the ship, it couldn't have been many yards away, and the third bomb apparently landed directly on it. From that distance, probably a thousand yards or more, one faint, but clearly discernible scream, high and shrill, and which actually did not reach them until after the geyser had already gone up, was heard by the men on shore, cut off and followed immediately by the sound wave of the explosion: some one nameless man's single instinctual and useless protest against the taking of his life and his own bad luck at being where he was instead of somewhere else, ridiculous, pointless, but not without a certain dignity, although, ironically, it was not heard, and appreciated, until after he himself no longer existed. His last scream had lived longer than he had.

When the spout of water had subsided so that they could see, there was nothing left of the LCI to be seen. At the spot where it had been a few figures bobbed in the water, and these rapidly became fewer. The two barges nearest them came about and made for the spot, reaching them before the little rescue boat that was standing by could get there. Losing way, they wallowed in the trough while infantrymen stripped off equipment and dived in to help both the injured and uninjured who had had no time to strip equipment and were being dragged under by it. The less seriously wounded and the uninjured were helped aboard the barges on little rope ladders thrown over the side by the pilots; the more seriously hurt were simply kept afloat until the rescue boat, which carried slings and baskets and was already on its way, could get there.

On shore, the watching men—the lucky ones, as the barge pilots had said, because they were out of it—tried to divide their attention between this operation and the planes still overhead. The bombers, having made their run, turned out toward the channel and headed back north. They made no attempt at strafing, they were too busy protecting themselves from the fighters, and the antiaircraft crews on the ships and shore could not fire either for fear of hitting their own fighters. The whole operation, except for the dropped bombs themselves, had taken place up there, high up in the air. Slowly, sedately, the bombers headed back into the north to where a protective blanket of their own fighters would be waiting for them, growing slowly and steadily smaller, as before they had grown slowly and steadily larger. The fighters still buzzed angrily around them, and before they were lost to sight a few more fell. All during the action the defending fighters had been hampered by having to break off and streak back to the air strip to renew fuel or ammunition. Replenished, they would return. But the number of fighters actually engaged was never as large as it might have been. Apparently the bombers were allowing for this factor. At any rate, slowly they dwindled to specks again, then to invisibility. Then finally, the fighters began to return. It was over. On the beach the work of unloading, which had never ceased during the attack, went right on.

Men who had been here longer and who were standing nearby to
C-for-Charlie, which still waited—and watched—from the edge of the
coconut grove, told them that there would probably be at least two more
attacks, now, during the day. The main thing was to get the damned
ships unloaded so they could get out of here and thus let things settle
back peacefully to normal. The unloading was the most important thing
of all. But it had to be finished by nightfall. The ships had to be out of
here as soon as it got dark, fully unloaded or not, rather than risk night
air attacks. If they weren't fully unloaded, they would leave anyway.

Already, long before the retreating bombers were out of sight, word
had circulated around the beach that the first transport had been damaged by the same bomb which had destroyed the bargeful of infantrymen. This was an even more important reason for the ships to get out.
The damage was slight, but the bomb had sprung some plates and she
was taking water, though not enough that the pumps could not handle
it. There had been some casualties aboard the ship, too, caused by bomb
fragments or pieces of flying metal from the barge among the densely
crowded men on deck; and one man, word had it, had had his face
smashed in by a helmet blown from the head of some man in the barge:
a complete, solid helmet, undented, undamaged. Such were the vagaries
of existence, the word had it. Pieces of meat and chunks of shattered
equipment had also been blown up onto the ship's deck from the barge,
the jagged riflestocks causing some little further injury. Apparently, word
from the ship said, the bomb had not landed directly in the barge itself,
but had hit right alongside its gunnel, between it and the ship. This was
the reason for the blast damage to the ship. On the other hand, had it
landed on the opposite side of the barge away from the ship, or even in
the barge, the men on deck would have been bombarded with a great
deal more meat and metal than they had been. As it was, the most of it
had—because of the bomb's position—been blown away from the ship
across the water. The casualties on board the ship, the word said, had
been seven dead and twenty-two injured, amongst which injured was the
man who had had his face smashed in by the helmet. All of these were
being cared for aboard in the ship's hospital.

C-for-Charlie heard this news with a strange feeling. This had been
their ship, these men now dead and injured their sailing companions.
The spot where the bomb fell had not been at all far from their own
debarkation position. They listened to the word-of-mouth reports with a
sort of mixture of awe and imaginative fear which they found completely
uncontrollable: If the bombers had been a few minutes earlier. Or if they
themselves had been only a few minutes later getting up on deck. Suppose one of the companies ahead of them had been much slower getting
off? Suppose, for that matter, the bomb hadn't landed some yards off in
the water? Suppose it had landed that number of yards toward the rail?
This sort of speculation was, of course, useless. As well as acutely painful.

But a strong awareness of this uselessness did not seem to help to make the speculation cease.

The survivors of the destroyed LCI were landed from the two barges and the rescue boat which had picked them up, not far away from C-for-Charlie company; so C-for-Charlie got to observe this action, too. With practical comments as to the extent of the various injuries in their ears from the nearby men who had been here longer, C-for-Charlie watched round-eyed as these men were tenderly led or carried up from the beach to where a field dressing station had been set up at dawn. Some of them were still vomiting sea water from their ordeal. A few were able to walk by themselves. But all of them were suffering from shock, as well as from blast, and the consummate tenderness with which they were handled first by their rescuers and then by the corpsmen was a matter of complete indifference to them and meant nothing. Blood-stained, staggering, their eyeballs rolling, the little party faltered up the slope of the beach to sit or lie, dazed and indifferent, and acquiescently allow themselves to be worked on by the doctors.

They had crossed a strange line; they had become wounded men; and everybody realized, including themselves, dimly, that they were now different. Of itself, the shocking physical experience of the explosion, which had damaged them and killed those others, had been almost identically the same for them as for those other ones who had gone on with it and died. The only difference was that now these, unexpectedly and illogically, found themselves alive again. They had not asked for the explosion, and they had not asked to be brought back. In fact, they had done nothing. All they had done was climb into a barge and sit there as they had been told. And then this had been done to them, without warning, without explanation, perhaps damaging them irreparably; and now they were wounded men; and now explanation was impossible. They had been initiated into a strange, insane, twilight fraternity where explanation would be forever impossible. Everybody understood this; as did they themselves, dimly. It did not need to be mentioned. Everyone was sorry, and so were they themselves. But there was nothing to be done about it. Tenderness was all that could be given, and, like most of the self-labeled human emotions, it meant nothing when put alongside the intensity of their experience.

With the planes which had done this to them still in sight above the channel, the doctors began swiftly to try to patch up, put back together, and save, what they could of what the planes had done. Some of them were pretty badly torn up, others not so badly. Some would yet die, so much was obvious, and it was useless to waste time on these which might be spent on others who might live. Those who would die accepted this professional judgment of the doctors silently, as they accepted the tender pat on the shoulder the doctors gave them when passing them by, staring up mutely from bottomless, liquid depths of still-living eyes at the doctors' guilty faces.

C-for-Charlie, standing nearby, and already counted off again into its true structural unity of platoons, watched this action at the aid station with rapt fascination. Each of its platoons and its company headquarters instinctively huddled together as though for warmth against a chill, seeking a comfort from the nearness of others which was not forthcoming, five separate little groups of wide-eyed spectators consumed with an almost sexual, morbid curiosity. Here were men who were going to die, some of them before their very eyes. How would they react? Would some of them rage against it, as they themselves felt like raging? Or would they simply all expire quietly, stop breathing, cease to see? C-for-Charlie, as one man, was curious to see: to see a man die. Curious with a hushed, breathless awe. They could not help but be; fresh blood was so very red, and gaping holes in bared flesh were such curious, strange sights. It was all obscene somehow. Something which they all felt should not be looked at, somehow, but which they were compelled to look at, to cluster closer and study. The human body was really a very frail, defenseless organism, C-for-Charlie suddenly realized. And these men might have been themselves. So might those others, out there now under the water over which the LCIs still scurried, and who would not be searched out and raised until the cessation of the unloading offered time and opportunity.

The wounded men, both those who would die and those who would not, were as indifferent to being stared at as they were to the tenderness with which they were treated. They stared back at their audience with lacklustre eyes, eyes which though lustreless were made curiously limpid by the dilation of deep shock, and if they saw them at all, which was doubtful, what they saw did not register. As a result, the whole of C-for-Charlie felt it, too: what all the others, with more experience, knew: These men had crossed a line, and it was useless to try to reach them. These had experienced something that they themselves had not experienced, and devoutly hoped they never would experience, but until they did experience it they could no longer communicate with them. An hour ago—even less than that—these had been like themselves; nervous, jumpy, waiting with trepidation at how they would behave, to be disembarked. Now they had joined company with—and had even gone beyond—those strange, wild-eyed, bearded, crazily dressed Marines and soldiers who had been fighting the Japanese here since August and who now stood around matter-of-factly, discussing professionally which of these wounds they thought might be fatal, and which might not.

Even the army itself understood this about them, the wounded, and had made special dispensations for their newly acquired honorary status. Those who did not die would be entered upon the elaborate shuttling movement back out from this furthermost point of advance, as only a short time back they had been entered upon the shuttle forward into it. Back out, and further and further back, toward that amorphous point of assumed total safety. It was as though, if each man's life in the army were looked upon as a graph, beginning at the bottom with his induction and rising steadily to this point, then this moment now—or rather the moment of the explosion itself, actually—could be considered the apex from which the line turned downward, back toward the bottom and his eventual discharge: his secret goal. Depending upon the seriousness of his condition and the amount of time required to heal him, his graph line would descend part, or all of the way, to the bottom. Some, the least injured, might never even get as far back as New Zealand or Australia, and might end their downward course at a base hospital in the New Hebrides and from there be sent back up again. Others, slightly more wounded, might get to New Zealand or Australia, but not back to the States, and so be sent forward again from there. Still others, more serious yet, might get to the States and yet not be discharged, so that they might be sent out again from there, toward this moving danger point of the front, either back this way, or to Europe. All of these graph lines would rise again, perhaps to an even higher apex. The dead, of course, would find that their graph lines stopped; at the apex itself, like those out there under the water, or else a little way below it like these men dying here.

It could all be worked out mathematically, young Corporal Fife thought suddenly when he discovered these thoughts running through his mind, and someone ought to do it. It would require a tremendous amount of work though, with all the men there were in all the armies of the world. But perhaps an electric brain could be constructed that would handle it.

At any rate, clearly the best way to be wounded, if one must be wounded at all, was to have a wound so bad that you would almost die, one that would leave you sick long enough for the war to get over, but which when you recovered from it would not leave you crippled or an invalid. Either that, or receive a minor wound which would incapacitate or cripple you slightly without crippling fully. Fife could not decide which he would prefer. He didn't really prefer any, that was the truth.

In the end, C-for-Charlie got to see three men die in the aid station, before the jeep with its route guide from regimental headquarters arrived to lead it to its bivouac. Of these three, two died very quietly, slowly sinking further and further into that state of unreality brought on by shock and by the ebbing of the functions so that the mind mercifully does not comprehend what is happening to it. Only one man raged against it, and he only for a moment, rousing himself briefly from his steadily encroaching hallucination to shout curses and epithets against what was happening to him and against everything which contributed to it, the doctors, the bomb, the war, the generals, the nations, before relapsing back quietly into the numbing sleep which would pass over into death with scarcely a transition. Others would die too here, certainly—as well as almost certainly still others on the plane out, or in the base hospital—but C-for-Charlie was not there to see them. They were already off on their six mile route march to their new bivouac.

From WWII

WAITING

My outfit had won a battle star for Midway. So had every other outfit serving in Hawaii at the time. Because of some geographical technicality, Hawaii had been included in the theater of operations. So that earned us the little bronze battle star—which, somebody or other told us, was to go on the orange, red-striped Asiatic-Pacific Campaign medal and ribbon; not on the yellow American Defense ribbon, where the battle star for Pearl Harbor was to be worn.

But, as somebody else pointed out, it appeared unlikely any of us would see any of those medals, or even the official campaign ribbons, for quite some little time. Maybe never. No one appeared scheduled to come around and bestow them. The same did not hold true for the commercial army-navy stores on the island, however. Almost before the news of Midway could be digested, the army-navy stores began displaying for sale, along with the American Defense ribbon and star, commercial copies of the Asiatic-Pacific ribbon with a star on it. None of us had even seen it. How they got them over from California, with all the severely restricted priority wartime shipping, no one knew. Somebody suggested maybe they made them on the island.

Around us Honolulu continued to grow and expand into a boom town. Troops, ships, workers, clerks, boatloads of supplies and matériel. Then it was announced the marines had invaded Guadalcanal in the Solomon Islands, and we knew where the carriers had gone.

On through the summer we had continued to maintain our anti-invasion guard on the beaches, with our puny .30-caliber watercooled MGs. (Nobody had had to tell us how ineffectual they would be against a serious invasion.) And as the hypothetical invasion threat shrank and then disappeared entirely with the victory at Midway, our guarding and guard inspections shrank in efficiency in direct ratio to the slackening of tension. We began to agitate for more passes. Some of the guys, who were lucky enough to be on beach positions which had suburban homes nearby, had found themselves wahine girlfriends in the neighborhood.

We were settling in. But that heavy cloud of waiting and wondering where we were going hung over us. Some of us who were not so lucky were on beach positions out of town farther east, in a string all the way to Makapuu Head where the southern exposure of Honolulu turns the corner to become the famous Windward Side, over which the easterly wind from the Mainland never ceases to blow, day or night.

But even we had our little windfalls. One day, when some of us were sitting on the wall of the scenic overlook in that wind, speculating on just when there would be tourists again, especially women tourists, to drive out in their rented cars to our scenic overlook, a half-Hawaiian gentleman with a good eye for business drove up in a pick-up truck with four wahines in the back. While our lieutenant and his staff sergeant looked the other way, the four girls, utilizing one of our five pillboxes and a sheltered ledge open to the wind directly behind it, managed to take care of the whole thirty-seven of us on the position in just over forty-five minutes. The lieutenant timed it, while ordering five men who had already been to go and relieve the five men on post in the pillboxes so they could go. The fee was ten bucks a man, and everybody was happy with the price.

But windfalls like that were rare. Word somehow got back to the company headquarters, and the man didn't come again. We went back to our more constant though less favorite pastime. Speculating on what was going to happen to us. Some rumors going around said we were going to Australia. That would mean combat against the Japanese, somewhere down there. Very few were really looking forward to that. Other, more hopeful rumors were that we were going to stay right there in Hawaii for the duration, as a former part of the old Hawaiian Division, and continue to take care of, guard and protect our dear friends the Islanders. Nobody quite believed that one.

And yet, strangely, if we had really found out we were actually going to stay on in Hawaii for the duration, we would not have been happy about it. We wanted to get into the act. On the other hand, if we had really found we were going to go south to combat, we would not have liked it at all. Thus, waiting, we teetered and swayed, pulled one way, then pulled another.

Then quite suddenly in mid-September we got orders to move back to Schofield Barracks for a period of reorganization and intensive training. Our beach positions would be taken over by a new, "green" division recently arrived from the States. We wondered what they thought we were, a "weathered" division, after our brief excitement of Pearl Harbor?

While we were at Schofield, whenever we had a free minute, which was seldom, we did what we had done all the past six months. We wondered, and we waited. Our training was neither intensive nor complete. It was woefully inadequate, and we knew it. But then these were the early days of the war. And perhaps it was impossible really to train a man for combat, without putting him actually in it. We jumped off some antique barges, already obsolete, and waded through shallow water and sand. We crawled on our bellies through mud under machine gun fire which was coming from MGs fixed between posts. We practiced throwing hand grenades, and practiced firing our rifles and various weapons. All this we had already done, except the barge part, innumerable times. For a week we had an hour of jiu-jitsu a day, and tried throwing each other on the ground. The rumor was still Australia.

Then, equally suddenly, the rest of our training schedule was cancelled, and we were loaded onto transports inside Pearl Harbor. The transports sailed out into the wastes of the trackless Pacific. We sat on the transports, and did what we had done at Schofield, in our few spare moments, the same as we had done all during the six months before. The rumor was still Australia.

*   *   *

GUADALCANAL

Long afterward, we found that our training schedule had been cut short because a big troop transport headed for Guadalcanal had run afoul of the Japs and been sunk, and men were urgently needed on Guadalcanal. But our original destination really had been Australia.

O, shades of splendid endeavor. Of youth's wild strenuous exertion and adventure. O, lost tropic beauty of sea and cocopalm and sand.

It is scarcely believable that I can remember it with pleasure, and affection, and a sense of beauty. But such are the vagaries of the human head. One can hardly credit that a place so full of personal misery and terror, which was perfectly capable of taking your life and on a couple of occasions very nearly did, could be remembered with such kindly feelings, but I do. The pervasive mud, and jungle gloom and tropical sun, when they are not all around you smothering you, can have a haunting beauty at a far remove. When you are not straining and gasping to save your life, the act of doing so can seem adventurous and exciting from a distance. The greater the distance, the greater the adventure.

But, God help me, it was beautiful. I remember exactly the way it looked the day we came up on deck to go ashore: the delicious sparkling tropic sea, the long beautiful beach, the minute palms of the copra plantation waving in the sea breeze, the dark green band of jungle, and the dun mass and power of the mountains rising behind it to rocky peaks. Our bivouac was not far from the ruined plantation house and quarters, and you could look at its ruin—not without awe—and imagine what it must have been like to live here before the armies came with their vehicles and numberless feet and mountains of supplies. Armies create their own mud, in actual fact. The jungle stillnesses and slimes in the gloom inside the rain forest could make you catch your breath with awe. From the mountain slopes in mid-afternoon with the sun at your back you could look back down to the beach and off across the straits to Florida Island and one of the most beautiful views of tropic scenery on the planet. None of it looked like the pestilential hellhole that it was.

The day we arrived there was an air raid, trying to hit our two transports. Those of us already ashore could stand in perfect safety in the edge of the trees and watch as if watching a football game or a movie. Around us marines and army old-timers would cheer whenever a Jap plane went smoke-trailing down the sky, or groan when one got through and water spouts geysered up around the transports. Soon we were doing it with them. Neither transport took a hit, but one took a near-miss so close alongside it sprang some plates, and had to leave without finishing unloading. Almost immediately after, a loaded barge coming in took a hit and seemed simply to disappear. A little rescue boat set out from shore at once, to pick up the few bobbing survivors. It seemed strange and curiously callous, then, to be watching and cheering this game in which men were dying.

Later, after our first time up on the line, we would sit in our bivouac on the hills above Henderson Field and watch the pyrotechnic display of a naval night battle off Savo Island with the same insouciance, and not feel callous at all. They took their chances and we took our chances.

Guadalcanal was the first American offensive anywhere, and as such got perhaps more than its fair share of notoriety, both in history and in the media of the time; more than later, perhaps tougher fights such as Tarawa and Peleliu. Fought at an earlier period of the war, when the numbers and matériel engaged were smaller, less trained and less organized, there was an air of adventure and sense of individual exploit about it (at least in the press) where small units of platoon and company strength still maintained importance, more than in the later battles of massed armadas, masses of newer equipment, and massed units of men in division and corps strength. It was still pretty primitive, Guadalcanal.

Everybody now knows, at least everybody of my generation, how the marines landed virtually unopposed on the 'Canal itself, after heavy fights on two smaller islands, Tulagi and Gavutu; how the Japanese, for reasons of their own deciding not to accept their first defeat, kept pouring men and equipment into the island; how Major General Vandegrift's tough First Marine Division, learning as they went along, fought them to a standstill, while the navy sank their loaded transports of reinforcements behind them—until in the end they were finally forced to evacuate it anyway. Not many, even of my generation, know that from about mid-November, 1942, on, U.S. infantry was doing much of the fighting on Guadalcanal, and from mid-December were doing it all. The doughty First Marine Division, dead beat, ill and tired, decimated by wounds and tropical diseases, but evolved into soldiers at last, had been relieved and evacuated.

The first elements of the Americal Division had landed in mid-October. The first elements of my outfit landed in late November, the rest in early December. No living soul looking at us, seeing us come hustling ashore to stare in awe at the hollow-eyed, vacant-faced, mean-looking First Marines, could have believed that in three months from that day we would be known as the famed Twenty-fifth Infantry Tropic Lightning Division, bearing the shoulder patch of the old Hawaiian Division Poi Leaf, with a streak of lightning running vertically through it. In the interim we had taken over from the First Marines, prosecuted the final offensive on the 'Canal, chased the Japanese to Tassafaronga in the whirlwind windup which gave us our name, and begun to move up to New Georgia for the next fight of our campaign. By then we would have had a fair amount of casualties and sick, and as a division and as individuals have made our own EVOLUTION OF A SOLDIER.

My own part in all of this was relatively undistinguished. I fought as an infantry corporal in a rifle company in a regiment of the Twenty-fifth, part of the time as an assistant squad leader, part of the time attached to the company headquarters. I went where I was told to go, and did what I was told to do, but no more. I was scared shitless just about all of the time. On the third day of a fight for a complex of hills called "The Galloping Horse" I was wounded in the head through no volition of my own, by a random mortar shell, spent a week in the hospital, and came back to my unit after the fight and joined them for the relatively little that was left of the campaign. I came out of it with a Purple Heart and a Bronze Star for "heroic or meritorious achievement" (not the V-for-Valor one), which was given to me apparently by a process as random as that of the random mortar shell that hit me. At least, I don't know anything I ever did to earn it. I was shipped out after the campaign for an injured ankle that had to be operated on.

It's funny, the things that get to you. One day a man near me was hit in the throat, as he stood up, by a bullet from a burst of MG fire. He cried out, "Oh, my God!" in an awful, grimly comic, burbling kind of voice that made me think of the signature of the old Shep Fields' Rippling Rhythm band. There was awareness in it, and a tone of having expected it, then he fell down, to all intents and purposes dead. I say "to all intents and purposes" because his vital functions may have continued for a while. But he appeared unconscious, and of course there was nothing to do for him with his throat artery torn out. Thinking about him, it seemed to me that his yell had been for all of us lying there, and I felt like crying.

Another time I heard a man yell out "I'm killed!" as he was hit. As it turned out, he was, although he didn't die for about fifteen minutes. But he might have yelled the same thing and not been killed.

One of the most poignant stories about our outfit was one I didn't see myself, but only heard about later. I was in the hospital when it happened. One of our platoon sergeants, during a relatively light Japanese attack on his position, reached into his hip pocket for a grenade he'd stuck there, and got it by the pin. The pin came out but the grenade didn't. No one really knows what he thought about during those split seconds. What he did was turn away and put his back against a bank to smother the grenade away from the rest of his men. He lived maybe five or ten minutes afterward, and the only thing he said, in a kind of awed, scared, very disgusted voice, was, "What a fucking recruit trick to pull."

A lot of the posthumous Medals of Honor that are given are given because men smothered grenades or shells with their bodies to protect the men around them. Nobody ever recommended our platoon sergeant for a Medal of Honor that I know of. Perhaps it was because he activated the grenade himself.

I think I screamed, myself, when I was hit. I thought I could vaguely remember somebody yelling. I blacked out for several seconds, and had a dim impression of someone stumbling to his feet with his hands to his face. It wasn't me. Then I came to myself several yards down the slope, bleeding like a stuck pig and blood running all over my face. It must have been a dramatic scene. As soon as I found I wasn't dead or dying, I was pleased to get out of there as fast as I could. According to the rules, my responsibility to stay ceased as soon as I was hurt. It really wasn't so bad, and hadn't hurt at all. The thing I was most proud of was that I remembered to toss my full canteen of water to one of the men from the company headquarters lying there.

SOLDIER'S EVOLUTION

What was it, really, this EVOLUTION OF A SOLDIER? What is it still? I've been talking about it all through this book, but I'm not sure I can explain or define it. I think that when all the nationalistic or ideological propaganda and patriotic slogans are put aside, all the straining to convince a soldier that he is dying *for* something, it is the individual soldier's final full acceptance of the fact that his name is already written down in the rolls of the already dead.

Every combat soldier, if he follows far enough along the path that began with his induction, must, I think, be led inexorably to that awareness. He must make a compact with himself or with Fate that he is lost. Only then can he function as he ought to function, under fire. He knows and accepts beforehand that he's dead, although he may still be walking around for a while. That soldier you have walking around there with this awareness in him is the final end product of the EVOLUTION OF A SOLDIER.

Between those two spectator episodes I described earlier, that first air raid we watched and cheered albeit guiltily, and the naval night battle we watched and cheered with callous pleasure, something had happened to us. Between those two points in time, somewhere during our first long tour up on the line, we changed. Consciously or unconsciously we accepted the fact that we couldn't survive. So we could watch the naval battle from the safety of the hills with undisguised fun.

There is no denying we were pleased to see somebody else getting his. Even though there were men dying. Being blown apart, concussed, drowning. Didn't matter. We had been getting ours, let them get theirs. It wasn't that we were being sadistic. It was just that we had nothing further to worry about. We were dead.

Now, not every man can accept this. A few men accept it immediately and at once, with a kind of feverish, self-destructive joy. The great majority of men don't want to accept it. They can accept it, though. And do accept it, if their outfit keeps going back up there long enough. The only alternative is to ask to be relieved and admit you are a coward, and that of course is against the law. They put you in prison.

And yet, strangely, for everyone, the acceptance and the giving up of hope create and reinstill hope in a kind of reverse-process mental photonegative function. Little things become significant. The next meal, the next bottle of booze, the next kiss, the next sunrise, the next full moon. The next bath. Or as the Bible might have said, but didn't quite, Sufficient unto the day is the existence thereof.

This is a hard philosophy. But then the soldier's profession is a hard profession, in wartime. A lot of men like it, though, and even civilian soldiers have been known to stay on and make it their life's work. It has its excitements and compensations. One of them is that, since you have none yourself, you are relieved of any responsibility for a future. And everything tastes better.

It is absolutely true, for example, that when you think, when you *know*, you are going off to die somewhere soon, every day has a special, bright, delicious, poignant taste to it that normal days in normal times do not have. Another perversity of the human mechanism?

Some men like to live like that all the time. Some are actually sorry to come home and see it end. Even those of us who hated it found it exciting, sometimes. That is what the civilian people never understand about their returned soldiers, in any war, Vietnam as well. They cannot understand how we could hate it, and still like it; and they do not realize they have a lot of dead men around them, dead men who are walking around and breathing. Some men find it hard to come back from their

EVOLUTION OF A SOLDIER. Some never come back at all, not completely. That's where the DE-EVOLUTION OF A SOLDIER comes in. Sometimes it takes at least as long to accomplish as its reverse process did.

Everything the civilian soldier learned and was taught from the moment of his induction was one more delicate stop along this path of the soldier evolving toward acceptance of his death. The idea that his death, under certain circumstances, is correct and right. The training, the discipline, the daily humiliations, the privileges of "brutish" sergeants, the living en masse like schools of fish, are all directed toward breaking down the sense of the sanctity of the physical person, and toward hardening the awareness that a soldier is the chattel (hopefully a proud chattel, but a chattel all the same) of the society he serves and was born a member of. And is therefore as dispensable as the ships and guns and tanks and ammo he himself serves and dispenses. Those are the terms of the contract he has made—or, rather, that the state has handed him to sign.

Most men in a war are never required to pay up in full on the contract for the life the state has loaned them. For every combat soldier there are about fifteen or twenty men required to maintain and service him who are never in much danger, if any. But everybody pays interest on the loan, and the closer to the front he gets the higher the interest rate. If he survives at all, it can take him a long time to get over the fact he isn't going to have to pay.

*   *   *

GREEN AND OBSCENE

The worst thing about being a seasoned soldier was they wouldn't let you go home. Your experience was needed, sorely needed, they told you. You yourself—that is, your body and its recently acquired skills—were at least ten times as valuable as when you were a green hand. So that the better you became, the less chance you had. About the only hope left was a serious wound.

It was probably simple vanity and pride which made Eisenhower, Marshall and company believe untested U.S. soldiers could go headlong straight on into the France of Hitler's "Fortress Europe" and win. The U.S. officer corps of those far-off days before the war lived in a sort of sealed-off plastic shell of their own making which could support such unrealistic dreams. The Great Depression years hurt them less than most citizens. Low-salaried though they were, their creature comforts were well seen to, by even lower-salaried enlisted slaves; and they could live well on their well-gardened, manicured posts and forts with booze and food at PX prices, and conduct their obsolete little training exercises with the same flair that they used to conduct the Saturday night Officers' Club dances. Polo was a great sport among them, for example, in those days when the use of horseless armor was just being understood. But they were brave men, and dedicated, and intelligent, great men a few of them, and with a Churchill and a Roosevelt to guide them, and some time in the field in a war to humble them a little, they could and would do great things to preserve the nation.

In the meantime, while the army leaders and the heads of state and their entourages gathered to debate the movement and the use of masses of lesser mortals and the millions of long tons of supplies needed to maintain them (gathered to decide, in fact, the actuarial statistics of death for tens and scores of thousands), the civilian soldier objects of this loving attention (and it was loving) themselves slogged on ahead, fighting and fearing one day, sleeping wet in mud the next. Gasping on the desert and in the hills (or puking and shaking with malaria in the jungles), his total horizon limited to from one to about five hundred yards in front of him, the private, non-com or junior officer knew little about what was going on or the grand design for his life for the next year. Or two years. Or three years.

There was no way for him to know. Strategic aims and planning, for simple reasons of security, could not be handed down to the rank and file. Even if he knew them, they wouldn't change his life much, or what he had to do. They might very well change his death date, but why tell him that. Anyway, he knew that (or suspected it) already.

The worst thing about being green was that he didn't know what to look for or listen for, or smell for. No amount of training behind his own lines could teach him what it was like to move out beyond them where there might be enemy. Where, eventually, there was sure to be enemy. But where? How did he look for them? What did he listen for? Those men seriously meant to kill him. Beyond the lines, a strange still breathlessness seemed to come down and settle on things: trees, roads, grass. Handling his fear was another problem. Learning to live with it, and to go ahead in spite of it, took practice and a certain overlay of bitter panache it took time to acquire. There were damned few fearless men. I knew, I think, two personally. But they were both crazy, almost certifiably so. That made them good soldiers.

But the human body, the animal human body, is incredibly adaptable. Did you ever begin using a new set of house and apartment keys? How you have to stop, and search, and look down till you find the right key for the right door? And how after several weeks or a couple of months, without any conscious participation on your part, you find that your hand itself is finding and selecting the right key by itself as the ring comes out of your pocket, without your even having to look? It was the same process which worked in the combat infantryman, almost entirely without conscious awareness, if he survived long enough to acquire it. (And the vast majority did survive: that was another thing he learned.)

But there was no way to learn it except by actual practice on the actual ground under the actual fire. Meantime, he exhausted himself daily. It's a pity the old men can't fight the wars. From the way they talk to the young we all know that they would love to do it. And they probably would be a lot more willing. At least, they have lived out a good part of their lives, and have some living chalked up behind them. But the truth is that physically they couldn't stand the gaff. I know from myself, now at fifty-three, that I couldn't possibly have stood the physical stresses I had to go through back then. And, secretly, I'm glad. But, of course, I won't admit it and will deny it with my last breath.

So there he stood—our once green, now obscene infantryman or tanker. Filthy, grimy, bearded, greasy with his own body oils (body oils aided by a thin film of dirt could make a uniform nearly completely waterproof, if it was worn long enough), dedicated to his own survival if at all possible, and willing to make it as costly as he could if it wasn't possible. He knew by the sound of incoming shells whether they would land near enough to be dangerous. He knew by the arc of falling aerial bombs if they would light nearby or farther out. He had learned that when fire was delivered, being thirty yards away could mean safety, and that fifty or a hundred yards could be pure heaven. He had learned that when the other guy was getting it a couple of hundred yards away, it had nothing to do with him; and that conversely when he was getting it, the other guy two hundred yards away wanted nothing to do with him, either. He had learned, maybe the most important of all for survival, that danger only existed at the exact place and moment of danger, and not before and not after.

He was about the foulest-mouthed individual who ever existed on earth. Every other word was fucking this or fucking that. And internally, his soul was about as foul and cynical as his mouth. He trusted nobody but his immediate outfit, and often not them. But everybody else, other outfits, he would cheerfully direct straight into hell. He had pared his dreams and ambitions down to no more than relief and a few days away from the line, and a bottle of booze, a woman and a bath.

But the green man had all this to go through yet. He had yet to serve his apprenticeship, to be accepted. Smart replacements soon learned that they got the dirtiest most-exposed jobs in the squad or platoon or section. They prayed for newer replacements to come in behind them, so that they might be, if not accepted, at least less noticed. The lucky, the tough, and the smart survived, and the rest were forgotten, shipped home, or buried. For the green hand the worst quality was the uncertainty and the total unfamiliarity with everything. And only time and lucky survival would change it to skill. On to Sicily! On to New Georgia!

* * *

HUMOR

It was the safety valve and saving factor of the "lower class" Fully Evolved Soldier. He wasn't really as lower class as all that, only comparatively so. America then as now has perhaps the biggest middle class in human history, mixed in there with its "proletarian" city-worker soldiers. But he was the kind of soldier who would never make an officer, let alone a colonel or a general. And his humor reflected his interest and preoccupation with the absurdities of privilege all around him, while he fought and died or lived in inconceivable daily misery in a war where he himself had none.

It was pretty rugged humor. And it got ruggeder and gruesomer as this middle period of a seemingly hopelessly long war wore on. There was the classic of the P-38 Lightning pilot shot down over the desert (or the jungle, or the Alaskan tundra) who, when rescue parties got to him, was clearly dying and a real mess. Both legs were twisted out at odd angles, both arms were smashed, his chest cavity was crushed by the forward edge of the cockpit, his face a mess of bloody hamburger. Every time he breathed a bloody froth of foam came out of the ruined mouth. They dragged him away from the wreckage, but the medic could only look at him helplessly. Finally he bent down and said inanely, "How do you feel?" From the bloody hamburger of his mouth, through the froth of blood, the pilot answered, "It only hurts when I laugh."

This story ran like wildfire across the world, through every theater, through every homeland camp, through every navy ship. And it never failed to crack everybody up who heard it. There were other more gruesome ones.

Then there was the ubiquitous Kilroy, his long pathetic hungry-looking nose hanging over the wall with the two peering eyes above it, always the spectator, never inside. "Kilroy was here." It was marked on the standing walls of ruined buildings, on latrine walls, on bars and whorehouses from Seattle to Miami and from Italy to Australia. No one ever knew who started it. Everybody understood it. If something bad had happened, Kilroy was responsible. If something good had happened, Kilroy had been across that wall, outside looking in.

It could be pretty rough humor. But then isn't all humor essentially cruel? A bunch of us were standing on an open hill one day, winded, after just having taken it against only token resistance, when one of our men facing toward the enemy on the next hill across a jungle ravine was hit by a ricochet. He had taken off his helmet to cool his head, and the bullet, traveling flat instead of by the point, struck him square between the eyes in the forehead, and went screaming off exactly as if it had hit a rock. Nobody knew where it came from. Nobody had heard the shot. It must have come from far off or it would have killed him anyway. Instead, it only knocked him half-way out. After no more fire came and we all got back on our feet (excepting, of course, the wounded man) the man who had just been standing with him started to yell for a medic, but then began to choke up with laughter and couldn't. Choking and gasping, he tried two or three times and failed, and then fell down on the ground, curled up and gasping, roaring with laughter. By that time someone else had called the medic. But then the wounded man sat back up beside his laughing buddy and looked around at all of us with a hurt look on his face. The skin on his forehead was torn, but the hot bullet must have partially cauterized the tear, because only a trickle of blood ran down onto his nose. This, plus the look on his face, sent his buddy off into fresh roars. And by this time the rest of us were laughing. Finally the buddy got himself stopped enough to tell what had happened. Standing with his back to the enemy hill, he had been looking right at his friend, talking, when the bullet hit him with a loud smack and went twanging off. Slowly the hit man's eyes had crossed themselves until the irises nearly disappeared beside his nose, and he had sat down and then fallen flat. If we could only have seen those eyes going crossed, he groaned, breaking out again and hugging himself. The medic had come up now, and looked at the slight tear on the hit man's forehead with disgust. "Christ, is this what you guys got me up here for?" He got the casualty on his feet, "Come on, I'll take you back to battalion. They'll give you some aspirin." By now there were six or eight of us roaring and paralyzed, on our knees or squirming on the ground or holding onto each other, as the medic led the stunned man off. "You sons of bitches, I coulda been killed," he called back irately at us. And we all broke out afresh.

Naturally, when he came back an hour later, he was immediately nicknamed "Irondome" and "Steelhead" and "Helmethead." Finally his nickname settled permanently: "Skillethead." And Skillethead he remained until he finally left the outfit.

It could be pretty basic humor, too. A man on a bare hillside who had to take a crap could do no better for privacy than to take an entrenching shovel and scoop out a hole and squat above it on the uphill side, while the men in the hollow below would whistle and make cowlike moans of false passion. One day when my company's forward platoon had just repelled a light, half-hearted Japanese attack, wild shouts of laughter and exclamations fell on the wind from the hill crest above us where the line was. When we called up to see what had happened, a soldier yelled down, "Jerry Marti's got a hard-on, for Chrissake. Right in the middle of an attack. He showed us. Won a five dollar bet from So-and-So."

A Polack in our outfit (nicknamed "Polack," naturally), who bore an unfortunately comic resemblance to a rhesus monkey, came down with a dose of clap in the middle of the Guadalcanal campaign. We had all of us been away from women for at least three months. Nobody knew how he could have caught it. He was accused of everything from buggering dead Jap corpses to getting himself up in a disguise as a monkey, so as to get in with a band of jungle monkeys. But Polack had the last laugh. His case was so bad it refused to respond to treatment and he had to be evacuated to New Zealand. We never saw him again, but used to curse him roundly for having such good luck as to get sent out for a dose of clap in a womanless jungle campaign. Later, the battalion surgeon gave it as a considered medical opinion that it was an old case never quite cured which was brought back on by strain and exertion.

The resilience of the human body is perhaps only exceeded by the comeback abilities of the human psyche. Hours after terror, and the hot dry mouth of fear, men back out of a fight or back off the line could begin to wrinkle their eyes a little and smile again. If the cynicism of each man's EVOLUTION OF A SOLDIER and the rawness of his humor grew proportionately with the trips up front he made, he was still able (after a relatively short period of relief) to perk up enough so that whenever he saw a reporter with a pencil or a photographer with a camera, he could be ready with the wisecrack and make the toothy smile for the folks back home.

It was amazing how little of his secret bitterness (as well as how little of his private humor) he allowed to filter through to the people at home as they worried, worked, and grew rich and fat on his war.

* * *

RESPONSIBILITY, BUT FOR WHAT?

So much has been written, and orated, and sermonized about the symbolic qualities of the atomic bomb and Hiroshima and the mushroom cloud, that it is difficult to separate out the military and political factors of its creation and use.

About the only thing that can be said without dispute is that had the United States not used its A-bomb the invasions of Kyushu and Honshu would have had to be carried out. At great cost. But even that has been disputed.

As for the A-bomb, probably no other nation had the technological facilities to develop it; we didn't ourselves, and had to create them as we went along, and it took us six years to develop one. Possibly Germany might have developed one. But we bombed their heavy water installations in Norway, and together with the British bombed out their research plants in Germany itself. It was Albert Einstein who first brought the United States the news in 1939 that the Germans were working on an atomic bomb, and suggested we had better build one first.

Politically, there seems to have been just about every reason to go ahead and use it. Harry Truman in his memoirs and to his dying day cheerfully accepted full responsibility for ordering its use, and said he considered it a military weapon and that was that. Japan had attacked us without any military provocation, and without warning. Japan had conducted her war in an incredibly savage way. And after the unconditional surrender of Germany, and the uncovering of the political cruelties and brutalities and genocide which had taken place within the German borders, could anything less than unconditional surrender be accepted from the Japanese?

Militarily, there was never any doubt that the atom bomb could and should be used. If only in counting casualties, there was clear reason to use it. The near ruin of Hiroshima (ironically, little of its war production potential was touched) and the partial destruction of Nagasaki were a small price to pay for an end to the war which must have exacted, at a minimum, five times as many casualties, and have taken months and perhaps two years to accomplish. In terms of destruction alone, the total annihilation of both cities (which was not accomplished in either case) was small compared to the destruction that would have taken place all over Japan had the war continued and the U.S. invasions been carried through.

Militarily and politically, it is impossible to point out reasons or make a sound argument for not using the A-bomb.

But at any rate the long war, for those who had fought it, as well as for those who had gotten rich off it, was over.

AN END TO IT

How did you come back from counting yourself as dead?

The plans called for nine million Americans to be demobilized between June, 1945, and June, 1946. The slow demobilization was necessary. Not only were large numbers required for the armies of occupation until they could be replaced, but the sheer physical logistics of transport made it necessary to string out the return. And what would happen to the happily humming economy, buzzing along, if you suddenly dumped nine million men on the job market? Already the "veterans" were a problem, even before they got to be "veterans." Many home-front assembly-line workers feared for their jobs, as the huge numbers of "vets" flooded back into the country.

If the "vets" were a problem to the economy and to the society as a whole, they neither minded nor cared. All they wanted was to get there: home. The combat men—the new "professionals"—of course got priority, or were supposed to. Out of the nine million very few had ever put their lives on the line, and fewer still had ever heard a shot fired in seriousness. There was a lot of payola under a lot of tables, but in general the plans were followed pretty closely. If out of nine million men a few tens of thousands got home earlier than they should have, who was going to worry about it, except the men they had got themselves squeezed in front of? And among such huge numbers, who would hear or listen to such a small number of voices? In Europe they started coming home even before it was finished in the Pacific.

Housing was a problem. President Truman begged the public to find living space for the veterans. Getting your old job back, or getting a new one, was less of a problem. And the civilian world went merrily on in its happy, dizzy whirl of prosperity in a booming economy. Articles appeared in women's magazines with titles like "What You Can Do To Help the Returning Veteran" and "Will He Be Changed?" *Good Housekeeping* said, "After *two or three weeks* [my italics] he should be finished with talking, with oppressive remembering. If he still goes over the same stories, reveals the same emotions, you had best consult a psychiatrist. This condition is neurotic." *House Beautiful* recommended that "home must be the greatest rehabilitation center of them all" and showed an apartment fixed up for some homecoming general. *Ladies' Home Journal* asked, in 1945, "Has your husband come home to the right woman?"

The answer, of course, was no. How could any woman be the right woman for a man who had just spent one year or two years as essentially a dead man, waiting, anticipating having his head blown off or his guts torn out? Even if she was the same woman he left (and most were not; how could they be?) she was not the right woman for such a man.

Instead of talking about it, most men didn't talk about it. It was not that they didn't want to talk about it, it was that when they did, nobody understood it. It was such a different way of living, and of looking at life even, that there was no common ground for communication in it.

It was like a Ranger staff sergeant I met in St. Louis years ago told me, "One day at Anzio we got eight new replacements into my platoon. We were supposed to make a little feeling attack that same day. Well, by next day, all eight of them replacements were dead, buddy. But none of us old guys were. We weren't going to send our own guys out on point in a damnfool situation like that. We knew nothing would happen. We were sewed up tight. And we'd been together through Africa, and Sicily, and Salerno. We sent the replacements out ahead." He gave me a sad smile, "But how am I going to explain something like that to my wife? She'd think it was horrible. But it was right, man, right. How were we going to send our own guys out into that?" We had some more drinks, got pretty drunk in fact, then he went home to his wife. Who, I am sure, was angry at him for getting drunk.

Another time an infantry sergeant who had fought in the Bulge told me how his platoon had taken some prisoners west of St. Vith. "There were eight of them, and they were tough old-timers, buddy. Been through the mill from the beginning. It was about the fourth or fifth day, and we needed some information. But they weren't talking, not those tough old birds. You had to admire them. So we took the first one off to the side, where they could see him, and shot him through the head. Then they all talked. They were eager to talk. Once they knew we were serious. Horrible? Evil? We knew all about Malmédy, man, and Stavelot. We needed that information. Our lives depended on it. We didn't think it was evil. Neither did they. But how am I going to tell my wife about something like that? Or my mother? They don't understand the problems." We went on getting drunk, and talking, until he felt he was ready to go home.

Slowly, bit by bit, it began to taper off. Men still woke up in the middle of the night, thrashing around and trying to get their hands on their wives' throats. Men still rolled out from a dead sleep, and hit the dirt with a crash on the bedroom floor, huddling against the bed to evade the aerial bomb or the artillery shells they had dreamed they heard coming. While their wives sat straight up in bed in their new frilly nightgowns bought for the homecoming, wide-eyed and staring, horrified. An old buddy would have roared with laughter. There is no telling what the divorce rate was then, in the early year or two. Certainly a lot higher than was ever admitted.

A number of men I knew slept with loaded pistols or unsheathed bayonets under their pillows for a number of months. Just made them feel more comfortable, they said shamefacedly, but it sure scared the shit out of their wives. And their wives' psychiatrists.

The DE-EVOLUTION OF A SOLDIER. It was longer in coming in some than in others. Some never did lose it, and some—a few—went off to the booby hatch. But not the vast majority. The majority, as they had survived the process of evolving into soldiers, now began to survive the process of de-evolving.

There was nothing the good old government could do about that. As with Uncle Sugar's expensive, astonishingly rich, lavish care which was being expended on the wounded and maimed, so with Uncle Sugar trying to fix things up for the returnee. Omar Bradley was put in charge of Veterans' Affairs, to modernize it and clean up its graft. Not only was the government sending everybody who wanted back to college, but it was sending anybody at all to college, anybody who asked, on their GI Bill of Rights. So much so that girls and civilian men who wanted to go had to score enormously high on the preschool exams, in order to get in. There simply wasn't room for them. But the government had never set up any DE-EVOLUTION OF A SOLDIER center, to match its induction centers. When you went in, they had the techniques and would ride you all the way to becoming a soldier. They had no comparable system when you came out. That you had to do on your own.

And with the de-evolving, as with the evolving, the first sign of change was the coming of the pain. As the old combat numbness disappeared, and the frozen feet of the soul began to thaw, the pain of the cure became evident. The sick-making thoughts of all the buddies who had died. The awful bad luck of the maimed. The next thing to go was the professionalism. How could you be a professional when there was no more profession? The only way was to stay in The Profession. And some, quite a few, did.

About the last thing to go was the old sense of *esprit.* That was the hardest thing to let go of, because there was nothing in civilian life that could replace it. The love and understanding of men for men in dangerous times, and places, and situations. Just as there was nothing in civilian life that could replace the heavy, turgid, day-to-day excitement of danger. Families and other civilian types would never understand that sense of *esprit,* any more than they would understand the excitement of the danger. Some old-timers, a lot of them, tried to hold onto the *esprit* by joining division associations and regimental associations. But the feeling wasn't the same, and never would be the same, because the motivation—the danger—was gone. Too many people lived too far away, and had other jobs and other interests, and anyway the drive was no longer there, and the most honest in their hearts had to admit it.

After all, the war was over.

When the veterans began to spend two nights a week down at the local American Legion, the families and parents and wives could heave a sigh of relief. Because they knew then that, after all, it—the war—was truly over.

PASS IN REVIEW!

How many times they had heard the old, long-drawn-out, faint field command pass down the long length of vast parade grounds, fading, as the guidons moved out front.

So slowly it faded, leaving behind it a whole generation of men who would walk into history looking backwards, with their backs to the sun, peering forever over their shoulders behind them, at their own lengthening shadows trailing across the earth. None of them would ever really get over it.

DUDLEY RANDALL
1914-

The black poet Dudley Randall served in the army in the South Pacific and after the war became an official in the public library system of the city of Detroit and a teacher of literature and writing at the University of Michigan. Espiritu Santo, the largest island of the New Hebrides, became an important military and naval base in 1942. There were cemeteries there.

From PACIFIC EPITAPHS

ESPIRITU SANTO

I hated guns,
Was a poor marksman,
But struck one target.

NORMAN MAILER
1923-

Mailer graduated from Harvard in 1943. A year later he found himself an enlisted man in the 112th Cavalry. He spent eighteen months overseas, in the Philippines and in occupied Japan.

His popular novel of the war, The Naked and the Dead *(1948), con-cludes with the agonies endured by Sergeant Croft's patrol, which pur-sues its mortal mission unaware that the battle has been won already and no longer needs its help. "We broke our ass for nothin'," as Polack says.*

From THE NAKED AND THE DEAD

On the same afternoon that Major Dalleson was mounting his attack, the platoon continued to climb Mount Anaka. In the awful heat of the middle slopes they bogged down. Each time they passed through a draw or hollow the air seemed to be refracted from the blazing rocks, and after a time their cheek muscles ached from continual squinting. It was a minor pain and should have been lost in the muscle cramps of their thighs, the sullen vicious aching of their backs, but it became the great-est torment of the march. The bright light lanced like splinters into the tender flesh of their eyeballs, danced about the base of their brains in reddened choleric circles. They lost all account of the distance they had covered; everything beneath them had blurred, and the individual tor-ments of each kind of terrain were forgotten. They no longer cared if the next hundred yards was a barren rock slope or a patch of brush and forest. Each had its own painful disadvantages. They wavered like a file of drunks, plodded along with their heads bent down, their arms slap-ping spasmodically at their sides. All their equipment had become leaden, and a variety of sores had farrowed on every bony knob of their bodies. Their shoulders were blistered from the pack bands, their waists were bruised from the jouncing of their cartridge belts, and their rifles clanked abrasively against their sides, raising blisters on their hips. Their shirts had long washed lines of white where the perspiration had dried.

They moved numbly, straggling upward from rock to rock, panting and sobbing with exhaustion. Against his will Croft was forced to give them a break every few minutes; they rested now for as long a period as they marched, lying dumbly on their backs, their arms and legs spread-eagled. Like the litter-bearers, they had forgotten everything; they did not think of themselves as individual men any longer. They were merely envelopes of suffering. They had forgotten about the patrol, about the war, their past, they had even forgotten the earth they had just climbed. The men around them were merely vague irritating obstacles into which they blundered. The hot glaring sky and the burning rock were far more intimate. Their minds scurried about inside their bodies like rodents in a maze, concentrating fruitlessly on first the quivering of an overworked limb and then on the smarting of a sore, became buried for many min-utes in the agony of drawing another breath.

Only two things ever intruded on this. They were afraid of Croft and this fear had become greater as they grew more exhausted; by now they waited for his voice, plunged themselves forward a few additional yards each time he flicked them with a command. A numb and stricken apprehension had settled over them, an unvoiced and almost bottomless terror of him.

And in opposition to that, they wanted to quit; they wanted that more than anything they had ever hungered for. Each step they advanced, each tremor of their muscles, each pang in their chests generated that desire. They moved forward with a dumb blistering hatred for the man who led them.

Croft was almost as exhausted; by now he appreciated the breaks as much as they did, was almost as willing to allow each halt to drag out to double its intended length. He had forgotten the peak of the mountain, he wanted to quit too, and each time a break ended he fought a quick battle with himself, exposed himself to all the temptations of rest, and then continued. He moved on because somewhere at the base of his mind was the directive that climbing this mountain was necessary. His decision had been made in the valley, and it lay as an iron warp in his mind. He could have turned back no more easily than he could have killed himself.

All through the afternoon they straggled forward, toiling up the gentler slopes, proceeding from rock to rock when the walls of the mountain became sheerer. They traveled from one ridge to another, stumbled painfully along the slanting inclines of minor knolls, slipped and fell many times when they passed over swatches of moist clay. The mountain seemed eternally to rear above them. They glimpsed its upper slopes through the fog of their effort, followed one another up the unending serpentines, and plodded along gratefully whenever their route was level for a time.

Minetta and Wyman and Roth were the most wretched. For several hours they had been at the tail of the column, keeping up to the men ahead with the greatest difficulty, and there was a bond between the three of them. Minetta and Wyman felt sorry for Roth, liked him because he was even more helpless than they. And Roth looked to them for support, knew in the knowledge of fatigue that they would not scorn him because they were only a little less prostrated than he.

He was making the most intense effort of his life. All the weeks and months Roth had been in the platoon he had absorbed each insult, each reproof with more and more pain. Instead of becoming indifferent or erecting a protective shell, he had become more sensitive. The patrol had keyed him to the point where he could not bear any more abuse, and he drove himself onward now with the knowledge that if he halted for too long the wrath and ridicule of the platoon would come down upon him.

But, even with this, he was breaking. There came a point where his legs would no longer function. Even when he stood still they were close to buckling under him. Toward the end of the afternoon he began to collapse. It was a slow process, dragging out through a series of pratfalls, a progression of stumbling and sliding and finally of dropping prostrate. He began to tumble every few hundred feet and the men in the platoon waited gratefully while he forced himself slowly to his feet, and staggered on again. But each fall came a little more quickly than the one that had preceded it. Roth moved forward almost unconsciously, his legs buckling at every misstep. After a half hour he could no longer get up without assistance, and each step he took was doubtful, uncertain, like an infant walking alone across a room. He even fell like an infant, his feet folding under him while he sat blankly on his thighs, a little bewildered that he was not still walking.

In time he began to irritate the platoon. Croft would not let them sit down and the enforced wait until Roth was able to walk again annoyed them. They began to wait for Roth to fall and the inevitable recurrence of it rasped their senses. Their anger began to shift from Croft to Roth.

The mountain was becoming more treacherous. For ten minutes Croft had been leading them along a rocky ledge up the side of a sheer bluff of stone, and the path in places was only a few feet wide. At their right, never more than a yard or two away, was a drop of several hundred feet, and despite themselves they would pitch at times close to the edge. It roused another fear in them, and Roth's halts made them impatient. They were anxious to get past the ledge.

In the middle of this ascent Roth fell down, started to get up, and then sprawled out again when no one helped him. The rock surface of the ledge was hot but he felt comfortable lying against it. The afternoon rain had just begun and he felt it driving into his flesh, cooling the stone. He wasn't going to get up. Somewhere through his numbness another resentment had taken hold. What was the point of going on?

Someone was tugging at his shoulder, and he flung him off. "I can't go on," he gasped, "I can't go on, I can't." He slapped his fist weakly against the stone.

It was Gallagher trying to lift him. "Get up, you sonofabitch," Gallagher shouted. His body ached with the effort of holding Roth.

"I can't. Go 'way!"

Roth heard himself sobbing. He was dimly aware that most of the platoon had gathered around, were looking at him. But this had no effect; it gave him an odd bitter pleasure to have the others see him, an exaltation compounded of shame and fatigue.

Nothing more could happen after this. Let them see him weeping, let them know for one more time that he was the poorest man in the platoon. It was the only way he could find recognition. After so much anonymity, so much ridicule, this was almost better.

Gallagher was tugging at his shoulder again. "Go 'way, I can't get up," Roth bawled.

Gallagher shook him, feeling a compound of disgust and pity. More than that. He was afraid. Every muscle fiber demanded that he lie down beside Roth. Each time he drew a breath the agony and nausea in his chest made him feel like weeping too. If Roth didn't get up, he knew he also would collapse.

"Get up, Roth!"

"I can't."

Gallagher grasped him under the armpits and tried to lift him. The dead resisting weight was enraging. He dropped Roth and clouted him across the back of his head. "Get up, you Jew bastard!"

The blow, the word itself, stirred him like an electric charge. Roth felt himself getting to his feet, stumbling forward. It was the first time anyone had ever sworn at him that way, and it opened new vistas of failure and defeat. It wasn't bad enough that they judged him for his own faults, his own incapacities; now they included him in all the faults of a religion he didn't believe in, a race which didn't exist. "Hitlerism, race theories," he muttered. He was staggering forward dumbly, trying to absorb the shock. Why did they call him that, why didn't they see it wasn't his fault?

And there was something else working. All the protective devices, the sustaining façades of his life had been eroding slowly in the caustic air of the platoon; his exhaustion had pulled out the props, and Gallagher's blow had toppled the rest of the edifice. He was naked another way now. He rebelled against it, was frustrated that he could not speak to them and explain it away. It's ridiculous, thought Roth in the core of his brain, it's not a race, it's not a nation. If you don't believe in the religion, then why are you one? This was the prop that had collapsed, and even through his exhaustion he understood something Goldstein had always known. His own actions would be expanded from now on. People would not only dislike him, but they would make the ink a little darker on the label.

Well, let them. A saving anger, a magnificent anger came to his aid. For the first time in his life he was genuinely furious, and the anger excited his body, drove him on for a hundred yards, and then another hundred yards, and still another. His head smarted where Gallagher had struck him, his body tottered, but if they had not been marching he might have flung himself at the men, fought them until he was unconscious. Nothing he could do was right, nothing would please them. He

seethed, but with more than self-pity now. He understood. He was the
butt because there always had to be a butt. A Jew was a punching bag
because they could not do without one.

His body was so small. The rage was pathetic, but its pitifulness was
unfair. If he had been stronger, he could have done something. And
even so, as he churned along the trail behind the men there was something different in him, something more impressive. For these few minutes he was not afraid of the men. His body wavering, his head lolling on
his shoulders, he fought clear of his exhaustion, straggled along oblivious
of his body, alone in the new rage of his person.

Croft, at the point, was worried. He had not taken part when Roth
had collapsed. For once he had been irresolute. The labor of leading the
platoon for so many months, the tensions of the three days with Hearn,
had been having their effect. He was tired, his senses rasped by everything that went wrong; all the sullenness of the men, their fatigue, their
reluctance to go on had been causing attrition. The decision he had
made after Martinez's reconnaissance had drained him. When Roth fell
down the last time Croft had turned to go back to him and then had
paused. At that moment he had been too weary to do anything. If
Gallagher had not struck him, Croft might have interfered, but for once
he was content to wait. All his lapses and minor failures seemed important to him. He was remembering with disgust his paralysis on the river
when the Japanese had called to him; he was thinking of the combat
since then, all the minor blank spots that had occurred before he could
act. For once he was uncertain. The mountain still taunted him, still
drew him forward, but it was with an automatic leaden response of his
legs. He knew he had miscalculated the strength of the platoon, his own
energy. There was only an hour or two until dark and they would never
reach the peak before then.

The ledge they were on was becoming narrower. A hundred feet
above them he could see the top of the ridge, rocky and jagged, almost
impossible to traverse. Farther ahead the ledge rose upward and crossed
the ridge and beyond should be the mountain peak. It could not be more
than a thousand feet above them. He wanted to have the summit in view
before they halted for the night.

But the ledge was becoming dangerous. The rain clouds had settled
over them like bloated balloons, and they traveled forward in what was
almost a fog. The rain was colder here. It chilled them and their feet slid
upon the damp rock. After a few more minutes the rain obscured the
ridge above them, and they inched along the ledge cautiously, their faces
to the rock wall.

The ledge was no more than a foot wide now. The platoon worked
along it very slowly, taking a purchase on the weeds and small bushes

that grew out of the vertical cracks in the wall. Each step was painful, frightening, but the farther they inched out along the ledge the more terrifying became the idea of turning back. They hoped that at any moment the ledge would widen again, for they could not conceive of returning over a few of the places they had already crossed. This passage was dangerous enough to rouse them temporarily from their fatigue, and they moved alertly, strung out over forty yards. Once or twice they would look down, but it was too frightening. Even in the fog they could see a sheer drop of at least a hundred feet and it roused another kind of faintness. They would become conscious of the walls, which were of a soft gray slimy rock that seemed to breathe like the skin of a seal. It had an odious fleshlike sensation which roused panic, made them want to hasten.

The ledge narrowed to nine inches. Croft kept peering ahead in the mist, trying to determine if it would become wider. This was the first place on the mountain that demanded some skill. Until now it has been essentially a very high hill, but here he wished for a rope or a mountain pick. He continued along it, his arms and legs spread-eagled, hugging the rock, his fingers searching for crevices to latch upon.

He came to a gap in the ledge about four feet wide. There was nothing between, no bushes, no roots to which they could cling. The platform disappeared and then continued on the other side. In the gap there was only the sheer drop of the ridge wall. It would have been a simple jump, merely a long step on level ground, but here it meant leaping sideways, taking off from the left foot and landing with the right, having to gain his balance while he teetered on the ledge.

He slipped off his pack carefully, handed it to Martinez behind him, and hesitated for a moment, his right leg dangling over the gap. Then he leaped sideways, wavering for a moment on the other side before steadying himself.

"Jesus, who the fug can cross that?" he heard one of them mutter.

"Just wait there," Croft said, "I'm gonna see if the ledge widens out." He traveled along it for fifty feet, and discovered it was becoming broader again. This gave him a deep sense of relief, for otherwise it would have meant turning back to find another route. And he no longer knew if he could rouse the platoon to go up again.

He leaned over the gap and took his pack from Martinez. The distance was short enough for their hands to touch. Then he took Martinez's pack and moved a few yards farther away. "Okay, men," he called, "let's start coming over. The air's a helluva sight better on this side."

There was a nervous snicker. "Listen, Croft," he heard Red say, "is that fuggin ledge any wider?"

"Yeah, more than a bit." But Croft was annoyed at himself for answering. He should have told Red to shut up.

Roth, at the tail of the column, listened with dread. He would probably miss if he had to jump, and despite himself his body generated some anxiety. His anger was still present, but it had altered into a quieter resolve. He was very tired.

As he watched them pass their packs across and leap over, his fear increased. It was the kind of thing he had never been able to do, and a trace of an old panic he had known in gym classes when he waited for his turn on the high bar rose up to torment him.

Inevitably, his turn was approaching. Minetta, the last man ahead of him, hesitated on the edge and then skipped across, laughing weakly. "Jesus, a fuggin acrobat." Roth cleared his throat. "Make room, I'm coming," he said quietly. He handed over his pack.

Minetta was talking to him as though he were an animal. "Now, just take it easy, boy. There's nothing to it. Just take it easy, and you'll make it okay."

He resented that. "I'm all right," he said.

But when he stepped to the edge and looked over, his legs were dead. The other ledge was very far away. The rock bluffs dropped beneath him gauntly, emptily.

"I'm coming," he mumbled again, but he did not move. As he had been about to jump he had lost courage.

I'll count three to myself, he thought.

One.

Two.

Three.

But he could not move. The critical second elongated, and then was lost. His body had betrayed him. He wanted to jump and his body knew he could not make it.

Across the ledge he could hear Gallagher. "Get up close, Minetta, and catch that useless bastard." Gallagher crawled toward him through Minetta's feet, and extended his arm, glowered at him. "C'mon, all you got to do is catch my hand. You can fall that far."

They looked weird. Gallagher was crouched at Minetta's feet, his face and arm projecting through Minetta's legs. Roth stared at them, and was filled with contempt. He understood this Gallagher now. A bully, a frightened bully. There was something he could tell them. If he refused to jump, Croft would have to come back. The patrol would be over. And Roth knew himself at this instant, knew suddenly that he could face Croft.

But the platoon wouldn't understand. They would jeer him, take relief from their own weakness in abusing him. His heart was filled with bitter-

ness. "I'm coming," he shouted suddenly. This was the way they wanted
it.

He felt his left leg pushing him out, and he lurched forward awkwardly, his exhausted body propelling him too feebly. For an instant he
saw Gallagher's face staring in surprise at him, and then he slipped past
Gallagher's hand, scrabbled at the rock, and then at nothing.

In his fall Roth heard himself bellow with anger, and was amazed that
he could make so great a noise. Through his numbness, through his
disbelief, he had a thought before he crashed into the rocks far below.
He wanted to live. A little man, tumbling through space.

*   *   *

When Roth missed the leap, the platoon was shattered. For ten minutes
they huddled together on the shelf, too stricken, too terrified, to move
on. An incommunicable horror affected them all. They stood upright,
frozen to the wall, their fingers clenched into the fissures of the rock,
their legs powerless. Once or twice Croft tried to rouse them, but they
shied away from the commands, petrified by his voice as though they
were dogs terrified by a master's boot. Wyman was sobbing in nervous
exhaustion, quietly, thinly, a small steady wailing, and into it fitted their
own voices, a grunt or a small moan or a hysterical curse, random things,
disconnected, so that the men who uttered them were hardly aware that
they had spoken.

Their will recovered enough for them to continue, but they moved at
a frantically slow pace, refusing to step forward for seconds at a time
before some minor obstacle, clinging to the wall ferociously wherever the
ledge became narrow again. After half an hour Croft finally brought
them out, and the ledge widened and crossed the ridge. Beyond was
nothing but another deep valley, another precipitous slope. He led them
down to the bottom, and started up the next ascent, but they did not
follow him. One by one they sprawled down on the ground, looked at
him with blank staring eyes.

It was almost dark, and he knew he could not drive them any more;
they were too exhausted, too frightened, and another accident might
occur. He called a halt, giving approval to what was already a fact, and
sat down in their midst.

On the next morning there would be the slope, a few gullies to traverse, and then the main ridge of the mountain to be crossed. They
could do it in two or three hours if . . . if he could stir them again. At that
moment he doubted himself seriously.

The platoon slept poorly. It was very difficult to find level ground, and
of course they were overtired, their limbs too tense. Most of them
dreamed and muttered in their sleep. To cap it all, Croft gave them each
an hour of guard, and some of them awoke too early and waited ner-

vously for many minutes before going on, found it difficult afterward to fall asleep. Croft had been aware of this, knew they needed the extra rest and knew it was virtually impossible there would be any Japanese on the mountain, but he had felt it more important not to break routine. Roth's death had temporarily shattered his command, and it was vital to start repairing it.

Gallagher had the last shift. It was very cold in the half hour before daylight and he woke up dazed, and sat shuddering in his blanket. For many minutes he was conscious of little, feeling the vast shapes of the mountain range about him as no more than a deeper border to the night. He only shivered and drowsed, waiting passively for the morning and the heat of the sun. A complete lethargy had settled over him, and Roth's death was remote. He drifted through a stupor, his mind almost inert, dreaming sluggishly of far-gone pleasant things as though deep within him he had to keep a small fire going against the cold of the night, the space of the hills, and the cumulative exhaustion, the mounting deaths of the platoon.

The dawn came slowly on the mountain. At five o'clock he could see the top of the mountain range clearly as the sky became lighter, but for a long half hour there was little change. Actually he could see nothing, but his body contained a tranquil anticipation. Soon the sun would struggle over the eastern ramparts of the mountain and come down into their little valley. He searched the sky and found a few tentative washes of pink streaming over the higher peaks, coloring the tiny oblong clouds of the dawn a purple. The mountains looked very high. Gallagher wondered that the sun could get over them.

All about him now it was getting lighter but it was a subtle process, for the sun still remained hidden and the light seemed to rise from the ground, a soft rose color. Already he could discern clearly the bodies of the men sleeping about him, and he felt a touch of superiority. They looked gaunt and bleak in the early dawn, oblivious to the approach of morning. He knew that in a short while he would be rousing them, and they would groan as they came out of their sleep.

In the west he could still see the night, and he recalled a troop train speeding across the great plains of Nebraska. It had been twilight then, and the night chased the train out of the east, overtook it, and passed on across the Rockies, on to the Pacific. It had been beautiful and it made him wistful now. He longed suddenly for America, wished so passionately to see it again that he could smell the odor of wet cobblestones on a summer morning in South Boston.

The sun was close to the eastern ridge-line now and the sky seemed vast, yet fresh and joyful. He thought of Mary and himself camping in a little pup tent in the mountains and he dreamt that he was waking with the velvet teasing touch of her breasts against his face. He heard her say,

"Get up, sleepyhead, and look at the dawn." He grunted drowsily, nuzzled against her in his fantasy and then popped open one eye as a grudging concession. The sun *was* clearing the ridge, and while the light in the valley was still faint, there was nothing unreal about it. The morning was here.

In that way Mary ushered in the dawn with him. The hills were shaking off the night mists and the dew was sparkling. For this brief moment the ridges about him appeared soft and feminine. All the men scattered around him looked damp and chilly, dark bundles from which mist rose. He was the only man awake for a distance of many miles, and he had the youth of the morning all to himself.

Out of the dawn, far on the other side of the mountain, he could hear artillery booming. It shattered his reverie.

Mary was dead.

Gallagher swallowed, wondering with a dumb misery how long it would be before he would stop tricking himself. There was nothing now to anticipate, and he was conscious for the first time of how tired he was. His limbs ached and his sleep seemed to have done him no good. The character of the dawn changed, left him shuddering in his blanket, damp and cold from the night's dew.

There was still his child, the boy he had never seen, but that did not cheer him. He believed he would never live to see him, and the knowledge was almost without pain, a dour certainty in his mind. Too many men had been killed. My number's coming. With a sick fascination, he envisioned a factory, watched his bullet being made, packed into a carton.

If only I could see a picture of the kid. His eyes misted. It wasn't so much to ask. If only he could get back from this patrol and live long enough for some mail to come with a picture of his kid.

But he was miserable again, certain he had tricked himself. He shivered from fright, looking about him uneasily at the mountains reared on every side.

I killed Roth.

He knew he was guilty. He remembered the momentary power and contempt he had felt as he bawled at Roth to jump, the quick sure pleasure of it. He twisted uncomfortably on the ground, recalling the bitter agony on Roth's face as he missed the step. Gallagher could see him falling and falling, and the image scraped along his spine like chalk squeaking on a blackboard. He had sinned and he was going to be punished. Mary was the first warning and he had disregarded it.

The mountain peak before them seemed so high. Gone now were the gentle outlines of the dawn; Anaka mounted before him, turret above turret, ridge beyond ridge. Near the peak he could see a bluff which encircled the crest. It was almost vertical and they would never be able to ascend it. He shuddered once more. He had never seen country like this; it was so barren, forbidding. Even the slopes of jungle and brush above them were cruel. He would never be able to make it today; already his chest ached, and when he slung his pack and began the climb again he would be exhausted in a few minutes. There was no reason to keep going; how many men had to be killed?

What the fug is it to Croft? he wondered.

It would be easy to kill him. Croft would be at the point and all he would have to do would be to raise his rifle, take aim, and the patrol would be over. They could turn back. He rubbed his thigh slowly, absorbed and uneasy from the force with which it appealed to him. Sonofabitch.

It was no way to think. His superstitious dread came back; each time he thought like this he was preparing his own punishment. And yet . . . It was Croft's fault that Roth had been killed. He really couldn't be blamed.

Gallagher heard a sound behind him and started. It was Martinez rubbing his head nervously. "Sonbitch, no sleep," Martinez said softly.

"Yeah."

Martinez sat down beside him: "Bad dreams." He lit a cigarette moodily. "Fall asleep . . . eeeeh . . . Hear Roth yell."

"Yeah, it hits ya," Gallagher muttered. He tried to reduce it to a more normal frame. "I never liked the guy particularly, but I never wanted him to get it like that. I never wanted nobody to get hit."

"Nobody," Martinez repeated. He massaged his forehead tenderly as if he had a headache. Gallagher was surprised how bad Martinez looked. His thin face had become hollow, and his eyes had a blank lusterless stare. He needed a shave badly, and dark streaks of grime had filleted all the lines in his face, making him appear much older.

"This is a rough deal," Gallagher muttered.

"Yah." Martinez exhaled some smoke carefully and they watched it glide away in the early morning air. "Cold," he muttered.

"It was a sonofabitch on guard," Gallagher said hoarsely.

Martinez nodded once more. His watch had come at midnight and he had been unable to sleep since then. His blankets had chilled; he had shuddered, twisted nervously for the rest of the night. Even now in the dawn, there was little release. His body still held the tension that had kept him awake, and he was bothered by the same diffused dread he had suffered all night. It had lain heavily on his body as though he were in fever. For over an hour he had been unable to rid himself of the expression on the face of the Japanese soldier he had killed. It was extremely vivid to him, and it reproduced the paralysis he had felt as he waited in the bushes with the knife in his hand. The empty scabbard clanked against his thigh, and he trembled delicately, a little shamefully. He fingered it with a twitching hand.

"Why the fug don't you throw the scabbard away?" Gallagher asked.

"Yah," Martinez said quickly. He felt embarrassed, meek. His fingers shook as he worked the hooks of the scabbard out of the eyelets in his cartridge belt. He tossed it away and winced at the empty clattering sound it made. Both of them started, and Martinez had a sudden gout of anxiety.

Gallagher could hear Hennessey's helmet spinning in the sand. "I'm gone to pot," he murmured.

Martinez felt automatically for the scabbard, realized it was gone, and with a sudden congealing of his flesh saw Croft telling him to be silent about his reconnaissance. Hearn had gone out believing . . . Martinez shook his head, choked by relief and horror. It wasn't his fault that they were on the mountain.

Abruptly the pores of his body opened, discharged their perspiration. He shivered in the cold mountain air, wrestling against the same anxiety he had suffered on the troopship the hours before they had invaded Anopopei. Against his will he stared up at the tessellated stones and jungle of the upper ridges, closed his eyes and saw the ramp of the landing boat going down. His body tensed, waiting for the machine-gun fire. Nothing happened and he opened his eyes, racked by an acute frustration. Something had to happen.

If only he could see a snapshot of his kid, Gallagher thought. "It's a goddam trap goin' up this mountain," he muttered.

Martinez nodded.

Gallagher extended his arm, touched Martinez's elbow for a moment. "Why don't we go back?" he asked.

"I don't know."

"It's fuggin suicide. What are we, a bunch of goddam mountain goats?" He rubbed the coarse itching hairs of his beard. "Listen, we'll all get knocked off."

Martinez wriggled his toes inside his boots, extracting a bleak satisfaction.

"You wanta get your fuggin head blown off?"

"No." He fingered the little tobacco pouch in his pocket where he kept the gold teeth he had stolen from the cadaver. Perhaps he should throw them away. But they were so pretty, so valuable. Martinez wavered, then left them there. He was struggling against the conviction that they would be an effective sacrifice.

"We ain't got a fuggin chance." Gallagher's voice shook, and as if he were a sounding board, Martinez resonated to it. They sat staring at each other, bound by their common fear. Martinez wished dumbly that he could assuage Gallagher's anxiety.

"Why don't you tell Croft to quit?"

Martinez shivered. He knew! He could tell Croft to go back. But the attitude was so foreign to him that he shied away from it fearfully. He could just ask him, maybe. A new approach formed for him naïvely. For a moment as he had hesitated before killing the Japanese sentry he had realized that he was only a man and the entire act had seemed unbelievable. Now the patrol seemed ridiculous. If he were just to ask Croft, maybe Croft would see it was ridiculous too.

"Okay," he nodded. He stood up and looked at the men bundled in their blankets. A few of them were stirring already. "We go wake him up."

They walked over to Croft, and Gallagher shook him. "Come on, get up." He was a little surprised that Croft was still sleeping.

Croft grunted, sprang to a sitting position. He made an odd sound, almost like a groan, and turned immediately to stare at the mountain. He had been dreaming his recurrent nightmare: he lay at the bottom of a pit waiting for a rock to fall on him, a wave to break, and he could not move. Ever since the Jap attack at the river he had been having dreams like this.

He spat. "Yeah." The mountain was still in place. No boulders had moved. He was a little surprised, for the dream had been vivid.

Automatically he swung his legs free of the blanket and began to put on his boots. They watched him soberly. He picked up his rifle, which he had kept beside him under the blankets, and examined it to see if it was dry. "Why the hell didn't you wake me earlier?"

Gallagher looked at Martinez. "We go back today, huh?" Martinez asked.

"What?"

"We go back," Martinez stammered.

Croft lit a cigarette, feeling the pungence of the smoke in his empty stomach. "What the hell you talkin' about, Japbait?"

"Better we go back?"

This was a shock to Croft. Was Martinez threatening him? He was stunned. Martinez was the only man in the platoon whose obedience he had never doubted. Croft's next reaction was rage. He stared quietly at Martinez's throat, restraining himself from leaping at him. His only friend in the platoon threatening him. Croft spat. There was no one you could trust, no one except yourself.

The mountain ahead had never looked so high and forbidding. Perhaps a part of him did want to turn back, and he flung himself from the temptation. Hearn was wasted if they turned back. And again the flesh on his back writhed under a play of nervous needles. The peak still taunted him.

He would have to go easy. If Martinez could do this, then the situation was dangerous. If the platoon ever discovered . . . "Goddam, Japbait, you turnin' on me?" he said softly.

"No."

"Well, what the hell's this talk? You're a sergeant, man, you don't go in for crap like that."

Martinez was caught. His loyalty was being questioned, and he hung sickly on Croft's next speech, waiting for him to say the thing he dreaded. A Mexican sergeant!

"I thought we were pretty good buddies, Japbait."

"Yah."

"Man, I thought they wasn't a damn thing you was afraid of."

"No." His loyalty, his friendship, his courage were all involved. And as he looked into Croft's cold blue eyes he felt the same inadequacy and shabbiness, the same inferiority he always knew when he talked to . . . to White Protestant. But there was even more this time. The undefined danger he always sensed seemed sharper now, closer upon him. What would they do to him, how very much would they do to him? His fear almost stifled him.

"Forget it. Japbait go with you."

"Sure." Croft's wheedling had hung awkwardly on him.

"Whadeya mean, you're goin' with him?" Gallagher asked. "Listen, Croft, why the hell don't you turn back? Ain't ya got enough fuggin medals?"

"Gallagher, you can shut your hole."

Martinez wished he could sidle away.

"Aaah." Gallagher pirouetted between fright and resolution. "Listen, I ain't afraid of you, Croft. You know what the fug I think of you."

Most of the men in the platoon had awakened and were staring at them.

"Shut your mouth, Gallagher."

"You better not keep your back to us." Gallagher walked away, trembling in the reaction from his courage. Any moment he expected Croft to come up behind him, spin him about, and strike him. The skin along his back quivered with anticipation.

But Croft did nothing. He was having a reaction from Martinez's unfaithfulness. The resisting weight of the platoon had never pressed more heavily upon him. He had the mountain to fight and the men dragging upon him. It accumulated in him for that moment, left him empty and without volition.

"All right, men, we're gonna move out in half an hour, so don't be fuggin around." A chorus of mutterings and grumblings answered him, but he preferred to single out none of them. He was extracting the last marrows of his will. He was exhausted himself and his unwashed body itched unbearably.

When they did get over the mountain what could they do? There were only seven of them left, and Minetta and Wyman would be worthless. He watched Polack and Red, who munched their food dourly, glaring back at him. But he forced these considerations away. He would worry about the rest of it once they had crossed the mountain. Now that was the only important problem.

Red watched him for several minutes afterward, noticing every move with a dull hatred. He had never loathed any man so much as Croft. As Red picked at the breakfast ration of tinned ham and eggs, his stomach rebelled. The food was thick and tasteless; when he chewed there was a balance between his desire to swallow it and his desire to spit it out. Each lumpful remained heavy and leaden for an interminable time in his mouth. He threw the can away at last, and sat staring at his feet. His stomach pulsed emptily, sickeningly.

There were eight rations left: three cheeses, two ham and eggs, and three beef and pork loafs. He knew he would never eat them; they were merely an added load in his pack. Aaah, fug this. He took out the ration cartons, slit the tops off each with his knife and separated the candy and cigarettes from the food tins, the crackers. He was about to throw the food away when he realized that some of the men might want it. He thought of asking, but he had an image of passing from man to man with the cans in his hand, having them jeer at him. Aaah, fug 'em, he decided, it's none of their goddam business anyway. He threw the food into some weeds a few feet behind him. For a time he sat there, so enraged that his heart was beating powerfully, and then he relaxed and began to make up his pack. That'll be lighter anyhow, he told himself, and his rage began again. Fug the Army anyhow, fug the goddam mother-fuggin Army. That stuff ain't fit for a pig. He was breathing very quickly once more. Kill and be killed for this lousy goddam food. So many images blurred in his mind, the mills where they stamped and pressured and cooked the food that went into the tins, the dull *thwopping* sound of a bullet striking a man, even Roth's shout.

Aaah, fug the whole goddam mess. If they can't feed a man, then fug 'em, fug 'em all. He was trembling so badly he had to sit down and rest. He had to face the truth. The Army had licked him. He had always gone along believing that if they pushed him around too much he would do something when the time came. And now . . .

He had talked to Polack yesterday, and they had both hinted about Hearn, both let it lay. He knew what he could do, and if he skipped out on it he was yellow. Martinez wanted them to go back. Since he had tried to convince Croft, Martinez must know something.

By now the sun was shining brightly on their slope, and the dark-purple shadows of the mountain had lightened to lavender and blue. He squinted upward toward the peak. They still had a morning's climb ahead of them, and then what? They would drop down among the Japs and be wiped out. They could never come back over the mountain again. On an impulse he walked over to Martinez, who was fixing his pack.

Red hesitated for an instant. Nearly all the men were ready, and Croft would shout at him if he delayed. He still had to put his blanket in his pack.

Aaah, fug him, Red thought again, ashamed and angry.

Before Martinez he paused, uncertain what to say. "How you doin', Japbait?"

"Okay."

"You and Croft couldn't work it out for a little while, huh?"

"Nothing the matter." Martinez averted his eyes.

Red lit a cigarette, disgusted with what he was doing. "Japbait, you're kind of chicken. You want to quit and you ain't even got the guts to say so."

Martinez made no answer.

"Listen, Japbait, we been around quite a while, we know what the hell the fuggin score is. You think it's gonna be fun goin' up that hill today? We're gonna have a coupla more men droppin' off on one of those ledges, maybe you, maybe me."

"Leave me alone," Martinez muttered.

"Let's face it, Japbait, even if we do get over, we'll just get a leg or an arm blown off on the other side. You want to stop a slug?" Even as he argued Red was bothered by a sense of shame. There was another way to do this.

"You want to be a cripple?"

Martinez shook his head.

The arguments filed naturally into Red's mind. "You killed that Jap, didn't you? Did ya ever know that brings your number a little closer?"

This was a powerful point to Martinez. "I don't know, Red."

"You killed that Jap, but did you say a goddam thing about it?"

"Yah."

"Hearn knew about it, huh, he walked into that pass knowing there was Japs?"

"Yah." Martinez began to shake. "I tell him, I try tell him, big damn fool."

"Balls."

"No."

Red was not completely certain. He paused, took another tack. "You know that sword I got with the jewels back at Motome? If you want, you can have it."

"Oh." The beauty of the sword shone in Martinez's eyes. "Free?"

"Yeah."

Croft shouted suddenly. "Come on, men, let's move out."

Red turned around. His heart was churning and he massaged his hands slowly against his thigh. "We ain't goin', Croft."

Croft strode toward him. "Made up your mind, Red?"

"If you want to do it so fuggin much, you can do it alone. Japbait'll take us back."

Croft stared at Martinez. "Changed your mind again?" he asked softly. "What are ya, a goddam woman?"

Martinez shook his head slowly. "I don't know, I don't know." His face began to work and he turned away.

"Red, get your pack ready and cut out this shit."

It had been wrong to talk to Martinez. Red saw it clearly. It had been disgusting, as though he had been arguing with a child. He had been taking the easy way and it wouldn't work. He would have to face Croft. "If I go up that hill, you'll be draggin' me."

Some of the men in the platoon were muttering. "Let's go back," Polack yelled, and Minetta and Gallagher joined him.

Croft stared at them all, and then unslung his rifle, cocked the bolt leisurely. "Red, you can go get your pack."

"Yeah, you would do somethin' when I ain't got a gun."

"Red, just get your pack and shut up."

"It ain't me alone. You gonna shoot all of us?"

Croft turned and gazed at the others. "Who wants to get lined up with Red?" None of them moved. Red watched, hoping numbly that one of them might pick up a rifle. Croft had turned away from him. Now was the time. He could leap at him, knock him down and the others would help out. If one man would move, they all would.

But nothing happened. He kept telling himself to jump at Croft and his legs wouldn't function.

Croft turned back to him. "Awright, Red, go get your pack."

"Fug you."

"Ah'm gonna shoot ya in about three-four seconds." He stood six feet away, his rifle raised to his hip. Slowly the muzzle pointed toward Red. He found himself watching the expression on Croft's face.

Suddenly he knew exactly what had happened to Hearn, and the knowledge left him weak. Croft was going to shoot. He knew it. Red stood stiff looking at Croft's eyes. "Just shoot a man down like that, huh?"

"Yeah."

It was worthless to temporize. Croft wanted to shoot him. For an instant he had a picture again of lying on his stomach waiting for the Japanese bayonet to strike into his back. He could feel the blood thumping in his head. As he waited, his will drained away slowly.

"How 'bout it, Red?"

The muzzle made a tiny circular motion as if Croft were selecting a more exact aim. Red watched his finger on the trigger. When it began to tighten he tensed suddenly. "Okay, Croft, you win." His voice croaked out weakly. He was making every effort to keep himself from trembling.

About him he could see the platoon relaxing. He felt as if his blood had slowed down, halted, and now had begun to flow again, outlining every nerve in his body. With his head down he strode over to his pack, rammed in the blanket, buckled the straps, and stood up.

He was licked. That was all there was to it. At the base of his shame was an added guilt. He was glad it was over, glad the long contest with Croft was finished, and he could obey orders with submission, without feeling that he must resist. This was the extra humiliation, the crushing one. Could that be all, was that the end of all he had done in his life? Did it always come to laying down a load?

He fell into line and trudged along in the middle of the platoon. He looked at nobody, and no one looked at him. All of them felt a wretched embarrassment. Each man was trying to forget the way he had been tempted to shoot Croft and had failed.

As they walked, Polack cursed continually in a low sullen voice, filled with self-loathing. Dumb yellow bastard. He was swearing at himself, frightened, a little shocked. The moment had been there, and he had let it go, had had his rifle in his hands, and had done nothing with it. Yellow . . . yellow!

And Croft at this point was confident again. This morning they would cross the mountain peak. Everything and everybody had tried to hold him back but there could be nothing left now, no obstacle at all.

The platoon climbed the slope, crossed another ridge, and descended over a stretch of scattered rocks into one more tiny valley. Croft led them through a small rock gorge onto another slope and for an hour they toiled upward from rock to rock, crawling sometimes for hundreds of yards on their hands and knees in a laborious endless progression which skirted the edge of a deep ravine. By midmorning the sun was very hot, and the men were exhausted once more. Croft led them much more slowly, halting every few minutes.

They topped a crest-line and jogged feebly down a gentle slope. Before them was a huge amphitheater, bounded in a rough semicircle by high sheer bluffs covered with vegetation. The cliffs of jungle rose almost vertically for five hundred feet, at least the height of a forty-story sky-scraper, and above them was the crest of the mountain. Croft had noticed this amphitheater; from miles away it looked like a dark-green collar encircling the neck of the mountain.

There was no way to avoid it; at either side of the amphitheater the mountain dropped for a thousand feet. They had to go forward and climb the jungle before them. Croft rested the platoon at the base, but there was no shade and the rest had little value. After five minutes they set out.

The wall of foliage was not so impossible as it had appeared from a distance. A crude stairway of rocks bedded in the foliage and zigzagged upward like a ramp. There were bamboo groves and bushes and plants, vines, and a few trees whose roots grew horizontally into the mountain and whose trunks bent upward in an L toward the sky. There was mud, of course, from all the rains that had trickled down the rocks, and leaves and plants and thorns restricted their passage.

It was a stairway, but not a convenient one. They carried the weight of a suitcase on their backs, and they had to climb what amounted to forty flights of stairs. To give an added fillip, the stairs were not of equal height. Sometimes they would clamber from one waist-high rock to another, and sometimes they would scrabble up a slope of pebbles and small rocks; sometimes indeed each rock was of a different height and shape than the one that had preceded it. And the stairway, of course, was littered, so that often they would have to push aside foliage or cut through vines.

Croft had estimated it would take an hour to ascend the wall of the amphitheater, but after an hour they were only halfway up. The men struggled behind him like a wounded caterpillar. They never traveled all at once. A few would advance over a rock and wait for the others to catch up. They advanced in ripples, Croft toiling ahead a few yards and the rest of the platoon filling the gap in a series of spasmodic lurches which traveled like a shock impulse. Often they would halt while Croft or Martinez hacked slowly through a tangle of bamboo. In a few places the stairway leaped upward in a big bound of seven or ten feet of muddy earth up which they climbed by clutching at roots.

Once more the platoon dropped from one layer of fatigue to another, but this had happened so often in the past few days that it was almost familiar, almost livable. With no surprise they felt their legs become numb, trail after them like a toy which a child drags on a string. Now the men no longer stepped from one high rock to another. They dropped their guns on the shelf above, flopped over and dragged their legs after them. Even the smallest rocks were too great to step over. They lifted their legs with their arms, and placed their feet on the step before them, tottered like old men out of their beds for an hour.

Every minute or two someone would stop and lie huddled on the rocks, weeping with the rapt taut sobs of fatigue that sound so much like grief. In empathy a swirl of vertigo would pass from one to the other and they would listen with a morbid absorption to the racking sounds of dry nausea. One or another of them was always retching. When they moved they were always falling. The climb up the rocks slippery with mud and vegetation, the vicious thorns of bamboo thicket, the blundering of their feet against the jungle vines, all blended into one vast torment. The men groaned and cursed, stumbled on their faces, reeled and skidded from rock to rock.

It was impossible to see more than ten feet ahead, and they forgot about Croft. They had discovered that they could not hate him and do anything about it, so they hated the mountain, hated it with more fervor than they could ever have hated a human being. The stairway became alive, personalized; it seemed to mock and deceive them at every step, resist them with every malign rock. Once more they forgot about the Japanese, forgot about the patrol, almost forgot about themselves. The only ecstasy they could imagine would be to stop climbing.

Even Croft was exhausted. He had the task of leading them, of cutting trail whenever the foliage became too thick, and he prostrated himself trying to pull them up the mountain. He felt not only the weight of his own body but the weight of all their bodies as effectively as if he had been pulling them in harness. They dragged him back, tugged at his shoulders and his heels. With all his physical exertion his mind fatigued him as greatly, for he was under the acute strain of gauging their limits.

There was another strain. The closer he came to the crest of the mountain the greater became his anxiety. Each new turn of the staircase demanded an excessive effort of will from him. He had been driving nearer and nearer to the heart of this country for days, and it had a cumulative terror. All the vast alien stretches of land they had crossed had eroded his will, pitched him a little finer. It was an effort, almost palpable, to keep advancing over strange hills and up the flanks of an ancient resisting mountain. For the first time in his life he started with fear every time an insect whipped into his face or an unnoticed leaf tickled his neck. He drove himself onward with the last sources of his endeavor, dropping at the halts with no energy left.

But each time the brief respite would charge his resolve again and he could toil upward a few yards more. He, too, had forgotten almost everything. The mission of the patrol, indeed even the mountain, hardly moved him now. He progressed out of some internal contest in himself as if to see which pole of his nature would be successful.

And at last he sensed that the top was near. Through the web of jungle foliage he could perceive sunlight as though they were approaching the exit of a tunnel. It spurred him on, yet left him exhausted. Each step he took closer to the summit left him more afraid. He might have quit before they reached it.

But he never had the opportunity. He reeled over a rock, saw a light-tan nest shaped something like a football, and in his fatigue he smashed into it. Instantly, he realized what the nest was, but too late. An uproar burst in it and a huge hornet, about the size of a half dollar, fluttered out, and then another and another after it. He watched dumbly as dozens of them flickered about his head. They were large and beautiful with great yellow bodies and iridescent wings; afterward he exhumed the memory as something completely apart from what followed.

The hornets were furious, and in a few seconds they raced down the line of men like a burning fuse. Croft felt one of them flutter at his ear, and he struck at it with a grunt, but it had stung him. The pain was maddening; it numbed his ear like frostbite, and traveled through his body with an acute shock. Another stung him and another; he bellowed with pain and struck at them frenziedly.

For the platoon this was the final unbearable distress. Perhaps five seconds they stood rooted, flailing dumbly at the hornets that attacked them. Each sting lashed through a man's body, loosing new frantic energies of desperation. The men were in delirium. Wyman began to bawl like a child, holding feebly to a rock, and swatting at the air in a tantrum.

"I can't stand it, *I can't stand it!*" he roared.

Two hornets bit him almost at once, and he hurled away his rifle, and screamed in terror. The shriek detonated the men. Wyman began to run down the rocks, and one by one they followed him.

Croft shouted at them to stop, but they paid no attention. He gave a last oath, swung impotently at a few of the hornets and then started down after them. In a last fragment of his ambition, he thought of regrouping them at the bottom.

The hornets pursued the men down the jungle wall and the rock ramp, goading them on in a last frenzy of effort. They fled with surprising agility, jumping down from rock to rock, ripping through the foliage that impeded them. They felt nothing but the savage fleck of the hornets, the muted jarring sensations of scrabbling from rock to rock. As they ran they flung away everything that slowed them. They tossed away their rifles, and some of them worked loose their packs and dropped them. Dimly they sensed that if they threw away enough possessions they would not be able to continue the patrol.

Polack was the last man ahead of Croft as the platoon poured into the amphitheater. He caught a quick glimpse of them, and the platoon was halting in confusion now that they had escaped the hornets. Polack threw a glance over his shoulder at Croft and burst among the men shouting, "WHAT THE HELL ARE YOU WAITING FOR? HERE COME THE BUGS!" Without pausing he ran past them, let loose a scream, and the platoon followed him, bolted in a new panic. They scattered over the floor of the amphitheater, continued on in the same spasm of effort over the next ridge, and down below to the valley, to the slopes of the rise beyond. In fifteen minutes they had fled beyond the point where they had started that morning.

When Croft finally caught up with the platoon, gathered them together, he discovered there were only three rifles and five packs left. They were through. He knew they could never make the climb again. He was too weak himself. He accepted the knowledge passively, too fagged to feel any regret or pain. In a quiet tired voice he told them to rest before they turned back to the beach to meet the boat.

The return march was uneventful. The men were wretchedly tired, but it was downhill work on the mountain slopes. Without any incident, they jumped the gap in the ledge where Roth had been killed, and by midafternoon descended the last cliffs, and set out into the yellow hills. All afternoon as they marched they heard the artillery booming on the other side of the mountain range. That night they bivouacked about ten miles from the jungle, and by the next day they had reached the shore and joined the litter-bearers. Brown and Stanley had come out of the hills only a few hours ahead of the platoon.

Goldstein told Croft how they had lost Wilson, and was surprised when he made no comment. But Croft was bothered by something else. Deep inside himself, Croft was relieved that he had not been able to climb the mountain. For that afternoon at least, as the platoon waited on the beach for the boats that were due the next day, Croft was rested by the unadmitted knowledge that he had found a limit to his hunger.

The boat picked them up the next day and they started on the journey back. This time the landing craft had been equipped with eighteen bunks along the bulkheads and the men put their equipment in the empty ones and stretched out to sleep. They had been sleeping ever since they had come out of the jungle the preceding afternoon, and by now their bodies had stiffened and become painful. Some of them had missed a meal that morning but they were not hungry. The rigors of the patrol had left them depleted in many ways. They drowsed for hours on the return trip, awaking only to lie in their bunks and stare out at the sky above the open boat. The craft pitched and yawed, spray washed over the sides and the bow ramp, but they barely noticed. The sound of the motors was pleasant, reassuring. The events of the patrol had receded already, become a diffused wry compound of indistinct memories.

By afternoon most of them were awake. They were still terribly fatigued but they could not sleep any longer. Their bodies ached and they felt no desire to walk about the narrow confines of the troop well, but still they were subtly restless. The patrol was over and yet they had so little to anticipate. The months and years ahead were very palpable to them. They were still on the treadmill; the misery, the ennui, the dislocated horror . . . Things would happen and time would pass, but there was no hope, no anticipation. There would be nothing but the deep cloudy dejection that overcast everything.

Minetta lay on his bunk, his eyes closed, and dawdled through the afternoon. There was one fantasy he kept indulging, a very simple one, a very pleasing one. Minetta was dreaming about blowing off his foot. One of these days while cleaning his gun he could point the muzzle right into the middle of his ankle, and press the trigger. All the bones would be mashed in his foot, and whether they had to amputate or not, they certainly would have to send him home.

Minetta tried to add up all the angles. He wouldn't be able to run again, but then who the hell wanted to run anyway? And as for dancing, the way they had these artificial limbs he could put on a wooden foot, and still hold his own. Oh, this was okay, this could work.

For a moment he was uneasy. Did it make any difference which foot it was? He was a leftie and maybe it'd be better to shoot the right foot, or were they both the same? He thought of asking Polack, and immediately dropped the idea. This kind of thing he'd have to play alone. In a couple of weeks, on a day when nothing was doing, he could take care of that little detail. He'd be in the hospital for a while, for three months, six months, but then . . . He lit a cigarette and watched the clouds dissolve into one another, feeling agreeably sorry for himself because he was going to have to lose a foot and it was not his fault.

Red picked at a sore on his hand, examining maternally the ridges and creases of his knuckles. There was no kidding himself any longer. His kidneys were shot, his legs would begin to break down soon, all through his body he could feel the damage the patrol had caused. Probably it had taken things out of him he would never be able to put back again. Well, it was the old men who got it, MacPherson on Motome, and then Wilson, it was probably fair enough. And there was always the chance of getting hit and coming out of it with a million-dollar wound. What difference did it make anyway? Once a man turned yellow . . . He coughed, lying flat on his back, the phlegm gagging him slightly. It took an effort of will to prop himself on his elbow and hawk the sputum out onto the floor of the boat.

"Hey, Jack," one of the pilots on the stern hatch yelled, "keep the boat clean. We don't want to scrub it after you guys."

"Aaah, blow it out," Polack shouted.

Croft called from his bunk, "Let's cut out that spittin', men."

There were no answers. Red nodded to himself. It was there, all right; he had waited a little anxiously for Croft to say something, had been relieved when Croft had not scolded him by name.

The bums in the flophouse who cringed when they were sober and cursed when they were drunk.

You carried it alone as long as you could, and then you weren't strong enough to take it any longer. You kept fighting everything, and everything broke you down, until in the end you were just a little goddam bolt holding on and squealing when the machine went too fast.

He had to depend on other men, he needed other men now, and he didn't know how to go about it. Deep within him were the first nebulae of an idea, but he could not phrase it. If they all stuck together . . .

Aaah, fug. All they knew was to cut each other's throats. There were no answers, there wasn't even any pride a man could have at the end. Now, if he had Lois. For an instant he hovered over the idea of writing her a letter, starting it up again, and then he threw it away. The least you could do was back out like a man. And there was the thought that maybe she'd tell him to go to hell. He coughed once more and spat into his hand, holding it numbly for several seconds before he wiped it surreptitiously on the canvas of his bunk. Let the boat pilot try to wash that out. And he smiled wryly, shamefully, at the satisfaction it gave him.

The sneak. Well, he'd been everything else in his time.

And Goldstein lay on his bunk with his arms under his head and thought dreamily about his wife and child. All the bitterness and frustration of losing Wilson had been tucked away in his brain, encysted temporarily by the stupor that had followed. He had slept for a day and a half, and the journey with the litter seemed remote. He even liked Brown and Stanley because they were a little uneasy with him and seemed afraid to bother him. He had a buddy too. There was an understanding between Ridges and him. The day they had spent on the beach waiting for the rest of the platoon had not been unpleasant. And automatically they had selected bunks next to each other when they got on the boat.

He had his moments of rebellion. The goy friend he got was such a goy—a peasant, an outcast himself. He *would* get somebody like that. But he was ashamed for thinking this, with almost the shame he felt whenever a random caustic thought about his wife slipped through his head. It ended by his being defiant. For a friend he had an illiterate, but so what? Ridges was a good man. There was something enduring about him. The salt of the earth, Goldstein told himself.

The boat wallowed along about a mile offshore. As the afternoon wore by the men began to move about a little, and stare over the side. The island skidded by slowly, always impenetrable, always green and opaque with the jungle skirting the water. They passed a small peninsula which they had noticed on the trip out, and some of them began to calculate how long it would be before they reached the bivouac. Polack climbed up on the rear hatch where the pilot was steering the boat and rested under the canvas canopy. The sun shifted over the water, reflecting brightly from each ripple, and the air held a subtle bouquet of vegetation and ocean.

"Jeez, it's nice out here," Polack said to the driver.

The man grunted. His feelings were hurt because the platoon had been spitting in the boat.

"Aaah, what's eatin' ya, Jack?" Polack asked.

"You were one of the wise guys who was giving me some lip before."

Polack shrugged. "Aaah, listen, Jack, you don' wanta take an attitude like that. We been t'rough a lot, our nerves are up in the air."

"Yeah, I guess you did have a rough go."

"Sure." Polack yawned. "Tomorrow they'll have our ass out on patrol, you watch."

"It's only mopping up."

"Where do ya get that stuff, moppin' up?"

The pilot looked at him. "Jesus, I forgot you men were out on patrol for six days. Hell, man, the whole fuggin campaign blew sky high. We killed Toyaku. In another week there won't be but ten Japs left."

"Wha . . . ?"

"Yeah. We got their supply dump. We're slaughtering them. I saw that Toyaku Line myself yesterday. They had concrete machine-gun emplacements. Fire lanes. Every damn thing."

Polack swore. "The whole thing's over, huh?"

"Just about."

"And we broke our ass for nothin'."

The pilot grinned. "Higher strategy."

Polack climbed down after a while and told the men. It all seemed perfectly fitting to them. They laughed sourly, turned over in their bunks, and stared at the side bulkhead. But soon they realized that if the campaign was over they would be out of combat for a few months at least. It confused them, irritated them, they didn't know whether the news pleased them or not. The patrol should have been worth something. In their fatigue this conflict brought them close to hysteria and then shifted them over to mirth.

"Hey, you know," Wyman piped, "before we went I heard a rumor they're going to send the division to Australia to make MPs out of us."

"Yeah, MPs." They roared at this. "Wyman, they're sendin' us home."

"Recon's gonna be personal bodyguard for the General."

"MacArthur is gonna have us build him another house at Hollandia."

"We're gonna be Red Cross girls," Polack shouted.

"They're puttin' the division on permanent KP."

Everything mixed in them. The boat, which had been almost silent, quivered from the men's laughter. Their voices, hoarse, trembling with mirth and anger, carried for a long distance over the water. Each time one of them said anything, it provoked new spasms of laughter. Even Croft was brought into it.

"Hey, *Sergeant*, I'm gonna be a cook, I hate to leave ya."

"Aaah, get the hell out, you're a bunch of goddam women," Croft drawled.

And this seemed funniest of all. They held weakly onto the stanchions of their bunks. "Do I have to leave now, Sergeant? There's a lot of water," Polack bawled. It rushed through them in a succession of confused waves like water ripples spreading out from a stone only to be balked by other wavelets formed by another stone. Every time someone opened his mouth they roared again, wild hysterical laughter, close to tears. The boat shook from it.

It died down slowly, erupted again several times like fire licking out from under a blanket, and finally wore itself out. There was nothing left but their spent bodies and the mild pleasure they found in releasing the tension upon their cheek muscles, soothing the ache of laughter in their chests, wiping their freshened eyes. And it was replaced by the flat extensive depression which overlay everything.

Polack tried to revive it again by singing but only a few of them joined him.

> *Roll me over*
> *In the clover.*
> *Roll me over,*
> *Lay me down*
> *And do it again.*
>
> *Ha' past three*
> *I had her on my knee.*
> *Lay me down,*
> *Roll me over,*
> *Do it again.*
> *Roll me over in the clover . . .*

Their voices piped out feebly, lost in the flat placid washes of the blue sea. Their boat chugged along, the motors almost smothering the sound.

> *Ha' past four*
> *I had her on the floor.*
> *Lay me down,*
> *Roll me over,*
> *Do it again.*

Croft got out of his bunk and peered over the side, staring moodily at the water. He had not been told the date on which the campaign had been won, and he made the error of assuming it was the day they had failed on the mountain. If they had been able to climb it, the campaign would have depended upon them. He did not even question this. It was a bitter certainty in his mind. His jaw muscles quivered as he spat over the side.

Ha' past five
We began to jive . . .

They sang as if they were playing chimes, Polack and Red and Minetta, gathered together at the stern. At every pause Polack would blow out his cheeks and go "Waah-waaaah," like a trumpet when it is fanned with a mute. Gradually it was catching the others. "Where's Wilson?" one of them shouted, and they all stopped for a moment. They had heard the news of his death but it hadn't registered. And suddenly he was dead. They understood it. The knowledge shocked them, loosed the familiar unreality of war and death, and the song wavered over a syllable or two. "I'm gonna miss that old sonofabitch," Polack said.

"C'mon, let's keep going," Red muttered. Guys came and guys went, and after a while you didn't even remember their names.

"Roll me *over* in the clover."

They passed a bend in the island and saw Mount Anaka in the distance. It looked immense. "Boy, did we climb that?" Wyman asked.

Some of them scrambled up the side, pointing out slopes of the mountain to each other, arguing whether they had climbed each particular ridge. They had a startled pride in themselves. "It's a big sonofabitch."

"We did okay to go as far as we did."

That was the main sentiment. Already they were thinking how they would tell it to their buddies in other platoons.

"We just got lost in the shuffle. Everybody's gonna have a story to tell."

"Yeah."

And that pleased them too. The final sustaining ironies.

The song was still going on.

Ha' past six
I had her doin' tricks.
Lay me down,
Roll me over,
Do it again.

Croft stared at the mountain. The inviolate elephant brooding over the jungle and the paltry hills.

It was pure and remote. In the late afternoon sunlight it was velvet green and rock blue and the brown of light earth, made of another material than the fetid jungle before it.

The old torment burned in him again. A stream of wordless impulses beat in his throat and he had again the familiar and inexplicable tension the mountain always furnished him. To climb that.
He had failed, and it hurt him vitally. His frustration was loose again. He would never have another opportunity to climb it. And yet he was wondering if he could have succeeded. Once more he was feeling the anxiety and terror the mountain had roused on the rock stairway. If he had gone alone, the fatigue of the other men would not have slowed him but he would not have had their company, and he realized suddenly that he could not have gone without them. The empty hills would have eroded any man's courage.

Ha' past seven
She thought she was in heaven . . .

In a few hours they would be back, pitching their pup tents in the darkness, getting a canteen cup of hot coffee, perhaps. And tomorrow the endless routine of harsh eventless days would begin once more. Already the patrol was unfamiliar, unbelievable, and yet the bivouac before them also was unreal. In transit everything in the Army was unreal. They sang to make a little noise.

. . . roll me over
And do it again.

Croft kept looking at the mountain. He had lost it, had missed some tantalizing revelation of himself.
Of himself and much more. Of life.
Everything.

KEITH DOUGLAS
1920–1944

Douglas was educated at Merton College, Oxford, where he struck observers as very intelligent and obstinate, impulsive and brutally honest. Commissioned in the army in 1940, he fought with the tanks in North

Africa, an experience he refracted in his classic memoir Alamein to Zem
Zem *(1946). He had been writing poems since boyhood, and those he
sent back from army service were published by his old college tutor, the
Great War poet and memoirist Edmund Blunden. Douglas's tank unit
went ashore in Normandy on June 6, 1944. Three days later, standing
outside his tank, he was hit by a tiny shell fragment from a tree-burst and
killed instantly. A year before he had written a friend, "To trust anyone
or to admit any hope of a better world is criminally foolish, as foolish as it
is to stop working for it."*

From ALAMEIN TO ZEM ZEM

I am not writing about these battles as a soldier, nor trying to discuss
them as military operations. I am thinking of them—selfishly, but as I
always shall think of them—as my first experience of fighting: that is
how I shall write of them. To say I thought of the battle of Alamein as an
ordeal sounds pompous: but I did think of it as an important test, which
I was interested in passing. I observed these battles partly as an exhibition—that is to say that I went through them a little like a visitor from
the country going to a great show, or like a child in a factory—a child
sees the brightness and efficiency of steel machines and endless belts
slapping round and round, without caring or knowing what it is all there
for. When I could order my thoughts I looked for more significant things
than appearances; I still looked—I cannot avoid it—for something deco-
rative, poetic or dramatic.

The geography of the country in which I spent those few months is
already as vague to me as if I had learnt it from an atlas much longer ago.
The dates have slipped away, the tactical lessons have been learnt by
someone else. But what remains in my mind—a flurry of violent impressions—is vivid enough. Against a backcloth of indeterminate landscapes
of moods and smells, dance the black and bright incidents.

I had to wait until 1942 to go into action. I enlisted in September
1939, and during two years or so of hanging about I never lost the
certainty that the experience of battle was something I must have.
Whatever changes in the nature of warfare, the battlefield is the simple,
central stage of the war: it is there that the interesting things happen.
We talk in the evening, after fighting, about the great and rich men who
cause and conduct wars. They have so many reasons of their own that
they can afford to lend us some of them. There is nothing odd about
their attitude. They are out for something they want, or their Governments want, and they are using us to get it for them. Anyone can understand that: there is nothing unusual or humanly exciting at that end of

the war. I mean there may be things to excite financiers and parliamentarians—but not to excite a poet or a painter or a doctor.

But it is exciting and amazing to see thousands of men, very few of whom have much idea why they are fighting, all enduring hardships, living in an unnatural, dangerous, but not wholly terrible world, having to kill and to be killed, and yet at intervals moved by a feeling of comradeship with the men who kill them and whom they kill, because they are enduring and experiencing the same things. It is tremendously illogical—to read about it cannot convey the impression of having walked through the looking-glass which touches a man entering a battle.

I had arrived in the Middle East in August 1941. As a result of passing a course on which I was sent by accident, I found myself posted away from my regiment to a Divisional staff. I still wanted to get into action, and probably looked impatiently at my colleagues and superiors on this staff. For eight months I honestly tried hard to make sense of the job I was given—in other words to persuade the staff colonel and major to whose department I was attached to give me some work to do. The situation emerged clearly and simply as the months passed. My job was to give camouflage training. The Staff officers of "G" staff, under the General, arranged training programmes: they invariably forgot to include camouflage. At first they airily agreed to my humble reminders with a wealth of condescending language—the General alone refrained from calling me "old boy" although he said good morning, good morning as civilly as Siegfried Sassoon's General.

After eight months of relative inaction, not being at any time a patient person, and having a hatred for wasted time, I tried to get back to my regiment. I could not be released: with the charm and politeness with which everyone on a staff always speaks to everyone else, I was told I was indispensable. Any disclaimer of this, any statement that I was doing nothing but waste Government petrol and money, appeared to strike them as a conventionally modest reply, equivalent to saying "I'm only doing my job, old boy." The offensive loomed very large in rumour, among so many officers living more or less inside the horse's mouth. I decided, if there were no other means of going into action with my regiment, to run away from divisional headquarters in my truck, and report to my colonel. I thought vaguely that this might be straightened out later. To plan this was the natural result of having the sort of little-boy mentality I still have. A little earlier, I might have wanted to run away and be a pirate. But it was surprising how easily the plan was realized and justified. For eight months I had done no mechanized training, my regiment was equipped with tanks, guns and wireless sets which I had never handled, scarcely seen, in my life; and it seemed possible, and even likely, that my colonel who had applied for me before the

battle, would not want an untrained officer to join him during action and
endanger everyone's life while learning his job. If he refused me I was
determined not to come back to Division but to drive away down the
coast road to Alexandria, and from there through Cairo and Ismalia and
across the Sinai desert to Palestine, to amuse myself until I was caught
and court-martialled.

The battle of Alamein began on the 23rd of October, 1942. Six days
afterwards I set out in direct disobedience of orders to rejoin my regiment. My batman was delighted with this manoeuvre. "I like you, sir,"
he said. "You're shit or bust, you are." This praise gratified me a lot.

I

Six days after I had heard rumbling on the western skyline, that famous
barrage that began it, I moved up from the rear to the front of the
British attack. Through areas as full of organization as a city of ants—it
happened that two days before I had been reading Maeterlinck's descriptions of ant communities—I drove up the sign-posted tracks until,
when I reached my own place in all this activity, I had seen the whole
arrangement of the Army, almost too large to appreciate, as a body
would look to a germ riding in its bloodstream. First the various headquarters of the higher formations, huge conglomerations of large and
small vehicles facing in all directions, flags, signposts and numbers standing among their dust. On the main tracks, marked with crude replicas of
a hat, a bottle, and a boat, cut out of petrol tins, lorries appeared like
ships, plunging their bows into drifts of dust and rearing up suddenly
over crests like waves. Their wheels were continually hidden in dustclouds: the ordinary sand being pulverized by so much traffic into a
substance almost liquid, sticky to the touch, into which the feet of men
walking sank to the knee. Every man had a white mask of dust in which,
if he wore no goggles, his eyes showed like a clown's eyes. Some did wear
goggles, many more the celluloid eyeshields from their anti-gas equip-
ments. Trucks and their loads became a uniform dust colour before they
had travelled twenty yards: even with a handkerchief tied like a cowboy's
over nose and mouth, it was difficult to breathe.

The lorry I drove was a Ford two-tonner, a commercial lorry designed
for roadwork, with an accelerator and springs far too sensitive for tracks
like these. I was thrown, with my two passengers, helplessly against the
sides and roof of the cab: the same was happening to our clothes and
possessions in the back. The sun was climbing behind us. As far as we
could see across the dunes to right and left stretched formations of
vehicles and weapons of all kinds, three-ton and heavier supply lorries of
the R.A.S.C., Field workshops with huge recovery vehicles and winches,

twenty-five-pounders and quads, Bofors guns in pits with their crews lying beside them, petrol fires everywhere, on which the crews of all were brewing up tea and tinned meat in petrol tins. We looked very carefully at all these, not having any clear idea where we should find the regiment. We did not yet know whether they were resting or actually in action. I realized that in spite of having been in the R.A.C. for two years, I had very little idea what to expect. I like to picture coming events to myself, perhaps through having been much alone, and to rehearse them mentally. I could not remember any picture or account which gave me a clear idea of tanks in action. In training we had been employed in executing drill movements in obedience to flag signals from troop leaders. We had been trained to fire guns on the move, and to adopt a vastly extended and exactly circular formation at night. But most of my training had been by lectures without illustrations: what few words of reminiscence I had heard from those who returned from actions in France and the desert, suggested that no notice was ever taken of the manoeuvres we had been taught in the field—which left me none the wiser. None of us had ever thought much of the drill movements and flag-signals. News films—just as later on that mediocre film "Desert Victory"—gave no idea where most of their "action" pictures were taken. Even my own regiment had been known to put their tanks through various evolutions for cameramen.

So feeling a little like the simple soul issuing from the hand of God, *animula blandula vagula,* I gazed on all the wonders of this landscape, looking among all the signs for the stencilled animal and number denoting my own regiment. I was not sure yet whether this was an abortive expedition—tomorrow might find me, with a movement order forged on my own typewriter, scorching down the road to Palestine. All my arrangements had been made to suit the two contingencies. I had dressed in a clean khaki shirt and shorts, pressed and starched a week or two before in an Alexandria laundry. My batman Lockett, an ex-hunt servant with a horseman's interest in turn-out and good leather, had polished the chin-strap and the brasses of my cap and belt till the brasses shone like suns and the chinstrap like a piece of glass laid on velvet. In the lorry, besides Lockett, rode a fitter from Divisional Headquarters, who was to drive it back there if Lockett and I stayed with the regiment.

The guns, such desultory firing as there was, sounded more clearly: the different noise of bombs was distinguishable now. The formations on either side were of a more combatant kind, infantry resting, heavy artillery and the usual light anti-aircraft. A few staff and liaison officers in jeeps and staff cars still passed, the jeeps often identifiable only by their passengers' heads showing out of enveloping dustclouds: but the traffic was now mostly supply vehicles moving between the combatant units and their "B" or supply echelons.

Fifteen miles from our starting point and about four miles in rear of the regiment, I found our "B" echelon, in charge of two officers whom I had known fairly well during my few months with the regiment, Mac— an ex-N.C.O. of the Scots Greys, now a captain; and Owen, a major; an efficient person with deceptive, adolescent manners, whom no one would suspect of being an old Etonian. It is difficult to imagine Owen at any public school at all: if you look at him he seems to have sprung, miraculously enlarged, but otherwise unaltered, from an inky bench in a private preparatory school. He looks as if he had white rats in his pockets. On these two I had to test my story.

I was afraid the idea of my running back to the regiment would seem absurd to them, so I began non-committally by greeting them and asking where the regiment was. "A few miles up the road," said Mac. "They're out of action at the moment but they're expecting to go in again any time. Have you come back to us?" I said that depended on the Colonel. "Oh, he'll be glad to see you," said Mac. "I don't think 'A' Squadron's got many officers left: they had a bad day the other day; I lost all my vehicles in B1 the same night—petrol lorry got hit and lit up the whole scene and they just plastered us with everything they had." In spite of this ominous news, I was encouraged by Mac's saying I was needed, and pushed on up the track until we came to the regiment.

Tanks and trucks were jumbled close together, with most of the men busy doing maintenance on them. A tall Ordnance officer whom I had never seen directed me to the same fifteen-hundredweight truck which had been the Orderly Room in the Training Area at Wadi Natrun. I left my lorry and walked, feeling more and more apprehensive as I approached this final interview. I looked about among the men as I went, but saw only one or two familiar faces; a regiment's personnel alters surprisingly, even in eight months.

I looked about for Edward, my squadron leader, and for Tom and Raoul, who had been troop leaders with me, but could not see them. The Colonel, beautifully dressed and with his habitual indolence of hand, returned my salute from inside the fifteen-hundredweight, where he was sitting with Graham, the adjutant, a handsome, red-haired, amiable young Etonian. I said to Piccadilly Jim (the Colonel), "Good evening, sir, I've escaped from Division for the moment, so I wondered if I'd be any use to you up here." "Well, Peter," stroking his moustache and looking like a contented ginger cat, "we're *most* glad to see you—er—as always. All the officers in 'A' Squadron, except Andrew, are casualties, so I'm sure he'll welcome you with open arms. We're probably going in early tomorrow morning, so you'd better go and get him to fix you up with a troop now." After a few more politenesses, I went to find Andrew, and my kit. The tremendous question was decided, and in a disconcertingly abrupt and definite way, after eight months of abortive efforts to rejoin. Palestine was a long way off and a few miles to the west, where the sounds of gunfire had intensified, lay the German armies.

II

I found Andrew, sitting on a petrol tin beside his tanks: I had met him before but when he looked up at my approach he did not recognize me. He was not young, and although at the moment an acting major about to go into action in a tank for the first time in his life, Andrew had already seen service in Abyssinia in command of the native mercenaries who had been persuaded to fight for Haile Selassie. From Abyssinia he had come to Cairo and fallen, through that British military process which penalizes anyone who changes his job, from colonel to major. Later, he had gravitated to base depot, and being unemployed, returned to his war-substantive rank of captain. As a captain he had come back to the regiment; it is not difficult to picture the state of mind of a man who knows he has worked well and receives no reward except to be demoted two grades. He now found himself second in command of a squadron whose squadron leader had been a subaltern under him before. What happened after that was probably inevitable. Andrew's health and temper were none the better for the evil climate and conditions of his late campaign. Someone who knew him before—which I did not—said that he went away a charming and entertaining young man, and returned a hardened and embittered soldier.

He was a small man with blond hair turning grey, sitting on a petrol tin and marking the cellophane of his map case with a chinagraph pencil. His face was brick-red with sun and wind, the skin cracking on his lips and nose. He wore a grey Indian Army flannel shirt, a pair of old corduroy trousers, and sandals. Round his mahogany-coloured neck a blue silk handkerchief was twisted and tied like a stock, and on his head was a beret. Like most ex-cavalrymen he had no idea how to wear it. To him I reported, resplendent—if a little dusty—in polished cap and belt.

He allotted me two tanks, as a troop, there not being enough on the squadron strength to make sub-units of more than two tanks. I drove my lorry with the kit on it to one of the tanks and began to unload and sort out my belongings. Lockett and I laid them out, together with the three bags of emergency rations belonging to the lorry. The Corporal, lately commander of this tank, departed, staggering under his own possessions barely confined by his groundsheet in an amorphous bundle.

Lockett was to go for the duration of the battle to the technical stores lorry where he had a friend and where he could make himself useful. To him I handed over the greater part of my belongings—the style in which I had travelled at Divisional Headquarters being now outmoded. I kept a half-share of the three bags of rations, which I distributed between my two tanks (this amounting to several tins of bully beef, of course, one or two of First American white potatoes, and some greater treasures, tins of American bacon rashers, and of fruit and condensed milk. A pair of clean socks were filled, one with tea, the other with sugar). I changed my peaked cap for a beret, and retained a small cricket bag with shirts, slacks, washing and shaving kit, writing paper, a camera and a Penguin Shakespeare's Sonnets. Rolled up in my valise and bedding were a suit of battledress, my revolver, and a British warm. In my pocket I had a small flask of whisky, and in the locker on the side of the tank, in addition to the rations, I put some tins of N.A.A.F.I. coffee and Oxo cubes, bought in Alexandria. I now felt the satisfaction of anyone beginning an expedition—or as Barbet Hasard might have said on this occasion, a Voyage— in contemplating my assembled stores, and in bestowing them. As soon as this was finished I began to make the acquaintance of my tank crews.

My own tank was a Mk. III Crusader—then comparatively new to us all. I had once been inside the Mk. II, which had a two-pounder gun and a four-man crew, and was now superseded by this tank with a six-pounder gun and only three men in the crew, the place of the fourth being occupied by the breech mechanism of the six-pounder. This tank is the best looking medium tank I ever saw, whatever its shortcomings of performance. It is low-built, which in desert warfare, and indeed all tank warfare, is a first consideration. This gives it, together with its lines and its suspension on five great wheels a side, the appearance almost of a speedboat. To see these tanks crossing country at speed was a thrill which seemed inexhaustible—many times it encouraged us, and we were very proud of our Crusaders; though we often had cause to curse them.

From underneath this particular tank a pair of boots protruded. As I looked at them, my mind being still by a matter of two days untrained to it, the inevitable association of ideas did not take place. The whole man emerged, muttering in a Glaswegian monotone. He was a small man with a seemingly disgruntled youngster's face, called Mudie. I found him, during the weeks I spent with him, to be lazy, permanently discontented, and a most amusing talker. In battle he did not have much opportunity for talking and was silent even during rests and meals; but at all other times he would wake up talking, as birds do, at the first gleam of light and long before dawn, and he would still be talking in the invariable monotone long after dark. He was the driver of the tank.

The gunner was another reservist. His name was Evan, and he looked a very much harder case than Mudie, though I think there was not much to choose between them. Evan scarcely spoke at all, and if drawn into conversation would usually reveal (if he were talking to an officer) a number of injustices under which he was suffering at the moment, introducing them with a calculated air of weariness and "it doesn't matter now," as though he had been so worn down by the callousness of his superiors as to entertain little hope of redress. In conversation with his fellows (I say fellows because he had no friends), he affected a peculiar kind of snarling wit, and he never did anything that was not directly for his own profit. Mudie would often do favours for other people. Evan would prefer an officer and then only if he could not well avoid it. Yet he was unexpectedly quick and efficient on two occasions which I shall describe.

We were at an hour's notice to move. This meant, not that we should move in an hour's time, but that, if we did move, we should have an hour in which to prepare for it. When I had sorted out my belongings, and eaten some meat and vegetable stew and tinned fruit, washed down with coffee, I lay down on my bedding with a magazine which someone had left on the tank, and glancing only vaguely at the pages, thought over the changes of the last few days, and confronted myself with the future. Desultory thumps sounded in the distance, occasionally large bushes of dust sprang up on the skyline, or a plane droned across, very high up in the blue air. Men passed and repassed, shouted to each other, laughed, sang, and whistled dance tunes, as they always did. Metallic clangs and the hum of light and heavy engines at various pitches sounded at a distance. Occasionally a machine-gun would sputter for a few seconds, as it was tested or cleared. The whole conglomeration of sounds, mixing in the heat of declining afternoon, would have put me to sleep, but for my own excitement and apprehensions, and the indefatigable flies.

But though I reflected, a little uncomfortably, on what might be happening to me in a few hours, I was not dissatisfied. I still felt the exhilaration of cutting myself free from the whole net of inefficiency and departmental bullshit that had seemed to have me quite caught up in Divisional Headquarters. I had exchanged a vague and general existence for a simple and particular (and perhaps short) one. Best of all, I had never realized how ashamed of myself I had been, in my safe job at Division until with my departure this feeling was suddenly gone. I had that feeling of almost unstable lightness which is felt physically immediately after putting down a heavy weight. All my difficult mental enquiries and arguments about the future were shelved, perhaps permanently. I got out my writing paper and wrote two letters, one to my mother and one to David Hicks in Cairo. Although in writing these letters (which, of course, got lost and were never posted) I felt very dramatic, the tone of them was not particularly theatrical. To my mother I wrote that I rejoiced to have escaped at last from Division and to be back with the regiment. I might not have time to write for a week or two, I added. To Hicks I sent a poem which I had written during my last two days at Division on an idea which I had had since a month before the offensive. I asked him to see that it got home as I had not got a stamp or an airgraph. He could print it in his magazine on the way, if he liked.

I had asked Andrew one or two questions in the hope of not showing myself too ignorant in my first action. But it was fairly plain that he knew nothing himself. "I shouldn't worry, old boy," was all he would say. "The squadron and troop leaders don't use maps much, and there are no codes at all, just talk as you like over the air—except for giving map-references of course—but you won't need them. You'll find it's quite simple." When I had written my letters I got into the turret with Evan and tried to learn its geography. My place as tank commander was on the right of the six-pounder. I had a seat, from which I could look out through a periscope. This afforded a very small view, and in action all tank commanders stand on the floor of their turrets so that their eyes are clear of the top, or actually sit in the manhole on top of their turret with their legs dangling inside. Behind the breech of the six-pounder is a metal shield to protect the crew against the recoil of the gun, which leaps back about a foot when it is fired. On my side of the six-pounder was a rack for a box of machine-gun ammunition, the belt of which had to run over the six-pounder and into the machine-gun mounted the other side of it. There were also two smoke dischargers to be operated by me. Stacked round the sides of the turret were the six-pounder shells, nose downwards; hand-grenades, smoke grenades and machine-gun ammunition. At the back of the turret on a shelf stood the wireless set, with its control box for switching from the A set to internal communication between the tank crew, and on top of the wireless set a pair of binoculars, wireless spare parts and tommy-gun magazines. There was a tommy-gun in a clip on Evan's side of the turret. On the shelf, when we were in action, we usually kept also some Penguin books, chocolate or boiled sweets if we could get them, a tin of processed cheese, a knife and some biscuits. We were lucky enough to begin the battle with a tin of Australian butter as well. About dusk the wireless sets in all tanks were switched on and netted into the regimental control station, to make sure everyone's set was as far as possible on the same frequency. Each station, like 2LO in early broadcasting, was known by a call sign, by which it announced itself and was called up by control stations. Before dark I went over to make sure that my other tank was ready to move, completely filled with rations, kit, petrol, oil, ammunition, and water. I stayed some time talking to the crew. The Corporal, Browning, had already been captured and recaptured during the first four days of the battle. He said the Germans had treated him very well, and seemed quite cheerful—so did his gunner and driver—at the prospect of going into action again. This was more than could be said of Evan and Mudie who grew dourer and more taciturn every minute.

I lay down to sleep in my clothes, covered with my British warm and blankets, for the nights were already beginning to be cold. Perhaps betrayed by the spectacle of the stars as clear as jewels on black velvet into a mood of more solemnity, I suddenly found myself assuming that I was going to die tomorrow. For perhaps a quarter of an hour I considered to what possibilities of suffering, more than of death, I had laid myself open. This with the dramatic and emotional part of me: but my senses of proportion and humour, like two court jesters, chased away the tragic poet, and I drifted away on a tide of odd thoughts, watching the various signs of battle in the lower sky. I persuaded myself that I had passed the worst ordeals of fear and that there would be no time for sharp, instantaneous fear in battle. If I thought so, I was not long to be so deceived. The moon, now grown much greater than when a week or two ago she had inspired me to write a poem on her ominous pregnancy, presided over a variety of lesser lights; starshells, tracers of orange, green, red, blue, and a harsh white, and the deeper colours of explosions. We were still at an hour's notice.

III

Someone shook me out of my sleep at four o'clock in the cold morning. Somewhat to my surprise I woke immediately with the full consciousness of where I was: for I had feared as I dropped asleep the morning might surprise me unpleasantly at my least heroic hour. The moment I was wakeful I had to be busy. We were to move at five: before that engines and sets had to be warmed up, orders to be given through the whole hierarchy from the Colonel to the tank crews. In the half light the tanks seemed to crouch, still, but alive, like toads. I touched the cold metal shell of my own tank, my fingers amazed for a moment at its hardness, and swung myself into the turret to get out my map case. Of course, it had fallen down on the small circular steel floor of the turret. In getting down after it I contrived to hit my head on the base of the six-pounder and scratch open both my hands; inside the turret there is less room even than in an aircraft, and it requires experience to move about. By the time I came up a general activity had begun to warm the appearance of the place, if not the air of it. The tanks were now half-hidden in clouds of blue smoke as their engines began one after another to grumble, and the stagnant oil burnt away. This scene with the silhouettes of men and turrets interrupted by swirls of smoke and the sky lightening behind them, was to be made familiar to me by many repetitions. Out of each turret, like the voices of dwarfs, thin and cracked and bodiless, the voices of the operators and of the control set come; they speak to the usual accompaniment of "mush," morse, odd squeals, and the peculiar jangling, like a barrel-organ, of an enemy jamming station.

   Probably as a result of some vacillation by higher authority, nobody moved before seven o'clock, when the Crusader squadron—my squadron—moved out and on to the other side of a main track running north to south. Here we halted, having left the heavy squadrons of Shermans and Grants still in our rest area, and were allowed to brew up. The immense moral satisfaction and recreation of brewing up was one I had never realized. As soon as the permission is given, all crews except those of tanks detailed for look-out duties swarm out of their turrets. The long boxes on the side of the tank are opened: tins of bacon or M. & V., according to the time of day, are got out, while someone is lighting a fire in a tin filled with a paste of sand and petrol. A veteran, blackened half of a petrol-tin, with a twisted wire handle, is unhooked from some extremity of the tank and filled with water for tea. Within five minutes a good crew has a cup of immensely strong and sweet hot tea and sandwiches (for example) of oatmeal biscuits fried in bacon fat and enclosing crisp bacon. If there is a little more time, it will probably be used to make another brew of tea from the same leaves, and to eat more biscuits spread with oleomargarine—to me, a horrible but wholesome synthetic—and Palestinian marmalade. This morning I found printed on my tin of marmalade the name of the communal settlement at Givat Brenner, where I had spent a day four or five months before. Thoughts of those quiet trees and that peaceful, industrious community induced a minute or two of nostalgia, and a less logical but more comfortable sense of friends following me. Soon after breakfast we were turned round and returned to camp—I never discovered why we made this excursion. We did not move again until late afternoon, when the regiment moved out, Crusaders leading, in single file on to the track up which I had come the day before. The head of the column turned westwards, only turrets and pennants, flown on the small aerials, showing above the billowing dust. I took a photograph of the column behind and in front of me.

That afternoon was still and sunny, the upper air clear, the ground churned everywhere into white dust by the endless traffic. This white dust lay very thickly rutted on the ground and mixed with the atmosphere, like a mist for a foot or two above the desert. Even without looking at the formations lying beside the track and stretching away from it, it was impossible not to feel immense subdued activity all over the area. On the track, besides our own column of tanks moving up slowly, screened and enveloped in their own dust, tanks and armoured cars passed us going out of battle, and a renewed traffic of staff cars and jeeps made it clear that the front line had advanced since the previous night when few of them were coming so far forward. These smaller vehicles bucketed in and out among the main streams of traffic.

Up above in the clear sky a solitary aeroplane moved, bright silver in the sunlight, a pale line of exhaust marking its unhurried course. The Bofors gunners on either side of us were running to their guns and soon opened a rapid, thumping fire, like a titanic workman hammering. The silver body of the aeroplane was surrounded by hundreds of little grey smudges, through which it sailed on serenely. From it there fell away, slowly and gracefully, an isolated shower of rain, a succession of glittering drops. I watched them descend a hundred feet before it occurred to me to consider their significance and forget their beauty. The column of tanks trundled forward imperturbably, but the heads of their crews no longer showed. I dropped down in the turret and shouted to Evan who was dozing in the gunner's seat: "Someone's dropping some stuff." He shouted back a question and adjusted his earphones. "Bombs!" I said into the microphone. Their noisy arrival somewhere on our right confirmed the word. Control called us over the air: "Nuts one, is everybody O.K.?" "Two O.K. off." "Three O.K. off." "Four O.K. off," said the troop leaders in turn. "Five O.K. off," I completed the group. The journey continued.

The view from a moving tank is like that in a camera obscura or a silent film—in that since the engine drowns all other noises except explosions, the whole world moves silently. Men shout, vehicles move, aeroplanes fly over, and all soundlessly: the noise of the tank being continuous, perhaps for hours on end, the effect is of silence. It is the same in an aircraft, but unless you are flying low, distance does away with the effect of a soundless pageant. I think it may have been the fact that for so much of the time I saw it without hearing it, which led me to feel that country into which we were now moving as an illimitably strange land, quite unrelated to real life, like the scenes in "The Cabinet of Doctor Caligari." Silence is a strange thing to us who live: we desire it, we fear it, we worship it, we hate it. There is a divinity about cats, as long as they are silent: the silence of swans gives them an air of legend. The most impressive thing about the dead is their triumphant silence, proof against anything in the world.

A party of prisoners now appeared marching on our left. They were evidently very tired but looked about them with a good deal of interest, particularly at our column. I thought of innumerable pictures of glowering S.S. men in Nazi tanks, and glared at them through my goggles in the hope of looking like part of an inexorable war machine myself. They must have been fairly impressed with the strength and concentration of our forces by the time they reached their cage at the rear. About two hundred of them passed us, in batches, as we continued our journey. We looked at them with an interest equal to their own. They did not look very fearsome: they were almost all Germans with shapeless green or khaki drill uniforms and floppy peaked caps with a red, white and black bull's-eye on them. The desert on either side of the track became more sparsely populated with vehicles, and at length there were none but derelicts. The column halted at last, so that my tank stood beside the burnt-out shell of a German Mk. IV Special, with its long gun and rows of little wheels. Most of one side of it had been torn out, probably by the explosion of its own ammunition. Some charred clothing lay beside it, but no equipment, and there was no sign of the crew. The whole thing made a disconcerting cautionary picture.

On the horizon to our front we could see two vehicles burning fiercely, from which expanding columns of black smoke slanted across the orange sky. We could see shells, visible by their traces as yellow or white lights, sailing in apparently slow curves across our front: they were being fired by tanks on our left, but were landing in dead ground to us. By now the light was ebbing perceptibly and soon the burning derelicts and the shell-traces gleamed against the sky. The traces of enemy shells could be seen flying from beyond the ridge ahead of us. We were now spectators of the closing stages of the day's battle.

IV

I dismounted and went to find Andrew, leaving Evan and Mudie silently examining the nearest derelict: apparently we were to leaguer for the night nearby, and Andrew went away into the growing obscurity to receive his orders from the Colonel. He told me to prevent the squadron moving away and getting lost before he came back. Eventually, however, he sent the Welsh sergeant, Thomas, to summon us back to him, and himself led us slowly, watching one another's red rear lights, into our position for the night.

The Crusaders were drawn up in two rows in front of the heavy tanks, and we were ordered to put out a guard, until a guard from our attached infantry came to relieve us, and to dig one slit trench per tank. I would have been quite content with the protection of my tank turret but passed on the orders, sending Evan over to help Sergeant Thomas with the slit trench for the guard. We began to try and make some impression on the stony ground. The burning derelicts were no longer visible, and for the moment there was a background of silence to our efforts.

After we had been digging about a minute, a projectile of some sort screamed over our heads and burst with an orange flame and a great deal of noise somewhere in the darkness behind us, apparently among the heavy tanks. Another followed it, and I decided it would be ridiculous to attempt digging a trench under H.E. fire, when the tank turret was already available for our protection. Evan came back from Sergeant Thomas's tank and scrambled into the turret. I told Mudie to get in, and as soon as they had made room, stepped in myself, trying not to hurry too much. There was silence for the next two minutes and I began to wonder if I had made an ass of myself. Sergeant Thomas's head appeared over the top of the turret. "Here, Evan," he said, "what are you skulking in there for, man? If you stop digging every time a bit of shit comes over, we'll never get finished. Come on out of it, now, and do a bit of bloody work. There's no reason to hop in the turret every time you get a bit of shit thrown at you." "All right," I said, giving in to Sergeant Thomas's greater experience, "get out and do some more digging." Evan and I climbed out on to the engine plates at the back of the tank and prepared to drop to the ground. But with a scream and a crash another shell arrived. Something glanced along the side of my boot and two or three more pieces hit on the tank with a clang. Evan rolled sideways off the back of the tank and fell to the ground. "Are you all right?" I asked him. "Yes, sir." "Well get back in the turret, I'm not going to muck about digging in this stuff." To my considerable satisfaction, I heard Sergeant Thomas also ordering his men to take cover: he was not going to recant entirely, however, but made them lie under the tank and begin to scoop a trench there. As I started to climb up on the tank again, I put my hand on one of the two-gallon water containers on the rack behind the engine. It was still very hot from the heat of the exhaust. I climbed back on to the turret and said to Evan and Mudie: "I'm going to make some coffee from the hot water at the back of the tank. You can stay there if you like, but I'm going underneath at the back." Evan remained inside, muttering something about not sticking his bloody neck out, but Mudie and I were underneath the rear end of the tank before the next shell arrived. Here we lay, drinking warm, if somewhat silty coffee, while the shelling continued irregularly—it was a solitary mortar which plagued us—for the best part of an hour. In one of the intervals I took a mug of coffee up to Evan, although I didn't wish him luck with it.

Andrew came back from the Colonel's tank and sent me over to it to do a spell as duty officer during the night. I rolled up my bedding, humped it on my back, and followed his directions until I saw the great bulk of the Grant in the increasing moonlight. John Simpson of "B" Squadron had arrived there on the same job, and I felt happier at seeing someone I knew. He was still the youngest officer in the regiment after two and a half years' commissioned service, a very tall, slim, young gentleman whose conversation was often informed with an entertaining sarcasm. He made some polite remark about being glad to see me back, and began to tell me that he had been "spending the evening in injecting morphia into our supporting infantry," most of whom, by his account, had crowded into the turret of his Sherman when the shelling started. The greater part of the shells had apparently landed among the infantry vehicles and heavy tanks at the back of the leaguer. "My tank is now a dressing station," he said, in a mock-serious voice which, so carefully did he maintain it, made it clear that it was an insurance against real seriousness. Although at the time it seemed to me—and I think to all of us—that we were behaving with admirable restraint, afterwards I realized how obvious that restraint would have been to anyone who, like a film audience, could have taken a detached view of us. In Sergeant Thomas's voice saying: "There's no reason to hop in the turret every time" there was a higher, more excitable note, an exaggeration of the usual Welsh singsong. In ordering Evan and Mudie back into the cover of the turret, I had enforced my order with two or three redundant blasphemies. And now John and I continued in this awful vein of banter as we went to look for a place to put our beds.

There were one or two German infantry positions and pits for vehicles to be driven into: beautifully finished and deep-cut trenches. John selected a deep narrow trench about the length and width of a bed, and was going to drop his blankets into it when I said: "I think there's some stuff in the bottom of it." "Oh!" John peered down into the murk. "I hope it's not a corpse." That was exactly why I had said "some stuff" instead of "something." But the object, whatever it was, was as long as a man and in a pose which suggested limbs. I stretched a tentative and reluctant hand down into the pit, wondering whether I should touch a stiffened arm, shoulder or leg. I had aimed at the centre of the mass to avoid contact with the face and teeth. Of course, after all this agony it was not a corpse, but someone else's bedding. We had been forestalled and had to sleep in a more open pit dug for a small truck.

When we had arranged our beds I walked back with John to his own tank. It was nearly double the size of my own, and impressed me that evening, seeing a Sherman at close quarters for the first time, as a massively safe stronghold. In a few days' time I would not willingly have changed my low-built and comparatively fragile Crusader for it. On the side of it was painted a huge eye. "The eye of Horus," said John. "He's the nearest thing in Egypt to the God of battles. I put it on with sump oil and the black of a brew-tin."

We found two infantrymen still sheltering in the turret, although the shelling had been over more than an hour. One explained quite lucidly that he was keeping the other company; his companion he explained being "took real bad." This I thought at first meant seriously wounded, but he was apparently suffering only from shock. We found a truck to take him to the M.O. and he was helped out of the turret and lowered down the front of the tank, shivering and moaning. The oblivion induced by John's morphia seemed to have left his head and nerve centres but not his limbs, which refused to support him. The infantry sentry who helped us get him down, disdaining John's device of banter, said honestly and plainly to me, "I'll be glad when this is over, won't you, sir?" While this was not a very clever thing to say, it was exactly what I was thinking, and I agreed with him sincerely. The exchange of banalities did us both good.

By the time John and I had got back to our beds, and had settled down, after sharing a packet of chocolate, the British twenty-five-pounders, spaced every twenty-five yards behind us, had opened a barrage lasting several hours. The noises of the shells, just as the noises of aeroplane engines, varied according to the angle at which they struck the ear. One gun which appeared to be firing more or less directly overhead sent a shell which whistled. Possibly at some part of the night there was some German counter-battery fire, or some heavier guns of our own joined in. At all events, there was every variety of noise in the sky, a whistling and chattering and rumbling like trains, like someone whispering into a microphone, or like the tearing of cloth. The sky was lit up almost without pause by the tremendous flashes on the horizon, and the noise was so continuous that we slept easily beneath it. Once I woke, providentially, in time to prevent the driver of a fifteen-hundredweight truck who had wandered into the area, from taking us and the pit in his stride.

As duty officer, with the last spell of duty—four o'clock until dawn—I had to wander about the area, visiting the various guards and pickets, deal with any messages received over the air by the duty operator, call the Colonel at five o'clock, and then rout the whole regimental group out of bed. The infantry had a machine-gun post out in front of the leaguer, which reported snipers out to their front. The fifteen-hundredweight which had almost run over me in bed had been one of a unit which had leaguered in front of us and had been withdrawn through us after having several casualties from these snipers. While I was talking to this picket, two bullets sang past in the darkness like innocuous insects; one struck a tank somewhere and rebounded whining into the darkness.

At five o'clock I woke the Colonel, who lay in his opulent sleeping-bag, in his pyjamas, his clothes and suede boots neatly piled beside him; a scent of pomade drifted from him as he sat up. I told him the time and about the snipers, and handed him over to his batman who already hovered behind me with a cup of tea. I went about stirring the sleeping cocoons of men with my foot. On the way I woke John and said, "Have some whisky. I suppose we've sunk pretty low, taking it for breakfast." Unfortunately there was no more chocolate.

By six o'clock the wireless in every tank was switched on, engines were running, and at six-fifteen, through a thick morning mist, the Crusader squadron began to move out in close formation ahead of the regiment. Andrew had relayed rather vague orders to me: but the only thing that seemed clear to me was that there was now no one between us and the enemy. If that were so, it seemed crazy to go swanning off into the mist; but I was fairly certain it was not free from doubt, because I knew there had been a traffic of one or two vehicles passing through our lines in the early morning—and they were soft skinned vehicles, not tanks. Presently, as I moved slowly forward, keeping one eye on the vague shape of Andrew's tank in the mist to my left, I saw on my right a truck, with its crew dismounted. I reported it to Andrew, and cruised across to investigate it. It was, of course, a British truck, whose driver told us there was a whole unit of soft vehicles ahead of us, and as far as he knew, no enemy in the immediate neighbourhood. There was no more mention of snipers, and I imagined these would have been part of some kind of patrol who had now returned to their own lines.

Andrew now began to call me impatiently over the air: "Nuts five, Nuts five, you're miles behind. Come on. Come on. Off." Speeding up, we saw the shape of a tank looming ahead of us again, and made for it. As we came nearer, it was recognizable as a German derelict. I had not realized how derelicts can complicate manœuvres in a bad light. We increased speed again; but there seemed to be no one ahead of us. I began to suppose we had passed Andrew in the mist, and realized that we were lost, without any information of our position or objective. In fact, the regiment had made a sharp turn left while we were halted, and if Andrew had mentioned this to me over the air we could have found them easily. As it was, we continued to move vaguely round until the mist cleared. Seeing some Crusaders on our left when it grew clear enough to pick up objects at a distance, we approached them: they belonged to one of the other regiments in the Brigade, and had no idea (although their colonel was in one of the tanks) on which side of them our regiment was moving. How all this came about I am not sure, because I afterwards found Brigade and regimental orders to be very clear, and there was never an occasion in later actions when every member of a tank crew did not know what troops were on his right and left. This was, however, only the third time the regiment had ever seen action as a tank unit, and I was probably not so far behind the others in experience as I felt.

Meanwhile we rushed eagerly towards every Crusader, like a short-sighted little dog who has got lost on the beach. Andrew continued to call up with such messages as: "Nuts three, Nuts three I still can't see you. Conform. Conform. Off." I perceived that two other tanks of the squadron had attached themselves to me and were following me slavishly about, although the other tank of my own troop was nowhere to be seen.

Another Crusader several hundred yards away attracted our attention, and we rushed towards it, floundering over slit trenches and passing through some of our own infantry. As we approached another trench, I was too late to prevent the driver from running over a man in black overalls who was leaning on the parapet. A moment before the tank struck him I realized he was already dead; the first dead man I had ever seen. Looking back, I saw he was a Negro. "Libyan troops," said Evan. He was pointing. There were several of them scattered about, their clothes soaked with dew; some lacking limbs, although no flesh of these was visible, the clothes seeming to have wrapped themselves round the places where arms, legs, or even heads should have been, as though with an instinct for decency. I have noticed this before in photographs of people killed by explosive.

The Crusader which had attracted our attention was newly painted, covered with bedding and kit: tin hats and binoculars hung on the outside of the turret, and a revolver lay on the turret flap. Although it was outwardly undamaged, we saw that it had been abandoned. As my own field-glasses were old and quite useless, I told Evan to get out and bring the ones hanging on the derelict. He was very reluctant. "It might be a booby trap, sir," said he, rolling his eyes at me. This seemed unlikely at that stage of the battle, and I said, not very sympathetically, "Well, have a look first and make sure nothing's attached to them. And if nothing is, get them." Very gingerly, he climbed on to the other turret, and returned with the glasses. While he was getting them, I had at last caught sight of the regiment and we moved across to them, with our two satellites.

We took position on the right, the Crusaders still lying in front of the regiment, and my own tank being near a derelict Italian M13, apparently no more damaged than the tank we had just left, and covered with a camouflage of scrub. Two burnt-out German tanks stood about fifty yards apart some four hundred yards away to our right front. The other Crusaders were spaced out away to the left of us and over into some dead ground. Nothing seemed to be happening at the moment of our arrival.

I had a look through my new field-glasses: they were certainly an improvement on the ones that had been issued to me. I thought I could make out some lorries and men moving about on the far skyline, and reported them. Two or three other tanks confirmed this and said they could see them too. Unfortunately, our R.H.A. Battery, which had been withdrawn for barrage work, was not yet back with us and these vehicles were out of range of our seventy-fives and six-pounders. So we continued to sit there. Evan produced a thriller and found his place in it. Mudie asked me to pass him a biscuit. I took one myself, and cut us a sliver of cheese each from the tin. I took off my greatcoat and draped it over the turret. We seemed to have settled down for the morning and I began to wonder when we should get a chance to brew up.

I was disturbed from a mental journey through the streets of Jerusalem by the shriek and crash of a shell which threw up dark grey smoke and flame near one of the heavy tanks. During the next hour these shells continued to arrive, with the same tearing and shunting noises as I had heard the night before. Among them, however, was a disturbing new kind of explosion, the air-burst, which the 88 mm. gunners often fired for ranging and to make the occupants of open tank turrets uncomfortable. By tinkering with their fuse they produced a sudden thunderclap overhead, which, beyond drawing a straight line of tiny puffs along the sand, hardly showed after the moment of bursting: so that the first time I heard the bang I was unable to find a dust cloud anywhere to account for it.

The flashes from these guns were not visible: they continued firing spasmodically for about two hours, distributing their fire between the Crusaders and heavy tanks. After a time they began to introduce some sort of oil-shell which burst with a much greater volume of flame and of black smoke. One of these set fire to the bedding strapped to the outside of a Sherman, but the crew soon extinguished this and climbed into their tank again. Apart from this short interlude of excitement, shells continued to arrive and to miss, and we to sit there in sulky silence, reading our magazines and books, eating our biscuits and cheese, and indulging in occasional backchat over the air, for the rest of the morning.

About midday, feeling that the futility of war had been adequately demonstrated to me, I arrived back among the supply vehicles, to refuel. We seized the opportunity to have a brew-up, and ate some of our tinned fruit. An infantry sergeant and three or four men had brought in a German prisoner, a boy of about fifteen, who looked very tired but still defiant. He had remained lying in a patch of scrub while our tanks passed him, and after the supply echelon had arrived, dismounted, brewed up, and settled down to wait for us to come back to them, he had started to snipe them. The sergeant, who regarded this as an underhand piece of work, was for executing the boy at once. "Shoot the bugger. That's what I say," he kept repeating. His more humane companions were for giving the prisoner a cup of tea and a cigarette, which he obviously needed. I think he got them in the end.

Having refreshed ourselves and our vehicles, we went back and sat beside the camouflaged derelict again. Presently an infantry patrol, moving like guilty characters in a melodrama, came slinking and crouching up to my tank. A corporal, forgetting his attitude for the time being, leant against the tank, saying: "You see them Jerry derelicts over there, them two?" He indicated the two burnt-out tanks to our right front and added: "They've got a machine-gun in that right-hand one. We can't get up to them. They open up on us and pin us down, see?" "Well, what would you like us to do?" "I should have thought you could run over the buggers with this," he said, patting the tank. "Well, we'll see. I'll have to ask my squadron leader." I indicated his tank, "Will you go over and tell him all about it?" "Very good, sir," said the corporal, suddenly deciding that I was an officer. He departed. His patrol, who had been slinking aimlessly round in circles, waiting for him, tailed on behind him.

Andrew's instructions were of the kind I was beginning to expect from him. "See what you can do about it. See if you can get those chaps out of it. But be very careful. I don't want you to take any risks." I interpreted this to mean: "If you make a mess of it, I wash my hands of you," and opened the proceedings by ordering Evan to spray the area of the derelict with machine-gun fire.

The machine-gun, however, fired a couple of desultory shots, and jammed; Evan cleared and re-cocked it. It jammed again. A furious argument followed, Evan maintaining that the trouble was due to my not passing the belt of ammunition over the six-pounder and helping it out of the box. I pointed out that the belt was free on my side. Our understanding of each other was not helped by the fact that while I was speaking into the i/c microphone, Evan removed his earphones because they hampered his movements. He then shouted to me, disdaining the microphone, words which I could not hear through my heavy earphones. At length the conversation resolved itself into a shouting match. Evan became more and more truculent, and I ordered the driver to begin advancing slowly towards the enemy. This had the effect I wanted. Evan stopped talking, and applied himself feverishly to mending the machine-gun. After about a hundred yards I halted and scrutinized the derelict through my glasses. I could see no movement. I wondered what the crew of the machine-gun felt like, seeing a tank slowly singling them out and advancing on them. Evan was stripping the gun in the bad light and confined space of the turret, skinning his fingers, swearing and perspiring. At this moment Andrew's voice spoke in my ear, saying airily that he was going to refuel: "Nuts five, I'm going back to the N.A.A.F.I. for lemonade and buns. Take charge. Off." So now I was left to my own devices.

Looking down for a moment at a weapon-pit beside us, I saw a Libyan soldier reclining there. He had no equipment nor arms, and lay on his back as though resting, his arms flung out, one knee bent, his eyes open. He was a big man: his face reminded me of Paul Robeson. I thought of Rimbaud's poem: "Le Dormeur du Val"—but the last line:

Il a deux trous rouges au côté droit

was not applicable. There were no signs of violence. As I looked at him, a fly crawled up his cheek and across the dry pupil of his unblinking right eye. I saw that a pocket of dust had collected in the trough of the lower lid. The fact that for two minutes he had been lying so close to me, without my noticing him, was surprising: it was as though he had come there silently and taken up his position since our arrival.

Evan's swearing approached a crescendo. "I'll have to take the bastard out," he said. "It's the remote control's bust. I'll fire it from the trigger." We got the biscuit tin off the back of the tank and mounted the gun on it loose, on the top of the turret. From this eminence, as we advanced again, Evan sprayed earth and air impartially, burning his fingers on the barrel casing, his temper more furious every minute. At length he succeeded in landing a few shots round the derelict tank. A red-faced infantry subaltern ran up behind us, and climbed on to the tank. He put his hands in his pocket and pulled out two grenades, the pins of which he extracted with his teeth. He sat clutching them and said to me: "Very good of you to help us out, old boy," in a voice much fiercer than his words. We were now only about thirty yards from the derelict, and saw the bodies of men under it. They did not move.

"There they are!" cried the infantryman suddenly. A few yards from the left of the tank, two German soldiers were climbing out of a pit, grinning sheepishly as though they had been caught out in a game of hide and seek. In their pit lay a Spandau machine-gun with its perforated jacket. So much, I thought with relief, for the machine-gun nest. But men now arose all round us. We were in a maze of pits. Evan flung down the Besa machine-gun, cried impatiently, "Lend us your revolver, sir," and snatching it from my hand, dismounted. He rushed up and down calling "Out of it, come on out of it, you bastards," etc. The infantry officer and I joined in this chorus, and rushed from trench to trench; I picked up a rifle from one of the trenches and aimed it threateningly, although I soon discovered that the safety-catch was stuck and it would not fire. The figures of soldiers continued to arise from the earth as though dragons' teeth had been sown there. I tried to get the prisoners into a body by gesticulating with my useless rifle. To hurry a man up, I pointed a rifle at him, but he cowered to the ground, like a puppy being scolded, evidently thinking I was going to shoot him on the spot. I felt very embarrassed, and lowered the rifle: he shot away after his comrades as though at the start of a race. I began to shout: "Raus, raus, raus," with great enthusiasm at the occupants of some trenches further back, who were craning their necks at us in an undecided way. Evan unluckily discouraged them by blazing off at them with a Spandau which he had picked up, and some high explosive began to land near the tank, which was following us about like a tame animal. Evan now found a man shamming dead in the bottom of a pit and was firing at his heels with my revolver, swearing and cursing at him. Another German lay on the ground on his back, occasionally lifting his head and body off the ground as far as the waist, with his arms stretched stiffly above his head and his face expressive of strenuous effort, like a man in a gymnasium. His companions gesticulated towards him and pointed at their heads, so that I thought he had been shot in the head. But when I looked more closely, I could see no wound, and he told me he was ill. Two of them assisted him away.

From the weapon pits, which were crawling with flies, we loaded the back of the tank with Spandaus, rifles, Luger pistols, Dienstglasse, the lightweight German binoculars, British tinned rations and the flat round German tins of chocolate.

As the main body of the prisoners was marched away under an infantry guard, the high explosive began to land closer to us. I did not feel inclined to attack the further position singlehanded, so I moved the tank back and tacked it on to the column of prisoners. The mortar stopped firing at us, and some of the infantry climbed on to the tank to ride back. I reported over the air that we had taken some prisoners.

"Nuts five, how many prisoners?" asked what I presumed to be Andrew's voice. "Nuts five wait. Off." I said, counting, "Nuts five about figures four zero. Over." "Bloody good. Most excellent." Apparently it was the Colonel talking. "Now I want you to send these chaps back to our Niner"—he meant the Brigadier—"so that you'll get the credit for this." This was unfortunately more than my conscience would stand. I felt that all the work had been done by Evan and the infantry officer, and said so. This was a bad thing to say to Piccadilly Jim, because it showed him that I did not agree with him about snatching little gobbets of glory for the regiment whenever possible. The infantry were in another Brigade, as Piccadilly Jim knew. Evan said: "You were a bloody fool to say that, sir. You've as good as thrown away an M.C." I said shortly that if I had, it was an undeserved one.

The reaction on me of all this was an overpowering feeling of insignificance. I went over to the infantry officers who were searching the prisoners and said: "You did most of the dirty work, so you'd better take them back to your Brigade." The one who had ridden on my tank replied. "Yes, we had orders to," in such a supercilious way that I almost decided to insist on my right to escort them after all. The man with a bad head was lying groaning on the ground. He clutched his head and waved it from side to side. I think perhaps he had ostitis: the pain made him roll about and kick his legs like a baby.

The turret, after the removal of the Besa, and our leaping in and out of it, was in utter confusion. During our struggles with the machine-gun the bottom of an ammunition box had dropped out, and the belt of it was coiled everywhere. The empty belt fired from the biscuit box mounting had fallen in whorls on top of this. The microphones, spare headphones, gunner's headphones and all their respective flexes were inextricably entwined among the belts. Empty cartridge and shell cases littered the floor. On the surface of this morass of metal reposed the Besa itself, and an inverted tin of Kraft cheese, which had melted in the sunlight. I rescued a microphone and a pair of headphones, and got permission to retire and reorganize. On my way back I was to call at the Colonel's tank. This I duly did, but my ears were singing so loudly that I could scarcely hear his kind words. As soon as the tank moved away from the prisoners, we were again fired on by a mortar, which followed us as we moved back, dropping shells consistently a few yards behind us. We brewed up in dead ground to the enemy behind a ridge; the mortar continued to search this ground with fire, but never got nearer than thirty yards, and that only with one shot.

We examined our trophies, and were shocked to find that the infantry had stolen all our German binoculars while enjoying our hospitality as passengers on the tank. We all bitterly reproached them, and I regretted ever having wished to give them extra credit. We had left, however, a large stack of machine-guns and rifles, which we dumped. Three Luger pistols, which we kept: these are beautiful weapons, though with a mechanism too delicate for use in sandy country. There were a few odds and ends of rations, cutlery, badges, knives, etc., which we shared out, eating most of the extra rations there and then in a terrific repast, with several pints of coffee. At last I decided we ought to rejoin the squadron, and reported we were on our way back.

After we had been back in our position about a quarter of an hour, someone on the right reported twelve enemy tanks advancing. A second report estimated twenty. Soon after this a very hot fire began to fall around us. Two petrol lorries were hit at once and began to blaze. The Germans came towards us out of the setting sun, firing, and supported by anti-tank and high-explosive fire. Some of the Crusaders, Andrew's tank included, began reversing. I moved back myself, but it was obvious that we should soon get moved up with the heavy tanks. I halted. Someone could be heard calling for smoke. Andrew was rating the squadron for bunching up and his own tank meanwhile avoided reversing into a Grant more by luck than judgment. There was a certain amount of incipient panic apparent in some of the messages coming over the air. The enemy fire grew more intense: it seemed incredible that only the two lorries had so far been hit. I crouched in the turret, expecting at any moment the crash which would bring our disintegration, seeing again the torn shell of the tank we had passed the previous evening—it seemed weeks ago. I could not see the enemy tanks any longer, and was not sure after so much reversing and milling around, exactly what the situation was. These were the intensest moments of physical fear, outside of dreams, I have ever experienced.

Control now instructed us: "Open fire on the enemy. Range one zero zero zero. Give the buggers every round you've got. Over." With, I think, some relief the various squadrons acknowledge. "One O.K. off"; "Two O.K. off"; "Three O.K. off." I ordered Davis to fire. "I can't see a muckin' thing," he protested. "Never mind, you fire at a thousand as fast as I can load." Every gun was now blazing away into the twilight, the regiment somewhat massed together, firing with every available weapon. I crammed shells into the six-pounder as fast as Evan could lay and fire it. Presently the deflector bag was full of shell cases, and Evan, who had now adjusted the Besa, blazed off a whole belt without a stoppage, while I tossed out the empty cases, too hot to touch with a bare hand. The turret was full of fumes and smoke. I coughed and sweated; fear had given place to exhilaration. Twilight increased to near-darkness, and the air all round us gleamed with the different coloured traces of shells and bullets, brilliant graceful curves travelling from us to the enemy and from him towards us. The din was tremendously exciting. I could see a trail of machine-gun bullets from one of our heavy tanks passing a few yards to the left of my tank, on a level with my head. Above us whistled the shells of the seventy-fives. Overhead the trace of enemy shells could be seen mounting to the top of their flight where, as the shell tilted towards us, it disappeared. Red and orange bursts leapt up beside and in front of us.

Darkness ended the action as suddenly as it had begun; the petrol lorries alone blazed like beacons, answered by distant fires in the direction of the enemy. Gradually we found our way into leaguer, creeping past the beacons after the dim shapes of our companions. My first day in action had been eventful enough: I felt as if I had been fighting for months.

I shall remember that day as a whole, separate from the rest of my time in action, because it was my first, and because we were withdrawn at two o'clock that morning for a four days' rest. We arrived about four o'clock and lay down to sleep at once. My last sensations were of complete satisfaction in the luxury of sleep, without a thought for the future or the past. I did not wake until ten o'clock next morning, and when I opened my eyes, still no one was stirring.

*   *   *

Vergissmeinicht

Three weeks gone and the combatants gone,
returning over the nightmare ground
we found the place again, and found
the soldier sprawling in the sun.

The frowning barrel of his gun
overshadowing. As we came on
that day, he hit my tank with one
like the entry of a demon.

Look. Here in the gunpit spoil
the dishonoured picture of his girl
who has put: *Steffi. Vergissmeinicht*
in a copybook gothic script.

We see him almost with content
abased, and seeming to have paid
and mocked at by his own equipment
that's hard and good when he's decayed.

But she would weep to see today
how on his skin the swart flies move;
the dust upon the paper eye
and the burst stomach like a cave.

For here the lover and killer are mingled
who had one body and one heart.
And death who had the soldier singled
has done the lover mortal hurt.

Homs, Tripolitania, 1943

GUY SAJER
1925–

Born in Alsace to a French father he hated and a half-German mother he adored, in 1942, aged seventeen, Sajer joined the German army and served on the Eastern Front, never rising above the rank of lance corporal. His book The Forgotten Soldier, *published in France in 1967, was translated into English by Lily Emmet in 1971. In his preface, he says, as so many soldiers can say, "A day came when I should have died, and after that nothing seemed very important."*

From THE FORGOTTEN SOLDIER

The snow was melting everywhere, and the cold was lessening as rapidly as it had increased—which seemed to be the way of Russian seasons. From implacable winter one was shifted into torrid summer, with no spring in between. The thaw did not improve our military situation, but made it worse. The temperature rose from five degrees below zero to forty degrees above, melting the unimaginable ocean of snow which had accumulated all winter.

Enormous pools of water and swampy patches appeared everywhere in the partly melted snow. For the Wehrmacht, which had endured the horrors of five winter months, this softening of the temperature fell like a blessing from heaven. With or without orders, we took off our filthy overcoats and began a general cleanup. Men plunged naked into the icy waters of these temporary ponds for the sake of a wash. No gunfire disturbed the tranquil air, which was sometimes even sunny.

The war itself, whose indefinable presence we still felt, seemed to have grown less savage. I had made the acquaintance of a sympathetic fellow, a noncom in the engineers, whose section was temporarily billeted in the hut opposite ours. He came from Kehl, right across the Rhine from Strasbourg, and knew France better than his own country. He spoke perfect French. My conversations with him, which were always in French, were like rest periods after the painstaking gibberish I was forced into with my other companions. Hals often joined us to improve his French in the same way I tried to improve my German.

Ernst Neubach—my new friend—seemed to be a born engineer. He had no equal in his ability to knock a few old boards into a shelter as weatherproof as one a fully-equipped mason might build. He made a shower from the gas tank of a large tractor, and it functioned miraculously, with a lamp-heater continuously warming its forty gallons of water. The first men to use this shower unfortunately received a tepid downpour of water flavored with gasoline. Although we rinsed the tank repeatedly, the water remained tainted for a long time.

In the evenings waiting to use the shower there was always a crowd of shouting, pushing men which often included our superiors. Priority was awarded to whoever produced the largest number of cigarettes, or a portion of the bread ration. Our feldwebel, Laus, once paid three hundred cigarettes. The showers always began after the five-o'clock meal and continued late into the night in an atmosphere of rowdy horseplay. Those who got through the showers first often found themselves tossed onto their backsides in the liquid mud which flooded the outskirts of the camp. Here we had no curfew or other barracks regulations. Once all the day's work was done, we were free to joke and drink for the whole night, if we wanted to.

We spent about a week in this way, with quiet, uneventful days. Each fatigue party obliged us to flounder through a sea of increasingly sticky mud. We made three trips back to the front; each time it was unbelievably quiet. On horseback or in carts, we took supplies to our troops, whose laundry was spread out to dry on all the parapets. Across the Don, the Russians appeared to be similarly engaged.

We spoke to a bearded soldier and asked him if everything was going well. He laughed. "The war must be over. Hitler and Stalin have made it up. I've never seen it so calm for so long. The Popovs do nothing but drink all day and sing all night. They have terrific nerve, too, walking around in the open air, right under our guns. Werk saw three of them going to get water from the river, just like that. Didn't you, Werk?" He turned to a sly-faced soldier who was washing his feet in a puddle.

"Yes," Werk said. "We just couldn't shoot them. For once, let's all stick our noses out without getting a bullet between the eyes."

A feeling of joy and hope had begun to take hold. Could the war be over?

"It really might be," Hals said. "The fellows on the front are always the last to be told anything like that. If it's true, we'll know in a few days. You'll see, Sajer. Maybe we'll all be going home soon. We'll have a terrific celebration. It's almost too good to be true!"

"Don't count your chickens before they're hatched," said one of the older men from the Rollbahn. His realism damped us down a little.

As usual, we set off down the track—more accurately, canal—of liquid mud which led to our camp. We stopped a moment to talk to Ernst, whose section was trying to restore the track to a usable condition.

"If it goes on this way," he said, "we'll have to take to boats. Two trucks came through here, and the stones we broke our backs shoving into the mud completely disappeared. It must be nice down in the trenches."

"They're in a mess," Hals said. "And their morale is really terrible, too. I wouldn't be at all surprised if they broke up their guns for kindling. Our fellows and the Popovs are having a real spree down there."

"Well let them make the most of it," Ernst said. "There's something funny going on. That radio truck over there is taking messages nonstop. And messengers all the time, too. The last one had to leave his scooter and wade in here to bring the Kommandant his message."

"Maybe it was congratulations for your showers," said Hals.

"That would be fine by me, but I doubt it. When those fellows run around like that, everybody else will too, before you know it."

"Defeatist," Hals shouted as we left.

When we got back to the camp, nothing seemed to have changed. We devoured the steaming mess the cook served up and prepared for another evening of larking. Then Laus blew the whistle for assembly.

"Lord," I thought. "Neubach was right. Here we go again."

"I'm not going to say anything about the way you look," Laus said. "Just pack up. We could be moving out of here any time now. Got it?"

"Fuck," someone said. "It was too good to last."

"You didn't think you could just sit here and fart, did you? There's a war on."

"Packing up" meant that we had to be ready for inspection, with our uniforms in impeccable order, and all our straps and buckles, polished and fastened in the prescribed manner. At least, that is what it had meant at Chemnitz and Bialystok. Here, of course, that kind of discipline was somewhat relaxed, but it all still depended on the humor of the inspecting officer, who could quibble at anything from the inside of a gun barrel to the state of our toes, and impose heavy details, or endless guard duty.

I could still remember only too well the four hours of punishment handed out to me a few days after I had arrived at Chemnitz. The lieutenant had drawn a circle on the cement of the courtyard, which was fully exposed to the sun. Then I had to put on the "punishment pack"—a knapsack filled with sand, which weighed nearly eighty pounds. I weighed one hundred and thirty. After two hours, my helmet was burning hot from the sun, and by the end I needed all my will power to keep my knees from buckling. I had nearly fainted several times. That is how I learned that a good soldier does not cross the barracks yard with his hands in his pockets.

So we rushed to get our gear in order, and frantically polished our sodden leather boots.

"And before we've walked ten yards, all this will be for nothing!"

It took us a good hour to make our kit more or less respectable. Then we had another twenty-four before our country holiday on the Don was transformed into a nightmare.

The day after our sprucing-up, I was put on guard duty and given the period from midnight until 2:30 A.M. I had summoned up all my patience, and was standing on the platform of empty munitions cases which had been put there so the sentry wouldn't sink into the mud. Beside the platform, a foxhole half filled with water was ready to receive the guard responsible for the stocks of gasoline—in this case, myself.

The night was mild. A rainy wind blew fat white clouds rapidly across the sky, occasionally revealing a large white moon. To my right, the outlines of our vehicles and the camp buildings stood out sharply. Ahead of me, the enormous dark, hilly horizon melted into the sky. As the crow flies, the Don lay about five miles from our first line of German reserves. Between us and the river, some thousands of men were sleeping in conditions of almost unimaginable squalor. The sound of engines came to us on the wind. Both sides used the dark for moving supplies and troops. Two of the sentries patrolling our perimeter came by, and we exchanged the usual formalities. One of the men told a joke. I was about to reply when the whole horizon, from north to south, was suddenly lit by a series of brilliant flashes.

Then there was a second series of flickering intensity, and I thought I felt the earth shake, as the air filled with a sound like thunder.

"Lord! It's an attack!" shouted one of the men on patrol. "I think it's them!"

We could already hear whistles in the camp and voices shouting orders through the still-distant noise of explosions. Groups of men went by on the run. Artillerymen who had been asleep were running to their guns on the edge of the abandoned airfield. As no one had told me to leave my post, I stayed where I was, wondering what would be asked of my comrades. A supply expedition through such a heavy bombardment would be an operation of an entirely different kind from the ones we had recently grown used to. The bursts of distant fire continued, mixed with the sound of our guns. Flashes of light, closer and more brilliant than before, turned the groups of men running through pools of water into shadow puppets.

It was as if a giant, in a fit of terrible fury, were shaking the universe, reducing each man to a ludicrous fragment which the colossus of war could trample without even noticing. Despite the relative distance of danger, I bent double, ready to plunge into my water-filled hole at a moment's notice. Two big crawler tractors came toward me, with all their lights out. Their wheels and treads had churned the mud into a kind of liquid sludge. Two men jumped down, and almost disappeared in it.

"Give us a hand, guard," one of them called. They were splattered with mud right up to their helmets.

The bombardment continued to enflame the earth and sky, as we loaded some drums of gasoline onto their machine.

"There's always something to fart in your face," one of them said to me.

"Good luck," I answered.

Further off, the soldiers in my unit were rounding up the nervous, jostling horses, which kept falling in the mud and whinnying frantically. Several times, trucks came to collect drums of gasoline, so that by daybreak, when my relief hadn't appeared, I wondered how much there was left for me to guard. The bombardment was almost as strong as ever. I felt exhausted and confused. A group of boys from my company came by, led by a sergeant who waved me over to join them. At that moment precisely, one of the first Soviet long-range shells landed about a hundred yards behind us. The explosion shook us, and we all started to run as hard as we could. I didn't ask any questions, but looked in vain for the broad shoulders of Hals.

Other projectiles were now falling on the camp, which was lit up everywhere. We had thrown ourselves onto the ground, and stood up again covered with mud.

"Don't dive like that," said the sergeant. "You're always late. Keep your eye on me, and do what I do."

A significant howl filled our ears, and all twelve of us, the sergeant included, plunged into the liquid mess. An enormous explosion sucked all the air from our lungs, and a simultaneous wave of mud washed over us.

We stood up again, soaked with filth, and wearing the pinched smiles of civilians who climb unscathed from a bad wreck. Three or four more bursts quite nearby forced us down again. Behind us, something was burning. As soon as we could, we ran to the nearest munitions dump.

The sight of this mountain of canvas-covered boxes made our stomachs turn over. If anything hit it, no one within a hundred yards would have a chance.

"Good God," said the sergeant. "There's nobody here. It's incredible."

With no apparent thought of danger, he climbed onto the hill of dynamite, and began to check the numbers on the boxes, which indicated their next destination. We stood and watched him, petrified, like condemned prisoners, with our feet apart, and our heads empty, waiting for orders. Two fellows soaked through, like us, came running up. The sergeant began to shout at them from his eminence. They snapped to attention despite the thunder of the guns.

"Are you supposed to be on duty here?"

"Yes, Herr Sergeant," they answered in unison.

"Then where were you?"

"The call of nature," one of them said.

"You went off to crap like that, both of you at once? Idiots! We've got too much trouble here for fun and games. Your names and units." The sergeant had not climbed down.

Silently, I cursed this animal with his niggling discipline, who stood there preparing a report, as if nothing unusual were happening. Fresh explosions which sounded very close threw us all onto the ground except the sergeant, who continued to provoke Providence.

"They're cleaning up our rear," he said. "They must have let loose their goddamned infantry. Get your fat tails up here and help me!"

Half paralyzed by fear, we climbed onto the volcano. The flashes of light all around us lit our bodies in a tragic glare. A few moments later, we were running as hard as we could, oblivious of the weight of the cases, in our anxiety to get away.

Daylight had now begun to rob the spectacle of some of its brilliance. The flashes of light were scarcely visible, and the horizon was shrouded by a dense cloud of smoke, irregularly punctuated by darker plumes. Toward noon, our artillery began to fire. We were still running from job to job, although we were nearly dropping with exhaustion. I can remember sitting in a huge crater which had been dried out by an explosion, staring at the long barrel of a 155 spitting fire with rhythmic regularity. I had found Hals and Lensen, and we were sitting together, with our hands over our ears. Hals was smiling, and nodding at each explosion.

For two days we had practically no sleep. The dance of death continued. We were carrying the growing number of wounded to shelters half filled with water, and laying them on hastily improvised stretchers made of branches. The orderlies administered first aid. Soon these rough infirmaries, filled with the groans of the wounded, were overflowing, and we had to put fresh casualties outside, on the mud. The surgeons operated on the dying men then and there. I saw horrifying things at these collection points—vaguely human trunks which seemed to be made of blood and mud.

On the morning of the third day, the battle intensified. We were all gray with fatigue. The shelling went on until dusk, and then, inside of an hour, stopped. Clouds of smoke were rising all along the battered front. We felt as if we could smell the presence of death—and by this I don't mean the process of decomposition, but the smell that emanates from death when its proportions have reached a certain magnitude. Anyone who has been on a battlefield will know what I mean.

Two of the eight huts that made up our camp had been reduced to ashes. The ones that remained standing were overflowing with wounded. Laus—who had a good heart when the chips were down—saw that we were foundering, and allowed us each an hour or two of sleep, as he could. We dropped to the ground wherever we were, as if felled by sleep. When our time was up, and we were shaken awake, we felt as though we'd only been asleep for a few minutes.

With exhaustion threatening to overwhelm us again, we returned to the nightmare of carrying agonized, mutilated men, or laying out rows of horribly burned bodies, which we had to search for their identity tags. These were then sent to the families of the deceased with the citation "Fallen like a hero on the field of honor for Germany and for the Führer."

Despite the thousands of dead and wounded, the last battle fought by the German army on the Don was celebrated the day after the shooting stopped. The mouths of dying men were pried open so that they could toast this Pyrrhic victory with vodka. On a front approximately forty miles long, General Zhukov, with the help of the accursed "Siberia" Army, which had just contributed to the German defeat at Stalingrad, had been trying to break the Don line south of Voronezh. Instead, the furious Russian assaults had broken against our solidly held lines. Thousands of Soviet soldiers had paid with their lives for this abortive effort—which had also cost us very dear.

Three-quarters of my company left that evening. The trucks were jammed with wounded, who were lying almost in piles. I was separated from Hals and Lensen for the moment: a separation I never liked.

Friendships counted for a great deal during the war, their value perhaps increased by the generalized hate, consolidating men on the same side in friendships which never would have broken through the barriers of ordinary peacetime life. I found myself alone with a couple of men who may have been more or less interesting, but with whom I never had the chance to talk. As soon as I could, I abandoned them for a truck seat on which I attempted to regain some of my strength.

The assembly whistle rang in my ears very early the next morning. I opened my eyes. The truck cab had made an excellent bed, more or less the right size, and I felt at last as though I'd had some sleep. But exhaustion had stiffened my muscles, and despite my sleep, I had a terrible time pulling myself onto my feet. Lining up outside, I saw the same exhausted, disheveled look on almost every face.

Even Laus wasn't feeling particularly energetic: he had slept with his equipment like all the rest of us. He told us that we were going to leave this area for a point farther west. As a preliminary, we should stand by to help the engineers load up, or destroy what we weren't taking with us. We filed past a big kettle from which we were served a hot liquid that made no pretense to being coffee, and went to join the engineers.

We were sent out with donkeys, under orders to range widely, picking up all the ammunition we could find, so that it wouldn't fall into the hands of the enemy. The departure seemed to be general. Long lines of infantry caked with filth were marching away from this sea of mud, to the west. At first we thought we were being replaced, but this proved to be untrue. The entire Wehrmacht along the western bank of the Don had been ordered to withdraw. We couldn't grasp the logic of following a heroic three-day resistance with retreat.

Most of us were unaware that the Eastern Front had entirely changed since January. After the fall of Stalingrad, a strong Soviet push had reached the outskirts of Kharkov, recrossed the Donets, and moved on to Rostov, almost cutting the German retreat from the Caucasus. Troops there had been forced to return to the Crimea by way of the Sea of Azov, with heavy losses. Our periodical *Ost Front und Panzer Wolfram* reported that there had been heavy fighting at Kharkov, Kuban, and even Anapa.

We never heard a frank admission of retreat, and as most soldiers had never studied Russian geography we had very little idea of what was happening. Nevertheless, a glance at any map was enough to inform us that the west bank of the Don was the easternmost German line in Russian territory. Luckily for us, the High Command ordered our retreat before an encirclement from the north and south could cut us off from our bases at Belgorod and Kharkov. The Don was no longer one of our defenses; it had been crossed both in the north and in the south. The thought that we might have been trapped, like the defenders of Stalingrad, still makes my blood run cold.

For two days, the landser had been pulling out—either on foot or loaded in trucks. Soon only a small section of the Panzergruppe was left at the nearly empty camp. The passage of vehicles and men had turned the Luftwaffe field into an extraordinary quagmire: thousands of trucks, tanks, tractors, and men rolled and tramped for two days and two nights through terrain running with streams of mud.

We were in the middle of this syrup, trying to reorganize the matériel we had to abandon. The engineers were working with us, preparing to dynamite the ammunition we had heaped against the huts, over the carcasses of eight dismantled trucks. Toward noon, we organized a fireworks display which any municipality might have envied. Carts, sleighs, and buildings were all dynamited and burned. Two heavy howitzers which the tractors hadn't been able to pull from the mire were loaded with shells of any caliber. Then we poured any explosive that came to hand into their tubes, and shut the breech as best we could. The howitzers were split in two by the explosions, scattering showers of lethal shrapnel. We felt exhilarated, filled with the spirit of destructive delight. In the evening, the spandaus stopped a few Soviet patrols, who had undoubtedly come to see what was happening. During our last hour, we were under light artillery fire, which caused us a certain emotion. Then we left.

After the period of light artillery fire, the troops covering the Panzergruppe signaled several enemy penetrations into our former positions. A hasty departure order was given. We were no longer organized to hold off the Russians for any length of time. I was carrying my belongings, looking for a vehicle, when our feld assigned me to a truck we had captured from the enemy which was now carrying our wounded.

"Step on the gas!" he shouted. "We're getting out!"

Every soldier in the Wehrmacht was supposed to know how to drive. I had been given some idea of how to handle military vehicles during my training in Poland, but on machines of a very different kind. However, as one never discussed orders, I jumped into the driver's seat of the Tatra. In front of me, the dashboard presented an array of dials whose needles uniformly pointed down, a few buttons, and a series of words in indecipherable characters. The engineers had just attached the heavy truck to the back of a Mark-4. We would be leaving instantly; it was essential that I get the wretched machine to start. I considered climbing out and confessing my incapacity, but repressed the idea on reflection that they might assign me to something more difficult, or even leave me behind, to get out on my own feet as best I could.

If I couldn't move, I would be captured by the Bolsheviks—a thought which terrified me. I pawed frantically at the dashboard, and was blessed by a miracle. My desperate eye fell on Ernst, who was clearly looking for a lift. I felt saved.

"Ernst!" I shouted. "Over here! I've got room!"

My friend joyfully jumped aboard.

"I was ready to hang on to the back of a tank," he said. "Thanks for the seat."

"Ernst," I asked in a voice of supplication. "Do you know how these damned things work?"

"You're a fine fellow, sitting here when you don't know the first thing about it!"

I had no time to explain. The powerful engine of the tank to which we were attached was already roaring. Hurriedly, we pulled at the controls. From the turret, one of the tank men signaled to me to put the truck in gear at the same time as the tank, to reduce the jolt for the wounded. Neubach pulled a lever under the dashboard, and we felt a responding throb from under the hood. I pressed down hard on the accelerator, and the engine made a series of loud bangs.

"Gently," the feld shouted at me. I smiled, nodded, and let up on the pedal. The chain stretched taut, and we increased our speed. How fast were we going? I had no idea. I knew with certainty only that we were not in reverse. The heavy truck took off with a brusque jolt, producing a chorus of groans and curses behind me.

Later on, in France, a pretentious bastard undertook to instruct me on a wretched Renault 4 CV, with all the airs of a commander of an ocean liner. I had to sit through a course of ludicrous demonstrations to receive a scrap of pink paper declaring me competent to drive an automobile. I didn't waste any time explaining that I had driven through Russia on a track which was more like a river than a road, fastened to a huge tank whose jolts were a constant threat to the front of my machine, which I felt certain would be wrenched off.

He would never have believed me. By that time I belonged to the Victorious Allies, who were all heroes, like every French soldier I met after the war. Only victors have stories to tell. We, the vanquished, were all cowards and weaklings by then, whose memories, fears, and enthusiasms should not be remembered.

The first night of retreat was complicated by a fine rain, which required of Ernst and me the agility and balance of acrobats simply to keep our Tatra in the wake of the Mark-4. Without the tank, we would never have been able to escape from that swamp. The driver stepped on the accelerator in fits of irritation, dragging the Tatra, which threatened to disintegrate. The tank treads churned the ground into a heavy syrup, which the rain thinned into soup. The windshield became completely caked with mud, and Ernst waded through the liquid ground to scrape it away with his hands.

The blacked-out headlight had been left with only a narrow strip uncovered. Within a few minutes this strip was sealed by mud, so that we had no light at all. I couldn't even see the back of the tank, although it was no more than five yards ahead of us. Our truck, more often than not at an oblique angle to the tank, was constantly being pulled back into line by the tightly stretched chain. Each time this happened, I wondered if we still had our front wheels.

Behind us, the wounded had stopped moaning. Maybe they were all dead—what difference did it make! The convoy moved ahead, and daylight dawned on faces haggard with exhaustion. During the night, the convoy had spread out. It no longer seemed to matter whether we were ahead of schedule or behind. The driver of our Panzer suddenly turned off to the right, leaving the track, which had become impassable even for a tank, and drove straight up the scrub-covered bank, crushing the sodden birches under his treads.

Our truck, whose wheels by this time were balls of mud, was pulled forward, while its engine rattled helplessly. Then everything came to a complete halt. This was the second stop since our departure. We had stopped once in the night to gas up. The poor bastards on the back of the tank jumped down among the broken branches. Their backsides had been burning all night on the hot metal over the engine, while the rest of their bodies froze in the cold rain. An exchange of shouted abuse which was nearly a fight broke out at once between a noncom in the engineers and the Panzerführer. Everyone else took advantage of this opportunity to crap and eat.

"One hour's rest!" shouted the noncom, who had taken on himself the leadership of the group. "Make the most of it!"

"Fuck you," shouted the Panzerführer, who had no intention of being pushed around by some half-baked engineer. "We'll leave when I've had enough sleep."

"We have to get to Belgorod this morning," the noncom said in a steely voice. He undoubtedly nourished dreams of being an officer. Then, putting his hand on the Mauser which hung at his side, he added: "We'll leave when I give the order. I've got the highest rank here, and you'll obey me."

"Shoot me if you like, and drive the tank yourself. I haven't slept in two days, and you're going to leave me the hell alone."

The other flushed crimson, but said nothing. Then he turned to us. "You two! Instead of standing there asleep on your feet, get into the truck and help the wounded. They have their needs, too."

"That's it," added the tank driver, who was clearly looking for trouble.

"And, when they're finished, the Herr Sergeant will wipe their asses."

"You watch it, or I'll report you," snorted the sergeant. He was now white with rage.

Inside the truck, the wounded had not died, despite the jolting of the journey. They were no longer making any noise, and we could see that some of their bandages were soaked with fresh blood. Fighting the exhaustion which made our hearts race, we helped them down and back as best we could—omitting only one man, who was missing both legs. They all asked us for something to drink, and in our ignorance we gave them as much water or brandy as they wanted. We certainly shouldn't have done this: two men died a short time later.

We buried them in the mud, with sticks and their helmets to mark their graves. Then Ernst and I curled up in the cab, to try to snatch a little sleep. But sleep wouldn't come, and we lay instead, with throbbing temples, talking of peace. Two hours later, it was the tank driver who gave the order to depart, as he had predicted. It was now midmorning. The day was clear and bright, and large chunks of snow fell slowly from the trees.

"Hah!" he said. "Our general left us all while we were asleep. Maybe he felt like taking a walk!"

It seemed that the noncom really was gone. He must have managed a ride in one of the trucks that had passed us during our rest.

"That shit has gone to make his report!" shouted the tank driver. "If I catch up with him, I'll drive right over him, flatten him out like a goddamned Bolshevik!"

It took us a while to extricate ourselves from the bank we had driven into. However, two hours later we arrived at a hamlet whose name I no longer remember, some five miles from Belgorod. It was filled with soldiers from every branch of the army. The few streets were perfectly straight, and lined with low houses; the way the roofs sat on the walls reminded me of heads with no foreheads, whose hair grows right into the eyebrows. There were swarms of soldiers, and a multitude of rolling equipment covered with mud, pushing through the shouting mob of soldiers, most of whom were looking for their regiments. The road at this point had been roughly resurfaced, and was much more negotiable.

We unhooked ourselves from the tank, and took on eight or ten of the engineers who had been riding on its back. Somewhat bewildered by this flood of soldiers, I had stopped the truck, and was looking for my company. Two M.P.s told me they thought it had gone on toward Kharkov, but as they weren't sure, they sent me to the redirection center which had been organized in a trailer and was staffed by three officers, who were tearing their hair. When I was finally able to catch their attention through the thousands of shouts and gesticulations besieging them, I was harshly reprimanded for straggling. They probably would have sent me to be court-martialed, if they'd had time. The disorder was incredible, and the landser, half furious, half joking, flooded into the Russian huts.

"We might as well sleep while we wait for all this to settle down."

All they wanted was a dry corner where they could lie down, but there were so many men crammed into each isba that there was almost no room left for the Russians who lived in them.

Not knowing what to do with myself, I went to find Ernst, who had gone to look for information. However, he had run into a truck hospital, and had returned to the Tatra with an orderly, who was checking over our wounded.

"They can go on as they are," he said.

"What?" Ernst asked. "But we've already buried two of them. At least we should give them fresh dressings."

"Don't be stubborn and stupid. If I label them 'urgent,' they'll have to wait their turn, lying in the street. You'll get to Belgorod quicker than that—and escape the trap that's closing on us."

"Is the situation serious?" Ernst asked.

"Yes."

So Ernst and I found ourselves responsible for twenty wounded men, some of them in critical condition, who had already been waiting several days for essential medical attention. We didn't know what to say when a man grimacing with pain asked us if he would soon be at the hospital.

"Let's get going," Ernst said, frowning anxiously. "Maybe he's right. If I'd ever thought it would be like this . . ."

I had been at the wheel for only a few minutes when Ernst tapped me on the shoulder. "Come on, little one, stop. You'll finish everybody off if it goes on like this. Hand over."

"But I'm supposed to drive, Ernst. I'm the one who's in the drivers' corps."

"Never mind. Let me do it. You'll never get us out of here."

It was true. Despite my best efforts, the truck was jolting and sliding from one side of the road to the other.

We arrived at the village exit point, where there was an interminable line of vehicles waiting for gas. Thousands of soldiers were walking up and down on either side of the road. An M.P. ran over to us.

"Why aren't you waiting like everybody else?"

"We've got to leave right away, Herr Gendarm. We're carrying wounded, and that's what the infirmary told us."

"Wounded? Serious cases?" He spoke in the doubting, disbelieving tone of every policeman in the world.

"Of course," said Ernst, who certainly wasn't exaggerating.

The policeman had to peer under the canvas anyway: "They don't look so bad to me."

There was a furious outburst of swearing. From time to time, wounded men availed themselves of their special position to abuse the police.

"You sonofabitch," groaned one man, who was missing a piece of his shoulder. "It's shits like you who should be sent to the front. Let us through, or I'll strangle you with the one good hand I have left."

The feverish landser was sitting up in spite of his pain, which made him frighteningly white. He seemed quite capable of putting this threat into action.

The policeman flushed, and his nerve faltered at the sight of these twenty battered wrecks. The position of a big-city policeman roaring at some pathetic bourgeois for going through a red light is a far cry from that of an M.P. behind the lines dealing with a gang of combat veterans who are holding their guts in with their hands, or have just bayoneted the guts out of somebody else. His display of bad temper turned into a set little smile.

"Get out of here," he said, with the air of someone who doesn't give a damn. When the wheels of the truck began to turn, he vented the last of his spleen: "Go and die somewhere else!"

It was hard to get even eight gallons of gas, and when we managed it our tank swallowed them in an instant. But we were glad to take what we could and get out. A feeble attempt had been made at surfacing the road, but there were still long stretches of bare ground which had become deep quagmires, to be avoided at all costs. We proceeded on the highway, or beside it, as circumstances required.

Far to the right, we could see another convoy struggling forward in a line parallel to ours. The men were dressed for battle, and seemed to be prepared for an encounter with the Soviets. We were stopped by a new set of police, who combed our papers to see if they could find any mistakes. They checked the truck, verified our I.D. cards and our destination . . . but when it came to the destination, they had to give us directions. One of them looked through the directory hanging around his neck, and told us, in a voice like a barking dog's, that we had to turn off the road a hundred yards ahead and proceed to Kharkov. We followed these instructions with regret, because the new road rapidly deteriorated into a ribbon of mire.

At our speed, we would soon have exhausted our supply of gas. We kept passing vehicles abandoned in the mud because of mechanical failure, or because they had run out of gas. A short distance along the new road, we were stopped by a group of about fifty landser, on foot, and in a state of unbelievable filth. They took our truck by storm. There were several wounded men among them. Some of them had ripped off their filthy dressings, and were walking with their wounds open to the air.

"Make room for us, fellows," they said, hanging on as hard as they could.

"You can see that we haven't got any room," Ernst answered. "Let go."

But we couldn't get rid of them. They swarmed over the tailgate, trampling on our wounded to try to make them move over. Ernst and I shouted at them, but it didn't do any good: they piled on everywhere.

"Take me," whimpered a poor devil scratching at my door with bloody hands. Another waved a pass which was already almost expired. The arrival of a steiner followed by two trucks restored order. An S.S. captain climbed out of the steiner.

"What's this ant heap? No wonder you've broken down! It's impossible! There must be at least a hundred men here."

The men scattered immediately, without asking for anything more. Ernst saluted, and explained the situation.

"Very good," said the captain. "You take five more along with your wounded. We'll take another five, and the rest will have to walk until the convoy comes by. Let's get going."

Ernst explained that we would be out of gas in a few minutes. The captain signaled to some soldiers on the steiner, who gave us six gallons. A few minutes later we were on our way again.

We kept passing groups of men wading through the mud who begged us to pick them up, but we didn't stop. Toward noon, with our last drop of gas, we reached a town where a unit was being assembled for the front. I escaped becoming an infantryman before my time by a hair's breadth.

We had to wait until the following day before we could use the reserve of five gallons of gas which Ernst was able to draw. We were about to leave, when an unexpected and unpleasant sound struck our ears. In the distance—still quite far away—we heard the booming of big guns. As we thought we were by now far from the front, we were both astonished and alarmed. We didn't know—and I didn't know until much later—that our course had been taking us parallel to the Belgorod-Kharkov line.

Nonetheless, after unloading two dying men to make room for three more wounded, we set off without delay. In the middle of that afternoon, everything went wrong again.

Our truck was more or less in the middle of a column of ten. We had just passed an armored unit whose tanks looked like a giant version of the slimy creatures that emerge on mud flats at low tide. They must have been on their way to meet the enemy, who seemed to be very close. We could hear artillery on our left, despite the loud laboring noises of the trucks. Ernst and I exchanged anxious looks. We were stopped by some soldiers who were setting up an anti-tank gun.

"Dig in, fellows," shouted an officer as we slowed down. "Ivan's getting pretty close."

This time, at least, they were telling us something. But I wondered how the Russians, who had been left some ninety miles behind, could already be in this district. Ernst, who was driving, stepped on the gas. Two other trucks did the same. Suddenly, five planes appeared in the sky, at a moderate altitude. I pointed them out to Ernst.

"They're Yak," he shouted. "Take cover!"

We were surrounded by bare mud, with occasional clumps of stunted brush. There was a sound of machine-gun fire from the sky. The column drove more quickly, toward a shallow fold in the ground which might give some protection. I was leaning out the window, trying to see through the flying mud spun by our wheels. Two Focke-Wulfs had appeared, and had shot down two of the Yaks, which crashed far to the west.

Until the final stages of the war, Russian aircraft were no match for the Luftwaffe. Even in Prussia, where Russian airpower was its most active, the appearance of one Messerschmitt-109, or one Focke-Wulf would make a dozen armored Ilyushin bombers turn and run. At this period, when German airpower still possessed important reserves, the lot of the Russian pilots was not enviable.

Two of the three remaining Yaks had taken flight, pursued by our planes, when the last dived straight at the convoy. One of the Focke-Wulfs was chasing him, and was plainly trying to get him in his sights.

We reached the dip in the road. The Soviet plane had come down very low, to use its machine guns. The trucks ahead of us had stopped short, and the able-bodied were jumping down into the mud. I was already holding the door open, and I jumped, with my feet together, plunging face downward, when I heard the machine guns.

With my nose in the mud, my hands on my head, and my eyes instinctively shut, I heard the machine gun and the two planes through a hellish intensity of noise. The sound of racing engines was followed by a loud explosion. I looked up, to watch the plane with the black crosses on its wings regain altitude. Three or four hundred yards away, where the Yak had crashed, there was a plume of black smoke. Everybody was getting up again.

"One more who won't give any trouble," shouted a fat corporal who was clearly delighted to be still alive.

Several voices joined in a cheer for the Luftwaffe.

"Anybody hit?" one of the noncoms called out. "Let's get going, then."

I walked over to the Tatra, trying to brush off the worst of the mud that clung to my uniform. I noticed two holes in the door I had opened to get out which appeared to have swung shut on its own momentum:

two round holes, each outlined by a ring of metal from which the paint
had been scraped away. Nervously, I pulled open the door. Inside, I saw a
man I shall never forget—a man sitting normally on the seat, whose
lower face had been reduced to a bloody pulp.

"Ernst?" I asked in a choking voice. "Ernst!" I threw myself at him.
"Ernst! What . . . ? Say something! Ernst!" I looked frantically for some
features on that horrible face. "Ernst!" I was nearly crying.

Outside, the column was getting ready to leave. The two trucks behind me were impatiently blowing their horns.

"Hey." I ran toward the first of the trucks. "Stop. Come with me. I've
got a wounded man."

I was frantic. The doors of the truck behind me swung open and two
soldiers stuck out their heads.

"Well, young fellow, are you going to move, or aren't you?"

"Stop!" I shouted louder than ever. "I've got a wounded man."

"We have thirty," one of the soldiers shouted back. "Get going. The
hospital isn't too far from here."

Their voices rose over mine, and the noise of their trucks, which had
pulled out, and were passing me, drowned my cries of desperation. Now
I was alone, with a Russian truck loaded with wounded men, and Ernst
Neubach, who was dead, or dying.

"You shits! Wait for me! Don't go without us!"

I burst into tears, and gave way to a mad impulse. I grabbed my
Mauser, which I'd left in the truck. My eyes were swimming, and I could
barely see. I felt for the trigger, and pointing the gun at the sky, fired all
five cartridges in the magazine, hoping that to someone in the trucks this
would sound like a cry for help. But no one stopped. The trucks continued to roll away from me, sending out a spray of mud on each side. In
despair, I returned to the cabin, and ripped open my kit to look for a
package of dressings.

"Ernst," I said. "I'm going to bandage you. Don't cry."

I was insane. Ernst wasn't crying: I was. His coat was covered with
blood. With the dressings in my hand, I stared at my friend. He must
have been hit in the lower jaw. His teeth were mixed with fragments of
bone, and through the gore I could see the muscles of his face contract-
ing, moving what was left of his features.

In a state of near shock, I tried to put the dressing somewhere on that
cavernous wound. When this proved impossible, I pushed a needle into
the tube of morphine, and jabbed ineffectually through the thicknesses
of cloth. Crying like a small boy, I pushed my friend to the other end of
the seat, holding him in my arms, and soaking in his blood. Two eyes
opened, brilliant with anguish, and looked at me from his ruined face.

"Ernst!" I laughed through my tears. "Ernst!"

He slowly lifted his hand and put it on my forearm. Half choked with emotion, I started the truck, and managed to begin moving without too great a jolt.

For a quarter of an hour, I drove through a web of ruts with one eye on my friend. His grip on my arm tightened and eased in proportion to his pain, and his death rattle rose and fell, sometimes louder than the noise of the truck.

Choking back my tears, I prayed, without reason or thought, saying anything that came into my head.

"Save him. Save Ernst, God. He believed in you. Save him. Show yourself."

But God did not answer my appeals. In the cab of a gray Russian truck, somewhere in the vastness of the Russian hinterland, a man and an adolescent were caught in a desperate struggle. The man struggled with death, and the adolescent struggled with despair, which is close to death. And God, who watches everything, did nothing. The breath of the dying man passed with difficulty through that horrible wound, making huge bubbles of blood and saliva. I considered every possibility. I could turn back and look for help, or force the men I was carrying to tend Ernst, at gunpoint if necessary, or even kill Ernst, to cut short his sufferings. But I knew very well I couldn't kill him. I had not yet been obliged to fire directly at anyone.

My tears had dried, leaving the trace of their passage on my filthy face, to betray my weakness to the world. I was no longer crying, and my feverish eyes stared at the knob on the radiator two meters in front of me, which cut hypnotically into the interminable horizon. For long moments, Ernst's hand would tighten on my arm, and each time I was overwhelmed by fresh panic. I couldn't look at that horrifying face. Several German planes passed overhead, through the cloudy sky, and in a desperate attempt at telepathy every fiber in my body appealed to them for help. But maybe they were Russian planes. It didn't matter; I had no time to spare. No time to spare: the expression assumed its full significance, as so many expressions do in wartime.

Ernst's hand gripped my arm convulsively. The pressure continued for so long that I slid my foot off the accelerator, and stopped, afraid of the worst. I turned and looked at the mutilated face, whose eyes seemed to be fixed on something the living can't see. Those eyes were veiled by a curious film. My heart was pumping so hard that I felt actual physical pain. I refused to believe what I could guess without difficulty.

"Ernst!" I shouted.

From the back of the truck my shout was answered by several others.

I pushed my companion down on the seat, imploring heaven to let him live. But his body fell heavily against the other side of the cabin.

Death! He was dead! Ernst! Mama! Help me!

In a delirium of terror, I leaned against the truck door, and then let myself drop, trembling, onto the runningboard. I tried to persuade my-self that none of this was happening, that it was all a nightmare from which I would wake to see another horizon.

As I sat and thought, I still had no idea of the extent of irremediable evil. I dreamed of what life would be like when I shook off this horrible nightmare in which my friend had just died. But my eyes could see only mud, sucking at my boots.

Two heads looked out from the back of the truck. They were saying something but I didn't hear them. I stood up, and turning my back on them, walked off a short distance. That small physical effort reawakened some sense of life and hope, and I tried to tell myself that all of this wasn't really serious, that it was only a bad dream I had to forget. I tried to impose an expression of smiling derision on my features. Two of the wounded men jumped down from the truck to relieve themselves. I stared at them unseeing, while the vitality of being alive beat back the darkness. I began to think with hope that surely all the German soldiers in Russia would be sent to help us, that something must be coming to help us. Suddenly I thought of the French. They were already on their way: all our newspapers said so. The first legionnaires had already set out. I had seen the photographs.

I felt a hot flush run through me. Ernst would be avenged: that poor fool who had never hurt a fly, who had spent his time making life more endurable for wretched soldiers shaking with cold. And his marvelous hot showers! The French would come, and I would run to embrace them. Ernst had loved them like his own compatriots. This surge of hope and joy could not be damped by facts I didn't know—like the fact that the French had decided on quite another course.

"What's happened?" asked one of the men, whose gray bandage was falling over his eyes. "Are we out of gas?"

"No. My friend has just been killed."

They looked into the cabin.

"Fuck . . . that's not so bad. At least he didn't have to suffer."

I knew that Ernst's agony had lasted for nearly half an hour.

"We ought to bury him," one of them said.

The three of us lifted out the body, which was already stiffening. I moved like an automaton, and my face was without expression. I saw a small rise of ground which was less trampled than everywhere else, and we took Ernst there.

We had no shovels, so we dug the grave with our helmets, rifle butts, and bare hands. I myself collected Ernst's identity tags and papers. The other two were already pushing back the dirt, and trampling it down with their boots when I looked my last on that mutilated face. I felt that something had hardened in my spirit forever. Nothing could be worse than this. We pushed in a stick at the head of the grave, and hung

Ernst's helmet on it. I slit the stick with the point of my bayonet, and slid in a piece of paper torn from the notebook Ernst always carried with him, inscribed naïvely in French: "Ici j'ai enterré mon ami, Ernst Neubach."

* * *

We drew up to a group of buildings, which first appeared as a vague, blurred mass in the dim, bluish light. We realized that an unusual rush of activity was taking place all around, and then gradually perceived that we were looking at a row of structures bordered on both sides by tree-lined roads jammed with innumerable vehicles. There were troops everywhere, on foot or arriving and leaving on high-speed motorcycles, and many officers and M.P.s. The trucks jerked to a sudden halt, and we were told to get off. Although we still understood that we'd been saved, we were beginning to feel that we'd had enough. We were famished and dropping with sleep.

We had to wait for another half hour before someone came to take charge of us. The rain fell steadily. Was it raining anywhere else? Was it raining in France? I tried to think of my house and my bed. Where were they now? In which direction? But I could only summon up confused and fragmented memories of the life I had left behind. My only world was the vast anonymity of Russia, which seemed to be engulfing all of us, absorbing entire regiments, so that even their names vanished.

Finally, a noncom came over to us. Our group leader handed him our papers, which he examined with a dimmed flashlight. Then he ordered us to collect our gear and follow him. At last, we entered the shelter of a roof, an amenity to which we'd grown so unaccustomed that we stared at it as if it were the ceiling of the Sistine Chapel.

"You'll be sent to your units later," shouted the noncom, who, like the rest of us, seemed to have had just about enough. "While you're waiting, try to get a little rest."

He didn't have to repeat himself. We explored the darkness of the hut with our pocket flashlights, and discovered that it contained a couple of benches and four or five large tables. Everyone stretched out where he could, making pillows of the nearest leg, or buttocks, or boot. The discomfort seemed unimportant beside the fact that at last we were out of the rain. Some fellows began to snore immediately. Others tried to pretend they were somewhere else. Despite our harsh reception, we all had a sense that from now on everything would go better, and that once again life was offering its possibilities. We all thought of the leave we would surely be getting, which was now only a question of patience.

However, soldiers fresh from the front cannot indulge the luxury of daydreams. The accumulated lack of sleep gripped our temples like an iron band. Like people suffering a serious illness, we dropped swiftly from consciousness into deep sleep.

We probably slept for a long time. It was broad daylight when a burst of noise suddenly woke us. Then a long blast of a whistle ordered us to our feet. We were all filthy and horribly crumpled. If the Führer had seen us, he would either have sent us all home or had us shot. The noncom who had waked us looked at us with an expression of surprise. Perhaps he too had never imagined that the German Army could be reduced to such a state. He spoke to us, but I no longer remember what he said. I was still only half awake, and understood that he was talking, without really listening to him. We gathered that we were to prepare for departure. We were going to be returned to our units.

One of the huts had been fitted with showers, but so many men were waiting that we clearly had no chance of getting inside. Instead, we were given some empty gasoline vats full of hot water. However, we all felt too exhausted to want to wash. Our days of training, when we were appalled by the smallest spot on our tunics, seemed very far away. Our concern had shifted from hygiene to something far more urgent. Furthermore, it was bitterly cold, and no one wanted to take anything off—not even the sacking draped over our shoulders.

I was so cold I was shivering, and I wondered if I was getting sick again. We had to go outside for food, and lined up like a column of tramps beside the field kitchen. A cold east wind was blowing damp patches of fog in from the river. Two cooks emptied large ladles of hot soup into our chipped and filthy mess tins. We had been expecting the usual ersatz, but it seemed that the time for that had long gone by. As a special gesture, they were serving us eleven-o'clock soup early. The burning-hot mixture made us feel much better.

A hauptmann stared at us as he walked by, and then turned back, obviously looking for our unit leader. The lieutenant who filled this position got up and walked over to him.

"Kamerad," the captain said, "you and your men have been given this opportunity to clean up. I think you should make the most of it."

"Jawohl, Herr Hauptmann."

The lieutenant ordered us over to the vats, which were standing under the eaves of one of the huts. We looked enviously across at the fellows who were going to get into hot showers. At least three hundred men were waiting for an experience which seemed like a blessing from heaven, so close to the front.

Those at the front of the line had more or less undressed, and were scratching the lice which had settled in a ring at the belt line, when we were suddenly ordered to prepare for immediate departure. For me, at least, this was a reprieve. Stripping in that icy air had begun to seem impossibly difficult. I much preferred to keep my lice relatively warm between my gray undervest and my stomach, which was rumbling with hunger. I was certainly ill again—I no longer had any doubts. I couldn't stop shivering, and felt cold right down to the soles of my feet. We piled into the open trucks, overloading them as usual. But no one complained. No matter how squashed we were, it was better than walking. However, I was soon caught in a grotesque predicament.

The trucks rolled off down a road which the rains had transformed into a swamp. The truck behind us gave off two sprays of liquid mud as steady and uniform as the sprays of a municipal fountain. I was strangely reminded of the retreat from the Don. Was Russia nothing but a vast sea of mud? As always, we were driving toward a northern horizon marked by dark forests. The echoes of occasional explosions drifted to us on the wind, but they didn't sound serious. The sky was overcast and threatened rain.

Huddled between two companions, I swayed to the slow rhythm of the trucks struggling through the mire. I felt more and more uncomfortable and ill. My lips and face seemed to be burning, and the slightest motion of the air felt like ice against my skin. My stomach was gripped by a brutal pain, which traveled outward through my body, in waves of violent shivers. At first I thought this must be an after-effect of the hard times we'd been through, especially as I had never entirely recovered from my illness at Konotop. I knew that I must look more cadaverous than ever. My intestines were twisting themselves in knots. Naturally, no one gave a damn, and besides I was certainly not the only one with a pain in my gut. Then my pain became so imperative that I tried to double over, despite the crowding and all my gear.

The fellow beside me noticed my restlessness, and leaned his hairy face toward me: "Take it easy, friend. . . . We'll soon be there." But he clearly had no more idea where we were going than I did.

"I've got a hell of a pain in the gut."

"And this is a hell of a time to crap."

Suddenly, I realized what was the matter with me. My stomach was churning with increasing violence and threatened to explode. I certainly couldn't stop a military convoy because my guts were about to turn inside out. I had to laugh at my predicament despite my shivers and cramps and salivating mouth. But I also had to try to think of a solution. The convoy was now in the middle of a forest, where there was no reason to stop. And, even if we came to a camp, I couldn't just leave my group the moment we arrived, without any apparent motive. If I did that, they might even shoot me as a deserter.

But could I hold out much longer? I tried desperately to think of something else, but failed. My pains increased, and I broke out in goose-flesh. Finally, my gut simply opened.

"Move over a little, fellow," I said, grimacing. "I've got terrible diarrhea, and I can't wait any more."

The truck was making a lot of noise, and no one seemed to hear me. I shoved with my elbows, and shouted louder. The fellows on either side of me moved back about four inches, but paid no further attention. I could feel myself blushing with embarrassment. I tried to undo my clothes, jostling one of my neighbors.

"What's the hurry?" he said. "You'll be able to crap when we get there."

"But I'm sick, damn it."

He muttered something and moved one of his feet, although there was really nowhere to put it. No one laughed; in fact, everybody seemed entirely indifferent to my plight. I struggled desperately with my clothes, but in the cramped space, encumbered with all my equipment, I was unable to free the lower half of my body. Finally, I realized there was nothing I could do. My bowels emptied, pouring a stream of vile liquid down my legs. No one seemed even to notice my condition, which left me in a state of indescribable misery. My stomach was knotted with pain, and I collapsed into a stupefied torpor which prevented me from appreciating the ridiculous aspects of my situation. In fact, the situation was not particularly funny. I was really seriously ill, and my head was spinning and burning with fever. This was the first attack of a chronic dysentery which has plagued me ever since.

Our journey continued for a considerable time, during which I suffered two further attacks of uncontrollable diarrhea. Although my state of filth was scarcely aggravated by these eruptions, I would gladly have exchanged ten years of my life for a chance to clean off and fall asleep in a warm bed. I was shaken by alternate fits of shivers and burning heat, and the pain in my intestines grew more and more intense.

After what seemed like an eternity, we arrived at our new camp, and I was dragged from the truck for roll call. My head was swimming, but, although fainting would have guaranteed the quickest route to the infirmary, I struggled to remain conscious. Somehow, I managed to stay upright among my comrades, each preoccupied with his own fate. However, my ghastly appearance did not escape the attention of the inspecting officer, and my gasping replies to his questions interrupted the regular rhythm of roll call.

"What's the matter with you?" he asked.

"I'm sick . . . I . . . I . . ." I was barely able to stammer a reply, and saw him only as a blurred and shifting silhouette.

"What's bothering you?"

"My stomach . . . I have a fever . . . Could I please go and wash, Herr . . ."

"Take him to the medical service as an urgent case," continued the officer, speaking to a subordinate.

The latter stepped forward and took me by the arm. Someone was actually trying to help me! I could hardly believe it.

"I've got acute diarrhea, and I have to clean off," I groaned as we tottered off.

"You'll find everything you need in the sanitary block, Kamerad."

At the infirmary, I stood in line behind some thirty other men. The pains in my abdomen tore at my entrails with an intensity which made me scream. I knew that my gut was about to pour out some more filth. I staggered from the line, trying to make my step firm, and followed the signs to the latrine. When that series of intestinal explosions was finished, I hesitated before pulling up my revolting trousers. Although I was in an incredible state of filth, I noticed that my excrement was streaked with blood. I went back to the infirmary to stand in line for another half hour. Then my turn came. One after the other, I peeled off my nauseating rags.

"My God, what a stink," exclaimed one of the orderlies, whose outlook was probably identical with that of the motto over the gate of our training camp: EIN LAUS, DER TOD!

I looked at the long table where members of the sanitary service were sitting like judges. The only plea I could possibly make was guilty.

"Dysenteric diarrhea," muttered one of the judges, obviously shocked by the shit which ran down below my knees.

"Get to the showers, you pig," the other said. "We'll look at you when you're clean."

"There's nothing I'd like better. You don't know how long I've been dreaming of a shower."

"Right over that way," said the first fellow, who was clearly anxious to be rid of me.

I threw my coat over my bony shoulders, and went across to the showers. Luckily, no one was there but a bewildered-looking boy who was scrubbing the floor.

"Any hot water in the showers?"

"Do you want hot water?" His voice was gentle and friendly.

"Do you have any?"

"Yes. Two big vats for 16th Company laundry. I could let you have some, though. The showers only run cold."

Through my fever, I saw him as another bastard who'd do a favor for cigarettes or something else.

"I don't have any cigarettes."

"That doesn't matter. I don't smoke."

I stood where I was, considerably surprised.

"Well, then, could you do it right away?"

But the fellow was already hurrying off. "Go in there," he said, pointing over his shoulder to an open cubicle. "You'll be more comfortable."

Two minutes later he was back, carrying two buckets of steaming water.

"Were you at the front?" he asked.

I looked at him, wondering what he was trying to find out. He was still smiling his foolish smile.

"Yes. And I've had enough of it, too, if you want to know. I'm sick and disgusted."

"It must be terrible . . . Feldwebel Hulf says that pretty soon now he'll be sending me off to get killed."

I went on with the extraordinary relief of washing off my backside, but looked up at him with some surprise.

"There are always fellows like that, who enjoy sending other fellows out to get it in the neck. What do you do?"

"I was called up three months ago. I left Herr Feshter, and after basic training in Poland was enrolled in the Gross Deutschland."

"That's a familiar story," I thought to myself.

"Who's Herr Feshter?"

"My boss. A little strict, but nice anyway. I've worked for him since I was a kid."

"Your parents sent you out so young?"

"I don't have any parents. Herr Feshter took me straight from the orphanage. There's a lot of work on his farm."

I stared at him: someone else whose luck had been a little thin. He was still smiling. I clutched my stomach, which once again felt as if it might explode.

"What's your name?"

"Frösch. Helmut Frösch."

"Thank you, Frösch. Now I must try to get into the infirmary."

I was preparing to leave when I noticed a short, thickset figure standing in the doorway watching us. Before I could say a word, the man shouted: "Frösch!"

Frösch spun around, and ran back to the wet rag he'd left on the floor. I went out slowly, trying to pass by unnoticed. But the feldwebel in any case was concentrating on Frösch.

"Frösch! You left your work. Why?"

"I was only asking him about the war, sergeant."

"You were forbidden to talk during punishment fatigue, Frösch, except to answer my questions."

Frösch was about to reply when a sonorous whack cut him short. I looked back. The feld's hand, which had just given it to Frösch full in the face, was still raised. I took myself off as fast as I could, as a torrent of abuse poured over my unfortunate companion.

"Bastard!" I shouted silently at the feld.

At the sanitary service, the aide looked at me without enthusiasm. I understood immediately that he was one of these fastidious fellows for whom a day of filthy scarecrows like myself was less than a pleasure, especially as he received no fees to encourage civility. He fingered all my parts, poking me a little all over, and concluded his examination by sticking his finger into my mouth to check the condition of my teeth. Then he added a string of numbers and letters to a card clipped to my papers, and I was sent down the line of tables to the surgical service. Five or six fellows there checked my documents and asked me to remove some of the clothes I'd thrown over my shoulders. A brute who must have been a wild man of the woods in civilian life gave me a shot in the left pectoral muscle, and I was taken to the hospital hut, where there were beds for the officially disabled. My papers were checked once again, and then, like a miracle, I was shown to a bed—which in fact was only a simple pallet covered with gray cloth. There were no sheets or blankets, but it was nonetheless a genuine bed on a wooden frame, in a dry room protected by a roof.

I collapsed onto the bed, to relish its comforts. My head was ringing with fever, and filled with a host of half-realized impressions. I had grown so used to sleeping on the ground that the degree of well-being a soft, clean mattress can induce struck me with astonishment. The room was full of cots like mine on which fellows were lying, whimpering and groaning. But I paid no more attention to them than one does to a hotel carpet which is not entirely to one's liking. I felt almost light-headed with well-being, despite the pain which tore at my entrails. I took off some of my clothes and spread my filthy coat and ground sheet over my body instead of blankets, burying myself in them and in the sense that I had been saved. I lay like that for a long time, trying to control the cramps which knotted my guts.

After a while, two orderlies arrived, carrying a cumbersome piece of equipment. Without a word of warning, they pulled off my covers.

"Turn over, kamerad, and let us have a look at your ass. We want to clean out your gut."

Before I understood what was happening, they had administered a copious enema, and moved on to the next patient, leaving me with some five quarts of medicated liquid gurgling painfully in my distended abdomen.

I don't know anything about medicine, but an enema has always struck me as a strange treatment for someone who is suffering from excessively frequent evacuations. The fact is that two repetitions of this operation enormously increased the misery of the next day and night, which I spent tottering to and from the latrine. This was situated some distance from the infirmary, which meant fighting the strong, icy wind which blew continuously. Any benefits I might have received from this amount of time ostensibly resting in bed were thus reduced to almost nothing.

Two days later, I was pronounced cured, and sent back to my company on rubber legs. My company—the one which had been organized as an assault group—was stationed in the immediate vicinity, only five or six miles from divisional headquarters, in a tiny hamlet which had been half abandoned by the Russian civilian population. Despite my intense joy at reuniting with my friends—all of whom were present, including Olensheim—my condition remained as precarious as it had been the day before I went to the infirmary.

My close friends, Hals, Lensen, and the veteran, made a special effort over me, and did everything they could to help me get well. Above all, they insisted on pouring large quantities of vodka down my throat— which, according to them, was the only reliable remedy for my complaint. However, my precipitate visits to the latrine continued despite these excellent attentions, and the sight of my bloody excrement worried even the veteran, who went with me on these trips in case I fainted. Twice, on the urging of my friends, I tried to re-enter the hospital, which was inundated with wounded from the battle of Kiev. But my papers, stating that I had been cured, presented an insuperable barrier.

I began to look like a tragic protagonist, made of some curious, white diaphanous substance, instead of flesh and blood. I no longer left the pallet which had been given to me in one of the isbas. Fortunately, a reduced service requirement allowed me to stay where I was. Several times, my friends took guard duty for me and did the other jobs which would ordinarily have been required of me. Everything was going well in the company, which was still commanded by Wesreidau. Unfortunately, we were still in a combat zone, which meant that at any minute we might be sent to some exposed position. Wesreidau knew that I would not be able to function in combat conditions as well as I knew it myself.

One evening, about a week after I'd left the infirmary, I became delirious, and was completely unaware of a fierce aerial battle which took place directly overhead.

"From some points of view, you're really the lucky one," Hals joked.

Hals even went to speak to Wesreidau about me. But, before he was able to explain himself, Wesreidau stood up and smiled.

"My boy, we'll be pulling out almost immediately. They're sending us to an occupied zone at least sixty miles farther west. We'll have a certain amount to do there, but even so it will seem like a holiday after this. Tell your sick friend to hang on for another twenty-four hours—and spread the news that we're moving. We'll all be better off."

Hals clicked his heels hard enough to shatter his shins, and burst out of Wesreidau's quarters like a hurricane. He looked into every hut he passed, shouting out the good news. When he reached us, he shook me from my torpor.

"You're saved, Sajer! You're saved!" he shouted. "We'll be leaving soon for a real rest." He turned to a couple of fellows who shared the hut with us. "We've got to get all the quinine we can for him. He has to hang on another twenty-four hours."

Despite my overwhelming weakness, Hals's intense joy communicated itself to me, and ran through me like a restorative balm.

"You're saved!" he said again. "And just think: with a fever like yours, they're bound to take you in a hospital—and they won't cut it off your leave either. You are a lucky dog!"

Every time I moved I felt it in my stomach, which seemed to be rapidly liquefying. Nonetheless, I began to collect my things. Everyone around me was doing the same. I put my packet of letters within easy reach. A voluminous backlog of correspondence had been kept for me by the divisional postal service. There were at least a dozen letters from Paula, which greatly eased my illness, as well as three from my parents, full of questions, anxiety, and reproaches about my long silence. There was even one from Frau Neubach. Somehow I found the strength to write everyone, although my fever undoubtedly interfered with the coherence of my messages.

Finally, we left. I was given a place in a small Auto-Union truck, and we drove to Vinnitsa on roads which belonged to the Carolingian era. Our faltering machines almost drowned in incredible quagmires, whose condition was aggravated by the rain. For a while I thought we had reached the notorious Pripet marshes, which were in fact not very far away. We avoided them by driving around them, on extraordinary wooden pavements which seemed to be floating on mud. These uneven roads made of split logs, on which one could obviously not drive very fast, were surprisingly effective in wet weather. However, it took us at least eight hours to travel ninety miles. The weather was cold and bad— snow flurries alternating with violent bursts of rain—but at least this protected us from Soviet aircraft, which were very active at that time.

When we arrived, I was sent immediately to a hospital, along with some six others from my company. Diarrhea was a common complaint at that time, and a group of specialists were able to stop mine very quickly. My friends were stationed some fifteen miles away, and I knew I would rejoin them once I was well.

The doctors had some trouble getting me on my feet again. I was told that because my complaint had not been attacked until late in the day my "intestinal flora" had been severely damaged.

In fact, it was a good two weeks before I was able to eat normally again. Every day I offered my backside to the orderly, who stabbed me as full of holes as a dressmaker's pincushion. Twice a day, the thermometer recorded my fever, which remained obstinately at 100°.

Winter had arrived, and I rejoiced as I watched the snow falling from behind the panes of a heated dormitory. I knew that for the moment my friends were out of danger, and, in a state of blissful ignorance, was unaware that over the whole front things were going from bad to worse. Our paper's coverage of news from the front was limited to photographs of smiling artillerymen installing themselves in a new position, or organizing their winter quarters, and articles which said nothing at all. Hals came to see me twice, bringing mail. He had managed to get himself made a postal assistant, which allowed him to visit me quite easily. He rejoiced at the slightest occasion for rejoicing, roaring with laughter whenever he missed me in a snowball fight. He was just as ignorant as I of the realities of our situation, which would soon involve us in an agonizing retreat, and acquaint us with the depths of horror.

When I had been in the hospital for about three weeks, I was given some marvelous news. I was told to go to the office to be checked for discharge. There an orderly inspected me, and told me that, since I was making a good recovery, he was going to authorize a leave for me.

"It occurs to me," he said, "that you would rather complete your convalescence at home than here in the hospital."

I replied that I would, restricting myself to mild assent, lest I offend that kindly angel with excessive exuberance. As a result, I found myself with a ten-day pass—a little shorter than the first one—which would go into effect as soon as it had been stamped. I thought immediately of Berlin and Paula. I would try to get permission for her to go with me to France. And, if that was impossible, I would stay in Berlin with her.

Despite the weakness, which still limited me severely, I was overjoyed. I got ready in record time, and left the hospital grinning broadly. I also wrote a note to my friends, excusing myself for not having visited them before I left. I thought they would surely understand.

My polished boots moved noiselessly across the snow as I walked to the station. I was so overflowing with happiness that I even nodded and spoke to the Russians I passed on the way. My linen and uniform had been cleaned and mended, and I myself felt neat and new. I forgot my bygone sufferings, and felt only gratitude to the German army and to the Führer for having made me into a man who knew the value of clean sheets and a watertight roof, and of friends who had nothing to offer but devotion, and offered that without reserve. I felt happy once again, and ashamed to have been despairing and afraid. I thought back, from a great distance, to some of the hard times I had experienced during my youth in France, which had sometimes made me think sourly of life. But was there anything that could sour me now? What disappointment could possibly darken things for me? Perhaps if Paula suddenly told me she no longer cared for me? . . . Yes, perhaps that.

But I felt as though I were now cured of a great many things. During some of my worst moments, I had imagined certain personal disasters—the death of my mother, for instance—and told myself that I could accept even that, if only the firing would stop. I had asked the pardon of every supernatural power for harboring such thoughts, but was prepared to pay that price if it would cut short the carnage by even a little.

The war seemed to have turned me into a monster of indifference, a man without feelings. I was still three months short of eighteen, but felt at least thirty-five. Now that I have reached that age, I know better.

Peace has brought me many pleasures, but nothing as powerful as that passion for survival in wartime, that faith in love, and that sense of absolutes. It often strikes me with horror that peace is really extremely monotonous. During the terrible moments of war one longs for peace with a passion that is painful to bear. But in peacetime one should never, even for an instant, long for war!

WILLIAM ELLISON

Lieutenant Ellison, a U.S. Marine Corps dive bomber pilot in the South Pacific, writes a friend in New York State.

To Elizabeth

Jan. 7, 1943

Dear Elizabeth:

Everything is quiet here these days and boring in comparison to a few weeks ago. I have read all the trash on the island.

I have been thinking of these guys and trying to see if they are in any way like the novels want them, most particularly the group in *Signed with Their Honour* by James Aldridge. It probably isn't a fair comparison because those people were English, and they were fighting a losing battle. But still there have been plenty of attacks when it looked like a losing battle and when our planes have been in such tough shape that they would not have been allowed off the ground ordinarily. Anyway, just looking at the flyers as such, all of them with combat hours, and forgetting the set-ups, these guys are not more like those than they are like the World War I pilots.

I'm not saying Aldridge's people weren't the way he says, but these seem a helluva lot more human, less pompous, and cold, more understanding of what the hell is going on, and they don't take themselves so damn seriously. They are not terse and bitter and full of meaningful glances, but they love to jabber about their flights, to exaggerate and make close calls sound funny—even the New Zealanders like to do this. Above all, they have a helluva lot more fun, even without love affairs, but I'll be damned if they like it any better. And there are plenty of chances not to have fun. One guy, who had the whole camp on edge waiting for news of his wife's expected twins, went out on an attack the night before the day they were due, and his plane crashed in Jap territory. Another guy, aged twenty-one, got a letter telling him his wife had been killed in an automobile accident, and two days later he went out, got caught in a storm, and went into the sea.

Another time a fighter pilot went nuts high above the clouds. He picked up his microphone and for fifteen minutes we heard through our headpieces the wildest, most devastating final speech, part raving and part sane—the most tragic thing I have ever heard—and then he came spinning down past us.

But still the people are human. There are pettinesses and absurdities; people get yellow and people get conceited, but yet they don't get pompous or self-righteous. They admit they are scared, everybody is scared at times, but they talk about it openly and laugh at it. They are as serious about wanting to live as anybody and are not frivolous nincompoops with cheesy tomorrow-we-die philosophies.

Everyone intends to do just as much as he can to get himself home, and everyone has an equal chance. I can't see anyone setting down and prattling about "You know, I have a rendezvous with death"; or "If I should die, I want you to think only this of me." Of course, those men were poets, much more sensitive and melancholic, but even a poet out here would not write like that. There is too much of another feeling out here for that—of guys who want to get home and raise damn good hell with their wives, or get back a job, or work on a farm (a lot of this), or buy an old airplane—much of it absurd, possibly, but not just bluster.

A writer might try to squeeze a whole lot of tragedy, highflown courage, longing and self-conscious significance out of this group, and he might find it wasn't the way he wanted it, and fling up his hands, saying, "You're all just a bunch of dumb, unfeeling bastards." But he would be wrong, and he wouldn't have seen what there is.

I cannot write any more. Something just happened. One of the guys in our tent brought in a whole case of Jacob Ruppert beer, pried from the Army. You don't know what this means. I have had two bottles of beer since I've been out on this island, and this is a whole damn case.

MAX HASTINGS
1945–

Hastings attended University College, Oxford, before joining the BBC as a documentary researcher and public affairs commentator. Later, active as a war correspondent for the BBC and the London Evening Standard, he wrote many works of military history, including accounts of D-Day and the battle for the Falkland Islands. His Bomber Command, *published in 1979, won the W. Somerset Maugham Award for nonfiction.*

From BOMBER COMMAND

COURAGE

Throughout the war, morale on British bomber stations held up astonishingly well, although there were isolated collapses on certain squadrons at certain periods—for example, during the heavy losses of the Battle of Berlin. Morale never became a major problem, as it did on some 8th Air Force stations during the terrible losses of 1943 and early 1944. An RAF doctor seconded to study aircrew spirit at one American station reported in dismay: "Aircrew are heard openly saying that they don't intend to fly to Berlin again or do any more difficult sorties. This is not considered a disgrace or dishonourable." Partly the Americans found the appalling business of watching each other die on daylight sorties more harrowing than the anonymity of night operations. Partly also, they were far from their homes, and many did not feel the personal commitment to the war that was possible for Englishmen.

But most of the crews of Bomber Command fought an unending battle with fear for most of their tours, and some of them lost it. Even today, the Judge-Advocate General of the Forces is implacably unhelpful on inquiries relating to the problems of disciplinary courts martial and "LMF"—lacking moral fibre—cases among wartime aircrew. I believe that around one man in seven was lost to operational aircrew at some point between OTU and completing his tour for morale or medical causes, merely because among a hundred aircrew whom I have interviewed myself, almost all lost one member of their crew at some time, for some reason. Few of these cases would be classified by any but the most bigoted as simple "cowardice," for by now the Moran principle that courage is not an absolute human characteristic, but expendable capital every man possesses in varying quantity, has been widely recognized. But in 1943 most men relieved of operational duty for medical or moral reasons were treated by the RAF with considerable harshness. There was great fear at the top of the service that if an honourable path existed to escape operations, many men would take it. "LMF could go through a squadron like wildfire if it was unchecked," says one of the most distinguished post-war leaders of the RAF, who in 1943 was commanding a bomber station. "I made certain that every case before me was punished by court martial, and where applicable by an exemplary prison sentence, whatever the psychiatrists were saying."

Command was enraged when stories emerged at courts martial of doctors in Glasgow or Manchester who for five pounds would brief a man on the symptoms necessary to get him taken off operations: insomnia, waking screaming in his quarters, bedwetting, headaches, nightmares. Station medical officers became notoriously unsympathetic to aircrew with any but the most obvious symptoms of illness. The Air Staff were in a constant dilemma about the general management of aircrew, who were intensively trained to fly their aircraft, yet for little else. Regular officers were exasperated by the appearance and off-duty behaviour of many temporary officers and NCOs. In their turn, the relentless pursuit of career opportunities by some regular airmen even in the midst of war did not escape the scornful notice of aircrew, especially when this took the form of officers burying themselves in Flying Training Command or in staff jobs rather than flying with operational squadrons.

The Air Ministry considered that morale and disciplinary problems were closely linked. In a 1943 report which attacked the practice of holding All Ranks dances at bomber stations, which noted that Harris's men had the highest rate of venereal disease in the RAF and No. 6 Group's Canadians a rate five times higher than anyone else's, the Inspector-General of the RAF noted with displeasure:

> Aircrew are becoming more and more divorced from their legitimate leaders, and their officers are forgetting, if they ever learnt them, their responsibilities to their men. Aircrew personnel must be disabused of the idea that their sole responsibility is to fly . . . and to do this, their leisure hours must be more freely devoted to training and hard work.

The Air Ministry never lost its conviction that gentlemen made the best aircrew, and a remarkable staff memorandum of late 1942 expressed concern about the growing proportion of Colonials in Bomber Command and suggested: "There are indications in a number of directions that we are not getting a reasonable percentage of the young men of the middle and upper classes, who are the backbone of this country, when they leave the public schools."

When Ferris Newton was interviewed for a commission, the group captain had already noted without enthusiasm that he owned a pub, and inquired whether it catered to the coach trade. Yet the Commonwealth aircrew, especially, believed that it was their very intimacy with their crews, their indifference to rank, that often made them such strong teams in the air. An Australian from 50 Squadron cited the example of a distinguished young English ex-public school pilot who was killed in 1943. This boy, he said, was a classic example of an officer who never achieved complete cohesion with his crew, who won obedience only by the rings on his sleeves and not by force of personality: "He simply wouldn't have known how to go out screwing with his gunners in Lincoln on a Saturday night." In his memoirs Harris argues that the English made the best aircrew, because they had the strongest sense of discipline. It was a difference of tradition.

To the men on the stations, the RAF's attitude to their problems often seemed savagely unsympathetic. One day on a cross-country exercise before they began operations, the bomb-aimer of Lindaas's crew at 76 Squadron fell through the forward hatch of the aircraft, which had somehow come loose. The rest of the crew thought at first that he had fallen out completely. Only after several seconds did they realize that he was clinging desperately beneath the aircraft. Only after several more seconds of struggle did they get the dinghy rope around him, and haul him back into the fuselage. When he returned to the ground, he said flatly that he would never fly again. He was pronounced LMF, and vanished from the station. Normally in such cases, an NCO was stripped of his stripes, which had been awarded in recognition of his aircrew status, and posted to ground duties. Only in incontrovertible cases of "cowardice in the face of the enemy," as at one 5 Group station where one night three members of a crew left their aircraft as it taxied to take-off, was the matter referred to court martial. A further cause of resentment against Permanent Commissioned Officers was that if they wished to escape operations, they could almost invariably arrange a quiet transfer to non-operational duties, because the service was reluctant to instigate the court martial that was always necessary in their case, to strip them of rank.

It was very rare for a case to be open and shut. The navigator of a

Whitley in 1941 ran amok and had to be laid out with the pilot's torch over Germany. The man disappeared overnight from the squadron— normal procedure throughout the war, to avoid the risk that he might contaminate others. But the pilot recounting this experience added: "Don't draw the obvious conclusion. The next time I saw the man's name, he was navigating for one of the Dambusting crews." Many men had temporary moral collapses in the midst of operational tours. The most fortunate, who were sensitively treated, were sent for a spell at the RAF convalescent home at Matlock in Derbyshire. A post-war medical report argues that many such men sincerely wanted to be rehabilitated and return to operations to save their own self-respect, while genuine LMF cases proved on close study to be men who should never have survived the aircrew selection process.

But the decisive factor in the morale of bomber aircrew, like that of all fighting men, was leadership. At first, it is difficult to understand what impact a leader can have, when in battle his men are flying with only their own crews over Germany, far out of sight and command. Yet a post-war 8 Group medical report stated emphatically: "The morale of a squadron was almost always in direct proportion to the quality of leadership shown by the squadron commanders, and the fluctuations in this respect were most remarkable." A good CO's crews pressed home attacks with more determination; suffered at least marginally lower losses; perhaps above all, had a low "Early Return" rate. Guy Gibson, the leader of the Dambusters, was one kind of legendary Bomber Command CO. Not a cerebral man, he represented the apogee of the pre-war English public schoolboy, the perpetual team captain, of unshakeable courage and dedication to duty, impatient of those who could not meet his exceptional standards. "He was the kind of boy who would have been head prefect in any school," said Sir Ralph Cochrane, his commander in 5 Group.

For the first four months of 1943, 76 Squadron was commanded by Leonard Cheshire, another of the great British bomber pilots of the war, of a quite different mould from Gibson, but even more remarkable. Cheshire, the son of a distinguished lawyer, read law at Oxford, then joined the RAF shortly before the outbreak of war. In 1940 he began flying Whitleys over Germany. By 1943, with two brilliant tours already behind him, he was a 26-year-old wing-commander. There was a mystical air about him, as if he somehow inhabited another planet from those around him, yet without affection or pretension. "Chesh is crackers," some people on the squadrons said freely in the days before this deceptively gentle, mild man became famous. They were all the more bewildered when he married and brought back from America in 1942 an actress fifteen years older than himself.

Yet Leonard Cheshire contributed perhaps more than any other single pilot to the legend of Bomber Command. He performed extraordinary feats of courage, studied the techniques of bombing with intense perception and intelligence, and later pioneered the finest precision marking of the war as leader of 617 Squadron. At 76 Squadron there was a joke about Cheshire, that "the moment he walks into a bar, you can see him starting to work out how much explosive it would need to knock it down." He was possibly not a natural flying genius in an aircraft like Micky Martin, but, by absolute dedication to his craft, he made himself a master. He flew almost every day. If he had been on leave and was due to operate that night, he went up for two hours in the morning to restore his sense of absolute intimacy with his aircraft. He believed that to survive over Germany it was necessary to develop an auto-pilot within himself, which could fly the aircraft quite instinctively, leaving all his concentration free for the target and the enemy. As far back as 1941 he wrote a paper on marking techniques. He had always been an advocate of extreme low-level bombing.

Cheshire himself wrote, "I loved flying and was a good pilot, because I threw myself heart and soul into the job. I found the dangers of battle exciting and exhilarating, so that war came easily to me." Most of those he commanded knew themselves to be frailer flesh, and he dedicated himself to teaching them everything that he knew. He never forgot that Lofty, his own first pilot on Whitleys, had taught him to know every detail of his aircraft, and he was determined to show others likewise. He lectured 76's crews on Economical Cruising Heights, Escape and Evasion techniques, and methods of improving night vision. They knew that he was devoted to their interests. On a trip to Nuremberg they were detailed to cross the French coast at 2,000 feet. He simply told Group that he would not send them at that height. It would be 200 feet or 20,000. He made his point.

A CO who flew the most dangerous trips himself contributed immensely to morale—some officers were derisively christened "François" for their habit of picking the easy French targets when they flew. Cheshire did not have his own crew—only Jock Hill, his wireless operator. Instead, he flew as "Second Dickey" with the new and nervous. Perhaps the chief reason that "Chesh" inspired such loyalty and respect was that he took the trouble to know and recognize every single man at Linton. It was no mean feat, learning five hundred or more faces which changed every week. Yet the ground crews chorused: "We are Cheshire cats!" because the CO spent so much of his day driving round the hangars and dispersals chatting to them and remembering exactly who had sciatica. It was the same with the aircrew. A young wireless operator, who had arrived at Linton the previous day, was climbing into the truck for the dispersals when he felt Cheshire's arm round his shoulder. "Good luck, Wilson." All the way to the aircraft, the W/Op pondered in bewildered delight: "How the hell did the CO know my name?" They knew that when Cheshire flew, it was always the most difficult and dangerous operations. He would ask them to do nothing that he had not done himself. It was Cheshire who noticed that very few Halifax pilots were coming home on three engines. He took up an aircraft to discover why. He found that if a Halifax stalled after losing an engine it went into an uncontrollable spin. After a terrifying minute falling out of the sky, Cheshire was skillful and lucky enough to be able to recover the aircraft and land, and report on the problem, which he was convinced was caused by a fault in the rudder design.

Handley Page, the manufacturers, then enraged him by refusing to interrupt production to make a modification. Only when a Polish testpilot had been killed making further investigations into the problem which Cheshire had exposed was the change at last made. His imagination and courage became part of the folklore of Bomber Command. He left 76 Squadron in April 1943 and later took command of 617, the Dambusters squadron. By the end of the war, with his Victoria Cross, three Distinguished Service Orders, Distinguished Flying Cross and fantastic total of completed operations, he had become a legend.

Cheshire left the squadron in April, to be succeeded by Wing-Commander Don Smith, a regular officer who came to Linton with a log-book which had been endorsed "exceptional" in every category of airmanship throughout his service career. Smith had flown fifty-eight successful operations in the Middle East while commanding two Blenheim squadrons in Aden in 1940 and 1941. He now began an eventful tour at 76 Squadron, flying the maximum twenty trips, sixteen on German targets. One July night, he and his crew were on the way home from Mont Beliard when

unexpected things began to happen. The two starboard engines cut out within five seconds of each other and Red muttered something about "fifteen gallons left." Steve looked at Pete, and Pete looked at Steve, and the one thought uppermost in the minds of both of them was just how many seconds the port engines were going to last out. Steve opened the hatch, and Pete went through with no trouble at all . . . They were somewhat shaken by the factory chimneys of Scunthorpe 200 feet below, but fortunately came to earth in the last field before the houses at the edge of the town. Instead of the motley array of pikes and pitchforks, which they were expecting, they were greeted on arrival by a deputation of Scunthorpe ladies in negligés, all very solicitous and all bearing cups of tea. Inside the aircraft, Red was having a pitched battle with the skipper, who refused to put on his chute and who in any case could not safely leave the controls even had he wanted to. So the skipper neatly hopped a couple of hedges and made another of his renowned belly-landings, this time in a potato field. He and "Dirts" Ashton went off to search for ham and eggs (and found them), leaving an equally hungry engineer to guard the remains of our third aircraft . . . We never found out just what started it all, but Red, at any rate, was exonerated.

Don Smith remained at Holme until the end of December, when he was awarded a DSO to add to the DFC he had won in May with 76 Squadron, and the Mention in Dispatches awarded to him for operations in the Middle East. He was then posted to instruct at an Operational Training Unit.

Yet whatever the quality of leadership and morale on a squadron, there was seldom any Hollywood-type enthusiasm for take-off on a bomber operation. One summer evening at Holme, 76 Squadron's crews were scattered at the dispersals, waiting miserably for start-up time before going to Berlin, the most hated target in Germany. The weather forecast was terrible, and the CO had been driving round the pans chatting to crews in an effort to raise spirits. Then, suddenly, a red Very light arched into the sky, signalling a "wash out." All over the airfield a great surge of cheering and whistle-blowing erupted.

A 76 Squadron pilot who later completed a second tour on Mosquitoes said that his colleagues on the light bombers "simply could never understand how awful being on heavies was." Some men simply found the strain intolerable. There were pilots who found themselves persistently suffering from "mag drop," so easily achieved by running up an engine with the magnetos switched off, oiling up the plugs. After two or three such incidents preventing take-off, the squadron CO usually intervened. One of the aircrew at 76 Squadron returned from every operation to face persecution from his wife and his mother, both of whom lived locally. "Haven't you done enough?" the wife asked insistently, often in the hearing of other aircrew. "Can't you ever think of me?" In the end the man asked to be taken off operations, and was pronounced LMF.

A 76 Squadron wireless operator completed six operations with one of the Norwegian crews before reporting sick with ear trouble. He came up before the CO for a lecture on the need for highly trained and experienced aircrew to continue flying, and was given a few days to consider his position. At a second interview, he told the CO he had thought over what had been said, but he wanted a rest. He felt that having volunteered "in" for aircrew duties, he could also volunteer "out." He was reduced to the ranks, stripped of his flying brevet, posted to the depot at Chessington which dealt with such cases, and spent the rest of the war on ground duties. So did Alf Kirkham's rear gunner:

After our first few trips together, which were very rough indeed [wrote Kirkham], he simply did not like the odds. He decided that he wanted to live, and told me that nothing anyone could do to him would be worse than carrying on with operations. He was determined to see the war out, and as far as I know he was successful.

Marginal LMF suspects, along with disciplinary cases who had broken up the sergeants' mess, had been discovered using high-octane fuel in their cars, or involved in "avoidable flying accidents," were sent to the "Aircrew Refresher Centres" at Sheffield, Brighton or Bournemouth. In reality these centres were open-arrest detention barracks, where they spent a few weeks doing PT and attending lectures before being sent back to their stations, or in extreme cases posted to the depot as "unfit for further aircrew duties." They were then offered a choice of transferring to the British army, or going to the coal mines. By 1943 the "Refresher Centres" were handling thousands of aircrew. One 76 Squadron rear gunner went from Sheffield to the Parachute Regiment, and survived the war. His crew were killed over Kassel in October.

F/Lt Denis Hornsey joined 76 Squadron in the autumn of 1943. He was among very many men who spent their war in Bomber Command fighting fear and dread of inadequacy, without ever finally succumbing. At the end of the war Hornsey wrote an almost masochistically honest and hitherto unpublished account of his experiences and feelings. At thirty-three, he was rather older than most aircrew and suffered from poor eyesight—he wore corrected goggles on operations—and almost chronic minor ailments throughout the war. He hated the bureaucracy and lack of privacy in service life, and was completely without confidence in his own ability as a pilot. After flying some Whitley operations in 1941, he was returned to OTU for further training, and his crew was split up. He then spent a relatively happy year as a staff pilot at a navigation school. He felt that he was an adequate flier of single or twin-engined aircraft, and repeatedly requested a transfer to an operational station where he could fly one or the other. But by 1943 it was heavy-aircraft pilots who were needed. Everybody wanted to fly Mosquitoes. Hornsey was posted to Halifaxes. He knew that he was by now being accompanied from station to station by a file of unsatisfactory reports. He began his tour at 76 Squadron with two "Early Returns," which made him more miserable than ever. Fear of being considered LMF haunted him almost as much as the fear of operations.

Each operation, in my experience, was a worse strain than the last, and I felt sure that I was not far wrong in supposing that every pilot found it the same. It was true that it was possible to get used to the strain, but this did not alter the fact that the tension of each trip was "banked" and carried forward in part to increase the tension of the next. If this were not so, the authorities would not have thought it necessary to restrict a tour to thirty trips.

There were men who were stronger than Hornsey, even men who enjoyed operational flying, but his conscious frailty was far closer to that of the average pilot than the nerveless brilliance of a Martin or Cheshire. The day after 76 Squadron lost four aircraft over Kassel and George Dunn's crew completed their tour, Hornsey recorded a conversation in the mess:

> "What chance has a man got at this rate?" one pilot asked plaintively. "Damn it all, I don't care how brave a chap is, he likes to think he has a *chance*. This is plain murder."
>
> "Better tell that to Harris," someone else suggested.
>
> "You needn't worry," I said, "you represent just fourteen bombloads to him. That's economics, you know."
>
> As it transpired, operations were cancelled at the eleventh hour, when we were all dressed up in our kit ready to fly. It was too late then to go out, so I went to the camp cinema and saw "Gun for Hire," a mediocre film portraying what I would have once thought was the dangerous life of a gangster. Now, by contrast, it seemed tame.
>
> That night, I found it difficult to settle down. There was much going on inside my mind that I wanted to express. I felt lonely and miserable, apprehensive and resigned, yet rebellious at the thought of being just a mere cog in a machine with no say in how that machine was used.
>
> But I was getting used to such attacks, which I learned to expect at least once in the course of a day, as soon as I found myself at a loose end. As I could now recognize, without fear of it adding to my mental discomfort, they merely signified an onset of operational jitters. So composing myself as best I could, I went to sleep as quickly as I could.

Hornsey's tragedy was that he was acutely imaginative. He pressed the Air Ministry for the introduction of parachutes that could be worn at all times by bomber aircrew, so many of whom never had the chance to put them on after the aircraft was hit. He made his crew practise "Abandon aircraft" and "Ditching" drill intensively, and protested violently when he found the remaining armour plate being stripped from his Halifax on Group orders, to increase bombload.

The men who fared best were those who did not allow themselves to think at all. Many crews argued that emotional entanglements were madness, whether inside or outside marriage. They diverted a man from the absolute single-mindedness he needed to survive over Germany. When a pilot was seen brooding over a girl in the mess, he was widely regarded as a candidate for "the chop list." Hornsey, with a wife and baby daughter, was giving only part of his attention and very little of his heart to 76 Squadron.

Cheshire argued emphatically that what most men considered a premonition of their own death—of which there were innumerable instances in Bomber Command—was in reality defeatism. A man who believed that he was doomed would collapse or bale out when his aircraft was hit, whereas in Cheshire's view if you could survive the initial fearsome shock of finding your aircraft damaged, you had a chance. Yet by the autumn of 1943, many men on 76 Squadron were talking freely of their own fate. One much-liked officer came fresh from a long stint as an instructor to be a flight commander. "You'd better tell me about this business, chaps," he said modestly in the mess. "I've been away on the prairies too long." After a few operations, he concluded readily that he had no chance of survival. "What are you doing for Christmas, Stuart?" somebody asked him in the mess one day. "Oh, I shan't be alive for Christmas," he said wistfully, and was gone within a week, leaving a wife and three children.

"The line between the living and the dead was very thin," wrote Hornsey. "If you live on the brink of death yourself, it is as if those who have gone have merely caught an earlier train to the same destination. And whatever that destination is, you will be sharing it soon, since you will almost certainly be catching the next one."

On the night of 3 November 1943, Hornsey's was one of two 76 Squadron aircraft shot down on the way to Düsseldorf. He was on his eighteenth trip with Bomber Command. It is pleasant to record that he survived and made a successful escape across France to England, for which he was awarded a DFC perhaps better deserved and more hardly earned than the Air Ministry ever knew.

RANDALL JARRELL
1914–1965

Poet, novelist, and critic, Jarrell was born in Nashville, studied at Vanderbilt, and taught English at Kenyon College. In 1942 he entered a pilot-training program in the Army Air Corps but washed out and served as a flight-controller instead. After the war he taught at Sarah Lawrence and at the Women's College of the University of North Carolina.

EIGHTH AIR FORCE

If, in an odd angle of the hutment,
A puppy laps the water from a can
Of flowers, and the drunk sergeant shaving
Whistles *O Paradiso!*—shall I say that man
Is not as men have said: a wolf to man?

The other murderers troop in yawning;
Three of them play Pitch, one sleeps, and one
Lies counting missions, lies there sweating
Till even his heart beats: One; One; One.
O murderers! . . . Still, this is how it's done:

This is a war. . . . But since these play, before they die,
Like puppies with their puppy; since, a man,
I did as these have done, but did not die—
I will content the people as I can
And give up these to them: Behold the man!

I have suffered, in a dream, because of him,
Many things; for this last saviour, man,
I have lied as I lie now. But what is lying?
Men wash their hands, in blood, as best they can:
I find no fault in this just man.

THE DEATH OF THE BALL TURRET GUNNER

From my mother's sleep I fell into the State,
And I hunched in its belly till my wet fur froze.
Six miles from earth, loosed from its dream of life,
I woke to black flak and the nightmare fighters.
When I died they washed me out of the turret with a hose.

LOSSES

It was not dying: everybody died.
It was not dying: we had died before
In the routine crashes—and our fields
Called up the papers, wrote home to our folks,
And the rates rose, all because of us.
We died on the wrong page of the almanac,
Scattered on mountains fifty miles away;
Diving on haystacks, fighting with a friend,
We blazed up on the lines we never saw.
We died like aunts or pets or foreigners.
(When we left high school nothing else had died
For us to figure we had died like.)

In our new planes, with our new crews, we bombed
The ranges by the desert or the shore,
Fired at towed targets, waited for our scores—
And turned into replacements and woke up
One morning, over England, operational.
It wasn't different: but if we died
It was not an accident but a mistake
(But an easy one for anyone to make).
We read our mail and counted up our missions—
In bombers named for girls, we burned
The cities we had learned about in school—
Till our lives wore out; our bodies lay among
The people we had killed and never seen.
When we lasted long enough they gave us medals;
When we died they said, "Our casualties were low."
They said, "Here are the maps"; we burned the cities.

It was not dying—no, not ever dying;
But the night I died I dreamed that I was dead,
And the cities said to me: "Why are you dying?
We are satisfied, if you are; but why did I die?"

BARRY BROADFOOT
1926–

A Canadian journalist, Broadfoot was born in Winnipeg and worked as a
reporter, columnist, and editor on newspapers there, in Vancouver, and
in Edmonton, as well as managing wire service bureaus in Montreal,
Toronto, and Calgary. He has produced several books about contempo-
rary Canadian experience and now lives in Vancouver. Like his Ameri-
can counterpart Studs Terkel, he has a remarkable ability to get people
talking without constraint, as he does in Six War Years, 1939–1945:
Memories of Canadians at Home and Abroad *(1974), a collection of*
anonymous utterances by all sorts of people.

From Six War Years, 1939–1945: Memories of
Canadians at Home and Abroad

DATES WHENEVER THEY WANTED

It was supposed to be a real class system. You know, the nicest girls went
in the air force and the mediocre ones went in the WRENS and the
scruff went in the army, that type of thing. That's the way people at
home thought of it.

That's not the way it was at all, though. I've seen some pretty awful air
force ones, and those navy girls, they were no darlings either. Some of
these could drink like you wouldn't believe. This business of air force,
navy and then army was so much hogwash and I know. I saw them all.

Girls around a bunch of men, hundreds of men, and dates whenever
they wanted, picking and choosing, all the booze—is it any wonder that
some of them got pretty tough? Spreading it around, they used to call it,
some of them. Hitting the mattress on every date.

And yet some were still incredibly naïve. Two or three girls in our
quarters got pregnant, and one girl said she thought it must have been

from some chap, apparently a real rotter, who had screwed her. I was making notes, of course, because I had a report to make, and when she said it was three years ago I nearly dropped my pen. Some didn't even know the score, and that was even after the lectures they got.

ESCAPE TO BELSEN

I escaped once. Not really an escape, but I broke away from the march at the end of the war. The Germans were marching us west towards the Americans and British, hoping, I guess, to try and negotiate a better settlement or peace by turning over thousands of prisoners. A way of showing good faith, I suppose, if you could follow some kind of Prussian reasoning. The march, by the way, started in Poland and our area was next and we kept picking up prisoners from other camps. Thousands, thousands.

I organized about 30 others to take off. Stupid, I guess, but we did it. Stupid because we were going home anyway, and we weren't heavily guarded and less guarded as we got closer to the Allied front, but we took off and headed north, up to Stettin, blundering around, not knowing where we were going, and as the senior officer I gave orders, and we were wandering into towns and villages, being fed by the Germans.

And then we blundered into Belsen. You know Belsen, the concentration camp. Gas ovens, tens of thousands of Jews killed. I remember being in this farmhouse near Belsen this night and I felt sick to my stomach although I didn't have that much on it, but finally I couldn't stand it any longer and I went outside and vomited. Threw up everywhere, and suddenly it came to me. There was a west wind blowing and it was blowing the stench of dead, of death, from the Belsen concentration camp, and this stink of death, which I well knew, filled the air. It was everywhere.

You must realize, of course, that I did not know what was happening to the Jews. I had been locked up for years. I did not know there *was* a Belsen. It was only later, after the war, when the news began to unfold, about the murder of millions of Jews, that I was able to connect that smell that night and my vomiting, to connect that with the town I had led my gang to, Belsen. The great death camp.

IT ONLY TOOK A MINUTE

I don't think we were any better than the Germans, I don't think that for one minute. We did a lot of things too. I've seen them. You couldn't be up to your arse in the thing and not know that what they were doing, we were doing too.

There's one man in this town—and I could point him out to you—who's killed lots of Germans. And he's one of the nicest guys I've ever met. Officer in the Legion. Helps with the kids' soccer league. Good, decent businessman. But I was in the same outfit with him. I know.

This was in Holland. There was a lot of snow on the ground. We were on patrol and we ambushed this bunch of Jerries. Eight of them. Two were Panzer officers, because they wore those black uniforms the captains of German tanks wore. The other guys with them were their crew. We saw them coming around the edge of this little forest, and they just walked in and that was it.

One officer was a young guy and his English was good and he said they had been trying to get back to their lines. I guess they didn't like the snow any more than we did, or the cold. He made a couple of little jokes, one about if they got the firewood then we could light the fire and we'd all stay warm. Another little joke he made was we could roast a pig, and we sort of laughed too. He said they'd passed a Dutch farmyard back a bit and there might be a pig and schnapps. The war was over for him, and I guess he was glad.

So we're standing there and I'm thinking that we'll have to take these prisoners back, so that would be the end of the patrol. And then this lieutenant, he just turned to the guy with the Bren and he said, "Shoot them."

Just like that. Shoot them down. I knew something had been bothering him for a few days and maybe this was when it all came out. But he just said, "Shoot them."

The officer with the blond hair, the one who was making the jokes, he sort of made a little run forward and put his arms across his chest and he said something and the guy with the Bren just cut loose. He just opened up. He just cut them down every which way, about chest level because he's shooting from the hip. There were two, I think, still flopping like gaffed salmon, and this guy we called Whitey from Cape Breton—we called him Whitey because he was always boasting how good a coalminer he was—he shot those two with a pistol the lieutenant let him carry. That was it.

It probably went into our history, I guess, as a German patrol wiped out. None of us really thought too much about it. They might have done the same to us. But I'll tell you this, a year before, if I'd been there, I'd have been puking up my guts. It only took a minute. Maybe less than that.

One of our guys who understood German said what the lieutenant said just before he was shot down was "Mother."

*   *   *

LEAVING HOME

I left for overseas on November 10, 1943. I guess that's one red circle on the old calendar I'll always remember. When you're twenty, well, what the hell. The thing is, you're only twenty and you've got those pilot wings. Manning pool, ground school, the Piper Cubs, advanced training. Hoo hah! Know what I mean. Telling this I feel like that kid again.

Oshawa isn't all that big a town and then it was smaller, and everybody on the street knew little old Jerry's leave was up, going away to serve the king. Fly the big bombers or *zoooooooom* [making a diving motion with his hand] a fighter. I'd been home, what was it, twelve days, fourteen.

I didn't seem to have many friends and it seemed most of the guys I knew in school were in the services anyway, so the last time home was just marking time. Walking around the neighbourhood. That was a pretty big deal in the morning. Downtown in the afternoon. The rink if there was a game at night. I might have a few beers with my father in the Legion.

I'm sort of setting the stage. Quite frankly, I was bored. Nothing to do. Nothing to talk about anyway. Do I talk about war, fighting, and have my mother get up from the table and go to her bedroom? That kind of stuff. They knew I was a pilot, and I knew I had three choices. If I went on coastal patrol it would be a piece of cake, just monotonous. Bomber Command and I had a good chance of going for a Burton. Casualties at that time were pretty fierce. And if I was a fighter pilot, glamourous as all get out, I could expect a good chance of seeing them thar Pearly Gates too. So I didn't talk about it.

The day came. Breakfast was as usual, and Dad stayed home. He worked in a department store. My sister worked at the phone company and she gave me a hug and said, "Look after yourself, Buddy, and write Mom and Dad, please. You know how they are." Then she left.

It was an hour until the taxi came at ten. A condemned man, I know what he goes through. We just sat in the parlour and I guess Mom asked me eight times if I'd like a cup of tea. My gear at the door. Coat on the chair, and hat too. I thought I'd better take a look around and see this place, because maybe it would be the last time. My home, you know. I don't think I was being dramatic or anything like that and certainly not heroic. At twenty? Even at that age you can get pretty realistic.

My mother, she was being brave. A bit trembly and you might say erratic, when she'd start a sentence and trail off and go over and spend a couple of minutes picking a couple of dead leaves off a rubber plant. Straightening a picture. Then asking if I wanted a cup of tea. She was wearing those old slippers from the Boer War and a mauve skirt and a sweater, wool, I think, brown, with a patched hole in the right sleeve. You can see, if I was a painter I could paint that room, that scene, the old mom and dad waiting for their son to go off to war.

My father. My dear father. He'd never missed more than five days off work in his life, I suppose. A real workhorse, loved the company and had a pride in his work, selling men's clothing. The first suit he'd pick off the rack, that would be the right one for the customer. There are men like that. And there he was sitting on the piano bench feeling guilty about missing half a day at the store and yet, here was his only son, first born, that sort of thing, and he had this duty. Stay and see him off. We talked fishing and he went into the back room and got out his notebook and there it all was, on April 19, Buddy had caught three trout, a pound, pound two ounces, a pound six. That passed a bit of time. Fishing data. My one big day. Three fish.

Remember that clock in the movie *High Noon?* Gary Cooper. The big clock going tick-tock tick-tock towards noon when the train with the killers on it would come? Same difference. Our grandfather's clock.

Finally it was ten and I stood up and said, "I gotta go." I put on my gaberdine and picked up my hat and fixed it at the hall mirror. You had to get that right angle. That was important. Off we go, into the wild blue yonder, flying high into the sky. Remember the song? Then the taxi beeped. Twice. I turned and hugged Mom and she had her arms tight around my neck, squeezing as hard as her little body could, and her face was in my shoulder and she said, and I'll remember this, she said, "Goodbye my darling son. Goodbye. Goodbye. Our prayers . . ." And then she gave me the Bible. I knew that Bible, it must have been 40 years old. It was the one she had when she came out to this country as a girl to work as a servant in the house of some mill owner in Stratford. That just about finished me there. Just about finished me.

Do you really want this kind of stuff? Okay.

Then it was Dad's turn. He stuck out his hand and said, "Good luck, son," and that's about what I expected. No nonsense. Just good luck. I grabbed him and hugged him and his eyes were glistening. The old goat. I loved him. I didn't know it until then, but I did. All the shit life had handed out to him, and he'd taken it and come back for more.

I picked up my little bag and said to my mother, "I'll read the guid booook, mither," imitating the Scots way of speech she had. Then I put my foot under the cat's belly and gave a heave. She'd go up in the air about three feet and come down and come over and brush her tail against my leg. She was a Persian and I'd done it a thousand times and I said, "Okay, Mugger, that's the last time you get boosted for a while."

I went out the door and said, "Bye, folks, I love you all to pieces," and got the hell out of there, down the walk, because I wasn't sure how much more I could take.

There was this old Mr. Lake across the street, an old busy-body if there ever was, and there he was, up against his gate and waiting, waving that old cane of his and yelling, "Give the buggers hell, Buddy. Shoot 'em out of the skies," and I had to laugh. I got in and looked back at the house and maybe it was just the skies, grey, November, remember, and I think it would be snowing in an hour or two, and my father and mother at the door, arms around each other as if they were like two old apple trees growing old together, branches wrapped about, and I waved and I could hear a sob. It was me, and I was crying, but it felt as if the tears were coming from everywhere, like out of my eyes and my forehead and my cheeks and as if my whole face was swimming in tears and I was fumbling around for a hankie as we drove away and I remember the cabbie saying, "Let them come, kid. It'll be over in a minute or two. Christ, I've seen guys ten times as tough as you suddenly start to overflow. Just sit back and let 'em come."

It's funny, you know, sitting here 30 years later, and remembering all this for the first time and being able to remember even that cab driver's words, but I do.

Anyway, end of story. I was glad when the cab turned the corner and the house was out of sight and we drove to the station. It was a damn funny feeling. Yes, I guess you could say I felt airborne. Everything in the past was over. Airborne.

* * *

WE'D JUST MADE LOVE

I was lying on the grass with this girl from the village where I was based. It was May, I remember, and it was one of those great English days, sunny, blue skies. There's no place in the world where you get bluer skies than jolly old England in May. There were flowers around us and we could smell them, and gun pits and barbed wire and all that junk around us, but where we were it was like a little hideaway.

We'd just made love and were on our backs, just looking up at the sky.

I heard this sound coming from the Channel and it's engine sound, and we sit up and look around and here comes a Heinkel. A bomber. That's one thing I could never figure. Jerry used to send these bombers over, just one, and it was certain death. No way he was ever going to get back. I remember the girl grabbed my hand and held on tight.

I wondered why the battery next door hadn't opened up and then I saw. Four Spitfires were above this Heinkel, just swanning about until he got in position, and they must have radioed to leave this one alone. No sense messing up the fields with a lot of flak, shrapnel from the guns. Besides the German was pretty low.

This one Spit just broke off and came down and in behind in an instant, and I could hear his guns banging away. I think I could almost see the bullets. Bits of the German flew off, metal, and then the bomber just dropped its nose and came down. Straight down. Like standing on a haystack and firing an arrow straight into the ground. He didn't have far to go, maybe 2,000 feet, and God, did he ever come down, and then he hit, in the next field and there was a shower of junk, like a big bit of fireworks going off and the ground shook and that was it.

It was as if that Heinkel and the crew had never existed, and all there was to say for it was a piece of English meadow black and burned, about the size of this restaurant. Nothing more.

Somebody could write a poem about that, I guess.

The girl was crying and I asked her why and she said she'd never seen a man die before.

* * *

CAUGHT IN A BURNING PLANE

Me and a buddy were walking behind an English pub once, going back to our base, and we saw this plane come over heading for an American base just across the valley. Its starboard engine was on fire, flames coming out, smoke streaming away, and we saw it hit. It didn't hit all that bad. It hit near us.

We didn't know if it was aborting a mission and it still had its bombs aboard or if it was coming back from Germany, so we didn't dare go near it. I ran and tried to phone the American bombing base, but I couldn't get through. The line just didn't work.

Fire brigades came from all over because England had a pretty good fire water system set up by that time, but nobody dared go near it because it was on fire and we couldn't find out if it still had its bombload and tanks full of gasoline fuel. The front of it had ploughed into this field and it had buckled up the fuselage so that the crew couldn't get out. We could hear the men inside screaming and pounding, pounding and yelling, and there was nothing anybody could do because of the bombs. They died, five of them.

Then we found out later it was on a training mission.

* * *

I THOUGHT SOMEBODY HAD DIED

It's easy for me to remember the blackest moment of the war in my house. That day I'd gone to a Boy Scout camp for the day somewhere north of Toronto. There was this log bridge, one log over this small ravine, and I slipped off the log but I caught myself and didn't fall, and I was busting to tell my parents about my great experience. I remember just a-bursting into that old house and my mother met me and shushed me. Quiet, be quiet. I remember I thought somebody had died, maybe my grandfather or Aunt Marion. My mother just said my dad wasn't feeling well and be quiet.

I remember going into the living room and it was kind of dark and Dad was sitting in his big easy chair. It always smelled of his Picobac pipe tobacco. There was a bottle sitting on the table beside him and it was nearly empty and he had this big glass in his hand. It was his Christmas whiskey. I knew that. The bottle his boss at the printing plant gave him every Christmas Eve and he always saved for special occasions. It had to be special. One year he didn't use it at all.

It was the first and last time I saw my father drunk.

He looked up and saw me and I remember him saying, "Gordie, turn that thing off, will you?" and he waved to our big radio and I did, and he said, "Come over here, laddie." I went over and he put his hand on my shoulder and tears were coming down his cheeks, rolling down, and he said, "They're gone. Both gone. Gone, just like that, and all those good men." He looked at me and I didn't know what he was talking about, and then he gave me a little shake and said, "Go and see your mother, Gordie, she'll give you a bite of supper."

I went into the kitchen and out on the porch and mother said my dad was so upset because the Japanese had sunk the *Wales* and the *Repulse.* That afternoon. The bulletin had come over about noon. I was only eleven but I knew what that meant. The *Prince of Wales* was a heavy cruiser and the *Repulse* a mighty battleship, and that was all we, I mean Britain, had in the Far East. But you just didn't knock out a battleship with a few lousy little planes. These things didn't happen.

I remember reading later that nothing shocked Mr. Churchill so much, nothing in all those tough and hard years, as the sinking of those two ships. I guess it finally brought home to him just the position we were in.

I know it did to my dad. He wasn't any great thinker, he was a compositor in a print shop, but he had been in the Royal Navy in the first world war and he knew. You're darn right he knew. That's why he got drunk, and believe me he got good and drunk. Right in his own living room.

* * *

NOT FIT FOR PIGS

Our regiment was the Seaforths, a pretty tough bunch, let me say that, and after being confined to camp for months, no passes, nothing, and I think the officers were stealing our packages from home, things were hair-trigger. Very, very dicey.

Anyway, things in this camp were real on edge. The food, you couldn't eat the stuff. Mutton, and you got about four or so ounces a day, and that counted the bone and fat too, and dehydrated potatoes. Ever had mutton—mutton that's maybe been frozen for a year anyway—and dehydrated potatoes and a gummy kind of pudding if you were lucky? I mean, day after day, after week after month?

We didn't have any food, see, so everything had to go in one mess tin. You kept the other, the fit-in half for coffee, with salt petre in it to keep us from raping the vicar's wife—not that she mightn't have liked it. So you'd go down the line, and this was what got to a lot of guys. *Slop*, in would go your ration of meat. No seconds. Just *plop*. Then on top, your potatoes. Dehydrated potatoes are mushy like guck. Then if you wanted gravy, in on top, and on days when there was pudding, in on top again. God, but it was a dog's breakfast.

Then you were supposed to eat this mess. I've seen guys just look at it and get up and dump it in the garbage cans.

One time the mess officers and these guys come along—swagger sticks under their arm, sharp as tacks, that sort of thing—and one says, "Everything all right, men?" It wasn't that we were in a rotten situation and that the food was worse than rotten; it was this fresh-faced little prig who'd probably come right out of university, right to officers' school, right into the King's uniform, this little bastard having the nerve to say anything like that. You could just see the bomb go up, in about five seconds when it sunk in to the guys.

One guy—I forget his name but he was killed in Italy, near Ortona—he jumped up and he yelled, "You call this shit food? This shit!" and he dumped the mess tin about half an inch from this lieutenant's polished brown boot and he looked him right in the eye and he yelled, "My father wouldn't even feed his pigs shit like this," and he got out of that tent and left. The officer did nothing, the sergeant did nothing, the orderly's bum boy couldn't do anything, so they all walked out through the tent and all the guys were laughing at them.

Nothing came of it. The guy wasn't charged, wasn't transferred, wasn't put on coal detail, four and four sentry walk or nothing. I guess they figured if they touched him the whole outfit would go up in smoke.

* * *

SHE WAS TORONTO, SHE WAS HOME

It's funny the things you remember, but I can remember one weekend clearly. This one just stays and stays in my mind and I can still be driving down the highway or mowing the lawn and suddenly there it is. It is just a weekend I spent with a CWAC in London. She was a girl I'd known at Collegiate in Toronto. I can't say I ever knew her well in high school or that I got to know her much better that weekend, but it is the one single memory I remember.

It was April 1944. I'd been on those big raids to Berlin and poor godforsaken Hamburg, which had been hit about three times by every single plane in Bomber Command. And then I get a 72-hour pass and I'm off to London.

I get in to Victoria Station about eleven in the morning and I slope off to my usual hotel in Ecclestone Square, and the old granny who ran it was glad to see me. A quid for the weekend, and she used to laugh and say, "I close my eyes and I sleep sound after pub closing, Canada," meaning, of course, what we did after that, she didn't care about. With girls, I mean. Women. London was full of them.

I wandered around. Along the Embankment. Into the Tate. Over to Trafalgar Square, to that madhouse of thousands of troops, sailors, airmen, girls, young and old. Into the National Gallery. Up to Piccadilly. Finding a pub open and having two or three pints and a bun. Just another airman on leave in a big town and not knowing anyone. God, but it is a lonely feeling, and I just wasn't one to make friends with some Yank or Aussie or hunt up some Canadian in a bar and make conversation.

And then I saw her. In Trafalgar Square, just standing on the steps there by the lions and I remember yelling, "Smitty!" and she spotted my arm waving and then my face, and she ran down the steps and into my arms. I can remember it now. Here was Smitty in London, a girl I'd gone to school with in Toronto, gone to Centre Island with on a picnic once, and with the class on a picnic up the Don Valley once. You know. She was in the army, a CWAC, and on leave. I can see her now. She wasn't a good-looking girl, but she did have an interesting face, lots of freckles and what you'd call a sardonic smile. I remember at school she had this dry wit. That's the only way I can describe it. She was tall, almost as tall as I was, and what you might call skinny. She wasn't pretty, but how many beautiful girls did you see in the service? Not many. But she had something.

And she was more. She was Toronto, she was home. She was talk, and she was a friend and she was fun and she knew the people I knew and, above all, she was home and I needed a good dash of home right then.

We became lovers immediately. Nothing was said. I didn't ask her if she had a date that night with the King of England. We were just lovers, and if I wanted to pay her a quid I'd buy her whiskey or dinner and not hand it over, as you did and have the tart stuff it in her handbag and pat you on the cheek and say, "Ta, ta, luv. Till we meet again." She wasn't a whore, she was a girl from Toronto and we'd met in London among six million people. We'd found each other.

There was something about England, London, that spring. Everybody knew the invasion was coming and it was kind of like a time, I suppose, when England knew the Spanish Armada was coming and everybody was excited.

We went to pubs, we went to dinner and we strolled through Green Park and looked at the children with their nannies and then we went down to Ecclestone Park and I boosted her over the fence. The park is locked, you know. It's for residents of the area. I think there was a vegetable garden in part of it, but we walked under the trees and then we went home, up three flights of narrow stairs, into that bedroom and we made love. I mean we really made love. This just wasn't a screw. And next morning old granny brought us our breakfast in bed, the lovable old sot.

Saturday we did the same, walked around, went to a picture show. *Mrs. Miniver.* Greer Garson. Britain at war. What a phony. You could hear the people muttering all around, making rude remarks about Greer Garson's clothes. Nobody dressed like that in Britain any more. We went out to Kew and then down into the East End to one of those singing pubs and we went back and made love, and then went out and spent an evening in a local, drinking beer and playing darts, and then we made love again and next morning too. You see, I can remember it all.

That afternoon she put me on the five o'clock train for my station in Kent and I kissed her out of the compartment window just like you used to see in old war movies, and that's the last I saw of her. We wrote a bit, saying we'd see each other back in Canada because the invasion was coming up fast by then, but we never did.

It was my fault, I guess. She didn't blame me, in her letters. It was just, I felt, that in those three days we had done everything we would have wanted to do for the rest of our lives or, anyway, for the rest of the war. And so it was enough. I felt that way, and she did too, I think. It was our own private and special wartime marriage.

*   *   *

SCREAMING, SCREAMING

I'll tell you a story and this is all you ever need to know about war. We were at Ortona and there were places where their lines and ours were fairly close together. Ortona is in Italy, over towards the Adriatic side. There was some terrible fighting there.

We'd send out patrols, they'd send out patrols. At night. If we got a chance, we'd grab a couple of them if we met, ambush, and they'd try the same. Or we'd try and knock a few over, and so would they. Or, and this happened, almost by gentlemen's agreement, we'd pass by. Like ships passing in the night. Nobody wanted to kill that night.

One night we had two patrols out and we knew they did, and about two in the morning we hear this terrible screaming. It's a guy screaming. On and on. I'm sure you could hear it for miles. Up and down, high and low, screaming, screaming. I can hear it now. Our lieutenant is with us and he says, "The poor bugger's taken some in the belly."

Now, I'm telling you this. It went on for two hours and it seemed like ten. You see, we thought he'd die. Not often did they last that long. But this one wouldn't die.

Finally a guy says he's going out there. He's an Indian, and I think he was from around Cochrane, near Calgary, or maybe his name is Cochrane. An Indian—he gets killed about a month later. Anyway, the lieutenant doesn't say anything and so this Indian slips out and Jeezus! it is one dark night and I ask the lieutenant if we should ask for a couple of flares, just to help him, and he says no.

In about fifteen minutes, all of a sudden the screaming stops. Just like that. Like shutting off a tap. A light switch. In about five minutes this Cochrane comes back and he says, "Damn it to hell. What a shitty way to earn a living."

The sergeant after a while asks who it was out there, and Cochrane says he doesn't know. Well, was it one of our guys? Cochrane says he doesn't know. Was it a German? He says how the hell should he know.

Then—and you might not think there are some very moving moments in a war in the mud and wet and shit—but Cochrane says, "All I know was that there was a dying soldier out there and I just put my hand on his forehead and said a little prayer and then I put the knife right into his throat. I was just helping a poor soldier along the way."

* * *

PURE HELL FOR A GUY NOT IN UNIFORM

Don't let anyone ever tell you it was all blue sky and sunshine for a guy not in uniform in those years. Sometimes it was pure hell.

Fellows who had tried to enlist and had been turned down, they got this little pin they could wear, and if people knew what it meant, then they were okay. I was a deferment, vital to the war effort. A classification like that meant I had no pin, and to a lot it looked like I was just running away from the whole thing.

Well, like hell I was. I was a master mechanic and stationary engineer and I worked in this little factory just outside Hamilton, and the family who owned it had wangled a job making parts for bearings for Liberty ships. If the government had given the contract to somebody bigger they'd have been better off, but as it was, we were vital to the war effort.

I was 29 and just ripe for a uniform, but there I was, keeping that damned plant going, running back and forth between the machine shop and the boiler room like an Olympic champion. Eighteen hours in a day and ten on Sunday was nothing, keeping that plant going. Every time I'd tell the boss to shove it—he was a canny old Scots bugger—he'd give me a raise and run off to the procurement board and get my deferment renewed. I couldn't have joined the army even if I'd wanted to.

That didn't help me, though. Look at me now. Well, back in 1943 I was still six-foot-one, and I was a good 195 pounds and none of it fat, but because I could make an engine part on a lathe out of scrap iron I'd find in the back of the shop, I was essential. And I took shit for it. Ask my wife.

We couldn't go to a dance. We'd be bumped on the floor by army and navy types. The air force wasn't too bad. But you'd hear all sorts of cracks like, "Maybe he's got a wooden leg," or, "Is that silver plate in his head where they pour the sawdust in?" and, "I guess his old man's got money," and on and on. Christ, if there were a thousand insults, I heard them all. We finally stopped going to dances. The wife just couldn't take it any more. She used to cry about it.

You got it on the streets, remarks you heard as you walked by, and I remember once on a streetcar I was sitting at the back and I felt something tapping the bottom of my foot and there was a paratrooper kicking me, and when I looked at him he gave me the up-yours sign. Sure, I could have got up and whaled him one, but he had two buddies with him and if you don't think that's what they were waiting for me to do, then you're wrong. You had to watch yourself.

There were thousands of us, I guess. Maybe we should have formed our own organization. A Mafia thing or something. For me, I just developed a hard shell. It got so I was immune, or I'm telling you now I was. I wasn't really. You kind of got the feeling of what it must be like to be a Negro in Georgia.

My father-in-law, who knew what I was doing at the foundry, he would hear these insults and he'd get madder than anyone. Once we were fishing near Guelph in that little river and some soldiers were down the bank with some girls drinking beer and playing around, and soon we heard a few remarks come up our way. Harry, my father-in-law, that scored him out and he went down and told them a thing or two, what I was doing, and I can still remember one of the girls laughing and saying, "Ah, fuck off, willya. We know exactly what he is."

It all ended pretty well when the war ended. A few of my friends when they got back from overseas would make the odd remark, joking, in a nonjoking kind of way, but that ended pretty soon too. But I can tell you now, right now, that I know I was more valuable in that plant patching up that equipment than if I'd killed five Germans a day.

"A PHOTO OF YOUR DEAD SON, PLEASE"

My first job at the Winnipeg *Tribune* was picking up pictures of casualties. I don't suppose there were jobs like it in Canada at that time. A job description written by a personnel manager would be a strange document to read. Remember, I was only seventeen. A very tender age.

I'd come on duty at four and about six-thirty I'd call a Moore's cab and I'd have a list of the casualties for the next day's paper. Every casualty had a firm release date—not to be released until such and such a date. It was stupid, really, because whether the person had been killed, wounded or was missing in action, his parents, next of kin had got the word, the telegram, the visit by the chaplain or officer about a month before.

That made my job easier. I mean I didn't have to go into a house cold, to say that Jim or John was dead. No, my job was to phone ahead and ask if they had a picture we could run and could I come out and get it. The answer, invariably, was yes. But if there was no phone—and many people didn't have phones—you just went out and knocked on the door. That could be a little rough.

I can see it all again, a thousand scenes. Say it was the north end of the city. Foreign, Jewish, Polish, strongly Ukrainian. You'd knock on the door of a small frame house, maybe with geraniums in the window boxes and heavy lace curtains in the windows. You'd be asked to come in. The mother was usually big, often a matriarchal type, strong and big-breasted. Big Momma type. The old man was often a stereotype too, work-worn, beaten-down, and his English might be poor or he might not speak English. In some of these households one person, usually the woman, would speak to the visitor and when business came up, they'd switch over to Ukrainian or Polish or whatever.

So there I'd be on the chesterfield. Would I like some coffee? Some cake? Even if I said no, I got it anyway. You couldn't refuse.

Out would come the photo album. Plenty of pictures, from baby to little boy to Boy Scout and on up. A picture of him in uniform, often air force at that time, because heavy army losses hadn't started to come in from Italy yet and D-day was far off. I can see them still. Uniform a bit large, but they meant it that way because they always said you'd fill out on service food. Hell, they just meant you would continue your natural process of growing up—service food had nothing to do with it. Stiff at attention, usually. Always very self-conscious. This type of photo would be the on-demand type. Mother demanding it be taken, his first in uniform, and she's proud.

There were others. Usually taken at graduation from gunnery school or when he finished pilot training. Head and shoulders, eight by eleven inches, and tinted. Christ, I always thought that a tinted photo made a guy look like he was in his coffin, made up with cosmetics and embalmed. They used to turn my stomach.

But this kind of photo, and I'm not trying to put these people down, this was the kind they wanted me to take. It looks so natural, they'd say. Often I'd have to pick out the one, and then the whole damned family would argue. Often in Yiddish or Ukrainian.

Sometimes the women would break down. Oh yes, many times I've had a woman just go to pieces, and if she was alone in the house I'd run next door and bring back a neighbour.

Or I'd have to sit and listen while they told me about the boy's life, and show me his report cards, his Y.M.C.A. swimming certificate, his Cub or Scout badges, things like that. I'd listen until hell froze over because I knew I was doing some good. They were talking, and accepting the inevitability of death.

But some didn't. No, some didn't. I'd hate to recall the number of times I've been asked, about a son killed in a bomber crash, wasn't it possible that the government had made a mistake? What was the sense of bullshitting these poor people? I could have, and walked out the door and left them to another month's torture, thinking that Nick or Mike or Steve was still alive. Sure, I could have done that. But no, I'd look at them straight and say something like the government doesn't make mistakes like this. I'm sorry, ma'am, but that's the way it is.

Or if he was missing. Then I could be a soothing balm. Yes, sure, often airmen came back. They'd parachute and be picked up by a friendly farmer or something. But I wasn't telling them much. They knew that. A hundred friends and neighbours and relatives had already told them the missing sometimes return. In fact, the newspapers used to give every one quite a play.

But there was one situation I never learned to cope with. Take a family with no phone. You drive up in the taxi and knock on the door. It's usually just after supper and a kid comes to the door, one of the brothers or sisters. I say I'd like to see your mother, or father. Usually the mother. The kid would yell and the old lady would come down the hall and see me and you'd see that look on her face. Just a flash. I'd say I was from the Winnipeg *Tribune* and I was calling about her son. Well!

Sometimes they'd shriek. Once one fell right into my arms. A Polish household can get pretty excited. And then it would take a few minutes to tell them I was just from the paper and wanted a picture of their son, the flyer, and I wasn't there to tell them that he was alive and well and coming home the next day.

You know, what I'm telling you is straight goods. Somebody could make a movie out of that period of my newspaper career, the butting into people's lives to get a lousy photograph so some layout editor could dress up an inside page with art on the casualty list. When you look at it that way, it was a pretty crummy job, I guess.

⸱ When you look at it the other way, I was doing good. I always felt I was doing good. You see, the name in the casualty list, the picture, the caption, killed over Europe, wounded or missing in Sicily, it brought the whole thing out into the open. There was no hiding any more from the inevitability of war, and no pretending that war doesn't mean death, but only means heroes and homecoming parades and medals and pretty girls.

I look at it that way now. Then I didn't. I won't say I was callow, unfeeling, because I wasn't. I listened, I put my hand on their shoulders when they wept again, wept for maybe the last time, and I ate their cake and drank their coffee and looked at the album and said what a good-looking guy he was, and for a while then, I was their friend.

And you've got to remember, I was only seventeen.

*   *   *

"YOU, YOU GET SHOVELS"

I didn't like doing burials, helping the padre. It was a volunteer job, like, "You, you, get shovels. The padre, you'll find him over by that shed." That would be the sergeant talking.

Sometimes you'd find three or four guys laid there and you dug the grave, in some stupid Italian farmer's yard and they were put in. The padre did all three. I mean, he would bury R.C.'s, Protestants and Jews. Or you'd just go and find them, that is if the battle had moved on.

Somebody would have marked them, mostly with a rifle stuck in the ground or a gas cape hanging on a stick. We usually buried them in their gas capes. We'd go through their pockets for the personal things, wrap them up in something, put them in their helmet, something like that. Or in their pack. We never carried much.

Dig the hole. Not deep, because they were gonna be dug up later. What we'd do, I'd put the shovel under the knees and the other guy would put the shovel under the shoulders and we'd sort of just easy, up she goes, and into the hole. Then the padre would say a few words. The right words, of course. Like in any burial. Usually there'd be nobody around.

I remember one chaplain we had once who carried four grenades in the shoulder bag he carried his prayerbooks in. To him, burying was just a business. He thought of himself mostly as a soldier.

DEAD MEN—WHAT THE HELL

The first time I saw one of our boys go down I thought he'd tripped. This is Normandy, on the beachhead, and there's shit flying loose and goosy and I think this guy has tripped. Of course, he's dead.

All the training in the world isn't going to help all that much when the Germans are over there and we're here, and those things are bullets coming at you. Nothing matters until you get into action and then, wow, you learn fast, and then faster, and then faster again. There is absolutely no substitute for action, and nothing in the world will bring reality home quicker than to see three or four guys draped across some fence all shot up, or a burned tank with a guy hanging out of it and he's burned like a pig caught in a burning grease pit. The first smell of that and, boy, it was a lesson about what war was all about.

And when it happened again and again, then shit, you never thought about it. If you see a hundred dead Jerries, or some of our dead, from the battalion, or maybe from some Yank outfit, you don't go into a big flap. Nothing like that seems to matter any more.

And then you come home, discharged, and a year later you see a dead dog on the boulevard, hit by a car, and you're all sympathies. But over there, dead dogs, dead horses, dead men, what the hell.

* * *

"GOD BLESS M FOR MOMSIE"

I don't think any of us actually ever got over the loss of a pal on squadron when his plane went down, but it was a thing that we never talked about much.

After a mission and after debriefing and breakfast—and, I remember, flight crews always got real bacon and fresh eggs on our station—if one of our boys had gone down there, we'd meet. There was no note passed around, no word of mouth saying the older fellows will meet in so-and-so's room for a bit. But on our squadron there were four or five old-timers, second time around on operations or that kind of thing, and they'd gradually drift into one chap's room in the hut. There would be the guys, and someone would haul out a bottle of whiskey and we'd sit around, stand around and pour ourselves drinks. And about the second or third drink, somebody would make a remark, oh, I don't know what, just something. A toast, you could call it. A toast to the dead pilot. It might be quite cynical like, "Well, I guess we'll see his D.F.C. turn up in the mail tomorrow," or, "Who wants to take a 72 [hour-leave] to go up to London to comfort his girlfriend?" Maybe something like that.

We never made any big fuss about it. No, it was usually some remark, a lift of the glasses, and bottoms up. Somebody might say, "God bless M for Momsie," or whatever his plane was, and that was it.

You learned to keep emotion at a very low level.

* * *

WELCOME TO THE WAR

When I first went into action, I didn't know what the score was. Nothing added up. In Canada they showed us plenty of films, but they were sweet bugger-all and we knew it. They really taught you nothing. The clock started when you got out of those big trucks and a runner from the front started to guide you towards the company position, and this was maybe eighteen or twenty days after D-day, so the shit was really flying. June and July, and boy, there was some tough going in Normandy then.

There was this little village—I mean what had been a village. There were about a dozen of us, and the captain put three of us in one platoon and scattered the rest around and told us to watch the other fellows, the guys who'd been there a few days. I remember him saying that in this place nobody wins or loses, you just survive. Well, that was okay with me.

The sergeant of our platoon, the second platoon, he was telling us his name, and the name of the lieutenant, and that things had been quiet so far that morning, and I heard an awful racket of gunfire and artillery over to our right and I asked what that was and he said, "That's an American combat team over there. Texans. It's their turn today. We got it yesterday." Casual as all hell.

Funny how you remember the little things, but this sergeant said, "You guys all got your pull-throughs? Those weapons get clogged up awful fast, so keep them clean." It seemed a funny remark right in the middle of a war, to keep our rifle barrels clean. Anyway, it makes sense now.

Just then, there's this goddamned church steeple or tower and it has
been three quarters knocked over, hit so there's mostly all but one side
gone and suddenly there is a *pow* sort of noise and down it comes. And
then a shell lands behind us, and another over to the side, and by this
time we're scurrying and the sarge and I and another guy wind up
behind a wall. The sergeant said it was an .88 and then he said, "Shit and
shit some more."

I asked him if he was hit and he sort of smiled and said no, he had just
pissed his pants. He always pissed them, he said, just when things started
and then he was okay. He wasn't making any apologies either, and then I
realized something wasn't quite right with me, either. There was something warm down there and it seemed to be running down my leg. I felt,
and it wasn't blood. It was piss.

I told the sarge, I said, "Sarge, I've pissed too," or something like that
and he grinned and said, "Welcome to the war."

*   *   *

"FLAK!"

Flak? It was two different things. At night it was one thing. If it was a
clear night you could actually see the .88-millimetre cannon, the classic
German aircraft cannon, firing at you. You could also see 20-mm. and
30-mm. cannon firing at you. It was even a bit nerve-racking with that
light stuff, even though you knew it wouldn't quite reach you. But the
heavy flak, the muzzles of the guns belching below, and then the crump
of the explosion, and if it was very close you'd hear the metal rattling like
heavy hail against your airplane and sometimes actually punching holes
in it—that was terrible.

If you got a direct hit, which you could, and survive, it would actually
seem like the plane might be coming apart. Of course, if the hit was in a
vital place, then that was it. The game was over. It could be sudden,
fatal, all over with, or it could be drawn out and you'd head for home
with your airplane falling apart. But it often was fatal.

And in daylight, and especially in our particular operations, the flak
was very nerve-racking because you just had to go down the old slot with
our gunners calling out where the bursts were, coming in on you, closer
and more accurate as the gunners down below got you in range, and I
would sometimes yell, "Shut up! I don't give a damn where they are!
There's nothing we can do about it." In other words, we had to fly that
one track in on this precision bombing, and so I'd say, "Shut up, I don't
want to hear about it."

But the rest of the crew, they'd be so tight about it—because it's a hell
of a feeling to see this stuff coming up at you and the next one could
destroy the airplane and everyone in it—they just felt they had to com-

municate. You see this hairy great ball just out there, and the next one bound to come closer, and you feel you want to warn everybody about it.

I remember the tail-end gunner once, and that's a hell of a lonely place to be, he once said over the intercom. "But I can't keep quiet. I've got to say something."

I remember once just after the war and my brother and I were sleeping on this porch at the cottage on the island, and suddenly there is this lightning and it must have landed very near, and he said I just leaped straight out of bed and screamed, "FLAK!"

*   *   *

I SHOOK HER HAND

I don't know if everybody expected us to be only 85 pounds and be wearing rags, but when we came to Canada they treated us like we were in cotton batting. They meant well, and I guess it was right that we should be grateful. Think of it, not everybody had spent one-sixth of their life in a Japanese prison camp. I was twenty when Hong Kong was captured and I was twenty-four when we got home.

Everything was a blur. I mean that. We didn't eat much but potato soup with some fish in it, but we stole more than our share of rice, and the Americans who first had us looked after us pretty well, so when I got home, I was in pretty fair shape. Except I was very nervous and I would cry sometimes over little things, and I didn't know what was happening. Canada was a changed place. The people were different, it seemed.

I remember coming home on the train. I don't know if we were the first Grenadiers to come home but they treated us pretty good and some reporters and photographers got on our coach at Brandon and rode with us to Winnipeg and it was one long string of asking questions and taking pictures and I was afraid. I don't know why, but I didn't say anything. Then this photographer came back and he said he'd done something wrong with his camera and he'd like to take another picture and I broke down and started to cry. The photographer looked like a nice guy and it was smoothed over.

Then we got into Winnipeg, the station across from the Fort Garry. I used to play in the old fort in the park there when I was a kid. I'd joined up when I was nineteen. I think there were lots of people in the station. Maybe the mayor, for all I know.

What I should be telling you now, if I can, is that I had a wife too, but I didn't know what she looked like. I mean I wasn't sure. The Japs had taken away our wallets and things and when I got mine back, or maybe it was my paybook, her picture was gone. Her name was Mary. We'd had a few dates. I couldn't afford much. We'd go bowling, five pins, and then have a Denver sandwich, and then I'd walk her to her boarding house and that would be it. Three weeks before I went to Hong Kong we got married, and I was afraid I wouldn't know what she looked like. I don't think my brain was working all that well.

I guess I should say that I didn't really know her. Hadn't heard from her, you see. We got no mail. A couple of guys did, but the Japs always seemed to lose mine.

I can't remember much about the station. Maybe there was a ceremony. There were a lot of people moving around and then, just like that, I hear this voice say, "Hello, Johnny." I turn around and there she is, and it's not the girl I thought it would be, because I honestly couldn't remember. It was all a blur.

You know what I did? I'm not kidding. I shook her hand. Like that, I shook her hand. She was a little thing.

I remember her saying, "C'mon, Johnny, we're going home. Have you got your bag?" and I had a little bag and I picked it up and walked out. It was October. The sun was shining. I remember that. About eleven in the morning. I could stretch this out and tell you other things, but all I remember is, I was crying and a taxi guy jumps out and opens the door and we get in. I couldn't remember if I'd been in a taxi in the past four or five years, but if I had I guess it was in Victoria or Vancouver. Wherever we landed. I can't, I don't think I can remember.

It was just a short trip, a few blocks. She just held my hand, and I must have just held hers and wiped my eyes with the other, with a hankie, and then we got out at the Garrick Hotel. I don't know if it is still there, but it was a funny little place. Little but tall, and we got out and she said, "Here's home for now, Johnny," and I got out and I remember when we were walking up the first flight of stairs the taxi driver comes charging up and he's got my bag. I'd left it. There was nothing in it anyway. I had nothing, just army stuff. Not even a gift. When he got to us he held out the bag to Mary and he squeezed my arm, right here where the muscle is, and he said, "Everything's gonna be fine. You wait and see." I'll always remember that guy.

We got to the room, just an ordinary hotel room in an ordinary hotel, you might say. It wasn't even a good room. A 2-dollar room, I'd say. I did some dumb things, like going to the dusty window and making knots-and-crosses in the dust, playing a game with myself. I asked her how her dad was and she said fine. I think I wasn't crying any more. Hell, this was 30 years ago. How can I remember everything?

I sat down on the bed and she went to her bag and brought out a bottle of Johnny Walker Red Label. Never forget it. She held it up and said, "You're home, Johnny. Johnny's home," and I got up and hugged her. That was the first time. I think, honestly, that that was when she just started to get through to me. That she just wasn't some little girl who had picked me up in the station.

I said we weren't altogether right. We looked okay, 150 pounds, new haircut, new uniforms, the medals we'd earned, and I guess I had about 3,000 bucks back pay coming and enough for a start, but we weren't right. We weren't right emotionally. We weren't ready for our wives. Know that?

I poured myself a drink and one for Mary and another and another and in about an hour we had finished the bottle. I mean I had. She had a couple, maybe three. Then I took off my tunic and lay down on the bed and zonk, that was it. Out. Before I went under I saw Mary taking off her blouse and her little skirt and she lay down beside me and she held me.

That was the start of my coming back to the world. I can't put it any other way. It took a long time and I was terrified a lot, but that was the start and that was it. The start.

JOHN FITZGERALD KENNEDY
1917–1963

Lieutenant (j.g.) Kennedy, commanding a patrol torpedo boat in the Pacific, wrote this letter home shortly after his boat was sunk off the Solomon Islands in the summer of 1943.

To His Parents

Dear Mother & Dad:

Something has happened to Squadron Air Mail—none has come in for the last two weeks. Some chowder-head sent it to the wrong island. As a matter of fact, the papers you have been sending out have kept me up to date. For an old paper, the New York Daily News is by far the most interesting . . .

In regard to things here—they have been doing some alterations on my boat and have been living on a repair ship. Never before realized how badly we have been doing on our end although I always had my suspicions. First time I've seen an egg since I left the states.

As I told you, Lennie Thom, who used to ride with me, has now got a boat of his own and the fellow who was going to ride with me has just come down with ulcers. (He's going to the States and will call you and give you all the news. Al Hamn). We certainly would have made a red-hot combination. Got most of my old crew except for a couple who are being sent home, and am extremely glad of that. On the bright side of an otherwise completely black time was the way that everyone stood up to it. Previous to that I had become somewhat cynical about the American as a fighting man. I had seen too much bellyaching and laying off. But with the chips down—that all faded away. I can now believe—which I never would have before—the stories of Bataan and Wake. For an American it's got to be awfully easy or awfully tough. When it's in the middle, then there's trouble. It was a terrible thing though, losing those two men. One had ridden with me for as long as I had been out here. He had been somewhat shocked by a bomb that had landed near the boat about two weeks before. He never really got over it; he always seemed to have the feeling that something was going to happen to him. He never said anything about being put ashore—he didn't want to go—but the next time we came down the line I was going to let him work on the base force. When a fellow gets the feeling that he's in for it, the only thing to do is to let him get off the boat because strangely enough, they always seem to be the ones that do get it. I don't know whether it's just coincidence or what. He had a wife and three kids. The other fellow had just come aboard. He was only a kid himself.

It certainly brought home how real the war is—and when I read the papers from home and how superficial is most of the talking and thinking about it. When I read that we will fight the Japs for years if necessary and will sacrifice hundreds of thousands if we must—I always like to check from where he is talking—it's seldom out here. People get so used to talking about billions of dollars and millions of soldiers that thousands of dead sounds like drops in the bucket. But if those thousands want to live as much as the ten I saw—they should measure their words with great, great care. Perhaps all of that won't be necessary—and it can all be done by bombing. We have a new Commodore here—Mike Moran—former Captain of the Boise—and a big harp if there ever was one. He's fresh out from six months in the States and full of smoke and vinegar and statements like—it's a privilege to be here and we would be ashamed to be back in the States—and we'll stay here ten years if necessary. That all went over like a lead balloon. However, the doc told us yesterday that Iron Mike was complaining of headaches and diarrhea—so we look for a different tune to be thrummed on that harp of his before many months.

Love,
Jack

HAROLD L. BOND
1920-1986

Bond was for many years a Professor of English at Dartmouth and an authority on the life and times of Edward Gibbon, the historian of the decline and fall of the Roman Empire, but during the war Bond was a young infantry officer in the 36th Infantry Division in Italy. Twenty years later he revisited his old battleground and wrote Return to Cassino: A Memoir of the Fight for Rome, *published in 1964.*

From Return to Cassino: A Memoir of the Fight for Rome

The colonel came in carrying his walking stick in one hand and a cup of hot coffee in the other. He seemed quite cheerful, saying that things were a bit confused right now but that they would straighten out soon. Everything was going to be all right, he said, but until it was he would have to keep me here at headquarters. Part of the regiment I was to join was across the river, possibly even the company to which I would be assigned. Then he added, "A replacement officer coming to them right now would only get in the way and might even get himself killed." With this felicitous observation from the colonel, I resigned myself to another day of nervous waiting and listening to reports of what was happening.

The sun did not penetrate the mist and smoke until nearly noontime, and then it shone sickly, whitish and weak through the gray-brown branches of the olive trees. Two or three times during the morning the crew of the howitzer was called into action to fire a few rounds, and then they went back to their cards and their coffee, which they seemed to drink endlessly. Reports from the river, which came in sporadically during the morning, were confused, even contradictory. No one had any clear idea of what was going on or of what was happening to the men. "Elements of two battalions," the colonel had said, "are pressing the attack across the river"; but even he did not have any notion of what his jargon meant. The routine reports on the strength of the division had to be based on the figures as they were prior to the present action. The sergeant fussed with official army documents at his field desk. From the window I could see the Italian girl come out of the hovel where she and her family lived and stare at the Americans who were washing and shaving around their howitzer. In the distance there was almost no small-arms firing, just an occasional enemy shell, landing with a sickening crunch down in the direction of the river.

Toward the end of the morning a young second lieutenant named F—— came into our room. He was wet, dirty, and he looked very tired, even sick. He sat near the stove, quietly soaking up as much heat as he could and drying his wet clothing. The colonel told him to wait there until the jeep came to take him to the rear. The lieutenant said simply, "Yes, sir," and went on warming himself. The sergeant and I stepped outside for a moment, and from him I learned that F—— was under arrest. He had come back from across the river and left his men on the other side. His excuse was that he had returned to get help. I later found out that F—— was not averse to talking about his experience; in fact, after he had warmed himself, he seemed eager to explain. It had been terrible over there, he said. The men were pinned down by machine-gun fire and could not move forward at all. Big shells came in on their positions. He thought that at least half of his company had been killed or wounded. He was a good swimmer, and so he had set out to get help. He could have sent one of his men back, he realized, but it was too danger-ous for the others to make the trip. When reaching his battalion com-mander, he was charged with deserting his troops and sent back to division headquarters, technically under arrest, to await the army's jus-tice. He was too tired really to care very much then, and still too fright-ened by the terrible night down in the fog and cold of the riverbank, with huge shells crashing nearby and with machine-gun fire everywhere, the sharp angry crack of bullets passing close, and the shattering explo-sion of field mines. "But I'm a good swimmer, I was the one to go," he protested again and again, "a good swimmer." He was a big man physi-cally and rather good-looking, one could tell, under the dirt and three days' growth of beard on his face. He had had a college education and was commissioned through R.O.T.C. His family was respected back home. Yet he had left his men and come back across the river. I did not say anything, for there was nothing I could say; but he broke out again, as if he were still speaking to his battalion commander. "You don't know what it was like over there. Germans everywhere, mortar shells crunch-ing down in front of us and behind us, the screams of the wounded men . . ." The only way to get help was to go back, he had thought. He should have been the one to risk it, get out in the open, swim the icy river, crawl up the far bank, and bring aid to his men. Wasn't this an officer's job? His men were in a bad—a terribly bad—spot, and he would try to save them. Why didn't his battalion commander see that? He was doing his duty. But all his battalion commander could see was that he had deserted, left his troops across the river when he should have stayed with them. And now he sat by the warm stove, the heat working its way slowly into his aching, shivering body, and he listened to the sound of small-arms fire in the distance, a morally broken man.

He tried to escape the truth, this I know, for some years later I met him back in the United States. I ran into him by chance in a hotel lobby. He wanted very much to have a drink with me so that he could explain yet again, to himself as much as to me, why he had come back. "My men were in a bad way. They needed help. . . ." Army justice had been merciful with him, and he had been reassigned to some quartermaster unit, far behind the lines and the fighting. As I watched him that morning in the staff officer's headquarters, I wondered if I, too, someday would come back across a river, and I began to understand for the first time that in war it is most often the strong and the brave who are killed, while the weaklings live on.

During the morning we learned from other reports than F——'s that the attack of last night had been a failure. Two regiments had attempted to make the crossing, the 143d Infantry at a site downstream from the little town of San Angelo, the 141st Infantry upstream from the town. If successful in their crossing, the regiments would meet behind the town and pinch it off. Despite the tremendous artillery preparation made by our guns, both regiments ran into very heavy German fire almost from the start of the assault. The 143d Infantry was successful in getting most of a battalion across in the initial stages and they erected two footbridges for their other infantry battalions; but the bridges were destroyed by enemy shelling as soon as daylight came, and the troops on the far side ran into such tough resistance that the battalion commander gave orders to withdraw. Upstream, the 141st Infantry had a similar experience. They, too, got most of a battalion across and were successful finally, despite constant shelling, in erecting their footbridge. But in the early morning the German artillery destroyed this too, as well as sections of the bridge which the engineers were bringing up for tanks to use in crossing. The battalion on the far side was pinned down by enemy fire in the low, wet meadows near the riverbank, and the enemy artillery was slowly destroying it. German machine gunners, from fortified positions which they had been building for two months, fired safely and accurately at anything that moved in front of them. With the Germans holding the high ground on the far side, our troops were utterly naked to enemy observation during daylight hours. Our chemical battalions tried to fill the valley with smoke, but a slight wind kept blowing away the screen. Division had ordered another attack to be made at 1400 hours (2:00 P.M.) that day, and the colonel seemed to think that this time the attack would succeed.

"Our boys are having a tough time now," he said, "but we'll break through them tonight."

The young officer who had come back across the river did not say a word as the colonel spoke.

The sergeant brought me some field rations for my lunch, and afterward I walked around the farmyard while waiting for the great barrage which was to precede the next attack to begin. The landscape was bleak enough, with the stark outlines of trees against the hazy sky. Mount Trocchio, between us and the river, was gray, without foliage, and covered with huge boulders. I had been warned not to try to climb to the top in a foolish attempt to see what was going on. Our artillery observers up there did not want fire drawn to them through too much movement on the slopes. Furthermore, the Germans, knowing that we would use the mountain for observation, had mined it heavily. The air was very smoky and the day continued cold. The January sun was low in the south, even at noontime, and it gave little heat. The farms round about were quiet, and I was suddenly aware of there being no birds or animals in sight, not even chickens. No doubt the Germans, and then the newly arrived Americans, found chickens much tastier than army rations. There had been considerable shooting in the morning, but now, except for some firing in the east, many miles up the river, there was an oppressive stillness in the air. The world seemed dead. I looked at my watch and saw that it was almost two o'clock. The barrage should start any minute now. But the gunners at the howitzer emplacements were sleeping, a few playing cards, one washing some clothes. When I returned to our headquarters the sergeant was still working at his desk, fussing with details for his reports. F—— was gone, and I was relieved that I would not have to talk to him any more. The sergeant did not volunteer any information as to why there had been no artillery barrage before the attack. When I finally asked him he explained that the attack had been postponed until 1600 hours (4:00 P.M.). The 141st Infantry was having trouble getting organized.

The rest of the afternoon was consumed in dull waiting. Nothing happened. Sometimes short bursts of fire from down on the river could be heard, and sometimes the howitzer crew had to leave their cards to fire a few rounds, but that was all. Around four o'clock firing picked up, but the attack was postponed a third time, and it was not until well after dark, around six, that the artillery pieces around us and from all over the valley began to fire in earnest preparation.

The sergeant put the blackout curtains up at the windows and lit the candles. With the big guns thundering outside, we waited around the stove together for some news. I learned that he was from San Antonio, Texas, and had been with the division since its mobilization three years ago. He told me of their training on Cape Cod in Massachusetts before coming overseas, and of their fighting at Salerno. The night before they were to land on the beaches, loudspeakers on all the ships broadcast the news of Italy's surrender. Loud cheers went up from all the men, and it was not until the next day on the shore and around the ancient Greek temples at Paestum that they learned the ugly truth: Italy's surrender had nothing to do with the Germans, who were determined to fight over every inch of Italian soil. The sergeant, whose job was to file reports on casualties and troop strength, was well aware of his good fortune in having a relatively safe job in an infantry division. He worked hard and conscientiously to keep it. He kept the headquarters scrupulously neat, sweeping it two or three times a day, and his records were diligently and accurately kept. A mile or two away from where we were talking, men were being killed and wounded who would become figures in his records on the next day's entry.

The big guns near our farmhouse were firing only occasionally now, but there had been such a heavy bombardment earlier that I did not see how any Germans could live through it. Nor did I know then that the Germans had been preparing their defensive positions for months, and that all the protection which sandbags, steel, and concrete could give was theirs. I had still much to learn about the skill and determination of the enemy. When the guns were fired, flashes of pale white light penetrated even the blackout curtains, followed almost instantly by the great clap of explosion. And now, as we sat there talking, I heard for the first time the German Nebelwerfer firing in return. It had a terrifying sound, for it could put six big shells into the air at one time. Holes were cunningly made in the sides of these shells so that they screamed as they came toward us. When they landed and exploded, instead of breaking into thousands of pieces of small deadly shrapnel, they broke into great jagged chunks of iron, which went whirling through the air with all the force of bullets. The American troops nicknamed the Nebelwerfers "Screaming Mimis." They had rocket propulsion and chilled the blood of our troops as they got under way: Whooooop, Whoooooop, Whoooooop, and then the sound of six huge shells screaming through the night sky toward our positions. The German name means "mist-thrower," and the weapon was originally designed for chemical warfare, to lay smoke screens or gas; but the enemy had quickly discovered their awful psychological effect, and now they used them with high explosives. A jagged fragment from one of these shells could, and sometimes did, decapitate a man or sheer off a limb. There must have been half a dozen

of the weapons on our front, and again and again, out of the cold blackness to the north, we would hear the spine-chilling Nebelwerfers launch-
ing their missiles and then the terrifying screams as six shells at once
sped toward us. From the sound of their explosions the sergeant thought
that they were landing on the crossing sites of the 141st and 143d
Infantry Regiments.

The branch of division headquarters I was in is not the place where
one gets first news of the fighting, and the evening dragged on without
our hearing a thing about the attack. Before trying to get to sleep I went
out in the farmyard for some air. It was another cold night, but one could
see no stars. There was, indeed, "husbandry in heaven" and all their
candles were out. To the south there was an occasional flash, as a big gun
back in the valley fired, but this was all the light. Toward the front, on
the other side of Mount Trocchio, there was the sound of automatic
weapon fire. The thought that probably tomorrow I would be down on
the river where all this firing was going on frightened me. Yet I knew,
too, and had known since I joined the army a year and a half earlier, that
this was what I was being trained for: to go down to some obscure river
with the others and try to destroy the Germans who were in front of us. I
thought of the boredom of the long months of training and wondered
again how fit I would be to command the men who were even now down
on the river. In some ways I had been eager to come overseas. I had deep
convictions that Hitler and the Nazi regime were thoroughly evil and
must be destroyed, and I knew, too, that war was the only way that this
could be done. My generation, brought up on *A Farewell to Arms, All
Quiet on the Western Front,* and plays such as *Journey's End,* was not
easily persuaded that modern war made any sense at all. Most certainly
none of us thought any longer of glory and military heroics. But one has
to fight against a clear and palpable evil; the Nazis were both vicious and
degrading, appealing as they did to the worst side of human nature. I had
volunteered to come overseas ahead of the time when I might have
expected to be sent over, in order to take the place of a young father of
two children whom the colonel had first selected to go. I thought then,
probably rationalizing my boredom with training camps, that young,
unmarried men should be the first ones to go. And now I found myself at
the end of that long journey, with the Rapido River only a mile away,
and my first assignment in battle probably coming in the morning. I
thought of my parents at home and wondered what they were doing on
this particular evening. I remembered my last sight of them as my train
pulled out of the South Station in Boston many months ago. How brave
they had been in keeping their spirits up! They knew full well that we
might never see each other again. I wondered now if the ground in
Boston was covered with snow.

But it was time to go in. I went back to the farmhouse and found the sergeant already asleep on his cot, peacefully at rest until morning. In his deep slumber I doubt that he dreamed, but even if he did, his wildest dreams could not have told him that the next day would bring into his office the most astonishing figures he would ever have to record. He would have to write down that on this night and the night before the fighting effectiveness of two American regiments was destroyed on the banks of the Rapido River. The casualties would number well over 1,600 men. There would be a great many names entered as "killed" and "wounded," and a large number would have to go down as "missing in action." I stretched out my bedroll and lay down, aware this night of the hardness of the floor. I listened to the guns until I finally dropped off.

The dirt road which took us around the west flank of Mount Trocchio toward the river passed through olive groves and some plowed fields. Nothing had been planted, however, and the landscape was utterly without life. The sun filtered through the mist, casting a dull light. The colonel had told me about 10:00 A.M. that he was sending me down that day. The attack had been a failure—that wasn't his word; he said that the division was regrouping—and since there would be a lull in the fighting, I could join my unit. I was driven to the command post of the 3d Battalion of the 141st Infantry in a jeep. We passed very few farmhouses, for most of the peasants in this area lived close together in tiny villages, as they had done for centuries. After a short, fast trip my driver pulled abruptly into the yard of a stone house and said, "Here you are, Lieutenant." He helped me get my carbine and pack out of the jeep and then drove hurriedly off.

In the yard, leaning against the wall of the house, sat three or four exhausted infantrymen, trying to get warm in the weak sunshine. Their eyes were closed, nor did they bother to stir as I approached. I went in through the low wooden door and was surprised to find the room full of soldiers. In the chimney place at one end of the room there was a slow, smoking fire which seemed to throw no heat at all. A lieutenant was sitting at the one table in the room looking at a map and talking quietly with a sergeant on his left. There was a steady hum of voices, but no one was talking loudly. In one corner I saw a captain, a tall, rawboned man in a very dirty uniform. He was busily talking to a tired-looking lieutenant. The 3d Battalion had lost its commander and executive officer on the first night of the attack, I learned, and since then all its company commanders except this one had been killed or wounded. He had been placed temporarily in command of the battalion. Stepping over the legs of some of the men who were sitting on the floor, I walked over to where the captain was. He had a canteen cup in his hand and was drinking some hot coffee. Clearly he had not shaved for at least three days, and his face showed marks of deep fatigue. I told him, as soon as I could get his attention, that I had been sent down to join his battalion. He was obviously annoyed.

"What in Christ's name did they do that for?" was his reply. And then he added, talking to himself, "As if I haven't got enough trouble with the goddamn river crossing, they have to send me a new officer now." He motioned for me to wait for a little and turned away, resuming his conversation with the lieutenant beside him.

I moved away, into the crowded room, until he should have a chance to finish. There were two small windows letting some light in, and I stood by one of them listening to the men talk. From what I heard, the battalion had been badly disorganized and severely hurt in the attack of the preceding night. Most of its men who got across the river never came back. The captain had been trying all morning to reorganize his companies, and word was still coming in about losses, deaths, wounds. Once in a while he ordered his sergeant to clear everyone out of the room who had no business there, and the sergeant tried; but the room was soon full again, as if the men, by some instinct of which they were unaware, wanted to be close together. After three or four attempts he did get the room almost empty of everyone except the badly depleted battalion staff. The captain had finished with his lieutenant, who was now the commander of I Company, and then he came over to see me.

"You'll have to wait until this afternoon, when I have a better idea of where we can best use you," he said. "We have very few officers left." Then he asked suddenly, "What are you trained for? Machines guns? Rifle platoon? We might use you for the mortars."

I murmured something about mortars, thinking that I could probably manage this duty better than I could a rifle platoon. He said that he would have to see and then asked me to wait outside. I told him that I was eager to help where I could. I had not realized how badly things had gone. He made no reply to this except to say that if he could not assign me permanently today he would send me to one of the company posts for the night to help keep watch. This would enable a few of the men to get some sleep. They needed it desperately.

I went out into the yard, glad to leave the stuffy room. The soldiers sitting in the sun had not moved all the time I had been inside, and I discovered that they really were asleep. Toward the river stretched a long, flat field, filled with large gnarled trees which cut down the view to about two hundred yards. The road down which I had come from division headquarters carried on past the farmhouse toward the river, but there was a guard posted at the house who let no vehicle through without a special pass. There was little firing anywhere along the front, and one could even hear small flies buzzing, despite the cold, in the dooryard where the exhausted soldiers were sleeping. Every now and again a few soldiers, in twos or threes, arrived at the command post, looking dirty and worn like everyone else who had been down near the river. They would go inside and talk to one of the officers or deliver a message to the battalion commander. Then they tried to stay around as long as they could, until the sergeant, at the repeated insistence of the captain, made them get out.

I put my carbine against the wall of the house and sat down on a low stone wall. Then I saw, and really for the first time, the great abbey of Monte Cassino. I had had a hurried glimpse of it through the smoke three days before, as we raced past the dead German on Highway 6, but then, as on this morning on my way down to battalion headquarters, we had traveled too fast, and I had been too nervous, to take much in. Now, at midday, in the small enclosure outside the doorway with nothing to do until dark, I had time to take a good look at it. Its size and location were surprising, for one does not expect to find a huge building perched high on the top of a steep mountain. Like the king's palace at Caserta, its stone walls were yellow and unexpectedly warm on that cold January day. The sun reflected from some of the glass in the windows, and the great towers and dome were nobly outlined against the sky. Like a lion it crouched, dominating all approaches, watching every move made by the armies down below. Some soldiers in the yard told me that the Germans were using it for an observation post, and that was the reason why they had been able to fire with such deadly accuracy on all of our positions. It was a strange feeling to know that the men up there, watching our movements through field glasses, could, if they thought us worth the trouble, bring down terrible artillery fire on our heads. The monastery was only a few miles away. One direct hit on the little farmhouse half an hour ago would have accounted for twenty or more lives. And yet the fire did not come. The Germans were possibly waiting for better, surer targets, like a battalion of infantry exposed in an open meadow trying to get across a flooded river. I did not know it then, but I was to spend most of the next month in the shadow of that huge monastery. I was to be among the first to drop mortar shells on it—I am not proud of that—and I was to see wave after wave of planes fly low over it and drop their bombs, leaving it a heap of rubble and monstrous fragments of stone. Before the Allies were through with the monastery, thousands would be dead on its slopes and in the town down below. Many thousands more would be wounded. For over fourteen hundred years the abbey had been a center of European culture. It had played an important role in the preservation of classical learning and in the revival of interest in it. The monks of Benedict had addressed themselves to the highest intellectual and spiritual needs of nearly a hundred generations, and their ministers had carried this spirit to every part of Western Christendom. But now the abbey stood in the path of a destructive war. Its libraries and art treasures had been carried away. Most of the monks had been sent to Rome, and the American soldiers, fighting miserably in the plains below, were just beginning to realize that the monastery was the key to the Battle of Cassino. Ironically, although it was a symbol of much that we thought we were fighting for, the abbey would, nonetheless, go up in smoke and flames before we were through, and we would be the ones to destroy it. *Haec sunt lacrimae rerum.*

Most of army life consists of waiting, and I learned this afternoon that even on the battlefield the statement holds true. It was almost dark before the acting battalion commander told me that he wanted me to spend the night at I Company's command post. I Company had lost all of its officers except the young lieutenant I had seen the captain talking with earlier in the day. The men were jumpy and exhausted. They had been so weakened by the fighting of the past two days that their commander had all he could do to get them to take defensive positions on the high ground overlooking the river. The acting company commander was utterly worn out and had to have some sleep. I was to take charge of the command post, receive calls on the field telephone from the platoons, and keep battalion headquarters informed of any enemy action. We were very vulnerable to a German counterattack just then, although the battalion commander thought it unlikely that the Germans would cross the river in any force.

The command post was located in a partly destroyed two-story house. The upper floor had been hit a number of times by artillery fire and half of the roof was gone. There was no glass left in any of the windows. Downstairs the men had covered the windows and the gaping holes in the walls with army blankets, and so were able to have a small fire to heat their rations. Broken plaster and shattered stone littered the floor. Most of what furniture was there had long since been smashed up for firewood. The company sergeant, a big blond man with a very dirty face and several days' stubble, was keeping the command post by himself when the messenger brought me down. We were within three hundred yards of the river, and between us and the Germans there were only forty-one tired, frightened soldiers, who would wait out the long night in pairs in their foxholes. They were all who remained of an infantry company with a normal complement of two hundred fighting men. The sergeant seemed grateful to have someone in the house to help him with the watch. He had some coffee which he gave me, and I heated my field rations on the small fire which he kept going. Outside it was completely dark except for the flashes of the guns which could be seen from the stairway leading to the exposed second floor. While I ate my supper the sergeant explained to me where the company positions were and what the ground was like between us and the river.

After eating, I went up the creaking stairs to get a look around the battlefield in the dark. A good bit of shooting had started up, and I could hear enemy fire passing over, some big shells landing in our rear and the crackle of bullets from small arms directly overhead. As I peered from the frame of a ruined window I could see bright flames from a burning haystack only two hundred yards away. Tracer bullets from German automatic weapons spat by, showing white streaks of light. Now and again a brilliant white flare went up and cast a cold, bright light over everything. And through it all there was the tremendous pounding of artillery fire, German and American, and the whoosh and crash of great shells, all very close now, and very frightening. The firing was vigorous and kept up a long time. While I was watching, I heard the telephone downstairs in the command post ring a short jingle. Two men in the first platoon had been wounded and wanted permission to go back for medical help. The sergeant asked some sharp questions to find out how badly they had been hurt. Then he told them that they had better stay where they were until morning. The medic on the spot could take care of them, and he did not want to weaken our position any more. They could still fight if they had to. Then he hung up. I listened to all this from upstairs, but then a big shell landed close to the house. The sergeant called out, "You'd better come down from there, Lieutenant." When I came down he said simply, "This house has been hit too often to make it safe."

The night passed very slowly for me. I was alert to every noise, and the sergeant was helpful in explaining what the different battlefield sounds were. Before he dropped off to sleep he told me a little of what had happened to the company on the preceding night. They had tried to cross the river and were supposed to aid the men of the 1st Battalion who had been pinned down by fire on the far side all day. Everything had started smoothly enough. The company had assembled just before dark in a small grove of trees about five hundred yards from the river. Even the rubber assault boats were there and the guides to lead the men through the mine field on this side. The beginning of their assault was quite different, the sergeant had heard, from the experience of the 1st Battalion two days ago, when the engineers had dumped some of their boats in the wrong place and one company spent the first two hours trying to find them. When that company finally did locate their boats, artillery fire had blown away or covered with dirt the white tape which showed the path through the mine field, and they stumbled into mines almost immediately after starting down to the river. The exploding mines showed the Germans exactly where they were, and heavy artillery fire had disorganized them so badly that only a few of them ever did get to the river. Their company commander was killed and the second in command severely wounded. In the confusion, one of the surviving officers attached the few men he could find to the 3d Battalion, which was waiting its turn to cross.

But I Company last night had found their boats and were finally ready, just after dark, to make the assault. This time the markers on the mine fields had been properly laid out, and the men had not hit any mines on the way down. But the Germans were now fully prepared for them. After yesterday's fighting they had the approaches to the crossing sites accurately zeroed in. At the first evidence of a renewed American assault, they brought down a terrific artillery barrage and opened up with every weapon they had right afterward. The company was caught in the open field which sloped down to the river and had no protection at all. Many of the rubber boats were punctured by shrapnel and made utterly useless. The officers, moving about in the dark, trying to control the men, were fatally exposed. Two of them were killed and the other badly wounded. The Germans kept up a steady fire, but the company was finally able to reorganize itself. Almost half of the men who were left did manage to cross the river, but another artillery barrage drove the rest of the men back to the shelter of the woods, just over the crest of a small hill, leaving their dead and wounded on the forward slope. Their casualties had been frightful, but the worst part of the failure was that the men who *had* been able to get across were now lost, along with the men of the 1st Battalion, captured or killed in the meadow on the far side. There was nothing that anyone could do to rescue them, for to attempt yet another attack was clearly suicidal. The men were demoralized and beaten, unable to do anything more than hold for a while the ground they now occupied. With only one officer left, the company had established a position back here, with a few riflemen to the front, protecting the command post.

The sergeant told me all this bitterly, blaming the people up above for getting his company into such a mess. Since landing at Salerno, four months ago, he had seen nothing like the disaster of the preceding night. He mentioned the names of some of his friends who had probably been killed. Certainly no one had seen them since they started with their clumsy assault boats to make the crossing. These were men he had trained with for the past three years. He missed some of the officers, too; they had been well liked by their troops. But then we got talking about home, and I foolishly told him how proud everyone back in the States was of men like himself and those in his company. He laughed bitterly and said, "I'd change places with any of them this minute, if only they'd let me."

Not long after this he dropped off to sleep, and I was left alone, temporarily in command of a company which had been mauled and beaten, reduced to less than a quarter of its strength. I smoked in front of the fireplace, waiting for the phone to ring to tell me that something had happened to one of the platoons, or that the enemy had crossed the river, or that someone was killed. The machine-gun firing kept up, and so did the artillery fire. Three times during the night the awful Nebelwer-fers fired on our positions. But inside the house the sergeant slept pro-foundly, slumped awkwardly in a decrepit chair, and I watched and waited. The platoons made routine reports over the field phone every hour, and as it got on to three and four in the morning the firing died down. The room of our command post was extremely cold, and I missed the warm clothes which had been stolen in my barracks bag. I took an extra blanket, left behind by one of the medics, and threw it around my shoulders. I did not discover until morning that it had a large stain of dried blood on it.

Gradually, over the next day or two, I was able to piece together what had happened to the regiment in the two-night disaster at the river. We had plenty of time to talk, for our orders now were simply to stay where we were and hold. As I got to know some of the men they willingly told me everything they could remember. I often visited them in their hastily constructed dugouts. The dank smell of newly dug earth reminded me, incongruously enough, of the times when, as a boy, I used to dig tunnels and make underground huts. The men seemed eager to recount their experiences, as if they were made better by being talked about, as if their dead friends seemed less dead when they lived in their stories. There was, also, the horrible fascination with how this man or that stepped on a mine, or how badly another was wounded, and what finally happened to their lieutenant or their sergeant.

The entire attack seemed to have been conceived in haste and im-properly planned. Preliminary reconnaissance had been inadequate. The men had barely more than a day to prepare for the assault. All of the complicated operations of the division were rushed forward without enough time for anyone to do his job thoroughly. The engineers got mixed up about their orders and left some of the assault boats in the wrong places. The company and battalion assembly areas were in some cases so far back from the river that the men could not help attracting attention as they laboriously carried their heavy equipment and boats through open fields and sparsely wooded forests. Most of these marches had to be made when it was still daylight, with those eyes, up near or in the monastery, watching all the while. Moreover, the engineers did not have time to clear the mine fields properly. When the first mines went off they brought a concentration of enemy fire directly on the crossing sites.

The river was flooded, and the swift current swept away a number of the boats which finally did get down to the water. The boats themselves were clumsy, even for men trained to use them. The heavily laden infan-trymen, without any training, quite understandably capsized a number of them in the darkness. The places chosen by the higher commanders for the crossings were well covered by the enemy. The water was over nine feet deep, and it raced by between steep banks which were four to five feet high. In some places the river bent so sharply that German machine gunners on the opposite bank actually could fire into the rear of the Americans before they had crossed. So far as anyone could tell, the crossing sites had been chosen without any of the responsible officers of the division ever seeing the terrain. Battalion and even regimental commanders were told what they were to do in full detail without having any say whatsoever in how and where they were to do it. The German emplacements defending the river were exceedingly strong, having been carefully and deliberately prepared over a period of several months. Protected in front by mine fields and barbed wire, these emplacements were deeply dug. The best firing positions had been selected and defensive barrages had been planned. Sitting snugly under their heavily sandbagged roofs, the Germans had little to fear from our artillery fire. When the fire lifted to let our men go forward, the enemy soldiers had merely to resume their positions and shoot. At worst, they were only a little shaken by the bombardment. The Fifth Army had thrown the division headlong into one of the strongest defensive positions the Germans were ever to have in Italy.

Despite the shelling and the confusion, the 141st Infantry on the right almost did establish a real bridgehead on the first night. Despite the thickly strewn mine fields on the far side and despite the murderous machine-gun fire, the men of the 1st Battalion had pushed almost five hundred yards past the river; but there was very little cover in the meadow, and when daylight came the Germans had the relatively easy task of killing or capturing the men who were across. The infantry footbridges which might have brought reinforcements were blown clear out of the water by the enemy artillery fire, and the Bailey bridge for the tanks was destroyed before it ever got to the river. On the second night considerable parts of the 2nd and 3d Battalions were able to cross to help those left in the 1st Battalion, but then they too were cut off by heavy enemy fire, and with the coming of daylight it was impossible to reach them. The men on the far side put up a good fight for as long as they could, but in addition to their other troubles they were running out of ammunition. Then the Germans mounted a counterattack. Gradually the sound of American weapons firing on the far bank of the river died out altogether, and the regiments on our side finally gave it up, leaving their dead and wounded scattered along the approaches to the river where they fell, or soaking in the soggy ground across the stream. The Rapido did not run red with the blood of the slain, but the 141st Regiment alone lost nearly a thousand men in those two nights.

And then a strange thing happened. It was in the early afternoon on the fourth day after the Rapido attack had started. I had been ordered forward from I Company's positions to set up an observation post overlooking the river and the town of San Angelo. I carried field wire with me and a telephone, and I strung the wire out behind me as I went. After walking about three hundred yards I came to the ruins of a garden which had been plowed up by shell fire, and beyond it was a hedge. The garden stood at the top of a slight rise, on the far side of which the ground sloped down to the river. From the hedge I was able to see the whole battlefield. Everything was silent, and out in front of me nothing moved. Down by the river I could make out what I thought were the bodies of our fallen troops, and there were more in the field just across the river. The silence was unnatural, for there was no firing at all. Behind me was a lone house which was being used by our artillery observers. I had talked to them earlier in the morning, and they had advised me to get out of the house. I was glad to go, for the building was an obvious landmark for the Germans. Even as I left, an enemy shell came over and hit the upper window through which one of the men had been observing and blew off part of the roof. My observation post in the hedge at least had the virtue of not being a clear target.

Across the river and on the far side of the valley the town of San Angelo lay gray and shattered in the early afternoon light. Off to my right the great monastery loomed. Behind it I could see Mount Cairo, with snow up near its summit. No vehicles could be seen on the roads across the river. Everything seemed at rest. Not even a bird flew. Then, suddenly, down at the east end of the town I saw people coming out of the buildings. I looked at them carefully through my glasses and saw that they were Germans. They were coming toward us. I hastily connected the wires to my telephone, called back to company headquarters, and asked them to put me through to battalion. I hoped that I might be able to get some mortar fire on the enemy. Yet I could not be sure, with the demoralization of the battalion, that the mortars had even been set up. I knew that I was the only forward observer that the battalion had at that moment. When I did get the battalion commander he questioned me very carefully about what I saw, how many men, what they were doing, and exactly where they were. I told him as accurately as I could, for the number of people moving about down near the river was now growing. He said that he would try to get some mortars ready and ordered me to stay right where I was to keep a good eye on what happened. He then rang off. I waited for almost fifteen minutes, watching all the while and wondering why the artillery was not shooting. The men, who seemed very small in the distance, were walking slowly in the fields, now stopping and bending down, now getting up and going on. I was astonished to see how many of them were exposing themselves, and I could not understand why no one shot at them. Then my phone gave a short ring. It was the battalion commander, who wanted to know if there had been any shooting. I told him that there had not, but there were many Germans down on the riverbank. He said, "Don't, for God's sake, let anyone shoot. They've called a truce so that we can get our wounded out of there, and we just now learned about it."

In this case our own inefficiency worked to our advantage. Had I had guns ready I should have fired as soon as possible, without ever questioning why Germans should expose themselves in the early afternoon in full view of our observers. The severe defeat of the division in the past few days had broken down all kinds of routine operations, and the companies overlooking the battlefield had not even been notified that there was to be a truce. Fortunately the word came now, but only after the most dangerous moments of the truce were over. We learned later that the German officers had been extremely courteous to our medics, whom I could now see emerging from the shelters on our side of the river. The Germans had marked out the most seriously wounded men for ready care. Those men still alive were evacuated to our lines, being carried across the river on the few black rubber boats left from our attack. Not only were the wounded to be taken out, but the dead bodies, too, had to be collected and evacuated, and there were many of them. The truce lasted a full two hours.

The sun was nearly down before the truce drew to a close. I saw the last of our medics come up the field toward our positions carrying a white flag tied onto a tall stick. He and his fellows had made many trips to the river and back that afternoon. Dusk was beginning to fall and mists were forming in the valley below. The Germans disappeared back into their positions. Hopefully, the valley was now emptied of all the seriously wounded men. Perhaps most of the dead had also been collected. As for those who had been captured, were they passing through Rome this night on their way to PW camps in Germany? When the medic carrying his white flag disappeared over the crest of the hill, the truce was officially over, but no one started firing as night came on. The whole front remained silent until it was dark. Everyone there seemed reluctant to break the short peace, when Germans had directed Americans to spots where their comrades lay. A faint moon was now visible rising slowly in the southeast. The cold mists of the river began to move down the valley. Then, as if both sides had been told to start things up again, the big guns started shooting. Shells went whistling over my head to land on the German positions at San Angelo, and to the north I heard the sound of the Nebelwerfer sending up its six screaming bombs. Once more we found ourselves

> on a darkling plain
> Swept with confused alarms of struggle and flight,
> Where ignorant armies clash by night.

I could see nothing out here any longer, and I started back, tired and discouraged, to what was left of I Company. I still did not know whether I was to stay with them or be assigned to another one of the broken companies of the battalion.

On my return to the company command post I heard for the first time that the American VI Corps had landed behind the German lines at a place called Anzio on the preceding night. The landing had been co-ordinated with our Rapido attack as part of a larger plan to break the German resistance before Rome. Thousands of troops were pouring onto the beachhead and soon they would be threatening the German lines of communication and supply to the south. But our Rapido attack had been a failure and, as it turned out, so was the Anzio landing. I could not know this at the time, and the news of the landings lifted my spirits a little. Yet that night, as I sat in the command post listening to the German shells landing outside, I do remember thinking it strange that the enemy soldiers should indicate so clearly that they intended to stay right where they were on the Rapido-Cassino front. Indeed, we were soon to learn that, instead of helping us take Cassino that winter, the Anzio landings would prove a distinct hindrance to that operation.

JOHN M. BENNETT

Major Bennett commanded a bombardment squadron of B-17s in the U.S. Eighth Air Force, whose mission was the destruction of Germany from the air.

TO HIS FATHER

Dear Father:

There is an old saying which goes somewhat like this, "Cowards die many deaths, but a brave man dies but once." If this saying be true, then I am not only a coward myself, but I am fighting this war with a lot of other cowards. A story in the 8th Air Force tells about a group commander who read an over-zealous advertisement in a magazine which asked the question, "Who's afraid of the new Focke-Wulf?" This group commander cut out the advertisement, signed his name to it and pinned it on the bulletin board. After all of the pilots in the group had confessed their fear by signing, the page was mailed back to the U.S. advertiser. We are all afraid and only liars or fools fail to admit it. There are a variety of possible deaths which face a member of a bomber crew and each man is free to choose his own pet fear. A tire could blow out or an engine could fail on take-off. The oxygen system or electric heating system might fail at high altitude. There is the fear of explosion or midair collision while flying formation. In addition to these there is the ever present possibility of being shot down by enemy fighters or anti-aircraft fire. In dealing with the enemy, there is a certain feeling of helplessness about the bomber business which I find to be very distasteful. Imagine, for a minute, that you are required to carry two five-gallon cans of gasoline down a dark alley. These cans weigh over 30 pounds each so your hands are full and you can't run very fast. As you pass a certain corner in this alley, you know that a number of thugs are waiting to club you as you pass. However, there is a policeman patrolling this beat (your fighter escort) and if he happens to be at the dangerous corner at the time you arrive, then everything will be O.K., unless, of course, there are more thugs than the policeman can handle. Some of the thugs don't attack with clubs, but stand back (out of sight) and throw firecrackers at your cans of gasoline.

The bomber pilot can't fight back, but must just sit there and take it. I believe this explains why there is such a difference between the bomber and fighter boys. The men in this latter group can match their skill against the enemy. He carries a club of his own with which to fight back. I do not find the light-hearted devil-may-care spirit on the bomber station which has been so often described in stories about pilots in the last war. Our men go about their grim business with sober determination. When we are alerted for a mission, the bar closes early and everyone goes to bed. To be sure, at our monthly parties if there is no mission the next day, the boys get pretty drunk. I do not discourage this as I feel it gives them a much needed chance to blow off some steam.

When a new crew arrives on the station I try to have a talk with the men during the first 24 hours after arrival. One of the points stressed is that we are all afraid. I tell them that the worst part of a mission is just before the take-off. If they can "sweat it out" through this period, they will get through the rest all right. The flight surgeons are particularly helpful in spotting men who are showing signs of anxiety. If a crew goes through a particularly rough mission and is badly shot up, we try to send it to the "flak house" (rest home) for a week. In fact all crews are sent to the "flak house" for a rest at some time during their combat tour. Although I never find time to get to one of these rest homes myself, I am told that they are well run and very successful.

Winston Churchill's personal physician, Lord Moran, wrote a book about courage in combat. I like his definition of courage: "a moral quality . . . not a chance gift of nature like an aptitude for games. It is a cold choice between two alternatives, the fixed resolve not to quit; an act of renunciation which must be made not once but many times by the power of the will . . . Some men were able to see more clearly that there was no decent alternative to sticking it out, to see this not in a hot moment of impulse but steadily through many months of trial. They understood on what terms life was worthwhile."

As leader of a group I am constantly inspired by the soldiers under me. Their heroic acts are always a challenge. I frequently ask myself what the men expect of me. Living up to what I think they expect and deserve is a driving force which is ever present. Another point which I always remember is that I asked to be sent to England and the 8th Air Force. My good friend Colonel "Chuck" Clark had warned me against it before I left Washington. Chuck had told me that this was the toughest of all theatres. Since I requested combat duty with the 8th Air Force, I am determined to see it through.

Although the losses in the 100th Bomb Group are high, they are by no means the highest in the 8th Air Force. The Century Bombers losses are nearly always spectacular. We might run along for four months with very low losses and then one day we might lose half of the group. This news spreads about the air force and men get the idea that we always have heavy losses. What the 100th lacks in luck it makes up in courage. The Men of the Century have fighting hearts.

Love,
John

CHARLES A. LINDBERGH
1902–1974

Before Pearl Harbor, Lindbergh opposed the approaching war vigorously at rallies of America First, a conservative non-interventionist organization. After Pearl Harbor, he became a civilian aviation consultant with the United States Navy and flew many unauthorized and risky combat missions in the South Pacific, recalled in his Wartime Journals, *published in 1970.*

From WARTIME JOURNALS

Wednesday, May 24 [1944]

Arranged to go on a reconnaissance and strafing mission this afternoon along the northeast coast of New Ireland. To Intelligence hut for briefing at 1:00. There are to be four planes—no restrictions on targets. . . .

Four Corsairs abreast, racing over the water—I am the closest one to land. The trees pass, a streak of green; the beach a band of yellow on my left. Is it a post a mile ahead in the water, or a man standing? It moves toward shore. It is a man.

All Japanese or unfriendly natives on New Ireland—everything is a target—no restrictions—shoot whatever you see. I line up my sight. A mile takes ten seconds at our speed. At 1,000 yards my .50-calibers are deadly. I know just where they strike. I cannot miss.

Now he is out of the water, but he does not run. The beach is wide. He cannot make the cover of the trees. He is centered in my sight. My finger tightens on the trigger. A touch, and he will crumple on the coral sand.

But he disdains to run. He strides across the beach. Each step carries dignity and courage in its timing. He is not an ordinary man. The shot is too easy. His bearing, his stride, his dignity—there is something in them that has formed a bond between us. His life is worth more than the pressure of a trigger. I do not want to see him crumple on the beach. I release the trigger.

I ease back on the stick. He reaches the tree line, merges with the streak of green on my left. I am glad I have not killed him. I would never have forgotten him writhing on the beach. I will always remember his figure striding over the sand, the fearless dignity of his steps. I had his life balanced on a muscle's twitch. I gave it back to him, and thank God that I did so. I shall never know who he was—Jap or native. But I realize that the life of this unknown stranger—probably an enemy—is worth a thousand times more to me than his death. I should never quite have forgiven myself if I had shot him—naked, courageous, defenseless, yet so unmistakably man.

MARTHA GELLHORN
1908-

*American journalist and novelist Gellhorn served as a war correspondent
in Spain during the 1930s and in England, Italy, France, and Germany
during the 1940s, when she was the wife of Ernest Hemingway. She
later covered the war in Vietnam. During the invasion of Normandy, she
was on a hospital ship, as she recalls in* The Face of War *(1959).*

From THE FACE OF WAR

June 1944

There were four hundred and twenty-two bunks covered with new blankets, and a bright, clean, well-equipped operating room, never before
used. Great cans marked "Whole Blood" stood on the decks. Plasma
bottles and supplies of drugs and bales of bandages were stored in handy
places. Everything was ready and any moment the big empty hospital
ship would be leaving for France.

The ship itself was painfully white. The endless varied ships clotted in
this English invasion port were gray or camouflaged and they seemed to
have the right idea. We, on the other hand, were all fixed up like a sitting
pigeon. Our ship was snowy white with a green line running along the
sides below the deck rail, and with many bright new red crosses painted
on the hull and painted flat on the boat deck. We were to travel alone,
and there was not so much as a pistol on board in the way of armament,
and neither the English crew and ship's officers nor the American medical personnel had any notion of what happened to large conspicuous
white ships when they appeared at a war, though everyone knew the
Geneva agreement concerning such ships and everyone wistfully hoped
that the Germans would take the said agreement seriously.

There were six nurses aboard. They came from Texas and Michigan
and California and Wisconsin, and three weeks ago they were in the

U.S.A. completing their training for this overseas assignment. They had been prepared to work on a hospital train, which would mean caring for wounded in sensible, steady railway carriages that move slowly through the green English countryside. Instead of which they found themselves on a ship, and they were about to move across the dark, cold green water of the Channel. This sudden switch in plans was simply part of the day's work and each one, in her own way, got through the grim business of waiting for the unknown to start, as elegantly as she could. It was very elegant indeed, especially if you remembered that no one aboard had ever been on a hospital ship before, so the helpful voice of experience was lacking.

We had pulled out of the harbor in the night, but we crossed by daylight and the morning seemed longer than other mornings. The captain never left the bridge and, all alone and beautifully white, we made our way through a mine-swept lane in the Channel. The only piece of news we had, so far, was that the two hospital ships which preceded us struck mines on their way over, fortunately before they were loaded with wounded soldiers and without serious damage to the personnel aboard. Everyone silently hoped that three would be a lucky number; and we waited very hard; and there was nothing much to see except occasional ships passing at a distance.

Then we saw the coast of France and suddenly we were in the midst of the armada of the invasion. People will be writing about this sight for a hundred years and whoever saw it will never forget it. First it seemed incredible; there could not be so many ships in the world. Then it seemed incredible as a feat of planning; if there were so many ships, what genius it required to get them here, what amazing and unimaginable genius. After the first shock of wonder and admiration, one began to look around and see separate details. There were destroyers and battleships and transports, a floating city of huge vessels anchored before the green cliffs of Normandy. Occasionally you would see a gun flash or perhaps only hear a distant roar, as naval guns fired far over those hills. Small craft beetled around in a curiously jolly way. It looked like a lot of fun to race from shore to ships in snub-nosed boats beating up the spray. It was no fun at all, considering the mines and obstacles that remained in the water, the sunken tanks with only their radio antennae showing above water, the drowned bodies that still floated past. On an LCT near us washing was hung up on a line, and between the loud explosions of mines being detonated on the beach dance music could be heard coming from its radio. Barrage balloons, always looking like comic toy elephants, bounced in the high wind above the massed ships, and invisible planes droned behind the gray ceiling of cloud. Troops were unloading from big ships to heavy cement barges or to light craft, and on the shore, moving up four brown roads that scarred the hillside, our tanks clanked slowly and steadily forward.

Then we stopped noticing the invasion, the ships, the ominous beach, because the first wounded had arrived. An LCT drew alongside our ship, pitching in the waves; a soldier in a steel helmet shouted up to the crew at the aft rail, and a wooden box looking like a lidless coffin was lowered on a pulley, and with the greatest difficulty, bracing themselves against the movement of their boat, the men on the LCT laid a stretcher inside the box. The box was raised to our deck and out of it was lifted a man who was closer to being a boy than a man, dead white and seemingly dying. The first wounded man to be brought to that ship for safety and care was a German prisoner.

Everything happened at once. We had six water ambulances, light motor launches, which swung down from the ship's side and could be raised the same way when full of wounded. They carried six litter cases apiece or as many walking wounded as could be crowded into them. Now they were being lowered, with shouted orders: "That beach over there where they've got two red streamers up." "Just this side of Easy Red." We lay at anchor halfway between those now famous and unhealthy beaches, Easy Red and Dog Red. "Take her in slow." "Those double round things that look like flat spools are mines." "You won't clear any submerged tanks, so look sharp." "Ready?" "Lower her!"

The captain came down from the bridge to watch this. He was feeling cheerful, and he now remarked, "I got us in all right but God knows how we'll ever get out." He gestured toward the ships that were as thick around us as cars in a parking lot. "Worry about that some other time."

The stretcher-bearers, who were part of the American medical personnel, started on their long back-breaking job. By the end of that trip their hands were padded with blisters and they were practically hospital cases themselves. For the wounded had to be carried from the shore into our own water ambulances or into other craft, raised over the side, and then transported down the winding stairs of this converted pleasure ship to the wards. The ship's crew became volunteer stretcher-bearers instantly. Wounded were pouring in now, hauled up in the lidless coffin or swung aboard in the motor ambulances; and finally an LST tied alongside and made itself into a sort of landing jetty, higher than the light craft that ran the wounded to us, but not as high as our deck. So the wounded were lifted by men standing on the LST, who raised the stretchers high above their heads and handed them up to men on our deck, who caught hold of the stretcher handles. It was a fast, terrifying bucket-brigade system, but it worked.

Belowstairs all partitions had been torn out and for three decks the inside of the ship was a vast ward with double tiers of bunks. The routine inside the ship ran marvelously, though four doctors, six nurses and about fourteen medical orderlies were very few people to care for four hundred wounded men. From two o'clock one afternoon until the ship docked in England again the next evening at seven, none of the medical personnel stopped work. And besides plasma and blood transfusions, re-dressing of wounds, examinations, administering of sedative or opiates or oxygen and all the rest, operations were performed all night long. Only one soldier died on that ship and he had come aboard as a hopeless case.

It will be hard to tell you of the wounded, there were so many of them. There was no time to talk; there was too much else to do. They had to be fed, as most of them had not eaten for two days; shoes and clothing had to be cut off; they wanted water; the nurses and orderlies, working like demons, had to be found and called quickly to a bunk where a man suddenly and desperately needed attention; plasma bottles must be watched; cigarettes had to be lighted and held for those who could not use their hands; it seemed to take hours to pour hot coffee, via the spout of a teapot, into a mouth that just showed through bandages.

But the wounded talked among themselves and as time went on we got to know them, by their faces and their wounds, not their names. They were a magnificent enduring bunch of men. Men smiled who were in such pain that all they really can have wanted to do was turn their heads away and cry, and men made jokes when they needed their strength just to survive. And all of them looked after each other, saying, "Give that boy a drink of water," or "Miss, see that Ranger over there, he's in bad shape, could you go to him?" All through the ship men were asking after other men by name, anxiously, wondering if they were on board and how they were doing.

On A deck in a bunk by the wall lay a very young lieutenant. He had a bad chest wound and his face was white and he lay too still. Suddenly he raised himself on his elbow and looked straight ahead of him, as if he did not know where he was. His eyes were full of horror and he did not speak. Later he spoke. He had been wounded the first day, had lain out in a field and then crawled back to our lines, sniped at by the Germans. He realized now that a German, badly wounded also in the chest, shoulder and legs, lay in the bunk behind him. The gentle-faced boy said very softly, because it was hard to speak, "I'd kill him if I could move." After that he did not speak for a long time; he was given oxygen and later operated on, so that he could breathe.

The man behind him was a nineteen-year-old Austrian. He had fought for a year in Russia and half a year in France; he had been home for six days during this time. I thought he would die when he first came on board, but he got better. In the early morning hours he asked whether

wounded prisoners were exchanged, would he ever get home again? I
told him that I did not know about these arrangements but that he had
nothing to fear, as he could see. The Austrian said, "Yes, yes." Then he
said, "So many wounded men, all wounded, all want to get home. Why
have we ever fought each other?" Perhaps because he came from a
gentler race his eyes were full of tears. He was the only wounded German
prisoner on board who showed any normal human reaction to this disaster.

An American soldier on that same deck had a head wound so horrible
that he was not moved. Nothing could be done for him and anything,
any touch, would have made him worse. The next morning he was
drinking coffee. His eyes looked very dark and strange, as if he had been
a long way away, so far away that he almost could not get back. His face
was set in lines of weariness and pain, but when asked how he felt, he
said he was okay. He was never known to say anything more; he asked for
nothing and made no complaint, and perhaps he will live too.

On the next deck there were many odd and wonderful men who were
less badly wounded and talked more. It was all professional talk: where
they had landed, at what time, what opposition they had met, how they
had got out, when they were wounded, how that happened. They spoke
of the snipers, and there was endless talk about the women snipers, none
of the talk very clear but everyone believing it. There were no French
officers with these men, who could have interpreted, and the Americans
never knew what the villagers were saying. Two men who thought they
were being volubly invited into an old woman's house to eat dinner were
actually being warned of snipers in the attic; they somehow caught on to
this fact in time. They were all baffled by the French and surprised by
how much food there was in Normandy, forgetting that Normandy is
one of the great food-producing areas of France. They thought the girls
in the villages were amazingly well dressed. Everything was confused and
astounding: first there were the deadly bleak beaches and then the villages where they were greeted with flowers and cookies and often snipers
and booby traps.

A French boy of seventeen lay in one of the bunks; he had been
wounded in the back by a shell fragment. He lived and worked on his
father's land, but he said the Germans had burned their house as they
left. Two of the American boys in bunks alongside were worried about
him. They were afraid he'd be scared, a civilian kid all alone and in pain
and not knowing any English and going to a strange country. They
ignored their respective smashed knee and smashed shoulder and worried about the French kid. The French boy was very much a man and
very tight-lipped, and he made no complaints and kept his anxiety inside
himself though it showed in his eyes. His family was still there in the

battle zone and he did not know what had happened to them or how he would ever get back. The American soldiers said, "You tell that kid he's a better soldier than that Heinie in the bunk next to him."

We did not like this Heinie who was eighteen years old and the most demanding Master Race aboard. Finally there was a crisp little scene when he told the orderly to move him as he was uncomfortable and the orderly said no, he would bleed if moved, and when I explained the German said angrily, "How long, then, am I to lie here in pain in this miserable position?" I asked the orderly what to say and the orderly answered, "Tell him there are a lot of fine boys on this ship lying in worse pain in worse positions." The American soldiers in the bunks around said, "What a Heinie," wearily, and then they began wondering how they'd find their old units again and how soon they'd get mail.

When night came, the water ambulances were still churning in to the beach looking for wounded. Someone on an LCT had shouted out that there were maybe a hundred scattered along there somewhere. It was essential to try to get them aboard before the nightly air raid and before the dangerous dark cold could eat into their hurt bodies. Going in to shore, unable to see, and not knowing this tricky strip of water, was slow work. Two of the launch crew, armed with boat hooks, hung over the side of the boat and stared at the black water, looking for obstacles, sunken vehicles, mines, and kept the hooks ready to push us off the sand as we came closer in. For the tides were a nasty business too, and part of the time wounded had to be ferried out to the water ambulances on men's shoulders, and part of the time the water ambulances simply grounded and stuck on the beach together with other craft, stranded by the fast-moving sea.

We finally got onto a cement troop barge near the beach called Easy Red. The water ambulance could not come inshore near enough to be of any use at this point, so it left us to look for a likelier anchorage farther down. We waded ashore in water to our waists, having agreed that we would assemble the wounded from this area on board a beached LST and wait until the tide allowed the water ambulance to come back and call for us. It was almost dark by now and there was a terrible feeling of working against time.

Everyone was violently busy on that crowded dangerous shore. The pebbles were the size of melons and we stumbled up a road that a huge road shovel was scooping out. We walked with the utmost care between the narrowly placed white tape lines that marked the mine-cleared path, and headed for a tent marked with a Red Cross just behind the beach. Ducks and tanks and trucks were moving down this narrow rocky road and one stepped just a little out of their way, but not beyond the tapes. The dust that rose in the gray night light seemed like the fog of war itself. Then we got off on the grass and it was perhaps the most surprising of all the day's surprises to smell the sweet smell of summer grass, a smell of cattle and peace and the sun that had warmed the earth some other time when summer was real.

Inside the Red Cross tent two tired unshaven dirty polite young men said that the trucks were coming in here with the wounded and where did we want to have them unloaded? We explained the problem of the tides and said the best thing was to run the trucks down to that LST there and carry the wounded aboard, under the canvas roof covering, and we would get them off as soon as anything floated. At this point a truck jolted up and the driver shouted out a question and was told to back and turn. He did not need to be told to do this carefully and not get off the mine-cleared area. The Red Cross men said they didn't know whether wounded would be coming in all night or not—it was pretty tough to transport them by road in the dark; anyway they'd send everything down to our agreed meeting place and everyone said, well good luck fella, and we left. No one wasted time talking around there. You had a feeling of fierce and driven activity, with the night only being harder to work in than the day.

We returned to our small unattractive stretch of the beach and directed the unloading of this truck. The tide was coming in and there was a narrow strip of water between the landing ramp of the LST and the shore. The wounded were carried carefully and laid on the deck inside the great whale's-mouth cavern of the LST. After that there was a pause, with nothing to do. Some American soldiers came up and began to talk. This had been an ugly piece of beach from the beginning and they were still here, living in foxholes and supervising the unloading of supplies. They spoke of snipers in the hills a hundred yards or so behind the beach, and no one lighted a cigarette. They spoke of not having slept at all, but they seemed pleased by the discovery that you could go without sleep and food and still function all right. Everyone agreed that the beach was a stinker and it would be a great pleasure to get the hell out of here sometime. Then there was the usual inevitable comic American conversation: "Where're you from?" This always fascinates me; there is no moment when an American does not have time to look for someone who knows his home town. We talked about Pittsburgh and Rosemont Pa. and Chicago and Cheyenne, not saying much except that they were sure swell places and a damn sight better than this beach. One of the soldiers remarked that they had a nice little foxhole about fifty yards inland and we were very welcome there when the air raid started if we didn't mind eating sand, which was unavoidable in their nice little foxhole.

A stretcher-bearer from the hospital ship thanked them for their kind invitation and said that on the other hand we had guests aboard the LST and we would have to stay home this evening. I wish I had ever known his name because I would like to write it down here. He was one of the best and jolliest boys I've met any place, any time. He joked no matter what happened, and toward the end of that night we really began to enjoy ourselves. There is a point where you feel yourself so small and helpless in such an enormous insane nightmare of a world, that you cease to give a hoot about anything and you renounce care and start laughing.

He went off to search for the water ambulances and returned to say there wasn't a sign of them, which meant they couldn't get inshore yet and we'd just have to wait and hope they could find this spot when it was black night. If they never found this place the LST would float later, and the British captain said he would run our wounded out to the hospital ship, though it would not be for hours. Suddenly our flak started going up at the far end of the beach and it was beautiful, twinkling as it burst in the sky, and the tracers were as lovely as they always are—and no one took pleasure from the beauty of the scene. "We've had it now," said the stretcher-bearer. "There isn't any place we can put those wounded." I asked one of the soldiers, just for interest's sake, what they did in case of air raids and he said, well, you could go to a foxhole if you had time, but on the other hand there wasn't really much to do. So we stood and watched and there was altogether too much flak for comfort. We could not hear the planes nor hear any bomb explosions but as everyone knows flak is a bad thing to have fall on your head.

The soldiers now drifted off on their own business and we boarded the LST to keep the wounded company. It seemed a specially grim note to be wounded in action and then have to lie helpless under a strip of canvas while any amount of steel fragments, to say nothing of bombs, could drop on you and complete the job. The stretcher-bearer and I said to each other gloomily that as an air-raid shelter far better things than the hold of an LST had been devised, and we went inside, not liking any of it and feeling miserably worried about our wounded.

The wounded looked pretty bad and lay very still; and in the light of one bare bulb, which hung from a girder, we could not see them well. Then one of them began to moan and he said something. He was evidently conscious enough to notice this ghastly racket that was going on above us. The Oerlikons of our LST now opened fire and the noise inside the steel hold was as if your own eardrums were being drilled with a rivet. The wounded man called out again and I realized that he was speaking German. We checked up then and found that we had an LST full of wounded Germans and the stretcher-bearer said, "Well, that is just dandy, by golly, if that isn't the payoff." Then he said, "If anything hits this ship, dammit, they deserve it."

The ack-ack lifted a bit and the stretcher-bearer climbed to the upper deck, like Sister Anne on the tower, to see where in God's name those water ambulances were. I clambered like a very awkward monkey up a ladder to the galley to get some coffee and so missed the spectacle of two German planes falling like fiery comets from the sky. They hit the beach to the right and left of us and burned in huge bonfires which lighted up the shore. The beach, in this light, looked empty of human life, cluttered with dark square shapes of tanks and trucks and jeeps and ammunition boxes and all the motley equipment of war. It looked like a vast uncanny black-and-red flaring salvage dump, whereas once upon a time people actually went swimming here for pleasure.

Our LST crew was delighted because they believed they had brought down one of the German planes and everyone felt cheerful about the success of the ack-ack. A soldier shouted from shore that we had shot down four planes in all and it was nice work, by God. The wounded were silent and those few who had their eyes open had very frightened eyes. They seemed to be listening with their eyes, and fearing what they would hear.

The night, like the morning, went on longer than other nights. Our water ambulances found us, and there was a lot of good incomprehensible Cockney talk among the boatmen while the wounded were loaded from the now floating LST to the small, bucking launch. We set out, happy because we were off the beach and because the wounded would be taken where they belonged. The trip across that obstacle-studded piece of water was a chatty affair, due to the boat crew. "Crikey, mate, wot yer trying ter do, ram a destroyer?" And "By God, man, keep an eye in yer head for God's sake that's a tank radio pole." To which another answered, "Expect me to see a bloody piece of grass in this dark?" So, full of conversation, we zigzagged back to the hospital ship and were at last swung aboard.

The raid had been hard on the wounded in the wards of the ship, because of the terrible helplessness of being unable to move. The ship seemed to lie directly under a cone of ack-ack fire, and perhaps it would have been easier if the wounded had heard the German planes, so that, at least through their ears, they would know what was happening. The American medical personnel, most of whom had never been in an air raid, tranquilly continued their work, asked no questions, showed no sign even of interest in this uproar, and handed out confidence as if it were a solid thing like bread.

If anyone had come fresh to that ship in the night, someone unwounded, not attached to the ship, he would have been appalled. It began to look entirely Black-Hole-of-Calcutta, because it was airless and ill lit. Piles of bloody clothing had been cut off and dumped out of the way in corners; coffee cups and cigarette stubs littered the decks; plasma bottles hung from cords, and all the fearful surgical apparatus for holding broken bones made shadows on the walls. There were wounded who groaned in their sleep or called out and there was the soft steady hum of conversation among the wounded who could not sleep. That is the way it would have looked to anyone seeing it fresh—a ship carrying a load of pain, with everyone waiting for daylight, everyone hoping for the anchor to be raised, everyone longing for England. It was that but it was something else too; it was a safe ship no matter what happened to it. We were together and we counted on each other. We knew that from the British captain to the pink-cheeked little London mess boy every one of the ship's company did his job tirelessly and well. The wounded knew that the doctors and nurses and orderlies belonged to them utterly and would not fail them. And all of us knew that our own wounded were good men and that with their amazing help, their selflessness and self-control, we would get through all right.

The wounded looked much better in the morning. The human machine is the most delicate and rare of all, and it is obviously built to survive, if given half a chance. The ship moved steadily across the Channel and we could feel England coming nearer. Then the coast came into sight and the green of England looked quite different from the way it had looked only two days ago; it looked cooler and clearer and wonderfully safe. The beaches along this coast were only lovely yellow sand. The air of England flowed down through the wards and the wounded seemed to feel it. The sound of their voices brightened and sharpened, and they began making dates with each other for when they would be on convalescent leave in London.

We saw again the great armada of the invasion, waiting or moving out toward France. This vast directed strength seemed more like an act of nature than a thing men alone could manage. The captain shouted down from the bridge, "Look at it! By God, just look at it!"

American ambulance companies were waiting on the pier, the same efficient swift colored troops I had seen working on the piers and landing ramps before we left. On the quay there were conferences of important shore personages and our captain and the chief medical officer; and a few of us, old-timers by now, leaned over the rail and joked about being back in the paper-work department again. Everyone felt happy and you could see it in all their faces. The head nurse, smiling though gray with weariness, said, "We'll do it better next time."

As the first wounded were carried from the ship the chief medical officer, watching them, said, "Made it." That was the great thing. Now they would restock their supplies, clean the ship, cover the beds with fresh blankets, sleep whatever hours they could, and then they would go back to France. But this first trip was done; this much was to the good; they had made it.

WILLIAM PRESTON

Corporal Preston was a tanker attached to the First Infantry Division,
which landed on Omaha Beach on June 6, 1944.

To His Father

France
June 21, 1944

Dear Dad:

This being fifteen days after the fateful June 6th, I am free to discuss what happened to me of a military nature on "D" Day. Here goes.

You remember from my last letter I said we were the assault wave which was the first to touch down on the beach. Then followed a day I shall never forget.

As has already been mentioned in the papers the landings were made at low tide. There were three rows of obstacles to get through. These were above the low water mark, but under water at high tide. Therefore we had to get through them before high tide. This we were able to do with the engineers' help, and our own guns.

In front of us were cliffs, and to the right there were two exits from our beach through the cliffs to higher ground. Both of these were mined and defended heavily. In the cliffs were a whole series of underground fortifications, mostly interconnecting machine gun nests. These played hell with our infantry and engineers as they came through the obstacles. Some never got through, some fell and were claimed by a rising tide, but others slowly worked their way past the high water mark to the base of the cliffs. It took real guts for these boys to advance. Ernie Pyle in his column said it was a miracle a foothold was ever established. Perhaps he's right. I know at times I thought we had had it. There were some

88's in open emplacements which could have ruined us, but shortly after they started to fire a shot from a destroyer put the one near us out of action.

I cannot say enough for the Navy, for the way they brought us in, for the fire power they brought to bear on the beach, for the coordination between us. Whenever any of us fired a burst of tracer at a target, the destroyers, standing in so close they were almost ashore, fired a shot immediately after us each time hitting what we were firing at on the nose the first shot. It was amazing and plenty encouraging to have those big shells pour in there. It might have been a different story without the Navy boys. Meanwhile we were sweating it out on the beach unable to move off of it because the engineers could not clear the way out. All this time not a single German plane in the sky. Nor did we see many of ours, I guess they were further inland. I expected a counter attack all the time we sat there like ducks unable to move forward or backward. We knew something wasn't going right. We were never supposed to be on the beach so long, yet I never considered the fact that we could fail, that we wouldn't soon get off that terrible strip of sand. Time flew by, before I realized it the tide had risen, fallen, and risen again. Night was approaching.

The infantry said they were thankful we were there, the feeling is mutual. Without them we would still be on the beach.

The Germans adopted an old Japanese custom. There were snipers everywhere. The country is very wooded, the foliage extremely thick. The result, perfect concealment for snipers. They also hid out in buildings as well as tying themselves in the trees and took an inevitable toll before they were sought out and destroyed.

Some of the women civilians tried their hand at the same trick. Apparently having acquired a slight Nazi veneer from their associates of four years. They would wave and flash the "V" sign, then take a shot at your back. They didn't last long. I spoke to some French people who live on the coast; they said the hun had been at his station for three days before we landed. During which time they were confined to their homes. This may, or may not be true. Whether they were expecting us momentarily is anyone's guess. There was certainly plenty of opposition. Farther in a woman told me the boche was terrified and sick of the war in that town, that the soldiers had broken their rifles and run away before we entered the town, that one of the officers had taken a walk to never show up again, that others changed into civilian clothes to disappear. That garrison's age was from 20 to 27, most of the soldiers being forced into service from Poland, Russia and there were even Mongols (very few). Definitely not the fanatical young Nazis we'll probably meet later on.

"D" Day evening we bivouacked about a mile in, still not feeling quite secure, as there were not visible an over abundance of troops. There was no counter attack, no bombing, no artillery fire that night on our positions. Others had seen to that I guess, a few Nazi planes came over but focused their attention on the shipping. Anti-aircraft barrage was magnificent to watch.

So ended "D" Day. I shall never forget that beach, it was some way to start combat, but I am satisfied we did a good job.

I need catsup and mayonnaise, if it is possible to get and send them, for we get our own meals with vegetables added from French gardens, and these brighten it up no end. Those small boxes from Altman's have begun to arrive, they really hit the spot, please order another set after this runs out.

Also would you send me the Life magazine with the story of the Invasion in it and subsequent issues, if they have good stories and pictures of the show. My love to all, please write soon.

Much love
Bill

To Phyll

France
July 1, 1944

Dearest Phyll:

That was a truly wonderful letter, yours of the 11th and the 12th, one which I read and reread. One really lives for letters from home out here. It's hard to express but mail gives me just that much greater desire to come back from each succeeding skirmish with the enemy, and it is never ending because you are always expecting more. Before you go you think to yourself you must come back this time because there are two or three letters you still haven't received. So you come back, receive and answer them and the whole thing goes on again.

You know I heard so much about the changes war makes in people, that they return so different after combat. "D" Day then should certainly have changed me, because I saw as much then to make me cynical, bitter, irreligious as I may ever see at one time, and yet today I find that I am just about the same person I was before it all, with the same philosophy, the same hopes, sadder that what happened did have to happen, but wiser because of it. To me now, dead men, especially enemy dead bring no emotion whatsoever. I was a bit shaken at first, but I soon became hardened to seeing the worst of casualties with no feeling because in the beginning I had a curiosity which made me see everything, so now I am not affected. When I see an American soldier I get angry and sad that here he should have died so unnatural a death. I wonder about him, what were his plans never to be fulfilled, what fate brought him to that spot at that moment, who was waiting for him at home? Yet there is not too much time for such idle reflection.

Horrible as this was, has been, I think we both have benefited in some small way from it. I don't think there is much we won't be able to adjust to in the future. I think we've learned how important it is to be open minded, to ban silly prejudices which contribute so greatly to warping your viewpoint on life, how important not to criticize until you know the whole story, which makes criticism difficult because it is so seldom we ever do know the whole story. I believe we've learned to appreciate things we might well before have taken for granted; that the present is important to a degree that we should not miss one chance to make it a happy present yet not to a degree that we live for it AND IT ALONE. We have found things out that I for one might only have learned after long years, and therefore, life cannot but be richer and fuller for our whole family.

The "Battle of the Hedgerows" continues as near to jungle fighting as anything I can think of. The small open fields surrounded by thick bushes and trees on all sides are only traps for the unwary, and as there are hundreds of these small meadows, so there are hundreds of traps to be sprung before the enemy is beaten. It makes advancing agonizingly slow, nor do I ever feel more like a goldfish in his bowl than when we advance across these fields from hedgerow to hedgerow. There is absolutely nothing in the books which covers this type of fighting. Every advantage of terrain lies with the enemy.

Sorry this letter isn't up to par. I think this rainy weather did it. My best to Tal. Love to the family,

Much love,
Bill

RUDOLF HÖSS
1900–1947

Höss became a Nazi in 1922 instead of the Catholic priest his family wanted him to be. In 1933 he joined the SS, and in 1940 he became the commandant of the concentration camp at Auschwitz, Poland, devoted to the extermination by gas of Jews, Poles, gypsies, and other "subhumans." Condemned after the war by a Polish court, he was hanged at Auschwitz, but to the end he remained proud of his military loyalty in conscientiously carrying out the orders of his superiors. He was persuaded to write an account of his experiences, published in 1951 as Commandant of Auschwitz.

From COMMANDANT OF AUSCHWITZ

By the will of the Reichsführer SS, Auschwitz became the greatest human extermination centre of all time.

When in the summer of 1941 he himself gave me the order to prepare installations at Auschwitz where mass exterminations could take place, and personally to carry out these exterminations, I did not have the slightest idea of their scale or consequences. It was certainly an extraordinary and monstrous order. Nevertheless the reasons behind the extermination programme seemed to me right. I did not reflect on it at the time: I had been given an order, and I had to carry it out. Whether this mass extermination of the Jews was necessary or not was something on which I could not allow myself to form an opinion, for I lacked the necessary breadth of view.

If the Führer had himself given the order for the "final solution of the Jewish question," then, for a veteran National-Socialist and even more so for an SS officer, there could be no question of considering its merits. "The Führer commands, we follow" was never a mere phrase or slogan. It was meant in bitter earnest.

Since my arrest it has been said to me repeatedly that I could have disobeyed this order, and that I might even have assassinated Himmler. I do not believe that of all the thousands of SS officers there could have been found a single one capable of such a thought. It was completely impossible. Certainly many SS officers grumbled and complained about some of the harsh orders that came from the Reichsführer SS, but they nevertheless always carried them out.

Many orders of the Reichsführer SS deeply offended a great number of his SS officers, but I am perfectly certain that not a single one of them would have dared to raise a hand against him, or would have even contemplated doing so in his most secret thoughts. As Reichsführer SS, his person was inviolable. His basic orders, issued in the name of the Führer, were sacred. They brooked no consideration, no argument, no interpretation. They were carried out ruthlessly and regardless of consequences, even though these might well mean the death of the officer concerned, as happened to not a few SS officers during the war.

It was not for nothing that during training the self-sacrifice of the Japanese for their country and their emperor, who was also their god, was held up as a shining example to the SS.

SS training was not comparable to a university course which can have as little lasting effect on the students as water on a duck's back. It was on the contrary something that was deeply engrained, and the Reichsführer SS knew very well what he could demand of his men.

But outsiders simply cannot understand that there was not a single SS officer who would disobey an order from the Reichsführer SS, far less consider getting rid of him because of the gruesomely hard nature of one such order.

What the Führer, or in our case his second-in-command, the Reichsführer SS, ordered was always right.

Democratic England also has a basic national concept: "My country, right or wrong!" and this is adhered to by every nationally-conscious Englishman.

Before the mass extermination of the Jews began, the Russian *politruks* and political commissars were liquidated in almost all the concentration camps during 1941 and 1942.

In accordance with a secret order issued by Hitler, these Russian *politruks* and political commissars were combed out of all the prisoner-of-war camps by special detachments from the Gestapo. When identified, they were transferred to the nearest concentration camp for liquidation. It was made known that these measures were taken because the Russians had been killing all German soldiers who were party members or belonged to special sections of the NSDAP, especially members of the SS, and also because the political officials of the Red Army had been ordered, if taken prisoner, to create every kind of disturbance in the prisoner-of-war camps and their places of employment and to carry out sabotage wherever possible.

The political officials of the Red Army thus identified were brought to Auschwitz for liquidation. The first, smaller transports of them were executed by firing squads.

While I was away on duty, my deputy, Fritzsch, the commander of the protective custody camp, first tried gas for these killings. It was a preparation of prussic acid, called Cyclon B, which was used in the camp as an insecticide and of which there was always a stock on hand. On my return, Fritzsch reported this to me, and the gas was used again for the next transport.

The gassing was carried out in the detention cells of Block II. Protected by a gas-mask, I watched the killing myself. In the crowded cells death came instantaneously the moment the Cyclon B was thrown in. A short, almost smothered cry, and it was all over. During this first experience of gassing people, I did not fully realise what was happening, perhaps because I was too impressed by the whole procedure. I have a clearer recollection of the gassing of nine hundred Russians which took place shortly afterwards in the old crematorium, since the use of Block II for this purpose caused too much trouble. While the transport was detraining, holes were pierced in the earth and concrete ceiling of the mortuary. The Russians were ordered to undress in an anteroom; they then quietly entered the mortuary, for they had been told they were to be deloused. The whole transport exactly filled the mortuary to capacity. The doors were then sealed and the gas shaken down through the holes in the roof. I do not know how long this killing took. For a little while a humming sound could be heard. When the powder was thrown in, there were cries of "Gas!," then a great bellowing, and the trapped prisoners hurled themselves against both the doors. But the doors held. They were opened several hours later, so that the place might be aired. It was then that I saw, for the first time, gassed bodies in the mass.

It made me feel uncomfortable and I shuddered, although I had imagined that death by gassing would be worse than it was. I had always thought that the victims would experience a terrible choking sensation. But the bodies, without exception, showed no signs of convulsion. The doctors explained to me that the prussic acid had a paralysing effect on the lungs, but its action was so quick and strong that death came before the convulsions could set in, and in this its effects differed from those produced by carbon monoxide or by a general oxygen deficiency.

The killing of these Russian prisoners-of-war did not cause me much concern at the time. The order had been given, and I had to carry it out. I must even admit that this gassing set my mind at rest, for the mass extermination of the Jews was to start soon and at that time neither

Eichmann nor I was certain how these mass killings were to be carried out. It would be by gas, but we did not know which gas or how it was to be used. Now we had the gas, and we had established a procedure. I always shuddered at the prospect of carrying out exterminations by shooting, when I thought of the vast numbers concerned, and of the women and children. The shooting of hostages, and the group executions ordered by the Reichsführer SS or by the Reich Security Head Office had been enough for me. I was therefore relieved to think that we were to be spared all these blood-baths, and that the victims too would be spared suffering until their last moment came. It was precisely this which had caused me the greatest concern when I had heard Eichmann's description of Jews being mown down by the Special Squads armed with machine-guns and machine-pistols. Many gruesome scenes are said to have taken place, people running away after being shot, the finishing off of the wounded and particularly of the women and children. Many members of the *Einsatzkommandos,* unable to endure wading through blood any longer, had committed suicide. Some had even gone mad. Most of the members of these *Kommandos* had to rely on alcohol when carrying out their horrible work. According to Höfle's description, the men employed at Globocnik's extermination centres consumed amazing quantities of alcohol.

In the spring of 1942 the first transports of Jews, all earmarked for extermination, arrived from Upper Silesia.

They were taken from the detraining platform to the "Cottage"—to Bunker I—across the meadows where later Building Site II was located. The transport was conducted by Aumeier and Palitzsch and some of the block leaders. They talked with the Jews about general topics, enquiring concerning their qualifications and trades, with a view to misleading them. On arrival at the "Cottage," they were told to undress. At first they went calmly into the rooms where they were supposed to be disinfected. But some of them showed signs of alarm, and spoke of death by suffocation and of annihilation. A sort of panic set in at once. Immediately all the Jews still outside were pushed into the chambers, and the doors were screwed shut. With subsequent transports the difficult individuals were picked out early on and most carefully supervised. At the first signs of unrest, those responsible were unobtrusively led behind the building and killed with a small-calibre gun, that was inaudible to the others. The presence and calm behavior of the Special Detachment served to reassure those who were worried or who suspected what was about to happen. A further calming effect was obtained by members of the Special Detachment accompanying them into the rooms and remaining with them until the last moment, while an SS-man also stood in the doorway until the end.

It was most important that the whole business of arriving and undressing should take place in an atmosphere of the greatest possible calm. People reluctant to take off their clothes had to be helped by those of their companions who had already undressed, or by men of the Special Detachment. The refractory ones were calmed down and encouraged to undress. The prisoners of the Special Detachment also saw to it that the process of undressing was carried out quickly, so that the victims would have little time to wonder what was happening.

The eager help given by the Special Detachment in encouraging them to undress and in conducting them into the gas-chambers was most remarkable. I have never known, nor heard, of any of its members giving these people who were about to be gassed the slightest hint of what lay ahead of them. On the contrary, they did everything in their power to deceive them and particularly to pacify the suspicious ones. Though they might refuse to believe the SS-men, they had complete faith in these members of their own race, and to reassure them and keep them calm the Special Detachments therefore always consisted of Jews who themselves came from the same districts as did the people on whom a particular action was to be carried out.

They would talk about life in the camp, and most of them asked for news of friends or relations who had arrived in earlier transports. It was interesting to hear the lies that the Special Detachment told them with such conviction, and to see the emphatic gestures with which they underlined them.

Many of the women hid their babies among the piles of clothing. The men of the Special Detachment were particularly on the look-out for this, and would speak words of encouragement to the woman until they had persuaded her to take the child with her. The women believed that the disinfectant might be bad for their smaller children, hence their efforts to conceal them.

The smaller children usually cried because of the strangeness of being undressed in this fashion, but when their mothers or members of the Special Detachment comforted them, they became calm and entered the gas chambers, playing or joking with one another and carrying their toys.

I noticed that women who either guessed or knew what awaited them nevertheless found the courage to joke with the children to encourage them, despite the mortal terror visible in their own eyes.

One woman approached me as she walked past and, pointing to her four children who were manfully helping the smallest ones over the rough ground, whispered:

"How can you bring yourself to kill such beautiful, darling children? Have you no heart at all?"

One old man, as he passed by me, hissed:

"Germany will pay a heavy penance for this mass murder of the Jews." His eyes glowed with hatred as he said this. Nevertheless he walked calmly into the gas-chamber, without worrying about the others.

One young woman caught my attention particularly as she ran busily hither and thither, helping the smallest children and the old women to undress. During the selection she had had two small children with her, and her agitated behaviour and appearance had brought her to my notice at once. She did not look in the least like a Jewess. Now her children were no longer with her. She waited until the end, helping the women who were not undressed and who had several children with them, encouraging them and calming the children. She went with the very last ones into the gas-chamber. Standing in the doorway, she said:

"I knew all the time that we were being brought to Auschwitz to be gassed. When the selection took place I avoided being put with the able-bodied ones, as I wished to look after the children. I wanted to go through it all, fully conscious of what was happening. I hope that it will be quick. Goodbye!"

From time to time women would suddenly give the most terrible shrieks while undressing, or tear their hair, or scream like maniacs. These were immediately led away behind the building and shot in the back of the neck with a small-calibre weapon.

It sometimes happened that, as the men of the Special Detachment left the gas-chamber, the women would suddenly realise what was happening, and would call down every imaginable curse upon our heads.

I remember, too, a woman who tried to throw her children out of the gas-chamber, just as the door was closing. Weeping she called out: "At least let my precious children live."

There were many such shattering scenes, which affected all who witnessed them.

During the spring of 1942 hundreds of vigorous men and women walked all unsuspecting to their death in the gas-chambers, under the blossom-laden fruit trees of the "Cottage" orchard. This picture of death in the midst of life remains with me to this day.

The process of selection, which took place on the unloading platforms, was in itself rich in incident.

The breaking up of families, and the separation of the men from the women and children, caused much agitation and spread anxiety throughout the whole transport. This was increased by the further separation from the others of those capable of work. Families wished at all costs to remain together. Those who had been selected ran back to rejoin their relations. Mothers with children tried to join their husbands, or old people attempted to find those of their children who had been selected for work, and who had been led away.

Often the confusion was so great that the selections had to be begun all over again. The limited area of standing-room did not permit better sorting arrangements. All attempts to pacify these agitated mobs were useless. It was often necessary to use force to restore order.

As I have already frequently said, the Jews have strongly developed family feelings. They stick together like limpets. Nevertheless, according to my observations, they lack solidarity. One would have thought that in a situation such as this they would inevitably help and protect one another. But no, quite the contrary. I have often known and heard of Jews, particularly those from Western Europe, who revealed the addresses of those members of their race still in hiding.

One woman, already in the gas-chamber, shouted out to a non-commissioned officer the address of a Jewish family. A man who, to judge by his clothes and deportment appeared to be of very good standing, gave me, while actually undressing, a piece of paper on which was a list of the addresses of Dutch families who were hiding Jews.

I do not know what induced the Jews to give such information. Was it for reasons of personal revenge, or were they jealous that those others should survive?

The attitude of the men of the Special Detachment was also strange. They were all well aware that once the actions were completed they, too, would meet exactly the same fate as that suffered by these thousands of their own race, to whose destruction they had contributed so greatly. Yet the eagerness with which they carried out their duties never ceased to amaze me. Not only did they never divulge to the victims their impending fate, and were considerately helpful to them while they undressed, but they were also quite prepared to use violence on those who resisted. Then again, when it was a question of removing the trouble-makers and holding them while they were shot, they would lead them out in such a way that the victims never saw the non-commissioned officer standing there with his gun ready, and he was able to place its muzzle against the back of their necks without their noticing it. It was the same story when they dealt with the sick and the invalids, who could not be taken into the gas-chambers. And it was all done in such a matter-of-course manner that they might themselves have been the exterminators.

Then the bodies had to be taken from the gas-chambers, and after the gold teeth had been extracted, and the hair cut off, they had to be dragged to the pits or to the crematoria. Then the fires in the pits had to be stoked, the surplus fat drained off, and the mountain of burning corpses constantly turned over so that the draught might fan the flames.

They carried out all these tasks with a callous indifference as though it were all part of an ordinary day's work. While they dragged the corpses about, they ate or they smoked. They did not stop eating even when engaged on the grisly job of burning corpses which had been lying for some time in mass graves.

It happened repeatedly that Jews of the Special Detachment would come upon the bodies of close relatives among the corpses, and even among the living as they entered the gas-chambers. They were obviously affected by this, but it never led to any incident.

I myself saw a case of this sort. Once when bodies were being carried from a gas-chamber to the fire-pit, a man of the Special Detachment suddenly stopped and stood for a moment as though rooted to the spot. Then he continued to drag out a body with his comrades. I asked the Capo what was up. He explained that the corpse was that of the Jew's wife. I watched him for a while, but noticed nothing peculiar in his behaviour. He continued to drag corpses along, just as he had done before. When I visited the Detachment a little later, he was sitting with the others and eating, as though nothing had happened. Was he really able to hide his emotions so completely, or had he become too brutalised to care even about this?

Where did the Jews of the Special Detachment derive the strength to carry on night and day with their grisly work? Did they hope that some whim of fortune might at the last moment snatch them from the jaws of death? Or had they become so dulled by the accumulation of horror that they were no longer capable even of ending their own lives and thus escaping from this "existence"?

I have certainly watched them closely enough, but I have never really been able to get to the bottom of their behaviour.

The Jew's way of living and of dying was a true riddle that I never managed to solve.

All these experiences and incidents which I have described could be multiplied many times over. They are excerpts only, taken from the whole vast business of the extermination, sidelights as it were.

This mass extermination, with all its attendant circumstances, did not, as I know, fail to affect those who took a part in it. With very few exceptions, nearly all of those detailed to do this monstrous "work," this "service," and who, like myself, have given sufficient thought to the matter, have been deeply marked by these events.

Many of the men involved approached me as I went my rounds through the extermination buildings, and poured out their anxieties and impressions to me, in the hope that I could allay them.

Again and again during these confidential conversations I was asked: is it necessary that we do all this? Is it necessary that hundreds of thousands of women and children be destroyed? And I, who in my innermost being had on countless occasions asked myself exactly this question, could only fob them off and attempt to console them by repeating that it was done on Hitler's order. I had to tell them that this extermination of Jewry had to be, so that Germany and our posterity might be freed for ever from their relentless adversaries.

There was no doubt in the mind of any of us that Hitler's order had to be obeyed regardless, and that it was the duty of the SS to carry it out. Nevertheless we were all tormented by secret doubts.

I myself dared not admit to such doubts. In order to make my subordinates carry on with their task, it was psychologically essential that I myself appear convinced of the necessity for this gruesomely harsh order.

Everyone watched me. They observed the impression produced upon me by the kind of scenes that I have described above, and my reactions. Every word I said on the subject was discussed. I had to exercise intense self-control in order to prevent my innermost doubts and feelings of oppression from becoming apparent.

I had to appear cold and indifferent to events that must have wrung the heart of anyone possessed of human feelings. I might not even look away when afraid lest my natural emotions got the upper hand. I had to watch coldly, while the mothers with laughing or crying children went into the gas-chambers.

On one occasion two small children were so absorbed in some game that they quite refused to let their mother tear them away from it. Even the Jews of the Special Detachment were reluctant to pick the children up. The imploring look in the eyes of the mother, who certainly knew what was happening, is something I shall never forget. The people were already in the gas-chamber and becoming restive, and I had to act. Everyone was looking at me. I nodded to the junior non-commissioned officer on duty and he picked up the screaming, struggling children in his arms and carried them into the gas-chamber, accompanied by their mother who was weeping in the most heart-rending fashion. My pity was so great that I longed to vanish from the scene: yet I might not show the slightest trace of emotion.

I had to see everything. I had to watch hour after hour, by day and by night, the removal and burning of the bodies, the extraction of the teeth, the cutting of the hair, the whole grisly, interminable business. I had to stand for hours on end in the ghastly stench, while the mass graves were being opened and the bodies dragged out and burned.

I had to look through the peep-hole of the gas-chambers and watch the process of death itself, because the doctors wanted me to see it.

I had to do all this because I was the one to whom everyone looked, because I had to show them all that I did not merely issue the orders and make the regulations but was also prepared myself to be present at whatever task I had assigned to my subordinates.

The Reichsführer SS sent various high-ranking Party leaders and SS officers to Auschwitz so that they might see for themselves the process of extermination of the Jews. They were all deeply impressed by what they saw. Some who had previously spoken most loudly about the necessity for this extermination fell silent once they had actually seen the "final solution of the Jewish problem." I was repeatedly asked how I and my men could go on watching these operations, and how we were able to stand it.

My invariable answer was that the iron determination with which we must carry out Hitler's orders could only be obtained by a stifling of all human emotions. Each of these gentlemen declared that he was glad the job had not been given to him.

Even Mildner and Eichmann, who were certainly tough enough, had no wish to change places with me. This was one job which nobody envied me.

I had many detailed discussions with Eichmann concerning all matters connected with the "final solution of the Jewish problem," but without ever disclosing my inner anxieties. I tried in every way to discover Eichmann's innermost and real convictions about this "solution."

Yes, every way. Yet even when we were quite alone together and the drink had been flowing freely so that he was in his most expansive mood, he showed that he was completely obsessed with the idea of destroying every single Jew that he could lay his hands on. Without pity and in cold blood we must complete this extermination as rapidly as possible. Any compromise, even the slightest, would have to be paid for bitterly at a later date.

In the face of such grim determination I was forced to bury all my human considerations as deeply as possible.

Indeed, I must freely confess that after these conversations with Eichmann I almost came to regard such emotions as a betrayal of the Führer.

There was no escape for me from this dilemma.

I had to go on with this process of extermination. I had to continue this mass murder and coldly to watch it, without regard for the doubts that were seething deep inside me.

I had to observe every happening with a cold indifference. Even those petty incidents that others might not notice I found hard to forget. In Auschwitz I truly had no reason to complain that I was bored.

If I was deeply affected by some incident, I found it impossible to go back to my home and my family. I would mount my horse and ride, until I had chased the terrible picture away. Often, at night, I would walk through the stables and seek relief among my beloved animals.

It would often happen, when at home, that my thoughts suddenly turned to incidents that had occurred during the extermination. I then had to go out. I could no longer bear to be in my homely family circle. When I saw my children happily playing, or observed my wife's delight over our youngest, the thought would often come to me: how long will our happiness last? My wife could never understand these gloomy moods of mine, and ascribed them to some annoyance connected with my work.

When at night I stood out there beside the transports, or by the gas-chambers or the fires, I was often compelled to think of my wife and children, without, however, allowing myself to connect them closely with all that was happening.

It was the same with the married men who worked in the crematoria or at the fire-pits.

When they saw the women and children going into the gas-chambers, their thoughts instinctively turned to their own families.

I was no longer happy in Auschwitz once the mass exterminations had begun.

I had become dissatisfied with myself. To this must be added that I was worried because of anxiety about my principal task, the never-ending work, and the untrustworthiness of my colleagues.

Then the refusal to understand, or even to listen to me, on the part of my superiors. It was in truth not a happy or desirable state of affairs. Yet everyone in Auschwitz believed that the commandant lived a wonderful life.

My family, to be sure, were well provided for in Auschwitz. Every wish that my wife or children expressed was granted them. The children could live a free and untrammelled life. My wife's garden was a paradise of flowers. The prisoners never missed an opportunity for doing some little act of kindness to my wife or children, and thus attracting their attention.

No former prisoner can ever say that he was in any way or at any time badly treated in our house. My wife's greatest pleasure would have been to give a present to every prisoner who was in any way connected with our household.

The children were perpetually begging me for cigarettes for the prisoners. They were particularly fond of the ones who worked in the garden.

My whole family displayed an intense love of agriculture and particularly for animals of all sorts. Every Sunday I had to walk them all across the fields, and visit the stables, and we might never miss out the kennels where the dogs were kept. Our two horses and the foal were especially beloved.

The children always kept animals in the garden, creatures the prisoners were forever bringing them. Tortoises, martens, cats, lizards: there was always something new and interesting to be seen there. In summer they splashed in the paddling pool in the garden, or in the Sola. But their greatest joy was when Daddy bathed with them. He had, however, so little time for all these childish pleasures. Today I deeply regret that I did not devote more time to my family. I always felt that I had to be on duty the whole time. This exaggerated sense of duty has always made life more difficult for me than it actually need have been. Again and again my wife reproached me and said: "You must think not only of the service always, but of your family too."

Yet what did my wife know about all that lay so heavily on my mind? She has never been told.

MARGUERITE DURAS
1914–

Born in French Indochina, Duras holds a law degree from the Sorbonne and is a novelist and memoirist. In her book The War *(1986) she considered the meaning of the German concentration and extermination camps.*

From THE WAR

There are an awful lot of them. There really are huge numbers of dead. Seven million Jews have been exterminated—transported in cattle cars, then gassed in specially built gas chambers, then burned in specially built ovens. . . . This new face of death that has been discovered in Germany—organized, rationalized—produces bewilderment before it arouses indignation. You're amazed. How can anyone still be a German? You look for parallels elsewhere and in other times, but there aren't any. . . . One of the greatest civilized nations in the world, the age-long capital of music, has just systematically murdered 11 million human beings with the utter efficiency of a state industry. The whole world looks at the mountain, the mass of death dealt by God's creature to his fellows. Someone quotes the name of some German man of letters who's been very upset and become very depressed and to whom these things have given much food for thought. If Nazi crime is not seen in world terms, if it isn't understood collectively, then that man in the concentration camp at Belsen who died alone but with the same collective soul and class awareness that made him undo a bolt on the railroad one night somewhere in Europe, without a leader, without a uniform, without a witness, has been betrayed. If you give a German and not a collective interpretation to the Nazi horror, you reduce the man in Belsen to regional dimensions. The only possible answer to this crime is to turn it into a crime committed by everyone. To share it. Just like the idea of equality and fraternity. In order to bear it, to tolerate the idea of it, we must share the crime.

LOUIS SIMPSON
1923–

Born in Jamaica, Simpson attended Columbia University and served in the 101st Airborne Division. After the war he worked first in publishing and then as a Professor of English at the University of California and the State University of New York at Stony Brook. In his poems he is fond of revealing, as he says, "the other side of glory."

CARENTAN O CARENTAN

Trees in the old days used to stand
And shape a shady lane
Where lovers wandered hand in hand
Who came from Carentan.

This was the shining green canal
Where we came two by two
Walking at combat-interval.
Such trees we never knew.

The day was early June, the ground
Was soft and bright with dew.
Far away the guns did sound,
But here the sky was blue.

The sky was blue, but there a smoke
Hung still a᠎bove the sea
Where the ships together spoke
To towns we could not see.

Could you have seen us through a glass
You would have said a walk
Of farmers out to turn the grass,
Each with his own hay-fork.

The watchers in their leopard suits
Waited till it was time,
And aimed between the belt and boot
And let the barrel climb.

I must lie down at once, there is
A hammer at my knee.
And call it death or cowardice,
Don't count again on me.

Everything's all right, Mother,
Everyone gets the same
At one time or another.
It's all in the game.

I never strolled, nor ever shall,
Down such a leafy lane.
I never drank in a canal,
Nor ever shall again.

There is a whistling in the leaves
And it is not the wind,
The twigs are falling from the knives
That cut men to the ground.

Tell me, Master-Sergeant,
The way to turn and shoot.
But the Sergeant's silent
That taught me how to do it.

O Captain, show us quickly
Our place upon the map.
But the Captain's sickly
And taking a long nap.

Lieutenant, what's my duty,
My place in the platoon?
He too's a sleeping beauty,
Charmed by that strange tune.

Carentan O Carentan
Before we met with you
We never yet had lost a man
Or known what death could do.

ON THE LEDGE

I can see the coast coming near . . .
one of our planes, a Thunderbolt, plunging down
and up again. Seconds later
we heard the rattle of machine guns.

That night we lay among hedgerows.
The night was black. There was thrashing
in a hedgerow, a burst of firing . . .
in the morning, a dead cow.

A plane droned overhead . . .
one of theirs,
diesel, with a rhythmic sound.
Then the bombs came whistling down.

———

We were strung out on an embankment
side by side in a straight line,
like infantry in World War One
waiting for the whistle to blow.

The Germans knew we were there
and were firing everything they had,
bullets passing right above.
I knew that in a moment the order would come.

There is a page in Dostoevsky
about a man being given the choice
to die, or to stand on a ledge
through all eternity . . .

alive and breathing the air,
looking at the trees, and sky . . .
the wings of a butterfly
as it drifts from stem to stem.

But men who have stepped off the ledge
know all that there is to know:
who survived the Bloody Angle,
Verdun, the first day on the Somme.

As it turned out, we didn't have to.
Instead, they used Typhoons.
They flew over our heads, firing rockets
on the German positions.

So it was easy. We just strolled
over the embankment,
and down the other side,
and across an open field.

Yet, like the man on the ledge,
I still haven't moved . . .
watching an ant
climb a blade of grass and climb back down.

THE BATTLE

Helmet and rifle, pack and overcoat
Marched through a forest. Somewhere up ahead
Guns thudded. Like the circle of a throat
The night on every side was turning red.

They halted and they dug. They sank like moles
Into the clammy earth between the trees.
And soon the sentries, standing in their holes,
Felt the first snow. Their feet began to freeze.

At dawn the first shell landed with a crack.
Then shells and bullets swept the icy woods.
This lasted many days. The snow was black.
The corpses stiffened in their scarlet hoods.

Most clearly of that battle I remember
The tiredness in eyes, how hands looked thin
Around a cigarette, and the bright ember
Would pulse with all the life there was within.

RICHARD EBERHART
1904–

*Eberhart has long been a Professor of English at Dartmouth. In the
Navy during the war, he taught aerial gunnery to "tens of thousands of
young Americans." And "all too soon," he adds, "their names would
come back in the death lists."*

THE FURY OF AERIAL BOMBARDMENT

You would think the fury of aerial bombardment
Would rouse God to relent; the infinite spaces
Are still silent. He looks on shock-pried faces.
History, even, does not know what is meant.

You would feel that after so many centuries
God would give man to repent; yet he can kill
As Cain could, but with multitudinous will,
No farther advanced than in his ancient furies.

Was man made stupid to see his own stupidity?
Is God by definition indifferent, beyond us all?
Is the eternal truth man's fighting soul
Wherein the Beast ravens in its own avidity?

Of Van Wettering I speak, and Averill,
Names on a list, whose faces I do not recall
But they are gone to early death, who late in school
Distinguished the belt feed lever from the belt holding pawl.

NORMAN LEWIS

British novelist and travel writer Norman Lewis served as a sergeant in the Field Security Service, the equivalent of the American Counter Intelligence Corps. In the fall of 1943 he went ashore with the American Fifth Army at Salerno and soon found himself performing bizarre investigative duties in Naples. He kept a diary then, and looking it over many years later, he said, "I was amazed that the episodes recalled by these notes, which had seemed so unexceptional at the time, should now appear so extra-ordinary." In 1978 he published a selection of the entries in a book titled Naples '44.

From NAPLES '44

OCTOBER 3

A gale of the kind no one ever expects of Italy blew down our tent in the middle of the night. Pitch darkness, hammering rain, the suffocating weight of waterlogged canvas over mouth and nostrils, muffled cries from all directions. A lake of water flooded in under the beds, and gradually rose to the level of the bottom of the mattress. It was several hours before we could be rescued. All my kit stowed under the bed was lost, and only my camera and notebooks in the drawer of the bedside table survived. One patient was killed by the main tent-pole falling across his bed.

OCTOBER 4

Discharged from hospital and kitted out temporarily as an American private with bucket helmet, hip-clinging trousers and gaitered boots, I picked up a lift in an American truck going in the direction of Naples, which had fallen three days before, and where I supposed the section would already be installed. At Battipaglia it was all change, with an opportunity for a close-quarters study of the effects of the carpet bombing ordered by General Clark. The General has become the destroying angel of Southern Italy, prone to panic, as at Paestum, and then to violent and vengeful reaction, which occasioned the sacrifice of the village of Altavilla, shelled out of existence because it *might* have contained Germans. Here in Battipaglia we had an Italian Guernica, a town transformed in a matter of seconds to a heap of rubble. An old man who came to beg said that practically nobody had been left alive, and that the bodies were still under the ruins. From the stench and from the sight of the flies streaming like black smoke into, and out of, the holes in the ground, this was entirely believable. No attempt had even been made to clear the streets of relics of the successful strike. So much so that while standing by the truck talking to the old man I felt something uneven under one foot, shifted my position, and then glancing down realized that what had at first seemed to be a mass of sacking was in fact the charred and flattened corpse of a German soldier.

Thereafter on through Salerno and across the base of the Sorrento peninsula in a second truck. This is a region on which all the guidebooks exhaust their superlatives, and the war had singed and scorched it here and there, and littered the green and golden landscape with the wreckage of guns and tanks, but happily no town had been large enough to warrant the General's calling in his Flying Fortresses. The only visible damage to most villages had been the inevitable sack of the post office by the vanguard of the advancing troops, who seem to have been philatelists to a man. Presently we were in the outskirts of Naples, which took the form of a number of grimy, war-husked towns: Torre Annunziata, Torre del Greco, Resina and Portici, which have grown together to form twelve miles of dismal suburb along the seafront. We made slow progress through shattered streets, past landslides of rubble from bombed buildings. People stood in their doorways, faces the colour of pumice, to wave mechanically to the victors, the apathetic Fascist salute of last week having been converted to the apathetic V-sign of today, but on the whole the civilian mood seemed one of stunned indifference.

Somewhere a few miles short of Naples proper, the road widened into something like a square, dominated by a vast semi-derelict public building, plastered with notices and with every window blown in. Here several trucks had drawn up and our driver pulled in to the kerb and stopped too. One of the trucks was carrying American Army supplies, and soldiers, immediately joined by several from our truck, were crowding round this and helping themselves to whatever they could lay hands on. Thereafter, crunching through the broken glass that littered the pavement, each of them carrying a tin of rations, they were streaming into the municipal building.

I followed them and found myself in a vast room crowded with jostling soldiery, with much pushing forward and ribald encouragement on the part of those in the rear, but a calmer and more thoughtful atmosphere by the time one reached the front of the crowd. Here a row of ladies sat at intervals of about a yard with their backs to the wall. These women were dressed in their street clothes, and had the ordinary well-washed respectable shopping and gossiping faces of working-class housewives. By the side of each woman stood a small pile of tins, and it soon became clear that it was possible to make love to any one of them in this very public place by adding another tin to the pile. The women kept absolutely still, they said nothing, and their faces were as empty of expression as graven images. They might have been selling fish, except that this place lacked the excitement of a fish market. There was no soliciting, no suggestion, no enticement, not even the discreetest and most accidental display of flesh. The boldest of the soldiers had pushed themselves, tins in hand, to the front, but now, faced with these matter-of-fact family-providers driven here by empty larders, they seemed to flag. Once again reality had betrayed the dream, and the air fell limp. There was some sheepish laughter, jokes that fell flat, and a visible tendency to slip quietly away. One soldier, a little tipsy, and egged on constantly by his friends, finally put down his tin of rations at a woman's side, unbuttoned and lowered himself on her. A perfunctory jogging of the haunches began and came quickly to an end. A moment later he was on his feet and buttoning up again. It had been something to get over as soon as possible. He might have been submitting to field punishment rather than the act of love.

Five minutes later we were on our way again. The tins collected by my fellow travellers were thrown to passers-by who scrambled wildly after them. None of the soldiers travelling on my truck had felt inclined to join actively in the fun.

OCTOBER 6

The city of Naples smells of charred wood, with ruins everywhere, sometimes completely blocking the streets, bomb craters and abandoned trams. The main problem is water. Two tremendous air-raids on August 4 and September 6 smashed up all the services, and there has been no proper water supply since the first of these. To complete the Allies' work of destruction, German demolition squads have gone round blowing up anything of value to the city that still worked. Such has been the great public thirst of the past few days that we are told that people have experimented with sea-water in their cooking, and families have been seen squatting along the sea-shore round weird contraptions with which they hope to distil sea-water for drinking purposes.

The Section has fallen on its feet. I arrived to find that we had been installed in the Palace of the Princes of Satriano at the end of Naples's impressive seafront, the Riviera di Chiaia, in the Piazza Vittoria. The four-storey building is in the Neapolitan version of Spanish baroque, and we occupy its principal floor at the head of a sweep of marble staircase, with high ceilings, decorated with mouldings, glittering chandeliers, enormous wall-mirrors, and opulent gilded furniture in vaguely French-Empire style. There are eight majestic rooms, but no bathroom, and the lavatory is in a cupboard in the kitchen. The view across the square is of clustered palms, much statuary, and the Bay of Naples. The FSO has done very well by us.

At first sight Naples, with the kind of work it is likely to involve, seemed unglamorous compared with North Africa. Gone forever were the days of forays into the mountains of Kabylie for meetings with the scheming Caïds and the holy men who controlled the tribes, and the secret discussions in the rose arbour in the Palace Gardens of Tunis. Life here, by comparison, promised to be hard-working, sometimes prosaic, and fraught with routines. There were military units by the dozen all round Naples who wished to employ Italian civilians and all of these had to be vetted by us as security risks. Nothing could have been easier than this operation. The Fascist police state kept close tabs on the activities of all its citizens, and we inherited their extensive archives on the top floor of the Questura—the central police office. Ninety-nine per cent of the information recorded there was numbingly unimportant, and revealed as a whole that most Italians lead political lives of utter neutrality, although prone to sexual adventures. In all, the unending chronicles of empty lives. A little more thought and effort would have to be devoted to the investigation of those few hundreds of persons remaining in the city who had been energetic Fascists, and whom—largely depending on our reports—it might be thought necessary to intern.

A suspects file had to be started, and this was a job that fell to me. Section members had already cleared out the German Consulate in Naples, removing from it a car-load of documents, all of which had to be studied. The work was increased as a deluge of denunciations began to flood in. They were delivered in person by people nourishing every kind of grudge, or even shoved into the hands of the sentry at the gate. Some of them were eccentric, including one relating to a priest who was claimed to have arranged shows of blue movies for the commander of the German garrison. Everything—from the grubbiest scrap of paper on which a name had been scrawled, and the single word "murderer" scribbled beneath, to a scrupulously typed document bearing the seal and signatures of the Comitato di Liberazione—had to be studied and recorded. The labour involved was immense, and exceedingly tedious, and was much complicated by the prevalence in Naples of certain family names—Espositos and Gennaros turn up by the hundred—and by the fact that material supplied by our own authorities for inclusion in the official Black Book was often vague. Quite frequently suspects were not even identified by name, but by such descriptions as "of medium height," "age between thirty and forty," "strikingly ugly," or in one case, "known to possess an obsessive fear of cats." However, the work went on; the filing system expanded, and the Black Book with its vagueness and its sometimes almost poetic idiocies, began to put on bulk.

Within days of settling in, three section members were sent out on detachment to Sorrento and the coastal towns, and Eric Williams, our best Italian speaker, became a solitary exile in the important town of Nola. Three more people, apart from the FSO, were tied down to administrative duties at HQ, leaving only four of us, Parkinson, Evans, Durham and myself, to confront the security problems of that anthill of humanity, the city of Naples itself.

First impressions of my colleagues under working conditions are favourable. They are hampered in several cases by their lack of Italian, but they are an industrious lot, and set to work with enthusiasm to learn the language. Like all sections, this has developed its own personality. It is less informal than most, and a little bureaucratic. I cannot imagine any member of 312 FSS being able to manœuvre himself into a position where he could turn up at an airfield, wave his pass about, and bamboozle some Airforce officer, British or American, into arranging a quick unofficial flight back to England—an achievement of the kind which has been possible in certain other sections. All my new friends have been issued with special officer's-type identity documents replacing the normal AB 64, but Captain Cartwright has clearly not wished to have these endorsed as in the case of those issued to 91 FSS—one of which I still carry—with the authorization to be in any place, at any time, and in any dress. Nor, so far, do section members wear civilian clothes. Army Books No. 466 (no erasures, no pages to be detached) are scrupulously carried, and daily entries condensed in the form of a log, handed in to the FSO first thing each morning, and discussed at a parade at nine, at which certain regimental formalities are carefully preserved. These things are quite new in my experience.

OCTOBER 8

Contact with the military units brought its inevitable consequences. The phone started ringing first thing in the morning and rarely stopped. An excited officer was usually on the line to report the presence in his area of an enemy agent, or a secret transmitter, or a suspected cache of abandoned German loot. All this information came from local civilians who poured into the nearest army HQ, anxious to unburden themselves of secrets of all kinds, but as not even phrase books had been issued to help with the language problem, mistakes were frequent. Today, being the only section member left in the office, I was sent hurriedly on the motor-bike, in response to the most urgent request, to Afragola, where an infantry major was convinced from local reports that a village woman was a spy. In this case evidence had been transmitted mostly by gestures which the Major had failed to interpret. It turned out that what the villagers had been trying to explain was that the woman was a witch, and that if allowed to cast her malefic gaze on the unit's water supply, she would make it undrinkable.

On my way to resolve this misunderstanding I saw a remarkable spectacle. Hundreds, possibly thousands of Italians, most of them women and children, were in the fields all along the roadside driven by their hunger to search for edible plants. I stopped to speak to a group of them, and they told me that they had left their homes in Naples at daybreak, and had had to walk for between two and three hours to reach the spot where I found them—seven or eight miles out of town. Here a fair number of plants could still be found, although nearer the city the fields had been stripped of everything that could be eaten. There were about fifteen different kinds of plants which were worth collecting, most of them bitter in flavour. All I recognized among their collections were dandelions. I saw other parties netting birds, and these had managed to catch a few sparrows and some tiny warblers which they said were common at this time of the year, attracted by the fruit in the orchards. They told me they had to face the hostility of the local people, on whose lands they were trespassing, and who accused them of raids on their vineyards and vegetable patches.

OCTOBER 9

This afternoon, another trip along the sea-front at Santa Lucia provided a similar spectacle of the desperate hunt for food. Rocks were piled up here against the sea wall and innumerable children were at work among them. I learned that they were prising limpets off the rocks, all the winkles and sea-snails having been long since exhausted. A pint of limpets sold at the roadside fetched about two lire, and if boiled long enough could be expected to add some faint, fishy flavour to a broth produced from any edible odds and ends. Inexplicably, no boats were allowed out yet to fish. Nothing, absolutely nothing that can be tackled by the human digestive system is wasted in Naples. The butchers' shops that have opened here and there sell nothing we would consider acceptable as meat, but their displays of scraps of offal are set out with art, and handled with reverence: chickens' heads—from which the beak has been neatly trimmed—cost five lire; a little grey pile of chickens' intestines in a brightly polished saucer, five lire; a gizzard, three lire; calves' trotters two lire apiece; a large piece of windpipe, seven lire. Little queues wait to be served with these delicacies. There is a persistent rumour of a decline in the cat population of the city.

OCTOBER 10

How lucky for all concerned that the liberation of Naples happened when it did—when the fruit harvests were still to be gathered in—and the perfect weather of early autumn helped hardships of all kinds to be more endurable. Day followed day of unbroken sunshine, although the heat of summer had gone. From where I sat sifting wearily through the mountains of vilification and calumny, I could refresh myself by looking down into the narrow street running along one side of the palazzo. This is inhabited to bursting-point with working-class families, whose custom it is to live as much as they can of their lives out of doors, for which reason this street is as noisy as a tropical aviary.

Quite early in the morning, a family living in the house opposite carried out a table and stood it in the street close to their doorway. This was briskly covered with a green cloth with tassels. Chairs were placed round it at an exact distance apart and on it were stood several framed photographs, a vase of artificial flowers, a small cage containing a goldfinch, and several ornate little glasses, which were polished from time to time as the day passed by to remove the dust. Round this table the family lived in what was in fact a room without walls; a mother, grandfather and grandmother, a girl in her late teens, and two dynamic boys, who constantly came and went. Here the mother attended to the girl's hair, washed the boys' faces, served something from a steaming pot at midday, sewed and did the family washing in the afternoon. There were a number of other such tables along the street, and constant social migrations took place as neighbours paid each other visits. The scene was a placid one. The green *persianas* hanging over all the upper windows and balconies breathed in and out gently in the mild breeze from the sea. People called musically to each other over great distances. A beggar with tiny, twisted legs was carried out by his friends and propped up in a comfortable position against the wall, where he started to strum a mandolin. Two lean, hip-swinging American soldiers, sharing a bottle of wine, passed down the street, and the girl at the table looked up and followed them with her eyes until they turned the corner and disappeared from sight.

There is no notice in the palazzo to say who we are and what we are doing here so it is hard to understand why people assume this to be the headquarters of the British Secret Police. However, they do and we are beginning to receive a stream of visitors, all of them offering their services as informers. No question ever arises of payment. Our visitors are prepared to work for us out of pure and unalloyed devotion to the Allied cause. In the main they are drawn from the professional classes, and hand over beautifully engraved cards describing them as *Avvocato, Dottore, Ingeniere* or *Professore.* They are all most dignified, some impressive, and they talk in low, conspiratorial voices. We received a visit, too, from a priest with a pocketful of denunciations who asked for a permit to be allowed to carry a pistol. These are the often shabby and warped personalities on which we depend. Once they were called by their real names, now they are officially "informants," and already there is a euphemistic tendency to turn them into "contacts." They are a special breed, the life's blood of Intelligence, and the world over they have an extraordinary thing in common: a strange and exclusive loyalty to one particular master. An informer is like a duckling newly freed from its shell and in need of fostering. He can be counted upon to attach himself permanently to the first person who is prepared to listen sympathetically to what he has to say, and prefers never to transfer his allegiance. In these first few days we all made half a dozen or so "contacts."

All names are checked as a matter of course with our rapidly expanding files, and we find to our amusement that several of these men who have come forward to assist us in every way they can, have been accused by their fellow citizens of being arch-collaborators. We have collected copies from the offices of the German Consulate of many servile and congratulatory letters written by Neapolitan worthies to Adolf Hitler himself. An outstanding example of these was from a Counsellor at the Naples Court of Appeal who had just called to offer his services. This assured the Führer of "my great admiration and sympathy for the soldiers of your country," and concluded, *"Con profonde devota osservanza."*

What is remarkable to us is the German bureaucratic rectitude with which all these communications, many of them highly nonsensical, have been conscientiously acknowledged, translated, and actually forwarded to the Chancery of the Nazi Party in Berlin, and fulsomely replied to by that office—the reply being returned via the German Embassy in Rome. One's imagination reels at the thought of the paperwork involved in dealing with thousands of such epistles from the toadies of occupied Europe.

*   *   *

Complaints are coming in about looting by Allied troops. The officers in this war have shown themselves to be much abler at this kind of thing than the other ranks. The charge has been made that officers of the

King's Dragoon Guards, to whom fell the honour of being the first British unit to enter Naples, have cut the paintings from the frames in the Princess's Palace, and made off with the collection of Capodimonte china. The OSS have cleaned out Achille Lauro's sumptuous house. Some of the bulkier items of booty are stated to have been crated up for return to England with the connivance of the Navy.

OCTOBER 13

A week in which our activities have been hampered, and even frustrated, by false alarms and scares of every conceivable kind. Anyone whose activities depart in any way from the standards of normality set by the city is regarded as a spy, and we have been involved in endless wild-goose chases. None of these forays out into the night produced results. The suspected spies were always harmless eccentrics. The mysterious stranger in the next flat tinkering with a powerful radio was not an enemy agent operating a transmitter, but a man trying to get the BBC. In houses said to contain caches of arms we found nothing more lethal than unemptied babies' chamberpots; while flashing lights in the night were always people on their way to the cess-pit at the bottom of the garden.

Now that the mail is operating normally again, a horde of censors are busily slitting open letters to probe for hidden meaning among the trivia of family and business correspondence, and when in doubt they fall back on us. Unhappily many telephone conversations are being monitored, too, and the typed out "intercepts" sent to us contain their fair share of absurdity. The prize example received so far was one solemnly headed "Illegal use of telescope." This referred to a passage in an overheard conversation between two lovers in which the girl had said, "I can't see you today because my husband will be here, but I'll admire you, as ever, through love's telescope." No. 3 District adds to these burdens by bombarding us with addenda for the Black Book, which serves as the rag-bag for everybody's paranoia. In one case we had to make an entry for a suspect about which nothing is known but his possession of three teats on the left breast, while another was described as "having the face of a hypocrite."

All these things encourage the growth of disbelief, so that when a few days ago reports began to come in about mysterious knocking sounds coming from the depths of the earth, we were unimpressed. But when yesterday the Italian Pubblica Sicurezza Police—sceptics like ourselves—were on the phone to talk about the knockings, adding that they had even been heard by a senior policeman, notice had to be taken. The knockings had been reported from a number of widely separated areas in the northern part of the city. It was the police's theory, supported by much rumour and some credible evidence, that a picked squad of German SS had volunteered to remain behind after the German retreat from Naples, and that they had hidden in the catacombs, from which they might at any time make a surprise sortie. There was also a likelihood, if this were the case, that their plans had gone wrong, and that they had lost themselves in the darkness of a vast and only partially charted labyrinth, in which case the knocking could be explained as their attempt to draw attention to their predicament.

Only a small part of the catacombs—the most extensive in Italy, and possibly the world—is accessible to visitors and the police had had some difficulty in finding an old map showing their full extent. There was no way of knowing how accurate this map remained after the damage of the earth tremors of the past and the subsidences they were certain to have caused. However, the map was studied in its relation to the location of the places where knocking sounds had been heard and, the general opinion being that the Germans were down there somewhere, a force numbering about fifty men was assembled, to include the Italian Police, the American Counter-Intelligence Corps and ourselves, to enter and explore the catacombs.

Of the two networks of catacombs under Naples, the principal one, which concerned us, is entered from the back of the church of San Gennaro. These catacombs are believed to date from the first century, and consist of four galleries, excavated one below the other, each gallery having numerous ramifications and lateral passages. The two nethermost galleries having partially fallen in, they have not been accessible in modern times.

It was decided to enter the catacombs shortly after dawn, and we arrived at the church in a dozen jeeps, lavishly equipped with gear of the kind used in cave-exploration, as well as all the usual weaponry. The monks in charge were already up and about, and showed us extreme hostility. One monk who planted himself, arms outstretched, at the entrance to the catacombs had to be removed by force, and then, when we went in, followed us, keeping up a resounding denunciation of our desecration of a holy place.

The Americans had equipped themselves with lamps like miniature searchlights; these shone on the walls of the anterooms through which we passed to reach the galleries, showing them to be so closely covered with frescoes—mostly in excellent condition after sixteen centuries—as to give the impression of colossal ikons. We were instantly confronted with the purpose for which the catacombs had been designed. Rows of niches forming burial chambers had been cut one above the other in the walls, and all these were crammed with skeletons, many said to have been plague victims of the sixteenth century. When somebody picked up a skull to examine it the angry monk trudging at our heels roared at him to put it back. Questioned about the possibility of Germans being in the catacombs, this man had answered in an evasive and suspicious way.

It soon became clear that we were looking for a needle in a haystack. We were in narrow, bone-choked streets, with innumerable side turnings to be explored, each with its many dark chambers in any one of which our quarry could have hidden, or from which they could have suddenly sprung out to ambush us, if they were still alive. These men, had they gone into the catacombs—and we were all still convinced they had—must have been in the darkness for nearly a fortnight since their torch batteries had finally given out. After which, groping their way, or crawling about among the bones, they would have encountered terrible hazards. Even in the second gallery we came suddenly to a black chasm. In the depths of this, where the whole roadway from wall to wall had caved in, the lights showed us a pile of dust from which protruded a few ancient rib-bones. We dangled a microphone into this pit and listened while the monk muttered at our backs, but the silence below was absolute.

We gave up and went back. It was two days now since the last knocking had been reported, and strange that the strength of men, however close to starvation, should have ebbed so suddenly that we could hear not even a moan or cry. The general opinion was that the monk knew more than he was prepared to say. There was even the possibility, the Police Commissario suggested, that he had gone into the catacombs and rescued the Germans. Whether or not this was so, it was unlikely that we should ever know.

* * *

IVOR ROWBERY

Private Ivor Rowbery, of the South Staffordshire Regiment, wrote this letter to his mother just before the Arnhem battle and placed it in an envelope on which he wrote, "To the Best Mother in the World." He was killed on September 17, 1944.

TO HIS MOTHER

Blighty
(Some time ago)
[undated]

Dear Mom,

Usually when I write a letter it is very much overdue, and I make every effort to get it away quickly. This letter, however, is different. It is a letter I hoped you would never receive, as it is just a verification of that terse, black-edged card which you received some time ago, and which has caused you so much grief. It is because of this grief that I wrote this letter, and by the time you have finished reading it I hope that it has done some good, and that I have not written it in vain. It is very difficult to write now of future things in the past tense, so I am returning to the present.

To-morrow we go into action. As yet we do not know exactly what our job will be, but no doubt it will be a dangerous one in which many lives will be lost—mine may be one of those lives.

Well, Mom, I am not afraid to die. I like this life, yes—for the past two years I have planned and dreamed and mapped out a perfect future for myself. I would have liked that future to materialize, but it is not what I will but what God wills, and if by sacrificing all this I leave the world slightly better than I found it I am perfectly willing to make that sacrifice. Don't get me wrong though, Mom, I am no flag-waving patriot, nor have I ever professed to be.

England's a great little country—the best there is—but I cannot honestly and sincerely say "that it is worth fighting for." Nor can I fancy myself in the role of a gallant crusader fighting for the liberation of Europe. It would be a nice thought but I would only be kidding myself. No, Mom, my little world is centred around you and includes Dad, everyone at home, and my friends at W'ton—*That* is worth fighting for—and if by doing so it strengthens your security and improves your lot in any way, then it is worth dying for too.

Now this is where I come to the point of this letter. As I have already stated, I am not afraid to die and am perfectly willing to do so, if, by my doing so, you benefit in any way whatsoever. If you do not then my sacrifice is all in vain. Have you benefited, Mom, or have you cried and worried yourself sick? I fear it is the latter. Don't you see, Mom, that it will do me no good, and that in addition you are undoing all the good work I have tried to do. Grief is hypocritical, useless and unfair, and does neither you nor me any good.

I want no flowers, no epitaph, no tears. All I want is for you to remember me and feel proud of me, then I shall rest in peace knowing that I have done a good job. Death is nothing final or lasting, if it were there would be no point in living; it is just a stage in everyone's life. To some it comes early, to others late, but it must come to everyone sometime, and surely there is no better way of dying.

Besides I have probably crammed more enjoyment into my 21 years than some manage to do in 80. My only regret is that I have not done as much for you as I would have liked to do. I loved you, Mom, you were the best Mother in the World, and what I failed to do in life I am trying to make up for in death, so please don't let me down, Mom, don't worry or fret, but smile, be proud and satisfied. I never had much money, but what little I have is all yours. Please don't be silly and sentimental about it, and don't try to spend it on me. Spend it on yourself or the kiddies, it will do some good that way. Remember that where I am I am quite O.K., and providing I know you are not grieving over me I shall be perfectly happy.

Well Mom, that is all, and I hope I have not written it all in vain. Good-bye, and thanks for everything.

Your unworthy son,
Ivor

EUGENE B. SLEDGE
1923–

Born in Mobile, Alabama, Sledge enlisted in the Marine Corps in December 1942. After the war he studied at Auburn and took a Ph.D. in Zoology at the University of Florida. In 1990 he retired from teaching biology at the University of Montevallo, Alabama. His account of his wartime experience in With the Old Breed at Peleliu and Okinawa *(1981) has earned him the respect of both the Marine Corps, which has asked him to speak at conferences on combat reality, and general readers in search of authentic and unflinching reports on the facts of battle.*

FROM WITH THE OLD BREED AT PELELIU AND OKINAWA

I griped as loudly as anyone about our living conditions and discipline. In retrospect, however, I doubt seriously whether I could have coped with the psychological and physical shock and stress encountered on Peleliu and Okinawa had it been otherwise. The Japanese fought to win. It was a savage, brutal, inhumane, exhausting, and dirty business. Our commanders knew that if we were to win and survive, we must be trained realistically for it whether we liked it or not. In the postwar years, the Marine Corps came in for a great deal of undeserved criticism, in my opinion, from well-meaning persons who did not comprehend the magnitude of stress and horror that combat can be. The technology that developed the rifled barrel, the machine gun, and high-explosive shells has turned war into prolonged, subhuman slaughter. Men must be trained realistically if they are to survive it without breaking mentally and physically.

ASSAULT INTO HELL

H-hour, 0800. Long jets of red flame mixed with thick black smoke rushed out of the muzzles of the huge battleships' 16-inch guns with a noise like a thunderclap. The giant shells tore through the air toward the island, roaring like locomotives.

"Boy, it must cost a fortune to fire them 16-inch babies," said a buddy near me.

"Screw the expense," growled another.

Only less impressive were the cruisers firing 8-inch salvos and the host of smaller ships firing rapid fire. The usually clean salty air was strong with the odors of explosives and diesel fuel. While the assault waves formed up and my amphibious tractor lay still in the water with engines idling, the tempo of the bombardment increased to such intensity that I couldn't distinguish the reports of the various types of weapons through the thunderous noise. We had to shout at each other to be heard. The big ships increased their fire and moved off to the flanks of the amtrac formations when we started in so as not to fire over us at the risk of short rounds.

We waited a seeming eternity for the signal to start toward the beach. The suspense was almost more than I could bear. Waiting is a major part of war, but I never experienced any more supremely agonizing suspense than the excruciating torture of those moments before we received the signal to begin the assault on Peleliu. I broke out in a cold sweat as the tension mounted with the intensity of the bombardment. My stomach was tied in knots. I had a lump in my throat and swallowed only with great difficulty. My knees nearly buckled, so I clung weakly to the side of the tractor. I felt nauseated and feared that my bladder would surely empty itself and reveal me to be the coward I was. But the men around me looked just about the way I felt. Finally, with a sense of fatalistic relief mixed with a flash of anger at the navy officer who was our wave commander, I saw him wave his flag toward the beach. Our driver revved the engine. The treads churned up the water, and we started in—the second wave ashore.

We moved ahead, watching the frightful spectacle. Huge geysers of water rose around the amtracs ahead of us as they approached the reef. The beach was now marked along its length by a continuous sheet of flame backed by a thick wall of smoke. It seemed as though a huge volcano had erupted from the sea, and rather than heading for an island, we were being drawn into the vortex of a flaming abyss. For many it was to be oblivion.

The lieutenant braced himself and pulled out a half-pint whiskey bottle.

"This is it, boys," he yelled.

Just like they do in the movies! It seemed unreal.

He held the bottle out to me, but I refused. Just sniffing the cork under those conditions might have made me pass out. He took a long pull on the bottle, and a couple of the men did the same. Suddenly a large shell exploded with a terrific concussion, and a huge geyser rose up just to our right front. It barely missed us. The engine stalled. The front of the tractor lurched to the left and bumped hard against the rear of another amtrac that was either stalled or hit. I never knew which.

We sat stalled, floating in the water for some terrifying moments. We were sitting ducks for the enemy gunners. I looked forward through the hatch behind the driver. He was wrestling frantically with the control levers. Japanese shells were screaming into the area and exploding all around us. Sgt. Johnny Marmet leaned toward the driver and yelled something. Whatever it was, it seemed to calm the driver, because he got the engine started. We moved forward again amid the geysers of exploding shells.

Our bombardment began to lift off the beach and move inland. Our dive bombers also moved inland with their strafing and bombing. The Japanese increased the volume of their fire against the waves of amtracs. Above the din I could hear the ominous sound of shell fragments humming and growling through the air.

"Stand by," someone yelled.

I picked up my mortar ammo bag and slung it over my left shoulder, buckled my helmet chin strap, adjusted my carbine sling over my right shoulder, and tried to keep my balance. My heart pounded. Our amtrac came out of the water and moved a few yards up the gently sloping sand.

"Hit the beach!" yelled an NCO moments before the machine lurched to a stop.

The men piled over the sides as fast as they could. I followed Snafu, climbed up, and planted both feet firmly on the left side so as to leap as far away from it as possible. At that instant a burst of machine-gun fire with white-hot tracers snapped through the air at eye level, almost grazing my face. I pulled my head back like a turtle, lost my balance, and fell awkwardly forward down onto the sand in a tangle of ammo bag, pack, helmet, carbine, gas mask, cartridge belt, and flopping canteens. "Get off the beach! Get off the beach!" raced through my mind.

Once I felt land under my feet, I wasn't as scared as I had been coming across the reef. My legs dug up the sand as I tried to rise. A firm hand gripped my shoulder. "Oh god, I thought, it's a Nip who's come out of a pillbox!" I couldn't reach my kabar—fortunately, because as I got my face out of the sand and looked up, there was the worried face of a Marine bending over me. He thought the machine-gun burst had hit me, and he had crawled over to help. When he saw I was unhurt, he spun around and started crawling rapidly off the beach. I scuttled after him.

Shells crashed all around. Fragments tore and whirred, slapping on the sand and splashing into the water a few yards behind us. The Japanese were recovering from the shock of our prelanding bombardment. Their machine gun and rifle fire got thicker, snapping viciously overhead in increasing volume.

Our amtrac spun around and headed back out as I reached the edge of the beach and flattened on the deck. The world was a nightmare of flashes, violent explosions, and snapping bullets. Most of what I saw blurred. My mind was benumbed by the shock of it.

I glanced back across the beach and saw a DUKW (rubber-tired amphibious truck) roll up on the sand at a point near where we had just landed. The instant the DUKW stopped, it was engulfed in thick, dirty black smoke as a shell scored a direct hit on it. Bits of debris flew into the air. I watched with that odd, detached fascination peculiar to men under fire, as a flat metal panel about two feet square spun high into the air then splashed into shallow water like a big pancake. I didn't see any men get out of the DUKW.

Up and down the beach and out on the reef, a number of amtracs and DUKWs were burning. Japanese machine-gun bursts made long splashes on the water as though flaying it with some giant whip. The geysers belched up relentlessly where the mortar and artillery shells hit. I caught a fleeting glimpse of a group of Marines leaving a smoking amtrac on the reef. Some fell as bullets and fragments splashed among them. Their buddies tried to help them as they struggled in the knee-deep water.

I shuddered and choked. A wild desperate feeling of anger, frustration, and pity gripped me. It was an emotion that always would torture my mind when I saw men trapped and was unable to do anything but watch as they were hit. My own plight forgotten momentarily, I felt sickened to the depths of my soul. I asked God, "Why, why, why?" I turned my face away and wished that I were imagining it all. I had tasted the bitterest essence of war, the sight of helpless comrades being slaughtered, and it filled me with disgust.

I got up. Crouching low, I raced up the sloping beach into a defilade. Reaching the inland edge of the sand just beyond the high-water mark, I glanced down and saw the nose of a huge black and yellow bomb protruding from the sand. A metal plate attached to the top served as a pressure trigger. My foot had missed it by only inches.

I hit the deck again just inside the defilade. On the sand immediately in front of me was a dead snake about eighteen inches long. It was colorful, somewhat like American species I had kept as pets when a boy. It was the only snake I saw on Peleliu.

Momentarily I was out of the heavy fire hitting on the beach. A strong smell of chemicals and exploding shells filled the air. Patches of coral and sand around me were yellowed from the powder from shell blasts. A large white post about four feet high stood at the edge of the defilade. Japanese writing was painted on the side facing the beach. To me, it appeared as though a chicken with muddy feet had walked up and down the post. I felt a sense of pride that this was enemy territory and that we were capturing it for our country to help win the war.

One of our NCOs signaled us to move to our right, out of the shallow defilade. I was glad, because the Japanese probably would pour mortar fire into it to prevent it being used for shelter. At the moment, however, the gunners seemed to be concentrating on the beach and the incoming waves of Marines.

I ran over to where one of our veterans stood looking to our front and flopped down at his feet. "You'd better get down," I yelled as bullets snapped and cracked all around.

"Them slugs are high, they're hittin' in the leaves, Sledgehammer," he said nonchalantly without looking at me.

"Leaves, hell! Where are the trees?" I yelled back at him.

Startled, he looked right and left. Down the beach, barely visible, was a shattered palm. Nothing near us stood over knee high. He hit the deck.

"I must be crackin' up, Sledgehammer. Them slugs sound just like they did in the jungle at Gloucester, and I figured they were hittin' leaves," he said with chagrin.

"Somebody gimme a cigarette," I yelled to my squad mates nearby.

Snafu was jubilant. "I toldja you'd start smokin', didn't I, Sledgehammer?"

A buddy handed me a smoke, and with trembling hands we got it lit. They really kidded me about going back on all my previous refusals to smoke.

I kept looking to our right, expecting to see men from the 3d Battalion, 7th Marines (3/7), which was supposed to be there. But I saw only the familiar faces of Marines from my own company as we moved off the beach. Marines began to come in behind us in increasing numbers, but none were visible on our right flank.

Unfamiliar officers and NCOs yelled and shouted orders, "K Company, first platoon, move over here," or "K Company, mortar section, over here." Considerable confusion prevailed for about fifteen minutes as our officers and the leaders from our namesake company in the 7th Marines straightened out the two units.

> From left to right along the 2,200-yard beach front, the 1st Marines, the 5th Marines and the 7th Marines landed abreast. The 1st Marines landed one battalion on each of the two northern White beaches. In the division's center, the 5th Marines landed its 1st Battalion (1/5) over Orange Beach One and its 3d Battalion (3/5) over Orange Beach Two. Forming the right flank of the division, the 7th Marines was to land one battalion (3/7) in the assault over Orange Beach Three, the southernmost of five designated beaches.
>
> In the confusion of the landing's first few minutes, K/3/5 actually got in ahead of the assault companies of 3/7 and slightly farther to the right than intended. As luck would have it, the two companies got mixed together as the right flank of the division. For about fifteen minutes we were the exposed right flank of the entire beachhead.

We started to move inland. We had gone only a few yards when an enemy machine gun opened up from a scrub thicket to our right. Japanese 81mm and 90mm mortars then opened up on us. Everyone hit the deck; I dove into a shallow crater. The company was completely pinned down. All movement ceased. The shells fell faster, until I couldn't make out individual explosions, just continuous, crashing rumbles with an occasional ripping sound of shrapnel tearing low through the air overhead amid the roar. The air was murky with smoke and dust. Every muscle in my body was as tight as a piano wire. I shuddered and shook as though I were having a mild convulsion. Sweat flowed profusely. I prayed, clenched my teeth, squeezed my carbine stock, and cursed the Japanese. Our lieutenant, a Cape Gloucester veteran who was nearby, seemed to be in about the same shape. From the meager protection of my shallow crater I pitied him, or anyone, out on that flat coral.

The heavy mortar barrage went on without slackening. I thought it would never stop. I was terrified by the big shells arching down all around us. One was bound to fall directly into my hole, I thought.

If any orders were passed along, or if anyone yelled for a corpsman, I never heard it in all the noise. It was as though I was out there on the battlefield all by myself, utterly forlorn and helpless in a tempest of violent explosions. All any man could do was sweat it out and pray for survival. It would have been sure suicide to stand up in that fire storm.

Under my first barrage since the fast-moving events of hitting the beach, I learned a new sensation: utter and absolute helplessness. The shelling lifted in about half an hour, although it seemed to me to have crashed on for hours. Time had no meaning to me. (This was particularly true when under a heavy shelling. I never could judge how long it lasted.) Orders then came to move out and I got up, covered by a layer of coral dust. I felt like jelly and couldn't believe any of us had survived that barrage.

The walking wounded began coming past us on their way to the beach where they would board amtracs to be taken out to one of the ships. An NCO who was a particular friend of mine hurried by, holding a bloody battle dressing over his upper left arm.

"Hit bad?" I yelled.

His face lit up in a broad grin, and he said jauntily, "Don't feel sorry for me, Sledgehammer. I got the million-dollar wound. It's all over for me."

We waved as he hurried on out of the war.

We had to be alert constantly as we moved through the thick sniper-infested scrub. We received orders to halt in an open area as I came upon the first enemy dead I had ever seen, a dead Japanese medical corpsman and two riflemen. The medic apparently had been trying to administer aid when he was killed by one of our shells. His medical chest lay open beside him, and the various bandages and medicines were arranged neatly in compartments. The corpsman was on his back, his abdominal cavity laid bare. I stared in horror, shocked at the glistening viscera bespecked with fine coral dust. This can't have been a human being, I agonized. It looked more like the guts of one of the many rabbits or squirrels I had cleaned on hunting trips as a boy. I felt sick as I stared at the corpses.

A sweating, dusty Company K veteran came up, looked first at the dead, and then at me. He slung his M1 rifle over his shoulder and leaned over the bodies. With the thumb and forefinger of one hand, he deftly plucked a pair of hornrimmed glasses from the face of the corpsman. This was done as casually as a guest plucking an hors d'oeuvre from a tray at a cocktail party.

"Sledgehammer," he said reproachfully, "don't stand there with your mouth open when there's all these good souvenirs laying around." He held the glasses for me to see and added, "Look how thick that glass is."

These sonsabitches must be half blind, but it don't seem to mess up their marksmanship any."

He then removed a Nambu pistol, slipped the belt off the corpse, and took the leather holster. He pulled off the steel helmet, reached inside, and took out a neatly folded Japanese flag covered with writing. The veteran pitched the helmet on the coral where it clanked and rattled, rolled the corpse over, and started pawing through the combat pack.

The veteran's buddy came up and started stripping the other Japanese corpses. His take was a flag and other items. He then removed the bolts from the Japanese rifles and broke the stocks against the coral to render them useless to infiltrators. The first veteran said, "See you, Sledgehammer. Don't take any wooden nickels." He and his buddy moved on.

I hadn't budged an inch or said a word, just stood glued to the spot almost in a trance. The corpses were sprawled where the veterans had dragged them around to get into their packs and pockets. Would I become this casual and calloused about enemy dead? I wondered. Would the war dehumanize me so that I, too, could "field strip" enemy dead with such nonchalance? The time soon came when it didn't bother me a bit.

Within a few yards of this scene, one of our hospital corpsmen worked in a small, shallow defile treating Marine wounded. I went over and sat on the hot coral by him. The corpsman was on his knees bending over a young Marine who had just died on a stretcher. A blood-soaked battle dressing was on the side of the dead man's neck. His fine, handsome, boyish face was ashen. "What a pitiful waste," I thought. "He can't be a day over seventeen years old." I thanked God his mother couldn't see him. The corpsman held the dead Marine's chin tenderly between the thumb and fingers of his left hand and made the sign of the cross with his right hand. Tears streamed down his dusty, tanned, grief-contorted face while he sobbed quietly.

The wounded who had received morphine sat or lay around like zombies and patiently awaited the "doc's" attention. Shells roared overhead in both directions, an occasional one falling nearby, and machine guns rattled incessantly like chattering demons.

We moved inland. The scrub may have slowed the company, but it concealed us from the heavy enemy shelling that was holding up other companies facing the open airfield. I could hear the deep rumble of the shelling and dreaded that we might move into it.

That our battalion executive officer had been killed a few moments after hitting the beach and that the amtrac carrying most of our battalion's field telephone equipment and operators had been destroyed on the reef made control difficult. The companies of 3/5 lost contact with each other and with 3/7 on our right flank.

As I passed the different units and exchanged greetings with friends, I was astonished at their faces. When I tried to smile at a comment a buddy made, my face felt as tight as a drumhead. My facial muscles were so tensed from the strain that I actually felt it was impossible to smile. With a shock I realized that the faces of my squad mates and everyone around me looked masklike and unfamiliar.

As we pushed eastward, we halted briefly along a North-South trail. Word was passed that we had to move forward faster to a trail where we would come up abreast of 3/7.

We continued through the thick scrub and heavy sniper fire until we came out into a clearing overlooking the ocean. Company K had reached the eastern shore. We had reached our objective. To our front was a shallow bay with barbed wire entanglements, iron tetrahedrons and other obstacles against landing craft. I was glad we hadn't tried to invade this coast.

About a dozen Company K riflemen commenced firing at Japanese soldiers wading along the reef several hundred yards away at the mouth of the bay. Other Marines joined us. The enemy were moving out from a narrow extension of the mangrove swamp on the left toward the southeastern promontory on our right. About a dozen enemy soldiers were alternately swimming and running along the reef. Some of the time only their heads were above the water as my buddies sent rifle fire into their midst. Most of the running enemy went down with a splash.

We were elated over reaching the eastern shore, and at being able to fire on the enemy in the open. A few Japanese escaped and scrambled among the rocks on the promontory.

"OK, you guys, line 'em up and squeeze 'em off," said a sergeant. "You don't kill 'em with the noise. It's the slugs that do it. You guys couldn't hit a bull in the ass with a bass fiddle," he roared.

Several more Japanese ran out from the cover of the mangroves. A burst of rifle fire sent every one of them splashing. "That's better," growled the sergeant.

The mortarmen put down our loads and stood by to set up the guns. We didn't fire at the enemy with our carbines. Rifles were more effective than carbines at that range. So we just watched.

Firing increased from our rear. We had no contact with Marine units on our right or left. But the veterans weren't concerned with anything but the enemy on the reef.

"Stand by to move out!" came the order.

"What the hell," grumbled a veteran as we headed back into the scrub. "We fight like hell and reach our objective, and they order us to fall back." Others joined in the grumbling.

"Aw, knock it off. We gotta gain contact with the 7th Marines," an NCO said.

We headed back into the thick scrub. For some time I completely lost my bearings and had no idea where we were going.

Unknown to the Marines, there were two parallel North-South trails about two hundred yards apart winding through the thick scrub. Poor maps, poor visibility, and numerous snipers made it difficult to distinguish the two trails.

When 3/5, with Company K on its right flank, reached the first (western-most) trail, it was then actually abreast of 3/7. However, due to poor visibility, contact couldn't be made between the two battalions. It was thought 3/5 was too far to the rear. So, 3/5 was ordered to move forward to come abreast of 3/7. By the time this error was realized, 3/5 had pushed 300–400 yards ahead of the 7th Marine's flank. For the second time on D day, K-3-5 was the forward-most exposed right flank element of the division. The entire 3d Battalion 5th Marines formed a deep salient reaching into enemy territory to the east coast. To make matters worse, the battalion's three companies had lost contact with each other. These isolated units were in critical danger of being cut off and surrounded by the Japanese.

The weather was getting increasingly hot, and I was soaked with sweat. I began eating salt tablets and taking frequent drinks of tepid water from my canteens. We were warned to save our water as long as possible, because no one knew when we would get any more.

A sweating runner with a worried face came up from the rear. "Hey, you guys, where's K Company's CO?" he asked. We told him where we thought Ack Ack could be located.

"What's the hot dope?" someone asked, with that same anxious question always put to runners.

"Battalion CP says we just gotta establish contact with the 7th Marines, 'cause if the Nips counterattack they'll come right through the gap," he said as he hurried on.

"Jesus!" said a man near me.

We moved forward and came up with the rest of the company in a clearing. The platoons formed up and took casualty reports. Japanese mortar and artillery fire increased. The shelling became heavy, indicating the probability of a counterattack. Most of their fire whistled over us and fell to our rear. This seemed strange although fortunate to me at the time. The order came for us to move out a short distance to the edge of the scrub. At approximately 1650 I looked out across the open airfield toward the southern extremities of the coral ridges—collectively called Bloody Nose Ridge—and saw vehicles of some sort moving amid swirling clouds of dust.

"Hey," I said to a veteran next to me, "what are those amtracs doing all the way across the airfield toward the Jap lines?"

"Them ain't amtracs; they're Nip tanks!" he said.

Shell bursts appeared among the enemy tanks. Some of our Sherman tanks had arrived at the edge of the airfield on our left and opened fire. Because of the clouds of dust and the shellfire, I couldn't see much and didn't see any enemy infantry, but the firing on our left was heavy.

Word came for us to deploy on the double. The riflemen formed a line at the edge of the scrub along a trail and lay prone, trying to take what cover they could. From the beginning to the end on Peleliu, it was all but impossible to dig into the hard coral rock, so the men piled rocks around themselves or got behind logs and debris.

Snafu and I set up our 60mm mortar a few yards behind them, across the trail in a shallow crater. Everyone got edgy as the order came, "Stand by to repel counterattack. Counterattack hitting I Company's front."

I didn't know where Company I was, but I thought it was on our left—somewhere. Although I had great confidence in our officers and NCOs, it seemed to me that we were alone and confused in the middle of a rumbling chaos with snipers everywhere and with no contact with any other units. I thought all of us would be lost.

"They needta get some more damned troops up here," growled Snafu, his standard remark in a tight spot.

Snafu set up the gun, and I removed an HE (high explosive) shell from a canister in my ammo bag. At last we could return fire!

Snafu yelled, "Fire!"

Just then a Marine tank to our rear mistook us for enemy troops. As soon as my hand went up to drop the round down the tube, a machine gun cut loose. It sounded like one of ours—and from the rear of all places! As I peeped over the edge of the crater through the dust and smoke and saw a Sherman tank in a clearing behind us, the tank fired its 75mm gun off to our right rear. The shell exploded nearby, around a bend in the same trail we were on. I then heard the report of a Japanese field gun located there as it returned fire on the tank. Again I tried to fire, but the machine gun opened up as before.

"Sledgehammer, don't let him hit that shell. We'll all be blown to hell," said a worried ammo carrier crouched in the crater near me.

"Don't worry, that's my hand he just about hit," I snapped.

Our tank and the Japanese field gun kept up their duel.

"By god, when that tank knocks out that Nip gun he'll swing his 75 over this away, and it'll be our ass. He thinks we're Nips," said a veteran in the crater.

"Oh, Jesus!" someone moaned.

A surge of panic rose within me. In a brief moment our tank had reduced me from a well-trained, determined assistant mortar gunner to a quivering mass of terror. It was not just that I was being fired at by a machine gun that unnerved me so terribly, but that it was one of ours.

To be killed by the enemy was bad enough; that was a real possibility I had prepared myself for. But to be killed by mistake by my own comrades was something I found hard to accept. It was just too much.

An authoritative voice across the trail yelled, "Secure the mortar."

A volunteer crawled off to the left, and soon the tank ceased firing on us. We learned later that our tankers were firing on us because we had moved too far ahead. They thought we were enemy support for the field gun. This also explained why the enemy shelling was passing over and exploding behind us. Tragically, the marine who saved us by identifying us to the tanker was shot off the tank and killed by a sniper.

The heavy firing on our left had about subsided, so the Japanese counterattack had been broken. Regrettably, I hadn't helped at all, because we were pinned down by one of our own tanks.

Some of us went along the trail and looked at the Japanese field gun. It was a well-made, formidable-looking piece of artillery, but I was surprised that the wheels were the heavy wooden kind typical of field guns of the nineteenth century. The Japanese gun crew was sprawled around the piece.

"Them's the biggest Nips I ever saw," one veteran said.

"Look at them sonsabitches; they's all over six foot tall," said another.

"That must be some of that 'Flower of the Kwantung Army' we've been hearing about," put in a corporal.

The Japanese counterattack was no wild, suicidal *banzai* charge such as Marine experience in the past would have led us to expect. Numerous times during D day I heard the dogmatic claim by experienced veterans that the enemy would *banzai*.

"They'll pull a *banzai*, and we'll tear their ass up. Then we can get the hell offa this hot rock, and maybe the CG will send the division back to Melbourne."

Rather than a *banzai*, the Japanese counterthrust turned out to be a well-coordinated tank-infantry attack. Approximately one company of Japanese infantry, together with about thirteen tanks, had moved carefully across the airfield until annihilated by the Marines on our left. This was our first warning that the Japanese might fight differently on Peleliu than they had elsewhere.

Just before dusk, a Japanese mortar concentration hit 3/5's command post. Our CO, Lt. Col. Austin C. Shofner, was hit while trying to establish contact among the companies of our battalion. He was evacuated and put aboard a hospital ship.

Companies I, K, and L couldn't regain contact before nightfall. Each dug in in a circular defense for the night. The situation was precarious. We were isolated, nearly out of water in the terrible heat, and ammunition was low. Lt. Col. Lewis Walt, accompanied by only a runner, came out into that pitch dark, enemy-infested scrub, located all the companies, and directed us into the division's line on the airfield. He should have won a Medal of Honor for that feat!

Rumor had it, as we dug in, that the division had suffered heavy casualties in the landing and subsequent fighting. The veterans I knew said it had been about the worst day of fighting they had ever seen. Casualty figures for the 1st Marine Division on D day reflected the severity of the fighting and the ferocity of the Japanese defense. The division staff had predicted D day losses of 500 casualties, but the total figure was 1,111 killed and wounded, not including heat prostration cases.

It was an immense relief to me when we got our gun pit completed and had registered in our gun by firing two or three rounds of HE into an area out in front of Company K. My thirst was almost unbearable, my stomach was tied in knots, and sweat soaked me. Dissolving some K ration dextrose tablets in my mouth helped, and I took the last sip of my dwindling water supply. We had no idea when relief would get through with additional water. Artillery shells shrieked and whistled back and forth overhead with increasing frequency, and small-arms fire rattled everywhere.

In the eerie green light of star shells swinging pendulumlike on their parachutes so that shadows danced and swayed around crazily, I started taking off my right shoe.

"Sledgehammer, what the hell are you doin'?" Snafu asked in an exasperated tone.

"Taking off my boondockers; my feet hurt," I replied.

"Have you gone Asiatic?" he asked excitedly. "What the hell are you gonna do in your stockin' feet if the Nips come bustin' outa that jungle, or across this field? We may have to get outa this hole and haul tail if we're ordered to. They're probably gonna pull a *banzai* before daybreak, and how do you reckon you'll move around on this coral in your stockin's?"

I said that I just wasn't thinking. He reamed me out good and told me we would be lucky to get our shoes off before the island was secured. I thanked God my foxhole buddy was a combat veteran.

Snafu then nonchalantly drew his kabar and stuck it in the coral gravel near his right hand. My stomach tightened and gooseflesh chilled my back and shoulders at the sight of the long blade in the greenish light and the realization of why he placed it within such easy reach. He then checked his .45 automatic pistol. I followed his example with my kabar as I crouched on the other side of the mortar, checked my carbine, and looked over the mortar shells (HE and flares) stacked up within reach. We settled down for the long night.

"Is that theirs or ours, Snafu?" I asked each time a shell went over.

There was nothing subtle or intimate about the approach and explosion of an artillery shell. When I heard the whistle of an approaching one in the distance, every muscle in my body contracted. I braced myself in a puny effort to keep from being swept away. I felt utterly helpless.

As the fiendish whistle grew louder, my teeth ground against each other, my heart pounded, my mouth dried, my eyes narrowed, sweat poured over me, my breath came in short irregular gasps, and I was afraid to swallow lest I choke. I always prayed, sometimes out loud.

Under certain conditions of range and terrain, I could hear the shell approaching from a considerable distance, thus prolonging the suspense into seemingly unending torture. At the instant the voice of the shell grew the loudest, it terminated in a flash and a deafening explosion similar to the crash of a loud clap of thunder. The ground shook and the concussion hurt my ears. Shell fragments tore the air apart as they rushed out, whirring and ripping. Rocks and dirt clattered onto the deck as smoke of the exploded shell dissipated.

To be under a barrage or prolonged shelling simply magnified all the terrible physical and emotional effects of one shell. To me, artillery was an invention of hell. The onrushing whistle and scream of the big steel package of destruction was the pinnacle of violent fury and the embodiment of pent-up evil. It was the essence of violence and of man's inhumanity to man. I developed a passionate hatred for shells. To be killed by a bullet seemed so clean and surgical. But shells would not only tear and rip the body, they tortured one's mind almost beyond the brink of sanity. After each shell I was wrung out, limp and exhausted.

During prolonged shelling, I often had to restrain myself and fight back a wild, inexorable urge to scream, to sob, and to cry. As Peleliu dragged on, I feared that if I ever lost control of myself under shell fire my mind would be shattered. I hated shells as much for their damage to the mind as to the body. To be under heavy shell fire was to me by far the most terrifying of combat experiences. Each time it left me feeling more forlorn and helpless, more fatalistic, and with less confidence that I could escape the dreadful law of averages that inexorably reduced our numbers. Fear is many-faceted and has many subtle nuances, but the terror and desperation endured under heavy shelling are by far the most unbearable.

The night wore on endlessly, and I was hardly able to catch even so much as a catnap. Toward the predawn hours, numerous enemy artillery pieces concentrated their fire on the area of scrub jungle from which Lt. Col. Lewis Walt had brought us. The shells screeched and whined over us and crashed beyond in the scrub.

"Whoo, boy, listen to them Nip gunners plaster that area," said a buddy in the next hole.

"Yeah," Snafu said, "they must think we're still out there and I betcha they'll counterattack right across through that place, too."

"Thank God we are here and not out there," our buddy said.

The barrage increased in tempo as the Japanese gave the vacant scrub jungle a real pounding. When the barrage finally subsided, I heard someone say with a chuckle, "Aw, don't knock it off now, you bastards. Fire all your goddamn shells out there in the wrong place."

"Don't worry, knucklehead, they'll have plenty left to fire in the right place, which is going to be where they see us when daylight comes," another voice said.

Supplies had been slow in keeping up with the needs of the 5th Marines' infantry companies on D day. The Japanese kept heavy artillery, mortar, and machine-gun fire on the entire regimental beach throughout the day; enemy artillery and mortar observers called down their fire on amphibian vehicles as soon as they reached the beach. This made it difficult to get the critical supplies ashore and the wounded evacuated. All of Peleliu was a front line on D day. No one but the dead was out of reach of enemy fire. The shore party people did their best, but they couldn't make up for the heavy losses of amtracs needed to bring the supplies to us.

We weren't aware of the problems on the beach, being too occupied with our own. We griped, cursed, and prayed that water would get to us. I had used mine more sparingly than some men had, but I finally emptied both of my canteens by the time we finished the gun pit. Dissolving dextrose tablets in my mouth helped a little, but my thirst grew worse through the night. For the first time in my life, I appreciated fully the motion picture cliché of a man on a desert crying, "Water, water."

Artillery shells still passed back and forth overhead just before dawn, but there wasn't much small-arms fire in our area. Abruptly, there swept over us some of the most intense Japanese machine-gun fire I ever saw concentrated in such a small area. Tracers streaked and bullets cracked not more than a foot over the top of our gun pit. We lay flat on our backs and waited as the burst ended.

The gun cut loose again, joined by a second and possibly a third. Streams of bluish white tracers (American tracers were red) poured thickly overhead, apparently coming from somewhere near the airfield. The cross fire kept up for at least a quarter of an hour. They really poured it on.

Shortly before the machine guns opened fire, we had received word to move out at daylight with the entire 5th Marine regiment in an attack across the airfield. I prayed the machine-gun fire would subside before we had to move out. We were pinned down tightly. To raise anything above the edge of the gun pit would have resulted in its being cut off as though by a giant scythe. After about fifteen minutes, firing ceased abruptly. We sighed in relief.

D PLUS 1

Dawn finally came, and with it the temperature rose rapidly.

"Where the hell is our water?" growled men around me. We had suffered many cases of heat prostration the day before and needed water or we'd all pass out during the attack, I thought.

"Stand by to move out!" came the order. We squared away all of our personal gear. Snafu secured the gun, took it down by folding the bipod and strapping it, while I packed my remaining shells in my ammo bag.

"I've got to get some water or I'm gonna crack up," I said.

At that moment, a buddy nearby yelled and beckoned to us, "Come on, we've found a well."

I snatched up my carbine and took off, empty canteens bouncing on my cartridge belt. About twenty-five yards away, a group of Company K men gathered at a hole about fifteen feet in diameter and ten feet deep. I peered over the edge. At the bottom and to one side was a small pool of milky-looking water. Japanese shells were beginning to fall on the airfield, but I was too thirsty to care. One of the men was already in the hole filling canteens and passing them up. The buddy who had called me was drinking from a helmet with its liner removed. He gulped down the milky stuff and said, "It isn't beer, but it's wet." Helmets and canteens were passed up to those of us waiting.

"Don't bunch up, you guys. We'll draw Jap fire sure as hell," shouted one man.

The first man who drank the water looked at me and said, "I feel sick."

A company corpsman came up yelling, "Don't drink that water, you guys. It may be poisoned." I had just lifted a full helmet to my lips when the man next to me fell, holding his sides and retching violently. I threw down my water, milky with coral dust, and started assisting the corpsman with the man who was ill. He went to the rear, where he recovered. Whether it was poison or pollution we never knew.

"Get your gear on and stand by," someone yelled.

Frustrated and angry, I headed back to the gun pit. A detail came up about that time with water cans, ammo, and rations. A friend and I helped each other pour water out of a five-gallon can into our canteen cups. Our hands shook, we were so eager to quench our thirst. I was amazed that the water looked brown in my aluminum canteen cup. No matter, I took a big gulp—and almost spit it out despite my terrible thirst. It was awful. Full of rust and oil, it stunk. I looked into the cup in disbelief as a blue film of oil floated lazily on the surface of the smelly brown liquid. Cramps gripped the pit of my stomach.

My friend looked up from his cup and groaned, "Sledgehammer, are you thinking what I'm thinking?"

"I sure am, that oil drum steam-cleaning detail on Pavuvu," I said wearily. (We had been together on a detail assigned to clean out the drums.)

"I'm a sonofabitch," he growled. "I'll never goof off on another work party as long as I live."

I told him I didn't think it was our fault. We weren't the only ones assigned to the detail, and it was obvious to us from the start (if not to some supply officer) that the method we had been ordered to use didn't really clean the drums. But that knowledge was slight consolation out there on the Peleliu airfield in the increasing heat. As awful as the stuff was, we had to drink it or suffer heat exhaustion. After I drained my cup, a residue of rust resembling coffee grounds remained, and my stomach ached.

We picked up our gear and prepared to move out in preparation for the attack across the airfield. Because 3/5's line during the night faced south and was back-to-back with that of 2/5, we had to move to the right and prepare to attack northward across the airfield with the other battalions of the regiment. The Japanese shelling of our lines began at daylight, so we had to move out fast and in dispersed formation. We finally got into position for the attack and were told to hit the deck until ordered to move again. This suited me fine, because the Japanese shelling was getting worse. Our artillery, ships, and planes were laying down a terrific amount of fire in front on the airfield and ridges beyond in preparation for our attack. Our preattack barrage lasted about half an hour. I knew we would move out when it ended.

As I lay on the blistering hot coral and looked across the open airfield, heat waves shimmered and danced, distorting the view of Bloody Nose Ridge. A hot wind blew in our faces.

An NCO hurried by, crouching low and yelling, "Keep moving out there, you guys. There's less chance you'll be hit if you go across fast and don't stop."

"Let's go," shouted an officer who waved toward the airfield. We moved at a walk, then a trot, in widely dispersed waves. Four infantry battalions—from left to right 2/1, 1/5, 2/5, and 3/5 (this put us on the edge of the airfield)—moved across the open, fire-swept airfield. My only concern then was my duty and survival, not panoramic combat scenes. But I often wondered later what that attack looked like to aerial observers and to those not immersed in the fire storms. All I was aware of were the small area immediately around me and the deafening noise.

Bloody Nose Ridge dominated the entire airfield. The Japanese had concentrated their heavy weapons on high ground; these were directed from observation posts at elevations as high as three hundred feet from which they could look down on us as we advanced. I could see men moving ahead of my squad, but I didn't know whether our battalion, 3/5, was moving across behind 2/5 and then wheeling to the right. There were also men about twenty yards to our rear.

We moved rapidly in the open, amid craters and coral rubble, through ever increasing enemy fire. I saw men to my right and left running bent as low as possible. The shells screeched and whistled, exploding all around us. In many respects it was more terrifying than the landing, because there were no vehicles to carry us along, not even the thin steel sides of an amtrac for protection. We were exposed, running on our own power through a veritable shower of deadly metal and the constant crash of explosions.

For me the attack resembled World War I movies I had seen of suicidal Allied infantry attacks through shell fire on the Western Front. I clenched my teeth, squeezed my carbine stock, and recited over and over to myself, "The Lord is my shepherd; I shall not want. Yea, though I walk through the valley of the shadow of death, I will fear no evil, for Thou art with me; Thy rod and Thy staff comfort me. . . ."

The sun bore down unmercifully, and the heat was exhausting. Smoke and dust from the barrage limited my vision. The ground seemed to sway back and forth under the concussions. I felt as though I were floating along in the vortex of some unreal thunderstorm. Japanese bullets snapped and cracked, and tracers went by me on both sides at waist height. This deadly small-arms fire seemed almost insignificant amid the erupting shells. Explosions and the hum and the growl of shell fragments shredded the air. Chunks of blasted coral stung my face and hands while steel fragments spattered down on the hard rock like hail on a city street. Everywhere shells flashed like giant firecrackers.

Through the haze I saw Marines stumble and pitch forward as they got hit. I then looked neither right nor left but just straight to my front. The farther we went, the worse it got. The noise and concussion pressed in on my ears like a vise. I gritted my teeth and braced myself in anticipation of the shock of being struck down at any moment. It seemed impossible that any of us could make it across. We passed several craters that offered shelter, but I remembered the order to keep moving. Because of the superb discipline and excellent esprit of the Marines, it had never occurred to us that the attack might fail.

About halfway across, I stumbled and fell forward. At that instant a large shell exploded to my left with a flash and a roar. A fragment ricocheted off the deck and growled over my head as I went down. On my right, Snafu let out a grunt and fell as the fragment struck him. As he went down, he grabbed his left side. I crawled quickly to him. Fortunately the fragment had spent much of its force, and luckily hit against Snafu's heavy web pistol belt. The threads on the broad belt were frayed in about an inch-square area.

I knelt beside him, and we checked his side. He had only a bruise to show for his incredible luck. On the deck I saw the chunk of steel that had hit him. It was about an inch square and a half inch thick. I picked up the fragment and showed it to him. Snafu motioned toward his pack. Terrified though I was amid the hellish chaos, I calmly juggled the fragment around in my hands—it was still hot—and dropped it into his pack. He yelled something that sounded dimly like, "Let's go." I reached for the carrying strap of the mortar, but he pushed my hand away and lifted the gun to his shoulder. We got up and moved on as fast as we could. Finally we got across and caught up with other members of our company who lay panting and sweating amid low bushes on the northeastern side of the airfield.

How far we had come in the open I never knew, but it must have been several hundred yards. Everyone was visibly shaken by the thunderous barrage we had just come through. When I looked into the eyes of those fine Guadalcanal and Cape Gloucester veterans, some of America's best, I no longer felt ashamed of my trembling hands and almost laughed at myself with relief.

To be shelled by massed artillery and mortars is absolutely terrifying, but to be shelled in the open is terror compounded beyond the belief of anyone who hasn't experienced it. The attack across Peleliu's airfield was the worst combat experience I had during the entire war. It surpassed, by the intensity of the blast and shock of the bursting shells, all the subsequent horrifying ordeals on Peleliu and Okinawa.

The heat was incredibly intense. The temperature that day reached 105 degrees in the shade (we were *not* in the shade) and would soar to 115 degrees on subsequent days. Corpsmen tagged numerous Marines with heat prostration as being too weak to continue. We evacuated them. My boondockers were so full of sweat that my feet felt squishy when I walked. Lying on my back, I held up first one foot and then the other. Water literally poured out of each shoe.

"Hey, Sledgehammer," chuckled a man sprawled next to me, "You been walking on water."

"Maybe that's why he didn't get hit coming across that airfield," laughed another.

I tried to grin and was glad the inevitable wisecracks had started up again.

Because of the shape of the airfield, 3/5 was pinched out of the line by 2/5 on our left and 3/7 on our right after our crossing. We swung eastward and Company K tied in with 3/7, which was attacking in the swampy areas on the eastern side of the airfield.

As we picked up our gear, a veteran remarked to me with a jerk of his head toward the airfield where the shelling continued, "That was rough duty; hate to have to do that every day."

We moved through the swamps amid sniper fire and dug in for the night with our backs to the sea. I positioned my mortar in a meager gun pit on a slight rise of ground about fifteen feet from a sheer rock bluff that dropped about ten feet to the ocean. The jungle growth was extremely thick, but we had a clear hole in the jungle canopy above the gun pit through which we could fire the mortar without having shells hit the foliage and explode.

Most of the men in the company were out of sight through the thick mangroves. Still short of water, everyone was weakened by the heat and the exertions of the day. I had used my water as sparingly as possible and had to eat twelve salt tablets that day. (We kept close count of these tablets. They caused retching if we took more than necessary.)

The enemy infiltration that followed was a nightmare. Illumination fired above the airfield the previous night (D day) had discouraged infiltration in my sector, but others had experienced plenty of the hellish sort of thing we now faced and would suffer every night for the remainder of our time on Peleliu. The Japanese were noted for their infiltration tactics. On Peleliu they refined them and practiced them at a level of intensity not seen in the past.

After we had dug in late that afternoon we followed a procedure used nearly every night. Using directions from our observer, we registered in the mortar by firing a couple of HE shells into a defilade or some similar avenue of approach in front of the company not covered by our machine-gun or rifle fire where the enemy might advance. We then set up alternate aiming stakes to mark other terrain features on which we could fire. Everyone lighted up a smoke, and the password for the night was whispered along the line, passed from foxhole to foxhole. The password always contained the letter *L*, which the Japanese had difficulty pronouncing the way an American would.

Word came along as to the disposition of the platoons of the company and of the units on our flanks. We checked our weapons and placed equipment for quick access in the coming night. As darkness fell, the order was passed, "The smoking lamp is out." All talking ceased. One man in each foxhole settled down as comfortably as he could to sleep on the jagged rock while his buddy strained eyes and ears to detect any movement or sound in the darkness.

An occasional Japanese mortar shell came into the area, but things were pretty quiet for a couple of hours. We threw up a few HE shells as harassing fire to discourage movement in front of the company. I could hear the sea lapping gently against the base of the rocks behind us.

The Japanese soon began trying to infiltrate all over the company front and along the shore to our rear. We heard sporadic bursts of small-arms fire and the bang of grenades. Our fire discipline had to be strict in such situations so as not to mistakenly shoot a fellow Marine. The loose accusation was often made during the war that Americans were "trigger happy" at night and shot at anything that moved. This accusation was often correct when referring to rear-area or inexperienced troops; but in the rifle companies, it was also accepted as gospel that anybody who moved out of his hole at night without first informing the men around him, and who didn't reply immediately with the password upon being challenged, could expect to get shot.

Suddenly movement in the dried vegetation toward the front of the gun pit got my attention. I turned cautiously around and waited, holding Snafu's cocked .45 automatic pistol at the ready. The rustling movements drew closer. My heart pounded. It was definitely not one of Peleliu's numerous land crabs that scuttled over the ground all night, every night. Someone was slowly crawling toward the gun pit. Then silence. More noise, then silence. Rustling noises, then silence—the typical pattern.

It must be a Japanese trying to slip in as close as possible, stopping frequently to prevent detection, I thought. He probably had seen the muzzle flash when I fired the mortar. He would throw a grenade at any moment or jump me with his bayonet. I couldn't see a thing in the pale light and inky blackness of the shadows.

Crouching low so as to see better any silhouette against the sky above me, I flipped off the thumb safety on the big pistol. A helmeted figure loomed up against the night sky in front of the gun pit. I couldn't tell from the silhouette whether the helmet was U.S. or Japanese. Aiming the automatic at the center of the head, I pressed the grip safety as I also squeezed the trigger slightly to take up the slack. The thought raced through my mind that he was too close to use his grenade so he would probably use a bayonet or knife on me. My hand was steady even though I was scared. It was he or I.

"What's the password?" I said in a low voice.

No answer.

"Password!" I demanded as my finger tightened on the trigger. The big pistol would fire and buck with recoil in a moment, but to hurry and jerk the trigger would mean a miss for sure. Then he'd be on me.

"Sle-Sledgehammer!" stammered the figure.

I eased up on the trigger.

"It's de l'Eau, Jay de l'Eau. You got any water?"

"Jay, why didn't you give the password? I nearly shot you!" I gasped.

He saw the pistol and moaned, "Oh, Jesus," as he realized what had nearly happened. "I thought you knew it was me," he said weakly.

Jay was one of my closest friends. He was a Gloucester veteran and knew better than to prowl around the way he had just done. If my finger had applied the last bit of pressure to that trigger, Jay would have died instantly. It would have been his own fault, but that wouldn't have mattered to me. My life would have been ruined if I had killed him, even under those circumstances.

My right hand trembled violently as I lowered the big automatic. I had to flip on the thumb safety with my left hand; my right thumb was too weak. I felt nauseated and weak and wanted to cry. Jay crept over and sat on the edge of the gun pit.

"I'm sorry, Sledgehammer. I thought you knew it was me," he said.

After handing him a canteen, I shuddered violently and thanked God that Jay was still alive. "Just how in the hell could I tell it was you in the dark with Nips all over the place?" I snarled. Then I reamed out one of the best friends I ever had.

HEADING NORTH

"Get your gear on and stand by to move out."

We shouldered our loads and began moving slowly out of the thick swamp. As I passed a shallow foxhole where Robert B. Oswalt had been dug in, I asked a man nearby if the word were true about Oswalt being killed. Sadly, he said yes. Oswalt had been fatally wounded in the head. A bright young mind that aspired to delve into the mysteries of the human brain to alleviate human suffering had itself been destroyed by a tiny chunk of metal. What a waste, I thought. War is such self-defeating, organized madness the way it destroys a nation's best.

I wondered also about the hopes and aspirations of a dead Japanese we had just dragged out of the water. But those of us caught up in the maelstrom of combat had little compassion for the enemy. As a wise, salty NCO had put it one day on Pavuvu when asked by a replacement if he ever felt sorry for the Japanese when they got hit, "Hell no! It's them or us!"

We moved out, keeping our five-pace interval, through the thick swamp toward the sound of heavy firing. The heat was almost unbearable, and we were halted frequently to prevent heat prostration in the 115-degree temperature.

We came to the eastern edge of the airfield and halted in the shade of a scrub thicket. Throwing down our gear, we fell on the deck, sweating, panting, exhausted. I had no more than reached for a canteen when a rifle bullet snapped overhead.

"He's close. Get down," said an officer. The rifle cracked again. "Sounds like he's right through there a little way," the officer said.

"I'll get him," said Howard Nease.

"OK, go ahead, but watch yourself."

Nease, a Gloucester veteran, grabbed his rifle and took off into the scrub with the nonchalance of a hunter going after a rabbit in a bush. He angled to one side so as to steal up on the sniper from the rear. We waited a few anxious moments, then heard two M1 shots.

"Ole Howard got him," confidently remarked one of the men.

Soon Howard reappeared wearing a triumphant grin and carrying a Japanese rifle and some personal effects. Everyone congratulated him on his skill, and he reacted with his usual modesty.

"Rack 'em up, boys," he laughed.

We moved out in a few minutes through some knee-high bushes onto the open area at the edge of the airfield. The heat was terrific. When we halted again, we lay under the meager shade of the bushes. I held up each foot and let the sweat pour out of my boondockers. A man on the crew of the other weapon in our mortar section passed out. He was a Gloucester veteran, but Peleliu's heat proved too much for him. We evacuated him, but unlike some heat prostration cases, he never returned to the company.

Some men pulled the rear border of their camouflaged helmet cover out from between the steel and the liner so the cloth hung down over the backs of the necks. This gave them some protection against the blistering sun, but they looked like the French foreign legion in a desert.

After a brief rest, we continued in dispersed order. We could see Bloody Nose Ridge to our left front. Northward from that particular area, 2d Battalion, 1st Marines (2/1) was fighting desperately against Japanese hidden in well-protected caves. We were moving up to relieve 1st Battalion, 5th Marines (1/5) and would tie in with the 1st Marines. Then we were to attack northward along the eastern side of the ridges.

On this particular day, 17 September, the relief was slow and difficult. As 3/5 moved in and the men of 1/5 moved out, the Japanese in the ridges on our left front poured on the artillery and mortar fire. I pitied those tired men in 1/5 as they tried to extricate themselves without casualties. Their battalion, as with the others in the 5th Marines, had had a rough time crossing the airfield through the heavy fire the previous day. But once they got across they met heavy resistance from pillboxes on the eastern side. We had been more fortunate: after getting across the airfield, 3/5 moved into the swamp, which wasn't defended as heavily.

With the relief of 1/5 finally completed, we tied in with the 1st Marines on our left and 2/5 on our right. Our battalion was to attack during the afternoon through the low ground along the eastern side of Bloody Nose, while 2/5 was to clean out the jungle between our right flank and the eastern shore.

As soon as we moved forward, we came under heavy flanking fire from Bloody Nose Ridge on our left. Snafu delivered his latest communiqué on the tactical situation to me as we hugged the deck for protection: "They need to git some more damn troops up here," he growled.

Our artillery was called in, but our mortars could fire only to the front of the company and not on the left flank area, because that was in the area of the 1st Marines. The Japanese observers on the ridge had a clear, unobstructed view of us. Their artillery shells whined and shrieked, accompanied by the deadly whispering of the mortar shells. Enemy fire grew more intense, until we were pinned down. We were getting the first bitter taste of Bloody Nose Ridge, and we had increasing compassion for the 1st Marines on our left who were battering squarely into it.

The Japanese ceased firing when our movement stopped. Yet as surely as three men grouped together, or anyone started moving, enemy mortars opened up on us. If a general movement occurred, their artillery joined in. The Japanese began to demonstrate the excellent fire discipline that was to characterize their use of all weapons on Peleliu. They fired only when they could expect to inflict maximum casualties and stopped firing as soon as the opportunity passed. Thus our observers and planes had difficulty finding their well-camouflaged positions in the ridges.

When the enemy ceased firing artillery and mortars from caves, they shut protective steel doors and waited while our artillery, naval guns, and 81mm mortars blasted away at the rock. If we moved ahead under our protective fire support, the Japanese pinned us down and inflicted serious losses on us, because it was almost impossible to dig a protective foxhole in the rock. No individual events of the attack stuck in my mind, just the severe fire from our left and the feeling that any time the Japanese decided to do so, they could have blown us sky high.

Our attack was called off late in the afternoon, and we were ordered to set up our mortar for the night. An NCO came by and told me to go with him and about four others from other platoons to unload an amtrac bringing up supplies for Company K. We arrived at the designated place, dispersed a little so as not to draw fire, and waited for the amtrac. In a few minutes it came clanking up in a swirl of white dust.

"You guys from K Company, 5th Marines?" asked the driver.

"Yeah, you got chow and ammo for us?" asked our NCO.

"Yeah, sure have. Got a unit of fire, water, and rations. Better get it unloaded as soon as you can, or we'll draw fire," the driver said as his machine lurched to a halt and he climbed down.

The tractor was an older model such as I had landed from on D day. It didn't have a drop tailgate; so we climbed aboard and hefted the heavy ammo boxes over the side and down onto the deck.

"Let's go, boys," our NCO said as he and a couple of us climbed onto the tractor.

I saw him gaze in amazement down into the cargo area of the tractor. At the bottom, wedged under a pile of ammo boxes, we saw one of those infernal fifty-five-gallon oil drums of water. Filled, they weighed several hundred pounds. Our NCO rested his arms on the side of the tractor and remarked in an exasperated tone, "It took a bloody genius of a supply officer to do that. How in the hell are we supposed to get that drum outa there?"

"I don't know," said the driver. "I just bring it up."

We cursed and began unloading the ammo as fast as possible. We had expected the water to be in several five-gallon cans, each of which weighed a little more than forty pounds. We worked as rapidly as possible, but then we heard that inevitable and deadly *whisshh-shh-shh.* Three big mortar shells exploded, one after the other, not far from us.

"Uh oh, the stuff's hit the fan now," groaned one of my buddies.

"Bear a hand, you guys. On the double," said our NCO.

"Look, you guys, I'm gonna hafta get this tractor the hell outa here. If it gets knocked out and it's my fault, the lieutenant'll have my can in a crack," groaned the driver.

We had no gripe with the driver, and we didn't blame him. The amtrac drivers on Peleliu were praised by everyone for doing such a fine job. Their bravery and sense of responsibility were above question. We worked like beavers as our NCO said to him, "I'm sorry, ole buddy, but if we don't get these supplies unloaded, it's *our* ass!"

More mortar shells fell out to one side, and the fragments swished through the air. It was apparent that the Japanese mortar crew was trying to bracket us, but was afraid to fire too much for fear of being seen by our observers. We sweated and panted to get the ammo unloaded. We unloaded the water drum with a rope sling.

"You fellows need any help?" asked a Marine who appeared from the rear.

We hadn't noticed him before he spoke. He wore green dungarees, leggings, and a cloth-covered helmet like ourselves and carried a .45 caliber automatic pistol like any mortar gunner, machine gunner, or one of our officers. Of course, he wore no rank insignia, being in combat. What astonished us was that he looked to be more than fifty years old and wore glasses—a rarity (for example, only two men in Company K wore them). When he took off his helmet to mop his brow, we saw his gray hair. (Most men forward of division and regimental CPs were in their late teens or early twenties. Many officers were in their mid-twenties.)

When asked who he was and what unit he was in, he replied, "Capt. Paul Douglas. I was division adjutant until that barrage hit the 5th

Marines' CP yesterday, then I was assigned as R-1 [personnel officer] in the 5th Regiment. I am very proud to be with the 5th Marines," he said. "Gosh, Cap'n! You don't have to be up here at all, do you?" asked one of our detail in disbelief as he passed ammo boxes to the fatherly officer. "No," Douglas said, "but I always want to know how you boys up here are making out and want to help if I can. What company are you fellows from?"

"From K Company, sir," I answered.

His face lit up, and he said, "Ah, you're in Andy Haldane's company." We asked Douglas if he knew Ack Ack. He said, yes, that they were old friends. As we finished unloading, we all agreed that there wasn't a finer company commander than Captain Haldane.

A couple more mortar shells crashed nearby. Our luck would run out soon. Japanese gunners usually got right on target. So we yelled, "Shove off," to the driver. He waved and clanked away in his unloaded amtrac. Captain Douglas helped us stack some of the ammo and told us we had better disperse.

I heard a buddy ask, "What's that crazy old gray-headed guy doing up here if he could be back at regiment?"

Our NCO growled, "Shut up! Knock it off, you eightball! He's trying to help knuckleheads like you, and he's a damned good man."

(Paul Douglas became a legend in the 1st Marine Division. This remarkable man was fifty-three years old, had been an economics professor at the University of Chicago, and had enlisted in the Marine Corps as a private. In the Peleliu battle he was slightly wounded carrying flamethrower ammunition up to the lines. At Okinawa he was wounded seriously by a bullet in the arm while carrying wounded for 3/5. Even after months of therapy, he didn't regain complete use of the limb.

Years after the war, I had the great pleasure of meeting and visiting with Senator Paul Douglas. I told him about the remark referring to him as the "crazy old gray-headed guy." He laughed heartily and expressed great pride in having served with the 1st Marine Division.)

Each man in our detail took up a load of supplies, bade Captain Douglas "so long," and started back to the company lines. Other men went back to bring up the rest of the supplies before dark. We ate chow and finished preparations for the night. That was the first night on Peleliu that I was able to make up a cup of hot bouillon from the dehydrated tablets in my K rations and a canteen cup of heated, polluted, oily water. Hot as the weather was, it was the most nourishing and refreshing food I had eaten in three days. The next day we got fresh water. It was a great relief after that polluted stuff.

Dug in next to our gun pit were 1st Lt. Edward A. ("Hillbilly") Jones, Company K's machine-gun platoon leader, and a salty sergeant, John A. Teskevich. Things were quiet in our area except for our artillery's harassing fire pouring over; so after dark obscured us from Japanese observers, the two of them slipped over and sat at the edge of our gun pit. We shared rations and talked. The conversation turned out to be one of the most memorable of my life.

Hillbilly was second only to Ack Ack in popularity among the enlisted men in Company K. He was a clean-cut, handsome, light-complexioned man—not large, but well built. Hillbilly told me he had been an enlisted man for several prewar years, had gone to the Pacific with the company, and had been commissioned following Guadalcanal. He didn't say why he was made an officer, but the word among the men was that he had been outstanding on Guadalcanal.

It was a widespread joke among men in the ranks during the war that an officer was made an officer and a gentleman by an act of Congress when he was commissioned. An act of Congress may have made Hillbilly an officer, but he was born a gentleman. No matter how filthy and dirty everyone was on the battlefield, Hillbilly's face always had a clean, fresh appearance. He was physically tough and hard and obviously morally strong. He sweated as much as any man but somehow seemed to stand above our foul and repulsive living conditions in the field. Hillbilly had a quiet and pleasant voice even in command. His accent was soft, more that of the deep South, which was familiar to me, than that of the hill country.

Between this man and all the Marines I knew there existed a deep mutual respect and warm friendliness. He had that rare ability to be friendly yet not familiar with enlisted men. He possessed a unique combination of those qualities of bravery, leadership, ability, integrity, dignity, straightforwardness, and compassion. The only other officer I ever knew who was his equal in all these qualities was Captain Haldane.

That night Hillbilly talked about his boyhood and his home in West Virginia. He asked me about mine. He also talked about his prewar years in the Marine Corps. Later I remembered little of what he said, but the quiet way he talked calmed me. He was optimistic about the battle in progress and seemed to understand and appreciate all my fears and apprehensions. I confided in him that many times I had been so terrified that I felt ashamed, and that some men didn't seem to be so afraid. He scoffed at my mention of being ashamed, and said that my fear had been no greater than anyone else's but that I was just honest enough to admit its magnitude. He told me that he was afraid, too, and that the first battle was the hardest because a man didn't know what to expect. Fear dwelled in everyone, Hillbilly said. Courage meant overcoming fear and doing one's duty in the presence of danger, not being unafraid.

The conversation with Hillbilly reassured me. When the sergeant came over and joined in after getting coffee, I felt almost lighthearted. As conversation trailed off, we sipped our joe in silence.

Suddenly, I heard a loud voice say clearly and distinctly, "You will survive the war!"

I looked first at Hillbilly and then at the sergeant. Each returned my glance with a quizzical expression on his face in the gathering darkness. Obviously they hadn't said anything.

"Did y'all hear that?" I asked.

"Hear what?" they both inquired.

"Someone said something," I said.

"I didn't hear anything. How about you?" said Hillbilly, turning to the sergeant.

"No, just that machine gun off to the left."

Shortly the word was passed to get settled for the night. Hillbilly and the sergeant crawled back to their hole as Snafu returned to the gun pit. Like most persons, I had always been skeptical about people seeing visions and hearing voices. So I didn't mention my experience to anyone. But I believed God spoke to me that night on that Peleliu battlefield, and I resolved to make my life amount to something after the war.

That night—the third since landing—as I settled back in the gun pit, I realized I needed a bath. In short, I stunk! My mouth felt, as the saying went, like I had gremlins walking around in it with muddy boots on. Short as it was, my hair was matted with dust and rifle oil. My scalp itched, and my stubble beard was becoming an increasing source of irritation in the heat. Drinking water was far too precious in those early days to use in brushing one's teeth or in shaving, even if the opportunity had arisen.

The personal bodily filth imposed upon the combat infantryman by living conditions on the battlefield was difficult for me to tolerate. It bothered almost everyone I knew. Even the hardiest Marine typically kept his rifle and his person clean. His language and his mind might need a good bit of cleaning up but not his weapon, his uniform, or his person. We had this philosophy drilled into us in boot camp, and many times at Camp Elliott I had to pass personal inspection, to the point of clean fingernails, before being passed as fit to go on liberty. To be anything less than neat and sharp was considered a negative reflection on the Marine Corps and wasn't tolerated.

It was tradition and folklore of the 1st Marine Division that the troops routinely referred to themselves when in the field as "the raggedy-ass Marines." The emphasis during maneuvers and field problems was on combat readiness. Once back in camp, however, no matter where in the boondocks it was situated, the troops cleaned up before anything else.

In combat, cleanliness for the infantryman was all but impossible. Our filth added to our general misery. Fear and filth went hand in hand. It has always puzzled me that this important factor in our daily lives has received so little attention from historians and often is omitted from otherwise excellent personal memoirs by infantrymen. It is, of course, a vile subject, but it was as important to us then as being wet or dry, hot or cold, in the shade or exposed to the blistering sun, hungry, tired, or sick.

KERMIT STEWART

Second Lieutenant Kermit Stewart took part in the reconquest of the Philippines with the 43rd Infantry Division.

To His Parents

New Guinea
5 Nov. '44

Dear Folks:

Well, you called the wrong shot this time. You will note that I am still sitting, safely and monotonously, here in New Guinea. Don't know how much longer it's going to last, but here I am . . .

Don't worry about the "literacy" of your letters. Remember that I censor a pile of letters every day, and it's an education about U.S. education to read them. Many are quite good, of course—but the rest!!?! It is also an interesting job (however boring) in that you learn that you are not the only person in the world who has troubles. Staying here, isolated this way, and comparatively inactive, is very depressing to everyone's morale. You can sense it in the letters. Worries about home affairs become magnified, lack of feminine companionship becomes unbearable, petty annoyances assume large proportions, the specter of a coming campaign becomes terrifying. In our small company alone the past 3 weeks two boys have been evacuated as psycho-neurotics. That's a polite name for going batty.

In a neighboring company a chap's wife became pregnant—by his father! He went completely nuts. One boy in our company died recently from natural causes. One of my jobs is to gather up personal belongings of evacuees or casualties and send them on. It's a depressing job to sort out the pitifully few trinkets and the mementoes of a frustrated life—and send them home where they will open old hurts anew. Hope I have very little of that to do. A few nurses have been shipped in recently with a hospital unit. I saw a couple of them from a distance the other day—the first women I've seen in months. There are just enough of them to be a nuisance. We have had to put canvas screens around showers, latrines, etc—and to wear bathing trunks on the beach. Gone is the life uninhibited. That's all for now. I enjoy your letters—Keep writing—

Love to all,
Kermit

To Guy

The Philippines
7 March 1945

Dear Guy:
    Your letter of Feb. 10th came yesterday—and left me with my mouth hanging open. Now I'm wondering what the hell I said that seemed to impress you all so much. I wrote that letter soon after the last hand-to-hand action I've had and when the memory of ten or twelve days of action was still vividly in mind. Much of it will always be vivid.
    Actual battle is the very essence of emotional drama. In some of the tightest places I've been in I've been aware of the stark drama of the situation. As a would-be writer I've become conscious of such things. Some of that drama and emotionalism must have communicated itself in my letter—although I remember very little of what I said. I hope people didn't think I was trying to dramatize myself. My role has been just that of any other infantry officer—and not in the least heroic. One of my boys did a fine job one day—and I've put him in for a Silver Star. One of the tank drivers was killed and we were trying to pull out of a position where we were under heavy fire. I yelled for an assistant driver—he stuck himself out of a hole and asked what I wanted. "Can you drive that tank out?"—then I noticed a huge bandage over his arm. "Jesus, are you hurt?"—"Just a scratch."—"Can you drive?"—"Sure!" So he hustles a hundred yards under fire—climbs into the tank—and drives it five miles one handed—and it was piled full of wounded men. The guy is still in the hospital with a cut to the bone through his biceps. I hope he gets a medal—"Just a scratch!"
    I don't care what you do with any of my letters—read or print—if they will help people to realize what the men go thru. I just don't want to

be thought of as trying to emphasize my part in this hell of a war.

We've been fighting again—I don't know how many days. I've had a lot of responsibility. I directed my cannon fire today—hundreds of rounds—and most of the time firing within one to two hundred yards of our own men. The least slip, and maybe twenty of your own men get killed. When you've sat thru 300 rounds—nerves like fiddle strings till each round hits—well, that's one thing that makes an old man of you.

You have to admire the guts of these little Japs sometimes. Our men were attacking a ridge. Thru my glasses, 2,000 yards away, I suddenly saw a dozen Japs' head and shoulders above the ridge, rifles ready, like tin soldiers in a toy shop. I put a round of 105 right in the middle of them. They ducked, and came up again. That happened 5 or 6 times.—Guts—Finally we got tired of that—so I adjusted time fire about ten yards over their heads and laid in a barrage. Fox holes or trenches—they couldn't have lived thru that—and we saw no more of them. We located a pill box near there and adjusted fire on it. The third shot knocked off a corner of it—and eight Japs—looking like animated dolls thru our glasses—came running out. Our infantry was a hundred yards away—and they mowed them down with rifle fire. Our next shot was directly on the box and threw logs sky-high. It burned for an hour. That's just one example of what is happening time and again in my job. And, of course, the Japs shoot back. Fortunately, they have no heavy guns in this position, and I'm personally fairly safe in this campaign—so far. The worst worry I've had is not to hit our own men—and so far we've been lucky—or rather, the GIs have been lucky.

I sometimes reflect with amazement on my role in this war. I used to be a music teacher—I was a pacifist—talked about the infinite value of the human personality—how barbaric it was to kill a man because he was in another color uniform. But here I am—and when we make a direct hit, we smile grimly at each other and phone a "well done" to the gun crew. One day a Jap who had been bypassed nearly killed one of my sergeants. He was in a hole in a river bank. I, and some of my boys, covered the sergeant (he got the honor) while he crept up and threw two grenades into the hole. Then the men dragged out the Jap, and poured a whole magazine of tommy-gun into him. After that it's my job to search the body for documents. And it doesn't bother me! Do you wonder that I say I'm sometimes amazed at myself? I'm more of a pacifist than I ever was, but as long as there are vermin like Japs and Nazis, they have to be exterminated—and it is hellish work. The cost in human lives, material and labor simply can't be estimated.

My love to Janice and Prudence—and thanks for your good letter.

Yours,
Kermit

JOHN GUEST
1911–

John Guest was a highly literary, sensitive young British artillery officer who kept a journal and sent it in installments to his friend Christopher Hassall (later, the biographer of Rupert Brooke). After the war, he worked as an editor in London publishing houses. The book he made from his wartime journal he published as Broken Images *in 1949.*

From BROKEN IMAGES

20TH NOVEMBER [1941]: GLASGOW

I'm afraid a good time has elapsed since I last wrote anything. I've felt singularly unproductive—not unhappy—just busy and dull. Several times I've sat down to write to you, but on each occasion I've dried up, and gone for a walk or gone to the cinema instead. Meantime the poisonous stain of the war is seeping over the whole surface of the earth. I find I cannot think clearly about it at all. It has become too big for comprehension. The only thing about it that touches me personally is the final absolute realisation that what is past is past. I've told myself so before, but I've always been unwilling really to believe it. What is happening now has torn the threads we clung to from our hands. We have cast off—or rather, been shoved off—and I am convinced there will be no return. There are times when I wonder what will become of us all if we are brought low as beasts. Perhaps it will be easier for the thugs than for us, but I am convinced that *we* shall need inexhaustible reservoirs *in ourselves* when the communal ones are blown up, requisitioned or poisoned. In all this change and disintegration the things which will survive are the perfectly self-contained things—you can't put Bach or Shakespeare into concentration camps—and these things, and our personal relationships, will be valuable salvage.

* * *

11TH JANUARY 1943: BEJA

To-night, as so often in England, I write to you because I must. This is the first time since I've been out here that I've had an acute attack of restlessness, of sheer spiritual disorder. I'm afraid that the instalments I wrote in England must often have been overcast just because I flew to writing as one rushes to the lavatory when one thinks one is going to be sick. This, of course, is a terrible confession. It means that I write to you from utterly wrong motives and, looking back, it seems that so much of my writing was done in this manner rather than from normal ebullience.

But my life has been uprooted, shredded and scattered. Some time ago I was pulled into battery, and the Battery Orderly Officer sent out for experience to my troop. Since then I've been harried from pillar to post. I've been looking after a party of reinforcements forty miles back, supervising another party making a road, getting Naafi stores up, chasing after yet another party of 3rd Echelon and, in between times, going forward to battery to report every two or three days. At the moment I've returned to pay and straighten out the lot here.

They are living in a disused granary in a blitzed town about twenty miles from the front. I live with a batman and a sergeant in a little villa opposite. It belonged originally to some Italians and was completely looted when the campaign started. But it still contains a few pieces of battered furniture, and has a little garden full of violets and hyacinths. I write now at a mahogany table by candlelight. Before me are two cigarette tins, one full of white intoxicatingly-scented hyacinths and the other of enormous purple violets which breathe out scent like notes from a violin. But I am unsettled and long for intimacy. If only all this would end.

When I came back on this job I had to leave my batman with the troop, but I managed to get another, a volunteer, from one of the rear parties. He was a very bad batman but so amusing that he more than made up for his lack of skill. We drove about the country together in a Utility, picnicking, buying wine and staying the night at various places. His obvious enjoyment of these excursions increased my own. He talked endlessly, laughed a lot and admired what there was to admire. To-day I had to post him away to another party, and I have been surprised, almost alarmed, to find how much I relied on his company.

It is at times such as to-night that I feel myself growing older. I look back and see nothing, absolutely nothing, done in my life. I wish I were married and had children, a home of my own—something (I must say it) to look forward to. Even the excitement of battle would be better than this nothingness. Churchill has promised a big drive: I hope it comes soon. So much has been written of the horror of war—so little of the boredom. Boredom is a word which conjures up drawing-rooms: there should be a word also for this sort of boredom which annihilates even the spirit. One can escape from "the hot water at ten" and the "closed car at four"—from this there seems to be absolutely no way out.

Do you know (and I have no qualms in saying this, and feel no pride, and am conscious of no conceit) I think I should be brave in battle. What I have seen so far cannot be called battle. But I have so very little to lose. I have never felt what so many healthy-minded people feel—a great tenacity to life. What I fear, and what they would despise in me, is physical pain. But to be instantly destroyed—"to leap into the thinnest air"—by a bomb, a shell or a bullet; surely it is an ideal death. No pain, no lingering anxiety, no consciousness of the sorrow of relatives: the most awful of all transitions accomplished (probably literally) in a flash. And people say it is morbid to talk like this. It is only, to my mind, because their own ideas on death are misplaced that they find it so. It is dying, not death, that I fear. And it is much the same thing with fear itself. So long as there is a chance of escape, so long as you can hear the breath and the padding footsteps of the pursuer behind you, so long as you know that you have not shaken him off, do you feel fear. But as soon as the hand descends on your shoulder and you know that you're caught, that you've "had it," then the worst is over, and with inevitability comes the indifference and resigned courage of the lost.

I wish I could send you a box of these violets beside me: they're singing like nightingales in the candlelight. I do often wonder what you are doing, not just vaguely but at this very moment, now. I hardly ever write to anyone nowadays. You will say that if I can find time to write all this I could find time to write to others, but it isn't so. Something happens to one out here—temporarily the life that goes with writing and talking stops, is laid aside, just as my green tweed suit has been left hanging in the wardrobe at home: it is all right, but it must wait. Of course my life here is a dream, the life in the cave of my skull constantly and infinitely more real to me than this boredom, even than the flashes of field guns, the obscene cactus, the ME.109's sliding through the clouds.

I hate to think of the time these bulletins take to reach you. Letters out here give one the greatest joy, but I know that to say so is a form of blackmail. Still, I should love to know that you have received this safely.

*   *   *

1ST FEBRUARY 1944: SANGRO BRIDGE

I am only too conscious of not having sent you anything for months; indeed, there have even been times when I began to wonder whether I should ever resume these bulletins. But at last I have begun to feel again a certain stirring, an "irritation" which I recognise with pleasure and which makes me feel that, perhaps, after all, I haven't been submerged completely. It may be because, for the first time since we arrived in Italy, we have been settled in one place long enough to have got things organised as a routine (there are now, of course, plans for an impending move). Perhaps it has something to do with the perfect weather, like an English Easter, which we've been having. At any rate, I've looked out of the window where I'm now sitting every day for the past six weeks, but never with such pleasure as at this moment.

Outside is a flat river valley with low hills on the far side beneath a blue evening sky. The land is fertile—dotted with olive trees, clusters of dry yellow bamboos and little winter fruit trees. There are ditches, but no hedges, and one can see where the fields end by the sharply defined colours of green, yellow and brown, or by the vines which are garlanded along the boundaries. Even at this hour there are many Italians working. The women are renewing the bamboo stakes for the vines, and the men are turning the acres of wild white arabis with their crude ploughs, pulled by lumbering pairs of slow white oxen. It is really a Werner Peiner scene; I have thought so especially during the day when one often sees pieces of brilliant blue and white cloth laid on the grass with, perhaps, a red handkerchief and a loaf and a few scarlet red-peppers for lunch. Though there are not many wild flowers yet, I have been astonished at the vivid colouring of the countryside—green boughs in orchards, the pink wands of willows, and pools reflecting the brilliant sky.

We have now got two rooms in a farmhouse, more like attics above a stable at home—bare whitewashed walls, no fireplace, and cobwebby rafters in the roof. Half of the space downstairs consists of stalls occupied by ten huge white oxen. I have noticed that invariably they all lie or stand together—never some doing one thing, some another. Many of the family sleep fully-clothed in the straw with the oxen, and hot dungy smells drift up the stairs at night. As always, I have suffered a good deal with fleas, but we put carbolic powder everywhere, even inside our clothes, to keep them at bay.

The Italians in this part of the country are extraordinarily poor, and have practically no personal belongings. The one room they occupy downstairs contains only an improvised table, a broken chair, some barrels, a pile of sacks and an open fireplace in which they boil water in any old cans they can scrounge. The fields are their lavatory, and there is, of course, no garden—just a muddy patch of ground, a tumble-down shed, a hay-rick and a wood-pile. During the day, until dark, the men work in the fields, and the women sit outside in the sun, de-lousing the children and making wicker baskets, or fetching and cutting wood. I have not yet managed to sort out the relationships in the household. Those who do not sleep in the stable lie on a pile of rugs and sacks in a sort of upstairs potting-shed which contains mounds of grain and dried beans, and a variety of desiccated fruits and vegetables dangling from the rafters. But they are kindly and do our washing for us, and make a surprisingly good job of it; in exchange we give them corned beef, salt, matches and candles, and occasionally a little chocolate for the lousy children who are nevertheless beautiful with great dark eyes and pale olive skins.

But I haven't yet told you why it is that we are living in a house instead of in our tent. The story goes back to the most terrible night of my life—and I say so without any reservations whatsoever—"the night of 1943–44" as we now call it. We were then living in our new I.P. tent which we had made reasonably comfortable by laying rushes on the floor and covering them with sand-bags. The first trial came when I received a signal, just after we had got into bed, that there was to be a rum issue immediately. As all the guns here are far off the road, at the end of long mud-tracks no longer negotiable by vehicles, and in some instances through mine-fields, it was necessary to go on foot. Outside, it was blowing a full gale and streaming with a horizontal mixture of snow, ice and rain. Having been unable to get torch batteries, we had to take hurricane lamps, and these, of course, blew out immediately. At last, in the early hours, having completed several miles thigh-deep in mud, we arrived back wet to the skin, frozen and filthy.

By this time we found that our own tent was in grave danger of collapsing; it lashed with reverberating cracks from side to side until I thought the ropes would snap. In the dark we drove the pegs into the sodden earth as best we could, and hung on to the poles. Pools of water had already formed on the floor, the tent was leaking at every seam, and the temperature was arctic. At any moment I expected the whole thing to be whipped away, and the gale was such that all our possessions would have been whirled off into icy darkness. Finally, one of my officers shouted above the din: "Well, you're the Captain. Do we abandon ship, or don't we?" There was nothing more to be done. If we abandoned the tent all would be lost; so, at three in the morning, utterly exhausted, we got into bed; and since we had all prayed, so far without result, the same man cried in a loud voice: "Kismet! Kismet! We await the end!"

The following morning, New Year's Day, I awoke with the first glimmerings of light and was conscious immediately of a sinister stillness, then of a tremendous weight on my body. It took me a moment to realise that the tent was leaning at an angle of forty-five degrees, and that a great balloon of ice and snow on the outside was pinning me down. But this was nothing to the horror of what I next saw—water lapping the edge of my pillow! There was two feet of water everywhere—clothes, boots, £15 worth of new Naafi issue, all our boxes, everything floating or sunk; all the codes and documents and precious lists of this and that—all beneath the flood! You know how valuable every single item is to one "in the field"; it was a stultifying blow. But, worst of all, the water was visibly rising. I just had time to see the face of one of the other officers, blissfully asleep, his bed almost totally submerged. The next moment they were awake and, though we were only three, cries of dismay filled the tent like a corner of the Inferno.

I hardly remember plunging about to find a pair of boots and trousers, but what I shall never forget is the sheer searing pain, like fire, of almost frozen water. It's hellish. To get out of the field on to the road we had to wade to the arm-pits through this swirling torture. In all, I made three journeys, carrying my bed and what belongings I could save. My legs and belly were shot through with such pain that, for ten minutes after the last journey, I was unable to speak.

The banked canal beside which we had pitched our tent had burst, and where had been fields were now acres of swiftly-flowing silvery-grey water. The first thing I did was to go to the Italian house, turn them out of a room upstairs into the stable, and commandeer the kitchen where there was a fire—and, in doing so, I felt no compunction. The rest of the day was chaotic. Wearing what clothes I could borrow, and with a cap-comforter on my head, I went round the guns. Desolation on every side. The men huddled together, standing in swirling water on petrol tins; wet to the skin, frozen by the wind. There was no question of making fires. The tents were torn to ribbons, the poles snapped like matches. Gun-pits flooded to the layers' seats. Rivers pouring over the roads—and *still* it rained and blew. In the end we got tea going at Troop H.Q. and organised relays for a drink and warm by the fire. Then, shortly before lunch, I found time to report to Battery H.Q. which was on a hillside and relatively intact. Here, a mere pinprick by now, I was severely reproved for appearing improperly dressed. As you can well imagine, it took us about a week to begin to recover. But, as it turned out, we found much of our stuff lying about the field when the floods abated, and on a final reckoning it was remarkable how little we lost.

Since then the weather has been perfect—frost at nights, but blue cloudless days with a silvery morning to golden evening light: and all the countryside so fresh and green and vivid, with something secretive and still in the air, as though the earth were preparing for spring as a surprise, working softly and furtively—but dropping little hints, clumsily, like a child—and you pretending not to notice. I *know*, although I have not even seen the buds, that violets are preparing; and I know too that, although I am forewarned, I shall still see with a thrill of surprise the first moth-wing leaves trembling out of the twigs to dry in the sunlight. That yellowy-green colour! The leaves so thin they seem scarcely to hold back the light.

But, in these banks and fields, where one might look for robins' nests, and larks' nests under the tufts, and the little woven dome of the willow-wren, are iron mines which, at a touch, leap into the air and blast men to a stained rag of battle-dress. I saw a leg standing in the mud here for a whole day before it was removed—and it did not shock or frighten me: it was just supremely disgusting, a jibe at humanity—the actual conclusion of a brutal thought.

It is getting late now, and I have just been out to our lavatory—a plank over a trench—which is situated in a grove of bamboos. I carried a hurricane lamp. It is very disagreeable sitting in the whistling wind, but also strange and eerie with the white bamboos illuminated against the surrounding black, and going up out of sight above, and all the dry spear-shaped leaves grating and squeaking and twittering in the wind. I can *not*, and I can't believe that I ever shall, get used to this open-air business, even after years and years.

The stars are particularly bright to-night; one especially pleases me— it twinkles like a piece of glass in a chandelier, changing from red to orange to yellow to green to blue to violet, as though it were hanging from a thread and turning slowly in the sky, reflecting brilliance from some great hidden light below the horizon.

As I write to you now I am drinking a last cup of tea. The other officers are in bed in our whitewashed room, talking. Outside, the wind flaps the shutters against the wall, the hurricane lamp flickers on the table, a batman who has just brought the tea stands and talks of his civilian job in a brewery.

✳   ✳   ✳

7TH DECEMBER [1944]: SILLARO VALLEY

I have had your note saying that you will be writing soon: in the mean-time I'll meet your letter by beginning this new bulletin. I have not very much energy, my hands are cold, and I hardly know where to begin—or what to say. As usual, I'm writing to get away for a few hours from this life.

I'll tell you first where I am. I'm sitting in an I.P. tent at a table covered with a looted table-cloth—a white cloth (now very dirty) which has fine coloured silk embroidery on it. Under the table is a Valor stove which warms my knees but not my feet. It is ten o'clock in the morning and I have—rare thing—deliberately postponed my visit to the guns until this afternoon. At the end of the tent our two beds are sunk in a trench beneath the level of the ground. There is a good deal of shell-fire here. The feet of the beds stand permanently in water. From the entrance of the tent I see the hillside on which we are pitched—grass, stones and a little harsh scrub. But I can only see at the most a hundred yards. There is a thick white mist, partly natural but mostly chemical. This smoke is released at the top of the valley all day long, since otherwise we would be under observation. When the wind is in the wrong direction the whole valley fills with it and everyone coughs—sheep in a mist—at the filthy taste in their throats.

The ground for fifty yards outside is MUD—six inches deep, glistening, sticky, holding pools of water. Great excavations in the mud, leaving miniature alps of mud, show where other tents have been pitched in the mud, and moved on account of the mud to other places in the mud. The cumulative psychological effect of mud is an experience which cannot be described. Vehicles grind along the road beneath in low gear. Either side of the road is a bank of mud, thigh-deep. The sides of the road collapse frequently and the huge trucks, like weary prehistoric animals, slide helplessly down into the ditches and stick there until dragged out by recovery teams. All the traffic gets held up and people sit in the vehicles clapping their gloved hands to keep warm, smoking, and making wan facetious remarks to the pedestrians who go slopping and slithering past in their gum-boots. My men stand in the gun-pits stamping their feet in the wet, their heads sunk in the collars of their greatcoats. When they speak to you they roll their eyes up because it makes their necks cold to raise their heads. Everyone walks with their arms out to help them keep their balance.

When the wind is in the right direction, and the smoke doesn't blow this way, the valley looks like the approach to Hell—a Doré illustration to Dante. Pinpoints of fire from the field guns flash viciously in all the gullies, the desolation, the *damage*—not a yard of ground that is not torn up: it is barely recognisable, like a corpse that has been flayed—the leafless bushes, the ugliness, the unnaturalness; a dead horse, half skeleton; and a human leg in a boot, gaiter and trouser, that has no more significance than a piece of wood; and, at the end of the valley, the screen of white smoke curling slowly, voluminously and endlessly into the broken blue and grey sky. And yet, one gets used to it. What I have written down is what I have seen and felt, but, by a sort of automatic shutter operating over the senses, one doesn't feel it continuously.

But these last few days I have been seriously unhappy. The reason chiefly is that one morning I found the gun teams of two sites in bed half an hour after "Stand Down", so I put all of them on to full manning for two days. This was a harsh punishment on top of their other difficulties, and I have tormented myself since, wondering whether I was justified. It has created an unpleasant atmosphere, making visiting the guns difficult;

but to relax the punishment would be a weakness that would, perhaps, in the long run cause even more trouble. I am completely stale and would welcome almost any change. Light A.A. has now become a farce, and the maintenance of morale and efficiency when one doubts if one will ever fire again is exhausting. But I mustn't continue in this vein. . . .

I have not told you but, for a period of two months before coming here, we were Infantry. I have written nothing about that and cannot resuscitate it all now—though I should like, for my own purposes, to have made some notes on what we did and felt. Nothing dangerous happened—we neither attacked nor were attacked—and there was only one casualty in my troop: a man shot, at night, in the leg (a muscle wound) by another member of the troop! Most of the time we were on mountains at a height of more than three thousand feet; it practically never stopped raining, and our only communication with the world was by mule, or oxen and sleigh, even for water. The worst part was the occupation of the positions—the gruelling march up in the dark with packs, ammunition, brens, mortars, rations. Men fainted from exhaustion. My most vivid memory? A horror again, I'm afraid. Please forgive me. I have no desire to nauseate you, but something impels me to write it. Perhaps it is a natural morbidity on my part—I doubt it—more, I think, because of the implied suffering. The whole subject of suffering occupies my serious thoughts, as indeed it must everybody's, more than any other.

A recce party, consisting of the Major, myself and two other officers, was going up a little mountain path ahead of the troops (they were following on after dark) to see our new positions. On the way up we passed about fifteen German prisoners, led by Indians, coming down. Then we met some stretcher bearers. The path was narrow, rocky and slippery. One of the stretchers, lurching cruelly, contained a figure completely covered by a blanket, one knee drawn up in the air. The whole stretcher was red with blood. That's all. As we went on up the mountain for several miles I saw the blood on the path—a drop every few steps— and ever drop seemed to be living. The path was edged with flowers, and the valley below filled with sunlight. This, I am fully aware, is nothing, *nothing* to what regular infantry troops experience continually—and I myself have seen many other casualties—but the one I have just described meant more to me.

When we arrived at the little mountain farm we were to occupy, there was a pile of stiff corpses waiting to be removed from our position. They were laid on the cobblestones of a yard beside a pig-sty, but they might have been no more than a wood-pile. Even a day or so later, seeing them being loaded, one either side of a mule, and it was a difficult job, I was still unmoved. The suffering was over.

As you know, I have been kicking against the pin-pricks of the Church for a long time and have also had periodical doubts regarding fundamental Christian beliefs. Recently, however, I have begun to feel rather differently. All these worries really came to the surface with my resentment at, and failure to understand, how the world—apparently full of decent people for the most part—has fallen into such an appalling mess. The discrepancy between things as they are and the Christian claims regarding God's activities has, at times, goaded me to blasphemy—or rather, fury with the Church (it's no good railing at events). I still don't understand it. We are told "Not a sparrow falls etc. . . ." and yet the most frightful fates overtake the innocent and good. The calm confidence with which parsons expound the Will of God when it suits their purpose seems to me astoundingly presumptuous: all the more so in view of the fact that when they come up against the inexplicable and countless tragedies and injustices which apparently redound to the discredit of God, they merely shake their heads and say that the ways of God are inscrutable. They talk about standards of right and wrong as though we could recognise them instinctively, yet, with the best will in the world and acting truly according to their consciences, godly men have committed, and do commit, the most cruel blunders in the name of Christianity; and ignorance is not always wickedness.

And I can't take all this talk about wickedness. Maybe I'm singularly deficient in a sense of sin, but I just don't apply it, with rare exceptions, to myself. I don't believe I am wicked and I don't believe the majority of people, Germans included, are either—certainly not wicked enough to have been deservedly overtaken by this war. And I hate the continual Christian emphasis on the benefits to be derived from suffering. The parsons seem to regard suffering and its beneficial effects as some sort of hideous medical treatment. Just look at the confusion which exists in the Church over the associations of happiness, pleasure and gaiety with evil; and spiritual agonies, physical mortification and even penury with good. It all seems to me merely a sad way of making the best of a bad show—just as the doctrine of free will so conveniently waives everything that might call for an otherwise difficult answer. I don't believe it, and I distrust it—it's too easy.

Another thing that annoys me about the Church is all the importance attached to abstract theological hypotheses—disputes as to whether God is Three in One, One, or Seven in Ten. There are many, many theologians who would not pass as Christians to my way of thinking, yet these very men regard as damned countless others because they haven't been baptised or confirmed. As for their attempts to expound the mysteries rationally, to fit them into our human scheme, you might as well try to gather a bowl-full of smoke. A mystery's a mystery, and that's that. Why not the Virgin Birth? Why not the Resurrection?

But, in spite of all this, as I said, I've begun recently to feel rather differently. What does strike me more and more forcibly is the urgent need for a return to Christian living—and I don't mean more baptisms and confirmations and mortifications, but merely Christian action, strengthened and based upon a simple faith in, and knowledge of, the New Testament. Whatever is the use of post-war plans for this and that without it. No plan on earth will work. So convinced am I of the absolute importance of this that faith in the Christianity of action is rapidly engendering or restoring faith in me for Christianity in all its aspects. I might even in time be prepared to listen to the theologians; but at this stage *they're in the way.* They're the trees for which the Church, and the people, can't see the wood. They have made of the simplest religion in the world a mountain of complexities and irrelevancies, and confused with theological theory the example of Christ's life and death. I have been writing with Protestants in mind, but the Catholics have done as much, so that now the Christian core of the Roman Church is all but obscured by the political, social, financial and theatrical débris of nearly two thousand years. On re-reading the above I seem to emerge as a complete Nonconformist, rather to my surprise!

And recently I have been suddenly, as it were, conscious of my age and found no comfort in this new realisation. Until, say, this year I had always felt—without ever considering the matter—that I was young, that I had plenty of time to develop, that there was no need to put myself out. Then, in the space of a few months, I found that time's wingéd chariot was at my back, and since then I have been constantly conscious of it—almost obsessed by the thought. A long time ago I remember writing to you that the war was like a bridge which we were crossing to a new country, and as we proceeded the arches behind us crumbled into the abyss. This horrid sensation that there is no turning back, that the past is irretrievable, is growing stronger.

When I think of my grandfather's house, and all the family anecdotes of my mother's youth, I realise that the formative atmosphere (excuse the rather grand phrase) of my own childhood was brought by my mother out of what is now *history.* Her own childhood's books which we used to read are almost of antiquarian interest to the present world. It is not so much the number of years involved as the phenomenal acceleration, concertina-ing, of events. Picnics in the woods at home, with the milk in a medicine bottle; my prep school, with the skylarks' nests in the sandhills, and the long seashore; Fettes, with the lights shining in the dark for early morning school, and Sunday evening chapel in the summer, the sunset blazing on the bad stained glass; Cambridge, with its terrible mixture of beauty and awful loneliness; the horror of tanneries and sordid streets and commercialism in Lancashire; the dreamlike holidays with my brother in Germany and Austria and France—all this is no more than old photo albums. I am cut off from it. There is no continuity—everything that one had collected and valued and used to pore over has suddenly been demolished in a whirl of dust and rubble. Perhaps when I get a room again with my books in it and my pictures on the wall and my photograph albums handy for reminiscent evenings, I shall feel differently. But the future! The problem of my own future nearly stuns me if I allow myself to think of it.

*   *   *

5TH MAY [1945]: FORLI

This is the culmination of a monster mental effort. I've been winding myself up daily for almost a fortnight to write to you, but every time I get out pen and paper there's a click and a whirr and I run down with a dying moan. Yesterday I wrote you two whole pages before the mechanism broke, and such was my obvious anxiety to keep going that what I wrote was barely intelligible—certainly of no interest—so I tore it up. The thing is, I suppose, that I've been winding myself up daily for five years, and now that it is all over I'm just incapable of further action. Never was anything such a flop for me as the end of this war.

We're in harbour area now—a long field bounded by trees garlanded with vines: the guns are down one side (dead camels under tarpaulins) and the tents down the other. A terrible stillness pervades everything. A little charging set is ticking away, just as the windscreen wiper which MacNeice saw ticked away six years ago. My batman cleans my jeep, and the rest of the camp is deserted. All the transport is away carrying this, that and the other, and all the men are shepherding vast hordes of prisoners from debussing areas to stations, and from stations to prisoner-of-war cages—drab, weary, negative, toad-coloured heaps of débris from the most shamed nation in history. But I'm not going to make any comments on the end of the war, the Germans, atrocities or anything else: I'm bored with the whole bloody business.

Now that it is all over, I do not see why I should not tell you what we've been doing. For the last six weeks of the war, as it touched us, I had a troop of 4.2-inch mortars in the mountains just outside Bologna. We were situated on a reverse slope, and the enemy were just over the top, half-way down the other side. On quiet days it was a most enjoyable spot. When we arrived, however, at the beginning of March, it was filthy. There were piles of tins and shit and rotting food everywhere; half-buried stinking carcases of mules and even a few bodies; torn branches, shell-holes, mud. Then suddenly the spring came. We burned the refuse, buried the tins and carcases, rebuilt the dug-outs, drained the muddy ground. Violets burst out everywhere; green grass and wild flowers covered the dirty scars. The men took their shirts off and got brown in the sun; we made a tennis-quoits court (games were violently interrupted by having to fling ourselves down at the sound of a coming shell!), and my excellent corporal cook began to turn out unbelievably good food. Pale green leaves settled like clouds of locusts on all the bushes and trees, hiding the white bone-splinters of the branches. But there was another side to it.

Just over the crest above us the machine-guns rattled away, and the shells and mortars banged and crashed—and not always on the other side. We were, of course, well in front of our own gun lines, and all day and all night our own shells went whirtering, whimpering, screaming or whispering over us. All night the sky flickered, flared or glowed with coloured lights. It's extraordinary how one gets to distinguish the different sounds. With shells one could nearly always say it's "a comer" or "a goer," and one could always say: "that's a Bren—or a Spandau—or a Vickers—or a grenade—or a mortar—or a rocket." We got a good many shells in the position itself though by the grace of God no one was hurt.

Sometimes at night it was particularly disagreeable. There was something horrifying about the way the shells rushed at one as though one had suddenly come face to face with an express train in wildly unexpected circumstances. First a tiny note, a whisper that gripped one's heart, then a fantastically sudden crescendo of noise and fear culminating in a tearing crash like a mental black-out; then silence and the patter of earth and stones. One's heart hurt beneath the ribs and already one was straining one's ears for the next faint whisper.

Do you remember, at Sevenoaks, the thought that was in our minds— God grant that we won't get mutilated or blinded? And now it's all over, and we're all right. I don't realise it properly yet, but I shall. Even writing this, I feel slightly uneasy: I dread having a car accident now, or treading on one of the many mines with which this country is strewn.

The nearest miss I had during the whole war occurred at the mortar point. My dug-out was next to the sergeants', divided from theirs by a wall of earth perhaps two feet thick. On this particular afternoon I was lying in bed, having a siesta. Outside, a sergeant was distributing Naafi to about six men. Suddenly there was a terrific woosh and a thump which shook the ground and brought earth showering down from the roof of my dug-out—but no explosion. I hurried out and found everyone picking themselves up from the ground and asking "what was it?" We looked here and there until finally I noticed that the earth at the entrance to the sergeants' dug-out was slightly disturbed. We prodded about but found nothing. Then we went into the sergeants' dug-out. At the entrance lay a greatcoat. I turned it over, and there, nestling against a bottle of whisky, smiling blandly (one might say) to itself, was an 88-mm. shell! It had landed about three feet from my head, and almost in the midst of the men sorting the Naafi. One man, in fact, when he heard it coming, dived into the dug-out and landed with his nose about six inches from it. God, how we laughed! Never has anything seemed so funny. We laughed for days about it, whenever it was mentioned. I picked it up, rather gingerly, and placed it in a deep hole we had just completed for a new latrine. It was hot, like a wounded animal, and seemed to have a malignant life of its own.

Nothing, I know, can be more boring than war stories, but I must tell you one other incident that happened at the mortar point. One morning, just as I was dressing, there was a terrific crash, very close, and I rushed out to see everything obscured in smoke and dust. I felt immediately, with an acute nausea, that one of the dug-outs had been hit. I ran over to the place, and there, hardly daring to look, I saw a hideous gaping hole where had been a dug-out. The metal ammunition boxes, which we had filled with earth and laid on the roof, were twisted and scattered like tissue-paper. Peering down into the hole I saw what I most feared—a sordid pile of blankets, leather jerkins and earth. Corpses look just like rotten old clothes. Feeling slightly sick I went into the next dug-out, and there, lying on the ground, with white lips and his eyes closed, was a young lad whom I have always specially liked. The others were crowded round, bending over him. His denims were torn and he was covered with earth and dust, but there was no blood. *He was unhurt.* He had been in the dug-out when it received a direct hit. Everything was ripped and peppered by steel splinters—and he was not touched. If ever I have seen a miracle, that was it. As we examined him, and the amazing fact gradually was realised, I had to restrain a sudden impulse to embrace him. That time we didn't laugh.

The other aspect of our job was the O.P. work. Our O.P.s were all houses and we could only reach them and get back from them after dark. I and my other officer took it in turn, taking a sergeant and a signaller with us, to stay in one or another of them for three days at a stretch. The one I used most contained a platoon of infantry: they slept during the day, except for lookouts, and deployed at night in positions round the house which was down the forward slope of the mountain I have described. The only approach was covered by fire from German machine-guns and mortars, and one didn't dawdle on the way. It was exactly level with a largish German position—up the slope, from their point of view—and about five hundred yards away from us with a small gulley in between. The "house" was actually little more than a pile of rubble. When I first saw it, creeping down towards it in the moonlight, my heart turned over. It was the epitome of all war paintings—a jagged outline of beams and shattered walls like a heap of splintered bones, almost phosphorescent in the cold blue light. Yet underneath all that rubble were rooms, or rather spaces, sand-bagged and shored up with timber, with crawl-holes tunnelled through the fallen masonry and debris.

The filth in these O.P.s was indescribable. We had been in the same positions for months, and as one could not show oneself at all or even give any evidence of occupation, everywhere inside was stacked high with refuse, rotting old food cans and putrid swill. It could not be exaggerated. As the hot weather came, we put down pounds and pounds of chloride of lime; still it made no difference. Mice—and I loathe them—scuttled about the sand-bags and even ran across my binoculars as I was observing during the day. At night they scuttered over one's face. And there were rats in abundance, too, though they left us alone, as there was already more than enough to eat. The moment you had finished a meal you had to cover your mess-tin, or you'd find a mouse in it cleaning up. I shall never forget the smell of those O.P.s.

From our position on the mountain-side we looked right out across the valleys and foothills occupied by the Germans; and in the distance, limitless on a clear day, shimmering in the heat, sparkling with white houses, towns and villages, veined with silver rivers and streams, was The Plain—The Promised Land. You can have no idea what The Plain meant to us. Just to say "The Plain" was to name the symbol of all our hopes. Only forward troops had seen it. When one came down from the O.P. the men would ask eagerly: "Can you see The Plain?" and the sergeant and the signaller who came down with me would tell the others: "We've seen The Plain." All our discomforts and disappointments were due to the mountains—that we had been held up in them for the bitter winter months, the appalling roads and tracks, the difficulties of working with mules and oxen, of getting to positions, of exhausting climbs carrying everything on our backs.

For the rest, the lovely hills and valleys were scattered with the ruins of farms and burnt-out haystacks beneath which the enemy tunnelled and burrowed and lay like mice, peering through the chinks at us. During the day one saw no movement at all: it was a country of the dead. Just occasionally, if one did see the odd German or a car tearing along one of the roads, one brought fire down on the spot immediately. The only activity was the smoke of shells and mortars as they pounded at the already ruined walls. Sometimes our fighter planes swooped over the crest above us and dived on some derelict farm, spattering it with a sparkle of bursting cannon-shells.

At night both sides came out and deployed in trenches. If one observed very carefully and patiently in the half-light, one sometimes saw Germans run from a building to scatter down nearby banks and ditches. After dark the patrolling began, the mine-laying and wiring, the improving of positions, the bringing up of supplies, the relieving of forward troops.

And now I have a confession to make to you—one which I've not been able to make to anyone out here, as I know no one well enough yet. When I was bringing fire to bear on a target—and our mortars had a very big bomb—I did so with a barely concealed nausea. As I saw the vicious flash and great cloud of smoke, I tried only to think of directing the fire and not of what the bombs themselves might be doing. I knew what it was like to be mortared and I was sick in myself at inflicting such hideous suffering. I had always to tell myself that only by continuing to fire would I help to end the greater suffering of the whole war. When the infantrymen in the O.P. sniped at the Germans, I tried not to think about it. I could not have fired myself, not at an unsuspecting man that I could see. This war has got us all into such a mess that I was glad to hear, in the service we had this morning, a prayer for forgiveness, penitence.

Only once did I order fire viciously. Early one morning the Germans started to mortar us in the O.P., and several rounds fell among the ruins, filling the room with the stench of fumes and dust, and rattling down stones and earth from the shored-up ceiling. I had already registered what I suspected to be several of his own O.P.s and mortar positions, so I got on the phone immediately and called down fire from heaven!

Did you happen to hear the broadcast recently of Dorothy Sayers's *Man Born To Be King?* One night I was on duty in the Command Post with one of the sergeants, when we tuned in to this on the wireless. I thought it extremely good, especially the last scene of the crucifixion. It was moving and at the same time horrifying—almost too much so, as they produced in detail even the sounds of hammering. I was, however, completely absorbed by it and quite imagined myself as one of the bystanders. When it was all over I was too abstracted to speak for a moment—but not so the sergeant. In a very bright, almost social, tone of voice, he said: "Shockin' affair, wasn't it!"

I can't quite finish this without telling you of one especially bad night. As luck would have it, I was in the O.P.—stuck out, as we were, in front of everyone. Jerry shelled and mortared the ridge for three and a half hours before putting in a largish attack. For the whole of this period a shell or a mortar landed unpleasantly close every few seconds, while the general noise all round us was continuous. In addition, we were expecting to be attacked at any moment and we just sat waiting for it. I laced my boots up tightly, collected a little pile of grenades where I could feel them in the dark, chain-smoked and chatted, rather over-brightly, to my little O.P. party, who behaved with complete, if resigned, composure.

Just before the attack came in, everything opened upon both sides. The lights that flashed and flared through the O.P. window were hellish—tracer, verey, flame-throwers, flares and explosions of every kind. Jerry was using rockets as well, which made a fiendish tearing noise followed by a tremendous crash. When the attack did come in, it was fortunately on our right: but they were undoubtedly the worst hours of the war for me—and in saying so I don't forget for one moment what a cushy time I've had. Most of the next day we watched the stretcher parties, draped with Red Cross flags, moving about the hillside between the lines, collecting the dead and wounded.

So much for the war—my war. I have little energy to put into it now and, in any case, it all seems such unsuitable stuff to tell you. Still, I wanted to get the gist of it down on paper, and if I don't tell you now I know that I never shall.

JAMES ROBESON

Private First Class James Robeson fought on Iwo Jima with the Fifth Marine Division, a platoon of which reached the top of Mt. Suribachi and raised the American flag there.

To His Parents

> *February 27, 1945*
> *Iwo Jima*
> *Suribachi Mt.*

Dear folks:

How is everyone? I am still fine. We have been on this island 9 days today and everything is coming along OK although there is still plenty fighting up at the other end. I have made it so far without even a scratch so I guess I'll not even get a purple heart.

Did you hear Thomas my platoon Sgt. made his speech over the radio? It was on a world wide hook-up. If you didn't well my platoon was the first one up on this mt., that is the top of it. We raised the Stars and Stripes for the first time over the real Japanese empire. I was the third man to the spot where we raised the flag too. My squad leader Snyder and my group leader Keller were the first two! All in all it has been a great experience. I was never scared so stiff in my life before. When the mortars and artillery (theirs) starts dropping I just can't help but shake like I was freezing but I guess everybody else does the same thing. I can't write much now as all I have is this Jap stationery and a Jap pencil. I found a pen to address the envelope but there is no ink and I would hate to use another man's all up. I have a few souvenirs, a wrist watch and several other little things. I haven't got my blankets here yet but the Japanese were kind enough to leave a nice brand new one all folded up in a cave. So I sleep pretty comfortable. I will write more when I get a chance. I have plenty of chow and feel swell so don't worry, everything ought to be over real soon. Write often. We ought to get mail in here soon.

Love to all,
Jim

STUDS TERKEL
1912–

Studs Terkel (born Louis Terkel in New York City) graduated from the University of Chicago and also took a law degree there. He has worked as a civil servant and an actor but is best known as a radio and TV interviewer and newspaper columnist in Chicago and the compiler of a number of books of interviews. For "The Good War" (1984) he solicited the memories of hundreds of people, ordinary and famous, Allied and Axis.

From "THE GOOD WAR"

JOHN GARCIA:

A broadcast came from Tokyo Rose: "Good evening, men of the Seventh Infantry. I know you're on your way to the Philippines." She was right. (Laughs.) We were there from October of '44 until March of '45. Totally combat.

I fought very carefully, I fought low. There were a couple of Japanese boys, our interpreters, who were a little bit heroic. They would climb on board a Japanese tank going by, knock on the things, converse in Japanese, and as soon as the door popped open, they'd drop a hand grenade—boom!

Our next stop was Okinawa. We landed there on April 1, '45. No opposition. Several days later, we got word that President Roosevelt had died. We were all sort of down—boom! They said a man called Truman replaced him. I said, "Who is Truman?" We were there eighty-two days. I did what I had to do. When I saw a Japanese, I shot at him and ducked. Shot and ducked, that's all I did. I was always scared until we took Hill 87.

We buried General Ushijima and his men inside a cave. This was the worst part of the war, which I didn't like about Okinawa. They were hiding in caves all the time, women, children, soldiers. We'd get up on the cliff and lower down barrels of gasoline and then shoot at it. It would explode and just bury them to death.

I personally shot one Japanese woman because she was coming across a field at night. We kept dropping leaflets not to cross the field at night because we couldn't tell if they were soldiers. We set up a perimeter. Anything in front, we'd shoot at. This one night I shot and when it came daylight, it was a woman there and a baby tied to her back. The bullet had all gone through her and out the baby's back.

That still bothers me, that hounds me. I still feel I committed murder. You see a figure in the dark, it's stooped over. You don't know if it's a soldier or a civilian.

I was drinking about a fifth and a half of whiskey every day. Sometimes homemade, sometimes what I could buy. It was the only way I could kill. I had friends who were Japanese and I kept thinking every time I pulled a trigger on a man or pushed a flamethrower down into a hole: What is this person's family gonna say when he doesn't come back? He's got a wife, he's got children, somebody.

They would show us movies. Japanese women didn't cry. They would accept the ashes stoically. I knew different. They went home and cried.

I'd get up each day and start drinking. How else could I fight the war? Sometimes we made the booze, sometimes we bought it from the navy. The sailors stole it from their officers. (Laughs.) Sometimes it cost us seventy-five dollars a bottle, sometimes it cost us a Japanese flag. You'd take a piece of parachute silk, make a circle on it, put a few bullet holes in it, give it to the navy, and they'd give you a bottle of whiskey.

I drank my last drink on the night of August 14, 1945, I think it was. When we heard from Swedish radio that the Japanese wanted to contact the Americans in order to end the war, we just went wild. Every soldier just took a gun and started shooting. I got into my trench and stayed there because the bullets were all over. Thirty-two men out of our outfit were killed that night by stray celebrating bullets.

I haven't touched a drop since. I wasn't a drinking man before. I started in the Philippines when I saw the bodies of men, women, and children, especially babies, that were hit by bombs. They were by the side of the road, and we would run over them with our tanks.

Oh, I still lose nights of sleep because of that woman I shot. I still lose a lot of sleep. I still dream about her. I dreamed about it perhaps two weeks ago. . . . (He lets out a deep breath; it's something more turbulent than a sigh.)

* * *

ROBERT RASMUS:

In Boston Harbor, we actually saw the first visible sign of the war: an Australian cruiser tied up next to the troop ship. There was a huge, jagged hole in the bow. The shape of things to come. There was a lot of bravado, kidding.

Our impression of France, those of us who grew up in the thirties, was French maids, French poodles, a frivolous type of people. So it was striking to see these stolid peasants walking behind horse-drawn plows. The area we were in had not yet been hit by the war. I was struck by the sheer beauty of the countryside, the little villages, the churches. This sort of thing the impressionists did.

Going to the front, I can remember the cities in Belgium: Liège, Namur. We were going through towns and villages. We were hanging out of the cars of the trains and on the roofs. We had all this extra candy from our K rations and would just throw them out to the kids. There was a sense of victory in the air. They had already been liberated. They were elated.

All of a sudden, the tone changes. You get off the train on the border in that little corner of Holland and Germany. We're near Aachen, which had been absolutely leveled by Allied bombings. Rubble, nothing but rubble. Here was the ancient city of Aix-la-Chapelle, just a sea of rubble. We've had forty-eight hours enjoying being part of the victorious army. Now the party's over. You're within a few miles of the front. You're off the train into trucks. You hear gunfire in the distance.

Everybody sobered up very rapidly. We drove on for a few miles and there was a second city, Düren, totally wiped out. It was one of the most bombed-out cities in Germany. Now we're moving forward on foot.

They moved us into what they called a quiet front. Our division occupied a frontage on the Rhine, south of Cologne. We simply relieved another division that had been there, the Eighth. We moved into the same foxholes. You know it's getting close. It's still sort of exciting. Nobody's gotten killed yet. To me, it was interesting because of the architecture. From the distance I could see the Cologne cathedral, with the twin towers.

We stayed in bombed-out buildings. It was almost surreal. Here's a cross-section of a four-story, where every room is open to the atmosphere on one side and there's another room that is still intact. This was true all the way through Europe.

The very first night, our squad was in comfortable quarters. Our one side was completely open, but on the other side were beds and kitchens and what-not. It was almost theatrical. Since the Germans were the enemy and evil, we never had any sense of guilt that we were in somebody's apartment. Any abuse of the apartment, like throwing dishes out the window, was what they deserved. Whatever was there in the way of food and drink, we would make use of.

One of the things we had was this old music box. It could play whole melodies. We had two disks. One was "Silent Night" and the other was "We Gather Together to Ask the Lord's Blessing." I had a typical Lutheran churchgoing background. Here am I hearing a Christmas carol and a hymn that I'd sung many times in church.

I was sort of schizophrenic all through this period. I was a participant, scared out of my wits. But I was also acutely aware of how really theatrical and surreal it was.

Three days later we pulled out, crossed the Rhine, and cut off a German pocket. As we were moving out of this area of sheared-off buildings, there were courtyards with fruit trees in blossom. And there were our heavy mortars blasting away across the river. I had been seeing shadowy figures moving around. Were they infiltrators or just a bush that I was imagining? And there in sight was the Cologne cathedral amidst all this wreckage.

We've seen a little of the war now. We've seen planes dropping bombs over on the other side. We've sent out patrols, have captured prisoners. But we really hadn't been in it ourselves. It was still fun and dramatics. When the truck took us from Cologne south through Bonn, for me it was, Hey, Beethoven's birthplace! But when we crossed a pontoon bridge and I saw a balloon of fire, I knew the real combat was going to begin. I had the feeling now that we were gonna be under direct fire, some of us were gonna be killed. But I was also enormously affected by the beauty of the countryside. We were in rolling hills and great forests. It stretched out for mile after mile. I could almost hear this Wagnerian music. I was pulled in two directions: Gee, I don't wanna get killed. And, Boy, this is gorgeous country.

Our uniforms were still clean. We were still young kids who hadn't seen anything. You could see these veteran troops. Their uniforms were dirty, they were bearded, there was a look in their eyes that said they'd been through a lot. A sort of expression on their faces—You're gonna find out now. A mixture of pity and contempt for the greenhorns.

We started seeing our first dead, Germans. You drew the obvious inference: if Germans were dead, the Americans were getting killed farther up the line. Night fell, we were up within a couple of miles of where the action would begin. We were passing through our artillery emplacements. Incessant firing. It was reassuring to see how much artillery we had, but disturbing to see all these German dead. I had never seen a dead body before, except in a funeral home.

We were told that the next morning we would be on the attack. I remember the miserable cold. By this time, I had taken up cigarette smoking, wondering what my mother would think when I came back. (Laughs.) I felt sickish, I was cold, I was scared. And I couldn't even get one last cigarette.

We were awakened before dawn. I honestly don't know whether I dreamed it or whether it really happened. I've asked buddies I've seen since the war: Can you remember these ambulances and army surgeons getting their gear out? I have such an absolute recollection of it, but nobody else remembers it. It had a dreamlike quality: just seeing surgeons ready to work. Here we were still healthy, still an hour or two away from actual combat. It added to the inevitability that really bad, bad things were going to happen.

Our platoon of thirty men was to take a small town. At the time, I was a bazooka man. I'll never forget that sense of unreality as we were moving through the woods to this village, which we could just see a few hundred yards away. There were sheep grazing in the fields. By now there's gunfire: machine guns, rifle fire, mortar shells.

You'd lost your sense of direction. This was not a continuous front. These were piercing, probing actions. You'd take a town, then to the next river, then across the river and then the next one. This was the first. Now I can see actual mortar shells landing in this meadow. German 88s. They were hitting the tile roofs of these houses and barns. My initial reaction: they're not hurting anything. Oh, a few tiles being knocked loose, but it's still a beautiful sunny day. The meadow is lovely. Here we are in a medieval village. This reaction lasted three seconds. These sheep started getting hit. You were seeing blood. Immediately you say, Soon it's gonna be us torn up like these animals. You sense all these stages you've gone through. And now (laughs), the curtain has gone up and you're really in it.

We captured that town without any casualties. I think the German troops had moved out. My confidence is coming back a little. Gee, we captured a town and didn't even see a German. Later that afternoon, we were moving up to take another town. We have a sense that things aren't going too well. We seem out of radio contact with the other rifle companies. I sense an apprehension by our officers.

All of a sudden, we spotted a group of German soldiers down by the slope of this hill, perhaps fifty. We were strung out, a couple of platoons. We would be on the ground, get up on command, and start firing right into this group of Germans. We did catch them by surprise. They responded quickly, firing back, machine guns and rifles. We had them well outnumbered, our company, about 240. We did the march-and-fire. It was a new maneuver we'd never done in training. We learned. I noticed that some of our guys were getting hit. It was all in a few minutes. We killed most of the Germans. A few might have gotten away, but we wiped them out. Our guys were getting killed, too. Irony again, the first one killed was our platoon sergeant.

You have to understand the culture of our company. Most of our privates were college types. They had been dumped en masse into these infantry divisions. The cadre of noncommissioned officers were old-timers. They were mostly uneducated country types, many of them from the South. There was a rather healthy mutual contempt between the noncoms and the privates. This sergeant was the most hated man. One of the nineteen-year-olds, during maneuvers, was at the point of tears in his hatred of this man who was so unreasonable and so miserable. He'd say, "If we ever get into combat, I'm gonna kill 'im. First thing I'll do." Who's the first one killed? This sergeant. I'm sure it was enemy fire. I would bet my life on it. I'm sure the guys who said they would kill him were horrified that their wish came true.

My best friend was leaning against a tree. We were waiting for further instructions. He had this sly grin on his face. I was so aghast. It didn't occur to me that one of our people had done it. I'm really sure we didn't. "I'm gonna kill 'im" is said a million times. Added to the horror of our first dead is that he's the one all of us hated so much.

I'm sure our company was typical. We had x percent of self-inflicted wounds. There's no question that a guy would blow his toe off to get out of combat. People would get lost. These combat situations are so confused that it's very easy to go in the other direction. Say you get lost, get sick, get hurt. By the time you get back to your outfit, a couple of days have gone by.

We remember examples of Caspar Milquetoast: ordinary people showing incredible heroism. But you have to accept the fact that in a cross section of people—in civilian life, too—you've got cowards and quitters. Our radio man shot up his radio: he thought we were going to be captured. Panic. I became a bazooka man because our bazooka man threw his weapon away and I picked it up. He ran off.

Our captain said, "Pick up the bodies. We don't leave our dead to the enemy." We're now cut off and have to join the rest of our battalion. We had to improvise stretchers. I took off my field jacket and turned the arms inside out. We poked rifles through the arms and fashioned a stretcher. We got the sergeant on ours and, jeez, half his head was blown off and the brains were coming out on my hands and on my uniform. Here's the mama's boy, Sunday school, and now I'm really in it.

I remember lying in that slit trench that night. It was a nightmare. I'd now seen what dead people look like, the color out of their face. I think each person in my squad went through this dream of mine. Daylight came and we moved out into another town. This is twenty-four hours of experience.

Those who really went through combat, the Normandy landings, the heavy stuff, might laugh at this little action we'd been in, but for me . . . We were passing people who were taking over from us, another company. We had one day of this. Our uniforms were now dirty and bloody and our faces looked like we'd been in there for weeks. Now *we* had the feeling: You poor innocents.

We weren't able to bring those bodies back with us. The mortar fire became too much. The next morning, our squad was assigned to go back and recover the bodies. It was sunshine and quiet. We were passing the Germans we killed. Looking at the individual German dead, each took on a personality. These were no longer an abstraction. These were no longer the Germans of the brutish faces and the helmets we saw in the newsreels. They were exactly our age. These were boys like us.

I remember one, particularly. A redhead. To this day, I see the image of this young German soldier sitting against a tree. This group was probably resting, trying to make their escape. The whole thing might have been avoided had we been more experienced and called down in German for them to surrender. They probably would have been only too glad. Instead, out of fear, there was this needless slaughter. It has the flavor of murder, doesn't it?

What I remember of that day is not so much the sense of loss at our two dead but a realization of how you've been conditioned. At that stage, we didn't hate the Germans just for evil the country represented, their militarism, but right down to each individual German. Once the helmet is off, you're looking at a teen-ager, another kid. Obviously you have to go on. There are many, many more engagements.

A few days later, we're in Lüdenscheid. It's near the Ruhr pocket. Two Allied armies had crossed the Rhine fifteen miles apart. It's a pincer movement, closing in a pocket of 350,000 Germans. Under Field Marshal Model, I believe. They just don't surrender overnight. They're gonna fight it out. Our job, all the way through Germany, was to move as fast as you could on trucks, on tanks, until you came up against resistance. Some towns fell without a battle. Others, quite a bit of resistance. You'd assume the worst.

You were constantly behind the lines and then moved up. You'd pass through your artillery and you knew you were getting closer. Pretty soon things would thin out. Just an hour earlier there were an awful lot of GIs around. As you got closer to action, it was only your platoon, and then it was your squad ahead of the other two. You were the point man for the squad.

I thought, This is incredible. We've got these great masses of troops, of quartermasters and truckers and tanks and support troops, and then all of a sudden it's so lonely. (Laughs.) You're out ahead of the whole thing.

In Lüdenscheid, we were in the hills looking down. It was dead silence in the town, except that you became aware of German ambulances with the big red crosses on the roofs. We didn't know whether it was a trick. There was something mysterious about that sight. The bells started tolling in the city. You didn't know what to make of it. Was this the opening of a major battle? Were they going away? There was very little resistance and we took the town.

Now I began to get an inkling of some other evil abroad. We were very much aware that the Germans had mobilized the Poles, the French, the captive countries, into workers on farms and in factories. As each town was captured, you were liberating Slavs, Poles, French, whatever. It was often highly emotional. The idea of those death camps still hadn't reached us at all. I marvel as I think back on it. When we took Lüdenscheid, our platoon stayed overnight in what was a combination beer hall, theater, festival-type thing, with a stage and a big dance floor. There in the middle of the floor was this mountain of clothing. I realize now that was probably the clothing they'd taken from the people that went to Dachau or another camp. It really didn't register with us what that might have been. You knew this wasn't just a Salvation Army collecting clothes. I remember it because that was the day Roosevelt died.

Every town had a certain number of slave laborers. It might range from handfuls to hundreds, depending on whether there was industry in that town. The final one we captured in the Ruhr was Letmathe. There was a large number of Italian laborers who worked in a factory. There were quite a few Russians. The military government hadn't yet moved in. I remember the Russians taking the horses and running them up and down the street to get their circulation up and then kill them for food. A Russian was going to kill the horse with a hatchet. I wasn't up to shooting the horse myself, but I let him use my pistol. We were aware of the starvation and the desperate measures they would take.

You had these spontaneous uprisings where the slave laborers and war prisoners the Germans had in these towns would just take over. It was very chaotic.

I remember where a Russian was in the process of strangling a German in the cellar of our building. This was a moment of truth for me. I was still nurturing the notion that every individual German was evil and the Russians were our allies. Somehow I got the picture that the Russian was carrying out vengeance. He claimed this German had killed his buddy. In that confused situation you couldn't tell whether it was true or whether it was a grudge carried out or what. It didn't take much deliberation to stop it. The Russian broke out in tears when I wouldn't let him kill the German. He just sobbed. Reflecting on it later, I had reason to believe his story was true. But I wasn't up to letting it happen.

We were aware that the Russians had taken enormous losses on the eastern front, that they really had broken the back of the German army. We would have been in for infinitely worse casualties and misery had it not been for them. We were well disposed toward them. I remember saying if we happen to link up with 'em, I wouldn't hesitate to kiss 'em.

I didn't hear any anti-Russian talk. I think we were realistic enough to know that if we were going to fight them, we would come out second best. We hadn't even heard of the atomic bomb yet. We'd just have to assume that it would be masses of armies, and their willingness to sacrifice millions of troops. We were aware that our leaders were sparing our lives. Even though somebody would have to do the dirty work in the infantry, our leaders would try to pummel the enemy with artillery and tanks and overpower them before sending the infantry in. If that was possible.

I've reflected on why people my age and with my experience don't have that spontaneous willingness to be part of the nuclear freeze. It's the sense that the Germans were willing to lose millions of men. And they did. Every German house we went to, there would be black-bordered pictures of sons and relatives. You could tell that most of them died on the eastern front. And the Russians lost twenty million.

Later, we were back in the States being retrained for the Japanese invasion. The first atom bomb was dropped. We ended halfway across the Pacific. How many of us would have been killed on the mainland if there were no bomb? Someone like me has this specter.

In the final campaign down through Bavaria, we were in Patton's army. Patton said we ought to keep going. To me, that was an unthinkable idea. The Russians would have slaughtered us, because of their willingness to give up so many lives. I don't think the rank of the GIs had any stomach for fighting the Russians. We were informed enough through press and newsreels to know about Stalingrad. I saw the actual evidence in those black-bordered pictures in every German household I visited. Black border, eastern front, nine out of ten.

I have more disapproval of communism today than ever. I think our government did try to stimulate a feeling about good Uncle Joe. The convoys to Murmansk. We had this mixed feeling: Gee, we're glad they did the lion's share, the overwhelming bulk of the dying, the breaking the back of the German armies. And individually, they can't be all that bad. In any case, we don't want to fight 'em. (Laughs.)

The thing that turned me against the Vietnam War was an issue of *Life* magazine in '68. It had a cover picture of the hundred men that died in Vietnam that week. I said, Enough. I don't want to stand here as a veteran of World War Two saying that we somehow took a stand that was admirable. We are bad as the rest if we don't think independently and make up our own minds. We were willing to go along as long as it seemed an easy victory. When it really got tough, we started re-examining.

World War Two was utterly different. It has affected me in many ways ever since. I think my judgment of people is more circumspect. I know it's made me less ready to fall into the trap of judging people by their style or appearance. In a short period of time, I had the most tremendous experiences of all of life: of fear, of jubilation, of misery, of hope, of comradeship, and of the endless excitement, the theatrics of it. I honestly feel grateful for having been a witness to an event as monumental as anything in history and, in a very small way, a participant.

* * *

DELLIE HAHNE:

While my conscience told me the war was a terrible thing, bloodshed and misery, there was excitement in the air. I had just left college and was working as a substitute teacher. Life was fairly dull. Suddenly, single women were of tremendous importance. It was hammered at us through the newspapers and magazines and on the radio. We were needed at USO, to dance with the soldiers.

A young woman had a chance to meet hundreds of men in the course of one or two weeks, more than she would in her entire lifetime, because of the war. Life became a series of weekend dates.

I became a nurse's aide, working in the hospital. Six or eight weeks of Red Cross training. The uniform made us special people.

I had a brother three years younger than I. He was a cadet at the Santa Ana Air Base. Your cadet got to wear these great hats, with the grommets taken out. Marvelous uniform.

I met my future husband. I really didn't care that much for him, but the pressure was so great. My brother said, "What do you mean you don't like Glenn? You're going to marry him, aren't you?" The first time it would occur to me that I would marry anybody. The pressure to marry a soldier was so great that after a while I didn't question it. I have to marry sometime and I might as well marry him.

That women married soldiers and sent them overseas happy was hammered at us. We had plays on the radio, short stories in magazines, and the movies, which were a tremendous influence in our lives. The central theme was the girl meets the soldier, and after a weekend of acquaintanceship they get married and overcome all difficulties. Then off to war he went. Remember Judy Garland and Robert Walker in *The Clock?*

I knew Glenn six weekends, not weeks. They began on Saturday afternoon. We'd go out in herds and stay up all night. There was very little sleeping around. We were still at the tail-end of a moral generation. Openly living together was not condoned. An illegitimate child was a horrendous handicap. It was almost the ruination of your life. I'm amazed and delighted the way it's accepted now, that a girl isn't a social outcast any more.

The OWI, Office of War Information, did a thorough job of convincing us our cause was unquestionably right. We were stopping Hitler, and you look back at it and you had to stop him. We were saving the world. We were allied with Russia, which was great at that time. Germany had started World War One and now it had started World War Two, and Germany would be wiped off the face of the map. A few years later, when we started to arm Germany, I was so shocked. I'd been sold a bill of goods—I couldn't believe it. I remember sitting on the back porch here, I picked up the paper, and I read that our sworn enemy was now our ally. The disillusionment was so great, that was the beginning of distrusting my own government.

Russia was the enemy from the time I was born right up to '40. Then Russia became our ally. It's funny nobody stopped to think that this was a complete turnabout. As soon as the war was over, we dropped Russia. During the war, I never heard any anti-Russian talk.

There was a movie and there were two Russian artillery women. This woman could not speak English. She had been obviously, painfully coached. The announcer said, "If you were to meet a German now, what would you do?" And she says, (very slowly) "My hand would not falter." And everybody cheers and claps. There were some who said, What bullshit is this? Even so, we knew the importance of loving the Russians and being told that what they were doing was great.

I had one of those movie weddings, because he couldn't get off the base. My parents approved. My mother had a talk with the head of the army base. She wanted to know why the guy I was to marry was restricted to quarters. He said they were having nothing but trouble with this guy. The major advised her to think twice before permitting her daughter to marry a man like this: he was totally irresponsible. My mother told me this, and we both laughed about it. He was a soldier. He could not be anything but a marvelous, magnificent human being. I couldn't believe for one minute what this major had said. He was given a weekend pass and we were married.

Shortly after that he was thrown out of the air force. This was my first doubt that he was magnificent. So he became a sergeant, dusting off airplanes. He was sent to various parts of the country: Panama City, Florida; Ypsilanti, Michigan; Amarillo, Texas. I followed him.

That's how I got to see the misery of the war, not the excitement. Pregnant women who could barely balance in a rocking train, going to see their husbands for the last time before the guys were sent overseas. Women coming back from seeing their husbands, traveling with small children. Trying to feed their kids, diaper their kids. I felt sorriest for them. It suddenly occurred to me that this wasn't half as much fun as I'd been told it was going to be. I just thanked God I had no kids.

We didn't fly. It was always a train. A lot of times you stood in the vestibule and you hoped to Christ you could find someplace to put your suitcase and sit down. No place to sleep, sit up maybe three, four nights. The trains were filthy, crowded.

You'd go live with your husband, far from home. In the town, provision was made for the service wife. They needed all the woman-power they could get. You'd work in a factory or a restaurant. In some towns, your husband had a regular day off. They would allow you to have that day off. The townspeople were accommodating because they needed us. But you never got the feeling that you were welcome. It was an armed truce.

In Amarillo, I went to the store to buy a loaf of bread. I am next. The woman deliberately waits on two or three women who are after me. She knows these women and I'm an outsider. I opened a checking account and they threw my check out without a word of explanation. Account closed. The landlady returned the check to me furious. It was the first check I had written my whole life. The bank manager told me, curt and cold, I had signed my signature card Dellie Hahne and I had signed my check Mrs. Dellie Hahne. In any other person, they'd say, "Look, you made a mistake. This is how you write a check." It was the immediate cold, contemptuous dismissal. I was an outsider.

I felt one step above a camp follower. In some cases, I was asked to produce my marriage license. Most cases, you paid your rent in advance. Lot of times you were told, leave your door open if, say, one of your husband's friends came over. We were looked down upon. Yet they got very rich on the soldiers.

On V-J Day, I went out in the street and all the people were milling around. I talked to a man who was so dazed I thought he was a psychiatric case. He said he lived on a farm and came to Panama City to work in the shipyards. The war ended, half an hour later he was dismissed. He said, "I don't have a dime saved up. I got a kid. I don't know where the hell to go."

I ran across a lot of women with husbands overseas. They were living on allotment. Fifty bucks a month wouldn't support you. Things were relatively cheap, but then we had very little money, too. It wasn't so much the cost of food as points. I suspected the ration system was a patriotic ploy to keep our enthusiasm at a fever pitch. If you wanted something you didn't have points for, it was the easiest thing in the world . . . Almost everybody had a cynical feeling about what we were told was a food shortage.

When it started out, this was the greatest thing since the Crusades. The patriotic fervor was such at the beginning that if "The Star-Spangled Banner" came on the radio, everybody in the room would stand up at attention. As the war dragged on and on and on, we read of the selfish actions of guys in power. We read stories of the generals, like MacArthur taking food right out of the guys' mouths when he was in the Philippines, to feed his own family. Our enthusiasm waned and we became cynical and very tired and sick of the bloodshed and killing. It was a completely different thing than the way it started. At least, this is the way I felt.

We had a catchphrase: The War Against Fascism. I remember a Bing Crosby movie. I think he's a cabdriver and some guy is dictating a letter in the cab to a secretary. Crosby's singing a song. The businessman says, "Will you cut it out?" And Crosby says, "The world would be a better place if we didn't have so many dictators." The catchwords and catchphrases again. This was the war to stop Hitler, stop Mussolini, stop the Axis.

There were some movies we knew were sheer bullshit. There was a George Murphy movie where he gets his draft induction notice. He opens the telegram, and he's in his pajamas and bare feet, and he runs around the house and jumps over the couch and jumps over the chair, screaming and yelling. His landlady says, "What's going on?" "I've been drafted! I've been drafted." Well, the whole audience howled. 'Cause they know you can feed 'em only so much bullshit.

If a guy in a movie was a civilian, he always had to say—what was it? Gene Kelly in *Cover Girl?* I remember this line: "Well, Danny, why aren't you in the army?" "Hell, I was wounded in North Africa, and now all I can do is keep people happy by putting on these shows." They had to explain why the guy wasn't in uniform. Always. There was always a line in the movie: "Well, I was turned down." "Oh, tough luck." There were always soldiers in the audience, and they would scream. So we recognized a lot of the crap.

There were some good books, *Mrs. Miniver* by Jan Struther. She asked herself why did it take a war to get government to paint its curb-stones white so that people wouldn't trip at night? Why did it take a war to bring out the poverty and injustice? There were a lot of people who didn't want to fight. Why the hell fight for this country? What did this country do for me? There was a book called *This Above All.* The theme was first we win the war, *then* we settle your poverty and your wretched childhood and your neglect and your want. You go overseas, you come back, you'll get . . . All they did get is the GI Bill of Rights, going to school. As for the rest of it . . .

Most soldiers were resentful of guys who were not in uniform. There was a term, 4-F bastards. If two guys in cars were fighting it out, the uniformed guy stuck his head out the window: "Oh, you 4-F bastard!" They didn't want to be handed a bill of goods that the men not in uniform were sorry, or the man in uniform was happy as a lark. He wasn't. He was sick of the whole damn thing.

The good war? That infuriates me. Yeah, the idea of World War Two being called a good war is a horrible thing. I think of all the atrocities. I think of a madman who had all this power. I think of the destruction of the Jews, the misery, the horrendous suffering in the concentration camps. In 1971, I visited Dachau. I could not believe what I saw. There's one barracks left, a model barracks. You can reconstruct the rest and see what the hell was going on. It doesn't take a visit to make you realize the extent of human misery.

I know it had to be stopped and we stopped it. But I don't feel proud, because the way we did it was so devious. How many years has it been? Forty years later? I feel I'm standing here with egg on my face. I was lied to. I was cheated. I was made a fool of. If they had said to me, Look, this has to be done and we'll go out and do the job . . . we'll all get our arms and legs blown off but it has to be done, I'd understand. If they didn't hand me all this shit with the uniforms and the girls in their pompadours dancing at the USO and all those songs—"There'll Be Bluebirds over the White Cliffs of Dover"—bullshit!

If only we had a different approach, that's all I'm asking for. If you have to live through a war, be truthful. Maybe you have to get people to fight a war, maybe you have to lie to them. If only they'd said that this isn't the greatest of all worlds, and there's graft and corruption in Washington, and kids are going without milk so some asshole can take a vacation in Florida. If they'd done that, I wouldn't feel so bad.

My brother was killed. Not even overseas. He was killed in North Carolina on a flight exercise. It ruined my mother, because she just worshipped my brother. He was the only boy. I don't think she ever recovered from it.

There was *one* good thing came out of it. I had friends whose mothers went to work in factories. For the first time in their lives, they worked outside the home. They realized that they were capable of doing something more than cook a meal. I remember going to Sunday dinner one of the older women invited me to. She and her sister at the dinner table were talking about the best way to keep their drill sharp in the factory. I had never heard anything like this in my life. It was just marvelous. I was tickled.

But even here we were sold a bill of goods. They were hammering away that the woman who went to work did it temporarily to help her man, and when he came back, he took her job and she cheerfully leaped back to the home.

There was a letter column in which some woman wrote to her husband overseas: "This is an exact picture of our dashboard. Do we need a quart of oil?" Showing how dependent we were upon our men. Those of us who read it said, This is pure and simple bullshit. 'Cause if you don't know if you need a quart of oil, drive the damn thing to the station and have the man show you and you'll learn if you need a quart of oil. But they still wanted women to be dependent, helpless.

I think a lot of women said, Screw that noise. 'Cause they had a taste of freedom, they had a taste of making their own money, a taste of spending their own money, making their own decisions. I think the beginning of the women's movement had its seeds right there in World War Two.

* * *

JEAN WOOD:

I was a dancer on the stage and just beginning to make my way. I was married and had one baby. My mother took care of her, so I was free and the world was my oyster. I was twenty-five. That war cut out my life till I was thirty-five.

Although the war ended after six years, we still had rationing and tightening our belts and, at one stage or another, no roof over our heads. My husband was in the Royal Artillery. He was wounded. He was never the same man again. He died from his war wounds, some years afterwards. I get a minute widow's pension.

I was due to have another baby when the blitz was at its height. That was 1940. We had a lull between 1939 and the summer of 1940. When the war broke out, I was dancing at a seaside resort. Ballet. I remember gazing out over the English Channel: how could people go to war on such a lovely day and kill each other? It was so unreal.

What was real was that everybody around me downed their tools and clambered to get to the recruiting office. Stores were left unattended, banks closed down. I'd left my little girl with my mother. I said to my husband, "For God's sake, let's get our little girl out of London." So we got her out. The government said, If you're out of London with a child, please stay put. You're more of a nuisance coming back to London.

I went back to seaside. They said there'd be a lull. They paid you to be evacuated. We were billeted in different people's homes. I had a terrible billet. The woman wouldn't even let me boil a kettle of hot water. She wouldn't let me iron my baby's clothes. She wouldn't let me keep the baby carriage in the house. She said, "Outside. It stays in the rain." I had to put the baby in a damp carriage.

The first day war was declared, the air-raid siren went off. People dived under the most ridiculous places, thinking the Luftwaffe was coming over. (Laughs.) They did feel silly when it was a false alarm. My God, is that what we're going to do? Fling ourselves down into the gutter and all that?

My husband said, "I'll go to the nearest big town and try to put the money down on a house. So at least you'll have your own roof and be safe." On the way, he volunteered to go into the army. He didn't have to go. He was thirty-four, and they weren't calling up that age yet. He said, "I may as well go in now and get it over with." I had to stay with this dreadful woman for a while. He went off and left me.

The war didn't start until the blitz. In October it started. First they bombed two schools in daylight. The kids were all laid out. We couldn't believe it. That was in Croydon.

The seaside was worse than London. When I'd been there, we'd had 109 dogfights overhead. I'd seen our Battle of Britain boys spiraling down. I'd also seen them do a victory roll when they shot a German airplane down. These boys went up day and night, in these Spitfires, almost stuck together with chewing gum. The mother of two of them lived quite near me. She lived in fear and trembling. We lived near the Spitfire airfield and we got terrible bombings. Here is where we were supposed to be safe.

One day I took my little girl shopping in the main little street. A German plane came down and started to machine-gun us. I ran into a store and put her and myself under the shop counter. I had my behind sticking out. (Laughs.) The machine gun was going bang! bang! bang! all up the road.

They had public underground shelters. They held maybe a couple of hundred. You could dodge in any time there was an air raid. There was no warning in these dogfights. You just looked up and saw planes coming down, machine-gunning. It was mostly bombers; our Spitfire boys were fighting back.

We also had our own air-raid shelter that the government issued. In the country, it was a steel table. You had it in your bedroom or living room. You all crawled underneath it. It was not very high, and if you were pretty big, it was awful to get under. (Laughs.) You'd stay under it for hours.

If you were in a big town, like London or Manchester, there was one in the garden. I don't know which was worse. The garden one was concrete or old tin and it was terribly damp. It used to be up to here with water. Such was the fortitude of the ordinary working class that they made little cozy living rooms in it. (Laughs.) They took their bird down there or their cat. The cat was always the last one: "Where's the cat?"

I had an aunt killed through coming up to make a cup of tea. The siren had just gone all clear. (Demonstrates pitch.) She came up the steps, said to her husband, "I'll make a nice hot cup of tea." They'd been there all night, listening to the crashing and bombing. She put the kettle on and with that, the bomb threw a direct hit on the house.

It was nothing to have the people who lived opposite's furniture blow through your window. We acquired all kinds of furniture we never owned. We ended up with a medley of furniture. Most people did. I had an old aunt of eighty who ended up like a film star's dressing table. How it shot into her garden, all that lovely furniture. (Laughs.)

You had air-raid wardens who were very good. These were men who weren't fit for service or worked in key jobs, and after they finished work, they'd be air-raid wardens. They would help you. They would drag the dead out. My husband once was coming home on leave through London. He was days late because he kept stopping at buildings, pulling out the dead. It was awful.

I had four daughters, all except one born during the war. When I went to have one of them, we didn't have ambulances. I had to go out into the blitz with all the fires raging, to try to get to a phone you could still use, call my doctor. He sent two men with a little truck, with a plank across it. I lay on it. There was no light and no signs, in case the Germans came. These two men were so hopeless, I almost gave birth in the truck. We fell down a big bomb crater and I almost tipped over. But you took it all in your stride. It looked as if you were going to live this way the rest of your life.

When I had my third baby, I stood in the room and said, "Please, God, if you're going to kill us with these bombs, let's all die together now, at night." One didn't know how many children to take under you, like a bird, put them under your wing. I thought if I had two here, and that one was over there, she might get killed and leave me with these two. You had to sort of lay on top of them, so that you'd all be killed together. Never thought I had it in me.

I never thought I could sit and read to children, say, about Cinderella, while you could hear the German planes coming. Sometimes a thousand a night came over, in waves. We had a saying, (says it staccato) I'm gonna getcha, I'm gonna getcha. That's how the planes sounded. You'd hear the bomb drop so many hundred yards that way. And you'd think, Oh, that missed us. You'd think, My God, the next one's going to be a direct hit. But you'd continue to read: "And the ugly sister said"—and you'd say, "Don't fidget, dear." And you'd think, My God, I can't stand it. But you bore up. And I wasn't the bravest of people, believe me.

You had hunches. About half past three you'd say, "I won't sleep over there tonight. I'll put them all over here 'cause I have a hunch that that part of the wall will come down." Or what few neighbors were left would say, "Why don't you bring all the kids over to me tonight and let's all sing and play cards. We won't bother with Jerry tonight." Now would it be safer that side of the road or this side? We'll go over there.

I did fire-watch. And that's frightening. You got up on the roof with a steel helmet on. You're supposed to have a protective jacket. The fire bombs were round balls. They'd come onto roofs and start fires. So the government gave you a bucket of sand and a shovel. Charming. (Laughs.) You stood there till the bomb fell. And you'd shovel it up quick and throw it into the bucket of sand. I didn't do that for long, because I fell pregnant again.

Most of the bombs were in working-class areas. I know there was a big thing about Buckingham Palace had a bomb, but they were all under a beautiful shelter. The working class caught it the worst because of the dock areas. And gasometers and electrical power stations. They aimed for those things. They thought if they demoralized the working class, they weren't going on with the war. For some reason, that never happened.

I had an aunt who was bombed out three times. My grandmother, who was eighty-odd, was bombed out and left clinging to the stairs, with her hair alight. The air-raid wardens got her out. She said, "I must go back for my hat." They took her in a truck with a lot of other elderly people to a safety zone.

I had to stay with my mother-in-law once. Sometimes the raids came before the siren went off, so you weren't down in the shelter. Land mines came down by parachute and laid whole streets low. It was like a bombed-out piece of land. This airplane was very low dropping the fire bombs, dropping them everywhere she was going. She did this terrific zigzag all across this field, hopping and leaping, hopping and leaping. Afterwards, people ran to get the parachute, 'cause with this parachute, we could make ourselves clothes. Clothes rationing was terribly strict. My husband got me a piece, and I made the children little dresses out of this nylon.

A lot of flowers grew on these bombed spaces, especially one in particular. It was a stalk with a lot of little red spots. It was like a weed, really. It was called London pride.

There was the blitz, when all London caught fire, except Saint Paul's

Cathedral, thank God. That's why every time I go to Saint Paul's, I say, Oh, you're still there, thank God. Everything was in flames that night. It was like daylight, the flames.

I saw schoolchildren killed one Saturday morning. No warning. That's when the V-2s came. They were like big telegraph poles that shot through the air. No pilot, no nothing. They went into a building and laid low a whole street. On this morning, kids were shopping at Woolworth's. You couldn't buy much. You couldn't buy candy without your coupons. My mother's house was two blocks over and we heard this terrible crash. We all ran out to see. It was this Woolworth's and all these kiddies' bodies were brought out. They said they buried them. They don't know what arms and legs belong to people's arms and legs. They had cardboard coffins. We made so many, but we never made enough.

Then we had the V-1s. They were the planes that came over belching fire. It was amazing when the first one came down—in a working-class area, as usual. The fire went *chuchuchu, chuchuchu*. When the fire stopped, they circled and circled. You could almost pinpoint where it's going to land. We all ran to see it. When's the pilot going to get out? We were going to take him prisoner. But there was no pilot.

After that, there was another lull while they thought up the next monstrosity: the V-2s. You had no warning of those. At least with the V-1s you could hear a *bububu, bububu* with the fire. You could see the fire. If the war had gone on ten days longer, they might have had the atom bomb. All these things were getting up to that. The blitz began in 1940 when the French let us down at Dunkirk, and lasted until the Normandy landing.

We had bouncing bombs, too. They dropped a bomb here and it didn't stay there. It bounced over a building.

There was a great camaraderie, too. People were down there with their sleeping blankets and their bags of goodies or rations. I don't know of one case where anybody took advantage of you. Even going to the bathroom, they might try to hang a little curtain or something. It was "After you, luv." "That's all right, duck, you go." People developed terrifically high morals.

Being a dancer and a singer, I took over an empty house with my bunch of evacuees. These were very poor people. They hadn't even the little things in life. They didn't know which way to turn. Their husbands were in the war. God knows if they were dying or what. So I said, "Come on, girls, let's all get together to scrub the place out." We managed to get a rickety old piano through these rich ladies. I used to play songs and keep 'em all singin' in the afternoon while another two ladies made cups of tea and served little cookies. That cheered 'em up. We'd say, "Come on, let's have a singsong." And we turned the top floor into a playpen with Girl Scouts taking care of the babies to give these poor mothers a break. They, who had babies by day and night, with landladies who were horrible to 'em.

One time when I was evacuated, I was given a house that people had just fled. It was a lovely place. I could never have had one like it in my normal life. These very upper-class people said, "You look a nice type. We know you'll take care of it, so we'll give it to you as long as we're gone." It had a swing in the garden and everything. It was all done through an evacuee council. They commandeered any empty house. In wartime they can make laws overnight, so people who left their property had it confiscated for the duration.

It was getting near D-Day. Normandy, 1944.

They let me stay in their house an extra five years after the war, because I didn't have anyplace to come back to in London. They were a vicar and his wife, who'd lost a son in a Nazi prison camp. The old vicar had died, and this lady was going to New Zealand and live with her daughter. I paid a very minimum rent. It just paid her taxes.

At that time, you were lucky if you had a corner in somebody else's room. There were no houses for people to come back to. It was surviving as best you could. I know Americans have never had the experience of being bombed out. I don't ever wish it on them, either. But I do wish they wouldn't be so keen to get into wars, because one day it will come back on your territory and God help you. I was sorry for the Germans, too. They must have suffered. You have such silly ideas when you're young: Oh, if I could see Adolf Hitler, I'd shoot him myself tomorrow. Oh, Hitler's dead, isn't that marvelous? But that's not the end of your troubles.

When the war ended, we thought it was going to be a better world. I remember feeling so elated, I really do. I don't think I've ever had such good feelings since. I could see everybody being kind to each other 'cause we'd been through such dreadful things.

The housing was terrible. When the men came back from service and found their wives sleeping in these subway shelters and weeks went on, they took over the Savoy Hotel and became squatters. It was the best hotel in London at the time. The working people rallied around them. They went to these big hotels and the servicemen would let down buckets on ropes and we all put what bits of food we had in them. They occupied those hotels for ages. The authorities were petrified. They thought it was going to be Bolshevism or something. The squatting went on spasmodically for about six months. Then they put up prefabricated houses. They built them in one day. Every available construction worker was busy putting up these houses.

At that time, our family had no home. So my husband said he'd be a sandwich man. You know? Wear a placard in front and back with a sign and parade up and down: You have houses for the tourists, but none for your servicemen. I called a newspaper and told them this is what he planned to do. Within two days, we were offered a nice place to live.

The war took a disastrous chunk out of my life. I gave up thinking about my profession. I had a war-wounded husband and four children. I became a different personality. Before the war, I saw everything through rose-colored glasses and lived for music and my dancing. After the war, I began to study things. I had to help educate my children. I had to adjust to never ever having any money, 'cause we existed on my husband's war pension. I put behind me looking into store windows, 'cause you knew you never were going to be able to buy anything in the way of pretty clothes. Never coveting anything off anybody, because that would only make you old and hateful-looking.

It's taken a lot of maybes and pleasures from me, but I began to see people and events in a certain light. I'm always looking for the economic reason why people do this or why a government does this. It's not always nice to know. (Laughs.)

Maybe I'm pessimistic. Maybe we'll see a lovely new era come. I'm so worried now for my grandchildren. I feel so sorry for them. But then, maybe somebody should have felt sorry for me, growing up in World War Two. (Laughs.) Yet with all its horrors, it made people behave better toward each other than they thought they could.

Housewives during the war were far better cooks than they've been ever since. Can you believe that? We had so little to manage with, we became inventive. If one managed to get a little bit of rice and you had a piece of chop meat, you would mix the two together and make it spread further. If you managed any sultanas or raisins, you scotched all the bits of bread you had together with water and made a gorgeous pudding. If you managed to get some syrup and some brown sugar, if you were lucky, you could make toffee for the kids. So we did fantastic swaps.

I had a very nice lady and her husband, neighbors. She was having her son on leave and she didn't have any meat for him. But that particular day, the butcher let me have some rabbit. In wartime, we et horsemeat and whale steaks, so rabbit was a taste treat. I didn't want the rabbit, 'cause I'd rather give my small children an egg, if I could get eggs. So I took the rabbit round to her. She was so thrilled. On that particular day, her son was killed. We could have flung the rabbit anywhere, for all we cared. He was such a nice boy, a young officer, nineteen years old.

* * *

ELLIOTT JOHNSON:

Four of us were in an upstairs Chinese restaurant in Portland, Oregon, when the little Chinaman came bursting through the double doors of the kitchen. He was carrying a portable radio and turning up the volume. We learned then that Pearl Harbor had been attacked. We were furious. No one's gonna come in our country. We immediately went to the marine recruiting headquarters.

There was a line over two blocks long. A marine was at a card table set up right at the front door. When it came to me, he said, "Step out of line, you're getting a Dear John letter from the President." The next day, Monday, I got a letter from the President of the United States. Greetings. On January 12, I was inducted into the army.

What about your three buddies?

One had poor vision. He tried to enlist in every branch of the service. He would not give up. He was going to do something for his country. That was the spirit that prevailed in those days. He ended up with the merchant marines. Another joined the Marine Corps, was at Guadalcanal. The third was too short, but he stayed in bed four days to put on an extra half-inch in height. His mother drove him and he laid out on the back seat all the way down there. He got on the scale and he hit the height. He was in. The air corps.

We arrived about one o'clock in the morning. It was snowing, and they showed us one of those perfectly horrid films on social disease. They fed us coffee, which I swear was laced with saltpeter. The man that issued my pants measured my waist and then to hell with it. I swear the man they made those pants for wore stilts. They dragged out eighteen inches in the back. There was a young GI who recognized this opportunity and he brought a sewing kit with him. He was right there when you tried the pants on—(clap hands)—just like that. He said, "For fifty cents I'll alter them." He fixed 'em beautifully and they fit like a top.

Some of the boys there were from the hills. They couldn't read or write. You may call them ignorant, but when it came to those guns, they could make us look stupid. They'd take the parts, put 'em in a bag, dump 'em on the floor, and put 'em back together again, blindfolded. Made up their own songs. The verses rhymed and they had a message. It was a real education for me.

At OCS I had another learning experience. We lived in half-tents in Fort Sill, Oklahoma. There were eight of us in each tent. I was stationed with seven other Johnsons. I was the only white. I kept that thing cleaned up. There wasn't any question what would happen if I didn't. I was in the minority and they had had the short stick for all their lives.

Was this your first acquaintance with black people?

There was one black boy in high school in Portland.

I reported for duty as a lieutenant at Camp Gordon, Georgia, where the captain made me stand at attention for so long. I could see him, in my peripheral vision, swinging back and forth in his swivel chair, staring at me. It was so hot. The perspiration came down my forehead, down my nose. He didn't return my salute. I was getting dizzy. Finally this voice said, "You a northerner?" I said, "I'm a westerner, sir." I heard him say, "Relax, fella." He got up and shook hands with me.

Now I'm in the artillery of the Fourth Infantry Division. We're a self-propelled unit, so we travel with the infantry. We trained intensively for a couple of years before we actually went into the invasion of Normandy. There were people who had been in the army for years. I had to learn to work those guns as good as any one of them.

We started for Normandy on June 3, I believe, or June 4. We lined up in long rows, vehicles under shade trees. Beautiful roads in the English countryside, with trees coming all the way across, making arches as you drive through. The English, I'm sure, knew why we were there and yet no word was said at all. The channel was very rough, so we turned around and came back.

On the morning of June 6, we took off. I can remember that morning. Who could sleep? A lot of the boys played poker all night. I wanted to take a bath. Don't ask me why, 'cause I can't explain it. It was against the rules, but I took a shower anyway.

I was on an LST, a landing ship tank. It was three hundred feet long. It had a great mouth in front of which was the ramp that let down the smaller craft. I remember going up to the highest part of that ship and watching the panorama around me unfold. In my mind's eye, I see one of our ships take a direct hit and go up in a huge ball of flames. There were big geysers coming up where the shells were landing and there were bodies floating, face down, face up.

The LST, as we vacated it, was to become a hospital ship. The boys who had gone first and been wounded were now being brought out. This continued my education: recognizing our body as finite. I remember one young boy who was so badly hurt he was gray, like a piece of flannel. I thought he was dead. They gave him a transfusion and I could see his color coming back. The relief I felt that this boy was gonna make it—I can't remember whether he was German or ours. It didn't matter. Isn't that interesting?

It came our turn to go into the little craft, and we went in. We had a young navy officer who wasn't gonna take us up that beach. I knew dang good and well that if we took our 155 off in that water, that would be all she wrote. We could swim ashore, but we'd never make it, we were loaded with so much paraphernalia. So I ended up taking my gun out on him. Shoved it in his mouth. Can you believe that? He wanted to get the hell out of there. He was the guy in *The Caine Mutiny,* the one rattling the steel balls in his hands. He wanted to dump us. Yeah, that's close enough, go on. He finally got us to where we were in about three feet of water and he said, "I just can't go any more." Fine, let down the ramp.

This self-propelled 155 is nothing but half a tank. Instead of a turret on top, it has a 155 howitzer. You don't have a steering wheel. You just pull on this and you go to the right. The other way, you pull to the left. Pull 'em both, you stop. For some reason, we got our signals crossed. Corporal Rackley was driving and watching me. I threw up my hand. He thought I meant stop. So I assaulted the beach of Normandy in the inglorious fashion of somersaulting through the air and landing on my back. All I could see was this tank out of which I had pitched. It couldn't stop in that soft sand. The guys for a long time teased me that they had never seen me move so fast. (Laughs.) I just got out of the way. It would have gone right over me. I've always contended that when the Germans saw that kind of clown-acting, it scared the hell out of them. (Laughs.)

I looked around and saw this causeway filling with water very fast. It would have locked us on the beach. I told Rackley to hit it. We made it to one area that was only under one foot of water. That became our road and we got across, off the beach.

Part of my job was standing near the driver because we had a .50-caliber machine gun mounted up there that I would operate if necessary. We looked back and there were the Germans. Beyond them were the Americans, still on the beach side. So I was able to shoot at the backs of the Germans.

We weren't the only ones that got across the water. There was an anti-aircraft crew. This was the dangedest thing. You can't imagine all this noise and all these shells exploding and fellows being hurt and killed, and here's this crew sitting smoking cigarettes and reading a comic book. I couldn't believe it. We stopped a hundred feet from them. I could see them out of the corner of my eye.

All of a sudden—wham!—they were galvanized into action. I looked up and nobody had to say anything. All of us dove out of that thing and crawled under, 'cause here came these three German aircraft. These guys didn't do any hiding. We did. It's a good thing we did. The Germans hit that thing with those .50-caliber machine guns. And these guys hit every one of those three German airplanes and knocked them down. Every one of them. Only two parachutes opened and we were yelling and jumping up and down: Where's the other parachute? Obviously, the boy was killed. We were rooting for him. Yeah, the German guy. Funny, eh?

I had a colonel who was a great instructor. He helped a lot of us. But he couldn't take combat. Long before we ever landed, he was just stoned out of his mind. He came walking by, hanging on to his command car because he was so drunk. He waved me down the road: "Git outa here, git outa here."

Now way down the road I saw, on my right, these dead German boys. On my left, going across the field, is a French peasant leading a cow, cradling its head in his arms, protecting it with his body as much as possible. He had come back to get his cow, leading it away from all the noise and death.

I looked up. There was a two-story house across the road to the woods. I could see this German boy silhouetted in the window. I finished laying the guns and with a couple of others went around to the right flank. We had incendiary grenades and set the house on fire. Pretty soon the boy came out. He was my first prisoner. I told him, "Take your shoes off." He didn't understand, so I got down and pulled them off. He had thrown his gun away. All you do is point him back down the road. What happens to him, you could care less. He's out of the war. Everybody that sees him knows he's been captured, as long as he's in uniform and barefoot.

On the way to the house, I had come across a paratrooper sergeant helplessly entangled in a tree. He had a broken leg, compound break, blood coming out of his pants. As soon as we sent the German boy down the road, we cut this boy down. He was so humiliated because he had been up there since before daybreak. It had been a shock to his system, so his bodily eliminations had functioned. He was so mortified he didn't want us to get near him. We just cut off his pants and gently washed him all over, so he wouldn't be humiliated at his next stop.

I was very calm in laying my battery. We got our first order to fire. There's 6,400 degrees in an aiming circle. We were 90 degrees off. We'll never know where those shells came down. I just hope and pray I didn't hurt anybody who was out of the war. I hope it went into the ocean.

This was the first day, all the first day. A lifetime in one day.

I wasn't scared until the third day. When we landed on the beach, our mission was to turn west and go all the way to Cherbourg and clean it out. We could then proceed across France. So I'm going to this huge old chateau. We heard there was a lot of good wine in the cellar.

I had to cross a road and I was learning already about the German 88. You could tell from the sound when it was pointed at you. I heard this *chok!* and I knew it was mine. I was right in the middle of this road. I gave a dive over this hedgerow and went straight down into a moat, all covered with green slime. That killed any desire I had for wine. I was through. All I wanted to do was get back. I raced across the road and got behind another hedgerow. Not before he took another shot at me. He was up in that church steeple and he had a telephone going straight down to that guy. When he'd say fire, the guy'd pull that lanyard. I was the target.

They were so fast and, oh, so accurate. They came close. I had one more road to cross. One more. He had been following me all the way across. This guy was a terrific shot. I began to realize I didn't have a chance. I got a running start from a crouch. He barely missed by being too low. I got a fragment right up here. (Indicates thigh.) It's the only wound I had in the war. I was so embarrassed I never told anybody. 'Cause I'm going after some booze and I get hurt. (Laughs.) The fear hit me a few days later. Fitzpatrick, a wonderful young man, was walking across one of those entrances and an 88 hit him direct and there was nothing left of him. Just exploded his whole body. Eighty-eight millimeters, a little howitzer and very versatile.

The fifth night we were there, we were in dug-in foxholes, in a very checkered position. There were Germans ahead of us and Germans in the back of us. Americans over there ahead of these Germans. The infantry and the artillery were side by side. There was no infantry out in front. When the infantry moved, we moved. There was no straight front line. It was a mess.

We were surrounded by hedgerow fences. One corner would be cut down so cattle could go and drink. In one such corner, there was a sniper. He was shooting at us. Every time, I'd stick my head out of the foxhole, I'd get shot at. I called two very dear friends on the telephone. We fanned out, each of us with a grenade. At a given point, we pitched our grenades and accomplished what we had to do.

I avoid using words like "kill a man" because I like to divorce myself from that. We recognized that we were in a war, but we recognized that they came from families like we came from families and that they had loved ones and they were good guys and they were bad guys. We were called on by our government, that our country was in jeopardy. Therefore we had to fight for it. Personally, I had no malice at any time toward the Germans.

There were only one or two times we ever had face-to-face confrontations with storm troopers. The SS. They were the elite. They were so brainwashed they were impossible to reason with. Those people made me angry.

The ordinary Germans, the boys we took prisoner, were so glad to be out of it. We'd take their shoes and they'd walk down the road. The last thing they'd do is come back and either shake hands with us or embrace us.

We were so mixed up, Americans and Germans. People were shooting at my dear friend Ed Bostick, our forward observer. This was on the second day or third. He jumped into a ditch on the side of the road. The only thing that saved him was a dead German boy who he pulled on top of him. He lay there for hours until he felt safe to move. When he came back, he fell in my arms. Imagine what he'd been through, using a dead boy as a shield.

I went back to my foxhole and I was suddenly drained. It was about one-thirty in the morning. I had to stay on duty until two. Ed was to come and relieve me. I couldn't stay awake. I was just plain exhausted. We never turned the crank or rang the bell on the telephone. When you are an officer—and this included the top noncoms—you went to sleep with your headset at your head. Instead of ringing the bell or speaking, we'd just go (whistles softly), and that would waken you from a sound sleep. This voice came on and said, "Yes, El?" I said, "Can you relieve me? I'm just bushed." He said, "I'll be right over." He came walking over to where I was and for some reason he began to whistle. I'll never know why. A young artillery man, one of ours, I'm sure had dozed off. The whistle wakened him. He saw a figure and fired.

I was out and running, and I caught Ed as he fell. He was dead in my arms. Call it foolish, call it irrational, I loaded Ed in a jeep. I had to take him in for proper care. Now! I went to our battalion headquarters, and I was directed to this drunken colonel. He came out and said, "Get that goddamn hunk of rotten meat out of here." You have no idea of my feeling toward him. It's remained with me for a long time, hard to get rid of. That was a very, very hard experience for me, even to think about now.

That was my fifth day.

At one point, I had been reassigned to be forward observer for the entire battalion. To live and work with the infantry, which I did for the major part of my combat career. One morning in December, it was very cold and snowing, about 2:00 A.M., we were on our way to crossing the Aare River. It was ice, water, and more ice. There was a steep slope on the other side with nothing but snow. We knew Germans were over there and it would be trouble. We had to get across the river. We had inflatable rubber boats to row very silently across. That was fine except for human nature. One of the boys had gotten his hands on some Calvados. He came down the river singing "Row, Row, Row Your Boat" at the top of his lungs. The sky absolutely exploded and the mortars came in on us. It was terrible. It seemed like half a day. Actually it was a few minutes. We made our way across. Oh yes, we had heavy casualties.

It was just beginning to be daybreak. There was a row of houses on each side of this little winding country road. We had to go through each house looking for German boys. We came to the last house. You get inside and you have the gut feeling there is someone in here. We had met some and they were perfectly willing to surrender, no trouble at all. But this one—I had a terrible feeling in my stomach. I searched the house. I knew I had to go into the basement. It was dark down there. No flashlight, no nothing. If he sees my silhouette first, he'll blow me away.

I went down into the cellar. It had windows. Daylight was just coming through. I could see two forms huddled over in the corner. It was a French peasant and his wife. He was holding a rooster to his breast. She was holding a hen. I said, "It's all right." They kind of understood me. The last I remember, they were walking down the road together holding on to their precious treasure.

As a forward observer, if I wanted to bring in an entire division, I called a singsong on a code word. If I wanted a huge amount of fire power, I'd call for a serenade.

I was looking down this steep bank into a very narrow valley, just wide enough for a road leading into a rectangle of heavy forest. All day long, I watched German tanks and vehicles move in. Enormous numbers. I asked for a serenade, the whole thing. I asked for one-half white phosphorus, which I hated and still hate today. And I called for one-half posit fuses. These would get so far from the earth and detonate. A rain of steel would come down. Just terribly destructive. If white phosphorus hit your flesh and started to burn, you couldn't stop it. I asked for I don't know how many rounds. The devastation on that little piece of land, the accuracy of those boys in firing, was incredible. It's one of my bad memories, the suffering.

A day or two later, I was in my foxhole. I was separated from the rest of the company. The snow had melted so I was in two, three inches of water. Night came and it started to freeze. My feet were ice, so I had to get up and walk around. Not ten feet away was a German lieutenant looking around to see what he could see. His back was to me. I just went down into my foxhole. (Laughs.) I just couldn't shoot him in the back. I had a Thompson submachine gun. He didn't have a chance. The next day, I thought I should have done it. And then I thought, how stupid to alert the world, here I am.

You'd have five days up and five days back. They never stayed with it. You'd go five days up, you'd come back, take a bath, change clothes, and the next morning you'd be back. That's because of the casualties. On the way back, I saw the little French peasant and his wife walking back to their house. They had survived with their chickens.

Altogether I was in combat from June of '44 to May of '45. France, Luxembourg, and Germany. We landed on June 6. On July 4, I was able to take my shoes and socks off and change clothes.

There were some cement bunkers I had to go through. There was a German boy. Reflex. Again, an unpleasant memory. It was my first experience with face-to-face combat. It was during the battle of Hürtgen Forest. Our worst, I believe. Our division had four hundred percent casualties.

One time I was sent back to get a truckload of replacements, young boys. They hadn't the benefit of the long training we had in the States. I told them, "If I hear anything coming in and if I tell you to jump, do exactly what I do." We had to be alert for interdiction fire, artillery shells lobbed at an intersection. We came near this intersection and I heard one in the distance going *chok!* I told the guys, Get out of here! I dove over the rail of the truck into the gutter beside the road. Out of the twenty or twenty-five boys I picked up that day, ten were dead.

I was a forward observer at Hürtgen Forest. I had a crew of three. All of us carried radio equipment. I was sent to a forester's tower. At the base of the tower, some trees had been knocked down by shells. We arranged two logs parallel and the others perpendicular to form a roof. We crawled under that and it was our house. When the shells came in and hit the trees and fragments of metal came down, we were protected by these logs.

The second day I was there, I saw another forester's tower. There was a German lieutenant looking right at me. We waved at each other. I marked him on the map. I got my guns zeroed in on him, and I know in my heart he did the same thing to me. He was also an artillery observer. Along my ridge was a road. German tanks rolled along there. My target. He would watch my shooting. He was interested in my effectiveness.

I was bringing the artillery in. One day there came several German vehicles in line. Three ambulances were in the middle. That was hands off. I was just watching them go by. Suddenly somebody started shooting artillery at them. I looked over at the lieutenant right away. I shook my head as hard as I could. He thought I called the fire on those ambulances. I saw him pick up his telephone and I hit the ladder. I barely got in my house and he laid it on us. Almost knocked the tower down. Just his precision shooting. After he lifted his fire, I went tearing up the ladder again. I had my hands up and I was waving and shaking my head: not me. He looked at me. Then he took off his helmet. That was his apology to me.

One day I went down the tower to the edge of the woods to urinate. A German boy was standing not five feet away, behind a tree. I'm holding my organ in my hand as I turned toward him. My friends never let me forget it: I pointed my gun at him. I sat him down, took his shoes off, and he handed me his gun.

I knew another forward observer. He went out with his crew. White phosphorus was thrown at them. Two of the men burned before his eyes. He came running to where I was in another part of Hürtgen Forest. I went down the road to meet him. He was sobbing and falling into my arms. He kept saying, "No more killing, no more killing, no more killing."

There were so many signs that the German surrender was near. I was sent on a route to do something with a jeep and a driver. I came into a meadow and there was an entire German division. No sense in being afraid now. I drove up to a German soldier and I said, "Where is your commandant?" He showed me the tent. This very fine general came walking out. I stood at attention and saluted him and he saluted me. He handed me his sidearm. He surrendered. I had no idea I'd run into this.

I radioed in and told them what happened. They said, "Take him to Bamberg." I led the caravan. He and I rode together. He spoke some English. We got along fine until we got to the prison camp. Everyone who entered those gates had to be deloused. He was furious that he was included.

There really was no celebration on V-E Day. A caravan came winding down a hill with their headlights on. I knew then it was over. Until that moment, it wasn't real.

I was raised in a house that believed in God. All right? But it took something like this to hammer it home to me: I am totally averse to killing and warfare. I saw it with my own eyes and it didn't do a dadratted thing. And the wonderful boys we lost over there. It took four years out of my life.

*   *   *

DR. ALEX SHULMAN:

I was in Belgium at the time of the Bulge. Winter, '44. I was doing neurosurgery, head surgery. This German youngster was brought in. He was fourteen, fifteen. Looked like a lost little boy. Hitler was takin' the kids and the old men. This kid was cut off from his outfit several weeks before, and he hid in a barn. He was a sad, dirty-looking kid, with a terrible gash in his head. It was actually a hole through his scalp and his skull.

When I first saw him, he was covered with old straw and manure and blood, and it was all caked together. I didn't know what to do with him. What is his injury? We always pictured Germans as having short-cropped hair. It was the GIs who had short-cropped hair. The German boys had long hair, long before our boys did. So did this kid, and his hair was matted together.

As I took him to the operating room, he started to cry. A little kid. I said, "Stop crying." I could speak a little bit of German, and a little bit of Yiddish helped. All I did was get a basin of hot water and some soap and washed his hair. Here was a captain in the United States Army washing the hair of a little German boy. I finally cleaned him up and looked at the wound. It wasn't bad. Nature had done quite a job healing it.

Then he really started to cry. I said, "What are you crying about?" He said, "They told me I'd be killed. And here you are, an American officer, washing my hands and face and my hair." I reminded him that I was a Jewish doctor, so he would get the full impact of it.

*   *   *

GRIGORI BAKLANOV:

Eight from my family went to the front. Three came back. We were a lucky family.

When my children ask, "Tell us about the war," I can't tell them anything. I don't like this reminiscing. A lot of people, who lived after the war quite a long life, start to recollect. It was miraculous, wonderful, how brave we were then, how close together we were. It is not a worthy occupation for a human being.

Of my generation, out of a hundred who went to fight, three came back. Three percent. One should not ask those of us who remained alive what war means to them.

I live life as if presented to me. I'm surprised that I have it. A friend asked me, "What's your attitude towards death?" It is absolutely zero. With much more surprise and excitement, I take the fact that I'm alive. I look at my children and my grandchildren and I think: only centimeters decided whether they should be on this earth or not. Whether the bullet went that way or this way. They don't understand that they live on this earth quite by accident. It was quite natural that I wouldn't be alive. But I lived and they happened. They can't understand that.

I think the world is divided into two parts. Half is alive and the other half is in the shadow. It doesn't exist but in the mind. In my short story, I recollect a phrase: "The bullet that killed us today goes into the death of centuries and generations, killing life which didn't come to exist yet."

I was the only one from our class of all the boys who went to the front who remained alive after that war. What else is there to say?

HARRY TOWNE

Corporal Harry Towne was with the U.S. Fifth Marine Division.

To His Mother

March 19, 1945
Central Pacific

Dear Mom:

I don't know if you have heard that I was wounded or not, Mom. I asked a Chaplain to write to you, so you probably know about it.

I am coming along fine now and expect to be in the States before long. I was wounded quite badly, Mother, but the Navy Medical Corps will fix me up like new again. In a year or less I shall be able to walk just as before.

Don't let this be a shock to you, Mother, I will be in almost as good shape as before now that they have these new artificial limbs. Yes, Mother, I have lost my right leg, but it isn't worrying me a bit. I shall receive a pension for the rest of my life and with the new artificial limb, you can hardly tell anything is wrong . . .

I lost my leg on the front lines of Iwo Jima on February 27, but have been moved around so much I couldn't write. I would like to write to Alma, but somehow I can't force myself to do it. You write and tell her, Mother. I'll try to write to her later on.

Don't worry, Mom, the war for me is ended and I should be seeing you by fall.

Love,
Bill

JAMES J. FAHEY
1918–

Fahey served as a Seaman First Class on the light cruiser USS Montpelier, *and although keeping diaries was against naval regulations, he kept an engaging account of events. After the war he returned to his job with the Department of Sanitation, Waltham, Massachusetts, and in 1963 he was named "Garbage Man of the Year" by the* Refuse Removal Journal of New York. *Always a modest man, on this occasion he commented, "It's an honorable profession and I'm happy." He was encouraged to publish his* Pacific War Diary, 1942–1945 *(1963) by Admiral Samuel Eliot Morison, and the Navy thought so highly of his achievements both literary and patriotic that it gave him a parade at Annapolis.*

From Pacific War Diary, 1942–1945

October 3, 1942: I enlisted in the U.S. Navy today. It looks like the Navy got the makings of a very poor sailor when they got me. I still get carsick and cannot ride on a swing for any length of time.

I took my physical examination at the Post Office Building in Boston, Mass., a distance of about ten miles from Waltham, Mass. A fellow next to me was rejected because he was color blind. They told him the Sea Bees would take him. On the way home I relaxed in the old trolley car and felt like the Fleet Admiral himself.

October 7, 1942: I got up early this morning for my trip to Boston, on my way to Great Lakes Naval Training Station in Chicago, Illinois.

Before leaving I shook my father's hand and kissed him goodbye.

It was a clear cool morning as my sister Mary, brother John and I headed for the bus at the corner of Cedar Street. The bus and trolley car were crowded with people going to work. When we reached the Post Office Building in Boston I shook John's hand and kissed Mary goodbye.

After a long tiresome day of hanging around we were finally on our way to the train station. The group was very large and they came from the New England states. We were called the Lexington Volunteers in honor of the carrier *Lexington*. It was sunk by the Japanese Navy May 7, 1942, in the battle of the Coral Sea.

With a big band leading the way we marched through downtown Boston before thousands of people. It took about half an hour to reach the North Station and at 5:30 P.M. we were on our way.

When the train passed through my city it was beginning to get dark and I could picture the folks at home having supper. There would be an empty place at the table for some time. It would have been very easy for me to feel sad and lonely with these thoughts in my mind but we should not give in to our feelings. If we always gave in to our feelings instead of our judgment we would fall by the wayside when the going got rough.

It will be a long tiresome trip and our bed will be the seat we sit in, two to a seat.

October 8, 1942: The long troop train stopped in the middle of nowhere today. It looked like a scene from a western movie in the last century. All you could see was wide open spaces with plenty of fields and a small railroad station. It felt good to get some fresh air and stretch our legs for a change after the crowded conditions on the train. Some of the fellows like myself mailed letters and cards home. The postmark on the mail was STRATHROY, Ontario, Canada. It was a warm sunny day so we sat on the side of the tracks while waiting for the train to get started again.

At Great Lakes: On the evening of Oct. 9 we pulled into the stockyards at Chicago and stayed there for some time. It gave us another chance to get some fresh air and walk around on solid ground for a change. All the people in the big tenement buildings were at their windows looking at us.

At last the train was on its final leg of the journey. We were a tired dirty lot when the train finally pulled into Great Lakes Naval Training Station in the early morning darkness. The weather was on the chilly side.

They got us up bright and early after a few hours sleep on the floor of a large drill hall. We were far from being in condition for a physical examination but that was the way we started the day and it took a long time. We went from one doctor to another upstairs and downstairs and from one room to another. They checked us from head to toe and even asked us our religion. At last it was over and our first shower in some time. It sure felt good.

We spent four weeks of training and lived in barracks. Our company number was 1291. A Chief Petty Officer was in charge of each company and our chief was liked by all.

Some of the Chiefs are hated because they go out of their way to make it as miserable as possible. They enjoy getting the fellows up at two in the morning and have them stand at attention in the cold for a long time with very little clothing.

The instructor who taught us judo enjoyed taking it out on the new recruits. He sent one of the boys from my company to the hospital in a stretcher. Our chief was boiling mad and if he could have gotten his hands on this punk he would have done a job on him.

You learned that your days of privacy were over while you were in the Navy and they would not return until you were back in civilian life again. When you ate, slept, took a shower, etc., you were always part of the crowd, you were never alone.

No one enjoyed sleeping in the hammocks because they were too tight. It was like sleeping on a tight clothesline. You felt like you were going to fall out if you turned over. You felt safe on your back but you can't sleep on your back all night.

We will never forget our first haircut. When the barber got through there was no hair to cut. It was shorter than short. It was funny to see a nice looking fellow with a beautiful crop of hair get into the barber's chair and leave with no hair at all.

Great Lakes is the largest naval training station in the world and they also have one of the best football teams in the country. I had the pleasure of talking to Bruce Smith the all-American back from Minnesota. He was the number one football player in the country in 1941. You could not help but like him. He slept in our barracks.

We always marched to the mess hall for our meals and kept in step by singing loud and strong.

I had to go to sick call one day because of a bad blow to the ribs I received in a boxing bout but they did not do anything for me even though the pain was killing me. They think everyone is a faker when he goes to sick call, that he just wants time off from work.

We were kept on the go at all times and at last our training was over. It was home sweet home for us. We were very proud of our uniform as we boarded the train for home. After a nine day leave we returned to Great Lakes and stayed here for two days before leaving for Norfolk, Virginia, our next stop.

November 23, 1942: Late Friday evening Nov. 21, a large group of us boarded a truck for the pier. It was a great feeling as I staggered up the gangway to the ship with my sea bag in one hand and the mattress cover loaded with blankets, mattress, etc., over my shoulder. The name of the ship is the U.S.S. *Montpelier.* It is a light cruiser. At last I have a home and a warship at that.

We slept in our hammocks in the mess hall at first but then we were assigned to divisions. I went to the 5th division. It is a deck division.

It will take some time before we know our way around this large ship. It is over 600 feet long and has many decks and compartments.

Today at eight in the morning we left Norfolk for the Philadelphia Navy Yard.

* * *

I will now tell what happened while we were in the Good Old U.S.A. August 22, 1944, we docked at Mare Island which is in Vallejo, Calif. Our section had first leave. We left Vallejo, Calif., on a warm, sunny morning by bus for the Army air base at Sacramento, Calif., about 70 miles away. We got there in the afternoon and had to wait about 4 hours before our plane took off. If you had been overseas 1 year or more, you can take the Army bombers, they carry freight and passengers and it will not cost you a cent. The only drawback is that you don't know how long it will take you to get home, because sometimes you have to get off to make room for the big crates of cargo. You are allowed to take so much with you and no more. They weigh your things before you get on the plane. They are 2 engine transports and cargo planes. When you get tired of sitting in the plane you go up on the crates and fall asleep. The crates are in the center of the plane, you sit on the sides. Your ears feel funny and every now and then you hit air pockets when the plane drops. On long trips it gets very tiresome and about every 3 hrs. the plane would land and the freight would go off or some would come on. They also had to fuel the plane. It is something like a C-47, with two motors.

It is a good size, it carries about 30 passengers plus plenty of freight which was secured to the floor in the center of the plane. We sat shoulder to shoulder facing the crates of cargo, we sat on both sides of the plane facing each other also. Every place we stopped there was a Red Cross stand for the men to get free food and drinks. They come in very handy because everyone was hungry and the planes only stay about ½ hour. We got as far as Omaha, Nebraska, the next morning, Aug. 24th. We were over halfway home, to Mass. Tony Freitas and myself had to get off and make room for more freight, so we did not wait for another plane because we might have to wait a long time.

We went to the station but our train did not leave until the afternoon so we took a walk around Omaha, to see the sights. This is a very large city and a nice place but we did not see any servicemen. Just the ones waiting for trains. Everyone here must be overseas. We had a big meal and took the train that left in the afternoon. That same evening we changed trains at Chicago and the next day, Friday, Aug. 25th, at 9 o'clock in the evening we finally pulled into the South Station, Boston, Mass. We walked up Washington St. and I was impressed to see it so quiet, that was something new for Boston. Everyone must be overseas. We tried to buy some tailor-made blues, but the stores were closed so we took a taxi to the Y.M.C.A. We took a shower and hit the sack. I was very careful that nothing happened to my Diary.

When I got off the train in Boston I felt like I never felt before, it was great. We got up the next morning at 10 A.M. and took a taxi to a clothing store and had a suit of tailor-made blues made. It only took about ½ hour to get them. A couple of shoeshine boys were outside and they gave our shoes a good polishing. It was a nice, warm morning as we headed for the Boston Common. I left Tony at the Common, because he had to get a bus for Fall River, I went below and got the subway for Newton Corner and then got on the bus for Waltham and home. I had 3 bags with me, my clothing and some Jap souvenirs. I got off the bus at the corner of my street, the place was deserted. I walked down the street and up the front steps, the place was deserted. It was a feeling you cannot explain. It was not only the idea of being away for almost 2 years so much but all the close calls we had and being able to come through them all without any harm. It was about 1 P.M. Saturday afternoon, Aug. 26, as I walked up the hall stairs and as I got close to the kitchen I could hear the radio playing. As I stepped into the kitchen my brother John saw me and you could have knocked him over with a feather, boy was he surprised to see me. No one knew I was in the States. I wanted to surprise them, they thought I was still in the Pacific. John put on his uniform and we went to Grant's store where my sister works. This was going to be a surprise for Mary. We locked the kitchen door and left for the store. I was so overjoyed I felt like running. We walked to the rear of the store where Mary worked and when she saw me she was going to cry, she was so overjoyed. The Boss gave Mary permission to take the day off and we headed for home.

On the way home I had to drop in and see one of my close friends, Mrs. Sweeney. She was surprised to see me, she gave me a big hug and kiss. She gave us some homemade pie and cake, it really hit the spot. It was my first home cooked meal in almost 2 years. Mary lives with the Sweeneys and goes home on weekends, because John usually has liberty. Mrs. Sweeney's son is also in the Navy. He is a doctor. We left the Sweeneys' and headed for home. That evening I had a meal that really hit the spot, you cannot beat home cooked meals. We expected a 30 day leave but had to settle for 23 days. That gave me 14 days at home, because I had to allow myself enough time to travel. The 14 days went very fast and before I knew it I was on my way back to the ship in Calif. I went everywhere and had a good time while I was home. The city was dead, nearly everyone was in the service. When you walked down the street there was no one to talk to, just women, old men, and 4F's. You might just as well be in the service with the rest of the fellows. We had almost 15 million in all branches of the military and when you came home you could see that it looked like everyone was in the service. The old gang was gone. But it felt good to walk around the city.

Our troops were making such progress in Europe that they said the war (over there) would be over in a couple of months. Well, Sunday afternoon Sept. 10th I started on my way back to the ship. It was about the 10th of Nov. 1942 that I left home for my 1st stay in the Pacific, and here I was again doing the same thing all over again almost 2 years later. I met Tony Freitas at the South Station, and said goodbye to Mary, John, and Alice Sweeney.

The next time I come home the war should be over. I kissed Mary goodbye and shook hands with John and Alice as I stepped into the train. The train was crowded as usual, and it took us some time before we found a seat. Everyone was in uniform. We got off the train at New York at 6 P.M. and headed for the Newark Airport. They told us that we could get a cargo plane about 2:30 A.M. Monday morning, for San Francisco, Calif. We told the man in charge that we were going to take a look at the city and that we would be back about 2 A.M. We walked around Newark and had something to eat. We also brought back some food to the plane for our trip. When we got back to the airport we took our dress blues off and put on our dungarees, because your clothes get wrinkled and dusty sleeping on the wooden crates. The waiting room was very quiet, only the man at the desk was there. We lay down on the bench and told the fellow at the desk to wake us up when our plane was ready to take off. About 3:45 A.M. Monday morning we got in the plane and took off for San Francisco, Calif.

We stopped about every 3 or 4 hours and it was the same routine, cargo coming and going off, new men coming on, some going off. Some of the places we stopped were Arizona, Texas, Oklahoma.

We stopped at Tucson, Arizona, early in the morning and took a stroll around the building. It looks like a good size house or hotel. We were hungry but could not get anything to eat, everyone was asleep. The air was great here and the only sound you could hear outside was the sound of insects. It was peaceful and quiet. We stopped in Texas early Tuesday morning about 2 A.M. and Tony left to see his brother who was at one of the Army camps.

He was about 40 miles from here. We made good plane connections so Tony could afford some time to see his brother. He went out on the highway and started to thumb a ride. A lady in the Red Cross trailer was the one who gave him the information about his brother. I waited here in Texas for the plane to get fuel. We could hear a radio playing Western songs. We had to wait 4 hours in Oklahoma City for a plane. This was a big Army Air Corps base. They had a few Big B-29 Super Flying Fortresses here, the kind that hit Tokyo. They are the largest in the world. We went inside and looked them over. They were very big, it was some plane. We also went to the mess hall and had something to eat. We reached Frisco about noon Tuesday. We stopped quite a few times and were held over for quite a while but still it only took us about 1 day and 9 hours. That was much better than a 4 or 5 day trip by train. I had a few days left for my leave so I took in Frisco and the other cities close by. My leave expired Sept. 15th/1944. The first few weeks we lived in barracks while the Navy yard crew worked on the ship and the chow was good. We also had 3 nights a week off. The last couple of weeks before we left the States we lived on the ship and things changed. We had to stand watches again, and we had one working party after another, as we took on hundreds of tons of supplies, such as food etc. We also unloaded about 15 freight cars of ammunition. The chow wasn't very good. It was a good thing that you could buy food in the Navy yard, the fellows were always eating. They might as well eat plenty now because once we leave the States it will stop.

We only got about one week end off while we were in the States. We usually handled ammunition on Sundays and had the evening off. If your section rated it. When a ship comes back to the States you get nothing but working parties. They want the ship ready for sea as soon as possible.

*   *   *

At 10:50 A.M. this morning General Quarters sounded, all hands went to their battle stations. At the same time a battleship and a destroyer were alongside the tanker getting fuel. Out of the clouds I saw a big Jap bomber come crashing down into the water. It was not smoking and looked in good condition. It felt like I was in it as it hit the water not too far from the tanker, and the 2 ships that were refueling. One of our P-38 fighters hit it. He must have got the pilot. At first I thought it was one of our bombers that had engine trouble. It was not long after that when a force of about 30 Jap planes attacked us. Dive bombers and torpedo planes. Our two ships were busy getting away from the tanker because one bomb-hit on the tanker and it would be all over for the 3 ships.

The 2 ships finally got away from the tanker and joined the circle. I think the destroyers were on the outside of the circle. It looked funny to see the tanker all by itself in the center of the ships as we circled it, with our guns blazing away as the planes tried to break through. It was quite a sight, better than the movies. I never saw it done before. It must be the first time it was ever done in any war. Jap planes were coming at us from all directions. Before the attack started we did not know that they were suicide planes, with no intention of returning to their base. They had one thing in mind and that was to crash into our ships, bombs and all. You have to blow them up, to damage them doesn't mean much. Right off the bat a Jap plane made a suicide dive at the cruiser *St. Louis,* there was a big explosion and flames were seen shortly from the stern. Another one tried to do the same thing but he was shot down. A Jap plane came in on a battleship with its guns blazing away. Other Jap planes came in strafing one ship, dropping their bombs on another and crashing into another ship. The Jap planes were falling all around us, the air was full of Jap machine gun bullets. Jap planes and bombs were hitting all around us. Some of our ships were being hit by suicide planes, bombs and machine gun fire. It was a fight to the finish. While all this was taking place our ship had its hands full with Jap planes. We knocked our share of planes down but we also got hit by 3 suicide planes, but lucky for us they dropped their bombs before they crashed into us. In the meantime exploding planes overheard were showering us with their parts. It looked like it was raining plane parts. They were falling all over the ship. Quite a few of the men were hit by big pieces of Jap planes. We were supposed to have air coverage but all we had was 4 P-38 fighters, and when we opened up on the Jap planes they got out of the range of our exploding shells. They must have had a ring side seat of the show. The men on my mount were also showered with parts of Jap planes. One suicide dive bomber was heading right for us while we were firing at other attacking planes and if the 40 mm. mount behind us on the port side did not blow the Jap wing off it would have killed all of us. When the wing was blown off it, the plane turned some and bounced off into the water and the bombs blew part of the plane onto our ship. Another suicide plane crashed into one of the 5 inch mounts, pushing the side of the mount in and injuring some of the men inside. A lot of 5 inch shells were damaged. It was a miracle they did not explode. If that happened the powder and shells would have blown up the ship. Our 40 mm. mount is not too far away. The men threw the 5 inch shells over the side. They expected them to go off at any time. A Jap dive bomber crashed into one of the 40 mm. mounts but lucky for them it dropped its bombs on another ship before crashing. Parts of the plane flew everywhere when it crashed into the mount. Part of the motor hit Tomlinson, he had chunks of it all over him, his stomach, back, legs etc. The rest of the crew were wounded, most of them were sprayed with gasoline from the plane. Tomlinson was thrown a great distance and at first they thought he was knocked over the side. They finally found him in a corner in bad shape. One of the mt. Captains had the wires cut on his phones and kept talking into the phone, because he did not know they were cut by shrapnel until one of the fellows told him. The explosions were terrific as the suicide planes exploded in the water not too far away from our ship. The water was covered with black smoke that rose high into the air. The water looked like it was on fire. It would have been curtains for us if they had crashed into us.

Another suicide plane just overshot us. It grazed the 6 inch turret. It crashed into Leyte Gulf. There was a terrific explosion as the bombs exploded, about 20 ft. away. If we were going a little faster we would have been hit. The Jap planes that were not destroyed with our shells crashed into the water close by or hit our ships. It is a tough job to hold back this tidal wave of suicide planes. They come at you from all directions and also straight down at us at a very fast pace but some of the men have time for a few fast jokes, "This would be a great time to run out of ammunition." "This is mass suicide at its best." Another suicide plane came down at us in a very steep dive. It was a near miss, it just missed the 5 inch mount. The starboard side of the ship was showered with water and fragments. How long will our luck hold out? The Good Lord is really watching over us. This was very close to my 40 mm. mount and we were showered with debris. If the suicide plane exploded on the 5 inch mount, the ammunition would have gone up, after that anything could happen.

Planes were falling all around us, bombs were coming too close for comfort. The Jap planes were cutting up the water with machine gun fire. All the guns on the ships were blazing away, talk about action, never a dull moment. The fellows were passing ammunition like lightning as the guns were turning in all directions spitting out hot steel. Parts of destroyed suicide planes were scattered all over the ship. During a little lull in the action the men would look around for Jap souvenirs and what souvenirs they were. I got part of the plane. The deck near my mount was covered with blood, guts, brains, tongues, scalps, hearts, arms etc. from the Jap pilots. One of the Marines cut the ring off the finger of one of the dead pilots. They had to put the hose on to wash the blood off the deck. The deck ran red with blood. The Japs were spattered all over the place. One of the fellows had a Jap scalp, it looked just like you skinned an animal. The hair was black, cut very short, and the color of the skin was yellow, real Japanese. I do not think he was very old. I picked up a tin pie plate with a tongue on it. The pilot's tooth mark was into it very deep. It was very big and long, it looked like part of his tonsils and throat were attached to it. It also looked like the tongue you buy in the meat store. This was the first time I ever saw a person's brains, what a mess. One of the men on our mount got a Jap rib and cleaned it up, he said his sister wants part of a Jap body. One fellow from Texas had a knee bone and he was going to preserve it in alcohol from the sick bay. The Jap bodies were blown into all sorts of pieces. I cannot think of everything that happened because too many things were happening at the same time.

These suicide or kamikaze pilots wanted to destroy us, our ships and themselves. This gives you an idea what kind of an enemy we are fighting. The air attacks in Europe are tame compared to what you run up against out here against the Japs. The Germans will come in so far, do their job and take off but not the Japs. I can see now how the Japs sank the two British battleships *Prince of Wales* and the *Repulse* at the beginning of the war at Singapore. You do not discourage the Japs, they never give up, you have to kill them. It is an honor to die for the Emperor. We do not know how many Jap planes were shot down or the total of planes that attacked us during all the action but they threw plenty of them at us. I have not heard how many planes our ship shot down but at one period of the attack our ship shot down 4 suicide planes within 2 minutes. I think most of the Jap planes that attacked us were destroyed. The attack lasted for 2 hours, we went to battle stations at 10:50 A.M. in the morning and secured at 2:10 P.M. in the afternoon. The action took place not too far from Leyte. Every ship had its hands full with the Jap planes during those 2 hours. The Japs started the attack with 30 planes but after that more planes kept joining them.

After we secured from General Quarters the men looked the ship over to see the damage. The ship was a mess, part of it was damaged, cables were down, steel life lines snapped and steel posts broken. Big pieces of Jap planes were scattered all over the ship, life rafts damaged. Our empty shell cases were everywhere. Some of the other ships were in worse condition than ours. The wounded were brought down to sick bay and some had to be operated on at once.

When it was all over the tanker was still in the middle of the circle and the Japs did not hit it.

Someone said a couple of rafts were in the water with some Japs in them and one of the Japs was in bad condition. We will get more information about this action later when all the reports are in. We had chow at 2:30 P.M. in the afternoon and at 6:30 P.M. we went to sunset General Quarters. The Japs did not come out tonight, guess they had enough action to hold them this afternoon for the day. We secured from General Quarters at 8 P.M. We got some rain this evening. I got the midnight to 4 A.M. watch. No sleep.

*   *   *

Wednesday, May 16, 1945: I left the ship this morning for a stores working party on the cruiser *Nashville*. It had just returned from the States. It had procured supplies at Manus for the *Montpelier* and the other ships in the harbor. It was raining as we left the ship in an LCT. We worked all day until 6 P.M. on stores. We loaded landing craft that transported them to the other ships. It was good to be able to eat chow in the mess hall on the *Nashville* with our sleeves rolled up. Our ship could learn some things from the *Nashville*. We would have been tagged with extra duty aboard the *Montpelier*.

I was talking to the crew of the *Nashville*. They told me that 168 men had been killed when a Jap suicide plane crashed into them with its bomb load. This had occurred on their way to Mindoro to take part in the invasion there. Seventy men had been wounded in the same action. The Executive Officer had his head blown off. Only four men in the Marine division had escaped death. The remainder had all been killed. A light cruiser carries 50 Marines in its complement. Her decks were covered with the dead and wounded. Nearly all of the machine gun mounts were knocked out of action by the explosion. A 5 inch mount and 95 of its live shells blew up, sending chunks of hot steel raining down upon the crew. They spent three months in the States for repairs. Each man on board was allowed a 28 day leave while there. They also told me that the carrier U.S.S. *Franklin* was docked stateside. It was a mess of tangled steel. They don't know how it ever reached there, it was in such bad condition. The *Franklin* was hit by Jap planes last Feb. about fifty miles off Japan. A Jap airplane had flown out of the clouds and crashed into the parked planes on the flight deck. Everything exploded, bombs, high octane gas, shells, etc. Over 1,600 casualties were reported. It was a miracle that it did not sink. We have a lot more ships damaged than they say.

Thursday, May 17, 1945: All hands on deck at 5 A.M. We left Subic Bay at 6:30 A.M. for Manila. We will stay there for four days. It was raining this morning when we arose. We dropped anchor in Manila Bay at 8:30 A.M. Our section rated liberty. We left the *Montpelier* at 12:15 P.M. in a landing craft. We can stay in Manila until 6 P.M.

Prices are very expensive in the city. A bottle of Coca-Cola costs $1.00 to $1.50 each, compared to five cents in the States. A small spoon of ice cream costs $1.00 also. In the center of the city, an Army truck loaded with Jap prisoners went by. The young Filipino children yelled and threw stones at them. American soldiers with machine guns were the guards. The Japs I saw on the truck were short and very husky. I talked to one of the nearby Filipino men. He seemed to be well educated. He had spent much of his time under Japanese rule, in the hills. While hiding out from the Japs, they were kept informed of the latest news by short wave radio. He had seen the infamous Death March. He said that an abhorable amount of cruelty had been shown our troops by the Japs. He had watched the American prisoners work on the docks, loading and unloading ships in the bay. The only clothes they wore were a pair of short pants and worn-out shoes. They were very weak and pale and thin. They only got a little rice to eat each day. Anytime a Jap soldier felt like sticking a bayonet into one of them, he would do so. The Jap army troops were a very poor lot, ignorant and uneducated. They had been recruited from the farms and rural areas of Japan. Whenever drunk, they committed obscenities unheard of before. They were like animals. The men in the Japanese Navy were of a better caliber, being educated, and their outrageous actions more limited. When they went in a place to drink they stayed by themselves and kept quiet. The Japs stripped Manila bare and sent all the good stuff to Japan. The Filipinos were left with nothing except their faith that the United States would liberate them from the oppressors. He told me that the city was left in rubble, but freedom again was enough to satisfy him. Everyone is overjoyed at being liberated.

The people in the States do not know how lucky they are. They have come out of this war very easy. The country is all in one piece, and they have clean homes to go to. Over here the people have nothing, the Japs took everything away from them, and the Japs brought bad habits upon the girls. It's a shame the way the girls make money. It's the same way all over the city. I never saw anything like it. Most of the girls are from 15 to 20. Little kids about nine years old are out drumming up business. They say about 70% of the females are diseased.

The whiskey that the fellows buy here is mostly homemade and it is very bad stuff to drink. I never saw so many fellows knocked out by it. Of course, being away from whiskey for eight months might explain that. It's very potent and smells like alcohol that is put in car radiators in the wintertime. A few have gone blind from drinking it, the last time we were here. Others had to be strapped in stretchers when brought aboard the *Montpelier*. They acted like crazy people.

*   *   *

Sunday, September 2, 1945: The Japs signed the peace papers on the battleship *Missouri* in Tokyo Bay. It was about 8 P.M. Sat. night on east coast.

Monday, September 3, 1945: This afternoon at 5:30 P.M. the word was passed that no more gun watches would be stood. Watches will be stood on guns only at sea. In port all guns will be secured. This is the first time the guns have not been manned. I sometimes thought that I would never see this day. After gunnery tomorrow most of the ammo will be removed from the shields. It looked good to see them lock the five inch mounts. I never saw them like that before.

MITCHELL SHARPE

Private First Class Mitchell Sharpe fought on the line with the 87th Infantry Division in France and Germany in 1944 and 1945.

To His Mother

2 May 1945
England

Dear Mom:

I couldn't possibly feel any worse if you had written one of the immediate family had died. Neal's death has hit me pretty bad for I know how he must have gone. I keep thinking of him like that kid with his M1 stuck in the ground with his helmet on it (a sign of death) lying off the path looking as if he were asleep. I see him lying on his back arms overhead with eyes and mouth open as if asking, "God, why?" To the people at home killed in action means one ceases to exist. Here it is different. One may be for days in a perpetual attitude of some form of physical expression—fear, sleep, laughter. I keep remembering all the letters from him. He had planned many things—"As soon as we get home." If you could only see us kids killed at eighteen, nineteen and twenty fighting in a country that means nothing to us, fighting because it means either kill or be killed not because you're making the world safe for democracy or destroying Nazism. Kids that have never had a crack at life. Some have never worked and earned money and felt proud, never finished their quest or insatiable thirst for knowledge, never felt the temporary exhilaration of being drunk, never slept with a girl. Each one of them has something just as precious to go back to at home—a slum district in New York, a farm in Kansas, a small town in Arkansas. Each one has so many dreams and plans. There's no *"if* I get home" it is always *"when* I get home." I'm convinced of one thing—Neal didn't go "like a quarry slave at night scourged to his dungeon" but he went proudly. Mom, Neal was proud of being a buck sergeant. At first he had the same position I have, but he looked down on it. He wanted to be first scout. He was made a buck sergeant assistant squad leader. He wrote me and I could tell he was full of pride at being made a sergeant. He took a special pride in fulfilling his duties because he was conscientious. He made me ashamed of the petty jealousies and quarrels that went on in our platoon. His death has made me despise the self-centered mundane, little creatures who because of their positions as officers assume, and state, "I'm God" attitudes. It has made me see what a hopeless and senseless mockery this war is. What we have now will never compensate for the thousands of Neals buried from Normandy to Munich. It will all have to be done again in fifty or so years. . . .

Write soon, love
Mitchell

DONALD BAIN

1922-

Bain attended Cambridge University and served with the Royal Artillery and the Gordon Highlanders. He published in Penguin New Writing *during the war and afterward became an actor.*

WAR POET

We in our haste can only see the small components of the scene;
We cannot tell what incidents will focus on the final screen.
A barrage of disruptive sound, a petal on a sleeping face,
Both must be noted, both must have their place;
It may be that our later selves or else our unborn sons
Will search for meaning in the dust of long deserted guns,
We only watch, and indicate and make our scribbled pencil notes.
We do not wish to moralize, only to ease our dusty throats.

HEINRICH BÖLL
1927–1985

Novelist and Nobel prize winner, Böll was born in Cologne to a pacifist,
Roman Catholic family. Drafted into the German army, he served on
both the Eastern and Western fronts, ending the war in an American
prisoner-of-war camp. His Letter to My Sons: War's End *was his last*
piece of writing, finished in May 1984.

A LETTER TO MY SONS: WAR'S END

Dear René, dear Vincent,
   If you should find in this the slightest trace of glorying in Germany's
survival and reconstruction, cross it out, laugh at it, put it down to irony
or anger; but believe me, I don't intend to fall into the tone of the older
generation, always out to tell their young listeners what a hard time "we"
had of it, and how easy it really is for them and always will be. Oh, those
plucky types with their sleeves rolled up: they've still got them rolled up,
even now—as I write, the notorious Amnesty Bill is being pushed
through Parliament by the most brazen of them—even now the crooks
are busy rolling over the Federal Republic.
   No, it's no easier for you than it was for us: don't let them tell you
otherwise. It was possible to survive the last war, and that's what I want
to tell you about: our experience of *the end of the war.* "Telling a story"
is a risky business—in every story-teller there invariably lurks a braggart
or a show-off; but in actual fact he's a true hero as well or at least a true
sufferer. Even the Odyssey is full of boasting, and what I want to tell you
about is like a little Odyssey. I've written enough about the war; read it
with a forgiving eye, and if you detect—as you may here—anything
accusatory in the tone, it's only the German Reich that I'm accusing, its
leaders and its people, never the victorious powers, never the Soviet
Union. I wouldn't have any grounds anyway on which to accuse the

Soviet Union. I was ill there a few times, and I was wounded there, but that's war, and it was always clear to me: no one *asked* us over there. It just so happens that in a war you get shot at—they had those mortars, "Stalin's organ pipes," and the like; and sometimes you had to eat and drink things that were unsafe or unfit for consumption. When you're half crazy with thirst (one lesson I will pass on to you—thirst is always worse than hunger!), you do drink from puddles and you forget all the warnings about germs and bacteria. You can tell I wasn't keen to fall into Soviet hands by the way that, from the autumn of 1944 onwards, I managed to keep to the west, although they would have liked to send me back eastwards. I did what I could. Anyway, soldiers—and I was one— shouldn't complain about the people they've been sent to fight against, only about those who sent them there.

* * *

Where should I start what is not a "story," but simply an account of how we experienced the *end of the war?* I suppose the best thing is to begin with my mother's death, on 3 November in Ahrweiler, while I was in hospital in Bad Neuenahr. I wasn't sick or wounded; I had been transferred from hospital in Ahrweiler to Dresden, then discharged from there and sent back to Ahrweiler. In order to get another spell in hospital after my leave had come to an end, I had once again helped Nature along a bit, with something I'd been given by a Cologne doctor who's still alive. After my mother's funeral we left the hotel in Ahrweiler, probably round the seventh or eighth November. Her death probably saved our lives. A few days after we moved out of the hotel, it was destroyed by a bomb with a direct hit. Our "move"? No, I shan't describe it. It would turn out as an adventure story, and there are enough of those already. One important thing, though: the lorry-driver was a saint—patient, gentle, friendly. We billeted ourselves rather forcibly, although by invitation, on my relations: Maria, Alois, Marie-Theres, Franz and Gilbert in Marienfeld, where your little brother Christoph is buried. Our welcome in our new home was appropriate enough: a bomb, the first to be dropped on the village since the war began. Nothing from me here about food and living conditions; all that's been done often enough. Six adults and three children in temporary accommodation. My father was almost seventy-five, and still fond of cigars. The only reliable source of tobacco was a Polish prisoner of war who worked as a joiner in the house next door. His name was Toni, and he was a perfect gentleman in dress and demeanour.

We had one wish only: to live, not exactly for ever, but preferably a while longer, and without the Nazi pestilence.

How many novels would it take to describe the time between 3 November 1944 and April 1945? Remember that the Minister of the Interior was Himmler, and that after 20 July he was also the Commander-in-Chief of the reserve army: *my, our,* Commander-in-Chief. The internal terror that prevailed between 20 July and the end of the war has yet to be described.

We not only had the frivolous desire to survive this horror, we were hungry as well; there were nine, sometimes ten or eleven of us to be fed. Ask Annemarie, your mother, ask her about it when you get the chance: she knitted gloves that would have delighted any boutique, and in exchange she would get half a bucketful of potatoes, a few of them already starting to rot. The winter was a cold one, like all the winters of the war. Why do we remember them all as so cold? I don't know what an objective, meteorological view would be. What else could we do but beg and steal? The stealing was confined to firewood, which had to be chopped by the women in a little wood nearby, up to their knees in the snow, under the strict supervision of your grandfather. Later, in the temporary accommodation for the nine of us, he sawed up the wood expertly on the kitchen table, after first, equally expertly, sharpening the saw. Do you know the sound of a saw being sharpened, one tooth at a time, with a saw-file? The wood was wet, and paper scarce; how could your grandfather, who always insisted on doing it himself, get a fire going? Well, our accommodation was the former vestry, only reachable from the street by a ladder, and in the loft above were stored the posts that carry the banners on Corpus Christi Day and other processions. The wood was dry, and the thickness of the posts ideal. We called them "pastors," because one of the banners in the procession at Corpus Christi read "Bless Our Pastor." Every so often one of the "pastors" would have to be secretly got down from the loft under the cover of darkness and sawn up into stove-sized lengths. We often asked ourselves whether the "pastors" would last us till the end of the war (later on in the prisoner-of-war camp, with the approach of Corpus Christi, I wondered what would happen when the villagers found out that their "pastors" had disappeared!). But you can't light a fire just with dry wood and a little paper; you need matches or a lighter, and we had neither. And so your grandfather would position himself at the gate at six o'clock on dark winter mornings, and wait for someone whose lighter he could use to light a twist of paper. Nevertheless he used to curse those farmers, who got up too late for his taste; he got up between five thirty and six all his life, to go to Mass.

Your uncle Alois, a "sponti" before his time, had the understandable, if also dangerous, inclination to absent himself from his unit on repeated occasions, which could quite easily have been taken as desertion. Officially he "served"—that is, did nothing—in the Hacketäuer barracks in

Cologne-Mülheim-of-wretched-memory. He would borrow or somehow get hold of a bicycle and just turn up, usually exhausted and drenched in sweat, having cycled via Much to Marienfeld. We sometimes had visits from the military police (known as "guard dogs"). The military police meant real danger, and not just for Alois, whom they could have shot, or strung up from the nearest tree—no, I too had reason to fear their visits, because I wasn't always able to keep my papers up to date, or have them properly falsified. Once I had to hide in the broom-cupboard, and the "guard-dogs" luckily didn't look in there. The three children were useful for camouflage and distraction. Also we brothers had the good fortune to resemble each other, so that the neighbours could never be quite sure whether there was just one of us, or both, around at any time. That's why we couldn't go out and help with chopping wood in the daytime.

At this point, I must mention Johann Peters, the farmer from Berz-bach near Much, who would not only give us two litres (!) of milk every day (!) in return for two worthless Kriegsmarks, but who would also—he was an amputee from the First World War, a Catholic and an anar-chist—welcome a couple of German deserters to his stove, and give us the odd pipe of tobacco to smoke, which was worth considerably more than two Kriegsmarks. Milk soups of the winter of '44, maybe it's to you and farmer Johann Peters that we owe our lives! Two litres of milk a day in a winter in the war. Our evening milk soup was the only meal we could depend on. Fetching the milk by daylight became a dangerous busi-ness—sometimes Annemarie and Marie-Theres could escape the low-flying fighter planes only by leaping off the road into the ditch.

Fear and hunger, hunger and fear of the Germans. Perhaps now, Vincent and René, you'll understand a bit more what we so often tried to explain to you: why even today shopping for me is always panic-buying, why I always get too much bread, too much milk, eggs and butter, and cigarettes preferably by the carton; and maybe you'll under-stand why I'm continually astonished that I didn't spend the rest of my life sitting by the stove, reading with a few cigarettes to hand. After all, I was married to a secondary-school teacher, decently well-off, whose sal-ary would, while modest, have been enough for us all. To sit by the stove and read; to be free for just a few hours from fear of the "guard-dogs" and of Herr Himmler, the Minister of the Interior, and Herr Himmler, the Commander-in-Chief, and his laws and his emissaries: it'll help you understand also how the merest hint of Fascism throws me into a panic; why I always keep my car filled up with petrol, why I like to have enough money in my pocket to last at least a week, and why I live within reach of the Dutch and Belgian border. Crazy, I know, crazy. And perhaps you'll understand that only fear can make you brave—only the situation where the choice is between being courageous and being destroyed—and that it was this fear that gave me the courage to exist on faked papers, which I then boldly handed in at some army office for genuine ones, to be faked in their turn. Don't take this as a tip or advice from me, René and Vincent, just as a statement on my behaviour, which at the time felt "historically correct," in view of the imminent *end of the war*—something historians will see entirely differently. If it should happen to you, it will happen quite differently. Advice isn't much use there.

The first time I falsified my papers was in the spring of '44, when I persuaded the girl who was making out my hospital discharge in a Hungarian hospital to leave a blank under the rubric "Destination." My fountain pen probably saved my life: in the toilet of the train, I wrote in *"Metz,"* the westernmost point still in Nazi hands. Otherwise I would have had to report for a front-posting in Debrečen—and the chaos in the Balkan theatre of war in the autumn of '44 you can read about in any account. From Hungary via Ahrweiler to Metz, from Metz via Ahrweiler to Dresden, from Dresden via Ahrweiler and Bad Neuenahr to Marienfeld. I want to describe *one* moment from all that time. It must have been September or October '44, and I was coming from Munich or Vienna to change trains in Remagen. As I went down the subway stairs to the Ahrweiler platform, your mother was coming down the opposite steps into the same subway—and we met in the tunnel! Can you understand how even after forty years our hearts still quake when we travel through Remagen?

I had gone to Marienfeld with genuine papers, my discharge from hospital in Neuenahr. As the expiry date came nearer, I panicked and travelled to Siegburg, having again first "doctored" myself, duly arrived there with a temperature, and got the document extended. The extension ran out, I changed the date; that date too elapsed and I presented myself, again with a temperature, to a civilian doctor in Much who extended the faked date, thereby making it almost "official" again. I faked the "officially" extended date, that too elapsed—and the scrap of paper became so tatty and so covered with typed-in corrections as to be unusable. Do I need to tell you that we weren't just longing for the Americans to get through, we used to pray, even curse them on their way? But they still didn't come. Do I have to describe our alarm when my brother Alois kept going on longer and crazier walkabouts away from his unit?

It occurred to me that I had one more card up my sleeve. After all, with three or four months in hospital and so many periods of illness at home I was still, in the German army's terms, a "reconvalescent," and thus before they could send me back to the war again I was still entitled—what "entitlements" did you have anyway, with Herr Himmler as

Minister of the Interior and Commander-in-Chief?—to some "convalescence leave." With my utterly tattered bit of bumf, the best thing seemed to me to return to the bosom of my damned unit, called a "reserve force," based in some miserable dump south of Mannheim. I went there. Yes, went. All the stations were like enormous caravanserais, swarming with exhausted, nervous, mostly filthy groups of people with their squalid baggage: civilians, "ordinary" travellers, bombed-out refugees, soldiers, POWs, policemen of all species . . . then I get a few things mixed up; the chronology isn't quite there, so I'll give you just a few guaranteed absurd details.

The reserve unit was quartered in a tobacco-village in Baden, I've forgotten its name. A company usually numbered just over a hundred men, but there were 800 in mine, and they stood there on parade, variously grumpy and cursing: some without an arm, others a leg, or both legs, or both legs and an arm, on crutches, with improvised artificial limbs, waiting for their pension-claims to be settled, decorated heroes queueing up for a dollop of dried vegetables. I suppose it was January or February, freezing cold, and you only got a coat if you put yourself down as "fighting fit." You slept in tobacco-sheds from which the tobacco had wisely been removed or confiscated. The false limbs were hung up at night from various hooks and nails on the wall; everything mouldy, foul coffee substitute, dry bread with a little jam. At least I'd got rid of my tatty, suspicious papers without any query and was legal again. I was cold and hungry, had to wait two days for my turn to eat. Evenings spent in farm-kitchens and the back-rooms of pubs, haggling over cigarettes; not a girl for miles, roll-calls barked out, shouting and swearing—oh, noble fatherland of mine, the way you treat your heroes, your crippled heroes (see *Märchen!*). Annemarie had lent me her wonderfully warm and light Turkish shawl for the trip and I'd created quite a stir with that, all draped in red. I straightaway got myself put down as "fighting fit," got a coat and, just as important, some genuine papers. I was given a "convalescence leave" note. Ask Annemarie about the years before that, the meeting in Remagen, the weeks in Metz, the Cologne apartments. Perhaps now you can understand what feelings and memories are set off in us by the stations at Remagen, Cologne, Bonn? When we visit the Kopelevs in Cologne, they live directly opposite the house in the Neuenhöfer Allee where we, newlyweds at the end of '42, experienced the worst of the bombing raids. One particular memory—the flat—surfaces irresistibly and unasked. I don't know how many times I stayed there, five or six or seven; the last was the night of 29 June 1943, when Cologne was almost totally demolished.

I can't locate the order given by Himmler in those last weeks of the war, allowing any soldier to shoot any other soldiers found "out of earshot of battle." That made every German into a potential summary court-martial for every other German—even though the one doing the finding would himself have to be "out of earshot of battle." The number of executions was enormous, running into tens of thousands. Now we know that Himmler gave this order shortly before he tried to arrange a separate peace through Count Bernadotte—of which Hitler was of course unaware—to save his own skin. His honour was his fidelity. (The SS slogan!) The Commander-in-Chief tried to save himself while all around him tens of thousands of men were shot and hanged on *his* orders. Between 20 July 1944 and the *end of the war*, Germany was completely terrorized by Himmler, the Minister of the Interior. And on the radio, Goebbels's screeching. Let me tell you that the American army shot *one* deserter in Europe, just one, and his widow sued the Pentagon for years afterwards, for decades. No one knows how many German soldiers were executed; certainly upwards of 30,000. And was there one single German widow, fiancée, mother or sister who tried to sue the German Reich or its successors, or one of the surviving Field-Marshals under whose jurisdiction the shooting or hanging took place? Of course there's no way of knowing how many of those who were executed found their way into the statistics of "war dead," and are possibly now immortalized on memorial plaques. . . .

I knew one "deserter" who was shot. It was in a village called Kaldauen near Siegburg, and he spoke to me briefly once when I was back with the army. He was an NCO with the unusual name of Schmitz, a quietly-spoken fellow, and he talked to me because he knew Maria and Alois. After the war I heard he'd been shot for desertion. He had left the front—Kaldauen is about three or four kilometres from the outskirts of Siegburg—to visit his parents, probably to have a cup of coffee with them, and one of those licensed German murderers must have caught up with him, "out of earshot" of the fighting. It wouldn't have taken long, and there was no fuss afterwards. A little later, in the early '50's, German women didn't oppose rearmament. I never understood that; maybe you can try.

Then things get a bit disorganized. I know for a fact that I was in Ludwigshafen at one stage. Why? What was I doing? Was I on the way to the tobacco-village in Baden? I suppose so.

I was also in Mainz, in February '45. As I hated hanging around in the gigantic mouldering station/caravanserais, I went into the town (yes, I can vouch for the truth of this "story"!), saw the sign "Area Command," went inside—don't ask me why—asked for the "legal officer" of all people and, with my faked leave in my pocket, had my name sent in to him. Was I suicidal? No, I still wanted to live. The officer, a major, had me shown in and I told him a whole string of lies: how on the way back to my unit I had heard of my mother's death (she was already dead four or five months), and had to attend the funeral, and I'd also heard that our flat in Cologne had been bombed (which in fact had happened a year and a half before), and so I had to go to Cologne as well as to the funeral to rescue my library and my papers, which were absolutely vital for me as I was finishing a doctorate (my official designation was the highly ambiguous "student," and of course the officer had no way of knowing or guessing, let alone checking, that I'd been called up during my first term at university). Well, this incredible man, a major or perhaps even a lieutenant-colonel, who looked terribly stern and Prussian, he *believed* me, or—this only occurred to me later—he pretended to believe me, because he knew the war was lost and wanted to save whatever lives he could. He allowed me a fortnight's leave, and there I was again with legitimate papers and time off. One thing you've experienced, perhaps, so you know it's not a boast, just a fact: I can be pretty cool-headed when I have to.

I know one other thing: it was this leave that expired on 2 March 1945, so it must have been mid-February that I found myself—for what reason I really couldn't say—in Mainz, *with* a coat.

A fortnight was generous, a fortnight was forever, and the Americans would have to get through some time. Those fourteen days, with a proper set of documents in my pocket, were just about carefree, except that I was afraid for my brother, who was in greater danger than the women of our family had realized. It was during that fortnight that I cycled to Cologne on Tilla's bicycle in order to check up on our flat and to buy some cigarettes on the black market. But after that, things get a bit confused again: I do know that on 2 March I stood on the Michaelsberg in Siegburg, and watched the gigantic clouds of dust that had once been Cologne roll over the plain towards Siegburg. Also, I'm absolutely certain that 2 March was the deadline of my very last legal leave, but did I alter this before Siegburg or after? Probably before, because in Siegburg that day I could easily have fallen into the hands of the *Heldenklau* (detachments which went around quite indiscriminately nabbing soldiers and taking them to the nearest fighting unit—that is, into the notorious "earshot of battle"). My falsification this time was to type in a "5" after the "2," using my father's old office typewriter: the "5" turned out crooked, and it was in a different typeface. A fake like that wouldn't have helped me much if I'd fallen into the hands of a proper criminologist; then—I don't know, daren't think about it—some German moron could have shot me quite easily. I still don't know why I didn't type in a "9" after the "2." I had gained twenty-three days, twenty-three eternities, but why not twenty-seven? Even unfaked, the papers weren't worth very much, because in this phase of the war no one was given five weeks' leave at a time. Perhaps we were just absolutely convinced that by then—at the very latest—the Americans, our liberators, would have got through. . . .

At some time I can remember going around bombed-out Bonn with Annemarie, probably to try and get into hospital again after "doctoring" myself once more. This time it didn't work. And once—yes, this is all like "Once upon a time"—once I was in Engelskirchen with my sister Mechtilde, where Tilla was arranging something again for Alois. It was the head-quarters of Field Marshal General Model, a feared murderer who at least had the decency to shoot himself in a wood between Duisburg and Düsseldorf, aged fifty-four—two years younger than his supreme commander and nine years older than Himmler (yes, in 1945 Himmler was just forty-five; when you have the time work out how many murders he committed for each minute of his life). Strafing raids, the roads crawling with soldiers, refugees, evacuees—if anyone wanted to make a film about this they would need hundreds of thousands of extras. Troops advancing, troops retreating: who could tell the front from the rear?

We knew of course from listening to foreign radio stations (punishable by death!) that the Americans had gone on down the *Autobahn* from Remagen as far as Hennef, and had reached the river Sieg, which was only twelve kilometres away from us. Well, they had other plans: they moved east as far as Kassel, and together with the British who had advanced from Arnheim, they formed a pocket in the Ruhr where they trapped a large part of the German army—but they didn't come to Marienfeld. So, the twenty-fifth came ever nearer, and this time there was nothing left to falsify and without valid papers and out of "earshot of battle" I'd have been strung up pretty smartly. Sometimes I think the chaos during and after the Thirty Years War couldn't have been as great as it was in this one. The geographical area covered was much the same, but its population had increased many if not thousands of times over and the potential for chaos was far greater. Also, our enemies weren't the advancing British and Americans: our enemies were the great death-and-chaos-specialists, one of whom called himself the Führer and sat in his concrete ivory tower in Berlin, and the other the Minister of the Interior and Commander-in-Chief of the reserve army, Herr Himmler; and they had transmitted their mania for destruction to subordinate organizations composed of great sections of the population. You'll always be able to tell a German by whether he refers to the eighth of May as a day of defeat or a day of liberation. *We* awaited our "enemies" as liberators. One of the surviving Field Marshal Generals wouldn't talk of "defeat" but of "lost victories." Don't read this as an adventure story, even though a few adventurous elements are unavoidable: read it as a crime-thriller, though it can't be *that* exciting since the main issue—do they catch him?—is settled irrefutably by my own survival. The most exciting question you could ask would be: How did he manage not to get caught?

The twenty-fifth March came and went without the Americans crossing the Sieg and liberating us; there was cold comfort in the fact that even a "9" after the "2" wouldn't have made much difference, since on the twenty-ninth they still hadn't.

There was nothing for it but to rejoin the German army. By now the question was: Where did you have a better chance of surviving, with the army or away from it? The answer we came up with, after giving it a great deal of thought, was with the army. Away from it, and without papers—that would have been dicing with death. But rejoining the army meant parting and further separation; a parting in wartime, and more especially in a *Nazi* war, could always be final, and it didn't help much that we were convinced it "really couldn't last much longer now." After all, it had gone on for two years after Stalingrad, and if they'd had the chance the Germans would have prolonged the famous "five past midnight" to the break of day.

So, we prolonged our farewells. Annemarie accompanied me to the nearest army headquarters, which was a couple of kilometres away near a village called Bruchhausen. It turned out to be a staff headquarters: lots of people with red stripes on their trousers, a nervous staff who couldn't make anything of this private who had just turned up and who weren't able to give me legal papers in exchange for my ill-omened fakes. I was told to go on to a village called Birk on the way from Siegburg to Much, and was given some proper marching-rations: bread, sausage, margarine, cigarettes—and we extended our farewell further by sharing these together somewhere off the road between Bruchhausen and Marienfeld: we were both hungry, and your mother was pregnant. Annemarie walked with me as far as Much, a long downhill journey that she would have to make back uphill again later, and then we said goodbye at the crossroads down in the valley, with hordes of soldiers and civilians streaming past each other, sometimes into each other. Germany was on the move, and I had those rotten documents in my pocket. Yes, goodbye. No descriptions. How should I describe fifty or even a hundred farewells? In Cologne, Ahrweiler, Marienfeld, Metz, Bitsch, St. Avold and elsewhere.

I trotted off towards Birk, with a wholly irregular walking-stick in my hand which caused an officer of the military police who was driving past to stop and give me a severe ticking-off for being turned out in a way unbefitting a German soldier. I was too upset even to feign remorse, told him where I was going—and he ordered me to get into his car. He looked stern and punctilious, and I was afraid—he was after all a military police officer—that he would ask to see my papers, or even take me in immediately. He did neither, but dropped me without a word outside the unit's orderly room in Birk, waited for me to go in, and drove on. I gave my name to the duty sergeant and presented my papers, but before he could study them he was called away into the next room. I grabbed the wretched scraps of paper, my *corpus delicti*, and when he came back and asked where they were I said, "But you took them with you." He was surprised and confused, but left it at that; I was incorporated into the company, and was once more legal. That ill-fated leave-note must still be around somewhere among my untidied war-letters, that document which probably saved my life.

On with the thriller. I felt relieved and depressed at the same time: after half a year, I was once more separated from Annemarie and the others, back with the German army. The excursions to the tobacco-village, to Mainz and elsewhere, had been risky, but more calculable in their consequences. I was pretty miserable, especially not being able to phone, which had always been a comfort in the earlier years of the war. In the evening I went for a walk in Birk, despairing, but still toying with the idea of simply slipping away—only where to? Then, in the main street in Birk, I bumped into the daughter of a Cologne shopkeeper whom we had bought food from many times—and on tick for years. A nice girl, whom unfortunately I have never seen since. She took me "home" with her: to temporary accommodation, where I met her father; they had left home just two days ago, fleeing to avoid being recruited into the *Volkssturm* territorials. We exchanged our news, and Herr Fog, as his name was, told me that he wanted to move nearer to the American lines to steer clear of the *Volkssturm*, and asked me whether he might hide for a day or two with my family in Marienfeld. I said of course, and he asked me if I would, as it were, book him in, and gave me as an advance a stout bag containing twenty-five pounds of sugar. Twenty-five pounds of sugar, at the end of March 1945! How could I get it to Marienfeld this late at night? Well, I was crazy, the girl lent me her bicycle, I jammed the sugar into the basket and set off. It was madness, and perhaps this sugar-transport, "quitting my unit"—like a subsequent bicycle-ride under similar circumstances that I'll come to later—was my only act of "heroism": sugar for Marienfeld! I cycled down minor roads; avoided dangerous crossroads where military police and the *Heldenklau* might be lurking, pushed sugar and bicycle up embankments, and finally reached Marienfeld bathed in sweat. That was some homecoming! A surprise, and yet still painful, and again the problem: whether to stay or go back. Finally, my "sense of honour" prevailed: I had promised the girl I would return her bike, and in these times a bicycle was worth more than a fleet of cars. Bicycles played a big part in determining my destiny, to the good as it turned out. So I rode off in the middle of the night, returned the bicycle, and crept back into our sleeping-quarters. Legal again.

Now the last phase begins, which I don't want to write about in detail because it's stuff you can read up on in any war book. In Kaldauen, I met Corporal Schmitz whom they later shot a few hundred yards from his parents' home; then I was transferred to Niederauel, facing the town of Blankenberg across the river. We were positioned facing the Americans, separated only by the Sieg, so that we could see with our own eyes the white, white bread—it shone like the moon. There was no shooting: it was forbidden, so to speak, because if a single German shot fell whole barrages of American artillery would be sent over in return. Dissolution, mayhem, barely any normal rations, stealing, milking cows, contriving to spend the night in barns and animal-sheds for the warmth—you may wonder why I didn't go over to the Americans right away and surrender to that white, white bread. The answer is simple: not only did I want to survive, I wanted if possible to survive without being imprisoned—a really frivolous wish. Alois and I had decided that we would go and hide in the little loft at home in Marienfeld, among the remaining "pastors," and "await developments" there. I wanted to be with Annemarie, at home, and besides I would have had to swim or ford the cold Sieg. I waited. Open talk of desertion: some had tried already—they had families living in American-occupied territory—and climbed and crawled their way along a ruined bridge—and were shot at, because they were taken for a reconnaissance patrol. No, I waited, and once more a bicycle led me into temptation.

Together with a few others I was ordered to escort our relief-detachment, a company from a bicycle-corps of Cologne policemen, from All-ner back to Niederauel at night. It wasn't far from Allner to Marienfeld—twelve, at most fifteen kilometres. I was able to persuade one of the policemen to part with his bicycle. He must have been a saint because, as I say, a bicycle was precious, and how could you trust anyone in early April 1945, at the worst moment of Germany's chaos? Well, he gave it to me (I don't know his name, otherwise I'd put up a monument to him, like farmer Peters), and I rode off into the night, as muddled and impulsive as I'd always accused Alois of being, got to Marienfeld, saw Annemarie, took my father a couple of cigars—and more discussion: should I go or stay? Up into the loft with the "pastors," or back to Allner, which was tantamount to going back to the front? By now the poor people had even had someone else "billeted" on them in the "temporary accommodation." My father had common sense and advised me to take to the loft, but I could see the policeman's decent, honest face in front of me. I'd promised to take the bicycle back to him, and so I set off back to

Allner, down side-roads in the dark night. Later on I heard that the entire company of policemen and their bicycles had been wiped out.

We, my unit, moved on, through the Bröl valley towards Waldbröl: an utter rabble, dragging this way and that. Once, I recall, we reached the edge of a village and saw white flags flying. Somehow—I can't remember exactly how it happened—the whole show broke up there and I set off home, until in the middle of nowhere I ran into this lieutenant who literally held a pistol to my head and forced me to join his own "unit," which bore the insane name "Garrison Brüchermühle": the tiny hamlet that gave its name to the last German army unit I belonged to must be situated somewhere between Denklingen and Waldbröl. I thought it best not to resist this madman, and so finally, after a few unpleasant days I came to be an American prisoner at Brüchermühle. Finally? I was surprised: we had begged, implored and cursed the Americans to come; it meant liberation, to be *finally rid of the Germans*—and yet, this was the surprise: I found it difficult to raise my hands. I found it difficult, but of course I did.

The rest doesn't matter so much now. A chilly night in an improvised camp in Rosbach on the Sieg, the Final Victory whisperings still going on. The thrilling drive through the Westerwald to Linz, across the Rhine to Sinzig, Namur, Attichy—a huge camp. Of course, it wasn't a rest home. I had feared the worst, but it really wasn't half so bad in the end. It had always been the Germans who were the real danger, holding trials and doing away with "defeatists" in the latrines—and all this in April 1945, while the Soviet and American armies were fraternizing on the Elbe. No, no complaints. The important thing is that I was able—don't ask me how, it's a mini-thriller in itself—to refuse the inducement of better rations, and not to do physical work. I thought to myself, If you do physical work now (it was absurd "work"), then you'll end up doing it for years, maybe decades into the future. Rather a few more months of hunger, I thought, than years of being a labourer somewhere. Perhaps that was the first occasion when I acted with "historical awareness." Still later, when the camp—200,000 men apparently—was broken up and handed over (sold) to the French, I was able, after a detailed test of suitability for work, to get categorized as "unable to do the work for which he is qualified." This was astonishing, as my occupation was "student." At this point, with about sixty out of 200,000 of us "unable to work," the Americans showed their sometimes surprising common sense: we were split off from the others, fed separately, almost well, and even got our own medics who gave us washing things, until we were moved on, this time to a British camp near Waterloo. The British were very different, less obsessed with hygiene than the Americans, but there was proper food and lots of tea with milk and sugar, which the Germans despised. To begin with, I wasn't a tea-drinker either, but I soon became one, acquired a taste for that incomparable English tea, and kept what was left over of it in a one-litre Belgian beer bottle that became my most precious possession. . . .

Too many things come back to me, and I must stop, otherwise I'll write a whole novel, and start "telling stories" and get into uncertain territory when I meant to stay on the "solid ground" of "true experience." Perhaps some things will be clearer for you now: why we're quite incapable of throwing bread away, why we hate pouring away tea or coffee, why I take what's left over of those precious commodities with me into my study after breakfast, and why I can't stop smoking cigarettes. And you should know that on my wanderings from 1939 to 1945, no Circe was able to lure me onto her rocks. The squalid sexuality in and around stations and trains at that time never held any attraction for me. Penelope was at once herself *and* Circe. You should also know that in the American camp were men with both legs amputated at the thigh who had been captured fighting with grenade-launchers: last ditch desperadoes. And that when a train full of British soldiers on their way home stopped next to ours at a station on the Lower Rhine, they passed us their half-smoked cigarettes.

Maybe now you'll understand why characters like Filbinger and Kiesinger—who smoothly, smirkingly survived everything, in untroubled bourgeois complacency—infuriated us most of all. And you should know that Adenauer's celebrated move to release POWs concerned mainly the senior officers, the ones who thought in terms of "lost victories" rather than "defeat" or "liberation," and who were useful in the rebuilding of the German army (now called the *Bundeswehr*) and who were a bigger drain on pension-money than some invalid or shot-up soldiers, because they lived longer. Perhaps you'll understand better why our many trips abroad always had about them an element of running away, running away from types like Filbinger, who couldn't remember having participated in the execution of a man he'd sentenced to death. (Just imagine: he couldn't remember!) How many Germans there are who can't remember: not all of them judges, but all potential executioners, into whose hands I might have fallen. And what about "German mothers," a much-lauded group—how many of them sent their fourteen- and seventeen-year-olds to their deaths, sacrificed to Hitler, without resistance, without undue grief, some even with enthusiasm? There was one called Ferdinand Schörner, one of Hitler's personal favourites—in March 1945, he promoted Schörner to Field-Marshal General—whose courts-martial were as notorious as Herr Model's; his soubriquet was "Bloodhound," his "disciplinary measures" the terror of his troops. He died not in 1945, like his beloved Führer, but in the Year of German

Grace 1973, in Munich. I think he was one of those whose release Adenauer secured.

Around sixteen years ago, dear Vincent, dear René, one of Rudolf Hess's sons wrote to me to ask if I would join the long list of those pleading for the release of Herr Hess. I couldn't do it. *My conscience wouldn't let me;* and even now that Hess is ninety, *my conscience doesn't let me.* As late as 1946, in Nuremberg, this peculiar dove of peace was insisting that Hitler was the greatest son that Germany's millennial history had brought forth. And I can't get that wheedling, fanatical racist's voice I heard on the radio as a sixteen-year-old out of my head, and I can't forget that face I saw in the cinema news: the piercing eyes that asked for sacrifice and obtained sacrifice. No, I wouldn't protest *against* his release, but I can't plead *for* it.

And you should know that I refused to participate in the clearing-up in Cologne, as was the declared duty of every returning man. I didn't lift a single *public* stone, but quietly and alone, knocking the plaster from every stone, I cleared the debris in my father's workshop on the Vondel- strasse, which Alois was running then. Not one *public* stone. . . .

A few days ago, around mid-July, as I was finishing this report, SS General Karl Wolff died at the age of eighty-four. He was quite a spec- tacular Nazi, who in 1937 was already a General in the SS, Himmler's personal chief-of-staff, but who by late February 1945 was nevertheless convinced that the war was lost (you may laugh: by late February!). After negotiations through intermediaries with Alan Dulles, the German army in Italy capitulated. Well, well. Later Wolff was sentenced to four years in a labour camp, of which he served *one week.* Accused subsequently of complicity in the deaths of 300,000 Jews, he denied all knowledge of the death camps (and this was Himmler's personal chief-of-staff!). He got fifteen years in prison, and was released after seven. Remission of sen- tence. And lived on another thirteen years afterwards! That isn't a joke, dear René, dear Vincent, that's what *happened.* That's German history.

Your Father

HOWARD NEMEROV
1920–

Nemerov went to Harvard and during the war flew for both the Canadian and American air forces. He is now a Professor of English at Washington University, St. Louis, where he generates poems he describes as "subversive."

REDEPLOYMENT

They say the war is over. But water still
Comes bloody from the taps, and my pet cat
In his disorder vomits worms which crawl
Swiftly away. Maybe they leave the house.
These worms are white, and flecked with the cat's blood.

The war may be over. I know a man
Who keeps a pleasant souvenir, he keeps
A soldier's dead blue eyeballs that he found
Somewhere—hard as chalk, and blue as slate.
He clicks them in his pocket while he talks.

And now there are cockroaches in the house,
They get slightly drunk on DDT,
Are fast, hard, shifty—can be drowned but not
Without you hold them under quite some time.
People say the Mexican kind can fly.

The end of the war. I took it quietly
Enough. I tried to wash the dirt out of
My hair and from under my fingernails,
I dressed in clean white clothes and went to bed.
I heard the dust falling between the walls.

VERNON SCANNELL
1922-

Scannell fought with the Gordon Highlanders.

WALKING WOUNDED

A mammoth morning moved grey flanks and groaned.
In the rusty hedges pale rags of mist hung;
The gruel of mud and leaves in the mauled lane
Smelled sweet, like blood. Birds had died or flown,
Their green and silent attics sprouting now
With branches of leafed steel, hiding round eyes
And ripe grenades ready to drop and burst.
In the ditch at the cross-roads the fallen rider lay
Hugging his dead machine and did not stir
At crunch of mortar, tantrum of a Bren
Answering a Spandau's manic jabber.
Then into sight the ambulances came,
Stumbling and churning past the broken farm,
The amputated sign-post and smashed trees,
Slow wagonloads of bandaged cries, square trucks
That rolled on ominous wheels, vehicles
Made mythopoeic by their mortal freight
And crimson crosses on the dirty white.
This grave procession passed, though, for a while,
The grinding of their engines could be heard,
A dark noise on the pallor of the morning,
Dark as dried blood; and then it faded, died.
The road was empty, but it seemed to wait—
Like a stage which knows the cast is in the wings—
Wait for a different traffic to appear.
The mist still hung in snags from dripping thorns;

Absent-minded guns still sighed and thumped.
And then they came, the walking wounded,
Straggling the road like convicts loosely chained,
Dragging at ankles exhaustion and despair.
Their heads were weighted down by last night's lead,
And eyes still drank the dark. They trailed the night
Along the morning road. Some limped on sticks;
Others wore rough dressings, splints and slings;
A few had turbanned heads, the dirty cloth
Brown-badged with blood. A humble brotherhood,
Not one was suffering from a lethal hurt,
They were not magnified by noble wounds,
There was no splendour in that company.
And yet, remembering after eighteen years,
In the heart's throat a sour sadness stirs;
Imagination pauses and returns
To see them walking still, but multiplied
In thousands now. And when heroic corpses
Turn slowly in their decorated sleep
And every ambulance has disappeared
The walking wounded still trudge down that lane,
And when recalled they must bear arms again.

WILLIE MORRIS
1934-

Morris, the Southern novelist, journalist, and editor, was a close friend of James Jones and of his son Jamie. He recalled times with Jones and his family in James Jones: A Friendship *(1978).*

From JAMES JONES: A FRIENDSHIP

One winter night Jim and Jamie and I were sitting around the kitchen table talking. We had been discussing something about the war. Jamie asked: "Why haven't you ever showed me your medals, Dad?"

"Because I don't believe in that shit," Jim said.

"Where are they?"

"Tucked away in some drawer in the attic, I guess."

"Well, I'd like to see them."

Reluctantly he trudged upstairs and rummaged for a while. Jamie and I heard the thud of big objects from the floors above. Then he came back with a box. He sat down at the table and brought out an assortment of ribbons and medals and blew the dust off them. Jamie wanted to know what each one was.

"This here's Good Conduct. They took that one away once and then give it back . . . This is for Guadalcanal." An orange-and-red-striped one was the Asiatic-Pacific campaign ribbon and medal, with a bronze star on it for Midway. Another was the yellow American Defense ribbon, with a battle star, he said, for Pearl Harbor.

"What's this pretty one?"

"That's the Bronze Star."

"And this one?"

"That there's the Purple Heart. But this one here, it's the only one we wore when we shipped home." He pointed to the replica of a rifle on a field of blue with a silver wreath around it. "It's the Combat Infantryman's Badge."

"Why is it the only one you ever wore?"

"Oh, shit, I don't know. It was a point of pride, you see—better than all the rest. It spoke for itself. It really meant something. It was just an unspoken rule. If you wore any of the others, the men would've laughed you out of town, or maybe whipped your ass."

PART IV
THE WARS IN ASIA

Obscenity Without Victory

The Korean War (1950–1953) and the Vietnam War (1961?–1975) are conveniently considered together, for both involved the artificial division of a distant country into warring north and south sections, in both the abstract enemy was the same ("communism"), and both ended in a non-victory puzzling and annoying to those accustomed to the unambiguous conclusions of previous "total" wars. Both left a residue of bitterness, and both seemed to suggest that traditional ideas of soldierly motivation and morale needed serious revision. That is, both wars revealed the unpleasant but very modern fact that without powerful patriotic motivation—difficult to generate unless the actual territory of the United States is jeopardized—American troops tend to refrain from immolating themselves, preferring comfort, safety, money-making, drugs, alcohol, and sexual pleasure to the more heroic values formerly associated with the profession of arms. When contemporary soldiers are motivated to fight, they will probably not be fighting for principles or abstractions but for each other. In the absence of a clear moral mission justifying their suffering, troops will become angry, and their anger will readily boil over into acts of sadism, destructiveness, and mutiny. To this degree both Asian wars are an embarrassment to the military, which has not yet quite figured out how to deal with this problem.

KOREA

The way one modern war can smoothly modulate into another is illustrated by the beginning of the Korean War. Korea had been a possession of the Japanese since 1904–1905, and when the Second World War ended, Soviet troops, by agreement with the other Allies, occupied Korea down to the 38th parallel of latitude, while the United States occupied the peninsula south of that line. As the Cold War began developing, each occupying power began to encourage its ideas of government in its sector, and each began to encourage a local military establishment there as well. By 1949, having devised a "Republic of

Korea" in their half, and having organized a local army, the Americans conceived their occupation duty completed and went home. Meanwhile, the Soviets were raising a much better army in their half, and on Sunday morning, June 25, 1950, the North Korean army, 80,000 strong, crossed the 38th parallel, aiming at reuniting the country under a Communist government. This army soon forced the weak South Korean forces into a deep retreat. In four days the North Koreans were in Seoul, the southern capital, and only a small part of the southern tip of the country remained in the hands of the Republic of Korea.

The new United Nations had been established precisely to prevent such aggression as this, and President Truman appealed to the Security Council to do something. It responded by accepting Truman's understanding of its obligation to mount a "police action," and before long it had persuaded twenty countries to contribute forces for a U.N. army to repel the invaders. The fact that many nations were involved gave the operation a U.N. color, although the United States, which ultimately fed eight divisions into the war, was by far the major belligerent. Britain sent two infantry brigades, Canada one, plus an artillery regiment. France sent a battalion, and so did Ethiopia, Greece, Thailand, and Belgium. Luxembourg came up with an infantry platoon. Italy contributed a field hospital, India an ambulance. The whole effort was commanded by General MacArthur, whose mandate was to drive the invaders back across the 38th parallel and restore the *status quo ante*. He speeded up the slow progress north of his forces by a shrewd and lucky amphibious landing at Inchon, the port of Seoul, which recovered the capital. Success emboldened MacArthur to quarrel with his mandate and to conceive his mission to be the reuniting of the whole country under a South Korean, free enterprise government. With this aim, he crossed the parallel and approached the Yalu River, the border with China, whereupon the Chinese army, quiescent until now, suddenly surged into Korea with 300,000 troops and drove the U.N. army back behind the dividing line, badly battered. It was all Truman and the U.N. could do to persuade MacArthur not to invade China itself ("There is no substitute for victory," he proclaimed), and his increasing recalcitrance and uncontrolled flag-waving bellicosity finally prompted Truman to fire him (in the military euphemism, "relieve" him). Former artillery captain Truman was not at all unhappy doing this, for a lifetime of service with the National Guard had given him a contemptuous view of regular army officers, especially West Pointers. They were, he believed, pompous, power-mad, and largely fraudulent ("Mr. Prima Donna," he called MacArthur).

The Korean belligerents gradually settled into a stalemate at roughly the 38th parallel, and armistice negotiations began in July 1951. They continued for two years before a peace treaty was signed. Having accomplished nothing, the war ended exactly where it began. The two sides still confront each other, staring across a No Man's Land from trenches and bunkers. The war, which largely ruined both halves of the country, caused 3 million civilian deaths and maimings, and the U.N. force had 180,000 killed and wounded, 80 percent of them American.

The Korean War was important in establishing the model for post-atomic-bomb, undeclared, limited wars. Like the Vietnam War, it ignored the constitutional expectation that a war be not unpopular and thus readily declared by a highly representative Congress. The Korean War established another precedent by ignoring evidence that attempts to repress "progressive" reform in Asia, with its hordes of the poor and deprived, were unlikely to succeed. But if it resembled the Vietnam War in these ways, in another way it is unique: it generated virtually no literature, perhaps one reason it seems to be, as Clay Blair has called it, The Forgotten War. It did produce some good reporting, like BBC correspondent René Cutforth's account of what he saw when the Chinese attacked across their border. He saw "young GIs of hardly nineteen or twenty, ill-trained and in total panic, throw down their weapons and run from the front, tears streaming down their faces." But the war produced little writing worth preserving for its own moral or artistic sake. The reasons why are puzzling. Was it because the war was so short, the fighting lasting only a little more than one year? Was it because, despite the presence of some scared draftees, the war was fought largely by regulars and reserve call-backs who were not confirmed civilians and instinctive pacifists and thus capable of being eloquently shocked by what they encountered? Was it because the concept "police-action poetry" lacks appeal? Perhaps the war followed too closely on the Second World War, so that the Korean horrors could seem already too familiar to require literary exposure. Whatever the reason, the paucity of Korean War literature is striking, and in a book like this, unignorable.

VIETNAM

It is not easy to date the beginning of the Vietnam War accurately. Struggle between the organized poor of French Indochina, as it used to be called, and various foreign occupiers had been standard for decades, but the United States first became involved in a small way in 1950, when Truman sent thirty-five noncombatant "advisers" to help the French maintain their colonial authority, menaced by the Viet Minh, a radical guerrilla army. After their defeat at Dien Bien Phu in 1954, the French began leaving the country, and a peace conference in Geneva divided the country at the 17th parallel, with Ho Chi Minh in charge of the Communist north and Ngo Dinh Diem Prime Minister of the non-Communist south. In 1956 more American advisers arrived to train a South Vietnamese army, and the first American killed, in 1961, was one of these. The administration of President Kennedy now began increasing support of the South Vietnamese army (ARVN, or Army of the

Republic of Vietnam), and by December 1961, American planes and helicopters were introduced into the scene and the number of American troops, increasingly conceived less as advisers than combatants, reached 15,000. By 1964, assisted by the famous Tonkin Gulf incident—the pugnacious Lyndon Johnson claimed an attack on American ships, which only doubtfully took place—the Americans had become more bellicose and were bombing North Vietnam, the motivator of its South Vietnamese guerrilla arm, the Viet Cong. At the same time, Viet Cong operations became more and more unsettling: mines secretly implanted, murders of civilians assisting the Americans, destruction by mortars and artillery of American airfields, planes, and bases. By 1965 American marines and soldiers were pouring into the country, their number finally amounting to half a million. They seemed to be doing not badly at establishing an atmosphere in which the South Vietnamese government could survive, until January 1968, when the Viet Cong chose Tet, the Vietnamese New Year, as the date for immensely destructive attacks on Saigon, the capital (including the United States Embassy), and forty other cities. In retrospect, Tet came to seem the Stalingrad of the Vietnam War. It was a turning point, the undeniable beginning of American defeat.

By the late 1960s, American opposition to the war grew strident. The war was illegal, many said; it was immoral, colonialist, cruel, and unnecessary, and those directing it were simply war criminals. Richard Nixon came into office promising to end the war. His plan was to withdraw American troops gradually, replacing them with beefed-up equivalent forces from the ARVN, and to increase the bombing of North Vietnam to persuade that country to make peace. By 1970 the war had spread to neighboring Laos and Cambodia, and in the early 1970s everything began to come apart. The My Lai massacre, when hundreds of unarmed civilians, including infants and old women, were shot to death by angry U.S. Army troops, became known and was perceived less as an aberration than as an entirely representative atrocity. Anti-war demonstrations became more indignant. Protesters were beaten and, at Kent State University, killed. Troop morale began to erode, and soldiers stepped up their rate of such subversive behavior as "combat refusals" (i.e., mutinies), open hard-drug dependence, and the killing of unpopular officers. In Washington the Watergate scandal, the result of the President's paranoia about "national security" leaks and anger at the apparently treasonous behavior of those opposing the war, brought down the government and removed from the war any pretense of legitimacy and appropriateness it ever had. In 1973 the last American troops left. Deprived of this support, ARVN collapsed, and in May 1975, the war ended when North Vietnamese troops and tanks entered Saigon and united Vietnam into one Communist country, or as some might say, replaced in the south one tyranny by another. At the end, the television audience at home was vouchsafed disgraceful scenes of wild terror in the too-long-delayed evacuation of right-wing Vietnamese and American diplomatic personnel. It was a fitting scandal to end a war which had seldom seemed less than a scandal.

The whole performance which, lasting for about fifteen years, constituted America's longest war, was costly: its price was almost 2 million dead in Vietnam, 200,000 in Cambodia, 100,000 in Laos. Over 3 million were wounded in Southeast Asia, and 14 million became refugees. Of the American troops and marines, 58,135 were killed. Over 300,000 people were wounded, of whom 33,000 are permanently paralyzed. The price in American civil disruption and the augmenting of cynicism and contempt for the government was high also. Thousands of young people evaded the draft either by enrolling in college—the law surprisingly permitted this open validation of privilege and the class system—or by fleeing the country for Canada or Sweden. By the end of the war more people than one might expect could agree with I. F. Stone that "Every government is run by liars and nothing they say should be believed."

The lies were largely about the virtues of the South Vietnamese government and the combat adequacy of the South Vietnamese army. The government was grossly unrepresentative, a Roman Catholic autocracy governing a Buddhist majority, and its armed forces seemed to fight with the knowledge that defeat was inevitable, and besides, pimping and selling supplies were more profitable than duty. Those familiar with the Second World War in Europe can appreciate what Vietnam became by imagining French civilians and soldiers secretly selling to the Germans weapons and supplies conveyed to them, often at mortal risk, by the Allies. One marine officer, whose unit fought alongside elements of ARVN, testifies: "Every, every, every, *every* firefight that we got into, the ARVN fucking ran." Until the My Lai episode became public, the lies also had to cover the noisome fact that the enemies being shot down by American troops often consisted of unarmed civilians suspected of sympathy toward the Viet Cong, and that often these civilians were women and children and the elderly living in villages thought to be centers of Viet Cong activity. The official lies had to gloss over feelings like those in a letter left at home by one soldier to be opened if he did not return. When he was killed, his parents opened the letter to read,

> Dear Mom and Dad:
>   The war that has taken my life, and many thousands of others before me, is immoral, unlawful, and an atrocity. . . .

And all along, until near the end when the Americans were obviously in flight, the lies had to assure the electorate that the United States was "winning," and that if it was leaving, it was placing the cause in the hands of the sturdy, honest, well-trained, and self-respecting South Vietnamese, who would surely win. The lies also had to conceal the number of ARVN officers who were really Viet Cong agents and the likelihood that some high government officials, like Truong Nhu Tang, were secretly aiding the Viet Cong because they sympathized with the cause of apparent social justice represented by the north.

The reasons for American defeat and humiliation were many. One was a complacent ignorance of Asian social and political conventions, languages, and history and a lack of imaginative identification with the miserable and the poverty-stricken. Another was reliance on a showy but inappropriate technology to fight a war essentially social and political. The American army was trained to fight wars like the last European one, where victory resulted from the seizure and occupation of enemy terrain and where the killing of the enemy was only incidental to this end. Confronted with a very different challenge, a war where anyone might be an enemy and where the enemy was unidentifiable and everywhere, the army had no solution but to kill people, uniformed or not, old or young, male or female, proven Viet Cong or not. It was almost as if the German practice in the Second World War of widespread massacres of guerrillas in the interest of "pacification" had now been embraced by the Americans, who seemed to advertise their contempt for human life in general by the technique of the announced "body count" of the presumed enemy. As one American public-relations official finally admitted, "We were looking for quantitative measurements in a war that was qualitative."

The Second World War provided the American Air Force with a rationale for its contribution, the saturation bombing of civilian targets in North Vietnam, despite evidence gathered by the Strategic Bombing Survey suggesting that the bombing of civilian targets actually increases the enemy's will to resist. Regardless, the Air Force dropped on the Communists three times the bomb tonnage dropped in the whole of the Second World War, with little more effect than to pockmark the agricultural countryside with craters. But if hamstrung by precedents from the Second World War, the military in Vietnam did make some changes in their procedures. One was in response to what the Second War had revealed about the inevitability of psychiatric breakdown if troops have to fight too long without hope of ultimate reprieve—except that provided by death or serious injury. In Vietnam a soldier served one year and then was returned to stateside duty. But while psychologically intelligent, this proved militarily inconvenient, for units now consisted not of men who knew each other from way back but of virtual visitors no one could count on absolutely. Another difference from earlier wars was the new emphasis on Rest and Recreation ("R and R") as a relief from the strain of combat. Every soldier was entitled to his holiday in the bars and whorehouses of Tokyo or Bangkok, where he found an atmosphere not refreshingly different from the one in Saigon.

R and R was especially required in this war because of the terrible things the troops had to do and see, and because of their anger at the Vietnamese, both North and South, and their frustration and fear at the absence of a front line and a locatable enemy. The American emphasis on the body count quite dehumanized the Viet Cong, making routine the behavior described by journalist Phillip Knightley:

> The Americans mutilated bodies. One colonel wanted the hearts cut out of dead Vietcong to feed to his dog. . . . Ears were strung together like beads. Parts of Vietnamese bodies were kept as trophies; skulls were a favorite and the then Colonel George Patton III—"I do like to see the arms and legs fly"—carried one about at his farewell party. The Americans photographed dead Vietnamese as if they were game trophies. . . . The Twenty-fifth Infantry Division left a "visiting card," a torn-off shoulder patch of the division's emblem, stuffed in the mouth of the Vietnamese they killed.

Condemned to sadistic lunacy like this, the troops developed the particular sardonic-joky style, half-ironic, totally subversive, which is the hallmark of Vietnam War rhetoric. One popular saying among the troops was "A sucking chest wound is nature's own way of telling you war is hell." They held up two fingers in a "V" as a peace signal, and they exhibited everywhere they could, on helmet covers, rifle stocks, or medallions worn around the neck, the nuclear-disarmament peace logo. Because the war seemed run along business lines, with quantitative results expected, and because killing became so routine, mock business cards and mock ads flourished, a satire of both management style and the fraudulence of publicity. One helicopter gunship commander dropped visiting cards on his victims reading, "Congratulations. You have been killed through courtesy of the 361st." Another helicopter company which named itself the Kingsmen issued cards designating its specialties—"VC Extermination," "People Sniffer and Defoliation"—and promised to provide "Death and Destruction 24 Hours a Day." It concluded: "If you care enough to send the very best, send THE KINGSMEN." This mode resembled the normal irony practiced by troops in modern war, but now the irony was twisted and turned by hatred and anger into something close to sarcasm. On one vehicle was neatly painted: "Vietnam: Love It or Leave It."

This sarcastic tendency suggests that in its style the Vietnam War may be more than a modern one. It may be a "post-modern" one. That term, denoting certain kinds of contemporary writing and art which

press beyond the "modern" to something even more skeptical, prob-
lematic, and even nihilistic, seems applicable to this war which so seriously damaged the remaining clichés of patriotism and heroism. "In the
end," says one observer, "I came to believe that the war was destroying
the U.S. Army." One characteristic of post-modern procedure in the arts
is a self-consciousness bordering on contempt about the very medium or
genre one is working in, amounting to disdain for the public respect and
even awe that normally attend such artifacts—the works of Andy War-
hol are a well-known example. The correspondent Eddie Adams remembers reporting and photographing techniques in Vietnam: "We used to
go out in teams," he recalls, "so that if one of us got blown away, the
other could cover it. A bit sick." That can suggest the way the troops
regarded their capture and degradation by the war. Lionel Trilling once
spoke of the "modern" movement in culture as "the legitimation of the
subversive"—and that definition applies with increasing intensity to the
tendency called post-modern.

Because of the lies the home-front audience had been fed, soldiers
returning finally from Vietnam had more trouble than usual trying to
persuade some civilians that the war had been shamefully nasty. One
paralyzed ex-marine lieutenant, addressing an audience on Long Island,
was trying to depict for them the war as it was:

> This woman stands up and says, "I object to your use of obscenity." I
> said, "What did I say?" A guy said, "You used the word bullshit." I said,
> "You know, it's amazing. I'm talking to you about the obscenity of war,
> about wholesale atrocities as a matter of policy, and what you relate to as an
> obscenity is the word bullshit. What would you do if I said, 'Fuck you'?"
> This was in a full auditorium. . . . It was total pandemonium. In the aisles,
> ranting and raving.

"In Vietnam," wrote journalist John Mecklin, "a major American
policy was wrecked, in part, by unadorned reporting of what was going
on." A lot of that unadorned reporting will be found in these selections.
All is courageous, and most is informed by an uncompromised moral
sense. There are also some memories of the combatants, in the form of
autobiography and poetry. These selections register in various ways a
confrontation with the monstrous and the unbelievable. That is what
writing about Vietnam had to be, but looking back one sees that that is
what writing about all modern war inevitably must be.

MARGUERITE HIGGINS
1920–1966

Stubborn and outspoken, Higgins came to war reporting by way of the University of California and the Columbia School of Journalism. In the Second World War she covered the European Theater for the New York Herald Tribune *and for* Mademoiselle *and later reported from Korea, where her work won a Pulitzer Prize, and Vietnam. Her book* War in Korea: The Report of a Woman Combat Correspondent *appeared in 1951.*

From WAR IN KOREA: THE REPORT OF A WOMAN COMBAT CORRESPONDENT

I met the Eighth Army commander, Lieutenant General Walton H. Walker, for the first time when I returned to the front in mid-July after MacArthur had lifted the ban on women correspondents in Korea. General Walker was a short, stubby man of bulldog expression and defiant stance. I wondered if he were trying to imitate the late General George Patton, under whom he served in World War II as a corps commander.

He was very much of a spit-and-polish general, his lacquered helmet gleaming and the convoy of jeeps that escorted him always trim and shiny. I shall never forget the expression on the faces of two United States marine lieutenants who, on driving up to the Eighth Army compound at Seoul, were told by the military policeman at the gate: "You can't drive that vehicle in here. It's too dusty. No dusty jeeps in here. General Walker's orders!"

"Well, I'll be damned," breathed the marine lieutenant with deliberately exaggerated astonishment. "Everything we've been saying about the United States Army *is* true."

General Walker was very correct and absolutely frank with me.

He said he still felt that the front was no place for a woman, but that orders were orders and that from now on I could be assured of absolutely equal treatment.

"If something had happened to you, an American woman," the general explained, "I would have gotten a terrible press. The American public might never have forgiven me. So please be careful and don't get yourself killed or captured."

General Walker kept his promise of equal treatment, and from then on, so far as the United States Army was concerned, I went about my job with no more hindrance than the men.

Despite large-scale reinforcements, our troops were still falling back fast. Our lines made a large semicircle around the city of Taegu. The main pressure at that time was from the northwest down the Taejon-Taegu road. But a new menace was developing with frightening rapidity way to the southwest. For the Reds, making a huge arc around our outnumbered troops, were sending spearheads to the south coast of Korea hundreds of miles to our rear. They hoped to strike along the coast at Pusan, the vital port through which most of our supplies funneled.

It was at this time that General Walker issued his famous "stand or die" order. The 1st Cavalry and 25th Division were freshly arrived. Like the 24th Division before them, the new outfits had to learn for themselves how to cope with this Indian-style warfare for which they were so unprepared. Their soldiers were not yet battle-toughened. Taking into account the overwhelming odds, some front-line generals worried about the performance of their men and told us so privately.

General Walker put his worries on the record and at the same time issued his "no retreat" order. In a visit to the 25th Division front at Sangju in the north, he told assembled headquarters and field officers, "I am tired of hearing about lines being straightened. There will be no more retreating. Reinforcements are coming, but our soldiers have to be impressed that they must stand or die. If they fall back they will be responsible for the lives of hundreds of Americans. A Dunkerque in Korea would be a terrible blow from which it would be hard to recover."

Immediately General Walker, in a massive straightening operation of his own, took the entire 25th Division out of the line there north of Taegu. He sent them barreling to the southwest front to bear the brunt of the enemy's attempt to break through to Pusan. The operation was skillfully done and the reshuffled troops arrived just in time.

To fill the gap vacated by the 25th Division, the 1st Cavalry and the South Koreans were pulled back in a tightening operation in which we relinquished about fifty miles, but we attained a smaller, better-integrated defense arc.

It is certainly a tribute to General Walker that in the period when he had so few troops on hand and no reserves at all he was able to juggle his forces geographically so as to hold that great semicircle from the coast down the Naktong River valley to Masan on the southern coast.

I reached the southwest front in time for the 25th's first big battle after the "stand or die" order. By luck, I happened to be the only daily newspaperman on the scene. The rest of the correspondents were at Pusan covering the debarkation of the United States Marines. My colleague on the *Herald Tribune* had selected the marine landing for his own. So I left Pusan and hitchhiked my way west.

At Masan, I borrowed a jeep from the 724th Ordnance and drove in the dusk over the beautiful mountains that wind west and overlook the deep blue waters of Masan Bay. The jewel-bright rice paddies in the long, steep-sided valley held a soft sheen and the war seemed far away. But only a few nights later the sharp blue and orange tracer bullets were flicking across the valley's mouth until dawn.

The valley leads to Chindongni, where the 27th (Wolfhound) Infantry Regiment had established its headquarters in a battered schoolhouse under the brow of a high hill. Windows of the schoolhouse were jagged fragments, and glass powdered the floor. For our big 155-millimeter artillery guns were emplaced in the schoolhouse yard, and each blast shivered the frail wooden building and its windows. The terrific effect of these guns is rivaled only by the infernal explosions of aerial rockets and napalm bombs, which seem to make the sky quake and shudder.

I had been looking forward with great interest to seeing the 27th in action. Other correspondents had praised both the regiment's commander, Colonel John ("Mike") Michaelis, Eisenhower's onetime aide, and the professional hard-fighting spirit of his officers and men.

The spirit of the 27th impressed me most in the anxious "bowling-alley" days when the regiment fended off platoon after platoon of Soviet Red tanks bowled at them in the valley north of Taegu. I will never forget the message that bleated through on a walkie-talkie radio to the regiment from Major Murch's hard-pressed forward battalion. Sent close to midnight, the message said: "Five tanks within our position. Situation vague. No sweat. We are holding."

On that first night at Chindongni, I found Colonel Michaelis in a state of tension. Mike Michaelis is a high-strung, good-looking officer with much of the cockiness of an ex-paratrooper. His ambition and drive have not yet been broken by the army system.

He has inherited from his onetime boss, "Ike"—or perhaps he just had it naturally—the key to the art of good public relations: complete honesty, even about his mistakes.

That night Mike Michaelis felt he had made a bad one. His very presence in Chindongni was technically against orders. He had turned his troops around and rushed them away from assigned positions when he heard the Reds had seized the road junction pointing along the southern coast straight at Masan and Pusan. There was nothing in their path to stop them. But, reaching Chindongni, his patrols could find no enemy. There were only swarms of refugees pumping down the road. And at the very point Michaelis had left, heavy enemy attacks were reported.

Miserably, Michaelis had told his officers: "I gambled and lost. I brought you to the wrong place."

But depression could not subdue him for long. He decided he would find the enemy by attacking in battalion strength. If the road really was empty, his men might recapture the critical road junction some twenty miles to the east.

Michaelis asked the 35th Regiment to the north to send a spearhead to link up with his troops approaching the junction on the coastal route, and ordered Colonel Gilbert Check to push forward the twenty miles. The advance turned into the first major counterattack of the Korean campaign.

Michaelis told me about it in the lamplit headquarters room where conversation was punctuated by roars from the 155 guns. Again he was unhappily belaboring himself for having made a bad gamble.

It appeared that the Reds had been on the coastal road after all. Disguised in the broad white hats and white linen garb of the Korean farmer, they had filtered unhindered in the refugee surge toward Chindongni. Then, singly or in small groups, they had streamed to collecting points in the hills, some to change into uniform and others simply to get weapons.

From their mountainous hiding places they had watched Colonel Check's battalion plunge down the road. Then they had struck from the rear. Mortars and machine guns were brought down to ridges dominating the road. This screen of fire—sometimes called a roadblock—cut the road at half a dozen points between Michaelis's headquarters and Colonel Check's attacking battalion. Rescue engineer combat teams had battered all day at the hills and roads to sweep them clean of enemy, but had failed. The worst had seemingly happened. The regiment was split in two; the line of supply cut. The 35th Regiment to the north had been unable to fight its way to the road junction.

The fate of Colonel Check's battalion showed that the enemy was here in force and proved that Michaelis had been right to wheel his forces south to block this vital pathway to Pusan. But he felt he had bungled in ordering the battalion to advance so far.

"I overcommitted myself," Michaelis said miserably. "Now Check's men are stranded eighteen miles deep in enemy territory. From early reports, they've got a lot of wounded. But we've lost all contact. I sent a liaison plane to drop them a message to beat their way back here. I'm afraid we've lost the tanks."

Colonel Check's tanks took a pummeling, all right, from enemy antitank guns. But the tanks got back. Colonel Check himself told us the remarkable story as his weary battalion funneled into Chindongni at one o'clock in the morning.

"Antitank guns caught us on a curve several miles short of our objective," Check said. "Troops riding on the tanks yelled when they saw the flash, but they were too late. The tanks caught partially afire and the crews were wounded. But three of the tanks were still operable. I was damned if I was going to let several hundred thousand dollars' worth of American equipment sit back there on the road. I yelled, 'Who around here thinks he can drive a tank?' A couple of ex-bulldozer operators and an ex-mason volunteered. They got about three minutes' checking out and off they went."

One of the ex-bulldozer operators was Private Ray Roberts. His partly disabled tank led Check's column through ambush after ambush back to safety. Men were piled all over the tanks, and the gunners—also volunteers—had plenty of practice shooting back at Reds harassing them from ridges. Once the tank-led column was halted by a washout in the road. Another time Colonel Check ordered a halt of the whole column so that a medic could administer plasma.

"It might have been a damn-fool thing to do," Colonel Check said, "and the kids at the back of the column kept yelling they were under fire and to hurry up. But—well, we had some good men killed today. I didn't want to lose any more."

That night I found ex-bulldozer operator Roberts in the darkness still sitting on the tank. He was very pleased to show me every dent and hole in it. But he dismissed his feat with, "I fiddled around with the tank a few minutes. It's really easier to drive than a bulldozer. You just feel sort of funny lookin' in that darn periscope all the time."

I was amused after the roadside interview when Roberts and several of the other volunteers came up and said, "Ma'am, if you happen to think of it, you might tell the colonel that we're hoping he won't take that tank away from us. We're plannin' to git ordnance to help us fix it up in the mornin'." Private Roberts and company graduated from dogfeet to tankmen that night, but no special pleas were necessary. There were no other replacements for the wounded crews.

The battalion at final count had lost thirty men. In their biggest scrap, just two miles short of the road junction, the battalion artillery had killed two hundred and fifty enemy soldiers.

"We counted them when we fought our way up to the high ground where they had been dug in," Colonel Check said. "And earlier we caught a whole platoon napping by the roadside. We killed them all."

As Check concluded, Michaelis, with a mock grimace on his face, sent for his duffel bag, reached deep into it, and produced a bottle of scotch whisky, probably the only bona fide hard liquor in southwest Korea at the time.

"Here, you old bum," he said. "Well done."

When Check had gone, Michaelis turned to Harold Martin of the *Saturday Evening Post* and myself. We had been scribbling steadily as the colonel told of the breakout from the trap.

"Well, is it a story?" Michaelis asked. "You've seen how it is. You've seen how an officer has to make a decision on the spur of the moment and without knowing whether it's right or wrong. You've seen how something that looks wrong at first proves to be right. F'rinstance, coming down here against orders. And you've seen how a decision that seems right proves to be wrong—like sending Check's column up that road without knowing for sure what it would face. And then you've seen how a bunch of men with skill and brains and guts, like Check and the kids who drove the tanks, can turn a wrong decision into a right one. But is it a story?"

I said it was a honey and that I'd head back to Pusan first thing the next morning to file it.

With an entire battalion swarming in and around the schoolhouse, regimental headquarters was in an uproar. Colonel Michaelis had been planning to move his command post farther forward. But due to the lateness of the hour and the exhaustion of the headquarters staff and the troops, he postponed the transfer.

It was another of those chance decisions on which victories are sometimes balanced. We found out the next morning how close we had shaved our luck—again.

Half a dozen regimental staff officers, myself, and Martin were finishing a comparatively de luxe breakfast in the schoolhouse (powdered eggs and hot coffee) when suddenly bullets exploded from all directions. They crackled through the windows, splintered through the flimsy walls. A machine-gun burst slammed the coffeepot off the table. A grenade exploded on the wooden grill on which I had been sleeping, and another grenade sent fragments flying off the roof.

"Where is the little beauty who threw that?" muttered Captain William Hawkes, an intelligence officer, as he grabbed at his bleeding right hand, torn by a grenade splinter.

We tried to race down the hall, but we had to hit the floor fast and stay there. We were all bewildered and caught utterly by surprise. It was impossible to judge what to do. Bullets were spattering at us from the hill rising directly behind us and from the courtyard on the other side.

Thoughts tumbled jerkily through my mind . . . "This can't be enemy fire . . . we're miles behind the front lines . . . that grenade must have been thrown from fifteen or twenty yards . . . how could they possibly get that close . . . My God, if they are that close, they are right behind the schoolhouse . . . they can be through those windows and on top of us in a matter of seconds . . . dammit, nobody in here even has a carbine . . . well, it would be too late anyway . . . why did I ever get myself into this . . . I don't understand the fire coming from the courtyard . . . what has happened to our perimeter defense . . . could it possibly be that some trigger-happy GI started all this . . ."

There was soon no doubt, however, that it was enemy fire. We were surrounded. During the night the Reds had sneaked past our front lines, avoiding the main roads and traveling through the mountain trails in the undefended gap between us and the 35th Regiment to the north. In camouflaged uniforms, they crept onto the hillside behind the school-house, while others, circling around, set up machine guns in a rice paddy on the other side of the schoolyard. This accounted for the vicious cross fire.

They had managed to infiltrate our defenses for several reasons. The GIs forming the perimeter defense were utterly exhausted from their eighteen-mile foray into enemy territory and some of the guards fell asleep. And at least one column of the enemy was mistaken, by those officers awake and on duty, as South Korean Police.

We had been warned the night before that South Koreans were helping us guard our exposed right flank. This was only one of the hundreds of cases in which confusion in identifying the enemy lost us lives. It is, of course, part of the difficulty of being involved in a civil war.

The Communist attack against the sleeping GIs wounded many before they could even reach for their weapons.

I learned all of this, of course, much later. On the schoolhouse floor, with our noses scraping the dust, the only thought was how to get out of the bullet-riddled building without getting killed in the process. A whimpering noise distracted my attention. In the opposite corner of the room I saw the three scrawny, dirty North Koreans who had been taken prisoner the night before. They began to crawl about aimlessly on their stomachs. They made strange moaning sounds like injured puppies. One pulled the blindfold from his eyes. On his hands and knees he inched toward the door. But the fire was too thick. The bullets of his Communist comrades cut off escape. When next I saw the three of them they were dead, lying in an oozing pool of their own blood that trickled out the room and down the hall.

The bullets cutting through the cardboard-thin walls ripped the floor boards around us, and we all kept wondering why one of us didn't get hit.

I mumbled to Harold that it looked as if we would have a very intimate blow-by-blow account of battle to convey to the American public. But he didn't hear me because one of the officers suddenly said, "I'm getting out of here," and dove out the window into the courtyard in the direction away from the hill. We all leaped after him and found a stone wall which at least protected us from the rain of fire from the high ground.

In the courtyard we found a melee of officers and non-coms attempting to dodge the incoming fire and at the same time trying to find their men and produce some order out of the chaos. Some of the soldiers in the courtyard, in their confusion, were firing, without aiming, dangerously close to the GIs racing in retreat down the hill. Many of them were shoeless, but others came rushing by with rifles in one hand and boots held determinedly in the other.

Michaelis, his executive officer, Colonel Farthing, and company commanders were booting reluctant GIs out from under jeeps and trucks and telling them to get the hell to their units up the hill.

A ruckus of yelling was raised in the opposite corner of the courtyard. I poked my head around in time to see an officer taking careful aim at one of our own machine gunners. He winged him. It was a good shot, and an unfortunate necessity. The machine gunner had gone berserk in the terror of the surprise attack and had started raking our own vehicles and troops with machine-gun fire.

By now the regimental phones had been pulled out of the town schoolhouse and were located between the stone wall and the radio truck. Division called, and the general himself was on the phone. I heard Colonel Farthing excusing himself for not being able to hear too well. "It's a little noisy," he told the general.

Almost immediately Lieutenant Carter Clarke of the reconnaissance platoon rushed up to report he had spotted a new group of enemy massing for attack in a gulch to the north. Another officer came up with the gloomy information that several hundred Koreans had landed on the coast a thousand yards beyond.

I started to say something to Martin as he crouched by the telephone methodically recording the battle in his notebook. My teeth were chattering uncontrollably, I discovered, and in shame I broke off after the first disgraceful squeak of words.

Then suddenly, for the first time in the war, I experienced the cold, awful certainty that there was no escape. My reactions were trite. As with most people who suddenly accept death as inevitable and imminent, I was simply filled with surprise that this was finally going to happen to me. Then, as the conviction grew, I became hard inside and comparatively calm. I ceased worrying. Physically the result was that my teeth stopped chattering and my hands ceased shaking. This was a relief, as I would have been acutely embarrassed had any one caught me in that state.

Fortunately, by the time Michaelis came around the corner and said, "How you doin', kid?" I was able to answer in a respectably self-contained tone of voice, "Just fine, sir."

A few minutes later Michaelis, ignoring the bullets, wheeled suddenly into the middle of the courtyard. He yelled for a cease-fire.

"Let's get organized and find out what we're shooting at," he shouted.

Gradually the fluid scramble in the courtyard jelled into a pattern of resistance. Two heavy-machine-gun squads crept up to the hill under cover of protecting rifle fire and fixed aim on the enemy trying to swarm down. Platoons and then companies followed. Light mortars were dragged up. The huge artillery guns lowered and fired point-blank at targets only a few hundred yards away.

Finally a reconnaissance officer came to the improvised command post and reported that the soldiers landing on the coast were not a new enemy force to overwhelm us, but South Korean allies. On the hill, soldiers were silencing some of the enemy fire. It was now seven forty-five. It did not seem possible that so much could have happened since the enemy had struck three quarters of an hour before.

As the intensity of fire slackened slightly, soldiers started bringing in the wounded from the hills, carrying them on their backs. I walked over to the aid station. The mortars had been set up right next to the medic's end of the schoolhouse. The guns provided a nerve-racking accompaniment for the doctors and first-aid men as they ministered to the wounded. Bullets were still striking this end of the building, and both doctors and wounded had to keep low to avoid being hit. Because of the sudden rush of casualties, all hands were frantically busy.

One medic was running short of plasma but did not dare leave his patients long enough to try to round up some more. I offered to administer the remaining plasma and passed about an hour there, helping out as best I could.

My most vivid memory of the hour is Captain Logan Weston limping into the station with a wound in his leg. He was patched up and promptly turned around and headed for the hills again. Half an hour later he was back with bullets in his shoulder and chest. Sitting on the floor smoking a cigarette, the captain calmly remarked, "I guess I'd better get a shot of morphine now. These last two are beginning to hurt."

In describing the sudden rush of casualties to my newspaper, I mentioned that "one correspondent learned to administer blood plasma." When Michaelis saw the story he took exception, saying that it was an understatement. Subsequently the colonel wrote a letter to my editors praising my activities in a fashion that, I'm afraid, overstated the case as much as I perhaps originally understated it. But that Mike Michaelis should take time out from a war to write that letter was deeply moving to me. I treasure that letter beyond anything that has happened to me in Korea or anywhere. And, wittingly or unwittingly, Michaelis did me a big favor. After the publication of that letter it was hard for headquarters generals to label me a nuisance and use the "nuisance" argument as an excuse for restricting my activities.

It was at the aid station that I realized we were going to win after all. Injured after injured came in with reports that the gooks were "being murdered" and that they were falling back. There was a brief lull in the fighting. Then the enemy, strengthened with fresh reinforcements, struck again. But Michaelis was ready for them this time. At one-thirty in the afternoon, when the last onslaught had been repulsed, more than six hundred dead North Koreans were counted littering the hills behind the schoolhouse.

We really had been lucky. The enemy had attacked the first time thinking to find only an artillery unit. We had been saved by Michaelis's last-minute decision of the night before to postpone the transfer of the command post and bed down Colonel Check's battle-weary battalion at the schoolhouse. Without the presence of these extra thousand men, the Reds would easily have slaughtered the artillerymen, repeating a highly successful guerrilla tactic.

The North Koreans didn't go in much for counter-battery fire. They preferred to sneak through the lines and bayonet the artillerymen in the back.

Michaelis's self-doubts were not echoed by his bosses. The series of decisions—some of them seemingly wrong at the time—that led to the battle of the schoolhouse resulted in a spectacular victory for the 27th Regiment. For Michaelis it meant a battlefield promotion to full colonel, and for Colonel Check a silver star "for conspicuous gallantry."

After the schoolhouse battle I usually took a carbine along in our jeep. Keyes, an ex-marine, instructed me in its use. I'm a lousy shot, but I know I duck when bullets start flying my way, even if they are considerably off course. I reasoned that the enemy had the same reaction and that my bullets, however wild, might at least scare him into keeping his head down or might throw his aim off. Since Keyes usually drove our jeep, I, by default, had to "ride shotgun."

Most correspondents carried arms of some kind. The enemy had no qualms about shooting unarmed civilians. And the fighting line was so fluid that no place near the front lines was safe from sudden enemy attack.

In those days the main difference between a newsman and a soldier in Korea was that the soldier in combat had to get out of his hole and go after the enemy, whereas the correspondent had the privilege of keeping his head down. It was commonplace for correspondents to be at company and platoon level, and many of us frequently went out on patrol. We felt it was the only honest way of covering the war. The large number of correspondents killed or captured in Korea is testimony of the dangers to which scores willingly subjected themselves.

Fred Sparks of the Chicago *Daily News,* pondering about the vulnerability of correspondents, once observed: "I was lying there in my foxhole one day after a battle in which the regimental command post itself had been overrun. I started thinking to myself, 'Suppose a Gook suddenly jumps into this foxhole. What do I do then? Say to him, "Chicago *Daily News*"!'" After that Sparks announced he, too, was going to tote "an instrument of defense."

At Chindongni, when the battle was finally over, I went up to Michaelis and asked if he had any message for the division commander.

"Tell him," said Mike, "that we will damn well hold."

And they did, in this and in many subsequent battles. So did the Marines, who replaced the 27th in that area, and the 5th Regimental Combat Team, who came after the Marines. Thousands of Americans "stood and died" to hold Chindongni and the emerald valley behind it.

In battles of varying intensity, the "stand or die" order was carried out all along the Taegu perimeter. The defense arc was ominously dented on many occasions, with the most critical period being the Red offensive early in September. But it never broke. And because the line held despite the great numbers of the enemy, the fabulous amphibious landing at Inchon was made possible.

JEAN LARTEGUY
1920–

French journalist Larteguy has spent his life fighting wars and writing about them, first in Spain, then in the Second World War (in France, Italy, and Germany), and later in Korea and French Indochina. He recalled his life of military action and perceptions in The Face of War: Reflections on Men and Combat *(1979). Beth de Bilio is the translator.*

From THE FACE OF WAR: REFLECTIONS
ON MEN AND COMBAT

The Korean War was of the "classical" type. Everything behind the front lines to a depth of fifteen kilometers had been cleared of all civilians. The military could thus at least be assured of no guerrilla activity in that zone.

The two enemy forces maintained their front lines as they'd been held in 1914–18, digging themselves more and more deeply into their trenches and leaving themselves at the mercy of artillery and air bombardments. At Bilan, 800,000 North Koreans were killed or wounded and 400,000 South Koreans. No one spoke of Chinese casualties. No one thought of counting them. Just as no one thought of counting the civilians who died of cold, of hunger, or who disappeared under the bombardments.

At least two million civilians died.

To no good end and for two years of palaver at Panmunjom.

The monster Stalin had to die before peace could finally come.

The North Koreans and their Chinese allies paid an especially heavy price for having let themselves be talked into fighting their "classical" war, for having let themselves be influenced by the Soviets, who placed their faith in heavy fighter battalions and in the kind of tank groups that had won the day on the Steppes.

Everyone wanted to go on and on waging the kind of war they'd won before: the French that of 1914–18; the Russians the great armored battles of the Steppes.

When I arrived in Korea the Chinese had just launched a huge attack in force, and hundreds of thousands of men swarmed down over the hills. The Americans and their allies—all those who'd sent brigades, such as the British and the Turks; or battalions, such as Belgium, France, and the Philippines—retired twenty or thirty kilometers to the rear in "Operation van," as it was called. It was a catastrophe for the Chinese. With bombs and with napalm, the American air force wiped out that ant hill of men.

Later I went along our lines and through those valleys of the dead, and what I witnessed was atrocious. The Chinese had not had time to dig any foxholes, hardly had time to scratch at the earth. They were taken completely by surprise, and their charred bodies lay strewn upon the ground by the thousands and thousands. They lay in blackened tatters of clothing, bodies hideously twisted and commencing to decompose, to stink of rotting flesh.

I imagine that later in those valleys the harvests were beautiful and plentiful. There had been enough good fertilizer!

Another face of war: Seoul and the ravages made on it by the American dollar. The green sickness which prevailed in Indochina and which caused the fall of South Vietnam.

In that city of Seoul, three-quarters destroyed, everything was up for sale. The GIs came in from the front and threw themselves with their dollars upon anything alcoholic or female, placing a premium on the market in schoolgirls—students either real or made to look real with their braids, their blue dresses, their flat shoes.

I'm no Puritan, far from it, but it does seem to me that nothing at all is served for one country to defend another militarily while at the same time destroying its very substance with currency.

The American soldiers had too much money, too much of everything. Life for them was too soft. Besides, they didn't at all like the wars they were obliged to fight. (And it took Pearl Harbor to make Roosevelt declare a state of hostility.) Their government considered America the world's policeman, but they remained essentially isolationist. Their world was the United States. They knew or cared little about the rest of the world. For them, communism represented only a vague threat somewhere else.

The United States at first sent only its professional army to Korea, but that wasn't enough. They had to mobilize contingent forces, draftees.

The selective service system that was carried out on college campuses and in universities was at one and the same time logical, functional, and unusually cruel. America would send to the war only its ignoramuses, the bright students to be kept precious and safe at home. Those students old enough to bear arms had to undergo a certain number of tests. As a questionnaire unrolled from a machine, in the space for each answer the students were to insert either a circle or a cross. Those whose answers were not good enough were sent to war.

One such student whose name was Montfort—probably of French origin—and who was the brightest student at his university—a "young lion"—refused to take the tests because the idea of them was abhorrent to him. He was automatically sent to Korea.

One morning upon orders, Lieutenant Montfort was leading his company in an attack on the slopes of what would come to be called "Heartbreak Ridge." A stupid, pointless attack, a banzai attack like those of the Japanese in the islands of the Pacific. He was killed. The next day all the reserve officers of the division—all those who'd failed their tests—went into mourning for their friend, despite the fury of their general, who saw their action as the beginning of subversion.

To return to the tests given at the schools: they were worthless. Einstein, who died four years later, secretly took one of the tests. On the basis of the results, if he'd been a student, he'd have been sent to the bloody hills of Korea. A failure!

In truth, those tests thought up by average men were only valid for average men. Too high an intelligence, too lively an imagination, too creative a spirit could not be pegged by those tests, by that form of selection. Even there, war knew what she was doing. She could never be content with half-wits. She had to have the best, the youngest, the handsomest, and often the most intelligent to feed upon. Only these satisfy her appetite.

Tests and surveys! What stupidities! Booby traps!

In Korea we fought a war of the rich in a land full of misery.

In the zone behind our lines—in that area cleared of all civilians—there were piles and piles of cases of rations and of munitions along all the roads. They were heaped in veritable walls two stories high. As you passed by, you helped yourself to whatever you needed or wanted. Eventually we became very hard to please among such an excess of supplies, opening a case of rations to find a can of fruit salad, then throwing the rest of the case away. An incredible mess! Meanwhile, at Seoul and at Fusan, the people were starving to death; and in the streets, sanitation crews gathered up the bodies of children and of old people.

How I sweated and struggled my way over those peaks of Korea! Forever climbing and crawling my way up, achieving one crest and then seeing from there all the other crests and mountains we'd have to take sooner or later; mountains that lifted themselves serenely into infinity all the way to Siberia.

The Americans weren't prepared for that hard mountain warfare. They'd have preferred to run about in jeeps. But they learned. They fought well, in fact, out of pure patriotism, out of loyalty. (It would take Indochina for that spirit to die.) And they left fifty-four thousand men on the mountains of Korea. All to return everything to the *status quo ante*.

That autumn was a magnificent one, and the country mornings were soft and lovely. Sheltered behind our sandbags, we watched the ballet of the planes in the sky as they attacked each position with bombs and rockets.

Talk of peace had begun. The front had been stabilized, and activity had been reduced to that of patrols—or so it was said.

We held all the mountaintops forming a sort of great arc that we called the basin, with the exception of a section to the north of us, a kind of spur dominating the area. It was this spur that would soon be known as "Heartbreak Ridge"—*"la Crète du coeur brisé."*

It disturbed the general commanding that sector, a perfectionist, that his men didn't hold that spur. It bothered him to see that tiny red spot on his battle plan neatly colored in blue.

So one day he decided on an attack on the hill—a futile attack on that red spot, on that spur, on Heartbreak Ridge, that was of no strategic value whatever.

Later, when peace had come to Korea, I climbed Heartbreak Ridge with two friends—two battalion captains who'd been wounded shortly before I had. The ambassador of France accompanied us.

At that time, Heartbreak Ridge was in the demilitarized zone, and we needed all kinds of authorizations from both North and South Koreans to get there.

I quote from an article I wrote at that time:

> It was only a hill like all the other scrub-covered hills. We came across some ruined blockhouses, some cartridge cases, a rusted helmet.
>
> And beyond that hill were other hills, thousands of hills disappearing into blue infinity. Higher and higher they climbed, all the way to Manchuria. It had served nothing, nothing at all, to take Heartbreak Ridge. . . .

In that month of October 1951, two entire American divisions were thrown into the assault on Heartbreak Ridge and were massacred. Fifteen hundred American corpses remained on its slopes. The Chinese and the North Koreans were solidly entrenched, and they put their artillery to its best use. It was impossible to cut it off. Individual artillery pieces were brought out from under cover—from a cave or overhang— one at a time. Each fired two or three rounds and then withdrew, while another took its turn. They were never grouped in a battery—were always isolated. Their losses were thus slight.

The North Vietnamese, molded and trained by the Chinese, employed the same tactics at Dien Bien Phu. Our 105s, which were set up in the cove and neatly lined up together, were useless against the strategy of the enemy; so useless that the colonel commanding the French artillery committed suicide by putting a bullet through his head. It's just too bad a few of the chiefs of staff didn't follow his example!

The colonel in question had even been sent reports from Korea on the new Chinese tactics. But no one on the general staff was interested in reading what had taken place somewhere else.

I saw the parts of the American units that had survived coming back down all the little twisting trails from Heartbreak Ridge. The GIs carried long bamboo poles on their shoulders and bore the bodies of their friends like hunting trophies. Many, many soldiers had gone mad. Stupefied by their experiences, some would suddenly begin to howl, or to leap about in a frenzy, until it became necessary to stun them in order to quiet them.

Then it was our turn to attack.

The First Company mounted an attack and took a licking. Then the Second. Finally, just before dawn, I and my men of the Third advanced into a charnel house. By some rare chance we made our way through a barrage of grenades and found ourselves on Heartbreak Ridge. I had no more than a dozen men left. The others were either dead, wounded, or had fled. A company of Americans that had come to our aid was pinned down.

At nine o'clock on that same morning, I left Heartbreak Ridge in a helicopter. I'd been hit in both legs by a grenade. My war was over.

I was operated on in a field hospital across the valley, and I was lucky. My life was saved.

Then followed Osaka, Tokyo, and Saint Luke's Hospital.

I participated in a curious kind of experiment in that hospital.

A team of doctors had been devoting themselves to research into the healing of wounds. They certainly had a remarkable choice of men for their experiments: young men wounded in battle, and from a wide variety of nations, such as Turkey, the Philippines, Portugal, Belgium, France, Greece, and the United States—Americans of every origin.

The doctors discovered that they couldn't break their research down along racial lines, or even just along lines of origin; they could, though, in large part, along national lines. Wounds didn't heal in the same way for all nationalities. All Americans, for example, unless they were Puerto Rican or were otherwise recently nationalized, healed more slowly than any others. Why? Because their dietary habits had been so altered in Korea? Not at all. They still had all they needed, all they were used to: their Coca-Colas, their fruit juices, their frozen turkey.

It was all in the mind. And this is what happened in an American soldier's mind: The United States of America was like a mother to him. For her he had done his duty, and he'd been wounded doing it. He depended on her entirely. He'd abandoned himself to her, if you prefer. Now, his wound was no concern of his, not his responsibility; it was hers—America's—and it was up to her to take care of it.

On the other hand, those who belonged to older nations, such as the Greeks, the Portuguese, the French, healed much more rapidly. And it was because—the doctors whom I interviewed confirmed this—they didn't have the same behavior patterns in relation to their countries, the same freedom from constraint, the same confidence. For the Latins, for all the men of the Mediterranean, the state is not a mother; she is the enemy. In no instance can he place any real confidence in her. He'd been lied to and fooled by her too many times.

As a consequence, his wounds become something that concerns him and him alone. You can't in any case count on anyone except your clan, your family. The farther away from you the state remains, the better off you are; too many times she has revealed herself to be a thief, a swindler, someone who preys on the helpless, a sadist who hides behind incomprehensible rules and regulations in order not to have to keep her promises to you. If she should happen not to take your life from you, she'll at least steal the shirt off your back.

Out of these centuries-old and deeply rooted sentiments of the Latins have sprung organizations like the Mafia, created as a sort of insurance against the enemy—the state.

BRYAN ALEC FLOYD
1940–

Floyd spent two years in the United States Marine Corps but did not fight in Vietnam. His vignettes of Marine characters there are imagined. He is now a teacher on Long Island.

LANCE CORPORAL PURDUE GRACE, U.S.M.C.

He went home when the new replacements arrived,
but before he left
he talked with several of them,
all of whom looked scared and a bit self-pitying.
They knew he had made it through his tour
without getting a cold much less a wound.
One of the braver replacements
told him they were all terrified.
The Lance Corporal told them, "To be scared is okay.
I've seen lots of men change their pants
more than once a day, they were so scared.
But don't expect sympathy.
Sympathy is a sad word found in the dictionary

somewhere between scab and syphilis.
Always remember to keep your head out of your ass
and your ass out of the air.
Know this about this fucked-up war
that will never unfuck itself—
Life in Vietnam is a sea of shit:
Some people sink.
Some people swim.
And some people go in boats."

JOHN CLARK PRATT
1932–

Pratt retired from the United States Air Force in 1974 after serving twenty years. He has been a Professor of English at the Air Force Academy and at Colorado State University. In 1984 he compiled Vietnam Voices, *one of the most comprehensive and eloquent collections of documents and memoirs about the Vietnam War.*

Private Thomas Kingsley began his Vietnam tour of duty in December 1970.

Michael Clodfelter served as an artilleryman in the 101st Airborne Division.

From VIETNAM VOICES

LETTERS OF THOMAS KINGSLEY (AND GENERAL KENNETH G. WICKHAM)

Dear Mom and Dad,

This country is so beautiful, I don't believe it! It reminds me of Canada. It's so calm, picturesque, and serene. Presently I'm at Cam Ranh Bay. It's like a small resort town.

Love,
Tom

Dear Mom and Dad,

It's hard to experience Christmas when it's 110 degrees out. However, in between beers I managed to dream what it was like on the morning of Christmas. We didn't have to work today—they gave us a special dinner and free beer—so if this letter sounds incoherent it's because I had more beer than dinner. Merry Christmas!

I bought myself a camera, so I should have a lot of good shots when I get back. As I said before, this place is really beautiful, and I was not surprised to find that many lifers bring their wives and families out here to live.

I spent Christmas with some close friends (you'd be surprised how fast you meet "friends"), listened to Bob Hope on the radio—he was about 30 miles away—and went to a show they had on our firebase. I still haven't reached my final destination, so don't try to write yet. It will be another week before I find out what I'll be doing and where.

So far everything has been real quiet and everything is going fine. There are always rumors flying around though. The lifers say the war is over and everyone is pulling out. We were told we would be pulling out the 15th of January—that doesn't mean me, specifically—it means my division, the 1st Cavalry; no telling when they'll get to my company.

By the way, I enjoyed Christmas a day earlier than you did.

Merry Christmas and Love,
Tom

Dear Mom and Dad,

You'll have to excuse the handwriting again; I'm using a single cracked board as a backboard, and my hands are terribly dirty.

I have finally reached my end destination (I don't mean that factiously!), a place called Mace Firebase. During the welcoming orientation it was stated only two men have been killed in the last six months from this battalion, which numbers about 600 men. So I guess I am in a fairly safe location.

The name Air Cavalry refers to air mobility. Wherever we go we are transported by helicopter. You know how I am afraid of height; well, these people are scaring the hell out of me! I guess these helicopters are safe, though, but it seems to me they are held together with string and chewing gum; they rattle, shake, and lurch something terrible. All kidding aside, though, these helicopters are really efficient. They carry rockets, machine guns, small bombs, and other assorted weapons. They fly both daytime and nighttime missions, by means of a large searchlight on the latter. Transport helicopters carry about ten men each and are flanked and protected by gunships (helicopters loaded with armament).

Before we go on a mission, artillery will clear out an area with heavy bombing. They will then shift their target to the perimeter of the area we are to land in, in case the enemy wishes to attack us. When we are dropped off, the gunships will hover in the area until our position is positively fortified; then it will make runs in the surrounding area up to a mile out looking for the enemy. Sounds pretty safe, doesn't it. I hope so!

Right now I am on guard duty. I sit in a bunker with three other guys and listen to what is happening on the other side of the barbed wire. The other side of the wire is off limits to everyone after six o'clock and you're supposed to shoot on sight. However, we never do—too many drunken GI's around. Just a while ago there were two kids playing about 100 yards from the wire. Naturally we didn't shoot them, even though they could have been VC, but instead called headquarters, who in turn sent a party out to question them. All was legitimate and the kids were sent on their way.

By the way, have a good time on New Year's Eve, even though this letter is late.

Well, it's getting dark now so I have to concentrate on my work.

Love,
Tom

Dear Mom and Dad,

We've been at the LZ now for two days. The only duty we have to do for the five days is guard duty nightly—which lasts for one hour per person. When we first arrived back from the jungle, there sitting in front of our little caves was a truck-load of beer and Coke. During the daytime we play football, softball, volleyball, and other games. The greatest joy is that we're served three hot meals a day.

I sent home three cartridges of film to be processed. Half of them probably won't come out—some were taken from helicopters, trees, mud holes, and all kinds of other hazards.

It's a shame I couldn't caption the pictures because you probably won't understand what they're about. But at least you'll see what we wear, our surroundings, and other insights. I couldn't get any good shots of how we sleep because it's always too dark; we always travel in triple canopy jungle (three levels of growth). Which is why the jungle is so safe—we have literally cut our way through and therefore have only one passageway to protect. We set up trip flares across the path (a wire across the path attached to a flare) and land mines. If the enemy attempts to come any other way we will hear them.

Our first mission was completely uneventful, which doesn't displease me in the least. Our leader explained that for TET we are going out into the jungle and hiding for 15 days. By the way, I've found the jungle is the safest place to be. No one knows where you're at, you can hear people

coming a mile away, and it's very easy to protect yourself and hide. No
one expects a large TET offensive this year. But enough of tactics.

Our LZ, which we have nicknamed Peggy, is about 25 miles northeast
of Bien Hoa. We never travel more than 10 miles in any direction from
Peggy.

If I'm not writing on the lines, take into consideration I'm writing this
by candlelight. I also lost my pen in the darkness—that's why the change
of color.

I expect to hear from you shortly.

Love,
Tom

Dear Bob,

The first month has passed unceremoniously and uneventfully, which
doesn't displease me in the least. There have been times, though, when I
have been scared to death—a couple of times I thought it was all over. I
look back now and laugh because it wasn't even close.

The first night on guard I almost shot up a firefly, which I thought was
a gook with a flashlight. The second night I heard someone yelling at me.
So I woke up the guys around me and they said it was a frog! Sounded
just like a person.

There is not supposed to be much of a TET offensive—encompassing
only mortaring of large cities. Our leader says we are just going into the
jungle and hide—staying in one position. Needless to say, he has a good
head on him. We never do the things we're supposed to.

Sooner or later, though, the fan has got to hit the shit. Companies all
around us are running into contact, and I firmly believe I will not leave
here without being shot or injured first. I hate to say it, but that's how it
is; the odds of finding trouble are too great, something's got to happen
sometime. And anyone who tells you the war is over is full of shit.

I'm so embittered I don't believe it—but there is nothing you can do.
I'm not nervous at all, but you just realize something's got to happen.
Right now we're laying in ambush for gooks coming our way that at-
tacked the company next to us, killing two.

And it seems no one gives a damn besides us grunts in the bush. You
people in the world don't know what's happening because the Army
won't let you know and the goddamn lifers in the Army could care
less—as long as the death count is reasonable—say under 40 a week.

It's really hell, man. I saw a medivac operation after a company had
been hit by our own artillery. Four dead—everyone was injured, most
just slightly. But it was sickening. They carry the dead by a rope hanging
from a helicopter (the dead man is inside a plastic bag) and just lower
him to the ground—then throw them on a truck!

The fourth one was still alive when he came in—he was in the copter—and died a while later. He had no right leg at all; and seeing it just turned me to jelly, man—and guys just sitting around crying—it really shakes you up. And for no goddamn reason at all!

The kids spit at you—there's a bitter hatred between us and the South Viet Nam troops because they carry new weapons and we don't; and we do all the goddamn fighting while they sit on their asses all the time. Man, it makes you burn.

And I haven't seen any action yet—none of my friends have been hurt and no one in my company has been injured. But it will only be a matter of time. And how do you react—how do you blow off steam? A lot of guys grow a hatred for all gooks—that's why we have My Lai. Others take it out on the Army; in Nam they average two frags a week (fragging is where a man simply pulls the pin on a hand grenade and tosses it at a lifer).

It's bigger than that, though—it's the whole goddamn country—to allow such an atrocity to happen. I suppose because nobody really realizes what's happening here or can't imagine or picture it. I know I couldn't.

But I'll tell you, man, if I ever get back there and hear someone say Viet Nam was worthwhile or it was our obligation—I'll hit him right in the face. Because this is nothing but a shame—such a big mistake at such a huge cost. You can't believe it till you see it.

Oh well, enough rambling. I'm writing this in the morning and last night I had a good cry—because I was thinking too much—that's why all the emotion. Don't tell Mom or Dad or Mary about this letter because they think everything is okay.

Usually I get lost in books or cards and don't do much thinking. It's hard writing letters to them, too, because you have to slant everything into a good light. You know, Mom hasn't been feeling well, so needless to say, my letters to her have been very light toned, showing enthusiasm, etc. It would really affect her if she knew the whole situation. So don't let on that her son is experiencing traumatic happenings.

I sent her home a lot of pictures to be developed, so if you want to see the kid wearing a lot of smiles, go visit Mom and Dad. They would appreciate your company.

I expect to get a lot of letters about trivia from you now 'cause, man, I sure need it. Need something to take my mind off this place.

Sorry about the tone of this letter, but as the old saying goes—"You can bullshit some of the people some of the time . . ." I'll be hearing from you.

Tarzan

Hi, old buddy,

I'm a little calmer today for no apparent reason. I guess I'm getting used to this crap. After I finished that last letter, we made contact three more times that day—I didn't sleep very well that night. Then we made contact once on each of the next two days. So I'm getting used to it. (That takes me right up to today.) A couple of guys got hurt and three gooks were killed, I think (no one knows for sure)—we found one. Although I was very teed off when I wrote the last letter, I still feel exactly the way I did then. When we get back to the LZ I'm sure one of the boys will do the commanding officer in. The two guys who got hurt were the fault of the CO again—the guy is completely ignorant. Enough of the war stories, though.

Yes, I can receive packages, but just remember everything I receive I have to carry on my back—don't have a locker to store it in—so don't be sending me 18 hardbacks.

I found an article in Playboy, an advertisement put out by a group that opposes the war (Viet Nam Veterans Against the War). My friend Bob and myself got the whole squad together and joined in each sending a contribution. We also all signed a petition stating our feelings and gave it to the CO.

You asked about the jungle. Well, I was really scared at first—you run into spiders (huge ones), an occasional snake, and other animals, but they never bother you. You can be sleeping and they'll run right over you, but unless you sit on one, they don't bite. The biggest spider out here couldn't kill a person—but it could sure lay you up for a while—but then I could use a couple of weeks out of the bush. I sleep in a hammock that's killing my back—you know what they are, tie each end of a giant rag to a tree!

I just had a great idea—what I could really use which would remind me of civilization, would be a bottle of rum. They send out a couple of Cokes on log day, so I'd have a mix. I could mix it in my canteen cup. (March 6th is my birthday)—hint.

Well, I have to get a letter off to Mary.

Take it easy,
Tom

(My Birthday)

Good morning,

It's about 10:00 and I'm just sitting around in my hammock—I don't know how much longer it's going to hold me. We're in the mountains, and it's absolutely beautiful! We're right at the very top and the sights are something else—I can see the Red China Sea from my hammock!

Another good thing, there are no gooks here because there is no water.

So, the next 10 days or so will be like a vacation. Rumor has it this will be our last jungle mission—after this we'll be pulling guard duty at Bien Hoa, which would please me greatly—I've been out here for three months now without a break. I guess the Army is trying to make the deadline of May 1, to extract all jungle forces out of combat positions. We would then be used as a back-up force (while pulling guard) so for me it's very important that Vietnamization works—otherwise it won't be much of a break if we have to keep bailing the ARVN's out. The 10,000 GI's in Laos are back-up forces, but little good that title is doing them! The first Air Cavalry Division will definitely not be sent to Cambodia or Laos because our obligations in this region are too demanding; plus we're located too far away. It will be interesting to see what effect this Laos thing will have on the whole war.

I imagine there will be a long lull after the Laos battles. On the last mission we were running into contact 2 or 3 times a week, but I would say ¾ of the gooks were unarmed. During that mission I felt there was actually no real danger—that if contact was made it was by our initiative—not that we go out looking for trouble, far from it. But I think they have orders not to engage our forces unless absolutely necessary. We run into gooks, though, while traveling down paths or something like that. Many orders of our gung ho, John Wayne-type commander are ignored or carried out with less than high enthusiasm if there's a chance of getting hurt. Like I said before, we just try to hide in the jungle.

I'll be sending a tape home soon.

Love,
Tom

Mr. and Mrs. Frederick E. Kingsley:

The Secretary of the Army has asked me to express his deep regret that your son, Private First Class Thomas E. Kingsley, died in Vietnam on 20 March 1971. He was on a military mission when an automatic explosive device placed by a friendly force detonated. Please accept my deepest sympathy. This confirms personal notification made by a representative of the Secretary of the Army.

Kenneth G. Wickham
Major General USA
The Adjutant General
Department of the Army
Washington, D.C.

MEMOIR BY MICHAEL CLODFELTER

I was a regular kid, and like all other kids in all other times and places, I had one foot in the backyard and the other in fantasyland. Where my friends' fantasies might include batting a ball out of Yankee Stadium or driving a race car past the checkered flag at Indianapolis, my fantasies were those of combat. I was going to be the greatest war hero in history. I was going to wear a general's star by the time I was thirty and make the victories of the Duke of Marlborough, Frederick the Great, and Napoleon pale next to mine. Every kid knows that the world is going to be his atop a silver platter; mine was going to come mounted atop a tank tread.

It was not that my dream was so weird or unique. In a way it was the dream of every American boy, maybe of every boy everywhere. My goals were glory, fame, status, just as they were for those who would use a bat or a pigskin or a race car or, for those more practical among us, a briefcase or a test tube, to achieve those aims. The one difference—and the big difference—was that the tools of my trade would be rifles and machine guns, not stick shifts or Louisville Sluggers.

But even in this respect I was not such an oddity. Playing soldier is at least as universal a boyhood game as playing fireman. But most boys grew out of their G.I. Joe phase by their teens, became more interested in girls, basketball games and hot rods than in generals, battles and tanks. But I didn't grow out of that phase, for to me, it was not some mere phase but a fascination.

In the summer of 1964, at the age of seventeen, I enlisted in the United States Army. After boot camp, AIT, and airborne training, I was assigned to an artillery unit in the 101st Airborne Division. In July 1965, thanks to the Domino Theory and LBJ, I found myself in the middle of a Southeast Asian jungle and at the threshold of what I was certain would be the fulfillment of my special destiny. It turned out to be both less and more than what I had expected. It was all an agony and an ordeal. I wanted it to end every moment I was there, and yet I wanted it to never end. I wanted it to be all over with and forgotten, and yet I wanted it to last forever and I knew that I would never be able to forget it. I wanted to go home and leave it all behind me, and yet I knew that at least a part of me would never go home and that when I did go I would take a lot of it home with me. And I realized, in some intuitive secret room within myself, that this strange, alien, deadly place had somehow become my real home and that for a long time all else would seem strange and foreign and unreal for me. Vietnam and its war had worked its insidious magic on me. The "real world," the one back home on the other side of the Pacific Ocean, had become a fantasy world—one that so many of my instincts of old urged me to try to reclaim, but one that a new, stronger and darker instinct pulled me away from with an all-encompassing lack of logic.

There was no doubt that they had tricked us, deceived us—them with their John Wayne charging up Mount Suribachi, with their Gary Cooper-as-Sergeant York rounding up half the German Army and sharpshooting to death the other half. Have you ever seen a two-hour-long war movie that shows for an hour and fifty-nine minutes a soldier climbing a muddy mountain under the weight of a sixty-pound pack and 110-degree heat, and for only the last minute scenes of combat? That was the way the war was for us, mud mixed with sweat, sprinkled with lice, and all added to a generous portion of boredom to make a bitter recipe, a hateful dish that a pinch of the spice of combat could do little to make more palatable. We had imagined a movie; we had envisioned a feast. What we got was a reality removed from all other realities; what we got was a garbage pail.

The Vietnam War from my level, from the slit-trench and spider hole view of the hundreds of thousands of grunts on both sides, was really two wars. First there was the war that the newspapers reported, that Walter Cronkite broadcast on the evening news, that the officers in Saigon with their pointers and maps, their starched khakis and starched minds, lied about daily at the Five O'Clock Follies in the new dialect of Pentagonese, that long-haired college students protested against and hardhat hardheads paraded for. That was the war of battles and skirmishes, of firefights and ambushes, of air raids and gunship sorties. But the other war, the war that the soldiers of Vietnam were much more familiar with, the war that was rarely reported, that held little interest, that could hardly stir protests against or rallies in support of—that was the real war. This was the war of heat and rain and mud and dust, of heat exhaustion and sunstroke, of malaria and jungle rot, of sandbags and sixty-pound packs, of waiting and boredom. This was the war that was fought every day with the enemy all around, but an enemy armed with stingers and bacteria, with humidity and harshness, with thorns and with thunder.

The war against the toil and the terrain, against the sense of hopelessness and exile, was an every-day conflict, but the war of men pitted against men, of rifles blazing and bullets cracking, was much more infrequent. At first, when I was in the artillery, it seemed as if the shooting war, the one made phony-familiar to me through movies and television and G.I. Joe comic books, was a fairy tale. Because my view of arms and armies was almost exclusively of our side, the side with such power and military muscle, because nearly all I saw were American uniforms and American guns and tanks and planes in the midst of a small, unthreatening-appearing race of Orientals, it seemed that it was a game, just another military exercise, more maneuvers out on the firing range. The rare moments of action were filtered through my consciousness as fragments of a dream, quickly shattered when dull drudgerous reality resumed its nearly constant reign.

Later, after I had transferred to the infantry and became a grunt and my encounters with the enemy became much more frequent and much more intense, the fairy tale became more like a horror story and the dreams degenerated into nightmares. But even then there was still a sense of unreality about it all. Marches and monotony were still more the routine than contact and combat. Even after months in the bush a part of me was still surprised when the enemy did materialize and combat commenced its narcotic dance of terror and temptation. And it remained that way to the end. The enemy and the war he brought us was a phantom and a fantasy—a fantasy that could and did kill, but never really took on substance and form. Maybe that was why, though at times in the cauldron of combat terror held sway over all my senses, I did not live with the day-to-day dread that the circumstances probably warranted; I did not walk with the weight of a sure sense of my own mortality. For if the war was a fantasy to me—or at least to that part of the mind that throws up such defenses to deal with the intimacy of death—then surely a fantasy was incapable of killing me.

The enemy was real though, however enigmatic he may have been. That was a big part of the problem—just trying to figure out exactly who the hell was the enemy. We were not unique in military annals in having to deal with the guerrilla; not even in American military history. Geronimo's Apaches, Aguinaldo's Filipinos, and Sandino's Nicaraguans had all given American troops a taste, and always a bitter taste, of insurgency warfare. And American conventional forces, like conventional forces everywhere, had been unable to fight the guerrilla clear and clean. But those events of the past were all minor affairs, while this was guerrilla war on a grand scale, a dozen dirty little wars merged into one, one of the great wars of the century but fought on the level of Geronimo's Apache campaigns.

Killing the enemy was not the problem; it was identifying him. Killing him was easy once you found him and identified him. In fact, sometimes it was much easier to do the killing first and the identifying afterwards. Where no answers were possible, no questions were necessary. For many G.I.s the equation became simple; they bored right through all the complexities and tagged all Vietnamese as the enemy, every damn one of them. . . . Kill them all and you know for damn sure you're killing the enemy. If they're not all VC now, they could fuckin' well become VC. Solve the problem before it starts. If they're not going to put on uniforms and helmets like us, and live in base camps and fight in battalions and brigades like us, if they're going to plant rice sheets during the day and punji stakes at night without ever changing those fuckin' baggy black pajamas, then why not fuckin' waste them all, wipe their silly fucking smiles off their faces for good, keep my balls and my buddies' balls intact and safe from their Bouncing Bettys.

Christ it was hard! You come to this country with all sorts of John Wayne movie preconceptions about combat and the enemy and they're all blown to hell. Sure, sure, they drill into us all this stuff about guerrillas and the insurgent fish in the insurgent sea of the population, but you're still seeing yourself in all those war movies and you're still expecting the enemy to act like an enemy, to wear a web belt and steel pot like you, to be waiting for you behind his line of sandbags just like you're waiting behind yours. You don't expect him to be some slyly grinning Yahoo bebopping along behind some bored-looking water buffalo while the sun is still up and then come slinking through all the slime come nightfall to maybe lob a few incoming in on your spider holes or string a nice nasty little surprise across the trail that your recon patrol is going to be walking next morning.

It wasn't that way all the time and everywhere. Up in the northern reaches of "Eye" Corps, where the Marines tangled almost exclusively with the NVA, up around Khe Sanh and in Hue, and in the Ia Drang Valley and on Hill 875 in II Corps, soldiers and leathernecks found their enemy in the big battalions and in the big battles. It was hell, but it was a hell made familiar and recognizable by history and myth. But the enemy we encountered for the most part, in the paddy fields and hamlets of Phu Yen Province, though no harder to destroy—probably much easier than the better trained and better armed North Vietnamese regulars—were much more difficult to define. Those of us fighting the guerrillas were thrown into a hell far different than those men fighting the big battalions and the big battles. It was a hell worse in many ways, worse for our souls and spirits anyway, not because the fires were any hotter, but because the smoke was so much thicker.

Sometimes the enemy seemed so much made of the monsoon mist that we even doubted that he really existed. We arrived in the country expecting to encounter uniformed communist hordes, but found instead this strange small people wearing peasant garb and those inscrutable smiles. We wondered about all this ordnance hurled about, all the napalm, the 750-pound bombs and High Explosive artillery shells; found it hard to believe that these weak, undernourished-looking peasants could really present a threat and a danger to all our battalions of big, husky, heavily armed G.I.s. It seemed a laughable country and a laughable war—until we started running into the explosive evidence of the enemy's existence, until we started seeing and becoming a part of the red results of their cunning and courage. And then, slowly, as fear mounted frustration and rode down a crippled confidence, as callousness started taking over from condescension in our attitude toward the Vietnamese, our vision blurred, clouded over, and refocused. Where before we had found it difficult to see the enemy anywhere, now we saw him everywhere. It was simple now; the Vietnamese were the Viet Cong, the Viet Cong were the Vietnamese. The killing became so much easier now.

As the value of Vietnamese life went down in your estimation, so too did the realization start to sink in that your body and your life was really of very little importance to the men and the machines who ran the war; that winning victories was their prime concern, not safeguarding the lives of the men who must win the victories for them; that your life had a value to generals and armies and nations and causes only in relation to what or how much its sacrifice can bring. Somehow, you've carried the wild notion around that all this firepower, all these arms and ammunition, have been assembled not so much to take enemy lives as to protect yours, that the military machine's topmost priority is to lead you safely from harm's way. But sooner or later you are made conscious of the truth. Like any other machine, the green machine is impersonal to your life and death. You are only another piece of equipment, like a tank or the M-16 you carry, and your loss would be counted and calculated only in those terms. The machine would not care that a man had died, only that another part of its inventory had been lost and would require replacement, like the destroyed tank. And like the totaled tank, the Army would simply put in another order at another factory—a boot camp, where your replacement was being tooled and trained on a different kind of assembly line. It was just exactly as hard and as heartless as that and it was a heavy thing to accept—though accept it we all inevitably did.

So what it all came down to was that my world became the war, that my extended family became Charlie Company of the Second Battalion of the 502nd Airborne Infantry of the First Brigade of the 101st Airborne Division, and that my immediate family became the men of the Second "Hard Core" Squad of the First Platoon. At the head of that immediate family, my surrogate father in the Nam, was our squad leader, Staff Sergeant Heywood "Bud" Welch. The sergeant was short in stature, but you really had to squint hard to notice that. Everything else about the man was tall, including his tales. Welch would recount his exploits and there wasn't a man among us who believed half of what he claimed, but neither was there a man who doubted that the half that was maybe not yet true he would eventually make true. The sergeant was only twenty-two years old, but all of us were convinced that he had lived and would always live forever. Welch could make a brave man bolder and inspire confidence in a coward. We would have followed him anywhere—and, unfortunately, we did. We would have taken on half the NVA with him as our head and heart. Instead we took on an unarmed old man. We could have been heroes, but the war never, or rarely, gave us the chance. So Welch helped make us into the next best thing this war could offer—we became killers.

There was another kind of man in the platoon, a man we all were sure was a world removed from men like Welch—but a man who turned out to be only the darker side of our indomitable squad leader, and a side toward which the sergeant increasingly inclined. The man's name was Moses Atticus Tate, a West Virginia mountain boy and a homicidal maniac. We tried putting Tate into a separate category. He wasn't like the rest of us, we said, not even like those of us who, under the burdens and blows we had to take, sometimes gave in to the temptation to cruelty. He enjoyed the killing; he reveled in it. He was the company crazy, the regulation madman; the one kill-happy psychotic that every unit seemed plagued with, as if required by some demonic T.O.&E. (Table of Organization and Equipment) chart: so many riflemen, so many machine gunners, so many noncoms, and one bad-ass, blood-craving killer.

But Tate was in all of us and in each of us. Tate was all of us distilled down and down into some dark devil brew at the bottom. Tate was each of us stripped layer by layer of all that muddied veneer of civilized, socially-acceptable behavior, stripped clean down to the core where that mean biting thing lived that existed only to snarl and snap and draw blood. We hated him because what he had done we could do, because what he had become we could also become. Maybe one more month in Nam, one more buddy blown apart by a booby trap, maybe then the Tate would come out in all of us.

It all came apart in the monsoon October of 1966 as we were conducting Operation Seward in the rice paddy valley north of Tuy Hoa in Phu Yen Province on the central coast. We had been out several days and all we had to show for our sweat and exertion were robes of mud and waves of frustration. It had been a month now since any "Hard Core" glory had come the way of the Second Squad and the body count itch was making life miserable for all the corpse counters all the way up to battalion C.O. Finally, the First Squad scored, wasting an unarmed straggler, and the body count competition intensified. Tate, who had been in on the kill, taunted us so unmercifully on our lack of scalps that several members of the Second Squad, their "Hard Core" honor at stake, resolved to count coup and even the score even if it required wasting a slopehead who became VC only after he was dead.

After another sodden, miserable night, Welch saddled up his seven-man Hard Core Squad and led a patrol down from our hilltop NDP (Night Defensive Position) into the paddy valley below. Passing through the mud and muck of a nearby hamlet, we rousted out a gray-goateed old man and his betel-nut-chewing wife from a hootch at the south end of the village. Our squad leader and point man interrogated the old man, who responded, in a voice cracked with age and apprehension, with a litany of "No VC here! No VC! No VC here!"

Leaving the frightened old man behind, we moved on toward the last houses in the hamlet. There we got our chance and blew it. Three potential marks on the body count ballet were lounging on the front porch of a bamboo bungalo, their weapons stacked to form a neat little teepee off to the side. A volley away from eternity, the yawning communists were just nestling into their dreams of a Vietnamese workers' paradise when one of them caught sight of our stalking point man and yelped an alert. The slippery slopes nipped out under an M-16 broadside and, though the sergeant and his point man both claimed hits, we found no wet red wreckage purpling the muddy ground to validate their scores.

The Charlies had escaped; an easy score had slipped from our black-muzzled clutches. One of the Hard Core hardasses had promised to bring back to Tate evidence of a kill in the form of the victim's ears. Now we had nothing to show for our effort and nothing to throw into the face of Tate's taunts. But all was not lost; our honor could still be salvaged. The old man with gray cat's whiskers still remained, and his ears, except for the scales of age, were as good as those attached to the skulls of the three nimble Victor Charlies who had escaped. Tate could have his ears, Welch could chalk up a body count, and the squad could maintain its reputation for ferocity. All it required was murder.

Welch and two of his Cossacks stomped back to the old man's hootch and hustled him outside. The rest of us took up defensive positions in a vegetable garden surrounding the hootch. I waited in dread and anticipation, and the humid breaths I sucked in burned as if I were inhaling the alien atmosphere of a distant planet. I crouched down in a corner of that garden in hell, protecting my comrades-in-arms as they wrestled the old man to his execution block. I tried to keep my eyes fixed on the paddies and thatched huts before me, but that beast's lust for blood within me clawed at my face to turn me back and behold my comrades' shame and my own shame—to stare in horror and gaze in rapture at this monster war had conjured up.

I couldn't quite believe that it would really happen. I tried telling myself that the executioners would stay the axe; that in the final moment of reckoning they would show that their bluster was nothing more than bluff and bravado carried almost too far.

But it was too late now for the killers to draw back and consider the act that they were about to commit, though doubt and hesitation rose like suffocating, sulfurous fumes among those who were about to draw blood. One of the paratroopers pointed his M-79 grenade launcher at the doomed peasant, whose eyes spoke the silent language of the already-dead. Hesitation locked the trooper in a sweating embrace, filled the garden with its strangling tension, seemed to stop the very rotation of the earth and the passage of time. The old man stood motionless on the cliff's edge of death, a squeeze on the trigger away from a red-metaled Nirvana.

My mind bolted, like the recoil of a bombarding howitzer. I arose from my morass of sweat and dread to scream out words of protest . . . words that I should have loosened at the first insane moments of this horror. A shot reared, drowning out my frantic shout of protest in its louder scream. I would, in effect, still be shouting those unheeded words of protest in dozens of anti-war marches for years after I left Nam. I am still screaming them out today . . . too late, far too late. That unheard scream will echo through my soul forever.

The dozen steel pellets from a M-79 buckshot round crashed into the bowed, black-shirted back of the gray victim. He crumpled, as if a condor's claw had ripped out his aged spine in one vicious swoop. The old man's back was shattered into a bloody pulp, his severed red vertebrae whipping like the tentacles of an octopus.

But the old man did not die quickly. Standing over their twitching victim, the slayers shuffled uneasily, waiting for the old man to die and remove a throbbing thorn from their consciences.

One Hard Core trooper complained to the grenadier who had fired the buckshot round, "Man, you'd better trade that '79 in for a fuckin' slingshot. Can't you even waste a fuckin' old man? Whadaya need? A mother-fuckin' howitzer?"

The grenadier replied, "Shit, you know how fuckin' hard it is to kill these slopes. If you're in so much pain over his suffering, why don't you finish the old fucker off?"

The other man's expression wrinkled into a portrait of reluctance, but his Hard Core creed demanded that he fight off any show of squeamishness. He swallowed whatever compassion was left to him and reaffirmed his fraudulent pride with a clattering volley of automatic rifle fire into the stricken figure laying at his feet.

But still the old man, awash in a thickening red gravy in the center of the garden and at the dead center of our souls, clung to life. Not until the same rifleman thrust the muzzle of his M-16 against the old man's skull to crash a leaden fist into his brain did the life that had lingered in agony flee the heap of bullet-ravaged flesh and bones. The old man was at last dead; the Second Squad could report back to the platoon leader the attainment of a body count.

The grenadier turned away to escape the shame that was corroding his conscience, but the rifleman grabbed his arm and reminded him, "Man, are you going to forget why we zapped that old fucker?"

"What's to forget?" asked the grenadier impatiently.

"The ears, man, the mother fuckin' ears," answered the rifleman. "Them cats in First Squad are expectin' some Hard Core trophies."

"Oh yeah, the ears," muttered the grenadier. "The god damn ears." The grenadier kneeled down to collect his bounty. He went to work with his bayonet and soon the ears were off to decorate the elastic camouflage cover band on his steel pot, like some obscene plume atop a Roman legionnaire's helmet.

As the squad prepared to retire to the platoon HQ laden with its spoils of war, rifle shots popped in the tops of the banana trees shadowing the scene of our atrocity. The Charlies who had fled the hamlet must have returned, but we had already earned an easier body count and so we did not linger. The squad hastily retraced its steps out of the tiny peasant burg to rejoin the platoon. Upon reaching the platoon position, the grenadier proudly displayed his trophies, still dripping blood, to a much impressed Tate. We had joined his ranks.

I did not join in the ensuing celebration for our success. I was appalled; appalled at what my comrades had done and at what I had failed to do. I determined that if ever I should find myself in a position of leadership—and my promotion to sergeant was due in a few weeks—at the head of a patrol, a fire team, a squad, whatever, I would exert whatever authority I might have to prevent another such incident, a recurrence of barbarity. It was all I could do to make amends; a weak resolution in the face of such strong savagery. It was too late to help the old man. I could never have pointed my M-16 at my comrades to warn them off. They would have known and I would have known that there was no way that I could have squeezed the trigger, no way would I have harmed one of my comrades to save the life of an old gook. I owned nothing in the world anymore of value other than the good will and loyalty of these men; I would have let the whole gook race die before I forfeited it. Reporting the incident, turning them in, was simply no alternative. I never considered it; it did not exist as an option. Not in my world. Without these men I would die, if not in body then surely in spirit. It was that simple. My dependence upon the men of my squad, of my platoon, their dependence upon me and each other, was total. I did not want to become an outcast from the only family that really mattered to me now. Malingering, cowardice, cruelty, nothing would earn my comrades' contempt more than disloyalty. Somewhere in me, something told me that there existed a loyalty greater than that I gave and received from the men of the First Platoon; a loyalty to truth and justice and conscience. And later it was all so obvious; but much later, after I had left this country, this war, this platoon. But back then, truth and justice and morality were only words, words that could not save me from death or madness or that slow sinking into a morass of fear and isolation. There was but one loyalty in Nam that counted and it was, without exception, colored olive drab.

Fifteen years later I still have trouble dealing with that old man. He confronts me sometimes in my dreams, his face always ill-defined, cloudy, because I've forgotten just what he looked like after all these years. But I haven't forgotten his final expression, the one frozen on his face and in my soul, the one that he carried with him out of this world of the living when that M-79 buckshot round shattered his back.

But the old man's image comes and goes, just as the guilt comes and goes. Sometimes I have to remind myself of it; sometimes I have to hide from myself because I can't get away from it. That's because part of me, the part that made me question the war, that made me turn against the war, that made me work against the war, that part of me finds me guilty, an accessory to the crime of murder, guilty through inaction, through acquiescence, through acceptance. But another part of me, the part that loved the thought of war, that even kept a little bit of that love for the experience of war, that part excuses my act of non-action, buries the guilt, tells me it's all understandable and forgivable, given the circumstances of war, given the savagery of war, given the strange but special loyalties of war.

Back then, when it happened, something bright and burning inside me flickered and went out, leaving not even a warm cinder, leaving only a pile of cold cold ashes.

I went home four months later. It was not a happy homecoming. I suppose I would have come out of any war disillusioned. Even when fought for the most glorious cause, even when resulting in the most magnificent victory, war can never be the creature of dash and daring, of adventure and admiration, that young minds might imagine. And to the misfortune of our egos and aspirations—though probably ultimately to the good fortune of our souls—the only war offered our generation was Vietnam, surely the most disillusioning war ever fought by Americans. Had it been World War II or Korea maybe we could have salvaged some scrap of our former favorable opinion of war; maybe we could have looked back as middle aged vets sitting in VFW clubs and recalled some higher purpose to our sacrifices and proposed a toast to the good fight, to "our war." But ours was not WWII or Korea; ours was Vietnam, and it would have required a far greater leap from reality—and a dishonest one at that—than that of our adolescent fantasies, now that our opinion was no longer based on ignorance, for us to bless a war that could bear no blessing.

Though separated geographically, the war stayed with me down through all the following years. In all that time, in all those years while I was either fighting in the Vietnam War or against it, I often found it difficult, if not almost inconceivable, to imagine that any American, or at least any American of my generation, could look upon the war as trivial to their own lives, as something outside of and as far removed from their own private and personal existences as, say, the chaos in the Congo in the early 6os was. I could not fathom how Vietnam could be anything to all Americans but the central concern of their lives; how it could be anything less than the dark sun around which we were all in unbreakable orbit as its doomed and somehow hopeless satellites. But I had to face the fact, the appalling fact, that to the vast majority of Americans, even those of my age, families and homes and careers, and even cars, cocaine, connections and the next piece of ass, were greater concerns than all that muck and madness in Southeast Asia. Vietnam and its war touched and tainted millions of Americans in one way or another, but it left greater millions untouched. For all that the war affected them, most of the children of the '6os might just as well have been children of the '5os. Most of my family, friends and acquaintances did not serve in the war or in the war against the war. For most of my family, friends and acquaintances, the war had an impact upon them similar to that made by a pebble dropped into the depths of the ocean.

But for me and for most of the men who fought there, the war was everything. It had been the worst experience of my life and it had been the best. I never wanted out of any place so bad as I wanted out of Vietnam. But after I left I felt an immediate and overwhelming sense of loss for Vietnam and its war. After all these years, this nostalgia, this strange yearning to return to it all, still persists, still haunts me. Looking at it in terms of good or bad is all wrong. It was simply the most awesome experience of my life and will probably remain so to the end of my years. It is a mountain range rising up abruptly and sharply from the more or less level plains that make up the topography of the rest of my life. These are heights desolate and depressing, more like the mountains of the moon than some snow-capped range, magic and majestic. They are there, undeniable and unscalable, and though time and fading memory may erode them to foothills, they will never entirely disappear from my life's landscape until the gray glacier of death wears everything down to dust.

*   *   *

GRAFFITI LEFT IN A MILITARY LATRINE, SAIGON:

America lost her virginity in Vietnam.

Added by another hand:

And she caught the clap, too.

SEYMOUR M. HERSH
1937–

*Seymour Hersh was born in Chicago, and after graduating from the
University of Chicago he joined the United Press and later the New
York Times. "I hate secrets," he has said, and his disclosures about
American behavior in Vietnam and Cambodia, as well as about the
character of Henry Kissinger, have earned him a reputation as one of the
most effective of investigative journalists. His exposure of the My Lai
scandal and cover-up brought him a Pulitzer Prize. His book* My Lai 4
appeared in 1970.

From My Lai 4

Nobody saw it all. Some, like Roy Wood, didn't even know the extent of
the massacre until the next day. Others, like Charles Sledge, who served
that day as Calley's radioman, saw more than they want to remember.

But they all remember the fear that morning as they climbed onto
helicopters at LZ Dotti for the assault on Pinkville. They all remember
the sure knowledge that they would meet face-to-face for the first time
with the enemy.

Calley and his platoon were the first to board the large black Army
assault helicopters. They were heavily armed, each man carrying twice
the normal load of rifle and machine-gun ammunition. Leading the way
was Calley, who had slung an extra belt of M16 rifle bullets over his
shoulder. There were nine helicopters in the first lift-off, enough for the
first platoon—about twenty-five men—and Captain Medina and his
small headquarters unit of three radiomen, some liaison officers and a
medic. It was sunny and already hot when the first helicopter started its
noisy flight to My Lai 4. The time was 7:22 A.M.; it was logged by a tape
recorder at brigade headquarters. A brief artillery barrage had already
begun; the My Lai 4 area was being "prepped" in anticipation of that

day's search-and-destroy mission. A few heavily armed helicopters were firing thousands of small-caliber bullets into the area by the time Calley and his men landed in a soggy rice paddy 150 meters west of the hamlet. It was harvest season; the green fields were thick with growth.

The first platoon's mission was to secure the landing zone and make sure no enemy troops were left to fire at the second wave of helicopters—by then already airborne from LZ Dotti. As the flight of helicopters hovered over the landing area, the door gunners began spraying protective fire to keep the enemy—if he were there—busy. One of the helicopter's pilots had reported that the LZ was "hot," that is, Viet Cong were waiting below. The first platoon came out firing. But after a moment some men noticed that there was no return fire. "I didn't hear any bullets going past me," recalled Charles Hall, a machine gunner that day. "If you want to consider an area hot, you got to be fired on."

The platoon quickly formed a perimeter and secured the landing zone. Sergeant Cowen spotted an old man. Sledge was a few yards to Cowen's right: "We came to a well and there was a VC. We thought it was a VC. He was standing and waving his arms. Cowen fell back and said, 'Shoot the so-and-so.' I fired once, and then my [rifle] magazine fell out." Paul Meadlo noted that "the gook was standing up shaking and waving his arms and then he was shot." Allen Boyce saw it a little differently: "Some guy was in a rice field, doing something to a rice plant. He looked up and he got it. That was the most confused operation I ever went on. Just everything was screwed up."

By this time those Viet Cong who were in the area had slipped away. Some local supporters of the guerrillas also left, but they did not go too far. They watched as Charlie Company went through My Lai 4.

After about twenty minutes the second flight of helicopters landed, and the fifty men of the second and third platoons jumped off. Gary Garfolo heard the helicopter blades make sharp crackling sounds as they changed pitch for the landing. "It was a 'pop, pop, pop' sound like a rifle. Lots of us never even heard a hot LZ before. We knew we were going into a hot place. This got their adrenalin going." The men were quickly assembled. Calley's first platoon and Lieutenant Stephen Brooks' second platoon would lead the sweep into the hamlet—Calley to the south, and Brooks to the north. The third platoon, headed by Lieutenant Jeffrey La Crosse, would be held in reserve and move in on the heels of the other men. Captain Medina and his headquarters unit would move with the third platoon and then set up a command post (CP) inside to monitor the operation and stay in touch with other units. Charlie Company was not alone in its assault; the other two companies of Task Force Barker set up blocking positions to the north and south. They were there to prevent the expected Viet Cong troops from fleeing.

The My Lai 4 assault was the biggest thing going in the American Division that day. To get enough airlift, Task Force Barker had to borrow helicopters from other units throughout the division. The air lanes above the action were carefully allotted to high-ranking officers for observation. Barker monitored the battle from the 1,000-foot level. Major General Samuel Koster, commanding general of the division, was allotted the air space at 2,000 feet. His helicopter was permanently stationed outside his door at division headquarters twenty-one miles to the north, waiting to fly him to the scene of any action within minutes. Oran K. Henderson, commander of the 11th Brigade, was given the top spot—at 2,500 feet. All of the helicopters were to circle counterclockwise over the battle area. Flying low, beneath the 1,000-foot level, would be the gunships, heavily armed helicopters whose mission was to shoot down any Viet Cong soldiers attempting to escape.

Brigade headquarters, sure that there would be a major battle, sent along two men from the Army's 31st Public Information Detachment to record the event for history. Jay Roberts of Arlington, Virginia, a reporter, and photographer Ronald L. Haeberle of Cleveland, Ohio, arrived with the second wave of helicopters and immediately attached themselves to the third platoon, which was bringing up the rear.

The hamlet itself had a population of about 700 people, living either in flimsy thatch-covered huts—"hootches," as the GIs called them—or in solidly made red-brick homes, many with small porches in front. There was an east-west footpath just south of the main cluster of homes; a few yards further south was a loose surface road that marked a hamlet boundary. A deep drainage ditch and then a rice paddy marked the eastern boundary. To the south of My Lai 4 was a large center, or plaza area—clearly the main spot for mass meetings. The foliage was dense: there were high bamboo trees, hedges and plant life everywhere. Medina couldn't see thirty feet into the hamlet from the landing zone.

The first and second platoons lined up carefully to begin the hundred-meter advance into My Lai 4. Walking in line is an important military concept; if one group of men gets too far in front, it could be hit by bullets from behind—those fired by colleagues. Yet even this went wrong. Ron Grzesik was in charge of a small first-platoon fire team of riflemen and a machine gunner; he took his job seriously. His unit was supposed to be on the right flank, protecting Calley and his men. But Grzesik's group ended up on Calley's left.

As Brooks' second platoon cautiously approached the hamlet, a few Vietnamese began running across a field several hundred meters on the left. They may have been Viet Cong, or they may have been civilians fleeing the artillery shelling or the bombardment from the helicopter gunships. Vernado Simpson, Jr., of Jackson, Mississippi, saw a man he identified as a Viet Cong soldier running with what seemed to be a weapon. A woman and a small child were running with him. Simpson fired . . . again and again. He killed the woman and the baby. The man got away. Reporter Roberts saw a squad of GIs jump off a helicopter and begin firing at a group of people running on a nearby road. One was a woman with her children. Then he saw them "shoot two guys who popped up from a rice field. They looked like military-age men . . . when certain guys pop up from rice fields, you shoot them." This was the young reporter's most dangerous assignment. He had never been in combat before. "You're scared to death out there. We just wanted to go home."

The first two platoons of Charlie Company, still unfired upon, entered the hamlet. Behind them, still in the rice paddy, were the third platoon and Captain Medina's command post. Calley and some of his men walked into the plaza area in the southern part of the hamlet. None of the people was running away; they knew that U.S. soldiers would assume that anyone running was a Viet Cong and would shoot to kill. There was no immediate sense of panic. The time was about 8 A.M. Grzesik and his fire team were a few meters north of Calley; they couldn't see each other because of the dense vegetation. Grzesik and his men began their usual job of pulling people from their homes, interrogating them, and searching for Viet Cong. The villagers were gathered up, and Grzesik sent Meadlo, who was in his unit, to take them to Calley for further questioning. Grzesik didn't see Meadlo again for more than an hour.

Some of Calley's men thought it was breakfast time as they walked in; a few families were gathered in front of their homes cooking rice over a small fire. Without a direct order, the first platoon also began rounding up the villagers. There still was no sniper fire, no sign of a large enemy unit. Sledge remembered thinking that "if there were VC around, they had plenty of time to leave before we came in. We didn't tiptoe in there."

The killings began without warning. Harry Stanley told the C.I.D. that one young member of Calley's platoon took a civilian into custody and then "pushed the man up to where we were standing and then stabbed the man in the back with his bayonet . . . The man fell to the ground and was gasping for breath." The GI then "killed him with another bayonet thrust or by shooting him with a rifle . . . There was so many people killed that day it is hard for me to recall exactly how some of the people died." The youth next "turned to where some soldiers were holding another forty- or fifty-year-old man in custody." He "picked this man up and threw him down a well. Then [he] pulled the pin from a M26 grenade and threw it in after the man." Moments later Stanley saw "some old women and some little children—fifteen or twenty of them— in a group around a temple where some incense was burning. They were kneeling and crying and praying, and various soldiers . . . walked by and executed these women and children by shooting them in the head with their rifles. The soldiers killed all fifteen or twenty of them . . ."

There were few physical protests from the people; about eighty of them were taken quietly from their homes and herded together in the plaza area. A few hollered out, "No VC. No VC." But that was hardly unexpected. Calley left Meadlo, Boyce and a few others with the responsibility of guarding the group. "You know what I want you to do with them," he told Meadlo. Ten minutes later—about 8:15 A.M.—he returned and asked, "Haven't you got rid of them yet? I want them dead." Radioman Sledge, who was trailing Calley, heard the officer tell Meadlo to "waste them." Meadlo followed orders: "We stood about ten to fifteen feet away from them and then he [Calley] started shooting them. Then he told me to start shooting them. I started to shoot them. So we went ahead and killed them. I used more than a whole clip—used four or five clips." There are seventeen M16 bullets in each clip. Boyce slipped away, to the northern side of the hamlet, glad he hadn't been asked to shoot. Women were huddled against their children, vainly trying to save them. Some continued to chant, "No VC." Others simply said, "No. No. No."

Do Chuc is a gnarled forty-eight-year-old Vietnamese peasant whose two daughters and an aunt were killed by the GIs in My Lai 4 that day. He and his family were eating breakfast when the GIs entered the hamlet and ordered them out of their homes. Together with other villagers, they were marched a few hundred meters into the plaza, where they were told to squat. "Still we had no reason to be afraid," Chuc recalled. "Everyone was calm." He watched as the GIs set up a machine gun. The calm ended. The people began crying and begging. One monk showed his identification papers to a soldier, but the American simply said, "Sorry." Then the shooting started. Chuc was wounded in the leg, but he was covered by dead bodies and thus spared. After waiting an hour, he fled the hamlet.

Nguyen Bat, a Viet Cong hamlet chief who later defected, said that many of the villagers who were eating breakfast outdoors when the GIs marched in greeted them without fear. They were gathered together and shot. Other villagers who were breakfasting indoors were killed inside their homes.

The few Viet Cong who had stayed near the hamlet were safely hidden. Nguyen Ngo, a former deputy commander of a Viet Cong guerrilla platoon operating in the My Lai area, ran to his hiding place 300 meters away when the GIs came in shooting, but he could see that "they shot everything in sight." His mother and sister hid in ditches and survived because bodies fell on top of them. Pham Lai, a former hamlet security guard, climbed into a bunker with a bamboo top and heard but did not see the shootings. His wife, hidden under a body, survived the massacre.

By this time, there was shooting everywhere. Dennis I. Conti, a GI from Providence, Rhode Island, later explained to C.I.D. investigators what he thought had happened: "We were all psyched up, and as a result, when we got there the shooting started, almost as a chain reaction. The majority of us had expected to meet VC combat troops, but this did not turn out to be so. First we saw a few men running . . . and the next thing I knew we were shooting at everything. Everybody was just firing. After they got in the village, I guess you could say that the men were out of control."

Brooks and his men in the second platoon to the north had begun to systematically ransack the hamlet and slaughter the people, kill the livestock and destroy the crops. Men poured rifle and machine-gun fire into huts without knowing—or seemingly caring—who was inside.

Roy Wood, one of Calley's men who was working next to Brooks' platoon, stormed into a hut, saw an elderly man hiding inside along with his wife and two young daughters: "I hit him with my rifle and pushed him out." A GI from Brooks' platoon, standing by with an M79 grenade launcher, asked to borrow his gun. Wood refused, and the soldier asked another platoon mate. He got the weapon, said, "Don't let none of them live," and shot the Vietnamese in the head. "These mothers are crazy," Wood remembered thinking. "Stand right in front of us and blow a man's brains out." Later he vomited when he saw more of the dead residents of My Lai 4.

The second platoon went into My Lai 4 with guns blazing. Gary Crossley said that some GIs, after seeing nothing but women and children in the hamlet, hesitated: "We phoned Medina and told him what the circumstances were, and he said just keep going. It wasn't anything we wanted to do. You can only kill so many women and children. The fact was that you can't go through and wipe out all of South Vietnam."

Once the first two platoons had disappeared into the hamlet, Medina ordered the third platoon to start moving. He and his men followed. Gary Garfolo was caught up in the confusion: "I could hear heavy shooting all the time. Medina was running back and forth everywhere. This wasn't no organized deal." So Garfolo did what most GIs did when they could get away with it. "I took off on my own." He ran south; others joined him. Terrified villagers, many carrying personal belongings in wicker baskets, were running everywhere to avoid the carnage. In most cases it didn't help. The helicopter gunships circling above cut them down, or else an unfortunate group ran into the third platoon. Charles West sighted and shot six Vietnamese, some with baskets, on the edge of My Lai 4: "These people were running into us, away from us, running every which way. It's hard to distinguish a mama-san from a papa-san when everybody has on black pajamas."

West and his men may have thought that these Vietnamese were Viet Cong. Later they knew better. West's first impression upon reaching My Lai 4: "There were no people in the first part . . . I seen bodies everywhere. I knew that everyone was being killed." His group quickly joined in.

Medina—as any combat officer would do during his unit's first major engagement—decided to move his CP from the rice paddy. John Paul, one of Medina's radiomen, figured that the time was about 8:15 A.M. West remembered that "Medina was right behind us" as his platoon moved inside the hamlet. There are serious contradictions about what happened next. Medina later said that he did not enter the hamlet proper until well after 10 A.M. and did not see anyone kill a civilian. John Paul didn't think that Medina ever entered the hamlet. But Herbert Carter told the C.I.D. that Medina did some of the shooting of civilians as he moved into My Lai 4.

Carter testified that soon after the third platoon moved in, a woman was sighted. Somebody knocked her down, and then, Carter said, "Medina shot her with his M16 rifle. I was fifty or sixty feet away and saw this. There was no reason to shoot this girl." The men continued on, making sure no one was escaping. "We came to where the soldiers had collected fifteen or more Vietnamese men, women and children in a group. Medina said, 'Kill every one. Leave no one standing.' " A machine gunner began firing into the group. Moments later one of Medina's radio operators slowly "passed among them and finished them off." Medina did not personally shoot any of them, according to Carter, but moments later the captain "stopped a seventeen- or eighteen-year-old man with a water buffalo. Medina told the boy to make a run for it," Carter told the C.I.D. "He tried to get him to run but the boy wouldn't run, so Medina shot him with his M16 rifle and killed him . . . I was seventy-five or eighty meters away at the time and I saw it plainly." At this point in Carter's interrogation, the investigator warned him that he was making very serious charges against his commanding officer. "What I'm telling is the truth," Carter replied, "and I'll face Medina in court and swear to it."

If Carter was correct, Medina walked first into the north side of My Lai 4, then moved south with the CP to the hamlet plaza and arrived there at about the same time Paul Meadlo and Lieutenant Calley were executing the first group of villagers. Meadlo still wonders why Medina didn't stop the shooting, "if it was wrong." Medina and Calley "passed each other quite a few times that morning, but didn't say anything. I don't know if the CO gave the order to kill or not, but he was right there when it happened . . . Medina just kept marching around."

Roberts and Haeberle also moved in just behind the third platoon. Haeberle watched a group of ten to fifteen GIs methodically pump bullets into a cow until it keeled over. A woman then poked her head out from behind some brush; she may have been hiding in a bunker. The GIs turned their fire from the cow to the woman. "They just kept shooting at her. You could see the bones flying in the air chip by chip." No one had attempted to question her; GIs inside the hamlet also were asking no questions. Before moving on, the photographer took a picture of the dead woman. Haeberle took many more pictures that day; he saw about thirty GIs kill at least a hundred Vietnamese civilians.

When the two correspondents entered My Lai 4, they saw dead animals, dead people, burning huts and houses. A few GIs were going through victims' clothing, looking for piasters. Another GI was chasing a duck with a knife; others stood around watching a GI slaughter a cow with a bayonet.

Haeberle noticed a man and two small children walking toward a group of GIs: "They just kept walking toward us . . . you could hear the little girl saying, 'No, no . . .' All of a sudden the GIs opened up and cut them down." Later he watched a machine gunner suddenly open fire on a group of civilians—women, children and babies—who had been collected in a big circle: "They were trying to run. I don't know how many got out." He saw a GI with an M16 rifle fire at two young boys walking along a road. The older of the two—about seven or eight years old—fell over the first to protect him. The GI kept on firing until both were dead.

As Haeberle and Roberts walked further into the hamlet, Medina came up to them. Eighty-five Viet Cong had been killed in action thus far, the captain told them, and twenty suspects had been captured. Roberts carefully jotted down the captain's statistics in his notepad.

The company's other Vietnamese interpreter, Sergeant Duong Minh, saw Medina for the first time about then. Minh had arrived on a later helicopter assault, along with Lieutenant Dennis H. Johnson, Charlie Company's intelligence officer. When he saw the bodies of civilians, he asked Medina what happened. Medina, obviously angry at Minh for asking the question, stalked away.

Now it was nearly nine o'clock and all of Charlie Company was in My Lai 4. Most families were being shot inside their homes, or just outside the doorways. Those who had tried to flee were crammed by GIs into the many bunkers built throughout the hamlet for protection—once the bunkers became filled, hand grenades were lobbed in. Everything became a target. Gary Garfolo borrowed someone's M79 grenade launcher and fired it point-blank at a water buffalo: "I hit that sucker right in the head; went down like a shot. You don't get to shoot water buffalo with an M79 every day." Others fired the weapon into the bunkers full of people.

Jay Roberts insisted that he saw Medina in My Lai 4 most of the morning: "He was directing the operations in the village. He was in the village the whole time I was—from nine o'clock to eleven o'clock."

Carter recalled that some GIs were shouting and yelling during the massacre: "The boys enjoyed it. When someone laughs and jokes about what they're doing, they have to be enjoying it." A GI said, "Hey, I got me another one." Another said, "Chalk up one for me." Even Captain Medina was having a good time, Carter thought: "You can tell when someone enjoys their work." Few members of Charlie Company protested that day. For the most part, those who didn't like what was going on kept their thoughts to themselves.

Herbert Carter also remembered seeing Medina inside the hamlet well after the third platoon began its advance: "I saw all those dead people laying there. Medina came right behind me." At one point in the morning one of the members of Medina's CP joined in the shooting. "A woman came out of a hut with a baby in her arms and she was crying," Carter told the C.I.D. "She was crying because her little boy had been in front of their hut and . . . someone had killed the child by shooting it." When the mother came into view, one of Medina's men "shot her with an M16 and she fell. When she fell, she dropped the baby." The GI next "opened up on the baby with his M16." The infant was also killed. Carter also saw an officer grab a woman by the hair and shoot her with a .45-caliber pistol: "He held her by the hair for a minute and then let go and she fell to the ground. Some enlisted man standing there said, 'Well, she'll be in the big rice paddy in the sky.' "

In the midst of the carnage, Michael Bernhardt got his first good look at My Lai 4. Bernhardt had been delayed when Medina asked him to check out a suspicious wood box at the landing zone. After discovering that it wasn't a booby trap, Bernhardt hurried to catch up with his mates in the third platoon. He went into the hamlet, where he saw Charlie Company "doing strange things. One: They were setting fire to the hootches and huts and waiting for people to come out and then shooting them. Two: they were going into the hootches and shooting them up. Three: they were gathering people in groups and shooting them. The whole thing was so deliberate. It was point-blank murder and I was standing there watching it. It's kind of made me wonder if I could trust people any more."

Grzesik and his men, meanwhile, had been slowly working their way through the hamlet. The young GI was having problems controlling his men; he was anxious to move on to the rice paddy in the east. About three quarters of the way through, he suddenly saw Meadlo again. The time was now after nine. Meadlo was crouched, head in his hands, sobbing like a bewildered child. "I sat down and asked him what happened." Grzesik felt responsible; after all, he was supposed to be a team leader. Meadlo told him Calley had made him shoot people. "I tried to calm him down," Grzesik said, but the fire-team leader couldn't stay long. His men still hadn't completed their sweep of My Lai 4.

Those Vietnamese who were not killed on the spot were being shepherded by the first platoon to a large drainage ditch at the eastern end of the hamlet. After Grzesik left, Meadlo and a few others gathered seven or eight villagers in one hut and were preparing to toss in a hand grenade when an order came to take them to the ditch. There he found Calley, along with a dozen other first platoon members, and perhaps seventy-five Vietnamese, mostly women, old men and children.

Not far away, invisible in the brush and trees, the second and third platoons were continuing their search-and-destroy operations in the northern half of My Lai 4. Ron Grzesik and his fire team had completed a swing through the hamlet and were getting ready to turn around and walk back to see what was going on. And just south of the plaza, Michael Bernhardt had attached himself to Medina and his command post. Shots were still being fired, the helicopters were still whirring overhead, and the enemy was still nowhere in sight.

One of the helicopters was piloted by Chief Warrant Officer Hugh C. Thompson of Decatur, Georgia. For him, the mission had begun routinely enough. He and his two-man crew, in a small observation helicopter from the 123rd Aviation Battalion, had arrived at the area around 9 A.M. and immediately reported what appeared to be a Viet Cong soldier armed with a weapon and heading south. Although his mission was simply reconnaissance, Thompson directed his men to fire at and attempt to kill the Viet Cong as he wheeled the helicopter after him. They missed. Thompson flew back to My Lai 4, and it was then, as he told the Army Inspector General's office in June, 1969, that he began seeing wounded and dead Vietnamese civilians all over the hamlet, with no sign of an enemy force.

The pilot thought that the best thing he could do would be to mark the location of wounded civilians with smoke so that the GIs on the ground could move over and begin treating some of them. "The first one that I marked was a girl that was wounded," Thompson testified, "and they came over and walked up to her, put their weapon on automatic and let her have it." The man who did the shooting was a captain, Thompson said. Later he identified the officer as Ernest Medina.

Flying with Thompson that day was Lawrence M. Colburn, of Mount Vernon, Washington, who remembered that the girl was about twenty years old and was lying on the edge of a dyke outside the hamlet with part of her body in a rice paddy. "She had been wounded in the stomach, I think, or the chest," Colburn told the Inspector General (IG). "This captain was coming down the dyke and he had men behind him. They were sweeping through and we were hovering a matter of feet away from them. I could see this clearly, and he emptied a clip into her."

Medina and his men immediately began moving south toward the Viet Cong sighted by Thompson. En route they saw the young girl in the rice paddy who had been marked by the smoke. Bernhardt had a ground view of what happened next: "He [Medina] was just going alone . . . he shot the woman. She seemed to be busy picking rice, but rice was out of season. What she really was doing was trying to pretend that she was picking rice. She was a hundred meters away with a basket . . . if she had a hand grenade, she would have to have a better arm than me to get us . . . Medina lifted the rifle to his shoulder, looked down the barrel and pulled the trigger. I saw the woman drop. He just took a potshot . . . he wasn't a bad shot. Then he walked up. He got up real close, about three or six feet, and shot at her a couple times and finished her off. She was a real clean corpse . . . she wasn't all over the place, and I could see her clothing move when the bullets hit . . . I could see her twitch, but I couldn't see any holes . . . he didn't shoot her in the head." A second later, Bernhardt remembered, the captain "gave me a look, a dumb shit-eating grin."

By now it was past 9:30 A.M. and the men of Charlie Company had been at work for more than two hours. A few of them flung off their helmets, stripped off their heavy gear, flopped down and took a smoke break.

THE DAY—PART II

Hugh Thompson's nightmare had only begun with the shooting of the girl. He flew north back over the hamlet and saw a small boy bleeding along a trench. Again he marked the spot so that the GIs below could provide some medical aid. Instead, he saw a lieutenant casually walk up and empty a clip into the child. He saw yet another wounded youngster; again he marked it, and this time it was a sergeant who came up and fired his M16 at the child.

Larry Colburn, who was just eighteen years old at the time, noticed that "the infantrymen were killing everything in the village. The people didn't really know what was happening. Some of them began walking out of there and the GIs just started going up to them and shooting them all in the back of the head." He added, "We saw this one woman hiding there. She was alive and squatting; she looked up when we flew over. We dropped a smoke marker. When we came back she was in the same position—only she was dead. The back of her head was blown off. It had to be point-blank."

Thompson was furious. He tried unsuccessfully to radio the troops on the ground to find out what was going on. He then reported the wild firings and unnecessary shootings to brigade headquarters. All the command helicopters flying overhead had multi-channel radios and could monitor most conversations. Lieutenant Colonel Barker apparently intercepted the message and called down to Medina at the CP just south of the plaza. John Kinch of the mortar platoon heard Medina answer that he "had a body count of 310." The captain added, "I don't know what they're doing. The first platoon's in the lead. I am trying to stop it." A moment later, Kinch said, Medina called Calley and ordered, "That's enough for today."

Harry Stanley was standing a few feet away from Calley near some huts at the drainage ditch when the call came from Medina. He had a different recollection: "Medina called Calley and said, 'What the fuck is going on?' Calley said he got some VC, or some people that needed to be checked out." At this point Medina cautioned Calley to tell his men to save their ammunition because the operation still had a few more days to run.

It is not clear how soon or to whom Medina's order was given, but Stanley told the C.I.D. what Calley did next: "There was an old lady in a bed and I believe there was a priest in white praying over her . . . Calley told me to ask about the VC and NVA and where the weapons were. The priest denied being a VC or NVA." Charles Sledge watched with horror as Calley pulled the old man outside: "He said a few more words to the monk. It looked like the monk was pleading for his life. Lieutenant Calley then took his rifle and pushed the monk into a rice paddy and shot him point-blank."

Calley then turned his attention back to the crowd of Vietnamese and issued an order: "Push all those people in the ditch." Three or four GIs complied. Calley struck a woman with a rifle as he pushed her down. Stanley remembered that some of the civilians "kept trying to get out. Some made it to the top . . ." Calley began the shooting and ordered Meadlo to join in. Meadlo told about it later: "So we pushed our seven to eight people in with the big bunch of them. And so I began shooting them all. So did Mitchell, Calley . . . I guess I shot maybe twenty-five or twenty people in the ditch . . . men, women and children. And babies." Some of the GIs switched from automatic fire to single-shot to conserve ammunition. Herbert Carter watched the mothers "grabbing their kids and the kids grabbing their mothers. I didn't know what to do."

Calley then turned again to Meadlo and said, "Meadlo, we've got another job to do." Meadlo didn't want any more jobs. He began to argue with Calley. Sledge watched Meadlo once more start to sob. Calley turned next to Robert Maples and said, "Maples, load your machine gun and shoot these people." Maples replied, as he told the C.I.D., "I'm not going to do that." He remembered that "the people firing into the ditch kept reloading magazines into their rifles and kept firing into the ditch and then killed or at least shot everyone in the ditch." William C. Lloyd of Tampa, Florida, told the C.I.D. that some grenades were also thrown into the ditch. Dennis Conti noticed that "a lot of women had thrown themselves on top of the children to protect them, and the children were alive at first. Then the children who were old enough to walk got up and Calley began to shoot the children."

One further incident stood out in many GIs' minds: seconds after the shooting stopped, a bloodied but unhurt two-year-old boy miraculously crawled out of the ditch, crying. He began running toward the hamlet. Someone hollered, "There's a kid." There was a long pause. Then Calley ran back, grabbed the child, threw him back in the ditch and shot him.

Moments later Thompson, still in his helicopter, flew by. He told the IG what happened next: "I kept flying around and across a ditch . . . and it . . . had a bunch of bodies in it and I don't know how they got in the ditch. But I saw some of them were still alive." Captain Brian W. Livingston was piloting a large helicopter gunship a few hundred feet above. He had been monitoring Thompson's agonized complaints and went down to take a look for himself. He told a military hearing: "There were bodies lying in the trenches . . . I remember that we remarked at the time about the old Biblical story of Jesus turning water into wine. The trench had a grey color to it, with the red blood of the individuals lying in it."

By now Thompson was almost frantic. He landed his small helicopter near the ditch, and asked a soldier there if he could help the people out: "He said the only way he could help them was to help them out of their misery." Thompson took off again and noticed a group of mostly women and children huddled together in a bunker near the drainage ditch. He landed a second time. "I don't know," he explained, "maybe it was just my belief, but I hadn't been shot at the whole time I had been there and the gunships following hadn't . . ." He then saw Calley and the first platoon, the same group that had shot the wounded civilians he had earlier marked with smoke. "I asked him if he could get the women and kids out of there before they tore it [the bunker] up, and he said the only way he could get them out was to use hand grenades. 'You just hold your men right here,' " the angry Thompson told the equally angry Calley, " 'and I will get the women and kids out.' "

Before climbing out of his aircraft, Thompson ordered Colburn and his crew chief to stay alert. "He told us that if any of the Americans opened up on the Vietnamese, we should open up on the Americans," Colburn said. Thompson walked back to the ship and called in two helicopter gunships to rescue the civilians. While waiting for them to land, Colburn said, "he stood between our troops and the bunker. He was shielding the people with his body. He just wanted to get those people out of there." Colburn wasn't sure whether he would have followed orders if the GIs had opened fire at the bunker: "I wasn't pointing my guns right at them, but more or less toward the ground. But I was looking their way." He remembered that most of the soldiers were gathered alongside a nearby dyke "just watching. Some were lying down; some of them were sitting up, and some were standing." The helicopters landed, with Thompson still standing between the GIs and the Vietnamese, and quickly rescued nine persons—two old men, two women and five children. One of the children later died en route to the hospital. Calley did nothing to stop Thompson, but later stormed up to Sledge, his radioman, and complained that the pilot "doesn't like the way I'm running the show, but I'm the boss."

Gregory Olsen, who had watched the encounter from his machine-gun position a few dozen meters away, said that "the next thing I knew Mitchell was just shooting into the ditch." At this point Grzesik and his fire team came strolling into the area; they had gone completely through the hamlet, had a break, and were now returning. It was about ten o'-clock. Grzesik saw bodies all over the northeastern quarter of My Lai 4. He glanced at the ditch. Suddenly Mitchell yelled, "Grzesik, come here." He walked over. Calley then ordered him to go to the ditch and "finish off the people." Grzesik had seen the helicopter carrying some wounded Vietnamese take off from the area a moment earlier; much later he concluded that Calley—furious with Thompson's intervention—wanted to make sure there were no more survivors in the ditch. Calley told Grzesik to gather his team to do the job. "I really believe he expected me to do it," Grzesik said later, with some amazement. Calley asked him again, and Grzesik again refused. The lieutenant then angrily ordered him to take his team and help burn the hootches. Grzesik headed for the hamlet plaza.

Thompson continued to fly over the ditch and noticed that some of the children's bodies had no heads. He landed a third time after his crew chief told him that he had seen some movement in the mass of bodies and blood below. The crew chief and Colburn began walking toward the ditch. "Nobody said anything," Colburn said. "We just got out." They found a young child still alive. No GIs were in the immediate area, but Colburn was carrying a rifle. The crew chief climbed into the ditch. "He was knee-deep in people and blood," Colburn recalled. The child was quiet, buried under many bodies. "He was still holding onto his mother. But she was dead." The boy, clinging desperately, was pried loose. He still did not cry. Thompson later told the IG, "I don't think this child was even wounded at all, just down there among all the other bodies, and he was terrified." Thompson and his men flew the baby to safety.

In other parts of My Lai 4, GIs were taking a break, or loafing. Others were systematically burning those remaining houses and huts and destroying food. Some villagers—still alive—were able to leave their hiding places and walk away. Charles West recalled that one member of his squad who simply wasn't able to slaughter a group of children asked for and received permission from an officer to let them go.

West's third platoon went ahead, nonetheless, with the killing. They gathered a group of about ten women and children, who huddled together in fear a few feet from the plaza, where dozens of villagers already had been slain. West and the squad had finished their mission in the north and west of the hamlet, and were looking for new targets. They drifted south toward the CP. Jay Roberts and Ron Haeberle, who had spent the past hour watching the slaughter in other parts of the hamlet, stood by—pencil and cameras at the ready. A few men now singled out a slender Vietnamese girl of about fifteen. They tore her from the group and started to pull at her blouse. They attempted to fondle her breasts. The old women and children were screaming and crying. One GI yelled, "Let's see what she's made of." Another said, "VC Boom, Boom," meaning she was a Viet Cong whore. Jay Roberts thought that the girl was good-looking. An old lady began fighting with fanatical fury, trying to protect the girl. Roberts said, "She was fighting off two or three guys at once. She was fantastic. Usually they're pretty passive . . . They hadn't even gotten that chick's blouse off when Haeberle came along." One of the GIs finally smacked the old woman with his rifle butt; another booted her in the rear.

Grzesik and his fire team watched the fight develop as they walked down from the ditch to the hamlet center. Grzesik was surprised: "I thought the village was cleared . . . I didn't know there were that many people left." He knew trouble was brewing, and his main thought was to keep his team out of it. He helped break up the fight. Some of the children were desperately hanging onto the old lady as she struggled. Grzesik was worried about the cameraman. He may have yelled, "Hey, there's a photographer." He remembered thinking, "Here's a guy standing there with a camera that you've never seen before." Then somebody said, "What do we do with them?" The answer was, "Waste them." Suddenly there was a burst of automatic fire from many guns. Only a small child survived. Somebody then carefully shot him, too. A photograph of the woman and child, with the young Vietnamese girl tucking in her blouse, was later published in *Life* magazine. Roberts tried to explain later: "It's just that they didn't know what they were supposed to do; killing them seemed like a good idea, so they did it. The old lady who fought so hard was probably a VC." He thought a moment and added, "Maybe it was just her daughter."

West was annoyed at the photographer: "I thought it was wrong for him to stand up and take pictures of this thing. Even though we had to do it, I thought, we didn't have to take pictures of it." Later he complained personally to Haeberle about it.

By now it was nearly 10:30 A.M. and most of the company began drifting aimlessly toward the plaza and the command post a few yards to the south. Their work was largely over; a good part of the hamlet was in flames. The villagers "were laying around like ants," William Wyatt remembered. "It was just like somebody had poisoned the water and everybody took a drink and started falling out."

Herb Carter and Harry Stanley had shed their gear and were taking a short break at the CP. Near them was a young Vietnamese boy, crying, with a bullet wound in his stomach. Stanley watched one of Captain Medina's three radio operators walk along a trail toward them; he was without his radio gear. As Stanley told the C.I.D., the radio operator went up to Carter and said, "Let me see your pistol." Carter gave it to him. The radio operator "then stepped within two feet of the boy and shot him in the neck with a pistol. Blood gushed from the child's neck. He then tried to walk off, but he could only take two or three steps. Then he fell onto the ground. He lay there and took four or five deep breaths and then he stopped breathing." The radio operator turned to Stanley and said, "Did you see how I shot that son of a bitch?" Stanley told him, "I don't see how anyone could just kill a kid." Carter got his pistol back; he told Stanley, "I can't take this no more . . ." Moments later Stanley heard a gun go off and Carter yell. "I went to Carter and saw he had shot himself in the foot. I think Carter shot himself on purpose."

Other children were also last-minute targets. After the scene with the women and children, West noticed a small boy, about seven years old, staring dazedly beside a footpath. He had been shot in the leg. "He was just standing there staring; I don't think he was crying. Somebody asked, 'What do we do with him?' " At this point West had remembered there had been an order from Captain Medina to stop the shooting. "I just shrugged my shoulders," West recalled, "and said, 'I don't know,' and just kept walking." Seconds later he heard some shots, turned around and saw the boy no longer standing on the trail.

Haeberle and Roberts were walking together on the edge of the hamlet when they also noticed the wounded child with the vacant stare. In seconds, Roberts said, "Haeberle, envisioning the war-torn-wounded-waif picture of the year, got within five feet of the kid for a close-up. He was focusing when some guy, just walking along, leveled his rifle, fired three times and walked away." Haeberle saw the shooting through the lens of his camera. "He looked up in shock," Roberts added. "He just turned around and stared. I think that was the thing that stayed in our mind. It was so close, so real, we just saw some kid blown away."

By then a helicopter, called in by Medina, had landed near the command post to fly out the wounded Carter. Sergeant Duong Minh, the interpreter who had angered Medina with his questions about the dead civilians, was also put aboard.

One of Haeberle's photographs shows the company medic, Nicholas Capezza of Queens, New York, bandaging Carter, with Medina and a radio operator, Rodger Murray of Waukegan, Illinois, in the background near a partially destroyed red-brick house. Medina was on the radio. William Wyatt remembered the scene; that was the first time he'd seen Medina that morning. Roy Wood also saw him then for the first time. Others recalled, however, that the captain had left his CP south of the plaza many times during the late morning to tour the northern and western sections, urging the men to stop the shooting and get on with the job of burning down the buildings. Some GIs from the second platoon, under Lieutenant Brooks, found three men still alive. Gary Crossley heard the GIs ask Brooks, "What do we do now?" The lieutenant relayed the question by radio to Medina. "Don't kill them," the captain said. "There's been too much of that already." Gary Garfolo remembered that Medina seemed frantic at times, literally dashing about the hamlet. "He was telling everybody, 'Let's start getting out—let's move out of here.' "

Roberts also thought that Medina "was all over." He and Haeberle had crossed from the south to the north side of the hamlet to look around, and saw the captain there. "Then Carter shot himself and Medina went back," Roberts said. At some point earlier in the morning, Roberts had watched some GIs interrogate an old man. He didn't know anything, and somebody asked the captain what to do with him. Medina "indicated he didn't care," Roberts said, "that the guy wasn't of any use to him, and walked away." The GIs shot the man. Sergeant Mitchell may have witnessed the same scene. He saw both Calley and Medina interrogating an old man; Mitchell thought he was a monk. "Four or five of us weren't far away. We were watching. The old monk mumbled something and Medina walked off. I looked away for a second, and when I looked back the old man had been shot and Calley was standing over him."

Richard Pendleton remembered Medina himself shooting a civilian that day. Pendleton was standing about fifty feet away from the captain sometime that morning—Pendleton isn't sure exactly when. Pendleton hadn't seen the captain earlier and he wondered what Medina thought about what was going on. "Medina was standing there with the rest of the CP. It was right there in the open. I was watching." There was a small Vietnamese child, "the only one alive among a lot of dead people." He said he watched Medina carefully aim his M16 rifle at the child. "He shot him in the head, and he went down."

Pendleton may have been mistaken. There was a child shot near the command post that day, after Carter shot himself. Charles Gruver of Tulsa, Oklahoma, remembered vividly how it happened: he saw a small boy, about three or four years old, standing by a trail with a wound in his arm. "He just stood there with big eyes staring like he didn't believe what was happening. Then the captain's RTO [radio operator] put a burst of 16 [M16 rifle fire] into him." Ronald Grzesik also saw it. He was just watching the child when he heard a rifle shot; he looked back and saw that the radio operator was still in braced firing position. But Medina, Grzesik recalled, "was around the corner" in the command post at the time. Roberts also witnessed the shooting; he thought the toddler was searching through the pile of dead bodies for his mother or father, or a sister. He was wearing only a shirt. The impact of the M16 flung the small body backward onto the pile.

After that incident Grzesik said he went up to John Paul, one of Medina's radiomen, and told him what had been going on inside My Lai 5. Paul promptly asked him to tell the captain. Grzesik declined, thinking that Medina "was going to find out anyway if he walked up a few feet."

There were some small acts of mercy. A GI placed a blanket over the body of a mutilated child. An elderly woman was spared when some GIs hollered at a soldier just as he was about to shoot her. Grzesik remembered watching a GI seem to wrestle with his conscience while holding a bayonet over a wounded old man. "He wants to stab somebody with a bayonet," Grzesik thought. The GI hesitated . . . and finally passed on, leaving the old man to die.

Some GIs, however, didn't hesitate to use their bayonets. Nineteen-year-old Nguyen Thi Ngoc Tuyet watched a baby trying to open her slain mother's blouse to nurse. A soldier shot the infant while it was struggling with the blouse, and then slashed at it with his bayonet. Tuyet also said she saw another baby hacked to death by GIs wielding their bayonets.

Le Tong, a twenty-eight-year-old rice farmer, reported seeing one woman raped after GIs killed her children. Nguyen Khoa, a thirty-seven-year-old peasant, told of a thirteen-year-old girl who was raped before being killed. GIs then attacked Khoa's wife, tearing off her clothes. Before they could rape her, however, Khoa said, their six-year-old son, riddled with bullets, fell and saturated her with blood. The GIs left her alone.

There were "degrees" of murder that day. Some were conducted out of sympathy. Michael Terry, the Mormon who was a squad leader in the third platoon, had ordered his men to take their lunch break by the bloody ditch in the rear of the hamlet. He noticed that there were no men in the ditch, only women and children. He had watched Calley and the others shoot into that ditch. Calley seemed just like a kid, Terry thought. He also remembered thinking it was "just like a Nazi-type thing." When one soldier couldn't fire any more and threw down his weapon, "Calley picked it up." Later, during lunch, Terry and his men saw that some of the victims were still breathing. "They were pretty badly shot up. They weren't going to get any medical help, and so we shot them. Shot maybe five of them."

James Bergthold saw an old man who had been shot in both legs: "He was going to die anyway, so I figured I might as well kill him." He took his .45-caliber pistol (as a machine-gun ammunition carrier, he was entitled to one), carefully placed the barrel against the upper part of the old man's forehead and blew off the top of his head. Carter had watched the scene and remembered thinking that Bergthold had done the old man a favor. "If me and you were together and you got wounded bad," Carter later told an interviewer, "and I couldn't get you to a doctor, I'd shoot you, too."

Most of the shooting was over by the time Medina called a break for lunch, shortly after eleven o'clock. By then Roberts and Haeberle had grabbed a helicopter and cleared out of the area, their story for the day far bigger than they wanted. Calley, Mitchell, Sledge, Grzesik and a few others went back to the command post west of My Lai 4 to take lunch with Captain Medina and the rest of his headquarter's crew. Grzesik recalled that at that point he'd thought there couldn't be a survivor left in the hamlet. But two little girls showed up, about ten and eleven years old. John Paul said they came in from one of the paddies, where they apparently had waited out the siege. "We sat them down with us [at the command post]," Paul recounted, "and gave them some cookies and crackers to eat." When a C.I.D. interrogator later asked Charles Sledge how many civilians he thought had survived, he answered, "Only two small children who had lunch with us."

In the early afternoon the men of Charlie Company mopped up to make sure all the houses and goods in My Lai 4 were destroyed. Medina ordered the underground tunnels in the hamlet blown up; most of them already had been blocked. Within another hour My Lai 4 was no more: its red-brick buildings demolished by explosives, its huts burned to the ground, its people dead or dying.

Michael Bernhardt later summarized the day: "We met no resistance and I only saw three captured weapons. We had no casualties. It was just like any other Vietnamese village—old papa-sans, women and kids. As a matter of fact, I don't remember seeing one military-age male in the entire place, dead or alive. The only prisoner I saw was in his fifties."

The platoons pulled out shortly after noon, rendezvousing in the rice paddies east of My Lai 4. Lieutenant Brooks' platoon had about eighty-five villagers in tow; it kept those of military age with them and told the rest to begin moving south. Following orders, Medina then marched the GIs northeast through the nearly deserted hamlets of My Lai 5 and My Lai 6, ransacking and burning as they went. In one of the hamlets, Medina ordered the residents gathered, and then told Sergeant Phu, the regular company interpreter, to tell them, as Phu later recalled, that "they were to go away or something will happen to them—just like what happened at My Lai 4."

By nightfall the Viet Cong were back in My Lai 4, helping the survivors bury the dead. It took five days. Most of the funeral speeches were made by the Communist guerrillas. Nguyen Bat was not a Communist at the time of the massacre, but the incident changed his mind. "After the shooting," he said, "all the villagers became Communists."

When Army investigators reached the barren area in November, 1969, in connection with the My Lai probe in the United States, they found mass graves at three sites, as well as a ditch full of bodies. It was estimated that between 450 and 500 people—most of them women, children and old men—had been slain and buried there.

* * *

On December 1, one week after Paul Meadlo's startling television confession, the *Wall Street Journal* published an informal poll on My Lai 4 that its reporters had taken in cities across the nation. The results were interesting. Many of those interviewed refused to believe that the mass killings had taken place; others wondered why the incident was attracting so much attention.

"It was good," exclaimed a fifty-five-year-old elevator starter in Boston. "What do they give soldiers bullets for—to put in their pockets?" In Cleveland a woman defended the shooting of children: "It sounds terrible to say we ought to kill kids, but many of our boys being killed over there are just kids, too." A Los Angeles salesman said, "I don't believe it actually happened. The story was planted by Viet Cong sympathizers and people inside this country who are trying to get us out of Vietnam sooner." A teletype inspector in Philadelphia also said he didn't think it happened: "I can't believe our boys' hearts are that rotten." Not all of the 200 persons interviewed had such extreme attitudes, but only a handful said that what happened at My Lai 4 had changed their minds on the war.

Much of America's anger at the disclosures was directed toward the newspapers and television stations publicizing them. The *Cleveland Plain Dealer*, on the morning it published Ron Haeberle's shocking photographs of My Lai 4, received more than 250 telephone calls. About 85 percent of them said that the photographs should not have been published. "Your paper is rotten and anti-American," one woman said. Another asked, "How can I explain these pictures to my children?"

When one of the photographs, depicting about twenty slain women and children in a ditch, was later published on the front page of the *Washington Star,* that paper received calls complaining that the photograph was obscene. The callers were alluding to the fact that some of the dead victims were unclothed. After his interview with Meadlo, CBS correspondent Mike Wallace received 110 telephone calls, all but two of them abusive. One viewer fired off a telegram saying: "Wallace is pimping for the protesters." A *New York Times* survey of some GIs serving in the Quang Ngai area near My Lai 4 found wholesale resistance to the idea that Charlie Company had massacred some civilians. "There's gotta be something missing," one GI complained. Another said, "The company must have been hit hard before the action."

In early December, American Legion members in Columbus, Georgia, home of Fort Benning, took a four-column newspaper advertisement in the local newspaper proclaiming support for Calley and Captain Medina. The advertisement accused newspapers and television of trying to "tear down America and its armed forces." A week later a group of former servicemen in Atlanta, Georgia, began a petition movement to get the Army to drop its charges against Calley. During a rally on December 14, James A. Smith, chief spokesman for the group, said that "no American would ever kill 109 people like that" and suggested that the Haeberle photographs were fake. About fifty to seventy-five persons attended the rally, far less than the two hundred expected, but Smith said his group had collected 3,000 signatures on the petition. A few days later Calley personally opened a bank account with the Fourth National Bank of Columbus to handle contributions to his defense. Within a month the bank received several hundred letters, and more than $1,200 was on deposit. Calley had by then reached the status of a celebrity in Columbus. Most of the citizens openly supported him; some used-car salesmen even put his name in lights in front of their lots, urging contributions to the Calley Defense Fund.

A statewide poll published shortly before Christmas by the *Minneapolis Tribune* showed that 49 percent of 600 persons interviewed there believed that the reports of mass murder at My Lai 4 were false. To another query, 43 percent said they were horrified when they first heard the story and decided that it wasn't true. A later *Time* magazine poll of 1,600 households indicated that 65 percent of the American public believed such incidents were bound to happen in any war; and an even greater percent of the public, asked about news media coverage, complained that the press and TV should not have reported statements by GIs prior to a court-martial. The Pentagon even produced a poll. Deputy Secretary of Defense David Packard showed a group of newsmen a public-opinion study which he said had been conducted in the upper half of South Vietnam, an area that includes Quang Ngai Province. It showed, Packard said, that "only 2.8 percent of the people disapprove of the behavior of American troops in their country."

By mid-January six American Legion posts in Jacksonville, Florida, announced plans to raise a $200,000 defense fund for Calley. The lieutenant was granted permission to leave Fort Benning and fly to Jacksonville for a fund-raising party. He was greeted like a hero. A few fellow passengers recognized him, tapped him on the shoulder as they climbed off the airliner and said, "Good luck, son." A newspaper poll of the citizens in Duval County (Jacksonville) showed that more than 71 percent thought the Army should drop its charges against Calley. Robert C. Lenten, commander of one of the local Legion posts, told newsmen, "We are not saying he is guilty or not guilty. We feel Lieutenant Calley has been condemned and vilified for performance of his duties in combat without benefit of the opportunity to defend himself." In February former Governor George Wallace of Alabama endorsed Calley publicly. They met for more than one hour in Montgomery, Alabama, on February 20, and then came out together to face a battery of reporters. Wallace said he was "proud" to meet Calley and added, "I'm sorry to see the man tried. They ought to spend the time trying folks who are trying to destroy this country instead of trying those who are serving their country." The 1968 Presidential aspirant said, "I've been shot at myself and there's nothing like it." Calley said little.

At Fort Benning, many of Calley's fellow officers were outraged by the murder charges. "They're using this as a goddamned example," one officer said. "He's a good soldier. He followed orders." Another said, "It could happen to any of us. He's killed and seen a lot of killing . . . killing becomes nothing in Vietnam. He knew that there were civilians there, but he also knew that there were VC among them." A third officer, a West Point graduate, added, "There's this question—I think anyone who goes to Nam asks it. What's a civilian? Someone who works for us at day and puts on Viet Cong pajamas at night?"

One veteran of Vietnam told his local newspaper, in the aftermath of the My Lai 4 controversy, how he had witnessed Viet Cong prisoners' being thrown out of helicopters during interrogation by U.S. GIs. He was quickly subjected to a barrage of abusive telephone calls. "You ought to take a helicopter ride with me," one man said. "I know just exactly what to do with guys like you. You should be the one taken up and dropped out." Another caller said, "Someone should burn your house down, and maybe they just will."

Protests were voiced also by the Hawks in Congress. Senator Allen Ellender, Louisiana Democrat, told a television interviewer that the Vietnamese who had been slain "got just what they deserved." Senator

Ernest Hollings, South Carolina Democrat, publicly wondered if all soldiers who made "a mistake in judgment" were going to be tried "as common criminals, as murderers."

Senator Peter H. Dominick, Colorado Republican, led a number of legislators in attacks on the reporters who disseminated the news about My Lai 4, repeatedly accusing the news media of sensationalism and trial by press. In doing so, he singled out the interview with Meadlo and the publication in _Life_ magazine of Haeberle's photographs. "They go too far," Dominick told the Senate on December 2, "when interviews of potential witnesses are carried on nationwide TV, when these interviews are republished in newspapers all across the country over and over, and when a nationwide magazine publishes photographs of a highly inflammatory, and, I might add, revolting nature . . ." He argued that the public's right to know was met in full by the Army's public release of the charges against Calley on September 6.

GLORIA EMERSON
?1929–

Emerson was a foreign correspondent for the New York Times _in Nigeria and Northern Ireland in 1968 and 1969, and from 1970 to 1972 she covered Vietnam. Her book_ Winners and Losers: Battles, Retreats, Gains, Losses and Ruins from the Vietnam War _was published in 1976 and won the George Polk Award for foreign reporting._

From WINNERS AND LOSERS: BATTLES, RETREATS, GAINS, LOSSES AND RUINS FROM THE VIETNAM WAR

Each year that it lasted Americans who took opposite sides on the war seemed to hate each other more than the Vietnamese who opposed us. The quarreling was fierce; sometimes it did not seem as if the war alone could be the reason for the hatred. I have a box of this bitterness: they are letters written to Seymour Hersh, who in 1969 was the first American journalist to write about the My Lai massacre and Lieutenant William Calley and Charlie Company. In 1970 he won a Pulitzer Prize and his book describing the massacre and the participants, *My Lai 4*, was published. He often appeared on national television. Some letters said he had written about the massacre of the Vietnamese because he was a Jew. Condemnations were often written by other Jews, who thought he would make trouble for all of them. Mr. Hersh read each of the letters once and did not answer any of them.

A woman named Rosenfeld wrote she had seen Mr. Hersh on NBC. "You Jewish boys are well known for making a buck on our poor fighting boys," she said. Another woman in Beverly Hills, California, asked: "How can you live with yourself when you are a Judas to our Army and country. Your face shows it! I'll bet you and your family never went to war." From New Orleans still another woman wrote: "How much did Hanoi pay you?"

One letter said: "You are a lousy stinking anti-American and should be kicked out of the U.S. You went on an ego trip on the My Lai affair, just to get your name in the papers. All lousy jews are alike. Give them protection and let them come into the Country, and immediately they start an underground revolution. Heads of every country know this and Hitler was wise to the Jews. Too bad he didn't get rid of them all—what a lovely planet this would be without them."

A retired captain in the Air Force wrote that his son had served with the Americal—the division of Lieutenant William Calley and of Charlie Company—in Chu Lai. His son only saw Jews at desk jobs. The father said: "One cheerful possibility remains however, that if and when we are attacked and overwhelmed by the Reds, the potion to be meted out to you so-called Jewish intelligentsia could well be another holocaust even as your widely-shouted six millions in Germany."

A letter from a doctor and his wife in Albuquerque, New Mexico, said that they "never for a minute doubted My Lai . . . We are sure there have been tens of thousands of similar 'atrocities' committed by our GIs and other fighting men in the history of this great Nation. A soldier is a murderer only when he kills his own allies, not in the line of duty." It was their feeling that President Nixon should award Lieutenant Calley the Medal of Honor and a presidential pardon. As for the protests over the bombing of North Vietnam, the couple wrote that in World War II the bombing of little German villages like Hildesheim ultimately "broke the spirit of the German people and won the war."

The most desperate letter came from Mrs. Anthony Meadlo from New Goshen, Indiana. Her son had been in Charlie Company when they went through My Lai and left hundreds of dead civilians. She said her son "looked just like he had been whipped" when he came home missing his right foot. Paul Meadlo told everything, first to Seymour

Hersh, and then, in a long interview on the air, to Mike Wallace of CBS. His mother wrote: "I only hope and pray that there will be a day coming that you will suffer for what you have done to us . . . You are so rotten you surely don't have a mother or heart . . . so now you got him in all this trouble, now see if you can get him out of it. Your no good your filthy low down. I only hope I meet you again someday."

*   *   *

When American troops first arrived in Vietnam most of them were sent to the 90th Replacement Battalion at Bien Hoa, twenty-two miles northeast of Saigon, for what the Army called "in-country processing." One of the first things they were ordered to do was to write their parents immediately saying they had arrived safely in Vietnam. Later, when they were no longer new troops, soldiers wrote home to their mothers to send them all sorts of things: garlic salt, machetes, wire cutters, wading boots, tennis socks, pickles and certain knives. Many of the mothers sent cookies; I saw a lot of chocolate chip cookies. In the rear, on the big bases, the PXs seemed bloated; at Cam Ranh Bay soldiers could buy Koolfoam pillows, Shag Time bath mats, brightly colored oversized beach towels, Chun King chow mein and garlic sausage. Vietnam was never the same place for the two million, six hundred thousand men who were sent to Vietnam.

There were always soldiers who found it hard to write home; it required too much concentration, it was too hard to explain what was happening or not happening, they did not know how to say it. In the field the soldiers wrote the names of their girl friends and their wives on their helmet liners or on the soft jungle hats—they were Phyllis, Monica, Susie, Wendy, Linda, Maryanne. They wrote too on the camouflage covers of their helmets: F.T.A. meant Fuck the Army. Peace, Peace, Peace, said the helmet covers, Love, Love, Love. It was sometimes a gaudy army: the soldiers wore love beads and peace symbols, crosses and bracelets woven out of black bootlaces, folded scarves or woven headbands around their foreheads, tinted sunglasses.

It was a defiant yet dispirited army. They were against the war, not because of political perceptions, but because it took away too much, it put them in danger, and they hated the nagging, the bullying, the hassling of the military. Everywhere we waved to each other by giving the peace symbol, the V, which meant getting out. The infantrymen—the II Bravos—liked to wear soft camouflaged hats; some hung the rings of grenades above the brim to show how many they had thrown. It was not permitted for the men to wear these hats when they went to a stand-down area or to the big bases. It meant they were out of uniform. It made them hate their superiors, who became the immediate, the visible enemy. On a C-130 from Cam Ranh to Saigon, just after Christmas, a Specialist 4 named James Blunt in the 23d Division, the Americal, kept talking about his boonie hat, as the infantrymen called it. Nothing he owned was so important. We were packed in as usual, shoulder to shoulder, knees almost touching in the long rows of web seats facing each other. Almost everyone except Blunt was going to sleep; there was no snoring, they all dozed quietly, like men who had been chloroformed.

"They're always trying to take it away from me but I won't let them," he said. Blunt was twenty-six and his platoon had called him the Old Man. The hat was discolored and smelled damp. "One lifer at Long Binh said to me that I couldn't wear it on the base and I told him I'd kill him on the spot if he tried to make me. He looked kind of startled. They won't let me wear it lots of places but I don't give a fuck. I do my job—I won't let anyone else walk point, only me, that's the way it is. This here"—the little hat was lifted up for me to see again—"is a kind of memento. There's my wife's name. She's my second wife. It's Donna, see. Well, when I wear it walking point, she's kind of leading me, see."

When Blunt the Old Man was wounded the platoon got the hat to him in the hospital.

In Saigon, I sent a telegram to the United States for a Lieutenant Alsup from Asheboro, North Carolina, whose wife had just given birth to a daughter whose name he did not know. The lieutenant was worried; his tour in Vietnam was almost over but he felt he should stay longer to be with his platoon to keep them alive. If the platoon got a new officer, a fool, or one who wanted medals, the men might be pushed hard to find the enemy and engage them. The lieutenant did not want any of his men put in greater risk. No one used the words "die" and "death." A man was hit, not wounded. If he was killed, they said wasted or blown away. He bought it, or he bought the farm. He was greased or lit-up. Death was the Max. Each year the language of the soldiers changed a little as the new bunch came in.

Even now, so many years later, I still have the scrap of paper the lieutenant wrote his message on. It says: "Michelle, I am thrilled about the baby stop I live day to day thinking of you stop I cannot bear to even peek two days ahead for there are so many left but not as many as before stop I love you Bill." But that day he could not make up his mind: to stay with the platoon or to go home to his wife.

The soldiers had a year in Vietnam, sometimes a little less. Over and over they counted each day gone and all the days left to get through. They counted all the time and told you fifty days were left, ten days, three days. The Army counted everything else, insisted that all things be counted, until the numbers meant nothing—but still the counting kept on. Sometimes there were contests for the troops which were based on points to be won and points that could be taken away. One contest in the 25th Division in 1969, called "Best of the Pack," was for the best rifle and the best weapons platoon in the 1st Battalion, 27th Infantry, which was known as the Wolfhounds. One award was a two-day pass for best weapons in Dau Tieng; the other, for best rifles a three-day pass in Cu Chi. "The platoon will also have exclusive permission to wear a special marked camouflaged jungle hat when not on operations," the announcement said. "Points will be awarded for the following":

5	Per man per day above 25 on an operation
10	Each possible body count
10	Each 100 lbs. of rice
15	Each 100 lbs. of salt
20	Each mortar round
50	Each enemy individual weapon captured
100	Each enemy crew served weapon captured
100	Each enemy Body Count
200	Each tactical radio captured
500	Each individual weapon captured
500	Perfect score on CMMI (inspection)
1,000	Each prisoner of war

Points will be deducted for the following:

50	Each U.S. WIA (wounded)
500	Each U.S. KIA (killed)

If a man was killed, his platoon was penalized and had less of a chance to win the pass.

Many men were desperate to get out of the field, but until they were sick or wounded there was nothing they could do except go crazy, but there was punishment for doing that. I knew some who drank bad water hoping to get a fever of unknown origin, others would not take their malaria pills. There were men who felt terrible, but it had nothing to do with their bodies. At Chu Lai, headquarters of the Americal, there was a mental hygiene clinic and a psychiatrist who saw men on the base and those who had been on the line. He had a tiny room: a table, two chairs, and another chair where I was allowed to sit in a corner. Each man had ten or fifteen minutes with the psychiatrist—a captain—who was young and had never seen combat. He had been drafted under the Berry Plan, which allowed him to finish his residency in psychiatry before induction. At any rate, the doctor let me sit in the room and take notes. The soldiers were asked if they minded this, but all they cared about was talking to him. Not one of them said they were ill from facing their own deaths, they only said how something was wrong. It did not take long to realize the doctor could only follow Army procedures, assure them that it was normal to be under stress, and let them be sent out again. Perhaps there was nothing he could do but give them ten or fifteen minutes, and some pills.

A platoon leader said he had been very dizzy and almost fainted during an attack and that an enlisted man had taken over. The doctor said that when you suffered from hyperventilation, it was good to do breathing exercises with your face inside a paper bag. The soldier looked hard at the doctor, turned his head to look at me, then we both looked at the doctor again.

He said: "Doc, we were taking fire."

"Yes, I understand, but how do you know this won't work unless you try it?" the doctor said. He told the platoon leader how to do the breathing—puff puff out, puff puff in—and that was that.

There was a very pale boy with blond hair that stuck up in back. He could not speak distinctly and for quite some time the three of us sat in the little room waiting for him to be able to begin. His trouble was that his best friend had been killed, but since then he had seen the best friend twice, standing close to him, smiling, looking as he had once looked. The doctor decided the boy should be put to bed for one day and one night and sedated so he could sleep.

"I want to call my parents," the boy said. He was not told yes or no. The psychiatrist said it was okay to let the boy go to bed for a while, but that was as far as the Army could let him regress. After that, the boy would have to go back on the line again.

JOHN KETWIG
1947–

Ketwig grew up in upstate New York, entered the army in 1966, and in 1967 was fighting in Vietnam. He recalled events there in his book And a Hard Rain Fell *(1985).*

From And a Hard Rain Fell

Life went on at home, and time dragged on in The Nam. I had arrived in early September. It was now mid-November. Over sixty days had passed, and my calendar showed fewer than three hundred Vietnamese sunrises remaining. Things were heating up, especially a hundred miles north near an outpost called Dak To. We had a small shop at Dak To. The surrounding hills were supposedly a staging area for North Vietnamese infiltrators coming off the Ho Chi Minh Trail; and Dak To was a base camp for the Fourth Infantry Division's search-and-destroy operations. In November of 1967, things went wrong for the Fourth Division. All around Dak To, Charley had sprung coordinated ambushes with surprising numbers of well-equipped troops. It became the largest battle of the war up to that point, and the tiny compound of Dak To came under siege. Mortars and rockets crashed in from the surrounding heights, disabling the airstrip. Before it was over, it would become impossible for a helicopter to land in the compound. Supplies had to be trucked in from Kontum and Pleiku.

One morning in late November, our first sergeant asked for volunteers to drive to Dak To. The cardinal rule of a soldier is, Don't ever volunteer, but I did. It was an impulse, not a considered decision; but I was relieved to have stepped forward. For two months I had been holding my breath as the war swirled around me. I knew it would inevitably swallow me. I couldn't be this close to such a mammoth event and expect it to avoid me; it had a kinetic energy that was crushing the life out of kids like myself throughout this Godforsaken land. Once, long ago, I had believed I might escape the draft, the army, and the war. Now, deep in my gut, I knew there would be no escape. In my comfortable youth, I had never been forced to face a situation of such awesome importance. The tension had grown unbearable. I had to know how I would act under fire; and the convoy offered the opportunity to find out. Today. In a few hours. The opportunity to end the agonizing waiting, and to face both Charley and myself, out on the road to Dak To, away from my friends. If I failed, I would not directly threaten the guys.

As I gathered my equipment, I was almost giddy. Archie was incredulous. I felt an exhilaration, a sense of adventure. I had a lot of confidence in my driving ability. In my mind, I was a Grand Prix racing driver at Watkins Glen, or Monza, or the Nurburgring. The Targa Florio. Mille Miglia. No speed limits, no radar traps. High-speed adventure on narrow overseas roads; sneering drivers defying death with scarves dancing merrily on the wind. Nuvolari. Ascari and Stirling Moss. I trembled with excitement. If I had to meet the Viet Cong, let it be at the steering wheel.

The great confrontation would come at the wheel of a dented deuce-

and-a-half, or two-and-a-half-ton stake-body truck. It looked tired, sagging beneath too many wooden cases of high explosive. In my mind's eye the faded olive-drab paint resembled British racing green, a color I had come to love as I had overlooked the pit straight at Watkins Glen. The interior was cramped and uncomfortable, like a Formula I Cooper or Porsche. A layer of sandbags on the floor was protection against shrapnel from mines, but I saw the interior of Surtees' Ferrari. I had seen Jimmy Clark, Graham Hill, Richie Ginther, Von Tripps, Bandini, and Gendebein before a race. Cool. Calculating. Contemplative. I stayed to myself until my shotgun introduced himself. He had been volunteered and was too short for this crap—under a hundred days, and he didn't relish riding with some green recruit.

"Gentlemen, start your engines!" They probably used other words, but those were the words I heard. The diesel engine responded slowly; the throw of the shifter was far too long. I practiced "split-shifting," simultaneously shifting the four-speed and the high-low range levers, double clutching to keep the rpms up. Like a parade lap, the column crawled out of the compound for the start of the Grand Prix of Vietnam. Soon we were on the open road, churning and grinding, sliding and crawling over a rutted dirt trail that was Highway One, Vietnam's finest highway. Through the torrents of rain and inadequate wipers I strained my eyes to watch the truck ahead, a tractor-trailer flatbed of ammo. Damned governor; I needed power. Shotgun sucked bourbon and pronounced me "fuckin' crazy."

I was getting the hang of the ponderous truck, making it work, feeling it become one with me and I with it. We passed ragged Vietnamese with crude carts pulled by water buffalo, a column of nearly naked Montagnards with their strange cylindrical baskets, the broken hulk of a bus. We roared through Kontum and beyond, across a pontoon bridge, past a devastated American armored personnel carrier. The army acronym for these boxes on tracks was APC, but we called them PCs. This one had taken a B-40 rocket in the side and was settled dejectedly into the mud, its rear hatch hanging open.

We were on a straight stretch with heavy jungle on both sides threatening to engulf the road. The engine roared. Clumps of mud clattered against the undercarriage, and the canvas top clattered against the wind. Shotgun was telling me about ice fishing in Minnesota, when everything disappeared. There was a giant confusion up ahead, a curtain of mud, a blinding flash, a roar unlike anything I had ever heard. I couldn't see. I couldn't hear. I existed in a slow-motion world turned upside down. The great barrier grew, fire and mud and smoke and noise, and the earth heaved, and I thought I had been shot in the head and what I was experiencing was the final spasm of torn and shattered brain tissue. The wiper cut through the wash of mud, and I glimpsed a dark hole and went for it. We plunged in, and we came out, and I was out of control, and there was a giant dark green truck stopped dead in the road. Nothing to do, nowhere to go, a dead-end tunnel; then limbs and leaves pounding against the windshield, popping, scraping, tearing; and I can't see; and . . . we were stopped. I sat, deflated and baffled. Frozen. I became aware of a frantic activity and confusion. I became aware that I was alive. Like a surreal movie, a face appeared to my right; a distorted, anguished face, obviously screaming, but I couldn't hear what it was saying. Where was Shotgun? I didn't remember him leaving. I couldn't hear! My hands went to my head, to my ears, and I realized I was hearing the most enormous, crushing, howling, roaring noise of my life. Little noise among the great noise. Crackling. My eyes were okay, I could see the seat, the dash, Shotgun's door hanging open. Where had he gone?

I lay across the seat to look out the door, to see where Shotgun had gone. There was a guy, lying in the mud, with a stick or . . . and an abstract swarm of golden insects flew away from his head, and I concentrated on the crackling sound because it must be a clue; the stick was his rifle, and he was shooting, and the insects were shell casings, and the roar was a lot of explosive, and we were hit. I was alive, and everybody was down there, and I was up here, where the hell was Shotgun, and what should I do now? Where was my rifle? On the sandbags, muddy. Gotta get down with those guys, gotta shoot. Can't see anything but muddy splotches on dark green leaves, and vines, and grass. What the fuck is going on? I don't see anybody. The noise. God damn the noise. My head aches. Won't somebody please be quiet? I don't see anybody to shoot at. Big, dark, noisy shadows overhead, the roar again, the mud is shaking and none of this makes sense.

Suddenly, it was quiet. Bodies stirred around me. I rolled over, lay on my back looking up into the gray rain. My head hurt. I felt it, felt wet mud in my hair, and checked my hand. Mud, not blood. Back to my head. There! My ears! There was that roaring sound that wouldn't go away. That's how it had started. What was that? What had happened? A face leaned over, smiled, held out a hand. Pulled me to my feet, and my knees didn't want to hold me up, and the hand held out my rifle. It tugged at my arm, but I'd lost Shotgun, and I didn't know how, so I staggered off to look for him. I had to ask him what that noise was. I'd never heard a noise like that before. I stumbled past the dark form of a truck, and guys were gathered, looking at something, so I should probably look too. There was a crater, a huge bowl-shaped hole, right square in the middle of the road. Wider than the road, stretching the jungle walls back. Twisted, shredded, dark forms, probably metal, a set of wheels, a grotesque steel ladder. Fireworks, or gunpowder. I smelled gunpowder. What was going on? Why hadn't I seen that great big hole? How could I have missed it? What had happened? Must be a clue there somewhere. All those guys, all strangers, all so quiet. Were they keeping a secret from me? No. Most of them looked bewildered too.

Suddenly Shotgun was there, screaming, hugging me, slapping my back, raving at the top of his lungs. ". . . motherfucker had our name on it, and you fuckin' drove that fuckin' truck and we fuckin' made it, and . . . and. . . . Fuckin' A! Fuckin' Christ, man, you fuckin' did it, you fuckin'-A did it, man, and . . ." I grabbed him, begged him to tell me what had happened. I felt very tired, very confused, and I just wanted to get this all sorted out and get on with it, get home. I didn't like this convoy shit, didn't understand it. What happened? Why were we stopped? What was that noise?

Shotgun stopped jabbering and looked at me. I guess, because he had been in The Nam so long, he realized that I had no idea what had happened. He lit two wrinkled cigarettes, put one in my lips, and explained. The flatbed just ahead of us had hit a mine. The whole load of ammo went off. Somebody said we went through it on two wheels, just from the force of the concussion. Blew that big fuckin' hole in the road. Dented the jungle. The guys in the truck? They were looking for them, for something to send home.

My knees gave out, and I knelt in the road. All the air had rushed out of me, as if some giant had squeezed me. My rifle lay beside me, in the goo. I saw it, but I had no control of my arms to reach over and pick it up. I was numb; everything was numb except my head, and it hurt so bad. I felt the cigarette fall from my lips, saw it land on the stinking mud. I started to tremble, then I started to shake, then I started to cry and to shake, and I almost fell over. Somebody put a bottle to my lips, and the fiery liquid seemed to cut through some of it, but I couldn't control the shaking. There was another cigarette, and they forced me to my feet, but I didn't want to walk. I didn't want to go anywhere, or do anything. Just think. Figure this out. They were screaming at me, and it wasn't my fault. "Go on." I didn't want to go on. "Got to. Got to."

Somehow, I went on. Choppers beat the air overhead. The truck was banged up bad. Shotgun's side of the windshield was gone, mine was starred and cracked. The canvas top hung low. The hood and left fender were buckled back. There were leaves and twigs and mud everywhere. I moved mechanically, stumbling without emotion. My blood had been drained; I was empty inside. The road cleared, the engine fired, and we rolled. Sheets of rain ripped in through Shotgun's broken windshield. He offered the bourbon, and it helped. I was thinking about driving over the torn road. Thought was returning. I went on. I'll never know how, but I went on.

I drove through a dream world. My head hurt, and I kept replaying those few moments. They didn't make sense, wouldn't make sense. My actions were mechanical. I saw my hands but didn't feel them. Just follow the truck ahead. I was shaking real bad, didn't know if I could breathe. Confused. It was happening all around me, and it was more than my mind could accept. Follow the truck ahead. Choppers overhead. Shotgun's booze. Confusion, and the headache. Wrestling the wheel.

We arrived at Dak To late in the afternoon. The noise was enormous, and it escalated as we got close. Chaos. Mud. There had been tanks, and PCs, and choppers. I could see a lot of activity, and I was driving into it, picking up momentum, a sense of urgency. Adrenaline flowing. Frantic, chaotic action. Noise, confusion, the smell of powder. Artillery roared. Incoming mortars whomped into the mud. There were squat, dark tents sinking into the goo, and men. Stooped, disheveled, frantic men. On the perimeter, firing with unbelievable ferocity. There was an emotion, a need, an intensity that seemed to grip me, as if the world had gone off its axis, and to do anything out of the ordinary might explode it all. It wasn't ordinary, just all-consuming, and you had to be a part of it because it was so enormous, so awesome. The endless rain seemed to beat against the place, driving it, and everyone in it, deeper into the depressing goo. The valley was sliced into horizontal thirds by a layer of blue-gray smoke accumulating fifty feet above the mud, and a huge, dark green hill loomed above the smoke. This was Hill 875, the focus of today's attention.

A muddied and rumpled man, his rank or unit unintelligible, leaped onto Shotgun's running board and screamed orders. In the roar and commotion most of what he said was lost, but Shotgun leaned over to yell, "No more than ten cases to each gun. I'll be working in graves registration. For Chrissake, don't leave without me." He punched my arm, hollered, "Keep your head down," and clambered out of the truck. After my cargo was unloaded, I would be on my own until the convoy formed up for the return trip in the morning. A nearby mortar round erupted in a huge geyser of mud and thunder, and I kicked the truck into motion.

Frantic men, distorted by wet and mud and fear, waved me toward the perimeter. Figures seemed to loom up out of the sound and fury, then disappear as if consumed by it. The roar never quieted. It banged inside my head in waves, drowning out my thoughts, and I lost all sense of where I was or where I was going. It didn't matter; it all looked the same. I managed to coax the tired truck through the slime to a gun emplacement. As the gun roared, steam rose, and brown, half-naked men struggled to load another shell. I hesitated, not knowing what to do. Two of the men clambered up onto the truck and hefted the ammo down to their buddies. I pulled the lever out of gear and went back to help. "Only ten cases!" They ignored me, tossing the heavy wooden crates into the soft goo. There was no stopping them. These weren't men; one look at their eyes told me that. These were frightened animals desperate to survive. A slap to my helmet startled me. A face, distorted by clods of wet mud, shouted and pointed at a round erupting about a

hundred yards away. "Go! Go! Get out of here!" The clear white of the
eyes seemed incongruous against the dull brown mask. "They're walkin'
'em in on ya!" Another round, closer this time, threw swamp into the air.
It was closer, and it was on a direct line toward us. Charley was adjusting
his aim round by round, closer and closer to me. I had to get out of there.
Sweat and debris seemed to cloud my eyes. I couldn't really see where I
was headed, but I made the truck lurch forward. Behind me, I heard
bumping and swearing as the gunners dived off. God, the noise was
awful! There was so much noise, so much action, but it was a kind of
action I had never seen, confusing, and I wished Shotgun had been there
to offer advice. I saw another gun crew, figured they could use ammunition, and forced the truck toward them. It bogged, refused to move. I
pulled levers, screamed at it, and it ground forward again. I lost sight of
the gun when a sea of brown swill washed over the broken windshield.
The wipers cut through, and I bounced toward my goal. I ground the
tired truck to a halt and burst out the door in such a hurry I went facefirst
into the slime. I pulled myself up and clambered onto the truck, fighting
the weight the mud had added to my loose-fitting jungle fatigues. The
ammo cases were heavy, bulky, slippery. I managed to get a couple over
the side before the guys arrived. Mud-soaked forms rose to help, only
their eyes and teeth showing color against the brown. I'm not sure why,
but I heard myself shouting, "Only ten! Only ten cases!" again and
again. Then the truck was empty and the men were back at the gun.
Smack! A blow to the side of my head knocked me off my feet and out
into space. I hit the mud on my back, and something heavy landed on
top of me, threatened to smother me. I fought.

"Get down, asshole! Get down!" One of the guys had knocked me off
the back of the truck, lost his footing, and tumbled on top of me. He put
his face inches from mine and screamed. "You okay? You okay?" I said I
was. "You were standing straight up in the back of that truck." He
needed a shave and a bath.

I was ashamed of my stupidity. "I'm okay. I thought I was shot. Next
time, just ask, or give me a shove."

He was grinning. His teeth were stained, and the wet pink of his
mouth stood out in striking contrast to the muddy face. His eyes were
red, tired. "I'd send ya a letter," he grinned, "but the mail hasn't been
dependable lately! You liked to got yourself killed. Where ya from?"

"New York. Rochester, New York."

He motioned toward the frantic bedlam at the wire. "Hell of a show,
ain't it? Fuckin' Charley don't give up. Four fuckin' days this been goin'
on. Hell of a show!"

A personnel carrier slithered across the slime, tracks rattling. "Do us a
favor," my new friend shouted against the noise. It wasn't so much a
question as a statement of fact. "Get that truck outta here. Charley likes

to drop mortars on trucks. Stick it over near those hootches, nobody gonna be sleeping in a hootch. Just get it away from here, then come back." I didn't want to move. I didn't want to get back in that truck. Every time I got in that truck, all hell broke loose. "C'mon!" he hollered, slapped the side of my helmet again, but with less force. "C'mon, get outta here. You gonna bring a whole buncha shit down on us!" There was a crazy, desperate look in his eyes. I struggled to the running board, then turned.

"You didn't say where you're from?"

"Ohio! Near Cleveland! Now get your young ass outta here, New York, and c'mon back so we can show ya how to fuck Charley's head up!" I pushed the lever into low and heard the tires growl.

I wrestled the truck into the little community of tents and struggled toward Ohio. Time after time I tripped or slipped, fighting to lift my sodden legs over ruts and out of puddles. It seemed I was moving in slow motion. The noise, that eternal, indistinguishable roar, seemed to be a wall. I felt the weight of the canteen on my hip, the cartridge clips in canvas pouches pulling the web belt lower. The pant legs seemed glued to my legs, stiff and heavy. I saw my rifle in my right hand, its familiar shape distorted by clods of mud. I felt grit in my mouth, sweat stinging my eyes. I tripped again. God damn it! An incoming round crashed on my right, a dull *whumpoom* threw up a cone of brown spray. I struggled forward, trying to keep my head down and still lift my legs high. My glasses were covered with filth, and I couldn't make out much of the scenario ahead. It all seemed to be closing in, swallowing me. I felt my right foot slip out from under me, the slow diving toward the muck. I watched the water splash away as I hit. I struggled to get my footing. I was straining, hurting, beginning to panic. Was there no escape. "C'mon, New York! C'mon! You're almost here. C'mon!" I saw the muddy barrel chest rise, the outstretched hand, the white teeth. I fell into the hole, disoriented. He held out that hand, helped me to my feet.

I didn't want to see. I didn't want to know what was going on around me. I wanted to crouch in the mud and slop, sink away, get away from all this. The noise was crushing me, squeezing in on my chest and my head. The weight of my limbs made me wonder if I had been shot, if the life was flowing out of me. Everything hurt, I couldn't pick out a specific pain. There was a glimpse of white, a flash near my head. I ducked so violently I smacked my head. Ohio was tugging me again, laughing. "Clean your glasses." He held out the white rag. It was damp and gritty, but I absentmindedly rubbed at the lenses. Ohio stuck a cigarette in my lips. They were quivering so badly it fell into the mud. "C'mon, New York! The fuckin' PX is closed. Get your shit together." He laughed, but there was a note of hurt in his voice. He held out another smoke. I held it carefully, pulled hard at it. God, it was good. My hands were shaking. Ohio held out a bottle. I swallowed, and my eyes cleared as my throat burned. I choked a little, then swallowed again. I could feel the heat in my gut now. Ohio had pushed gobs of mud off my rifle, wiping it with the rag. He lifted it over the sandbags, pointed it away, and squeezed off a few rounds without looking to see where they were going. I tipped the bottle again, leaned back against the sandbags. I struggled to control the shaking, lost it, felt heat on my thighs and belly, smelled urine. The bottle again. "Hey, that shit's harder to come by than cigarettes," and Ohio reached for it. "C'mon, meet the guys." The cigarette was soggy, but I sucked at it once more before I threw it away. We met the guys; most had naked torsos stained to the color of the mud. Everyone's hair seemed blond and wet. Stubble sparkled on their chins. I wasn't enthusiastic. They assigned me a post on the sandbags, looking out and downhill across the wire and mud to a dark line of trees. The noise had died somewhat, and the rain slowed to a drizzle. The blue layer of smoke seemed a canopy, pressing down, making it seem we were overlooking the entrance to a huge tunnel. It was nearly dark, but I thought I saw a human form.

"Ohio!"

He was a few feet to my left. "Yeah?"

"Is that a body out there?"

"On the wire? Yeah, patrol got hit last night. Shit got heavy, and that kid tried to make it back. There's about six of 'em right on the edge of that tree line. Probably a few gooks, too."

"You mean that's a GI?" I felt a chill.

"Yeah." Silence.

"How many were there?"

"Gooks? Or the patrol?"

"The patrol? How many American guys are out there?"

"Twelve. Maybe fifteen. I dunno. Poor fuckers got fucked up bad!"

"Hey, Ohio!"

"Yeah?"

"Got another cigarette? Mine got kinda wet."

A voice came out of the darkness behind us. "They're bad for your health!"

The darkness came fast. The incredible noise had died away, grown more distant. Occasionally a flare would pop and swing down on its silken parachute. The golden glow emphasized shadows. As soon as the dark returned, they seemed to move. I tried to make my eyes avoid that dark form by the wire, but they wouldn't obey. Somewhere, up above the smoky gray ceiling, a distant battle raged. Someone offered a box of C rations. Ham and lima beans. Shit! I lifted the dog tag chain over my head and set about opening a can of pears with my P-38 folding can opener. It was cold and damp now, the drizzle was getting heavier. Someone brought me a cup of coffee, two packages of C-ration Lucky Strikes, and a poncho. I wrapped the plastic poncho around me and swallowed the hot coffee, wondering how long eight cigarettes might last. I shivered and lit one. My mind struggled to comprehend the enormous events of the day. The explosion on the road seemed long ago. The sounds of distant firing and chopper blades seemed to set a mood, like music for dinner. The chaos of this place was overwhelming. Thousands of guys like myself, torn away from home and family, crouched in the mud, wishing they weren't here. How could all this happen? I pulled at the cigarette and finished the coffee. I moved two steps to the right and peed. What difference would it make? I pulled the poncho closer.

"Ohio?"

"Yeah?"

"You drafted?"

He moved toward me, dug into a thigh pocket and offered the bottle again. "Nightcap?" I needed the warmth. "I enlisted. My wife's brother was wasted last year, down in the delta somewhere. I wasn't doing much and wanted to get even. At the time, it seemed like a decent thing to do. She's stayin' with her folks, and I thought I was doing the right thing. Shit!" He swallowed from the bottle. "I was in-country six days and saw half my company get it. Three weeks later they send us here. I got three hundred 'n' seventeen days to go in this motherfucker, and I oughtta write to my wife, but I don't know what to say. She thinks her brother was a big fuckin' hero, ya know, and I'm gonna tell her about this?"

Did he really want an answer? Before I decided what to say, a voice from the darkness got me off the hook.

"Ho!"

Ohio looked up. Someone was splashing toward us. One of the guys hollered back, and a form dropped into the trench. There was excited whispering, then he moved to Ohio and me. Ohio nodded a greeting. "Lieutenant."

"How ya doin'?"

"All right, sir. Cold, wet, and hungry. What's up?"

"PC's going out after the patrol." He whispered, but belched loudly. "They want to get them in before they swell up and burst. Got some more near the gate. It's beehives at point-blank, right?"

"Got it."

The lieutenant splashed on down the trench. I realized how quiet it had become. Ohio shrugged. "Back to work."

"What's going on? What's a beehive?"

Ohio grinned. "Shit, New York, your education's been sadly neglected. C'mon, I'll show ya." We crept through the darkness to the gun. Ohio turned around to face me, holding something my mind interpreted as a watermelon. My eyes had tricked me. It was an artillery shell, about four inches in diameter and eighteen inches long, to be fired from a 105-millimeter Howitzer. "This is a beehive. Inside there are a couple thousand little steel arrows, about an inch long. Each one as sharp as a tack, and has four little steel quills. We use 'em for human waves. This sucker'll pin gooks to a tree forty deep. None of 'em'll be more than an inch thick. They're goin' out in a PC; try to bring that patrol in. The shit's apt to get pretty thick. If Charley gets pissed and comes at us, it's gonna be for real. There's a whole North Vietnamese division out there, shootin' up and gettin' half crazy. Somebody shouts, 'Go!' and there ain't no stopping them." He patted the dark cylinder. "This'll stop 'em."

I was chilled and shivering. My bones ached. I was bone-weary, and wet and dirty. Mostly, I was scared. Human waves? Visions of an army of drug-crazed Orientals in black pajamas, of John Wayne playing Davy Crockett at the Alamo, of hand-to-hand combat all ravaged my imagination. I was getting the shakes again, feeling the cold deep in my gut. In all my nineteen years, I had never seen anything like this. Hell, I had never imagined this might happen. Maybe it was a nightmare, and I would wake up and go to work. This couldn't be happening. I fought to remember my hand-to-hand combat training at Fort Dix. I had never paid that much attention, never dreamed I might have to rely on that training to stay alive. I wished I had a cup of coffee, a shower, or a few hours' sleep. I wanted to tuck into clean sheets, pull the pillow over my head to make the noise go away, and wake up in the morning to find myself home. As if to answer my thoughts, a flare popped and lit the slope in a golden glow. I saw the muddy hill, devoid of plants, streaming away toward the tangled wire. The tree line was a black wall now, an impenetrable black pit that led to the depths of hell. The sounds of war were distant now, but all around us. Surely, as they approached, we would be caught in the middle till Charley squeezed the life out of us. There was no place to go, no place to hide. Thousands of guys were kneeling in the mud, peering into the shadows and awaiting death, and none of them wanted to be here. What power could put so many American kids into a position like this? Why hadn't they told us about this while we were growing up? To my left a voice cut through the damp fog. "Holy Mary, Mother of God . . ." Were the others as scared as I? They were such a disheveled bunch, brawny and tough, it was hard to think of them as scared.

"Ohio?"

"Yeah?"

"You scared?"

"Fuckin' A I'm scared. I've been scared since I got off the plane at Cam Ranh Bay. Anybody that ain't scared shitless in a place like this is crazy as hell. You want a belt?"

I moved closer to him, thankful for the bottle. "Where the hell do you get this stuff? We been hittin' this bottle all day, and it never goes dry. You making your own or something?"

"Walker swapped some ammo to some Green Beanies, got us a whole case of it. At the time, we didn't think we'd need the ammo."

"Somebody coulda got killed."

"Yeah, but anything you do in this fuckin' place can get somebody killed. The Beanies must've really needed it, to give up a case of booze. So maybe we saved a life; who knows? Ain't it funny how little you know about what's goin' on around ya here? I mean, there's some heavy shit comin' down. Just listen. And what's it all about? No-fuckin'-body knows! It's fuckin' crazy. If somebody would just tell me what the fuck is going on around here, what they hope to gain, or what they stand to lose, or something . . . but, no! You see guys all blown to shit, and you don't know why." He tipped the bottle up and drank hard and long. "Hardest thing's gonna be goin' home, and seeing the wife and her family, and her kid brother got blown away over here, and I don't know what to tell them about it. I mean, how the fuck can you describe this to somebody's sister?"

"Yeah, but you're married to her. It'll come." For such a big man, he seemed very vulnerable. I tried to lift him up but didn't know how.

Ohio lit a cigarette. "Supposing we die tonight. What happens then? They put what's left in a body bag and ship you home, and some lifer in a dress uniform tells your wife you died for your country. They have a funeral, and they fold up a flag and present it to her, and they draft the kid next door!"

I hadn't thought about it. If I went home in a box, I didn't want the army involved in my funeral. Fuck 'em. I hadn't asked for any of this. I wasn't a hero. I would have to write to the folks, tell them not to allow a military funeral. Ohio flipped away the cigarette.

"How old are you, New York?"

"Nineteen."

"I was twenty, four days before I left home. The lieutenant's twenty-three, and he's the only guy older than I am. There's nineteen guys, and I'm the oldest. Only three of us are married. Can you imagine? My wife went to the recruiting office with me, and I enlisted to go to The Nam, and she just sat there and listened to the whole thing, and it was almost like she didn't have any emotion. So it's my birthday, right, and we're at her folks', and she brings out this cake with all the candles and says, 'Make a wish.' I wished, just once before I had to leave, that she would say she didn't want me to go. I blew out the candles, but I never got my wish. Look at this fuckin' place, would ya? My wife wanted me here! She thinks I'm doin' some kind of patriotic duty, and it's wonderful. What the fuck am I ever gonna have to say to her? She wanted me to come over here! I've been here a little over a month, and I'm not sure I love her anymore. I can't tell her what it's like, and I can't forgive her for wanting me to be here. Haven't written her a letter in weeks. How the fuck you gonna describe this? Shit! I don't know if I want to see her again. She'd tell her friends I was some kind of fuckin' hero, and I'd have to just tell her to shut the fuck up. I just hope if Charley fucks my shit up he does it right, 'cause I don't want to spend the rest of my life with her pushing me around in a wheelchair, telling people I did what I had to do. If she had asked me not to go, I would have stayed home. I don't need this shit! I don't need to hear what a fuckin' hero I am. I just need a bath, and a drink, and some good pussy. She can keep her mouth shut and her legs open, and we'll get along fine. I mean, I feel bad about her brother, but what fuckin' good am I doin' for him? He's dead, and I'm about to be, too, and I ain't seen anything getting a bit better because of it!"

My thoughts drifted away. There wasn't anything I could say to make it better. I thought about Jimmy Rollins, and my family. How would I talk to them? I heard an engine growl behind us, the clatter of tracks. Too much booze on an empty stomach. I had to pull my shit together. Thinking could get in the way. One more cigarette while the PC was going out; then I'd better have my shit together. God damn the rain!

The personnel carrier hung close to the trees, moving parallel to us. The sound of its engine, its General Motors three-speed automatic transmission seemed too loud, as if it were inviting the Cong to try something. Suddenly there was small-arms fire, then an explosion of firing. The PC zigzagged, bouncing and churning a haphazard dance from shadow to shadow. It accelerated, slowed, turned 180 degrees, stopped, accelerated again. The machine gun on top was hurling red tracers into the tree line. Ohio touched my arm, leaned close to whisper. "They find a body, and drive over it. Some poor bastard opens the back door a crack and leans out with a rope; ties it around a wrist or an ankle. They play out about ten feet of rope and slam the door, and go looking for the next one. Drag the whole string around; sometimes run over them with the tracks. They'll be all beat to shit, but you can't leave 'em out there. Charley'll crawl in, cut off their heads and stick 'em on poles with their balls in their mouth. In the morning the sun comes up and they're lookin' at ya all day long. Just be glad you aren't in graves registration tonight. They gotta bag 'em up to be shipped home; identify them and everything. Those guys are up to their ass in puke and guts and shit. I'd rather be here." I remembered Shotgun. That's where they had sent him.

A tremendous explosion erupted near the PC. "Mine." Ohio said it without emotion. "They pull a string to trigger it. Charley's timing sucks!" The armored carrier moved to the right, became obscured by rain and fog. The firing died down, and the sound of the grinding tracks was washed out by the clatter of a chopper overhead. A flare popped. Occasional rifle fire made sleep impossible. About three in the morning a heavy mortar barrage fell behind us. It was amazing. You could actually hear the rounds sizzling overhead. I hadn't expected the explosions to be so loud. In the cold and wet, I was shaking again. I had to pee. I unbuttoned my fly and let go against the sandbags, never taking my eyes off the misty slope. Dawn brought a few more mortar rounds, again over our heads. Ohio suggested breakfast. I was a guest here. There was no question; I got ham and lima beans again. The lieutenant got the beans and franks. A short-timer got the fruit cocktail. We built a small fire and heated coffee in canteen cups, added a shot of booze and a little sugar. Breakfast was the best meal of the day. It meant you had survived the night, you were one day shorter. Two F-4 Phantom jets screamed across the sky, pulled up sharply. We heard a muffled *whuuumppff*. Dak To was open for business.

The sounds of fighting on Hill 875 were intensifying as we got the word to saddle up. I shook Ohio's muddy hand. I was searching for words when he spoke first. "You keep your head down, New York, and thanks for the ammo." I wasn't eager to go back out onto Highway One. "C'mon, asshole." Ohio was grinning. "You don't want to stay here, do ya? Shit, in a few hours you'll be taking a hot shower back in Pleiku. In a few days you'll be eating Thanksgiving turkey and all this'll seem unreal. You're over the hard part. Shit, you're a battle-scarred veteran. Now get down that fuckin' road, 'fore ya smoke up all our cigarettes. We'll see ya again." He held out the bottle, and I tipped the neck his way before I drank.

"Hey, Ohio?"

"Yeah?"

"Hell of a party! You take care. Thanks, man."

I ran across the morass to the truck. Shotgun was already in his seat, and he started when I opened the door. His eyes were wild.

He looked away. I pushed the starter button. "Ready?"

He spoke out the open window, softly. "Just get us the fuck outta here!"

"You all right?"

"I don't think I'll ever be all right again, but get us the fuck outta here." He was crying. If graves registration did this to an experienced, hardened short-timer, I resolved to avoid it at all costs.

We ground up out of that stinking valley, leaving the sounds of battle behind us. Helicopters clattered overhead, and I kept a big distance between us and the truck ahead. Shotgun stared straight ahead, tears streaking his cheeks. We were rolling hard when he leaned out the window and puked. He was silent all the way back to Pleiku. It was an uneventful trip, if five hours of utter terror can be uneventful. No mines or ambushes, you had to feel fortunate. We ground to a halt at Camp Holloway. Shotgun punched my shoulder and spoke softly. "Good job. Hope ya make it." Then he just walked away, and I looked for a ride back to my compound.

I was in the shower when the shaking started. I thought about Ohio, how he had said I was over the hard part. Suddenly thirty hours of terror exploded in my stomach, and I started bawling like a baby. I rushed outside, stark naked, and threw up, on my knees in the mud. It all unwound out of me, like a coil spring. Unraveled. Came apart. I saw the explosion on the road again, the crater, the personnel carrier bouncing around in the dark, the disjointed body hanging on the wire. I heard the sound, that crushing roar that squeezed your ears till your brain went blank. I smelled the powder and the diesel fuel and the rot and the death. I went back into the shower, and I scrubbed till my skin was red, but it wouldn't come clean. Back at the hootch, I drank too much Scotch and fell on the bunk. When I closed my eyes I saw the road explode. I put the pillow over my head, tucked it tight against my ears, but the roar wouldn't go away. I felt very cold, got the uncontrollable shivers, pulled the heavy wool blanket tight around me. I saw the dump trucks loaded with bodies, the dark shadows trailing behind the PC. Christ, they must have hauled them right in to Shotgun. Never did know his name, or Ohio's. They never asked mine. Imagine experiencing something like that two feet from another guy, and you don't even know his name. You'll never see him again. Either of them. Wouldn't volunteer for another convoy if it was going to San Francisco! My volunteering days are over.

The guys burst into the tent, waving mail and laughing. I made believe I was sleeping. Archie shook me. "Jawn. Jawn." Damned Boston accent, leave me alone. "C'mawn, you gotta eat. Got a meal fit for a king." He whistled for an imaginary dog. "Here, King. Here, boy." How the hell could I ignore that? I sat up.

Archie looked at me kind of funny. "You look like hell. Pretty bad, huh?" I nodded. "Know what you need? Powdered potatoes! Stick to your ribs, give you intestinal fortitude to face the adversities of life in The Nam. Powdered potatoes'll fix anything. Half the bricks in Saigon are glued together with the army's powdered potatoes. C'mon, get dressed." He screwed up his face, made that handlebar mustache twist into a ridiculous caricature of a silent movie star. I had to laugh.

"Anybody ever tell you you're fuckin' crazy?"

He stepped back in mock horror, his eyebrows arched. "Sorry, fella, you got the wrong guy. Just 'cause I enlisted, you don't have to make disparaging remarks."

We ate, and I felt better. We talked about Dak To. I didn't go into detail; no need to get him upset. Every time I thought I was going to lose it, Archie clowned and got me over it. We smoked and drank too much, and went to bed early. The next day I would be back at the old grind.

* * *

As Christmas drew closer, we struggled for a suitable means of celebrating. The elite Green Berets, in order to make them "resourceful," were issued nothing. They had to steal and deal for their needs. The strict army code authorized them nothing. They needed truck parts. We needed a case of steaks for Christmas dinner. A deal was struck.

Two of us loaded the specified parts into a three-quarter-ton truck. We had stripped them off the skeletons in the boneyard, offering to share our booty with the "cannibals" if they looked the other way. This cumshawing was a way of life in The Nam, an elaborate system of collaboration for the common good. The Green Beanies were dug in at a firebase near the Cambodian border. There would be no convoy, no air cover, not even a radio. They assured us it would be safe. I hadn't volunteered; I was drafted. We roared and bounced across roads that were little more than rutted trails for about three nervous hours. Only when we arrived did we find three small holes behind the passenger's door.

The firebase was a hole in the sea of vegetation. Like the eye of a hurricane, a clearing, a grassy meadow had been ringed with barbed wire and sandbags. Near the center, two big guns hunkered down into the soft ooze. M-60 machine guns and automatic rifles stood vigilant at the perimeter, perched on sandbagged bunkers like guard posts on the corners of the stockade in a cowboys-and-Indians movie. I imagined painted Apaches on horseback circling the free-fire zone. There were no hootches, no outhouses, no mess hall. There were only mud and dirt and brackish puddles. A handful of ARVN troops in camouflage fatigues lounged about, their eyes insolent. Numerous vehicles, obviously tired and spent, were scattered in disorganized abandon. To our left we could see the Green Berets, gathered near a conglomeration of boxes, crates, tents, and an olive-drab, dilapidated fire truck. A fire truck? It was, because of its color and the streaked coating of mud, almost logical. Almost, but not quite! In fact, the incongruity of it all made me stop and laugh. Here we were, unprotected, in the middle of nowhere, without a building in sight, let alone a refrigerator. We were after beefsteak and found a fire truck! It was absurd!

Insane laughter rolled out of me in a release of tensions. We had made it. A giant man approached, grinning broadly. Naked to the waist, he bulged with power. The hair had probably been red once. Now it was bleached and streaked with white. His face was wrinkled and weathered, but the eyes were warm and inviting. He seemed really glad to see us. I had been uncomfortable about meeting these legendary men on their own turf. I had seen them before; wild, uncontrolled men whose sole purpose in life seemed to be violence. Someone once said, "Hell hath no fury like a drunk Green Beret." They marauded, they destroyed, they killed with a fury so intense it was sometimes unleashed upon their countrymen. Proximity could be a capital offense. They were Green Berets because they didn't fit the normal mold, and we could never fit theirs.

"Hey! Good to see you! We've been expecting you! Merry fuckin' Christmas!" His warmth simply melted my reservations. My shotgun found the bullet holes, and we discussed the implications. We were nervous. Our host, who had introduced himself as Lieutenant Frost, scoffed. "Charley can't hit shit. Best you can hope for is a gook tryin' to shoot ya. Can't hit shit!" Nervousness faded away. We were accepted. Frost looked over the truck parts. I was impressed. He was soft-spoken, down-to-earth. He seemed to appreciate the pieces that would get his men mobile again. It had been rough lately. He had lost a lot of men. No longer were the Cong the main problem. There were a lot of NVA around, heavy firepower. "They're bringing in tanks!" he said, his voice tired. "Can you imagine? How's a place like this supposed to stop tanks?" He looked older. We started walking toward the group of Berets.

"How's it going?" As Frost spoke, the circle opened. In its center were three whores, hands bound, eyes defiant. Someone said, "No good." An ARVN, obviously with rank, chattered at one of the girls in Vietnamese. From the tone of his voice it was obvious he was interrogating her. He was growing agitated, angry. It was like something out of the movies. All that was missing was the swinging light bulb. The ARVN officer was frustrated. His hand snaked out to slap the girl's face. Her head snapped. Tears rushed to her eyes. He struck again. They had words; hot, emotional words. She was defiant. The ARVN got to his feet, lit a cigarette. A Green Beret spoke to him in his native tongue. He answered, then turned back to the girl at his feet. There was obviously a question. She spat back an answer. He nodded to two of the Americans. They pulled the girl to her feet, tore her silken blouse open, removed her gaudy brassiere. Their giant hands closed on her upper arms. The ARVN dragged at his cigarette, stepped forward, and pushed the cherry tip to her nipple. I couldn't believe I was watching this. I looked at Jerry, my shotgun. We had never gotten along real well, but we communicated now. His eyes were wide. Frost noticed our discomfort. "You guys don't get to see this stuff where you are." He spoke factually, unemotionally. "One of our guys visited these ladies for a shot of cock. We found his head with his cock in his mouth! Haven't found the rest of him. We tore that place apart. Lots of papers, NVA stuff. These worthless cunts fucked our buddy up bad! Now, we know something big is coming. Real big! These babes are gonna tell us what Uncle Ho is up to, and they're gonna pay for what happened to Timmy. Timmy didn't deserve that shit. You guys want to leave, I'll get the shit outta your truck. You wanna see the war, stick around!" I looked at Jerry. He looked back at the girl. She hadn't uttered a sound. Her eyes were moist, but burning with hatred and defiance. Someone nudged me, handed me a joint. I took a deep hit. My feet were planted. I couldn't have moved if I wanted to. I looked at Jerry. He was staring, mouth open. I took another drag at the joint, passed it back. Somebody handed me a cold can of Coke. It shocked me a little as it touched my hand. I could feel the marijuana. I sat on the sandbags to watch the war. Jerry was swigging bourbon.

The girl was on her back now, and naked. Her bound wrists were over her head, held by a swarthy GI. The ARVN had backed away. There was a flurry of activity. I jumped at the sound of the starter as it brought the fire truck to life. "I couldn't believe a fire truck in a place like this!" I was laughing. Giggling. Frost's voice came from my right. "That's our water supply. We got tired of trying to catch rainwater. Cumshawed the thing in Qui Nhon. There's underground water, so we borrowed a drill and drilled us a well, and that's our pump. Got enough pressure, we shoot it straight up and all get a shower."

The girl's legs were held apart. A burly black stood over her, screaming. "Where Timmy? Where da resta Timmy? Cunt! Whore! You gonna die, oh, you gonna die bad, Mama-san! You gonna wear you cunt in you mouth, Mama-san! Talk t'me, woman!" He raged. He stormed. He paced back and forth. A geyser of water erupted from the fire truck, falling on us, shaking us out of the spell. Everyone gathered round, moving closer to watch the fun. It was obvious the mood was rising toward a crescendo. The girl lay still, impassive. The ARVN officer barked at the other two, his eyes glued to the scene unfolding. The other two whores had the same detached, faraway look in their eyes. The huge hose was brought into the circle. The giant black, still raging, shook it in front of the girl's face. The ARVN called to her. She closed her eyes, shuddered a little. The tarnished brass nozzle was forced between her legs, forced against the resilient folds of flesh. Her eyes started open. A scream started from her throat, a sound unlike any other! Red and pink and brown and white and green, a torrent of mixed flesh and high-pressure steam knocked the intimate circle back. The white flood of water died away, the lifeless hose was discarded.

It didn't matter what the Green Berets thought. I was sick. The sweetness of the Coke seemed to seep up my throat, through my nose. It gripped the back of my tongue, gagging me. I heaved until my insides ached.

Jerry and I talked about it on the way back. We were afraid of those men, afraid to say anything. We had seen "the real war." We made a pact to keep it a secret between the two of us. If that was the way it was, we weren't able to change it. We were just relieved to have been assigned to the relative civilization of Pleiku. "Aww, shit!" Jerry whispered. "They're gonna take a shower out of that hose tonight." It was the last time either of us mentioned the incident.

RON KOVIC
1946–

Ron Kovic, a paralyzed Vietnam veteran, was present at the 1972 Republican National Convention at Miami Beach that renominated President Richard Nixon. He registered the scene in his book Born on the Fourth of July *(1976).*

From BORN ON THE FOURTH OF JULY

It was the night of Nixon's acceptance speech and now I was on my own deep in his territory, all alone in my wheelchair in a sweat-soaked marine utility jacket covered with medals from the war. A TV producer I knew from the Coast had gotten me past the guards at the entrance with his press pass. My eyes were still smarting from teargas. Outside the chain metal fence around the Convention Center my friends were being clubbed and arrested, herded into wagons. The crowds were thick all around me, people dressed as if they were going to a banquet, men in expensive summer suits and women in light elegant dresses. Every once in a while someone would look at me as if I didn't belong there. But I had come almost three thousand miles for this meeting with the president and nothing was going to prevent it from taking place.

I worked my way slowly and carefully into the huge hall, moving down one of the side aisles. "Excuse me, excuse me," I said to delegates as I pushed past them farther and farther to the front of the hall toward the speakers' podium.

I had gotten only halfway toward where I wanted to be when I was stopped by one of the convention security marshals. "Where are you going?" he said. He grabbed hold of the back of my chair, I made believe I hadn't heard him and kept turning my wheels, but his grip on the chair was too tight and now two other security men had joined him.

"What's the matter?" I said. "Can't a disabled veteran who fought for his country sit up front?"

The three men looked at each other for a moment and one of them said, "I'm afraid not. You're not allowed up front with the delegates." I had gotten as far as I had on sheer bluff alone and now they were telling me I could go no farther. "You'll have to go to the back of the convention hall, son. Let's go," said the guard who was holding my chair.

In a move of desperation I swung around facing all three of them, shouting as loud as I could so Walter Cronkite and the CBS camera crew that was just above me could hear me and maybe even focus their cameras in for the six o'clock news. "I'm a Vietnam veteran and I fought in the war! Did you fight in the war?"

One of the guards looked away.

"Yeah, that's what I thought," I said. "I bet none of you fought in the war and you guys are trying to throw me out of the convention. I've got just as much right to be up front here as any of these delegates. I fought for that right and I was born on the Fourth of July."

I was really shouting now and another officer came over. I think he might have been in charge of the hall. He told me I could stay where I was if I was quiet and didn't move up any farther. I agreed with the compromise. I locked my brakes and looked for other veterans in the tremendous crowd. As far as I could tell, I was the only one who had made it in.

People had begun to sit down all around me. They all had Four More Years buttons and I was surprised to see how many of them were young. I began speaking to them, telling them about the Last Patrol and why veterans from all over the United States had taken the time and effort to travel thousands of miles to the Republican National Convention. "I'm a disabled veteran!" I shouted. "I served two tours of duty in Vietnam and while on my second tour of duty up in the DMZ I was wounded and paralyzed from the chest down." I told them I would be that way for the rest of my life. Then I began to talk about the hospitals and how they treated the returning veterans like animals, how I, many nights in the Bronx, had lain in my own shit for hours waiting for an aide. "And they never come," I said. "They never come because that man that's going to accept the nomination tonight has been lying to all of us and spending the money on war that should be spent on healing and helping the wounded. That's the biggest lie and hypocrisy of all—that we had to go over there and fight and get crippled and come home to a government and leaders who could care less about the same boys they sent over."

I kept shouting and speaking, looking for some kind of reaction from the crowd. No one seemed to want to even look at me.

"Is it too real for you to look at? Is this wheelchair too much for you to take? The man who will accept the nomination tonight is a liar!" I shouted again and again, until finally one of the security men came back and told me to be quiet or they would have to take me to the back of the hall.

I told him that if they tried to move me or touch my chair there would be a fight and hell to pay right there in front of Walter Cronkite and the national television networks. I told him if he wanted to wrestle me and beat me to the floor of the convention hall in front of all those cameras he could.

By then a couple of newsmen, including Roger Mudd from CBS, had worked their way through the security barricades and begun to ask me questions.

"Why are you here tonight?" Roger Mudd asked me. "But don't start talking until I get the camera here," he shouted.

It was too good to be true. In a few seconds Roger Mudd and I would be going on live all over the country. I would be doing what I had come here for, showing the whole nation what the war was all about. The camera began to roll, and I began to explain why I and the others had come, that the war was wrong and it had to stop immediately. "I'm a Vietnam veteran," I said. "I gave America my all and the leaders of this government threw me and the others away to rot in their V.A. hospitals. What's happening in Vietnam is a crime against humanity, and I just want the American people to know that we have come all the way across this country, sleeping on the ground and in the rain, to let the American people see for themselves the men who fought their war and have come to oppose it. If you can't believe the veteran who fought the war and was wounded in the war, who can you believe?"

"Thank you," said Roger Mudd, visibly moved by what I had said. "This is Roger Mudd," he said, "down on the convention floor with Ron Kovic, a disabled veteran protesting President Nixon's policy in Vietnam." . . .

Suddenly a roar went up in the convention hall, louder than anything I had ever heard in my life. It started off as a rumble, then gained in intensity until it sounded like a tremendous thunderbolt. "Four more years, four more years," the crowd roared over and over again. The fat woman next to me was jumping up and down and dancing in the aisle. It was the greatest ovation the president of the United States had ever received and he loved it. I held the sides of my wheelchair to keep my hands from shaking. After what seemed forever, the roar finally began to die down.

This was the moment I had come three thousand miles for, this was it, all the pain and the rage, all the trials and the death of the war and what had been done to me and a generation of Americans by all the men who had lied to us and tricked us, by the man who stood before us in the convention hall that night, while men who had fought for their country

were being gassed and beaten in the street outside the hall. I thought of
Bobby who sat next to me and the months we had spent in the hospital
in the Bronx. It was all hitting me at once, all those years, all that
destruction, all that sorrow.

President Nixon began to speak and all three of us took a deep breath
and shouted at the top of our lungs, "Stop the bombing, stop the war,
stop the bombing, stop the war," as loud and as hard as we could, looking
directly at Nixon. The security agents immediately threw up their arms,
trying to hide us from the cameras and the president. "Stop the bombing, stop the bombing," I screamed. For an instant Cronkite looked
down, then turned his head away. They're not going to show it, I
thought. They're going to try and hide us like they did in the hospitals.
Hundreds of people around us began to clap and shout "Four more
years," trying to drown out our protest. They all seemed very angry and
shouted at us to stop. We continued shouting, interrupting Nixon again
and again until Secret Service agents grabbed our chairs from behind
and began pulling us backward as fast as they could out of the convention hall. "Take it easy," Bobby said to me. "Don't fight back."

I wanted to take a swing and fight right there in the middle of the
convention hall in front of the president and the whole country. "So this
is how they treat their wounded veterans!" I screamed.

A short guy with a big Four More Years button ran up to me and spat
in my face. "Traitor!" he screamed, as he was yanked back by police.
Pandemonium was breaking out all around us and the Secret Service
men kept pulling us out backward.

"I served two tours of duty in Vietnam!" I screamed to one newsman.
"I gave three-quarters of my body for America. And what do I get? Spit
in the face!" I kept screaming until we hit the side entrance where the
agents pushed us outside and shut the doors, locking them with chains
and padlocks so reporters wouldn't be able to follow us out for interviews.

All three of us sat holding on to each other shaking. We had done it.
It had been the biggest moment of our lives, we had shouted down the
president of the United States and disrupted his acceptance speech.
What more was there left to do but go home?

I sat in my chair still shaking and began to cry.

TIM O'BRIEN
1946–

O'Brien was born in Minnesota and studied at Macalester College and (after the Vietnam War) at Harvard. In the war he was an army sergeant, an experience he recorded in his memoir of 1973, If I Die in a Combat Zone.

From IF I DIE IN A COMBAT ZONE

I grew out of one war and into another. My father came from leaden ships of sea, from the Pacific theater; my mother wore the uniform of the WAVES. I was the wrinkled, swollen, bloody offspring of the great campaign against the tyrants of the 1940's, one explosion in the Baby Boom, one of millions of new human beings come to replace those who had just died. My bawling came with the first throaty note of a new army in spawning. I was bred with the haste and dispatch and careless muscle-flexing of a rejuvenated, splendidly triumphant nation giving bridle to its own good fortune and success. I was fed by the spoils of 1945 victory.

I learned to read and write on the prairies of southern Minnesota, in towns peering like corpses' eyeballs from out of the corn.

Along the route used by settlers to people South Dakota and the flatlands of Nebraska and northern Iowa, in the cold winters, I learned to use ice skates.

My teachers were brittle old ladies, classroom football coaches, flushed veterans of the war, pretty girls in sixth grade, memories of hot-blooded valor.

In patches of weed and clouds of imagination, I learned to play army games. Friends introduced me to the Army Surplus Store off main street. We bought dented relics of our fathers' history, rusted canteens and olive-scented, scarred helmet liners. Then we were our fathers, taking on the Japs and Krauts along the shores of Lake Okabena, on the flat fairways of the golf course, writhing insensible under barrages of shore batteries positioned under camouflage across the lake. I rubbed my fingers across my father's war decorations, stole a tiny battle star off one of them and carried it in my pocket.

Baseball was for the summertime, when school ended. My father loved baseball. I was holding a bleached Louisville Slugger when I was six. I played a desperate short-stop for the Rural Electric Association Little League team; my father coached us, and he is still coaching, still able to tick off the starting line-up of the great Brooklyn Dodgers teams of the 1950's.

Sparklers and the forbidden cherry bomb were for the Fourth of July: a baseball game, a picnic, a day in the city park, listening to the high school band playing "Anchors Aweigh," a speech, watching a parade of American Legionnaires. At night, sometime after nine o'clock, fireworks erupted over the lake, reflections.

It had been Indian land. Ninety miles from Sioux City, sixty miles from Sioux Falls, eighty miles from Cherokee, forty miles from Spirit Lake and the site of a celebrated massacre. To the north was Pipestone and the annual Hiawatha Pageant. To the west was Luverne and Indian burial mounds.

Norwegians and Swedes, a few Dutch and Germans—*Giants in the Earth*—had taken the plains from the Sioux. The settlers must have seen endless plains and eased their bones and said, "here as well as anywhere, it's all the same."

The town became a place for wage earners. It is a place for wage earners today—not very spirited people, not very philosophic people.

Among these people I learned about the Second World War, hearing it from men in front of the courthouse, from men who had fought it. The talk was tough. Nothing to do with causes or reason; the war was right, they muttered when asked, it had to be fought. The talk was about bellies filled with German lead, about the long hike from Normandy to Berlin, about close calls and about the origins of scars just visible on hairy arms. Growing up, I learned about another war, a peninsular war in Korea, a gray war fought by the town's Lutherans and Baptists. I learned about that war when the town hero came home, riding in a convertible, sitting straight-backed and quiet, an ex-POW.

The town called itself Turkey Capital of the World. In September the governor and some congressmen came to town. People shut down their businesses and came in from their farms. Together we watched trombones and crepe-paper floats move on a blitzkrieg down mainstreet. The bands and floats represented Lismore, Sheldon, Tyler, Sibley, and Jackson.

Turkey Day climaxed when the farmers herded a billion strutting, stinking, beady-eyed birds down the center of town, past the old Gobbler Cafe, past Woolworth's and the Ben Franklin store and the Standard Oil service station. Feathers and droppings and popcorn mixed together in tribute to the town and the prairie. We were young. We stood on the curb and blasted the animals with ammunition from our peashooters.

We listened to Nelson Rockefeller and Harold Stassen and the commander of the Minnesota VFW, trying to make sense out of their words, then we went for twenty-five-cent rides on the Octopus and Tilt-A-Whirl.

I couldn't hit a baseball. Too small for football, but I stuck it out through junior high, hoping something would change. When nothing happened, I began to read. I read Plato and Erich Fromm, the Hardy boys and enough Aristotle to make me prefer Plato. The town's library was quiet and not a very lively place—nothing like the football field on an October evening and not a very good substitute—nothing like screaming for blood, nothing like aching with filial pride, nothing like hearty masculine well-being.

I watched the athletes from the stands and cheered them at pep rallies, wishing I were with them. I went to homecoming dances, learned to drive an automobile, joined the debate team, took girls to drive-in theaters and afterward to the A & W rootbeer stand.

I took up an interest in politics. One evening I put on a suit and drove down to the League of Women Voters meeting, embarrassing myself and some candidates and most of the women voters by asking questions that had no answers.

I tried going to Democratic party meetings. I'd read it was the liberal party. But it was futile. I could not make out the difference between the people there and the people down the street boosting Nixon and Cabot Lodge. The essential thing about the prairie, I learned, was that one part of it is like any other part.

At night I sometimes walked about the town. "God is both transcendent and imminent. That's Tillich's position." When I walked, I chose the darkest streets, away from the street lights. "But is there a God? I mean, is there a God like there's a tree or an apple? Is God a being?" I usually ended up walking toward the lake. "God is Being-Itself." The lake, Lake Okabena, reflected the town-itself, bouncing off a black-and-white pattern identical to the whole desolate prairie: flat, tepid, small, strangled by algae, shut in by middle-class houses, lassooed by a ring of doctors, lawyers, CPA's, dentists, drugstore owners, and proprietors of department stores. "Being-Itself? Then is this town God? It exists, doesn't it?" I walked past where the pretty girls lived, stopping long enough to look at their houses, all the lights off and the curtains drawn. "Jesus," I muttered, "I hope not. Maybe I'm an atheist."

One day in May the high school held graduation ceremonies. Then I went away to college, and the town did not miss me much.

The summer of 1968, the summer I turned into a soldier, was a good time for talking about war and peace. Eugene McCarthy was bringing quiet thought to the subject. He was winning votes in the primaries. College students were listening to him, and some of us tried to help out. Lyndon Johnson was almost forgotten, no longer forbidding or feared; Robert Kennedy was dead but not quite forgotten; Richard Nixon looked like a loser. With all the tragedy and change that summer, it was fine weather for discussion.

And, with all of this, there was an induction notice tucked into a corner of my billfold.

So with friends and acquaintances and townspeople, I spent the summer in Fred's antiseptic cafe, drinking coffee and mapping out arguments on Fred's napkins. Or I sat in Chic's tavern, drinking beer with kids from the farms. I played some golf and tore up the pool table down at the bowling alley, keeping an eye open for likely-looking high school girls.

Late at night, the town deserted, two or three of us would drive a car around and around the town's lake, talking about the war, very seriously, moving with care from one argument to the next, trying to make it a dialogue and not a debate. We covered all the big questions: justice, tyranny, self-determination, conscience and the state, God and war and love.

College friends came to visit: "Too bad, I hear you're drafted. What will you do?"

I said I didn't know, that I'd let time decide. Maybe something would change, maybe the war would end. Then we'd turn to discuss the matter, talking long, trying out the questions, sleeping late in the mornings.

The summer conversations, spiked with plenty of references to the philosophers and academicians of war, were thoughtful and long and complex and careful. But, in the end, careful and precise argumentation hurt me. It was painful to tread deliberately over all the axioms and assumptions and corollaries when the people on the town's draft board were calling me to duty, smiling so nicely.

"It won't be bad at all," they said. "Stop in and see us when it's over."

So to bring the conversations to a focus and also to try out in real words my secret fears, I argued for running away.

I was persuaded then, and I remain persuaded now, that the war was wrong. And since it was wrong and since people were dying as a result of it, it was evil. Doubts, of course, hedged all this: I had neither the expertise nor the wisdom to synthesize answers; most of the facts were clouded, and there was no certainty as to the kind of government that would follow a North Vietnamese victory or, for that matter, an American victory, and the specifics of the conflict were hidden away—partly in men's minds, partly in the archives of government, and partly in buried, irretrievable history. The war, I thought, was wrongly conceived and poorly justified. But perhaps I was mistaken, and who really knew, anyway?

Piled on top of this was the town, my family, my teachers, a whole history of the prairie. Like magnets, these things pulled in one direction or the other, almost physical forces weighting the problem, so that, in the end, it was less reason and more gravity that was the final influence.

My family was careful that summer. The decision was mine and it was not talked about. The town lay there, spread out in the corn and watching me, the mouths of old women and Country Club men poised in a kind of eternal readiness to find fault. It was not a town, not a Minneapolis or New York, where the son of a father can sometimes escape scrutiny. More, I owed the prairie something. For twenty-one years I'd lived under its laws, accepted its education, eaten its food, wasted and guzzled its water, slept well at night, driven across its highways, dirtied and breathed its air, wallowed in its luxuries. I'd played on its Little League teams. I remembered Plato's *Crito*, when Socrates, facing certain death—execution, not war—had the chance to escape. But he reminded himself that he had seventy years in which he could have left the country, if he were not satisfied or felt the agreements he'd made with it were unfair. He had not chosen Sparta or Crete. And, I reminded myself, I hadn't thought much about Canada until that summer.

The summer passed this way. Gold afternoons on the golf course, a comforting feeling that the matter of war would never touch me, nights in the pool hall or drug store, talking with towns-folk, turning the questions over and over, being a philosopher.

Near the end of that summer the time came to go to the war. The family indulged in a cautious sort of Last Supper together, and afterward my father, who is brave, said it was time to report at the bus depot. I moped down to my bedroom and looked the place over, feeling quite stupid, thinking that my mother would come in there in a day or two and probably cry a little. I trudged back up to the kitchen and put my satchel down. Everyone gathered around, saying so long and good health and write and let us know if you want anything. My father took up the induction papers, checking on times and dates and all the last-minute things, and when I pecked my mother's face and grabbed the satchel for comfort, he told me to put it down, that I wasn't supposed to report until tomorrow.

After laughing about the mistake, after a flush of red color and a flood of ribbing and a wave of relief had come and gone, I took a long drive around the lake, looking again at the place. Sunset Park, with its picnic table and little beach and a brown wood shelter and some families swimming. The Crippled Children's School. Slater Park, more kids. A long string of split level houses, painted every color.

The war and my person seemed like twins as I went around the town's lake. Twins grafted together and forever together, as if a separation would kill them both.

The thought made me angry.

In the basement of my house I found some scraps of cardboard and paper. With devilish flair, I printed obscene words on them, declaring my intention to have no part of Vietnam. With delightful viciousness, a secret will, I declared the war evil, the draft board evil, the town evil in its lethargic acceptance of it all. For many minutes, making up the signs, making up my mind, I was outside the town. I was outside the law, all my old ties to my loves and family broken by the old crayon in my hand. I imagined strutting up and down the sidewalks outside the depot, the bus waiting and the driver blaring his horn, the *Daily Globe* photographer trying to push me into line with the other draftees, the frantic telephone calls, my head buzzing at the deed.

On the cardboard, my strokes of bright red were big and ferocious looking. The language was clear and certain and burned with a hard, defiant, criminal, blasphemous sound. I tried reading it aloud.

Later in the evening I tore the signs into pieces and put the shreds in the garbage can outside, clanging the gray cover down and trapping the messages inside. I went back into the basement. I slipped the crayons into their box, the same stubs of color I'd used a long time before to chalk in reds and greens on Roy Rogers' cowboy boots.

I'd never been a demonstrator, except in the loose sense. True, I'd taken a stand in the school newspaper on the war, trying to show why it seemed wrong. But, mostly, I'd just listened.

"No war is worth losing your life for," a college acquaintance used to argue. "The issue isn't a moral one. It's a matter of efficiency: what's the most efficient way to stay alive when your nation is at war? That's the issue."

But others argued that no war is worth losing your country for, and when asked about the case when a country fights a wrong war, those people just shrugged.

Most of my college friends found easy paths away from the problem, all to their credit. Deferments for this and that. Letters from doctors or chaplains. It was hard to find people who had to think much about the problem. Counsel came from two main quarters, pacifists and veterans of foreign wars.

But neither camp had much to offer. It wasn't a matter of peace, as the pacifists argued, but rather a matter of when and when not to join others in making war. And it wasn't a matter of listening to an ex-lieutenant colonel talk about serving in a right war, when the question was whether to serve in what seemed a wrong one.

On August 13, I went to the bus depot. A Worthington *Daily Globe* photographer took my picture standing by a rail fence with four other draftees.

Then the bus took us through corn fields, to little towns along the way—Lismore and Rushmore and Adrian—where other recruits came aboard. With some of the tough guys drinking beer and howling in the back seats, brandishing their empty cans and calling one another "scum" and "trainee" and "GI Joe," with all this noise and hearty farewelling, we went to Sioux Falls. We spent the night in a YMCA. I went out alone for a beer, drank it in a corner booth, then I bought a book and read it in my room.

By noon the next day our hands were in the air, even the tough guys. We recited the proper words, some of us loudly and daringly and others in bewilderment. It was a brightly lighted room, wood paneled. A flag gave the place the right colors, there was some smoke in the air. We said the words, and we were soldiers.

I'd never been much of a fighter. I was afraid of bullies. Their ripe muscles made me angry: a frustrated anger. Still, I deferred to no one. Positively lorded myself over inferiors. And on top of that was the matter of conscience and conviction, uncertain and surface-deep but pure nonetheless: I was a confirmed liberal, not a pacifist; but I would have cast my ballot to end the Vietnam war immediately, I would have voted for Eugene McCarthy, hoping he would make peace. I was not soldier material, that was certain.

But I submitted. All the personal history, all the midnight conversations and books and beliefs and learning, were crumpled by abstention, extinguished by forfeiture, for lack of oxygen, by a sort of sleepwalking default. It was no decision, no chain of ideas or reasons, that steered me into the war.

It was an intellectual and physical stand-off, and I did not have the energy to see it to an end. I did not want to be a soldier, not even an observer to war. But neither did I want to upset a peculiar balance between the order I knew, the people I knew, and my own private world. It was not that I valued that order. But I feared its opposite, inevitable chaos, censure, embarrassment, the end of everything that had happened in my life, the end of it all.

And the stand-off is still there. I would wish this book could take the form of a plea for everlasting peace, a plea from one who knows, from one who's been there and come back, an old soldier looking back at a dying war.

That would be good. It would be fine to integrate it all to persuade my younger brother and perhaps some others to say no to wars and other battles.

Or it would be fine to confirm the odd beliefs about war: it's horrible, but it's a crucible of men and events and, in the end, it makes more of a man out of you.

But, still, none of these notions seems right. Men are killed, dead human beings are heavy and awkward to carry, things smell different in Vietnam, soldiers are afraid and often brave, drill sergeants are boors, some men think the war is proper and just and others don't and most don't care. Is that the stuff for a morality lesson, even for a theme?

Do dreams offer lessons? Do nightmares have themes, do we awaken and analyze them and live our lives and advise others as a result? Can the foot soldier teach anything important about war, merely for having been there? I think not. He can tell war stories.

*   *   *

In advanced infantry training, the soldier learns new ways to kill people.

Claymore mines, booby traps, the M-60 machine gun, the M-70 grenade launcher. The old .45-caliber pistol. Drill sergeants give lessons on the M-16 automatic rifle, standard weapon in Vietnam.

On the outside, AIT looks like basic training. Lots of push-ups, lots of shoe-shining and firing ranges and midnight marches. But AIT is not basic training. The difference is inside the new soldier's skull, locked to his brain, the certainty of being in a war, pending doom that comes in with each day's light and stays with him all the day long.

The soldier in advanced infantry training is doomed, and he knows it and thinks about it. War, a real war. The drill sergeant said it when we formed up for our first inspection: every swinging dick in the company was now a foot soldier, a grunt in the United States Army, the infantry, Queen of Battle. Not a cook in the lot, not a clerk or mechanic among us. And in eight weeks, he said, we were all getting on a plane that would fly to a war.

The man who finds himself in AIT is doomed, and he knows it and thinks about it. There are no more hopes of being made into a rear-echelon trooper. The drill sergeant said it when we formed up for our first inspection: every swingin' dick in the company was now a foot soldier, a grunt in the United States Army. Not a cook or typist in the lot. And in eight weeks, he said, we were all getting on a plane bound for Vietnam.

"I don't want you to mope around thinkin' about Germany or London," he told us. "Don't even think about it, 'cause there just ain't no way. You're leg men now, and we don't need no infantry in Piccadilly or Southampton. Besides, Vietnam ain't all that bad. I been over there twice now, and I'm alive and still screwin' everything in sight. You troops pay attention to the trainin' you get here, and every swingin' dick will be back in one piece, believe me. Just pay attention, try to learn something. The Nam, it ain't so bad, not if you got your shit together."

One of the trainees asked him about rumors that said we would be shipped to Frankfort.

"Christ, you'll hear the crap till it makes you puke. Every swingin' dick is going to Nam, every big fat swingin' dick."

* * *

During the first month, I learned that FNG meant "fuckin' new guy," and that I would be one until the Combat Center's next shipment arrived. I learned that GI's in the field can be as lazy and careless and stupid as GI's anywhere. They don't wear helmets and armored vests unless an officer insists; they fall asleep on guard, and for the most part, no one really cares; they throw away or bury ammunition if it gets heavy and hot. I learned that REMF means "rear echelon motherfucker"; that a man is getting "Short" after his third or fourth month; that a hand grenade is really a "frag"; that one bullet is all it takes and that "you never hear the shot that gets you"; that no one in Alpha Company knows or cares about the cause or purpose of their war: it is about "dinks and slopes," and the idea is simply to kill them or avoid them. Except that in Alpha you don't kill a man, you "waste" him. You don't get mangled by a mine, you get fucked up. You don't call a man by his first name—he's the Kid or the Water Buffalo, Buddy Wolf or Buddy Barker or Buddy Barney, or if the fellow is bland or disliked, he's just Smith or Jones or Rodríguez. The NCO's who go through a crash two-month program to earn their stripes are called "instant NCO's"; hence the platoon's squad leaders were named Ready Whip, Nestle's Quick, and Shake and Bake. And when two of them—Tom and Arnold—were killed two months later, the tragedy was somehow mitigated and depersonalized by telling ourselves that ol' Ready Whip and Quick got themselves wasted by the slopes. There was Cop—an Irish fellow who wanted to join the police force in Danbury, Connecticut—and Reno and the Wop and the College Joe. You can go through a year in Vietnam and live with a platoon of sixty or seventy people, some going and some coming, and you can leave without knowing more than a dozen complete names, not that it matters.

Mad Mark was the platoon leader, a first lieutenant and a Green Beret. It was hard to tell if the name or the reason for the name came first. The madness in Mad Mark, at any rate, was not a hysterical, crazy, into-the-brink, to-the-fore madness. Rather, he was insanely calm. He never showed fear. He was a professional soldier, an ideal leader of men in the field. It was that kind of madness, the perfect guardian for the Platonic Republic. His attitude and manner seemed perfectly molded in the genre of the CIA or KGB operative.

This is not to say that Mad Mark ever did the work of the assassin. But it was his manner, and he cultivated it. He walked with a lanky, easy, silent, fearless stride. He wore tiger fatigues, not for their camouflage but for their look. He carried a shotgun—a weapon I'd thought was out-lawed in international war—and the shotgun itself was a measure of his professionalism, for to use it effectively requires an exact blend of cour-age and skill and self-confidence. The weapon is neither accurate nor lethal at much over seventy yards. So it shows the skill of the carrier, a man who must work his way close enough to the prey to make a shot, close enough to see the enemy's retina and the tone of his skin. To get that close requires courage and self-confidence. The shotgun is not an automatic weapon. You must hit once, on the first shot, and the hit must kill. Mad Mark once said that after the war and in the absence of other U.S. wars he might try the mercenary's life in Africa.

He did not yearn for battle. But neither was he concerned about the prospect. Throughout the first month, vacationing on the safe beaches, he did precisely what the mission called for: a few patrols, a few am-bushes, staying ready to react, watching for signs of a rocket attack on Chu Lai. But he did not take the mission to excess. Mad Mark was not a fanatic. He was not gung-ho, not a man in search of a fight. It was more or less an Aristotelian ethic that Mad Mark practiced: making war is a necessary and natural profession. It is natural, but it is only a profession, not a crusade: "Hunting is a part of that art; and hunting might be practiced—not only against wild animals, but also against human beings who are intended by nature to be ruled by others and refuse to obey that intention—because war of this order is naturally just." And, like Aris-totle, Mad Mark believed in and practiced the virtue of moderation, so he did what was necessary in war, necessary for an officer and platoon leader in war, and he did no more or less.

He lounged with us during the hot days, he led a few patrols and ambushes, he flirted with the girls in our caravan, and, with a concern for only the basics of discipline, he allowed us to enjoy the holiday. Lying in the shade with the children, we learned a little Vietnamese, and they learned words like "motherfucker" and "gook" and "dink" and "tit." Like going to school.

It was not a bad war until we sent a night patrol into a village called Tri Binh 4. Mad Mark led it, taking only his shotgun and five other men. They'd been gone for an hour. Then came a burst of fire and a radio call that they'd opened up on some VC smoking and talking by a well. In ten minutes they were out of the village and back with the platoon.

The Kid was ecstatic. "Christ! They were right out there, right in the open, right in the middle of the ville, in a little clearing, just sitting on their asses! Shit, I almost shit! Ten of 'em, just sitting there. Jesus, we gave 'em hell. Damn, we gave it to 'em!" His face was on fire in the night, his teeth were flashing, he was grinning himself out of his skin. He paced back and forth, wanting to burst.

"Jesus," he said. "Show 'em the ear we got! Let's see the ear!"

Someone turned on a flashlight. Mad Mark sat cross-legged and unwrapped a bundle of cloth and dangled a hunk of brown, fresh human ear under the yellow beam of light. Someone giggled. The ear was clean of blood. It dripped with a little water, as if coming out of a bathtub. Part of the upper lobe was gone. A band of skin flopped away from the ear, at the place where the ear had been held to a man's head. It looked alive. It looked like it would move in Mad Mark's hands, as if it might make a squirm for freedom. It seemed to have the texture of a hunk of elastic.

"Christ, Mad Mark just went up and sliced it off the dead dink! No wonder he's Mad Mark, he did it like he was cuttin' sausages or something."

"What are you gonna do with it? Why don't you eat it, Mad Mark?"

"Bullshit, who's gonna eat a goddamn dink. I eat women, not dead dinks."

"We got some money off the gook, too. A whole shitload." One of the men pulled out a roll of greasy piasters, and the members of the patrol split it up and pocketed it; then they passed the ear around for everyone to look at.

Mad Mark called in gunships. For an hour the helicopters strafed and rocketed Tri Binh 4. The sky and the trees and the hillsides were lighted up by spotlights and tracers and fires. From our position we could smell the smoke coming from Tri Binh 4. We heard cattle and chickens dying. At two in the morning we started to sleep, one man at a time. Tri Binh 4 turned curiously quiet and dark, except for the sound and light of a last few traces of fire. Smoke continued to billow over to our position all night, however, and when I awakened every hour, it was the first thing to sense and to remind me of the ear. In the morning another patrol was sent into the village. The dead VC was still there, stretched out on his back with his eyes closed and his arms folded and his head cocked to one side so that you could not see where the ear was gone. Little fires burned in some of the huts, and dead animals lay about, but there were no people. We searched Tri Binh 4, then burned most of it down.

* * *

The days in April multiplied like twins, sextuplets, each identical. We played during the days. Volleyball. Gin. Tag. Poker or chess. Mad Mark had fun with his riot gas grenades, tossing them into a bunker and watching the artillery officer scramble out in tears. Captain Johansen and the battalion commander, Colonel Daud, flew overhead in a helicopter, dumping gas grenades onto the LZ. It was a training exercise. The idea was to test our reaction time, to make sure our gas masks were functioning. Mostly, though, it was to pass away the month of April.

At night we were supposed to send out ambushes, orders of Colonel Daud. Sometimes we did, other times we did not. If the officers decided that the men were too tired or too restless for a night's ambush, they would prepare a set of grid coordinates and call them into battalion headquarters. It would be a false report, a fake. The artilleryman would radio phony information to the big guns in the rear. The 105's or 155's would blast out their expensive rounds of marking explosives, and the lieutenant would call back his bogus adjustments, chewing out someone in the rear for poor marksmanship. During the night's radio watch, we would call our nonexistent ambush, asking for a situation report. We'd pause a moment, change our voice by a decibel, and answer our own call: "Sit Rep is negative. Out." We did this once an hour for the entire night, covering the possibility that higher headquarters might be monitoring the net. Foolproof. The enlisted men, all of us, were grateful to Alpha's officers. And the officers justified it, muttering that Colonel Daud was a greenhorn, too damn gung-ho.

* * *

In the next days it took little provocation for us to flick the flint of our Zippo lighters. Thatched roofs take the flame quickly, and on bad days the hamlets of Pinkville burned, taking our revenge in fire. It was good to walk from Pinkville and to see fire behind Alpha Company. It was good, just as pure hate is good.

We walked to other villages, and the phantom Forty-eighth Viet Cong Battalion walked with us. When a booby-trapped artillery round blew two popular soldiers into a hedgerow, men put their fists into the faces of the nearest Vietnamese, two frightened women living in the guilty hamlet, and when the troops were through with them, they hacked off chunks of thick black hair. The men were crying, doing this. An officer used his pistol, hammering it against a prisoner's skull.

Scraps of our friends were dropped in plastic body bags. Jet fighters were called in. The hamlet was leveled, and napalm was used. I heard screams in the burning black rubble. I heard the enemy's AK-47 rifles crack out like impotent popguns against the jets. There were Viet Cong in that hamlet. And there were babies and children and people who just didn't give a damn in there, too. But Chip and Tom were on the way to Graves Registration in Chu Lai, and they were dead, and it was hard to be filled with pity.

* * *

The Bouncing Betty is feared most. It is a common mine. It leaps out of its nest in the earth, and when it hits its apex, it explodes, reliable and deadly. If a fellow is lucky and if the mine is in an old emplacement, having been exposed to the rains, he may notice its three prongs jutting out of the clay. The prongs serve as the Bouncing Betty's firing device. Step on them, and the unlucky soldier will hear a muffled explosion; that's the initial charge sending the mine on its one-yard leap into the sky. The fellow takes another step and begins the next and his backside is bleeding and he's dead. We call it "ol' step and a half."

More destructive than the Bouncing Betty are the booby-trapped mortar and artillery rounds. They hang from trees. They nestle in shrubbery. They lie under the sand. They wait beneath the mud floors of huts. They haunted us. Chip, my black buddy from Orlando, strayed into a hedgerow and triggered a rigged 105 artillery round. He died in such a way that, for once, you could never know his color. He was wrapped in a plastic body bag, we popped smoke, and a helicopter took him away, my friend. And there was Shorty, a volatile fellow so convinced that the mines would take him that he spent a month AWOL. In July he came back to the field, joking but still unsure of it all. One day, when it was very hot, he sat on a booby-trapped 155 round.

When you are ordered to march through areas such as Pinkville—GI slang for Song My, parent village of My Lai—the Batangan Peninsula or the Athletic Field, appropriately named for its flat acreage of grass and rice paddy, when you step about these pieces of ground, you do some thinking. You hallucinate. You look ahead a few paces and wonder what your legs will resemble if there is more to the earth in that spot than silicates and nitrogen. Will the pain be unbearable? Will you scream or fall silent? Will you be afraid to look at your own body, afraid of the sight of your own red flesh and white bone? You wonder if the medic remembered his morphine. You wonder if your friends will weep.

It is not easy to fight this sort of self-defeating fear, but you try. You decide to be ultracareful—the hard-nosed, realistic approach. You try to second-guess the mine. Should you put your foot to that flat rock or the clump of weed to its rear? Paddy dike or water? You wish you were Tarzan, able to swing with the vines. You try to trace the footprints of the man to your front. You give it up when he curses you for following too closely; better one man dead than two.

The moment-to-moment, step-by-step decision-making preys on your mind. The effect sometimes is paralysis. You are slow to rise from rest breaks. You walk like a wooden man, like a toy soldier out of Victor Herbert's *Babes in Toyland.* Contrary to military and parental training, you walk with your eyes pinned to the dirt, spine arched, and you are shivering, shoulders hunched. If you are not overwhelmed by complete catatonia, you may react as Philip did on the day he was told to police up one of his friends, victim of an antipersonnel mine. Afterward, as dusk fell, Philip was swinging his entrenching tool like a madman, sweating and crying and hollering. He dug a foxhole four feet into the clay. He sat in it and sobbed. Everyone—all his friends and all the officers—were very quiet, and not a person said anything. No one comforted him until it was very dark. Then, to stop the noise, one man at a time would talk to him, each of us saying he understood and that tomorrow it would all be over. The captain said he would get Philip to the rear, find him a job driving a truck or painting fences.

Once in a great while we would talk seriously about the mines. "It's more than the fear of death that chews on your mind," one soldier, nineteen years old, eight months in the field, said. "It's an absurd combination of certainty and uncertainty: the certainty that you're walking in mine fields, walking past the things day after day; the uncertainty of your every movement, of which way to shift your weight, of where to sit down.

"There are so many ways the VC can do it. So many configurations, so many types of camouflage to hide them. I'm ready to go home."

The kid is right:

The M-14 antipersonnel mine, nicknamed the "toe popper." It will take a hunk out of your foot. Smitty lost a set of toes. Another man who is now just a blur of gray eyes and brown hair—he was with us for only a week—lost his left heel.

The booby-trapped grenade. Picture a bushy shrub along your path of march. Picture a tin can secured to the shrub, open and directed toward the trail. Inside the can is a hand grenade, safety pin removed, so that only the can's metal circumference prevents the "spoon," or firing handle, from jumping off the grenade and detonating it. Finally, a trip wire is attached to the grenade, extending across the pathway, perhaps six inches above the dirt. Hence, when your delicate size-eight foot caresses that wire, the grenade is yanked from its container, releasing the spoon and creating problems for you and your future.

The Soviet TMB and the Chinese antitank mines. Although designed to detonate under the pressure of heavy vehicles, the antitank mine is known to have shredded more than one soldier.

The directional-fragmentation mine. The concave-faced directional mine contains from 450 to 800 steel fragments embedded in a matrix and backed by an explosive charge—TNT or petnam. The mine is aimed at your anticipated route of march. Your counterpart in uniform, a gentle young man, crouches in the jungle, just off the trail. When you are in range, he squeezes his electronic firing device. The effects of the mine are similar to those of a twelve-gauge shotgun fired at close range. United States Army training manuals describe this country's equivalent device, the Claymore mine: "It will allow for wider distribution and use, particularly in large cities. It will effect considerable savings in materials and logistics." In addition, they call the mine cold-blooded.

The corrosive-action-car-killer. The CACK is nothing more than a grenade, its safety pin extracted and spoon held in place by a rubber band. It is deposited in your gas tank. Little boys and men of the cloth are particularly able to maneuver next to an unattended vehicle and do the deed—beneath a universal cloak of innocence. The corrosive action of the gasoline eats away the rubber band, releasing the spoon, blowing you up in a week or less. Although it is rarely encountered by the foot-borne infantryman, the device gives the rear-echelon mine finder (REMF) something to ponder as he delivers the general's laundry.

In the three days that I spent writing this, mines and men came together three more times. Seven more legs were out on the red clay; also, another arm.

The immediacy of the last explosion—three legs, ten minutes ago—made me ready to burn the midsection of this report, the flippant itemization of these killer devices. Hearing over the radio what I just did, only enough for a flashing memory of what it is all about, makes the *Catch-22* jokes into a cemetery of half-truths. "Orphan 22, this is . . . this is Yankee 22 . . . mine, mine. Two guys . . . legs are off . . . I say again, legs off . . . request urgent dust-off, grid 711888 . . . give me ETA . . . get that damn bird." Tactical Operations Center: "You're coming in distorted . . . Yankee 22? Say again . . . speak slowly . . . understand you need dust-off helicopter?" Pause. "This is Yankee 22 . . . for Chri . . . ake . . . need chopper . . . two men, legs are . . ."

But only to say another truth will I let the half-truths stand. The catalog of mines will be retained, because that is how we talked about them, with a funny laugh, flippantly, with a chuckle. It is funny. It's absurd.

Patent absurdity. The troops are going home, and the war has not been won, even with a quarter of the United States Army fighting it. We slay one of them, hit a mine, kill another, hit another mine. It is funny. We walk through the mines, trying to catch the Viet Cong Forty-eighth Battalion like an unexperienced hunter after a hummingbird. But he finds us far more often than we do him. He is hidden among the mass of civilians or in tunnels or in jungles. So we walk to find him, stalking the mythical, phantomlike Forty-eighth Battalion from here to there to here to there. And each piece of ground left behind is his from the moment we are gone on our next hunt. It is not a war fought for territory, not for pieces of land that will be won and held. It is not a war fought to win the hearts of the Vietnamese nationals, not in the wake of contempt drawn on our faces and on theirs, not in the wake of a burning village, a trampled rice paddy, a battered detainee. If land is not won and if hearts are at best left indifferent; if the only obvious criterion of military success is body count and if the enemy absorbs losses as he has, still able to lure us amid his crop of mines; if soldiers are being withdrawn, with more to go later and later and later; if legs make me more of a man, and they surely do, my soul and character and capacity to love notwithstanding; if any of this is truth, a soldier can only do his walking laughing along the way and taking a funny, crooked step.

After the war, he can begin to be bitter. Those who point at and degrade his bitterness, those who declare it's all a part of war and that this is a job which must be done—to those patriots I will recommend a postwar vacation to this land, where they can swim in the sea, lounge under a fine sun, stroll in the quaint countryside, wife and son in hand. Certainly, there will be a mine or two still in the earth. Alpha Company did not detonate all of them.

MICHAEL HERR
1940–

Herr covered the Vietnam War for Esquire *in 1967. He wrote the screenplay for Francis Coppola and John Milrus's film* Apocalypse Now *(1979) and currently works in publishing. William Burroughs commented on his work: "All the façades of patriotism, heroism, and the whole colossal fraud of American intervention fall away to the bare bones of fear, war, and death." He was talking about Herr's book* Dispatches, *published in 1977.*

From DISPATCHES

Airmobility, dig it, you weren't going anywhere. It made you feel safe, it made you feel Omni, but it was only a stunt, technology. Mobility was just mobility, it saved lives or took them all the time (saved mine I don't know how many times, maybe dozens, maybe none), what you really needed was a flexibility far greater than anything the technology could provide, some generous, spontaneous gift for accepting surprises, and I didn't have it. I got to hate surprises, control freak at the crossroads, if you were one of those people who always thought they had to know what was coming next, the war could cream you. It was the same with your ongoing attempts at getting used to the jungle or the blow-you-out climate or the saturating strangeness of the place which didn't lessen with exposure so often as it fattened and darkened in accumulating alienation. It was great if you could adapt, you had to try, but it wasn't the same as making a discipline, going into your own reserves and developing a real war metabolism, slow yourself down when your heart tried to punch its way through your chest, get swift when everything went to stop and all you could feel of your whole life was the entropy whipping through it. Unlovable terms.

The ground was always in play, always being swept. Under the ground was his, above it was ours. We had the air, we could get up in it but not disappear in *to* it, we could run but we couldn't hide, and he could do each so well that sometimes it looked like he was doing them both at once, while our finder just went limp. All the same, one place or another it was always going on, rock around the clock, we had the days and he had the nights. You could be in the most protected space in Vietnam and still know that your safety was provisional, that early death, blindness, loss of legs, arms or balls, major and lasting disfigurement—the whole rotten deal—could come in on the freakyfluky as easily as in the so-called expected ways, you heard so many of those stories it was a wonder anyone was left alive to die in firefights and mortar-rocket attacks. After a few weeks, when the nickel had jarred loose and dropped and I saw that everyone around me was carrying a gun, I also saw that any one of them could go off at any time, putting you where it wouldn't matter whether it had been an accident or not. The roads were mined, the trails booby-trapped, satchel charges and grenades blew up jeeps and movie theaters, the VC got work inside all the camps as shoeshine boys and laundresses and honey-dippers, they'd starch your fatigues and burn your shit and then go home and mortar your area. Saigon and Cholon and Danang held such hostile vibes that you felt you were being dry-sniped every time someone looked at you, and choppers fell out of the sky like fat poisoned birds a hundred times a day. After a while I couldn't get on one without thinking that I must be out of my fucking mind.

Fear and motion, fear and standstill, no preferred cut there, no way even to be clear about which was really worse, the wait or the delivery. Combat spared far more men than it wasted, but everyone suffered the time between contact, especially when they were going out every day looking for it; bad going on foot, terrible in trucks and APC's, awful in helicopters, the worst, traveling so fast toward something so frightening. I can remember times when I went half dead with my fear of the motion, the speed and direction already fixed and pointed one way. It was painful enough just flying "safe" hops between firebases and lz's; if you were ever on a helicopter that had been hit by ground fire your deep, perpetual chopper anxiety was guaranteed. At least actual contact when it was happening would draw long raggedy strands of energy out of you, it was juicy, fast and refining, and traveling toward it was hollow, dry, cold and steady, it never let you alone. All you could do was look around at the other people on board and see if they were as scared and numbed out as you were. If it looked like they weren't you thought they were insane, if it looked like they were it made you feel a lot worse.

I went through that thing a number of times and only got a fast return on my fear once, a too classic hot landing with the heat coming from the trees about 300 yards away, sweeping machine-gun fire that sent men head down into swampy water, running on their hands and knees toward the grass where it wasn't blown flat by the rotor blades, not much to be running for but better than nothing. The helicopter pulled up before we'd all gotten out, leaving the last few men to jump twenty feet down between the guns across the paddy and the gun on the chopper door. When we'd all reached the cover of the wall and the captain had made a check, we were amazed to see that no one had even been hurt, except for one man who'd sprained both his ankles jumping. Afterward, I remembered that I'd been down in the muck worrying about leeches. I guess you could say that I was refusing to accept the situation.

"Boy, you sure get offered some shitty choices," a Marine once said to me, and I couldn't help but feel that what he really meant was that you didn't get offered any at all. Specifically, he was just talking about a couple of C-ration cans, "dinner," but considering his young life you couldn't blame him for thinking that if he knew one thing for sure, it was that there was no one anywhere who cared less about what *he* wanted. There wasn't anybody he wanted to thank for his food, but he was grateful that he was still alive to eat it, that the motherfucker hadn't scarfed him up first. He hadn't been anything but tired and scared for six months and he'd lost a lot, mostly people, and seen far too much, but he was breathing in and breathing out, some kind of choice all by itself.

He had one of those faces, I saw that face at least a thousand times at a hundred bases and camps, all the youth sucked out of the eyes, the color drawn from the skin, cold white lips, you knew he wouldn't wait for any of it to come back. Life had made him old, he'd live it out old. All those faces, sometimes it was like looking into faces at a rock concert, locked in, the event had them; or like students who were very heavily advanced, serious beyond what you'd call their years if you didn't know for yourself what the minutes and hours of those years were made up of. Not just like all the ones you saw who looked like they couldn't drag their asses through another day of it. (How do you feel when a nineteen-year-old kid tells you from the bottom of his heart that he's gotten too old for this kind of shit?) Not like the faces of the dead or wounded either, they could look more released than overtaken. These were the faces of boys whose whole lives seemed to have backed up on them, they'd be a few feet away but they'd be looking back at you over a distance you knew you'd never really cross. We'd talk, sometimes fly together, guys going out on R&R, guys escorting bodies, guys who'd flipped over into extremes of peace or violence. Once I flew with a kid who was going home,

he looked back down once at the ground where he'd spent the year and
spilled his whole load of tears. Sometimes you even flew with the dead.

Once I jumped on a chopper that was full of them. The kid in the op
shack had said that there would be a body on board, but he'd been given
some wrong information. "How bad do you want to get to Danang?"
he'd asked me, and I'd said, "Bad."

When I saw what was happening I didn't want to get on, but they'd
made a divert and a special landing for me, I had to go with the chopper
I'd drawn, I was afraid of looking squeamish. (I remember, too, thinking
that a chopper full of dead men was far less likely to get shot down than
one full of living.) They weren't even in bags. They'd been on a truck
near one of the firebases in the DMZ that was firing support for Khe
Sanh, and the truck had hit a Command-detonated mine, then they'd
been rocketed. The Marines were always running out of things, even
food, ammo and medicine, it wasn't so strange that they'd run out of
bags too. The men had been wrapped around in ponchos, some of them
carelessly fastened with plastic straps, and loaded on board. There was a
small space cleared for me between one of them and the door gunner,
who looked pale and so tremendously furious that I thought he was angry
with me and I couldn't look at him for a while. When we went up the
wind blew through the ship and made the ponchos shake and tremble
until the one next to me blew back in a fast brutal flap, uncovering the
face. They hadn't even closed his eyes for him.

The gunner started hollering as loud as he could, "Fix it! Fix it!"
Maybe he thought the eyes were looking at him, but there wasn't anything I could do. My hand went there a couple of times and I couldn't,
and then I did. I pulled the poncho tight, lifted his head carefully and
tucked the poncho under it, and then I couldn't believe that I'd done it.
All during the ride the gunner kept trying to smile, and when we landed
at Dong Ha he thanked me and ran off to get a detail. The pilots jumped
down and walked away without looking back once, like they'd never seen
that chopper before in their lives. I flew the rest of the way to Danang in
a general's plane.

*   *   *

When the 173rd held services for their dead from Dak To the boots of
the dead men were arranged in formation on the ground. It was an old
paratrooper tradition, but knowing that didn't reduce it or make it any
less spooky, a company's worth of jump boots standing empty in the dust
taking benediction, while the real substance of the ceremony was being
bagged and tagged and shipped back home through what they called the
KIA Travel Bureau. A lot of the people there that day accepted the boots
as solemn symbols and went into deep prayer. Others stood around
watching with grudging respect, others photographed it and some just
thought it was a lot of bitter bullshit. All they saw out there was one

more set of spare parts, and they wouldn't have looked around for holy ghosts if some of those boots filled up again and walked.

Dak To itself had only been the command point for a combat without focus that tore a thirty-mile arc over the hills running northeast to southwest of the small base and airfield there from early November through Thanksgiving 1967, fighting that grew in size and fame while it grew more vicious and out of control. In October the small Dak To Special Forces compound had taken some mortar and rocket fire, patrols went out, patrols collided, companies splintered the action and spread it across the hills in a sequence of small, isolated firefights that afterward were described as strategy; battalions were sucked into it, then divisions, then reinforced divisions. Anyway, we knew for sure that we had a reinforced division in it, the 4th plus, and we said that they had one in it too, although a lot of people believed that a couple of light flexible regiments could have done what the NVA did up and down those hills for three weeks, leaving us to claim that we'd driven him up 1338, up 943, up 875 and 876, while the opposing claims remained mostly unspoken and probably unnecessary. And then instead of really ending, the battle vanished. The North Vietnamese collected up their gear and most of their dead and "disappeared" during the night, leaving a few bodies behind for our troops to kick and count.

"Just like goin' in against the Japs," one kid called it; the heaviest fighting in Vietnam since the Ia Drang Valley two years before, and one of the only times after Ia Drang when ground fire was so intense that the medevacs couldn't land through it. Wounded backed up for hours and sometimes days, and a lot of men died who might have been saved. Resupply couldn't make it in either, and the early worry about running out of ammunition grew into a panic and beyond, it became real. At the worst, a battalion of Airborne assaulting 875 got caught in an ambush sprung from behind, where no NVA had been reported, and its three companies were pinned and cut off in the raking fire of that trap for two days. Afterward, when a correspondent asked one of the survivors what had happened he was told, "What the fuck do you *think* happened? We got shot to pieces." The correspondent started to write that down and the paratrooper said, "Make that 'little pieces.' We were still shaking the trees for dog tags when we pulled back out of there."

Even after the North had gone away, logistics and transport remained a problem. A big battle had to be dismantled piece by piece and man by man. It was raining hard every day now, the small strip at Dak To became overloaded and unworkable, and a lot of troops were shuttled down to the larger strip at Kontum. Some even ended up as far out of their way as Pleiku, fifty miles to the south, for sorting and transport back to their units around II Corps. The living, the wounded and the dead flew together in crowded Chinooks, and it was nothing for guys to walk on top of the half-covered corpses packed in the aisles to get to a seat, or to make jokes among themselves about how funny they all looked, the dumb dead fuckers.

There were men sitting in loose groups all around the strip at Kontum, hundreds of them arranged by unit waiting to be picked up again and flown out. Except for a small sand-bagged ops shack and a medical tent, there was no shelter anywhere from the rain. Some of the men had rigged up mostly useless tents with their ponchos, a lot lay out sleeping in the rain with helmets or packs for pillows, most just sat or stood around waiting. Their faces were hidden deep inside the cover of their poncho hoods, white eye movement and silence, walking among them made you feel like you were being watched from hundreds of isolated caves. Every twenty minutes or so a helicopter would land, men would come out or be carried out, others would get on and the chopper would rear up on the strip and fly away, some toward Pleiku and the hospital, others back to the Dak To area and the mop-up operations there. The rotors of the Chinooks cut twin spaces out of the rain, forcing the spray in slanting jets for fifty yards around. Just knowing what was in those choppers gave the spray a bad taste, strong and briny. You didn't want to leave it on your face long enough to dry.

Back from the strip a fat, middle-aged man was screaming at some troops who were pissing on the ground. His poncho was pulled back away from the front of his helmet enough to show captain's bars, but nobody even turned around to look at him. He groped under his poncho and came up with a .45, pointed it into the rain and fired off a shot that made an empty faraway pop, like it had gone off under wet sand. The men finished, buttoned up and walked away laughing, leaving the captain alone shouting orders to police up the filth; thousands of empty and half-eaten ration cans, soggy clots of *Stars and Stripes*, an M-16 that someone had just left lying there and, worse, evidence of a carelessness unimaginable to the captain, it stank even in the cold rain, but it would police itself in an hour or two if the rain kept up.

The ground action had been over for nearly twenty-four hours now, but it was still going on in compulsive replay among the men who'd been there:

"A dead buddy is some tough shit, but bringing your own ass out alive can sure help you to get over it."

"We had this lieutenant, honest to Christ he was about the biggest dipshit fool of all time, all time. We called him Lieutenant Gladly 'cause he was always going like, 'Men . . . Men, I won't never ask you to do nothing I wouldn't do myself gladly,' what an asshole. We was on 1338 and he goes to me, 'Take a little run up to the ridge and report to me,' and I goes like, 'Never happen, *Sir.*' So he does, he goes up there himself and damned if the fucker didn't get zapped. He said we was gonna have a real serious talk when he come back, too. Sorry 'bout that."

"Kid here [not really here, "here" just a figure of speech] gets blown away ten feet in back of us. I swear to God, I thought I was looking at ten different guys when I turned around. . . ."

"You guys are so full of shit it's coming out of your fucking *ears!*" one man was saying. PRAY FOR WAR was written on the side of his helmet, and he was talking mostly to a man whose helmet name was SWINGING DICK. "You were pissing up everything but your fucking toenails, Scudo, don't you tell *me* you weren't scared man, don't you fucking *dare,* 'cause I was right fucking *there* man, and I was scared *shit!* I was scared every fucking minute, and I'm no different from any body else!"

"Well big deal, candy ass," Swinging Dick said. "You were scared."

"Damn straight! Damn straight! You're damn fucking straight I was scared! You're about the dumbest motherfucker I ever met, Scudo, but you're not that dumb. The *Marines* aren't even that dumb man, I don't care, all that bullshit they've got in the Marine Corps about how Marines aren't ever afraid, oh wow, I'll fucking bet. . . . I'll bet the Marines are *just as scared!*"

He started to get up but his knees gave under him. He made a quick grasping spasm out of control, like a misfire in the nervous system, and when he fell back he brought a stack of M-16's with him. They made a sharp clatter and everyone jerked and twitched out of the way, looking at each other as though they couldn't remember for a minute whether they needed to find cover or not.

"Hey baby, hey, watch where you're goin' there," a paratrooper said, but he was laughing, they were all laughing, and Pray For War was laughing harder than any of them, so hard that it filled suddenly with air and cracked over into high giggles. When he lifted his face again it was all tracked with tears.

"You gonna stand there, asshole?" he said to Swinging Dick. "Or are you gonna help me up on my fucking feet?"

Swinging Dick reached down and grabbed his wrists, locking them and pulling him up slowly until their faces were a couple of inches apart. For a second it looked like they were going to kiss.

"Looking good," Pray For War said. "Mmmm, Scudo, you are really looking good, man. It don't look to me like you were scared at all up there. You only look like about ten thousand miles of bad road."

* * *

One afternoon I mistook a bloody nose for a headwound, and I didn't have to wonder anymore how I'd behave if I ever got hit. We were walking out on a sweep north of Tay Ninh City, toward the Cambodian border, and a mortar round came in about thirty yards away. I had no sense of those distances then, even after six or seven weeks in Vietnam I still thought of that kind of information as a journalists' detail that could be picked up later, not something a survivor might have to know. When we fell down on the ground the kid in front of me put his boot into my face. I didn't feel the boot, it got lost in the tremendous concussion I made hitting the ground, but I felt a sharp pain in a line over my eyes. The kid turned around and started going into something insane right away, "Aw I'm sorry, shit I'm sorry, oh no man I'm *sorry.*" Some hot stinking metal had been put into my mouth, I thought I tasted brains there sizzling on the end of my tongue, and the kid was fumbling for his canteen and looking really scared, pale, near tears, his voice shaking, "Shit I'm just a fucking oaf, I'm a fucking clod, you're okay, you're really okay," and somewhere in there I got the feeling that it was him, somehow he'd just killed me. I don't think I said anything, but I made a sound that I can remember now, a shrill blubbering pitched to carry more terror than I'd ever known existed, like the sounds they've recorded off of plants being burned, like an old woman going under for the last time. My hands went flying everywhere all over my head, I had to find it and touch it. There seemed to be no blood coming from the top, none from the forehead, none running out of my eyes, my *eyes!* In a moment of half-relief the pain became specific, I thought that just my nose had been blown off, or in, or apart, and the kid was still going into it for himself, "Oh man, I'm really fucking sorry."

Twenty yards in front of us men were running around totally out of their minds. One man was dead (they told me later it was only because he'd been walking forward with his flak jacket open, another real detail to get down and never fuck with again), one was on his hands and knees vomiting some evil pink substance, and one, quite near us, was propped up against a tree facing away from the direction of the round, making himself look at the incredible thing that had just happened to his leg, screwed around about once at some point below his knee like a goofy scarecrow leg. He looked away and then back again, looking at it for a few seconds longer each time, then he settled in for about a minute, shaking his head and smiling, until his face became serious and he passed out.

By then I'd found my nose and realized what had happened, all that had happened, not even broken, my glasses weren't even broken. I took the kid's canteen and soaked my sweat scarf, washing the blood off where it had caked on my lip and chin. He had stopped apologizing, and there was no pity in his face anymore. When I handed his canteen back to him, he was laughing at me.

*   *   *

We were all strapped into the seats of the Chinook, fifty of us, and something, someone was hitting it from the outside with an enormous hammer. How do they do that? I thought, we're a thousand feet in the air! But it had to be that, over and over, shaking the helicopter, making it dip and turn in a horrible out-of-control motion that took me in the stomach. I had to laugh, it was so exciting, it was the thing I had wanted, almost what I had wanted except for that wrenching, resonant metal-echo; I could hear it even above the noise of the rotor blades. And they were going to fix that, I knew they would make it stop. They had to, it was going to make me sick.

They were all replacements going in to mop up after the big battles on Hills 875 and 876, the battles that had already taken on the name of one great battle, the battle of Dak To. And I was new, brand new, three days in-country, embarrassed about my boots because they were so new. And across from me, ten feet away, a boy tried to jump out of the straps and then jerked forward and hung there, his rifle barrel caught in the red plastic webbing of the seat back. As the chopper rose again and turned, his weight went back hard against the webbing and a dark spot the size of a baby's hand showed in the center of his fatigue jacket. And it grew—I knew what it was, but not really—it got up to his armpits and then started down his sleeves and up over his shoulders at the same time. It went all across his waist and down his legs, covering the canvas on his boots until they were dark like everything else he wore, and it was running in slow, heavy drops off of his fingertips. I thought I could hear the drops hitting the metal strip on the chopper floor. Hey! . . . Oh, but this isn't anything at all, it's not real, it's just some *thing* they're going through that isn't real. One of the door gunners was heaped up on the floor like a cloth dummy. His hand had the bloody raw look of a pound of liver fresh from the butcher paper. We touched down on the same lz we had just left a few minutes before, but I didn't know it until one of the guys shook my shoulder, and then I couldn't stand up. All I could feel of my legs was their shaking, and the guy thought I'd been hit and helped me up. The chopper had taken eight hits, there was shattered plastic all over the floor, a dying pilot up front, and the boy was hanging forward in the straps again, he was dead, but not (I knew) really dead.

It took me a month to lose that feeling of being a spectator to something that was part game, part show. That first afternoon, before I'd boarded the Chinook, a black sergeant had tried to keep me from going. He told me I was too new to go near the kind of shit they were throwing around up in those hills. ("You a reporter?" he'd asked, and I'd said, "No, a writer," dumbass and pompous, and he'd laughed and said, "Careful. You can't use no eraser up where you wanna go.") He'd pointed to the bodies of all the dead Americans lined in two long rows near the chopper pad, so many that they could not even cover all of them decently. But they were not real then, and taught me nothing. The Chinook had come in, blowing my helmet off, and I grabbed it up and joined the replacements waiting to board. "Okay, man," the sergeant said. "You gotta go, you gotta go. All's I can say is, I hope you get a clean wound."

* * *

In April I got a call telling me that Page had been hit again and was not expected to live. He had been up goofing somewhere around Cu Chi, digging the big toys, and a helicopter he was riding in was ordered to land and pick up some wounded. Page and a sergeant ran out to help, the sergeant stepped on a mine which blew his legs off and sent a two-inch piece of shrapnel through Page's forehead above the right eye and deep into the base of his brain. He retained consciousness all the way to the hospital at Long Binh. Flynn and Perry Young were on R&R in Vientiane when they were notified, and they flew immediately to Saigon. For nearly two weeks, friends at Time-Life kept me informed by telephone from their daily cables; Page was transferred to a hospital in Japan and they said that he would probably live. He was moved to Walter Reed Army Hospital (a civilian and a British subject, it took some doing), and they said that he would live but that he'd always be paralyzed on his left side. I called him there, and he sounded all right, telling me that his roommate was this very religious colonel who kept apologizing to Page because he was only in for a check-up, he hadn't been wounded or anything fantastic like that. Page was afraid that he was freaking the colonel out a little bit. Then they moved him to the Institute for Physical Rehabilitation in New York, and while none of them could really explain it medically, it seemed that he was regaining the use of his left arm and leg. The first time I went to see him I walked right past his bed without recognizing him out of the four patients in the room, even though he'd been the first one I'd seen, even though the other three were men in their forties and fifties. He lay there grinning his deranged, uneven grin, his eyes were wet, and he raised his right hand for a second to jab at me with his finger. His head was shaved and sort of lidded now across the forehead where they'd opened it up ("What did they find in there, Page?" I asked him. "Did they find that quiche lorraine?") and caved in on the right side where they'd removed some bone. He was emaciated and he looked really old, but he was still grinning very proudly as I approached the bed, as if to say, "Well, didn't Page step into it this time?" as though two inches of shrapnel in your brain was the wiggiest goof of them all, that wonderful moment of the Tim Page Story where our boy comes leering, lurching back from death, twin brother to his own ghost.

That was that, he said, *fini Vietnam,* there could be no more odds left, he'd been warned. Sure he was crazy, but he wasn't *that* crazy. He had a bird now, a wonderful English girl named Linda Webb whom he'd met in Saigon. She'd stayed with him in the Long Binh hospital even though the shock and fear of seeing him like that had made her pass out fifteen times on the first evening. "I'd really be the fool, now, to just give that one up, now, wouldn't I?" he said, and we all said, Yes, man, you would be.

On his twenty-fifth birthday there was a big party in the apartment near the hospital that he and Linda had found. Page wanted all of the people to be there who, he said, had bet him years ago in Saigon that he'd never make it past twenty-three. He wore a blue sweat suit with a Mike patch, black skull and bones, on his sleeve. You could have gotten stoned just by walking into the room that day, and Page was so happy to be here and alive and among friends that even the strangers who turned up then were touched by it. "There's Evil afoot," he kept saying, laughing and chasing after people in his wheelchair. "Do no Evil, think ye no Evil, smoke no Evil. . . . Yesh."

A month went by and he made fantastic progress, giving up the chair for a cane and wearing a brace to support his left arm.

"I've a splendid new trick for the doctors," he said one day, flinging his left arm out of the brace and up over his head with great effort, waving his hand a little. Sometimes he'd stand in front of a full-length mirror in the apartment and survey the wreckage, laughing until tears came, shaking his head and saying, "Ohhhhh, fuck! I mean, just *look* at that, will you? Page is a fucking hemi-plegic," raising his cane and stumbling back to his chair, collapsing in laughter again.

He fixed up an altar with all of his Buddhas, arranging prayer candles in a belt of empty .50-caliber cartridges. He put in a stereo, played endlessly at organizing his slides into trays, spoke of setting out Claymores at night to keep "undesirables" away, built model airplanes ("Very good therapy, that"), hung toy choppers from the ceiling, put up posters of Frank Zappa and Cream and some Day-Glo posters which Linda had made of monks and tanks and solid soul brothers smoking joints in the fields of Vietnam. He began talking more and more about the war, often coming close to tears when he remembered how happy he and all of us had been there.

One day a letter came from a British publisher, asking him to do a book whose working title would be "Through with War" and whose purpose would be to once and for all "take the glamour out of war." Page couldn't get over it.

"Take the glamour out of war! I mean, how the bloody hell can you do *that?* Go and take the glamour out of a Huey, go take the glamour out of a Sheridan. . . . Can *you* take the glamour out of a Cobra or getting stoned at China Beach? It's like taking the glamour out of an M-79, taking the glamour out of Flynn." He pointed to a picture he'd taken, Flynn laughing maniacally ("We're winning," he'd said), triumphantly. "Nothing the matter with *that* boy, is there? Would you let your daughter marry that man? Ohhhh, war is *good* for you, you can't take the glamour out of that. It's like trying to take the glamour out of sex, trying to take the glamour out of the Rolling Stones." He was really speechless, working his hands up and down to emphasize the sheer insanity of it.

"I mean, you *know* that, it just *can't be done!*" We both shrugged and laughed, and Page looked very thoughtful for a moment. "The very *idea!*" he said. "Ohhh, what a laugh! Take the bloody *glamour* out of bloody *war!*"

KEITH WALKER
1934–

Walker is a painter and filmmaker who lives in California. While making a photo essay about Vietnam veterans, he became interested in women veterans and began interviewing them. He published twenty-six of the interviews in A Piece of My Heart *(1985).*

From A Piece of My Heart

(Rose Sandecki was a nurse at evacuation hospitals in Vietnam, and later became the director of a center assisting veterans of the war.)

A story from Cu Chi, another example of the sort of rude awakening to my military naiveté. I got a phone call on the ward from the chief nurse, saying, "You've got a patient there that is going to get an award. Make sure that the bed has clean sheets, the area is straightened up, and the ward looks good." Which really turned me off to begin with: Let's clean up the ward because we've got VIPs coming in. Well, the VIP happened to be the general of the 25th Infantry Division along with his aide and an entourage of about twelve people. And this patient, when he came through the recovery room the day before, had remembered me. This was his second visit to us. He had been there three months before with frag wounds, had been sent back to the jungle, and came back this time with both of his legs blown off—he was all of about twenty years old. When he was waking up from the anesthesia, he remembered me. He started kidding me about how I had made him cough and deep-breathe so he wouldn't come down with pneumonia. We were kidding around, and he said, "Don't you remember me, ma'am?" I said, "Oh, yeah." But I really didn't because there were just so many of them. . . . The entourage was coming to give him an award because he happened to be number twenty thousand to come through the 12th Evac Hospital. In 1968 there were twenty-four Army evac hospitals in Vietnam, and he was number *twenty thousand* through *one* of twenty-four Army hospitals. We are not talking about the Air Force hospitals, the Navy hospitals . . . but twenty thousand through one hospital. So, for this distinction, the general comes in and gives him a watch. They have this little ceremony, give him a Purple Heart and the watch. I'm standing off in the corner watching all this, and as the general handed him the watch—"From the 25th Infantry Division as a token of our appreciation"—the kid more or less flings the watch back at him and says something like, "I can't accept this, sir; it's not going to help me walk." I couldn't really see the expression on the general's face, but they all left after this little incident. I went over and just put my arms around him and hugged him . . . and if I remember correctly, I started crying . . . and I think he was crying. I really admired him for that. That was one time that I let the feelings down and let somebody see what I felt. It took a lot for him to do that, and it sort of said what this war was all about to me . . .

(Linda J. McClenahan, a WAC, worked in communications in Vietnam.)

I had just turned twenty-one and had met this buck sergeant with the 199th. Ski and I were becoming closer all the time. In August, he and his buddy, Rowdy, and another guy came to pick us up, and that night I was the only woman who could make it. The three of us were riding in the back, drinking Wild Turkey and joking around when Ski had to go to the bathroom. The truck stopped and he jumped down and started to jog into the bushes. He stepped on a mine. . . . He was gone. . . . All we could do was continue on and report it—someone with detectors would have to come and get him. I remember we got back in the truck, and Rowdy took a drink from the bottle, passed it to me, and quietly said, "I gotta stop making friends over here." I was filled with guilt; I was the only woman on the truck. He wouldn't have gone into the bushes if I hadn't been there. . . . I never told anyone about that . . . not anyone. For twelve years I believed it was my fault that Ski was dead. Now I know I didn't kill Ski. . . . The war did. The war got Rowdy too, about a week later during their next outing. Except for R&R and coming home, I never left the Long Binh compound again.

(Pat Johnson was a surgical nurse in Vietnam.)

I'm not going to talk about the severity of the wounds and things like that. I can talk about some of the things that I felt, you know, by being a nurse there. One of the things that used to come back to me all the time while I was there is that these kids were so young. And many of them didn't want to be there. I remember having really angry feelings about the people who had gotten out of being there, because a lot of these kids in Vietnam were really young, and they were so far away from their families. They were so brave and they would come in. . . . They were really hurting, and they were really afraid. Many of them hadn't had a good home-cooked meal or even a good meal—you know, they'd been eating C-rations and stuff for such a long time—and their fatigues were so dirty. I remember one kid in particular; both of his legs had gone through a grenade thing. And I remember him saying, "I'm okay, so why don't you look at someone else?" Another thing that would just amaze me is that they would hardly ever ask for anything for pain. I'd worked in the emergency room in the States, and people come in with the smallest things just screaming out in pain and wanting something. And here are these kids with really horrendous injuries. I think they were just so happy to be alive and to be somewhere safe that they would never complain about their pain. I just remember feeling so sad for them.

(Bobbie Jo Pettit entertained the troops in Vietnam as a member of "The Pretty Kittens," an all-girl band.)

Another time, I remember we were sitting in an airport and a GI came in. He had a bush hat on with a lot of lines on it. I didn't know what that was at the time. The thing that drew me to him was that he was very singular; you could tell he was very independent, and he had an "over-and-under," an M-16 with a grenade launcher on it. I mean, he made John Wayne look like . . . John Wayne didn't look tough compared to this guy. So I talked to him for a while, and he told me he had been there for three years, didn't want to go home. His brother had been killed over there. He explained that all these lines on his hat were kills. And he was somebody that was . . . like, he was gentle. He said poetry to me right there in the airport. It was incredible. I got a letter from him when we were both back—that's the only contact I had with him—and it was a poetic letter about turning swords into plowshares, a lot of that kind of stuff. . . . But that was like what people's perceptions were on a level with. Granted that I grew up in America, in Los Angeles. You know, miniskirts and convertibles cruising the ice-cream shops . . . that was the mentality that we all went over there with. . . . That was what was so

. . . well, a lot like the movie *Deer Hunter,* which I think was the common story.

(Maureen Walsh was a Navy nurse in Vietnam.)

In August of 1966 I took my oath in the new Federal Building in downtown Boston. After women's officer school, I went to Quonset Point, Rhode Island, to the naval air station there and spent two years, which was a varied experience, being around the planes and the ships as well as the naval station hospital. I had a lot of experience flying in the planes and went through the low pressure chambers so I could fly in jets. I got to spend a lot of time on the ships, especially the carriers. I was head nurse in the dependents' units and also the emergency room there, and then, because we were near Groton, Connecticut, got involved with submarine medicine as well.

At that point I was rather addicted to military nursing, and of course, the social life wasn't any small part of it as well. Vietnam was starting to become prominent in the military picture, and I decided that I would volunteer to go over, much to my mother's dismay. My chief nurse discouraged me. She said, "You know, you're very young. They're only taking people who are very experienced, and you shouldn't go near Vietnam unless you've had a lot of experience." I decided after I got to Vietnam that there was nothing in the United States that could ever prepare me for that, absolutely nothing. But I was adventuresome, and I decided, what the heck, might as well go. So, I entreatied the chief nurse to endorse my request. She did, and said, "I do it with a lot of reservation. I know that you can do the work, but I really worry about your lack of experience." Sure enough, three months later, I received orders. She was more surprised than anybody, but I wasn't; I said I knew I'd be going anyway, because that was my intent. Ever since I was a little kid I wanted to be a Navy nurse and be stationed at the naval academy—of course, I had all of this glamour idea. The other thing, I wanted to be in a war zone or someplace where I could really experience my skills, et cetera. . . .

Well, that bubble burst after I got over there. It was September of '68. The memory is very vivid. I remember coming in to the airport at Da Nang, and it was raining of course—we were coming into the monsoon season. We got off the plane and really went through a culture shock. Everybody had guns; people were lining up; there were people in the airport sleeping all over the place. There was nothing but artillery from one end of the airport to the next. There were a lot of Vietnamese people walking around very, very depressed-looking. Off in the distance we could hear the guns exploding, and I thought to myself, "My God, this is like a John Wayne movie." You could actually see the explosions going off in the hills. But the eerie thing about it was, people were walking around like automatons. The explosions were going on, but nobody was paying any attention. Every time something would explode, I could just feel my heart skip a beat; it was both exciting and very frightening.

We unloaded at what seemed to be an old courthouse. It was dusty but it was the only place where the inside was dry. We sat down to write out the endless papers that you have to fill out when you go from one place to another in the military. As the explosions were going on, the desks or the tables that we were writing on would raise up off the floor. And the guy who was talking to us was talking nonstop like this was just ordinary traffic going by outside.

Anyway, we got to our quarters, which was in the east end of Da Nang, right along the South China Sea. It was a beautiful place, paradoxically, very beautiful and very hostile at the same time. We were right off the beach, where Seabees were on one end of the compound and the Marine engineers on the other. Across the street there were helicopters and the Marine airfield, and then beyond that was the beach. Marble Mountain was to the left as we were looking out to sea and to the right was Monkey Mountain. Behind us there was a Vietnamese village, and probably about ten miles out there was another mountain range, Hivan Pass. The hospital was made up of Quonset huts. It was the largest combat casualty unit in the world at the time. I don't remember how many personnel were there. There were hundreds; it was like a little city in itself. We lived in a Quonset hut and, according to the standards of Vietnam, lived rather luxuriously. I mean, we had our own toilets—we even had a washing machine! We each had an individual room with the metal military beds and a desk, but at least we had privacy. The Marines and Seabees had made a patio out in the back with a fence surrounding it. We would often pull up a chair, grab a beer, and watch the war as we could see it going on in the mountains north and south of us. Our chief nurse let us rest for about twenty-four hours to go through the jet lag, and then we were hustled onto the wards.

Each unit, which was one Quonset hut, had five corpsmen, with about thirty to sixty patients. And each of the huts would be divided into orthopedics, surgery, medicine, intensive care, or whatever. There were several of these huts lined up, and each had a walkway entrance to it so we could get from one to the next. The walkways had bunkers along them. The Navy nurses, because we had so many corpsmen in each ward, would be responsible for like three hundred to three hundred fifty patients, and what we'd have to do is go from one building to the next, get the report from the corpsmen, and take care of the sickest patients.

The first two nights I was there we didn't have any incoming or anything, though we could hear it in the peripheral areas. But my introduction to Vietnam nursing was on the third night as I was walking outside, going from one building to the next, checking the patients—and I was feeling overwhelmed as it was. From the mountains behind us, the Viet Cong were sending in mortars and rockets, and I heard this tremendous roar go over my head. I never heard a rocket in my life. I didn't know whether it was a plane, or a helicopter—I couldn't imagine what it was. Phew! This red, flaming thing came flying over, and I thought, "Oh, my God, that thing's from outer space." Well, when I heard that whoosh I went into one of the bunkers, and I know that I did not reach the bottom, because I felt all this stuff crawling around down there. I think I hit bottom and bounced right back out. I knew they were rats; they had to be rats! I said to myself, "Dear God, am I going to get bit by a rat and have to go home, or am I going to get hit by the shrapnel up here?" I decided it would be more honorable to be hit by the shrapnel, such a choice! So I just kind of buried into the sidewalk, and as I was kissing the concrete I looked up to watch all of this action. As I turned my head to the right—we were sort of on a hill on a sand dune—I could see the Marine base receiving rockets. As they went in I could see the planes explode. Oh, my God, this was like a movie! I couldn't conceive that I was really there. I was a participant, but I still didn't feel like I was going to get hit, because I really wasn't there; it was total denial.

Finally, everything stopped and I didn't know whether to get up. Navy nurses wore white uniforms over there, and we were walking targets. The Vietnamese village—we called it "the vill"—the Viet Cong vill was right behind us. Often times our people would take sniper fire at night. I didn't know about the sniper fire—that came a few days later—but I took my white hat off. If I had had something to put around me I would've, because I knew instinctively I was a sitting duck out there. So I just got up and said, "Well, I guess I'm in Vietnam, and I've got to do the best I can," looked down to make sure I hadn't wet my pants, went on to the next building, and walked into the ward. Some of my corpsmen had been there six or seven months, and this was a routine night to them. I must've looked as white as my uniform, and they started laughing as I came into the unit. They started teasing me about getting into a little action already. I could've clobbered them. So I guess I got my initiation; that was it. I was frightened as hell, and I was excited, yet on the other hand, if I let the emotions run away with me, I would've been totally incapacitated.

As it was, I was fighting inexperience; my former chief nurse was right. I was really flying by the seat of my pants as far as going into these units and checking the patients. To make up for my inexperience, I'd read the chart, check all the IVs, dressings, and casts several times for each patient. Each person had enough "plumbing" to make the average plumber marvel. I mean, there were machines on every person—suction, respirators, monitors of all sorts—everybody had multiple intravenous fluids infusing, catheters, and all sorts of sundry tubes and drains. By the time you weed through that to find the poor individual under it all, you couldn't really make him out. It was incredible!

I really had to stifle the emotions in order to be able to focus in on what was happening to each and every one of those patients and to keep all of that data in mind, write everything down, as well as talk to all of the corpsmen. I didn't even know all of the corpsmen at that point; I didn't know all of the patients. I would hope and pray every time I would leave a unit to go to the next one that I wouldn't find so much devastation, because already I was overwhelmed from the other wards. But I found similar situations on every ward. I think I had five wards that were my responsibility. And that's what we did when we worked the night shift. I had so much responsibility and so much to do on each of the units that I couldn't worry about the extraneous goings on outside.

Nights were especially difficult because this was the time when people who were wounded would be very frightened—moaning and groaning and calling out. Marines were incredibly stoic. It was surprising that they didn't cry out more than they did. There were a lot of times when they died on us at night. I mean, I would go from one unit to the next and have three, four, five Marines die maybe in the period of one night. Some of them in my arms. I'd be holding them, and they'd be hanging on—"Oh, I don't want to die!" You have to say, "Well, God, I can't get involved, I can't get involved," but it's pretty damn hard not getting involved when you see a nineteen- or twenty-year-old blond kid from the Midwest or California or the East Coast screaming and dying. A piece of my heart would go with each! You knew that their families would be getting a visit from the Marine Corps two days later. It was all I could do to hold back the tears, and we did hold back a lot, which I think was very unhealthy. It started very early; we had no way to really let loose with each other. One of the things we found is that we were all so extremely busy that we didn't have *time* to let loose with each other. The other aspect was that there was some sort of a feeling with nurses at the time that we were all volunteers that went over there. Since we were volunteers, we had to take what we got and not complain about it. The "shut up and do your work" mentality.

We also had to put up with the hostile environment as well. Besides the incoming, there were the rats, there were the snakes, there were the monsoons. We would often go down to a ward that was flooded from the monsoons. We were taking care of patients . . . There'd be rats in the water; sometimes there'd be snakes there. That bothered me more than anything. . . . We also took care of the Viet Cong and the NVA. This brought us down to the realities of war—there were young men there from the opposite side. They were the same age as our own fellas; most of them were even younger. They didn't want to be there any more than we did.

It took me about two days to realize that it was such a mistake being over there. We were so pumped up when we went to Vietnam, so patriotic, so full of American idealism, and when we got over there, it was nothing but a sham. The war was going on—there was no sense to it, there was no sense of "Okay, we're going into a battle. We're going to take over some of the geography; we're going to hold it, then we'll go on to the next part; we'll take over that. Then there will be peace." Our guys would go in to a hill or a village, get the hell beat out of them, and then we would receive the casualties. The next day they would be pulled out of there. Then they'd go back another week; we'd take more casualties. It was like that for the entire time we were over there. Marines were getting shot, they were getting mutilated, and there was no purpose; there was no rhyme nor reason to it.

So besides dealing with our own emotions and then dealing with that, we were in conflict between anger and grief constantly. There was just no resolution to any of that. Even when we went into town there was evidence of the Vietnamese taking advantage of us. The black markets were set up all over the place; they were milking us from every single angle that you could imagine. But we took care of *them,* we took care of them well. I remember the Viet Cong were like jungle rats, surviving in the jungles. Their skin was scarred like leather. They were very unsocialized. The average twenty-year-old looked like he was forty, fifty, sixty years old. Some of them I became quite attached to. The NVA were more educated, and a lot of their officers were very fluent in English; some of them had studied in the States. God, they didn't want to be there any more than we did. What we found was that the women, the NVA and VC women, were very, very vicious in behavior. I remember one night I brought a dinner tray to one of them, and she was on a bed with two casts on her legs, having had abdominal and eye surgery and all of the usual plumbing. I gave the woman a tray and turned around to get a sheet, and she had picked up a fork and was going right into my back. I just turned around in time and knocked it out of her hand. That was typical of the female behavior—they never gave up; they tenaciously fought to escape.

I want to talk about the intensive care unit. The other units were nothing compared with what the intensive care units were like. Many times when we were on duty and there were a lot of casualties coming in, the doctors would necessarily be taken to the triage area. That left the nurses and the corpsmen to do the best we could on the units. We couldn't call the doctors to do some of the things that were physician-related. For instance, patients would pop bleeders on the ward; they would start bleeding under their dressings. What we would have to do is make decisions about . . . We'd have to go in and clamp off bleeders. And it was rather a touchy situation because, you know, it looks pretty clear when you're in the laboratory or the operating room, but if you're not a surgeon, it's pretty hard to tell one artery from a ureter. It was anxiety-producing, to say the least.

Several times when we would have incoming, the mortars would blow out our regular and emergency generators. Of about twenty patients in the ICU, there were usually ten to fifteen on respirators, with chest tubes, and when the electricity went off, you can just imagine what chaos ensued. We often had to do mouth-to-mouth or trach-to-trach breathing for these people until the emergency power came on. We would have a few ambubags. We'd be throwing them around like footballs from one end of the unit to the other. So we lost people that way too. It was so frustrating, and a lot of times we'd have to give up breathing because we were so exhausted we would have passed out. That happened four or five times when I was on duty.

One night I was walking through one of the units that was right off the helicopter pad, when a mortar came in and exploded. Shrapnel came in the door—went right by me, under my legs. Another piece came in as I was counting narcotics for one of the corpsmen at the medicine cabinet near the door. The shrapnel went through his eye and through his head, went through the medicine cabinet, exited through the unit on the other side, and lodged in the wall. God, that was awful, that was awful to see that.

Another night that we had some incoming, we were walking along the walkway and I saw one of the mortars hit smack-dead on one of our units; it exploded. There was not a lot of screaming and yelling, but mostly what really hit me was the stench, the burning flesh. The Marines never screamed, which is incredible, their training is incredible. I remember going into the ward. The lights were all out, so I couldn't see a thing, but we knew there was a lot of activity. I'm not so sure I would've been prepared to see immediately what was happening. I had a flashlight with me . . . opened the flashlight and there was just chunks of flesh and blood all over the wall. Wounded men had been wounded again in the unit. Four of our corpsmen were killed that night. One of our nurses that was out going from one unit to another got down just in time. The way the shrapnel came it would've decapitated her had she not been down. I don't know how any of our nurses missed getting hit—by some miracle.

There were times when, as I say, the doctors weren't immediately available, and we had to make major life-saving decisions. One night, as a typical example, I was on a neurosurgery unit. We had a lot of casualties, and the doctors were all tied up in triage. I had a young man that was put on the unit, and the doctor said, "You've got to do the best you can with him." As soon as the doctor left, he went into respiratory distress, and I had to do a tracheostomy on him, and God, there was no equipment on the unit to do something like that—most of our patients went to the operating room to have something like that done. I just had to put a slit in his throat, and all I had was a ball-point pen; I had to unscrew that and put the tube of the pen into the trachea, which is a common thing actually—it's the only thing you had on you. There were a lot of those kinds of things going on that we had to do, things that we were never taught.

I'll never forget this one night. I was sitting next to this bed, and a young corpsman came in . . . and I looked at his name, of course. I had known him in the States. He was one of the fellows that was at the naval air station with me, but when I had seen him, I didn't recognize him because his wounds were so severe and numerous. There's no way you can save somebody like that, but the most incredible thing is that he was clear—he was talking with me; he knew who I was. I was holding the one hand that he had left, and as I was talking with him, he said, "I know I'm not going to live." . . . I remember him telling me to contact his mother, and he was telling me how much he enjoyed our friendship, and he said, "Please don't leave me." This young man was losing blood at a tremendously quick rate, and what amazed me is that he was still so clear. He grabbed my hand and I talked to him for as long as possible, and I just felt that grip loosening and loosening and loosening. The only thing I could do was sit there and pray with him. I knew he was going to leave this holocaust; he was lucky. I just told him good-bye.

Many times I'd have fellows that would come in the ward—especially the Navy corpsmen, some of whom I had trained—and some of them had been stationed with me at the units back at Quonset Point. That was horrible, seeing those men come in wounded. They were just like brothers to us, because the Navy nurses and the Navy corpsmen and the Corps WAVES had a very close bond. We worked very very closely and went through a great deal together. You knew their families, where they came from—you knew everything about them. And to see them come in—they were just like having your own family, own brothers, get killed. Those are some of the memories in the intensive care unit.

It sounds like there was a lot of gore over there, but there were good times as well, in between. We used to have lulls in the war. When we had time, we played. When we were not too tired we used to go over to the officers' club. Once in a while, in the one day we had off a week—if we did have the day off—we would go over on the beach.

We did a lot of things, also, in the community. I volunteered to go on the civil action patrols. We went out a number of times with some of the corpsmen, Marines and physicians that used to volunteer to go into the villages to see patients. And my eyes were opened out there too—people living in these slovenly, dirty huts—dirt floors—with the chickens and the ducks. We'd go in there and deliver babies in the filth and the crap. We went to the orphanages, played with the kids, and took them to the beaches every now and then.

Some of us got in to town; it was more or less off limits—you know, we had to deal with the sniper fire and everything else. Most of the time we didn't tell the chief nurse we were going in. I had a friend who was a Korean; he would pick me up on his motorcycle, and we would go to the different restaurants downtown. It was a dead giveaway that I had been there, because of all the garlic and kim chee and everything else that they used—it was awful-smelling.

The saddest thing that happened for me over there too, among all those other things, was I lost my fiancé. He was a Marine pilot, and I was with him the night that he died; he was going on a mission. I was sitting in the officers' club, and I knew he wasn't coming back. I practically begged him not to go, but there's no way he couldn't go. It was his job; he had to go. And he was shot down. The worst thing was that I was not allowed to grieve for the whole time that I was there. . . . I don't know if any of the other nurses really knew about it. I told them, but it was just one of those things that you didn't—you couldn't share because everybody else had their own little world of grief. Quite frankly, each of my friends, each of the nurses out there, was just totally saturated with their problems, with their own fatigue. . . . And again, the stiff upper lip-type martyr syndrome of nursing didn't allow for that to happen. I think I was more able to talk to the other Navy and Marine friends that I had out there. We had quite a relationship with the Marines that were around us; they were always in our club or took us out. They were more or less our confidants. I think my Marine friends knew more about me than the people that I actually worked with. They used to pick us up with their jeeps. I remember going out on a date with somebody riding shotgun . . . rather a lot of fun. I'll never forget, one night I was going out to the officers' club with one of my friends, and it was kind of a strange sensation having somebody go on a date with a .45 around his waist and a rifle on the dash of the jeep. We went through this village and somebody took a potshot at us, and I remember the bullet coming in and over my head and behind his and out through the other end of the jeep. The attitude that we had: we looked at each other and laughed. What else could you do?

Well, what I can say is, I did come back from the holocaust, from that horrific experience over there, with a very peaceful philosophy, a very changed value system about life and death. We came into California—

when I saw that Golden Gate Bridge I wanted to reach down and hug it. And by God, when we got to Travis Air Force Base I got down on the ground and kissed it. I remember having to stop there overnight and going to this swimming pool where all the officers' wives and everybody were chitchatting about the day's events. I thought to myself, "My God, I have been in hell. These women are sitting around talking, and they have no concept of what is going on over there." I was extremely depressed. But I knew I was coming home the next day. I was met in Boston by my folks. It was great to see them. I had requested to come to Annapolis to fulfill my dream, but it was for a different reason this time—it was to come back here for peace and quiet. I didn't want to go back to one of these huge hospitals. I didn't want to see any more carnage. There's nothing more pastoral and more quiet and soothing than this water around here.

I had injured my back when I was about three weeks away from coming home. I didn't tell anybody. What had happened is that the rockets came in and I belly flopped on the floor and really tore up the back. It gave me a lot of trouble when I came here to the States, shortly after I started working on the units. The horrible part about it was that I had a lot of pain and problems that I was going through, and I couldn't get anybody to believe me. You know, they were essentially saying, "Well, you're just a baby" or "It's all in your head." For about three years I went through all this pain. I had gotten orders from Annapolis to Bethesda Naval Hospital, and I finally went through surgery. They found a lot of damage in the back, so at least that vindicated me, but still I decided right then and there I was going to get out of the service.

I really didn't know what I wanted to do. I had reached the epitome of what it was to be a nurse. There was nothing I could possibly do in the United States that would equal that experience. My fellow nurses that had been over there, incredibly, never asked me what I went through. We went through an ignominious kind of a situation where, a couple times in Annapolis and in Bethesda, I did some things on the units that were not considered nursing responsibilities—but out of reaction, you know, gut-level reactions—and got chastised for it. There was no level of understanding that maybe I knew what I was doing, maybe it was okay for me to do what I was doing even though it wasn't accepted protocol. It was clear to me that I could never go back to being the kind of nurse I was before I left for Vietnam.

When I had my back surgery, I was temporarily retired from the service, and I went back to school at the University of Maryland to get my degree in nursing. It just so happened that one of my professors had had acupuncture, and she had suggested that I go through it, because even after surgery, I still had a lot of pain. The Navy kind of wrote me off and said, "You know, it's a degenerative process. It's just going to get worse. You have a choice—you can retire; we'll separate you from the service—you have a choice." I accepted the fact that I wanted to be separated from the service, because I couldn't see a future in the Navy anymore. Somehow all the, as I call it, "poop and circumstance" didn't mean anything anymore. It was a lot of . . . bullshit as far as I was concerned.

I started having the acupuncture treatments, and pretty soon things started coming together for me—and things started unraveling at the same time. A lot of the old stuff had started coming back—from the war zone, you know, as it often does. Things clear out when you start taking a natural therapy such as that. I was getting better and better, and finally I realized that, "Hey, I went through my hell, went through my training and education; all of the experiences were for me to do something like this." I went back to school to study acupuncture. I went to England to study at the College for Traditional Acupuncture in Oxford. Then I came back and did some clinical work in acupuncture and decided that I needed to deal with the spiritual role in healing as well. I went to Loyola College and got my master's degree in pastoral psych counseling to add to my bachelor's degree in nursing and the degrees I was getting in England for acupuncture.

I am now in my own private practice—doing nursing as well, but the kind of nursing that I know and feel ought to be done. I'm doing acupuncture and I'm doing counseling. I have one patient now who is a World War II veteran. He's gone through a lot of hell; he was a Navy man on a ship and had seen a lot of killing and wounding around him. This man is in his sixties, and he was still having these horrible, horrible dreams about the war. I sat down with him and listened to him and said, "Look, I know where you are; I know what you're feeling. I've been there." He looks at me as if saying, "I can't believe this is a woman who understands." Since he started treatments, he hasn't had any more of those dreams—after thirty, forty years. But it's because of my own feelings of where I need to deal with him—the holocaust he has been through—I can put myself in that position.

It really hurts every Veterans Day, when I see the Vietnam veterans rising up and getting so upset about not getting benefits and so forth. It starts opening wounds. You never forget what you've gone through. When the prisoners from Iran came back, I was shattered. It seems every time I get to a point where things have healed, or I think they have healed, something comes up in the news, and all the wounds start opening like Pandora's box. My question is, when is it all going to end? How much do you keep? I don't think you ever get rid of it. From all experiences, one can either become shattered or take the experience and incorporate it, learn from it, and make a positive thing from it. As a nurse, I really feel for the Vietnam veteran that came back to nothing. Most of us nurses were able to come back to professions; we weren't ostracized by bosses. We were just ignored, but we weren't ostracized in the fact that we were Vietnam veterans and therefore second-class citizens. I don't know, I have not really talked to any of my compatriots out there—surprisingly. I don't know what they're feeling or what they've done with their lives.

I was just thinking that my formative years in nursing have all been spent in the Navy. Whatever I've learned and gained and experienced, whether good, bad, or indifferent, I've learned in the Navy. That's what I took out into civilian life. A lot of my philosophy and the way I deal with problems is based on what I learned in the Navy. I may get upset at little things, but major crises—I'm just right there, cool, calm, collected. The ironic part is that when I came back I was supposed to forget the skills and the responsibility that had become second nature, so ingrained in me. I don't feel any regrets; I feel like I've pulled myself up. I've gone through school, I'm doing what I want to do, and I'm using the experiences probably with a deeper understanding than I ever would have, had I not gone over there.

With each person who goes out of my office from the acupuncture treatments in harmony, if they feel more peaceful, then somehow I've vindicated the war. I guess what I'm doing vicariously through them is coming to peace, coming to terms in a creative way. I certainly haven't prolonged the agony, I haven't prolonged the war, I haven't prolonged the chaos, but in fact have chosen something that is creating harmony, and I guess that's the testimony to my life now.

(Micki Voisard was a flight attendant for a civilian airline servicing Vietnam.)

I took on the job as a flight attendant with a civilian airline flying into Vietnam because I heard the money was good. It was, and somewhere along the way I convinced myself that this would be a perfect opportunity to save some money to continue my education. This was in 1969. I knew there was a war going on and that I would be flying in and out of the war zone on a regular basis.

I went through six interviews in two weeks, going from one to another, and there was a process of elimination. I didn't know what that process was until we had completed the six weeks of training and some of the girls didn't make it. It was like going through your final vows in the convent or something; you had to complete all this training, get the shots and pass the tests, then you still might not make it. I found out only after graduation that we were actually selected through handwriting analysis! I remember writing several stupid little paragraphs on why I wanted to be a stewardess, and they were using these to find out your personality traits, to see if you could handle this kind of thing.

I was real good at what I did because I have been cheerleading all of my life. I really was a cheerleader in high school, and it just seemed to carry on through; I still am at times. When we went through the training they didn't give us any beauty training, like they did in the other airlines. I would come across other crews and would talk about their training, and they would say, "Oh, we spent three weeks doing things on our hair." And I went, "God, we never spent three hours doing that." But, one thing about the company I worked for, they really were up on emergency procedures; I mean, that was essential. They were trying their hardest to prepare us for something that they themselves did not know was going to come about.

What they didn't prepare us for, and did very little work on, was how to work with 215 GIs on board the airplane, and I don't think anybody can prepare you for that. We would ask questions—you know, "What are they going to be like?" Their typical response would be "Boys will be boys; men will be men." That is the way it was left, and thinking back, what people are calling sexual abuse today was what went on all the time on those airplanes. I think it was up to you as an individual. When something happened to you, you reacted to it. The second time it happened, you had a choice of acting or reacting . . . and there is a big difference there. I learned that as a survival method. Whether anybody had any personal contact with you or not, you understood where you fit in. And it wasn't always in the best light; I never saw women as being in the best light with a lot of the men in the military.

Our headquarters was in Los Angeles, but the main stewardess headquarters was in San Francisco, and we had a contract with Travis AFB. We were connected with the Military Air Command (MAC), which is their airlift. During the war, the military needed their transports to fly equipment rather than troops, so this was contracted out to private companies like Continental, Flying Tigers, Pan Am, TIA, World, et cetera. My second home base was in Japan. The company had a hotel there and we had privileges at the Air Force bases.

Our trips lasted seven to fourteen days, during which time your whole life had to change. Your social life went with you like your suitcase did; you had to make it happen right there. And you couldn't wait until you got home because the company ended up screwing you, making sure that if you planned something, it wasn't going to happen: those two weeks skiing in Tahoe would suddenly become a turnaround flight back to Vietnam. It happened all the time.

We flew from Japan into Cam Ranh Bay, Bien Hoa, Da Nang, Tan Son Nhut, and generally they were seventeen-hour round trips. You flew

in, waited for them to clean the plane and reload passengers, and then
flew out. It was a long haul. That was if nothing happened. Sometimes
you flew in and didn't come out until a couple of days later because of
mechanical problems with the airplane or rocket attacks.

The very first flight into Vietnam I was in awe of what we were doing.
I was walking around with my mouth open, going, "Wow!" A limousine
came to take some dignitaries who were on the flight and then a school
bus for the officers. The draftees were herded into this big, open cattle
truck and were driven away, just like cattle going away to slaughter.
There was no glory, no John Wayne stuff; this was war. . . . This is what
people are so willing to do today, and it angers me, but if every mother
could see her son going off like that they wouldn't accept it. It was a
disgusting sight.

On the average trip you would see twelve hundred to fifteen hundred
guys, and to this day, being the visual person that I am, my mind is filled
with faces that I can bring back any time. I call them the faces of
Vietnam. It was interesting to me when *Life* magazine came out with an
issue called "The Faces of Vietnam." It became a turning point in my
life as a flight attendant going into the war zone. We were flying from
Yokota, Japan, to Travis AFB, taking a group of guys back from Vietnam. I had galley duty; it was real late at night, and I had nothing to do
so I picked up a magazine, and on the cover was the face of a GI. *Life*
was dedicating that issue to ending the war. So I started looking through
page after page of faces until one of them was very familiar. A guy I had
gone through school with. I looked at it and thought, "He can't be
dead." I started reading all the captions under the photographs. Then it
hit me that he was dead. . . . He was the hometown all-American boy.
Every girl in my high school was in love with him; he was the special one.
He was president of the student body and was the quarterback on the
football team; he had a scholarship. The whole town gave him a send-off
party . . . to Vietnam. . . . They sent him off to war. And when he was
killed, it was amazing what happened. His father committed suicide; his
mother had to be institutionalized. People just couldn't accept this.
They mourned for weeks. When I saw his picture, it just hit me—so
many of the guys on these flights who weren't going home, so many of
those faces.

On one flight, we got caught in a B-52 bombing mission. It's interesting, I think if I had given it any more thought, I wouldn't be here today;
I'd be in an institution, I'm sure. We were just outside of Da Nang,
heading to Japan, filled up with troops going home. I was looking out of
the porthole of the aft galley door, just admiring the view, and thought I
saw something go by real fast. And when you are up in the air you feel a
little uncomfortable about that; there is just not enough room up there
for something that close going that fast. . . . Then I saw it again. I looked

down the center aisle of the airplane, and all the people who were window-watching were pointing to something. Then the captain came on and said, "That was a B-52 bomber that just flew by us." It turned out that they were flying above us. They were in a bombing raid and were maintaining radio silence. One of them dropped down to see what this blip was on their radar, and it was us. So, it had to go through the chain of command for them to stop and let us through. (This is my interpretation of it—what we were picking up from the captain.) I remember going up front and seeing the looks on the passengers' faces. They had just gone through thirteen months of horror; they were going home in a civilian aircraft and are put under this stress . . . How could this happen?

Well, at first you couldn't see or hear them; then we got to this point where you could look out the window and see the bombs down there, hitting below us about thirty thousand feet. It was so silent—so clean—it was incredible. And for a good half an hour we sat there, strapped to our seats, waiting on pins and needles for our plane to clear the bombing area. We just wanted to do a right-hand turn and get the hell out of there! You felt like a mosquito in a shower: how are you not going to get wet?

In those years, I was three different people, three personalities. I had to be a cheerleader for the guys going over. Then on the way home, I had to tell them about things that I didn't want to tell them. The country was not welcoming heroes any more. They were so happy to be going home; you didn't want to break their hearts and say, "But, it's not going to be good. It's not going to be what Mom and your sisters have been writing. They are going to expect you to be the same guy that left."

I would go home, and my parents would say, "It's okay now, Micki. Why don't you forget it while you are on vacation?" Even if what I wanted to talk about was terrible, I still needed to do it, but nobody wanted to listen. One time—the first time I had ever been shelled, in Cam Ranh Bay—I came home twenty-four hours later, and my boyfriend had tickets to the play *Hair.* He called me up and said, "Can you be ready in half an hour?" I said, "You won't believe this—I just had a terrible experience. I don't think I want to go." And he said, "Every time you go on your trips all you do is talk about that stuff. . . . I spent twenty-five dollars on these tickets, and I hope you are going to be ready." I was stupid; you know, I put on my clothes and went. So, I'm sitting there looking around the room, thinking, "Just twenty-four hours ago, I was in a bunker, and here I am watching this antiwar play. . . . What am I doing? Am I crazy?" I walked out.

And I began wondering what the hell I was doing. I was flying over there, getting paid to be in the war. I'd come home and find myself going to Berkeley and marching in the antiwar demonstrations. And, after reading the *Stars and Stripes* newspaper, which I had to hand out to each seat on the return flights, I couldn't believe what they were passing off. I had to do that because it was my job, but I justified it by taking a whole bunch of those newspapers home and burning them at a demonstration. Everybody was burning their draft cards, I burned *Stars and Stripes* newspapers. That felt good to me. For three years I was playing so many different roles; it was so confusing. Why? How could anybody stay in there that long? And it was no longer the money. I mean, I wasn't even saving money. The guilt that I've had the last fifteen years is, Why in the hell *did* I stay for that long? Well, I was twenty-one. Who knows what you do when you are twenty-one years old. And if I look at my cultural background—I'm Catholic. I remember going into confession and making up my sins. I felt guilty that I didn't have all the sins down so I could give my penance, so I made them up as I went along. Then one day, I was talking to a couple of friends, and they said, "Well, who doesn't make up their sins?" Nobody believed in it, but they still went in there and did it. We didn't question those things. And I believed in the president . . . believed that there was somebody in charge. That was a big slap in the face—as I went through the war, I discovered there was never anybody in charge of that war. . . .

Cam Ranh Bay was a target because it was a main artillery base, and Charlie figured that out in a short period of time. Every time we would bring ships in, they probably were sitting there with their binoculars, watching them hauling in all this ammunition and putting it in the warehouses and Quonset huts around Cam Ranh Bay. Then they would go, "Okay," and they would blow them up. On one particular flight Cam Ranh was under fire when we came in; we didn't have a choice because we were low on fuel and couldn't go to an alternative airport. It was take your chance while you have it. The captain told us that there was all kinds of junk on the runway; they didn't know what to expect.

He did a great job landing, and then we sat there. All the lights were off in the airplane, the air conditioning is off, everybody is sweating, and you couldn't see faces because it was so dark. . . . You can feel 215 people in there. . . . I had to wait for six rings from the captain and then pull the emergency door, and the emergency slide is supposed to inflate. I'm flying number two position, sitting in the front jump seat and straining to hear six rings through all this "pow, pow!" And the plane is shaking. . . . I'm going, "One, two . . . I think I hear . . ." Finally the six rings come, and as I jumped out of the seat, I got my leg caught in the seat springs somehow. I had this feeling like I had my dress stuck, and being in such a frantic situation, I just ripped myself out and grabbed for the door. The slide didn't open—it just fizzled out! I am panicking because I could see everybody else letting their guys out. I have about fifty guys just sitting there in this dark coffin, waiting. There were three officers in front of me, and one said, "Let's go hand over hand." So, they went down and made, like, a chain ladder, and about halfway through he said, "It's your turn." I said, "I'm supposed to be the last one off the airplane." He says, "Get down there, lady!" and they practically threw me down. Then on the tarmac, I'm going, "Where am I? Is this Cam Ranh Bay?" In training they had shown slides of where there were bunkers at the various air bases. We had that information, but the troops on the airplane didn't know there were bunkers. They are saying, "Where do we go now?" And you go, "Oh, I saw slides of them once . . ." I mean, I remember the slides, and they showed the blue coral reefs in the background, and you thought, "Oh, that should be easy to find." You didn't realize that none of this is going to happen during the day—it is going to be dark. . . . Who is going to be looking for blue coral reefs?

Then some guy pointed in one direction, and I remember looking back at the airplane and seeing reflections in it like the whole earth was blowing up . . . lights, explosions . . . I thought, "Oh, Micki, you blew it. You were supposed to be the last one off that airplane. . . . The rules said . . ." I was even going to go back; you know, I had seen too many Goddamn John Wayne movies—"Oh, leave me here, you go ahead"— type stuff. I didn't know that I was hurt. I had cut my foot down to the muscle, and I ran on that foot through all the glass and debris on the tarmac. But the only thing I remember when we were running was the smell of sulfur everywhere. We got into the bunkers and stayed there for two hours—stood there, it was so tight. Then finally they moved us into a warehouse, and that's when I discovered my foot was hurt. Some guy said, "Eeew, you've got blood all over your pantyhose." Here we are, there are rockets going off outside, and the guy is still looking at my legs. I'm going, "Goddamn it! Some guys are . . ." But he was just trying to tell me that I was hurt. There was a medic right there, and he said, "Let me look at that. You do have blood on your pantyhose." I looked down at my foot and almost fainted!

After it was over, they refueled the airplane and got our crew on board. The medic had reported my injury to the senior stew, and she wrote it up. When we got to Yokote, I went into the hospital on Tachikawa air base and spent the night. Then the company flew us home, since our plane was damaged and was going to be worked on in Japan. We flew home thinking, "Oh, we'll probably get two weeks off, maybe a bonus. . . ." They gave us a turnaround! I was back in Vietnam in forty-eight hours! I mean, any excuse you would give them was not good enough, or bad enough. I called them up and said, "God, last night we were shelled in Vietnam. I'm really not feeling very good." They would go, "When can you be back on the line?" It was amazing. It was nothing to them. . . . You meant nothing to them. So, that was gnawing at me:

"Well, why the hell did you stay there then, Micki?" I lived with that for years. The reasons I came up with, in addition to my Catholic background, was I knew I was on to something. . . . Having a journalistic background, I was intrigued. It kept me going. I knew that the discrepancies were just too great, and that I had privileged information in my position. I could walk around as freely as can be, photographing and talking with people. I could ask any person what their side of the story was. . . . It was amazing . . . the stories, the confusion; nothing made sense, nothing.

The value was more than I could ever pay for, and the time that I spent in Vietnam was a significant and valuable period in my life. It haunts me to this day. I would not have traded it for anything. I was not injured over there to an extent where I was incapacitated, I didn't see my best friend die—or a lot of things that people saw over there—but I had my life on the line every time I flew in there.

And I had to deal with sexual abuse. I saw men masturbating all the time on the airplanes. I remember when I was new, having one stewardess tell me, "Never take a blanket off a sleeping GI." Then, once in a while, someone in Los Angeles who had forgotten we were hauling troops would put sanitary napkins on board, so we had to check out the lavs to see if there were any sanitary napkins. But there were times when we forgot or the guys would bring them on themselves. They would put ketchup down the center of the napkin, lay it in the middle of the aisle, and wait for your reaction. The first time it happened to me I was real embarrassed. Then there was the guy who got stuck in his seat belt; you were to save the day, helping him with it while he sits there with a big smile on his face and everybody around him is laughing. So, you learn the art of seat belt deployment by verbal command. Or, the guy who asks for a pillow and, as you reach up to get one, he has his hand up your dress. . . . You learned to never do things impulsively. You won't believe this one: the guy who follows you to the john to see if you locked the door. They would wait until you got comfortable, then jerk the door open, and everybody down the aisle could see you! So, to me right now, thinking of those things, it seems incredible, but it got to be routine. There were a lot of bad apples, but there were also guys that would let you know that they didn't approve of what they saw going on. A lot of them would come up and say, "I'm real sorry that happened to you." They weren't all older guys either; some were just young kids. You saw where respect came from.

Even now I have a way with men that . . . Fortunately I came out of it not hating them. I knew a lot of girls that ended up that way. They were having difficulty dealing with the men on the flights. I was able to function and talk with the GIs the whole time; it's just that I found myself giving commands all the time. In order to survive, I had to challenge them. They would challenge you, and if you could speak louder and be more authoritarian, then they would buckle under to you. Just my sense of survival, I guess.

Then there is the story about the bomb on our airplane. It was a pressurized bomb which, they figured, was supposed to go off above twelve thousand feet. It had been planted by one of the Vietnamese who cleaned out the airplane. We used to just stroll off the airplane and go down to the beach while they worked. . . . Well, that stopped real fast! The military started coming on board and standing there with M-16s pointed at these guys while they cleaned the plane.

I was in the aft galley with another girl, whose jump seat was right in front of the coffee maker, and on takeoff, it came out and hit her in the back of the head. She was actually holding it in place with her head—this big, heavy thing. We started pushing and shoving on it, trying to get it back in place and asked a couple of guys who were sitting near there to help us. Finally, we called the flight engineer, and he came back to check it out. We were all milling around, getting things ready for meal service, and meanwhile the plane is climbing. The flight engineer looks in behind the coffee maker with his trusty flashlight and says, "Oh, my God, everybody get out of here, right now!" Here is this happy-go-lucky-type guy who suddenly goes into instant fear. He says, "There's a bomb here." I remember standing there with all this coming back to me. I had been pushing on it, hitting it! Now, all of a sudden, I can't move; I can't even walk past that thing.

The captain came back, they discussed it, then went forward and talked with somebody on the radio in Cam Ranh. They were pretty sure it was a pressurized bomb and told us to level off and stay at our altitude until they could get some kind of a bomb squad together down there. Then we had to return, and it was up to the captain to bring that baby in as light as can be . . . and not make any drastic changes in altitude . . . slowly bring it down. The captain left the door of the cockpit open, and everybody on board was included. He let us hear the communication of he and the ground crew. They were joking and discussing this openly. Everybody felt 100 percent better because they were able to participate in this. He let that thing just glide into Cam Ranh Bay and landed. Everybody cheered! There were a lot of different kinds of heroes in that war.

I was telling someone this story, and they said, "Oh, you mean the *North* Vietnamese planted the bomb." I said, "No, a South Vietnamese." They said, "But we were fighting *for* the South Vietnamese." It was just amazing how people thought the war was that black and white: "Here is the north; all the bad guys live over here. Here is the south, and all the good guys live there, and we are saving the good guys, keeping communism away."

Then you come home, and they give the body count each night at dinnertime. They say, "North Vietnam lost fifteen hundred and we lost thirty. Isn't that great!" You know, to me that's where we really lost it, on that body count. Because people would be sitting there watching the six o'clock news, saying, "That's not too bad, only thirty guys. . . . They lost fifteen hundred. We are doing a good job over there." Nobody thought of thirty individuals. . . . Those guys got lost in there, somehow. Fifty-eight thousand people got lost in that body count.

(Doris I. ["Lucki"] Allen, a black member of the WAC, served in Vietnam in military intelligence units.)

The story of my life began fifty-six years ago; I'm almost fifty-seven. On Friday the thirteenth, 1950, I went in the military. I'd been teaching school, and I went to Jackson, Mississippi, and told them I wanted to join the military. I was going to be an officer at first, and I said, "No, I'm not going to be an officer. I'll go through the ranks." At any rate, they let me in—that's the way they put it: they let me in.

After basic training they asked what MOS I would like to be, and I wanted to join the band; I was qualified. So they sent three of us black women over for an audition with the WAC band, that's Women's Army Corps Band. I was playing trumpet, one woman was playing clarinet, the other was playing percussion. They gave me the fourth trumpet part, they gave the other lady the fourth clarinet part, and the percussionist was doing whatever she was doing. But if you know anything about music—those are really the hardest parts. You really have to concentrate, and you have to know what you're doing to be doing this du-pity-du-pity-du or whatever. As we were playing, the commander of the band, Chief Warrant Officer Allen—no kin, believe me—had made some prearranged signal with the rest of the band. She was standing up there directing us—we were playing "Under the Double Eagle," I think—and on the signal the rest of the band stopped. Then you heard nothing but this fourth trumpet part du-pity-du and this fourth clarinet part do-do-do-do-do and the drum going oom-ba, oom-ba. We kept playing because the director was still directing. She was getting so exasperated that we kept going, following her directions. To us it was, you know, follow directions, do what you're directed to do. I wish I could show you how Miss Allen looked. Afterwards, the regular members in the band congratulated us and said, "Yeah, you guys did real well." And we know we were in the band, right? Miss Allen called us in and told us that we did fine, but sorry, they couldn't have any Negroes in the band. So, well, that was my first real touch with how they want you but they don't want you.

Right after that rejection, they sent us to become entertainment specialists, which entailed nothing but putting on soldier shows. One of the fortunate things was that I did get a chance to play a gig with André Previn—just messing around at the Presidio in San Francisco.

I went to Japan within a year after joining the military, and when I came back I was stationed at Camp Stoneman, California. My sister, Jewel L. Allen, was my commander. I caught lots of flak from that because they thought we were colluding or doing something or going with each other or something. But when they closed Camp Stoneman, they wanted her to go to one end of the earth and me to another end of the earth. And I think that's because as sisters, we were real loving sisters, but when it came to being soldiers, we were soldiers.

Oh, there was another incident at Stoneman which was downright prejudice. I had been editor of a newspaper when I was in Japan. They didn't have an editor for the newspaper, so I was a college graduate and I spoke English well and they said, "Okay, you're it." Here I am a PFC, and I had all these other high ranks working—in a sense, working for me because they were doing the reporting and I was doing all the editing. When I got back to Stoneman I was supposed to be on newspapers, and I went in and told the sergeant, "Hey, I'm supposed to be doing some kind of newspaper work." The captain called me into his office and directed me to "go empty those inkwells." They were on his desk, those old-time inkwells. One had red ink in it, and the other, green. Why call me? I was a corporal. There were five men, PFCs, in the office. I was a woman, and he called me in to empty the inkwells. I picked them up, took them outside, in my very starched dress, washed them out, careful not to get dirty, brought them back in, set them on his desk, saluted him, and walked out. I went directly to the sergeant and told him that he had other people in here of lower rank who were not trained like I was and that I did not appreciate that. I think that was one of my first really assertive acts, knowing it's all right to assert yourself in the military and say, "Hey, I don't want to do that."

Another important time in my life, in the intervening seventeen years before I got to Vietnam, was at Fort Monmouth, New Jersey. I was running the education center and doing public information, and my boss wanted me to go out with him. And I said, "No, I don't mix business with pleasure." So he saw to it that I didn't get promoted. Even though there were not that many promotions to be had, there were what they called blood stripes. In other words, if somebody did something wrong and they lost their stripe, somebody else could get it if you were highly recommended. He never recommended me because I wouldn't go out with him. We had a good working relationship, but I . . . Well, I didn't get promoted for twelve years. I was sergeant then. I was stagnating and in that same no-win situation while I was at Fort Monmouth, and I said,

"Well, I'm going to have to do something." I applied for lots of things, lots of places, and they would always tell me, "Well, no, your MOS is too important. It's critical, so we can't send you."

They finally, though seemingly reluctantly, let me go to language school. I went to the language school in Monterey, California, to learn French. I was no longer in public information. I had become a French linguist when I finished school. I just knew I was going to go to France. But that was during the time that President de Gaulle said that he did not want Americans in his country any longer, so I didn't get a chance to go to France.

I went to Fort Bragg in North Carolina, where I had a problem, again, getting promoted. What eventually happened there was, one day I saw all these guys walking in, thirty-two of them to be exact, walking past my desk and standing there in their class A uniforms, looking sharp, and I said, "Geez, I had no wind of a formation today. Why are you guys dressed up?" They said, "We're going before the board." I said, "Come on, what board?" They said, "We're going before the promotion board." And me, in my naiveté—if you can use that term—said to myself, "Well, hey, Lucki, your stuff is so together; you're a good soldier. They know how good you are, how efficient and professional you are. You don't have to go before the board." Then I sat there and started thinking, and I jumped out of my complacency and got very upset. I told the sergeant major I wanted to speak to the colonel. I always walked in informally, but this time I *marched* into the colonel's office, saluted him, and forty-five minutes later I walked out of there. While I was in there, I was telling him how good I really was, how well trained I was, and my mother and dad raised no idiots . . . the whole bit; I expounded respectfully, but I was really venting. When the board is convened for promotion, that's the only board for that month; you just couldn't change that. This was on a Wednesday. Well, I guess about five minutes after I went back and sat at my desk, the colonel came through my office and went out the door—where he went, I don't know. When he came back he looked as if he was sort of in a huff. He called the sergeant major in, very formally, and the sergeant major came to my desk and said, "There will be a promotion board held for you on Friday."

What had happened in all of that—and this is not just reflection; I knew then what was happening—had I not said anything, had I just let it go, I'd probably still be the same rank I was then. When I did go before the board I came out fifth out of the thirty-three people. I would've been first but they threw out all of the education points for promotion because they looked at mine and I just messed up the curve completely. You know, I was already a college graduate, I'd taught school, I'd taken everything that the Army had to offer as far as extension courses, I took extra college courses in speech and a few other things I hadn't had. Too many. So they threw all of them out. I still came out number five. But the point being that you have to have the sense of how they were going to promote everybody else and not include me and just not say anything about it. Maybe it would've gone along and I'd have had to wait another month; this might have happened again. I believe that my assertiveness paid off. So I finally got promoted there.

Another important incident happened. When the Dominican Republic uprising happened, I was stationed in Fort Bragg, North Carolina. I was in military intelligence by then: a prisoner of war interrogator, a French linguist, and I also spoke Spanish. I had all the skills that they really needed. But for whatever reason they had, I was not sent to the Dominican Republic. It wasn't that I was asking to be sent, but according to my records, I was one of the highest qualified persons. Why not send me there, okay? They didn't do that.

At any rate, in 1967, I volunteered to go to Vietnam. I was working in strategic intelligence at that time. I wanted to go because I kept hearing what I thought must have been lies—all of this couldn't be true, the information that was coming back to me. And I got information not only through regular intelligence channels, but also from overseas newspapers and the regular media. There was a lot of conflict for me in knowing who was telling the truth, so I said, "Well, I know whatever it is I know, and I may as well be there too. I'm gonna be a part of this." Instead of just sitting back here and knowing that I had an expertise that was needed, it was better for me to be there. Not to fight and not to shoot guns and not to kill people, but I looked at it rather that my intelligence would save lives, as opposed to taking lives. Two months prior to the time that I left Fort Bragg, I did not read anything having to do with Vietnam. I didn't read reports; I didn't read newspapers; I almost didn't listen to the news. I'd kind of close it off when it came to what was happening in Vietnam. The reason I did this is because when I got to Vietnam, I wanted to be open-minded and unbiased and be able to work from there.

When I got to Vietnam, my paranoia started really showing. I don't remember the day I got to Vietnam, but it was either the thirteenth, fourteenth, or fifteenth of October, 1967. Going over, I was the only woman on the plane with all the other GIs. What I spent my time doing while I was on the plane is reading newspapers and doing the entire order of battle. This was possible because in newspapers they had given locations of all of the American troops from division headquarters down to platoon-size units, exactly where they were in all of Vietnam. So I kept saying to myself, "Here I am sitting on the plane being able to figure out where all of our troops are." I said, "My God, the enemy must be . . . They know!" I think I got paranoid reading that paper, you know. But I already had my cover story—"When I get to Vietnam I won't know anything about anything, and if I get captured, I'll be okay." The cover story I had made up was that I was an expert on the M-16. I knew why it jammed, when it jammed, what was wrong with it; I knew everything about it. I don't know a thing about the M-16 right now, but I had that weapon so heavy in my mind . . . And if they got me I was going to tell them that the only thing I did was take complaints about the M-16. I was going to say, "You know yourself it's a horrible weapon and that your AK-47 is much better than our M-16." Wow, listen to that fantasy!

When I got to Saigon, to Tan Son Nhut airport, dressed in my nice, clean cord uniform, I was looking sharp. They were calling off all these units and all these names, and I did not hear my name once. I don't care where you are, you hear your own name. I was just standing here, and all of a sudden the airport was clearing out, right? But I don't see it clearing out because I'm standing with head against the wall, because when I got there I see all these people that I knew were Vietnamese, okay? For whatever reason, I knew they were Vietnamese, and I saw these cameras, and people are clicking their cameras, and why are these people in here taking pictures? Oh, my God. Not realizing this is their airport—it wasn't military; we just happened to land there. I was standing with my face against the wall—"I hope they don't take a picture of me, oh, God." And that kind of wore out, but that was my introduction. Then I finally found somebody, and I said, "Listen, I'm here, you know, you must have a place for me." And I didn't want to tell them I was military intelligence. . . . Well, anyway, that was all my own anxiety.

They finally decided where I belonged, and I went down to wherever that place was where all the other Army women were sent, and they'd given me this white towel and white washcloth, so I could take a shower. And I think I have a beautiful brown color, right? I got in the shower and started washing, and I said, "Oh, my God, what's happening?!" My washcloth, absolutely, so help me God, was brown, and I thought I was turning white. You don't know how panicky that is—this is the honest truth. I just got panicky, and I almost started crying. . . . Do you realize how dusty and dirty Vietnam was? And this was a matter of being there just a few hours. Imagine, the first day there, and all my black's coming off. Well, I got over that.

The next day I started working. I was in intelligence. For my first year in Vietnam, I worked in the Army Operations Center (AOC), Headquarters, United States Army, Vietnam (USARV). I was the only specialist-7 at the time; there were only twenty-two spec-7s in the military. I was in the "Two Shop" in the AOC and was the only woman in there. I remember one of my humors came up one day. When the general walked in, nobody, none of the men in there, wanted to tell him that his fly was open. I told him his fly was open, and everybody glared at me. I don't think they liked that. The general says, "Oops, thank you," and zips his pants up.

Another general, Air Force General Ryan from Pacific Command in Hawaii, came for an orientation. I was directed to give the orientation, which included a complete rundown of the current military operations throughout Vietnam. I remember it kind of disturbed me, because they put five very plush chairs for the general and his staff to sit in, and I was wondering, "This is Vietnam. Why are you putting plush chairs there for somebody to sit in? I'm talking about war!" When I finished briefing General Ryan, he walked over to me and said, very loudly so that everybody in the AOC could hear it, "I've been CINCPAC for"—whatever time it was—"and I've had lots of reports from over here in Vietnam and been all over Vietnam, and this is the best and most honest report I've had yet, because you stood up here and dared to tell the truth." And everybody else was very excited about this. I think there was a lot of anxiety behind the fact that I was the only spec-7 in there. Well, being spec-7 had the connotation of, you're either really great or you're something special. Being a woman had lots to do with that. My credibility was with me—I had it—but a lot of people couldn't believe, or didn't want to believe, that a woman could actually be making decisions or analyses—and their being correct.

I think the first time I was really tested was when I called the Tet offensive. I had been looking at my notes and reading everything. I had all these reports that I'd read through; I was pouring over them and really into it. Then I wrote a paper, and I titled it "50,000 Chinese." What it said was, we had better get our stuff together because this is what is facing us, this is what is going to happen, and it's going to happen on such and such a day, around such and such a time. I had never heard the word *Tet;* it just wasn't part of my vocabulary. I didn't know that there was a Tet celebration, like maybe a lot of people in foreign countries don't know that we celebrate Easter or Christmas. But I put the date down and said it's going to happen around this particular date. When I took it in to the G-2, the intelligence officer said, "Well, I don't know about this." And I said, "We need to disseminate this. It's got to be told." Well, he sort of believed it and said, "I'll tell you what to do. I want you to take it up to Saigon and run it through and see what they think there, what the G-2 at MACV thinks about it." I said okay, and I got in my jeep and went on up to Saigon.

When I walked in I knew that it had to go through and be scrutinized by about fifteen people. It seemed like that, but it really went through only four or five. When I walked in there, the sergeant came up to me and said, "Can I help you?" And I said, "Yes, I'd like to see the G-2. I have something et cetera, et cetera." The captain came out: "What do you have?" I said, "I'd like to see the G-2 et cetera, et cetera." And he said, "Just a minute." A major came out, and I showed it to the major, and he said, "Well, just a minute." He handed it back to me, this paper

I'd written. I guess it was a page and a half. He walked back in there and said, "Maybe you better go talk to the colonel." The colonel came out, got the paper, took it back in the back, they discussed it, I imagine, and they came back out and said, "Well, we really don't know if this is . . . No, I don't think we better, no . . ." I know that they knew there was substance in it. . . . I don't know why I said that—I don't know, but they must have, because too many people took too much time to discuss it, whatever it was. Maybe they just saw it as logic, I don't know. I did this at least thirty days ahead of when this was supposed to be, and I think one of the things that might have scared them off was that I titled the report "50,000 Chinese," and there were not supposed to be any Chinese in the country; these were supposed to be Vietnamese, Viet Cong, North Vietnamese Army, okay? Maybe calling them Chinese made it unacceptable to our headquarters. At any rate, the date came, and I was right . . . but Tet, believe me, is history. Tet is history. Well, I'm not an "I told you so" person, but I most certainly felt very good for having at least tried to warn our brass, and even though we lost so much, I felt inside myself that I had done what I was supposed to do.

Another incident. The order came to send a convoy up to Song Be, and I warned the colonel that they shouldn't because of a possible ambush. I outlined enemy locations and the site of a possible ambush. "Well, ahh, I'm sorry, we're going to send it anyway." They sent the convoy up. . . . We're talking about five flatbed trucks blown up, nineteen wounded, and three killed. We lost a lot. You know, when you're talking about a flatbed, you're talking about lots and lots of ammunition that gets wasted because it got caught in an ambush. I even told them the probable location of the ambush. About two days later, when it was time to send out another convoy, the colonel came in and asked me, "Hey, by the way, do you think we ought to send this convoy up there today?" What happens with that is, somewhere your credibility is being questioned. Not that I had to establish any more credibility. As far as I was concerned, I was doing a sincere, caring, very professional job. So the onus was not on me to prove my credibility; the onus was on them to listen.

I guess the things that really stick about Vietnam is knowing you give them something and what you give is reliable and valid, but biases can creep through. There are a lot of things that they might have been biased about me with. I was a specialist as opposed to being a sergeant. I was black instead of being something else. I was enlisted instead of being an officer—especially in the milieu where there were only two enlisted people, and I was one of them. There was a master sergeant and myself; the other twenty-eight were officers. Being a WAC, whew! You know, "Women have no business over here, WACs especially." You know, there were a lot of things at my age—let me see how old I was, about ten years ago, I was in my forties. Ten years ago?? That's almost fourteen, fifteen years ago, wow, geez! How vivid it is! But somehow you have to say, "I'm going to either keep doing it, or I'm going to get bitter and I'm not going to even bother with this anymore."

Two more incidents—I'll make them short. One had to do with a chemical round (82-millimeter mortar) I heard about. A friend up in Tay Ninh called me up and said, "Hey, we've got something out here that's different." I found out that there was a chemical round, and it was the first time we knew about a chemical round in Vietnam. I made a couple of phone calls and a couple of little "calisthenics" and came up with the fellow who defused it. I brought him down to my headquarters, and we sat and he told me all he knew about it. I got it all drafted up in this big picture, telling exactly what one should expect if a "dud" 82-millimeter mortar round hit an area. I published it in a document called "Weekly Intelligence Estimate Update," which went out everywhere in Vietnam. Sometimes people don't read things—they throw them in trash cans; sometimes people do read things.

It happens that a Marine commander at Qua Viet, the 3d MAF area, up by the DMZ, happened to read it like he was supposed to. He read this article on Wednesday, and on Friday they were attacked. And the enemy was using the chemical round. He said, "Do not touch it," and they didn't touch the round. They found out later that it was actually a chemical round. The 3d MAF commander called back down to the USARV and asked, "Who put out the information on the chemical round? I think whoever it was should be credited with saving a hundred and one lives and be given at least the Legion of Merit." Well, my colonel was quite amenable to that, but by the time it got watered down I don't remember if I even got a thank-you. I did get a big thank-you from myself again for having done something that was really productive. Later they said I couldn't have a Legion of Merit because number one, I was a woman; number two, I was enlisted; and number three, it was not in actual combat—it wasn't in a shooting situation.

Another incident that was . . . Geez, I think about these years later . . . it was Tet of 1969. Almost the same thing was happening, but I had wind from my sources that rockets were being planted outside of our perimeter around Long Binh. They were using 122-millimeter rockets. What they were doing is just laying them on the ground and covering them with earth. They intended to use these ground mounds as launchers. They would put them down there, cover them up, and you just couldn't really see them from the air. This information was coming in to us; we had agents out there—we had woodcutters just like they had woodcutters, so to speak. I had been getting all these things across my desk and talking to all my friends that would call me on the hotline— that I was not authorized to have at my workplace—saying, "Hey, by the way, did you hear about such and such?" And the reason they'd talk to me is because when they'd talk to somebody else, nobody would want to do anything about anything. I wrote up a report saying that I figured there were at least five hundred rockets spread out around our perimeter. Something hit me all at once, and I said, "Jesus, this has got to be told right now." So I went down to II Field Force to the operations center—I was the only woman that normally ever went down there— and I was telling the sergeant major standing beside me what was happening, and he said, "Just a minute." Then a lieutenant came over. I don't know why they always did that with me; I went through more echelons and chains. So I said, "What are you guys doing about all this stuff?" "Ahh, there's nothing out there" was the reply. And it went on up the line. The colonel comes out, asks me, "Do you have an SI clearance?" I said, "No, but I'm not talking about SI clearances. I'm talking about what's happening right now," you know. He says, "I'm sorry, we can't talk to you. We don't have anything to do with that."

By that time, I'm really worried—these rockets were pointed at our compound. I have always thought that if I take care of me and you're riding with me, then you're taken care of. If I'm safe, you're safe. That was the first time in Vietnam I ever cried absolute tears. I was so angry when I walked out of there. I was angry that I knew what I was talking about and they didn't listen. This happened on the eighth of whatever month it was. On the tenth.they put out a couple rounds of duster fire, 40-millimeter duster fire, and they had a couple of secondary explosions. The next night, they did a flyover and got four more secondary explosions, okay? On the twelfth, they put out whatever they put out, but they got 117 secondary explosions up to a hundred feet high in the area that I was talking about. And I sat back and, again, felt very smug and snug and comfortable and thanking God, because had they not done it, we might have been hit again, another Tet. And I think a lot of people would have been killed. The things that I did were not big, in one sense, but had I not been assertive behind whatever it was I was saying—and I'm not saying that a lot of other people did not come to some conclusions—I don't know what more could have happened. What I am saying is that a person must be assertive enough to say, *"Do* something about it, please!" or even be willing to say, "I don't care what you do with the information, just here it is." If fifty million people take credit for it, I don't care.

Well, I stayed in Vietnam for three years. I came home a couple times during that. I came home on leave, had a marvelous time. I don't want to give the impression that all my time in Vietnam was spent . . . well, all my time was spent working. A lot of my time was spent really enjoying the camaraderie. There was a togetherness in Vietnam you wouldn't believe; most of the prejudices, for a while, went away. Even though blacks were into their black-power salute and a few whites had their confederate flags and stuff, there was a togetherness that I think you can only get in times of peril, if I can use that term.

I kept getting orders to go to Fort Bragg, North Carolina. I got five sets of orders to go to Fort Bragg while I was in Vietnam. I kept telling them, "I'm not going to Fort Bragg. I'll stay here." I was living in a hotel in Saigon my last six or seven months, and I had to walk to work. That was a trip, a combat tour in itself, walking up and down the streets of Saigon. But it got so bad I used to . . . They didn't want us to carry weapons in Vietnam; women couldn't carry weapons. Doris I. Allen carried her weapon. Make no mistake, I carried a .45. A couple others of us, friends of mine, carried weapons. That .45 was mine and I loved it, and I'm going to say it now: I still have it. I used to be able to cock that thing behind my back—maybe I was getting skittish or whatever. I had seen my name on captured enemy documents as one of the persons to be eliminated, and that's scary. The first time they told me that they had found a document with my name on it, it was on a list of intelligence personnel to be done away with, to be eliminated. I felt kind of, well, important—"Hey, tell all your friends how important you are," you know. Then the second time, I actually saw it. It was on a captured enemy document. The third time I saw it I happened to be assigned to the translation branch, in charge of the interpreters section at the Combined Documents Exploitation Center (CDEC) in Saigon. And one of my supervisors said, "Come here, Ms. Allen," and he put the captured document in my hand. I told him two and a half months later I was going home. It really got kind of scary. Then when cowboys on motorbikes would come by me and try to rip off my briefcase, it was just time to come home. I was getting skittish, getting nervous, and I might have blown somebody's head off. . . .

But at any rate, they finally got me back to Fort Bragg anyway. You know, when people want you, they get you. When I got back to Fort Bragg, I put on my uniform and I walked in, and I know I was looking good—a new warrant officer, WO-1. I had three rows of good stuff here on my chest—you know, all those pretty little five-cent ribbons you put on your chest on this side—and I had three ribbons over here. I walked into the office, and the colonel was sitting behind his desk, and in his office were sitting five other colonels. He says, "We have just the place for you. We're going to put you in CONTIC." The same outfit I was in before! I said, "Just a moment, sir," and he says, "Yes?" I said, "I must say this: I'm not given to vulgarity, and I'm not given to profanity, but I think I've spent my time in hell." And he says, "What? What do you mean?" I said, "I just got back here from Vietnam, where I spent three years. Before I went to Vietnam, I spent four years at Fort Bragg, North Carolina, and I think that's enough time in hell." He said, "Oops. Okay, where do you want to go?" Okay, that was another example of "if you don't tell him, you don't get it." I'm not saying that other women haven't told what they wanted, you know, and been assertive, but I'm saying that if we don't do that, then we are doomed as far as I'm concerned. And I think that's one of the reasons that I was able to do thirty years in the military—because had I not been able to talk for myself and not feel afraid to do that, then I think I could not have survived as well.

When I got back from Vietnam, I guess I did not have the problems that some people had. Maybe that was because, as I told you, my sister had been my commanding officer back at Camp Stoneman and she was very in tune to me. I became an instructor at the intelligence school in Fort Holabird, Maryland. About a year later we moved the intelligence school to Fort Huachuca, Arizona, and within a matter of a year, I became a full-time special agent. So my life was all working when I got back, as opposed to being put out on the street—put out to pasture, so to speak—and being left to the mercies and the tenderness of those people who did not like Vietnam vets, especially here in the state of California. Some people went home to some places, and they were heroes, and that's not that they were looking to be heroes, they were just looking to come home and—"Please welcome me home. I've been away." I think it was easier for me because of my sister on the one hand and the fact that I was really working on the other.

Actually one of the biggest shocks to me was that I had less money to spend. Within a month of leaving Vietnam I had been promoted to warrant officer. As a spec-7 having as much time in service as I did, I made more money than a warrant officer-one, newly promoted. So I lost that money. I was also collecting combat pay and interrogator specialty pay, so my shock was more like coming back and "Geez, I'm broke!" I wasn't eating as well—over there it was good steaks. Make no mistake, I ate very well in Vietnam. All that heat—I had an air conditioner in my room. I worked hard but I played hard. I had a nice, nice fellow who thought the world of me, and I thought the world of him. Every day he'd bring me a quart of Crown Royal. I didn't usually drink the whole bottle every day—unless I had to go to the bunker.

But that was a different time. . . . You had to sort of get crazy over there. Then when you got home, there was a lot of camaraderie lost. Nobody even really rapped about these things, and then things start going through your head. A good friend of mine, a nurse, told me that when she got back and saw that she was not being welcomed back, she internalized it and put it upon herself and said, "The only reason I'm feeling that way is 'cause I left that guy on the gurney, and I got to go back and take care of him." I think a lot of Vietnam vets have not been able to air and say what was happening. Again I'm very fortunate to have my sister that, even right now when I try to get crazy or whatever, says,

"Come on, knock it off" or "Hey, this is what's happened to you." I think we all needed that somewhere.

After I retired in 1980, I never had to go out there on the street and look for a job. A friend of mine called me a month before I got out. I hadn't talked to him for five years, and he says, "Congratulations on your retirement." We had a nice conversation, and he said, "By the way, what I really called about is, I'd like you to come work for me." So the bottom line of that is that I did become a private investigator with his company, and we still work together. The other thing that really helped me is that I'm working on my Ph.D. So what I've been doing—I've been working; I haven't given myself a chance to fall. . . . It's still there in my mind, but it has not come out to really haunt me, okay? Like I say, I keep busy, and now that I'll finish my Ph.D. next year, I'll have to find something to do, something to keep me going. Another thing I haven't been willing to do in one sense is to walk the picket line, but I might have to go start doing that.

Now you have the story of my life, my entire life.

TRUONG NHU TANG
1923–

A lawyer and politician, born in Saigon and educated at the Sorbonne, Truong Nhu Tang was an economics expert for the government of South Vietnam while secretly serving the Viet Cong. Bitterly disillusioned by the repression occasioned by the victory of Hanoi, he decamped to Paris, where he now lives. His book A Viet Cong Memoir *(1985) was written with David Chanoff and Doan Van Toai.*

From A VIET CONG MEMOIR

Infiltrating into areas under secure government control to see wives and children who had often been marked as Vietcong dependents was a chance business. To get around this, from time to time we would be able to bring families out to the jungle, something that was done for soldiers as well as cadres. But such meetings were necessarily brief and dangerous themselves. (Vo Van Kiet's wife and children were killed on their way to one such rendezvous, when they were caught in a B-52 raid.) More often than not these men went for extended periods without any contact at all with their families.

But for all the privations and hardships, nothing the guerrillas had to endure compared with the stark terrorization of the B-52 bombardments. During its involvement, the United States dropped on Vietnam more than three times the tonnage of explosives that were dropped during all of World War II in military theaters that spanned the world. Much of it came from the high altitude B-52s, bombs of all sizes and types being disgorged by these invisible predators. The statistics convey some sense of the concentrated firepower that was unleashed at America's enemies in both North and South. From the perspective of those enemies, these figures translated into an experience of undiluted psychological terror, into which we were plunged, day in, day out for years on end.

From a kilometer away, the sonic roar of the B-52 explosions tore eardrums, leaving many of the jungle dwellers permanently deaf. From a kilometer, the shock waves knocked their victims senseless. Any hit within a half kilometer would collapse the walls of an unreinforced bunker, burying alive the people cowering inside. Seen up close, the bomb craters were gigantic—thirty feet across and nearly as deep. In the rainy seasons they would fill up with water and often saw service as duck or fishponds, playing their role in the guerrillas' never-ending quest to broaden their diet. But they were treacherous then too. For as the swamps and lowland areas flooded under half a foot of standing water, the craters would become invisible. Not infrequently some surprised guerrilla, wading along what he had taken to be a familiar route, was suddenly swallowed up.

It was something of a miracle that from 1968 through 1970 the attacks, though they caused significant casualties generally, did not kill a single one of the military or civilian leaders in the headquarters complexes. This luck, though, had a lot to do with accurate advance warning of the raids, which allowed us to move out of the way or take refuge in our bunkers before the bombs began to rain down. B-52s flying out of Okinawa and Guam would be picked up by Soviet intelligence trawlers plying the South China Sea. The planes' headings and air speed would be computed and relayed to COSVN headquarters, which would then order NLF or Northern elements in the anticipated target zones to move away perpendicularly to the attack trajectory. Flights originating from the Thai bases were monitored both on radar and visually by our intelligence nets there and the information similarly relayed.

Often the warnings would give us time to grab some rice and escape by foot or bike down one of the emergency routes. Hours later we would return to find, as happened on several occasions, that there was nothing left. It was as if an enormous scythe had swept through the jungle, felling the giant teak and go trees like grass in its way, shredding them into billions of scattered splinters. On these occasions—when the B-52s had found their mark—the complex would be utterly destroyed: food, clothes, supplies, documents, everything. It was not just that things were destroyed; in some awesome way they had ceased to exist. You would come back to where your lean-to and bunker had been, your home, and there would simply be nothing there, just an unrecognizable landscape gouged by immense craters.

Equally often, however, we were not so fortunate and had time only to take cover as best we could. The first few times I experienced a B-52 attack it seemed, as I strained to press myself into the bunker floor, that I had been caught in the Apocalypse. The terror was complete. One lost control of bodily functions as the mind screamed incomprehensible orders to get out. On one occasion a Soviet delegation was visiting our ministry when a particularly short-notice warning came through. When it was over, no one had been hurt, but the entire delegation had sustained considerable damage to its dignity—uncontrollable trembling and wet pants the all-too-obvious outward signs of inner convulsions. The visitors could have spared themselves their feelings of embarrassment; each of their hosts was a veteran of the same symptoms.

It was a tribute to the Soviet surveillance techniques that we were caught aboveground so infrequently during the years of the deluge. One of these occasions, though, almost put an end to all our endeavors. Taken by surprise by the sudden earthshaking shocks, I began running along a trench toward my bunker opening when a huge concussion lifted me off the ground and propelled me through the doorway toward which I was heading. Some of my Alliance colleagues were knocked off their feet and rolled around the ground like rag dolls. One old friend, Truong Cao Phuoc, who was working in the foreign relations division, had jumped into a shelter that collapsed on him, somehow leaving him alive with his head protruding from the ground. We extricated him, shoveling the dirt out handful by handful, carefully removing the supporting timbers that were crisscrossed in the earth around him. Truong had been trapped in one of the old U-shaped shelters, which became graves for so many. Later we learned to reinforce these dugouts with an A-frame of timbers that kept the walls from falling in. Reinforced in this manner, they could withstand B-52 bomb blasts as close as a hundred meters.

Sooner or later, though, the shock of the bombardments wore off, giving way to a sense of abject fatalism. The veterans would no longer scrabble at the bunker floors convulsed with fear. Instead people just resigned themselves—fully prepared to "go and sit in the ancestors' corner." The B-52s somehow put life in order. Many of those who survived the attacks found that afterward they were capable of viewing life from a more serene and philosophical perspective. It was a lesson that remained with me, as it did with many others, and helped me compose myself for death on more than one future occasion.

But even the most philosophical of fatalists were worn to the breaking point after several years of dodging and burrowing away from the rain of high explosives. During the most intense periods we came under attack every day for weeks running. At these times we would cook our rice as soon as we got out of our hammocks, kneading it into glutinous balls and ducking into the bunkers to be ready for what we knew was coming. Occasionally, we would be on the move for days at a time, stopping only to prepare food, eating as we walked. At night we would sling our hammocks between two trees wherever we found ourselves, collapsing into an exhausted but restless sleep, still half-awake to the inevitable explosions.

Pursued relentlessly by such demons, some of the guerrillas suffered nervous breakdowns and were packed off for hospital stays; others had to be sent home. There were cases too of fighters rallying to the Saigon government, unable to cope with the demands of life in the jungle. Times came when nobody was able to manage, and units would seek a hopeful refuge across the border in Cambodia.

*   *   *

The first months of 1970 were a precarious time. Even before the new year began, intelligence sources in Phnom Penh informed us that Cambodia's Prince Sihanouk was coming under increased American pressure to allow stepped-up bombing of our Cambodian sanctuaries. Through the years of war, Sihanouk had bravely and ingeniously maintained Cambodia's neutrality, in part by turning a blind eye toward happenings in the border region. Indications that the Americans were looking for a more formal acquiescence to their strikes against our bases and supply routes were ominous indeed. Coupled with this information, Soviet and Chinese sources inside the Cambodian government were now sharing with us intimations they had been receiving of a possible anti-Sihanouk coup.

In preparation for whatever might eventuate, all our headquarters units began fine-tuning their contingency plans. The escape routes we would use if necessary led west across the Vam Co River and into Cambodia's Prey Veng Province, then north toward Kratie. Depending on circumstances, we could take up positions there, on the west bank (the far side) of the Mekong, or continue north up the Ho Chi Minh Trail toward Laos. Strong elements of the NLF's 5th, 7th, and 9th Divisions were brought into the area to provide security for any movements we might be forced to make.

Then, on March 18, 1970, while Sihanouk was vacationing in France, his opponents struck, deposing him as head of the Cambodian government. Sihanouk's removal was for us a cause of instant anxiety, as we now looked over our shoulders at Cambodia, not as a refuge but as a potential danger. With Sihanouk's less-than-farsighted minister Lon Nol in power, Phnom Penh immediately began to stare in our direction with undisguised hostility. Sensing the possibility of entrapment between a Saigon/American offensive from the east and Royal Cambodian Army pressure from the west, COSVN did not wait to monitor developments in the Cambodian capital. On March 19 the permanent staff moved out toward positions that had been readied deep inside Kratie. By the time troops from the American 25th Division struck the headquarters area during the American/Cambodian incursion, the COSVN command staff had been gone almost two months.

With these portentous events as background, the NLF, PRG, and Alliance complexes readied themselves for emergency withdrawal. As we reviewed defensive measures and logistical planning, the B-52 raids reached a peak of frequency. Each day massive explosions rumbled in the distance, shaking the ground under us as the bombers incessantly probed the surrounding jungle. Then on March 27 at four in the morning, we were awakened by the familiar thunder—nearer now than it had been in recent days. All the officials and guards made for the shelters, listening intently. The concussive *whump-whump-whump* came closer and closer, moving in a direct line toward our positions. Then, as the cataclysm walked in on us, everyone hugged the earth—some screaming quietly, others struggling to suppress attacks of violent, involuntary trembling. Around us the ground began to heave spasmodically, and we were engulfed in a monstrous roar. Then, abruptly, it stopped, leaving behind it nearly a hundred dazed Maquis, shaking their heads in an attempt to clear the pressure from their ears. The last of the bomb craters had opened up less than a kilometer away. Again, miraculously, no one had been hurt. But we knew that the time had come. Following advance groups, which had already crossed the Vam Co, the main body—all the ministries and command units spread out over a fifty- or sixty-kilometer arc—began the trek into Cambodia.

By March 30 the Justice Ministry was already established in one of the sanctuary complexes, working and sleeping inside bunkers. Early that morning, three days after the near miss by the B-52s, I was thrown out of my cot onto the bunker floor by a series of explosions rocking the area. Glancing quickly out through the bunker opening, my guards and I saw helicopters hovering just above the trees, maneuvering in to land. I could make out the faces of ARVN soldiers and gun barrels protruding from the open doorways. By this time, fire was stuttering out from the dugouts and shelters as our security people began loosing a fusillade of small-arms and machine gun fire at the attackers. Over the radio, voices crackled through with news that the other ministries were also under attack.

Hour followed hour as the firing surged, died down, then flared up again. All day long I hunkered down in the shelter, my two bodyguards watching the fighting closely, occasionally letting off a volley from their AK47s through the embrasures. Squirming around on my stomach, I gathered together the most important papers, knowing that, whatever the cost, we would have to break through the encirclement when night came. It was a matter of desperation; none of us had any question that we would be captured the following day if we were still in the complex.

With darkness, pressure from the Saigon troops eased off. They undoubtedly knew that our main force units were in the area, and they were afraid of being trapped themselves. At the signal, my guards and I slipped out of the bunker under the dying glow of a flare. There was no firing as we headed westward into the jungle along one of the prearranged escape routes toward the security corridor the 7th Division was setting up. I ran as far as I was able, then slowed into a kind of shuffling trot, gasping for breath. Some of the ministry officials were on the trail in front of me. I could hear other people hurrying behind. From the bunker complex the firing was picking up, filling the night with the staccato bursts of AK47s and M-16s.

Behind us the security teams fanned out, screening our flight and deflecting pursuit. Half-running, half-walking between my guards, I made my way along the trail, unable to see a thing in the blackness of the jungle. All night we slogged along, unsure of what was happening in back of us but determined to keep moving. As the initial rush of adrenalin wore off, my legs began to feel leaden, and my throat ached with thirst. When word was finally passed that we could stop, I slumped to the ground where I was, stupefied with exhaustion. Just before I passed out, I managed to scoop up a few handfuls of water from a stagnant pool next to the trail.

When I awoke it was 6 A.M. The first thing I noticed was that the swampy puddle from which I had drunk the previous night was the repository of several large piles of buffalo excrement. But I hardly had time to reflect on this unpleasant surprise before we heard the shriek of approaching jets. We dived into the jungle just as several American planes shot by, machine-gunning the trail. Under sporadic bombing and strafing attacks, we moved ahead all morning, an entire column by this time made up of the NLF, PRG, and Alliance ministries and support personnel. Though it was impossible to get firm information, it seemed as if we had not incurred any serious losses in the maelstrom of the previous day's assault.

As we walked, our troop strength was more and more in evidence. General Hoang Van Thai had deployed his defense forces to create a secure corridor from the rendezvous point (the place we had stopped for a few hours of sleep) and the Cambodian province of Kratie, our destination to the north. Though as we trudged along, the situation was unclear, there was no doubt at all that Thai's arrangements were undergoing a serious test. We knew that the Saigon troops had launched a thrust against us from the east while Lon Nol's Royal Cambodian forces were moving in from the west along Route 7, a road that intersected the corridor. Knowing that we were in great danger, we walked as fast as we could all day, our only food the cold rice balls we ate as we marched. Meanwhile, the 9th Division threw up a screen against the ARVN drive, while the 5th moved to block the Cambodians on our left. Along the corridor between them the headquarters and government personnel fled, closely shielded by units from the 7th.

Toward the end of the next day, April 2, a motorcycle driver picked me out of the line of march. He had been sent by PRG President Phat to take me to the 7th Division's headquarters farther to the north, where the rest of the NLF, PRG, and Alliance leadership was already assembled, including Mme. Nguyen Thi Dinh, deputy commander of the NLF armed forces. Early the following morning, we all moved out toward Route 7 only a few miles to our north, aware now that the highway was already under attack.

Fighting to break through the PLAF blocking forces, the ARVN and Cambodian vanguards were struggling to gain control of the highway before we could get there, which would cut off our escape and seal us into southern Cambodia, where we could be surrounded and cut apart. We were not sure whether the forces trying to head us off were aware of exactly who or what they were after, and to this day I do not know whether American and Saigon government military analysts realized how close they were to annihilating or capturing the core of the Southern resistance—elite units of our frontline fighters along with the civilian and much of the military leadership. But as we hurried through the corridor, *we* at least were quite clear about the stakes involved in breaking out. Our efforts were thus tinged not only with the desperation of men fleeing the grasp of a merciless foe, but with anxiety for the very existence of our struggle.

It was at this point that Dr. Hoa, seven months pregnant and supported on one side by her husband, on the other by a bodyguard, went into labor. It had been expected that she would require a cesarean section, so a surgical team had accompanied her on the move into Cambodia. But as it turned out, whether because of the constant walking or for some other reason, the birth came normally—and precipitously. On a square of nylon laid out on the jungle floor, the minister of health gave birth to a baby boy, noisy and apparently well, despite his ill-timed appearance and the confusion into which he had been born. Carrying this new addition to the revolutionary forces, we neared Route 7, listening intently for incoming artillery rounds amidst the sounds of battle to our right and left.

Just before we got to the highway, word passed down the column that our line blocking the Cambodians was holding—at least for the moment—and that the 9th Division had counterattacked Saigon forces at Krek, about ten kilometers to the east. Buoyed by this news we crossed 7 and pushed northward in the first of what would become a series of forced marches.

Before long our relief at having avoided entrapment was submerged in an exhaustion beyond description. As day, then night, then day again passed with constant harassment, little sleep, and cold dinners eaten for the most part on the trail, the middle-aged and elderly ministers, with their middle-aged civilian staffs, all of them weakened by disease and half-famished, began to break down physically. As we walked, the rains, typical for that time of year, poured down continuously, turning the red Cambodian earth to a sticky clay that sucked at our rubber sandals, until the last of them had been lost or discarded. Barefoot, pants rolled up above our knees, we shuffled ahead in the ankle-deep mud, each step an energy-draining struggle. Those who had bicycles abandoned them beside the muck of the trail. Like robots, we made our way through the downpour, each man grasping the shirt of the man in front of him for support and direction.

For five days it rained without letup. By this time I could barely stand, let alone walk. I moved along in a slow-motion daze, conscious only of the man in front of me—whose shirt I continued to clutch—and the mortar rounds and artillery shells that crashed sporadically into the jungle alongside our column, from time to time sending us sprawling face first into the mud. At night we slung our hammocks from the rubber trees, propping our nylon squares over us in a useless attempt to keep off the torrents of water. When morning came, it was difficult for any of us to tell if we had slept or had simply lapsed temporarily comatose.

But as we continued northward, we all sensed that there was less urgency to our movement. At some unidentifiable point we realized that no more shells were exploding dully in the sodden trees. At last, in the jungles outside Kratie, 150 kilometers or so north of Route 7, we were able to stop and rest. For several days we did little other than sleep and enjoy the luxuries of hot tea and prepared food, items we hadn't seen for a week and a half. With an opportunity to relax and begin recuperating from this ordeal, spirits started to revive. COSVN's Pham Hung and

General Trung joked that "Even though we ran like hell, still we'll win," sentiments that Henry Kissinger anticipated in his 1968 *Foreign Affairs* article: "Guerrillas win if they don't lose. A standard army loses if it does not win."

In taking stock of the situation, we had not in fact lost a great deal. In terms of casualties, our luck had continued to hold. Despite the close escape and the rigors of the march, all of the leadership had managed to arrive at Kratie unharmed. Here we linked up with the COSVN staff, which had previously been evacuated to the region, also without loss. In the expanses of Cambodia's northern provinces, we were less vulnerable to the B-52s and relatively immune to assault, since our forces had de facto control over the region (and had had for some time).

The ARVN attacks that we had so narrowly survived were a precursor to the large-scale American incursion into Cambodia that jumped off a month later. The wider war that resulted from these actions was an almost immediate benefit to us. The American/ARVN attack indeed caused damage and disrupted supply lines. But our antagonists had no staying power in Cambodia. The United States at this point was already in the process of a staged unilateral withdrawal, which could not be truly compensated for by increased air activity. The Saigon forces by themselves were hard-pressed to meet the military challenge they faced in South Vietnam, without adding Cambodia to their burden, while Lon Nol's army was quite simply unprepared for the kind of warfare it now had to face.

Nixon and Kissinger had gambled that a limited foray into our base areas and supply routes would have a telling effect. But they had seriously exaggerated their own ability to inflict damage relative to their opponents' elasticity and durability. Unwisely, they had traded a few immediate and short-term military gains for the unpredictable consequences of intruding into an already volatile Cambodia and for severe, long-term political debits at home. To our analysts, monitoring the American domestic scene, it seemed that the Cambodian invasion had stimulated a divisiveness equaled only perhaps by the Tet Offensive two years earlier. We had indeed, as Pham Hung said, run away, but Nixon had paid dearly for our temporary discomfiture by sustaining major political losses. Kissinger's argument that the invasion had gained a year may be true. But to our way of looking at it—from a political and diplomatic perspective as well as militarily—the United States action had resulted in a resounding victory for the Front.

BRUCE WEIGL
1949-

Weigl was in the First Air Cavalry in Vietnam. He has taught writing at Old Dominion University and now teaches at Pennsylvania State University.

MINES

1

In Vietnam I was always afraid of mines:
North Vietnamese mines, Vietcong mines,
French mines, American mines,
whole fields marked with warning signs.

A Bouncing Betty comes up waist high—
cuts you in half.
One man's legs were laid
alongside him in the Dustoff,
he asked for a chairback, morphine,
he screamed he wanted to give
his eyes away, his kidneys,
his heart . . .

2

Here is how you walk at night: slowly lift
one leg, clear the sides with your arms, clear the back,
front, put the leg down, like swimming.

HAYDEN CARRUTH
1921–

Carruth served in the U.S. Army Air Corps during the Second World War. He has written over twenty-five books of poetry and literary criticism.

ON BEING ASKED TO WRITE A POEM
AGAINST THE WAR IN VIETNAM

Well I have and in fact
more than one and I'll
tell you this too

I wrote one against
Algeria that nightmare
and another against

Korea and another
against the one
I was in

and I don't remember
how many against
the three

when I was a boy
Abyssinia Spain and
Harlan County

and not one
breath was restored

to one
shattered throat
mans womans or childs
not one not

one
but death went on and on
never looking aside

except now and then like a child
with a furtive half-smile
to make sure I was noticing.

PART V

AFTERWORDS

WILLIE MORRIS
1934–

*James Jones, his friend Willie Morris, and their two boys toured the
battlefields of the American Civil War in February 1976. In James
Jones: A Friendship, Morris has remembered their visit to Antietam,
where one day in 1862, 23,000 men and boys were killed and wounded.*

From JAMES JONES: A FRIENDSHIP

Jim wore a slouch hat and walking boots and tarried in the cold wind
with a pair of binoculars. It was melancholy land with its hollows and
ravines and outcroppings which snipers used, and they could hide a
whole brigade in some of those places. "It was a damned general's paradise," he said, as he peered through the binoculars at the ground where
Stonewall Jackson hid his men, "but very hard on the legs of the troops.
One of the things most people don't understand is the physical hardship
a soldier goes through even when he's not being shot at. The average
person couldn't climb that hill at Burnside's Bridge just to get there.
And going downhill is sometimes even more draining than going uphill.
If you've been a soldier you look at all that, I guess."

"If we'd been living then and been here, we'd probably have fought
against each other," I said.

"Yeah. I guess that's true."

The day waned on in its fog and rain, and we worked our way from
Nicodemus Hill down the Smoketown Lane and past the Roulette
Farmhouse, and now we were at the Sunken Road, which at the time
became known as Bloody Lane. Here, along a line of a thousand yards,
the Confederate center took its stand, thousands of them firing at close
quarters against the Federal troops charging across the crest of a ridge. It
lasted three hours, and the dead Confederate soldiers lay so thick here
that as far as the eye could see a man could walk upon them without once

touching ground, and the bodies of the attackers lay strewn in piles across the whole ridge.

We walked down the road for a while, and gazed out every so often from behind the wooden fences at the crest where the attackers came. Our two boys were quiet now also, and for a moment they looked silently at the monument only a few feet to the south of the road, dedicated to an Ohio brigade, and at the top of this was the stone silhouette of a boy who seemed to be no more than eighteen, raising his cap in one hand, holding a flag in the other. To the right of the Sunken Road was an observation tower, evil-smelling with the reek of urine. We climbed to the top of it. The view from here was spectacular, the blue mountains at the horizon, the sweeping sky, the landscape below in the mist, the Sunken Road itself sweeping almost to the opposite skyline.

"The way men go to die," Jim said, looking down at the ridge before us. "It's incredibly sad. It breaks my heart. You wonder why it was necessary, why human beings have to do that to each other. This reminds me a little of Europe, where every blade of grass has twenty-one drops of human blood on it. That's why Europe's so goddamned green."

Why do men do it, one of the boys wondered. Why did they do it here?

"Well . . ." He paused, to the sound of rain on the roof. "I think it's more because they didn't want to appear unmanly in front of their friends."

PAUL DEHN
1912–1976

Born in Manchester and educated at Oxford, Dehn was a poet, an anthologist, and a writer of screenplays. During the Second World War he was with the British Special Operations Executive.

ARMISTICE

It is finished. The enormous dust-cloud over Europe
Lifts like a million swallows; and a light,
Drifting in craters, touches the quiet dead.

Now, at the bugle's hour, before the blood
Cakes in a clean wind on their marble faces,
Making them monuments; before the sun,

Hung like a medal on the smoky noon,
Whitens the bone that feeds the earth; before
Wheat-ear springs green, again, in the green spring

And they are bread in the bodies of the young:
Be strong to remember how the bread died, screaming;
Gangrene was corn, and monuments went mad.

HARRISON E. SALISBURY
1908–

*Minneapolis-born journalist and author Salisbury was long associated
with* The New York Times. *During the Second World War he managed
the Moscow office of the United Press. In his memoir* A Journey for Our
Times *(1983), he reports what he saw in the Crimea in the spring of
1944.*

From A JOURNEY FOR OUR TIMES

I had become part of the Metropol world and half the time I was away
with the Red Army. I crossed the Ukraine and crossed it again. I had
never seen mud so deep, no bottom at all, thousands of German trucks,
tanks, gun mounts, troop carriers lost in the *chernozöm,* the famous

black soil. But the Red Army was moving—on foot, on horseback, in carts, in *telyagas*, peasant wagons, by old buggies pulled by horses, mules, donkeys, cows, oxen, an occasional camel and many snorting farm tractors—a helter-skelter movement, relentlessly westward. Nothing would stop them, and I thought the quickest way to Berlin was to stick with the Russians.

We went to the Crimea, the Germans finally driven out, corpses bobbing on the rock shore of the slim peninsula where the last stand was made, and over the stony land the Limburger stench of putrescent bodies; heavy, it got into your clothes, it clogged your throat, it hung in the air like plague. Here I inhaled the essence of war. I saw the pig-bellied bodies, eyes starting out of rotting heads, flaxen hair like wigs on a Kewpie doll, and the smell of piss-clotted uniforms, pants cruddy with excrement, with the pale worms of intestines, dirt, slime, paper, paper everywhere, brown-stained toilet paper, brown-stained newspapers with their Gothic print, broken bottles, jagged edges sparkling in the sun, rusty cans, the sleek white wood of ammo boxes, coppered coils of machine gun bullets, unmailed postcards, photos of girls stained with blood, here a splintered bone, the flesh torn like cotton rags, orders, commands, penalties, sentences (a sergeant sentenced to be shot; he had been apprehended trying to copulate with the captain's mare on the village street), surrender leaflets, bits of green grass and dandelions, stinking fish floating in the gentle waves beside corpses gas-filled, buttons burst from faded green uniforms.

The Crimea did it. I had seen the winter corpses at Katyn, at Leningrad, in the Ukraine. Death in winter is clean. The bodies freeze in rigid forms. There is little stench. Except for the horses. The horses were the worst, winter or summer. They blew up like titanic counterfeits, the eyes still alive with terror. Snow quickly covered the winter dead. Now in the Crimea the dead were omnipresent.

German prisoners with dead eyes stumbled among the corpses, carting them off to endless trenches under the tommy guns of sullen Red Army men. I could not tell whether either Russians or Germans knew what they were doing. The Germans moved like sleepwalkers. The hardest thing, they told us, was the moment of surrender. Unless you were in a big group, a hundred or a thousand, you didn't have a chance. The Soviet tommy gunners just mowed you down. The Nazis had been waiting for the boats to take them off, the boats that never came.

This was war and now I understood it. War was the garbage heap of humanity. It was shit and piss and gas from the rump; terror and bowels that ran without control. Here Hitler's Aryan man died, a worse death than any he devised in the ovens of Auschwitz, anus open, spewing out his gut until a Red tommy gunner ended it with a lazy sweep of his chattering weapon.

DOUGLAS MACARTHUR
1880–1964

General of the Army Douglas MacArthur, a hero in the First World War and later Superintendent of West Point, Army Chief of Staff, Field Marshal of the Army of the Philippines, Medal of Honor Winner, and the conqueror, ruler, and reformer of Japan, at the age of eighty-two says a final goodbye to the West Point cadets.

From ADDRESS TO THE CORPS OF CADETS, WEST POINT, MAY 12, 1962

You are the leaven which binds together the entire fabric of our national system of defense. From your ranks come the great captains who hold the nation's destiny in their hands the moment the war tocsin sounds. The Long Gray Line has never failed us. Were you to do so, a million ghosts in olive drab, in brown khaki, in blue and gray, would rise from their white crosses thundering those magic words—Duty-Honor-Country.

This does not mean that you are war mongers. On the contrary, the soldier, above all other people, prays for peace, for he must suffer and bear the deepest wounds and scars of war. But always in our ears ring the ominous words of Plato, that wisest of all philosophers, "Only the dead have seen the end of war."

The shadows are lengthening for me. The twilight is here. My days of old have vanished tone and tint; they have gone glimmering through the dreams of things that were. Their memory is one of wondrous beauty, watered by tears, and coaxed and caressed by the smiles of yesterday. I listen vainly, but with thirsty ear, for the witching melody of faint bugles blowing reveille, of far drums beating the long roll. In my dreams I hear again the crash of guns, the rattle of musketry, the strange mournful mutter of the battlefield. But in the evening of my memory, always I come back to West Point. Always there echoes and re-echoes in my ears—Duty-Honor-Country.

Today marks my final roll call with you. But I want you to know that when I cross the river my last conscious thoughts will be of the Corps—and the Corps—and the Corps.

I bid you farewell.

PETER PORTER
1929-

Born in Brisbane, Australia, Porter has worked in journalism and advertising and written many volumes of poetry, mainly satiric.

YOUR ATTENTION PLEASE

The Polar DEW has just warned that
A nuclear rocket strike of
At least one thousand megatons
Has been launched by the enemy
Directly at our major cities.
This announcement will take
Two and a quarter minutes to make,
You therefore have a further
Eight and a quarter minutes
To comply with the shelter
Requirements published in the Civil
Defence Code—section Atomic Attack.
A specially shortened Mass
Will be broadcast at the end
Of this announcement—
Protestant and Jewish services
Will begin simultaneously—
Select your wavelength immediately
According to instructions

In the Defence Code. Do not
Take well-loved pets (including birds)
Into your shelter—they will consume
Fresh air. Leave the old and bed-
ridden, you can do nothing for them.
Remember to press the sealing
Switch when everyone is in
The shelter. Set the radiation
Aerial, turn on the geiger barometer.
Turn off your Television now.
Turn off your radio immediately
The Services end. At the same time
Secure explosion plugs in the ears
Of each member of your family. Take
Down your plasma flasks. Give your children
The pills marked one and two
In the c.d. green container, then put
Them to bed. Do not break
The inside airlock seals until
The radiation All Clear shows
(Watch for the cuckoo in your
perspex panel), or your District
Touring Doctor rings your bell.
If before this, your air becomes
Exhausted or if any of your family
Is critically injured, administer
The capsules marked "Valley Forge"
(Red pocket in No. I Survival Kit)
For painless death. (Catholics
Will have been instructed by their priests
What to do in this eventuality.)
This announcement is ending. Our President
Has already given order for
Massive retaliation—it will be
Decisive. Some of us may die.
Remember, statistically
It is not likely to be you.
All flags are flying fully dressed
On Government buildings—the sun is shining.
Death is the least we have to fear.
We are all in the hands of God,
Whatever happens happens by His Will.
Now go quickly to your shelters.

James Robeson: Letter from *Lines of Battle: Letters of American Servicemen, 1941–1945*, edited by Annette Tapert. Copyright © James Robeson. We have made diligent efforts to contact the copyright holder to obtain permission to reprint this selection. If you have information that would help us, please write W. W. Norton & Co., 500 Fifth Avenue, New York, NY 10110.

Isaac Rosenberg: "Break of Day in the Trenches," from *Collected Works*, edited by Ian Parsons, Parsons, N.Y.: Oxford University Press, 1979.

Ivor Rowbery: Letter from *Despatches from the Heart*, edited by Annette Tapert. Reprinted by permission of Times Books.

Antoine de Saint-Exupéry: From *Wind, Sand, and Stars*. Copyright © 1939 by Antione de Saint-Exupéry and renewed 1967 by Lewis Galantiere. Reprinted by permission of Harcourt Brace Jovanovich, Inc.

Guy Sajer: From *The Forgotten Soldier*, by Guy Sajer. Copyright © 1967 by Robert Laffont; 1968 Translation by Harper & Row, Publishers, Inc. Reprinted by permission of Harper & Row, Publishers, Inc.

Harrison E. Salisbury: From *A Journey for Our Times*, by Harrison E. Salisbury. Copyright © 1983 by Harrison E. Salisbury. Reprinted by permission of Harper & Row, Publishers, Inc.

Siegfried Sassoon: "Blighters," "How To Die," "The General," "Lamentations," "Glory of Women," from *Collected Poems*. Reprinted by permission of Viking-Penguin, New York.

Siegfried Sassoon: From *Diaries, 1915–1918*, by Siegfried Sassoon. Reprinted by permission of Faber & Faber (Publishers) Ltd., London.

Vernon Scannell: "The Great War," "Walking Wounded," from *New and Collected Poems*. Reprinted by permission of Robson Books Ltd., London.

Louis Simpson: "Carentan O Carentan," from *A Dream of Governors*. Copyright © 1959 by Louis Simpson. Reprinted by permission of University Press of New England. "The Battle," from *Selected Poems, 1965*, by Louis Simpson. Reprinted by permission of the author.

Louis Simpson: "On the Ledge," from *Caviare at the Funeral*, by Louis Simpson. Reprinted by permission of Franklin Watts.

Eugene B. Sledge: From *With the Old Breed at Peleliu and Okinawa*, by E. B. Sledge. Reprinted by permission of Presidio Press.

Stephen Spender: "Two Armies," "Ultima Retio Regum," from *Collected Poems*. Copyright © 1942 and renewed 1970 by Stephen Spender. Reprinted by permission of Random House, Inc.

Kermit Stewart: Letters from *Lines of Battle: Letters of American Servicemen, 1941–1945*, edited by Annette Tapert. Copyright © Kermit Stewart. We have made diligent efforts to contact the copyright holder to obtain permission to reprint this selection. If you have information that would help us, please write W. W. Norton & Co., 500 Fifth Avenue, New York, NY 10110.

Truong Nhu Tang (with David Chanoff and Doan Van Toai): From *A Viet Cong Memoir* (1985). Reprinted by permission of Harcourt Brace Jovanovich.

Daniel J. Sweeney: Letter from *Despatches from the Heart*, edited by Annette Tapert. Reprinted by permission of Times Books.

Studs Terkel: From *"The Good War": An Oral History of World War Two*, by Studs Terkel. Reprinted by permission of Pantheon Books, a division of Random House, Inc.

Edward Thomas: "In Memoriam (Easter, 1915)," "This Is No Case of Petty Right or Wrong," "A Private," from *Collected Poems*, by Edward Thomas. Reprinted by permis-

INDEX